EDISON HIS LIFE AND INVENTIONS

By Frank Lewis Dyer

General Counsel For The Edison Laboratory And Allied Interests

And

Thomas Commerford Martin

Ex-President Of The American Institute Of Electrical Engineers

CONTENTS

INTRODUCTION

PRIOR to this, no complete, authentic, and authorized record of the work of Mr. Edison, during an active life, has been given to the world. That life, if there is anything in heredity, is very far from finished; and while it continues there will be new achievement.

An insistently expressed desire on the part of the public for a definitive biography of Edison was the reason for the following pages. The present authors deem themselves happy in the confidence reposed in them, and in the constant assistance they have enjoyed from Mr. Edison while preparing these pages, a great many of which are altogether his own. This co-operation in no sense relieves the authors of responsibility as to any of the views or statements of their own that the book contains. They have realized the extreme reluctance of Mr. Edison to be made the subject of any biography at all; while he has felt that, if it must be written, it were best done by the hands of friends and associates of long standing, whose judgment and discretion he could trust, and whose intimate knowledge of the facts would save him from misrepresentation.

The authors of the book are profoundly conscious of the fact that the extraordinary period of electrical development embraced in it has been prolific of great men. They have named some of them; but there has been no idea of setting forth various achievements or of ascribing distinctive merits. This treatment is devoted to one man whom his fellow-citizens have chosen to regard as in many ways representative of the American at his finest flowering in the field of invention during the nineteenth century.

It is designed in these pages to bring the reader face to face with Edison; to glance at an interesting childhood and a youthful period marked by a capacity for doing things, and by an insatiable thirst for knowledge; then to accompany him into the great creative stretch of forty years, during which he has done so much. This book shows him plunged deeply into work for which he has always had an incredible capacity, reveals the exercise of his unsurpassed inventive ability, his keen reasoning powers, his tenacious memory, his fertility of resource; follows him through a series of innumerable experiments, conducted methodically, reaching out like rays of search-light into all the regions of science and nature, and finally exhibits him emerging triumphantly from countless difficulties bearing with him in new arts the fruits of victorious struggle.

These volumes aim to be a biography rather than a history of electricity, but they have had to cover so much general ground in defining the relations and contributions of Edison to the electrical arts, that they serve to present a picture of the whole development effected in the last fifty years, the most fruitful that electricity has known. The effort has been made to avoid technique and abstruse phrases, but some degree of explanation has been absolutely necessary in regard to each group of inventions. The task of the authors has consisted largely in summarizing fairly the methods and processes employed by

Edison; and some idea of the difficulties encountered by them in so doing may be realized from the fact that one brief chapter, for example,--that on ore milling--covers nine years of most intense application and activity on the part of the inventor. It is something like exhibiting the geological eras of the earth in an outline lantern slide, to reduce an elaborate series of strenuous experiments and a vast variety of ingenious apparatus to the space of a few hundred words.

A great deal of this narrative is given in Mr. Edison's own language, from oral or written statements made in reply to questions addressed to him with the object of securing accuracy. A further large part is based upon the personal contributions of many loyal associates; and it is desired here to make grateful acknowledgment to such collaborators as Messrs. Samuel Insull, E. H. Johnson, F. R. Upton, R. N Dyer, S. B. Eaton, Francis Jehl, W. S. Andrews, W. J. Jenks, W. J. Hammer, F. J. Sprague, W. S. Mallory, and C. L. Clarke, and others, without whose aid the issuance of this book would indeed have been impossible. In particular, it is desired to acknowledge indebtedness to Mr. W. H. Meadowcroft not only for substantial aid in the literary part of the work, but for indefatigable effort to group, classify, and summarize the boundless material embodied in Edison's note-books and memorabilia of all kinds now kept at the Orange laboratory. Acknowledgment must also be made of the courtesy and assistance of Mrs. Edison, and especially of the loan of many interesting and rare photographs from her private collection.

EDISON HIS LIFE AND INVENTIONS

CHAPTER I

THE AGE OF ELECTRICITY

THE year 1847 marked a period of great territorial acquisition by the American people, with incalculable additions to their actual and potential wealth. By the rational compromise with England in the dispute over the Oregon region, President Polk had secured during 1846, for undisturbed settlement, three hundred thousand square miles of forest, fertile land, and fisheries, including the whole fair Columbia Valley. Our active "policy of the Pacific" dated from that hour. With swift and clinching succession came the melodramatic Mexican War, and February, 1848, saw another vast territory south of Oregon and west of the Rocky Mountains added by treaty to the United States. Thus in about eighteen months there had been pieced into the national domain for quick development and exploitation a region as large as the entire Union of Thirteen States at the close of the War of Independence. Moreover, within its boundaries was embraced all the great American gold-field, just on the eve of discovery, for Marshall had detected the shining particles in the mill-race at the foot of the Sierra Nevada nine days before Mexico signed away her rights in California and in all the vague, remote hinterland facing Cathayward.

Equally momentous were the times in Europe, where the attempt to secure opportunities of expansion as well as larger liberty for the individual took quite different form. The old absolutist system of government was fast breaking up, and ancient thrones were tottering. The red lava of deep revolutionary fires oozed up through many glowing cracks in the political crust, and all the social strata were shaken. That the wild outbursts of insurrection midway in the fifth decade failed and died away was not surprising, for the superincumbent deposits of tradition and convention were thick. But the retrospect indicates that many reforms and political changes were accomplished, although the process involved the exile of not a few ardent spirits to America, to become leading statesmen, inventors, journalists, and financiers. In 1847, too, Russia began her tremendous march eastward into Central Asia, just as France was solidifying her first gains on the littoral of northern Africa. In England the fierce fervor of the Chartist movement, with its violent rhetoric as to the rights of man, was sobering down and passing pervasively into numerous practical schemes for social and political amelioration, constituting in their entirety a most profound change throughout every part of the national life.

Into such times Thomas Alva Edison was born, and his relations to them and to the events of the past sixty years are the subject of this narrative. Aside from the personal interest that attaches to the picturesque career, so typically American, there is a broader aspect in which the work of the "Franklin of the Nineteenth Century" touches the welfare and progress of the race. It is difficult at any time to determine the effect of any single invention, and the investigation becomes more difficult where inventions of the first class have been crowded upon each other in rapid and bewildering succession. But it will be admitted that in Edison one deals with a central figure of the great age that saw the invention and introduction in practical form of the telegraph, the submarine cable, the telephone, the electric light, the electric railway, the electric trolley-car, the storage battery, the electric motor, the phonograph, the wireless telegraph; and that the influence of these on the world's affairs has not been excelled at any time by that of any other corresponding advances in the arts and sciences. These pages deal with Edison's share in the great work of the last half century in abridging distance, communicating intelligence, lessening toil, improving illumination, recording forever the human voice; and on behalf of inventive genius it may be urged that its beneficent results and gifts to mankind compare with any to be credited to statesman, warrior, or creative writer of the same period.

Viewed from the standpoint of inventive progress, the first half of the nineteenth century had passed very profitably when Edison appeared--every year marked by some notable achievement in the arts and sciences, with promise of its early and abundant fruition in commerce and industry. There had been exactly four decades of steam navigation on American waters. Railways were growing at the rate of nearly one thousand miles annually. Gas had become familiar as a means of illumination in large cities. Looms and tools and printing-presses were everywhere being liberated from the slow toil of man-power. The first photographs had been taken. Chloroform, nitrous oxide gas, and ether had been placed at the service of the physician in saving life, and the revolver, guncotton, and nitroglycerine added to the agencies for slaughter. New metals, chemicals, and elements had become available in large numbers, gases had been liquefied and solidified, and the range of useful heat and cold indefinitely extended. The safety-lamp had been given to the miner, the caisson to the bridge-builder, the anti-friction metal to the mechanic for bearings. It was already known how to vulcanize rubber, and how to galvanize iron. The application of machinery in the harvest-field had begun with the embryonic reaper, while both the bicycle and the automobile were heralded in primitive prototypes. The gigantic expansion of the iron and steel industry was foreshadowed in the change from wood to coal in the smelting furnaces. The sewing-machine had brought with it, like the friction match, one of the most profound influences in modifying domestic life, and making it different from that of all preceding time.

Even in 1847 few of these things had lost their novelty, most of them were in the earlier stages of development. But it is when we turn to electricity that the rich virgin condition of an illimitable new kingdom of discovery is seen. Perhaps the word "utilization" or "application" is better than discovery, for then, as now, an endless wealth of phenomena noted by experimenters from Gilbert to Franklin and Faraday awaited the invention that could alone render them useful to mankind. The eighteenth century, keenly curious and ceaselessly active in this fascinating field of investigation, had not, after all, left much of a legacy in either principles or appliances. The lodestone and the compass; the frictional machine; the Leyden jar; the nature of conductors and insulators; the identity of electricity and the thunder-storm flash; the use of lightning-rods; the physiological effects of an electrical shock--these constituted the bulk of the bequest to which philosophers were the only heirs. Pregnant with possibilities were many of the observations that had been recorded. But these few appliances made up the meagre kit of tools with which the nineteenth century entered upon its task of acquiring the arts and conveniences now such an intimate part of "human nature's daily food" that the average American to-day pays more for his electrical service than he does for bread.

With the first year of the new century came Volta's invention of the chemical battery as a means of producing electricity. A well-known Italian picture represents Volta exhibiting his apparatus before the young conqueror Napoleon, then ravishing from the Peninsula its treasure of ancient art and founding an ephemeral empire. At such a moment this gift of despoiled Italy to the world was a noble revenge, setting in motion incalculable beneficent forces and agencies. For the first time man had command of a steady supply of electricity without toil or effort. The useful results obtainable previously from the current of a frictional machine were not much greater than those to be derived from the flight of a rocket. While the frictional appliance is still employed in medicine, it ranks with the flint axe and the tinder-box in industrial obsolescence. No art or trade could be founded on it; no diminution of daily work or increase of daily comfort could be secured with it. But the little battery with its metal plates in a weak solution proved a perennial reservoir of electrical energy, safe and controllable, from which supplies could be drawn at will. That which was wild had become domesticated; regular crops took the place of haphazard gleanings from brake or prairie; the possibility of electrical starvation was forever left behind.

Immediately new processes of inestimable value revealed themselves; new methods were suggested. Almost all the electrical arts now employed made their beginnings in the next twenty-five years, and while the more extensive of them depend to-day on the dynamo for electrical energy, some of the most important still remain in loyal allegiance to the older source. The battery itself soon underwent modifications, and new types were evolved--the storage, the double-fluid, and the dry. Various analogies next pointed to the use of heat, and the thermoelectric cell emerged, embodying the application of flame to the junction of two different metals. Davy, of the safety-lamp, threw a volume of current across the gap between two sticks of charcoal, and the voltaic arc, forerunner of electric lighting, shed its bright beams upon a dazzled world. The decomposition of water by electrolytic action was recognized and made the basis of communicating at a distance even before the days of the electromagnet. The ties that bind electricity and magnetism in twinship of relation and interaction were detected, and Faraday's work in induction gave the world at once the dynamo and the motor. "Hitch your wagon to a star," said Emerson. To all the coal-fields and all the waterfalls Faraday had directly hitched the wheels of industry. Not only was it now possible to convert mechanical energy into electricity cheaply and in illimitable quantities, but electricity at once showed its ubiquitous availability as a motive power. Boats were propelled by it, cars were hauled, and even papers printed. Electroplating became an art, and telegraphy sprang into active being on both sides of the Atlantic.

At the time Edison was born, in 1847, telegraphy, upon which he was to leave so indelible an imprint, had barely struggled into acceptance by the public. In England, Wheatstone and Cooke had introduced a ponderous magnetic needle telegraph. In America, in 1840, Morse had taken out his first patent on an electromagnetic telegraph, the principle of which is dominating in the art to this day. Four years later the memorable message "What hath God wrought!" was sent by young Miss Ellsworth over his circuits, and incredulous Washington was advised by wire of the action of the Democratic Convention in Baltimore in nominating Polk. By 1847 circuits had been strung between Washington and New York, under private enterprise, the Government having declined to buy the Morse system for $100,000. Everything was crude and primitive. The poles were two hundred feet apart and could barely hold up a wash-line. The slim, bare, copper wire snapped on the least provocation, and the circuit was "down" for thirty-six days in the first six months. The little glass-knob insulators made seductive targets for ignorant sportsmen. Attempts to insulate the line wire were limited to coating it with tar or smearing it with wax for the benefit of all the bees in the neighborhood. The farthest western reach of the telegraph lines in 1847 was Pittsburg, with three-ply iron wire mounted on square glass insulators with a little wooden pentroof for protection. In that office, where Andrew Carnegie was a messenger boy, the magnets in use to receive the signals sent with the aid of powerful nitric-acid batteries weighed as much as seventy-five pounds apiece. But the business was fortunately small at the outset, until the new device, patronized chiefly by lottery-men, had proved its utility. Then came the great outburst of activity. Within a score of years telegraph wires covered the whole occupied country with a network, and the first great electrical industry was a pronounced success, yielding to its pioneers the first great harvest of electrical fortunes. It had been a sharp struggle for bare existence, during which such a man as the founder of Cornell University had been glad to get breakfast in New York with a quarter-dollar picked up on Broadway.

CHAPTER II

EDISON'S PEDIGREE

THOMAS ALVA EDISON was born at Milan Ohio, February 11, 1847. The State that rivals Virginia as a "Mother of Presidents" has evidently other titles to distinction of the same nature. For picturesque detail it would not be easy to find any story excelling that of the Edison family before it reached the Western Reserve. The story epitomizes American idealism, restlessness, freedom of individual opinion, and ready adjustment to the surrounding conditions of pioneer life. The ancestral Edisons who came over from Holland, as nearly as can be determined, in 1730, were descendants of extensive millers on the Zuyder Zee, and took up patents of land along the Passaic River, New Jersey, close to the home that Mr. Edison established in the Orange Mountains a hundred and sixty years later. They landed at Elizabethport, New Jersey, and first settled near Caldwell in that State, where some graves of the family may still be found. President Cleveland was born in that quiet hamlet. It is a curious fact that in the Edison family the pronunciation of the name has always been with the long "e" sound, as it would naturally be in the Dutch language. The family prospered and must have enjoyed public confidence, for we find the name of Thomas Edison, as a bank official on Manhattan Island, signed to Continental currency in 1778. According to the family records this Edison, great-grandfather of Thomas Alva, reached the extreme old age of 104 years. But all was not well, and, as has happened so often before, the politics of father and son were violently different. The Loyalist movement that took to Nova Scotia so many Americans after the War of Independence carried with it John, the son of this stalwart Continental. Thus it came about that Samuel Edison, son of John, was born at Digby, Nova Scotia, in 1804. Seven years later John Edison who, as a Loyalist or United Empire emigrant, had become entitled under the laws of Canada to a grant of six hundred acres of land, moved westward to take possession of this property. He made his way through the State of New York in wagons drawn by oxen to the remote and primitive township of Bayfield, in Upper Canada, on Lake Huron. Although the journey occurred in balmy June, it was necessarily attended with difficulty and privation; but the new home was situated in good farming country, and once again this interesting nomadic family settled down.

John Edison moved from Bayfield to Vienna, Ontario, on the northern bank of Lake Erie. Mr. Edison supplies an interesting reminiscence of the old man and his environment in those early Canadian days. "When I was five years old I was taken by my father and mother on a visit to Vienna. We were driven by carriage from Milan, Ohio, to a railroad, then to a port on Lake Erie, thence by a canal-boat in a tow of several to Port Burwell, in Canada, across the lake, and from there we drove to Vienna, a short distance away. I remember my grandfather perfectly as he appeared, at 102 years of age, when he died. In the middle of the day he sat under a large tree in front of the house facing a well-travelled road. His head was covered completely with a large quantity of very white hair, and he chewed tobacco incessantly, nodding to friends as they passed by. He used a very large cane, and walked from the chair to the house, resenting any assistance. I viewed him from a distance, and could never get very close to him. I remember some large pipes, and especially a molasses jug, a trunk, and several other things that came from Holland."

John Edison was long-lived, like his father, and reached the ripe old age of 102, leaving his son Samuel charged with the care of the family destinies, but with no great burden of wealth. Little is known of the early manhood of this father of T. A. Edison until we find him keeping a hotel at Vienna, marrying a school-teacher there (Miss Nancy Elliott, in 1828), and taking a lively share in the troublous politics of the time. He was six feet in height, of great bodily vigor, and of such personal dominance of character that he became a captain of the insurgent forces rallying under the banners of Papineau and Mackenzie. The opening years of Queen Victoria's reign witnessed a belated effort in Canada to emphasize the principle that there should not be taxation without representation; and this descendant of those who had left the United States from disapproval of such a doctrine, flung himself headlong into its support.

It has been said of Earl Durham, who pacified Canada at this time and established the present system of government, that he made a country and marred a career. But the immediate measures of repression enforced before a liberal policy was adopted were sharp and severe, and Samuel Edison also found his own career marred on Canadian soil as one result of the Durham administration. Exile to Bermuda with other insurgents was not so attractive as the perils of a flight to the United States. A very hurried departure was effected in secret from the scene of trouble, and there are romantic traditions of his thrilling journey of one hundred and eighty-two miles toward safety, made almost entirely without food or sleep, through a wild country infested with Indians of unfriendly disposition. Thus was the Edison family repatriated by a picturesque political episode, and the great inventor given a birthplace on American soil, just as was Benjamin Franklin when his father came from England to Boston. Samuel Edison left behind him, however, in Canada, several brothers, all of whom lived to the age of ninety or more, and from whom there are descendants in the region.

After some desultory wanderings for a year or two along the shores of Lake Erie, among the prosperous towns then springing up, the family, with its Canadian home forfeited, and in quest of another resting-place, came to Milan, Ohio, in 1842. That pretty little village offered at the moment many attractions as a possible Chicago. The railroad system of Ohio was still in the future, but the Western Reserve had already become a vast wheat-field, and huge quantities of grain from the central and northern counties sought shipment to Eastern ports. The Huron River, emptying into Lake Erie, was navigable within a few miles of the village, and provided an admirable outlet. Large granaries were established, and proved so successful that local capital was tempted into the project of making a tow-path canal from Lockwood Landing all the way to Milan itself. The quaint old Moravian mission and quondam Indian settlement of one hundred inhabitants found itself of a sudden one of the great grain ports of the world, and bidding fair to rival Russian Odessa. A number of grain warehouses, or primitive elevators, were built along the bank of the canal, and the produce of the region poured in immediately, arriving in wagons drawn by four or six horses with loads of a hundred bushels. No fewer than six hundred wagons came clattering in, and as many as twenty sail vessels were loaded with thirty-five thousand bushels of grain, during a single day. The canal was capable of being navigated by craft of from two hundred to two hundred and fifty tons burden, and the demand for such vessels soon led to the development of a brisk ship-building industry, for which the abundant forests of the region supplied the necessary lumber. An evidence of the activity in this direction is furnished by the fact that six revenue cutters were launched at this port in these brisk days of its prime.

Samuel Edison, versatile, buoyant of temper, and ever optimistic, would thus appear to have pitched his tent with shrewd judgment. There was plenty of occupation ready to his hand, and more than one enterprise received his attention; but he devoted his energies chiefly to the making of shingles, for which there was a large demand locally and along the lake. Canadian lumber was used principally in this industry. The wood was imported in "bolts" or pieces three feet long. A bolt made two shingles; it was sawn asunder by hand, then split and shaved. None but first-class timber was used, and such shingles outlasted far those made by machinery with their cross-grain cut. A house in Milan, on which some of those shingles were put in 1844, was still in excellent condition forty-two years later. Samuel Edison did well at this occupation, and employed several men, but there were other outlets from time to time for his business activity and speculative disposition.

Edison's mother was an attractive and highly educated woman, whose influence upon his disposition and intellect has been profound and lasting. She was born in Chenango County, New York, in 1810, and was the daughter of the Rev. John Elliott, a Baptist minister and descendant of an old Revolutionary soldier, Capt. Ebenezer Elliott, of Scotch descent. The old captain was a fine and picturesque type. He fought all through the long War of Independence--seven years--and then appears to have settled down at Stonington, Connecticut. There, at any rate, he found his wife, "grandmother Elliott," who was Mercy Peckham, daughter of a Scotch Quaker. Then came the residence in New York State, with final removal to Vienna, for the old soldier, while drawing his pension at Buffalo, lived in the little Canadian town, and there died, over 100 years old. The family was evidently one of considerable culture and deep religious feeling, for two of Mrs. Edison's uncles and two brothers were also in the same Baptist ministry. As a young woman she became a teacher in the public high school at Vienna, and thus met her husband, who was residing there. The family never consisted of more than three children, two boys and a girl. A trace of the Canadian environment is seen in the fact that Edison's elder brother was named William Pitt, after the great English statesman. Both his brother and the sister exhibited considerable ability. William Pitt Edison as a youth was so clever with his pencil that it was proposed to send him to Paris as an art student. In later life he was manager of the local street railway lines at Port Huron, Michigan, in which he was heavily interested. He also owned a good farm near that town, and during the ill-health at the close of his life, when compelled to spend much of the time indoors, he devoted himself almost entirely to sketching. It has been noted by intimate observers of Thomas A. Edison that in discussing any project or new idea his first impulse is to take up any piece of paper available and make drawings of it. His voluminous note-books are a mass of sketches. Mrs-Tannie Edison Bailey, the sister, had, on the other hand, a great deal of literary ability, and spent much of her time in writing.

The great inventor, whose iron endurance and stern will have enabled him to wear down all his associates by work sustained through arduous days and sleepless nights, was not at all strong as a child, and was of fragile appearance. He had an abnormally large but well-shaped head, and it is said that the local doctors feared he might have brain trouble. In fact, on account of his assumed delicacy, he was not allowed to go to school for some years, and even when he did attend for a short time the results were not encouraging--his mother being hotly indignant upon hearing that the teacher had spoken of him to an inspector as "addled." The youth was, indeed, fortunate far beyond the ordinary in having a mother at once loving, well-informed, and ambitious, capable herself, from her experience as a teacher, of undertaking and giving him an education better than could be secured in the local schools of the day. Certain it is that under this simple regime studious habits were formed and a taste for literature developed that have lasted to this day. If ever there was a man who tore the heart out of books it is Edison, and what has once been read by him is never forgotten if useful or worthy of submission to the test of experiment.

But even thus early the stronger love of mechanical processes and of probing natural forces manifested itself. Edison has said that he never saw a statement in any book as to such things that he did not involuntarily challenge, and wish to demonstrate as either right or wrong. As a mere child the busy scenes of the canal and the grain warehouses were of consuming interest, but the work in the ship-building yards had an irresistible fascination. His questions were so ceaseless and innumerable that the penetrating curiosity of an unusually strong mind was regarded as deficiency in powers of comprehension, and the father himself, a man of no mean ingenuity and ability, reports that the child, although capable of reducing him to exhaustion by endless inquiries, was often spoken of as rather wanting in ordinary acumen. This apparent dulness is, however, a quite common incident to youthful genius.

The constructive tendencies of this child of whom his father said once that he had never had any boyhood days in the ordinary sense, were early noted in his fondness for building little plank roads out of the debris of the yards and mills. His extraordinarily retentive memory was shown in his easy acquisition of all the songs of the lumber gangs and canal men before he was five years old. One incident tells how he was found one day in the village square copying laboriously the signs of the stores. A highly characteristic event at the age of six is described by his sister. He had noted a goose sitting on her eggs and the result. One day soon after, he was missing. By-and-by, after an anxious search, his father found him sitting in a nest he had made in the barn, filled with goose-eggs and hens' eggs he had collected, trying to hatch them out.

One of Mr. Edison's most vivid recollections goes back to 1850, when as a child three of four years old he saw camped in front of his home six covered wagons, "prairie schooners," and witnessed their departure for California. The great excitement over the gold discoveries was thus felt in Milan, and these wagons, laden with all the worldly possessions of their owners, were watched out of sight on their long journey by this fascinated urchin, whose own discoveries in later years were to tempt many other argonauts into the auriferous realms of electricity.

Another vivid memory of this period concerns his first realization of the grim mystery of death. He went off one day with the son of the wealthiest man in the town to bathe in the creek. Soon after they entered the water the other boy disappeared. Young Edison waited around the spot for half an hour or more, and then, as it was growing dark, went home puzzled and lonely, but silent as to the occurrence. About two hours afterward, when the missing boy was being searched for, a man came to the Edison home to make anxious inquiry of the companion with whom he had last been seen. Edison told all the circumstances with a painful sense of being in some way implicated. The creek was at once dragged, and then the body was recovered.

Edison had himself more than one narrow escape. Of course he fell in the canal and was nearly drowned; few boys in Milan worth their salt omitted that performance. On another occasion he encountered a more novel peril by falling into the pile of wheat in a grain elevator and being almost smothered. Holding the end of a skate-strap for another lad to shorten with an axe, he lost the top of a finger. Fire also had its perils. He built a fire in a barn, but the flames spread so rapidly that, although he escaped himself, the barn was wholly destroyed, and he was publicly whipped in the village square as a warning to other youths. Equally well remembered is a dangerous encounter with a ram that attacked him while he was busily engaged digging out a bumblebee's nest near an orchard fence. The animal knocked him against the fence, and was about to butt him again when he managed to drop over on the safe side and escape. He was badly hurt and bruised, and no small quantity of arnica was needed for his wounds.

Meantime little Milan had reached the zenith of its prosperity, and all of a sudden had been deprived of its flourishing grain trade by the new Columbus, Sandusky & Hocking Railroad; in fact, the short canal was one of the last efforts of its kind in this country to compete with the new means of transportation. The bell of the locomotive was everywhere ringing the death-knell of effective water haulage, with such dire results that, in 1880, of the 4468 miles of American freight canal, that had cost $214,000,000, no fewer than 1893 miles had been abandoned, and of the remaining 2575 miles quite a large proportion was not paying expenses. The short Milan canal suffered with the rest, and to-day lies well-nigh obliterated, hidden in part by vegetable gardens, a mere grass-grown depression at the foot of the winding, shallow valley. Other railroads also prevented any further competition by the canal, for a branch of the Wheeling & Lake Erie now passes through the village, while the Lake Shore & Michigan Southern runs a few miles to the south.

The owners of the canal soon had occasion to regret that they had disdained the overtures of enterprising railroad promoters desirous of reaching the village, and the consequences of commercial isolation rapidly made themselves felt. It soon became evident to Samuel Edison and his wife that the cozy brick home on the bluff must be given up and the struggle with fortune resumed elsewhere. They were well-to-do, however, and removing, in 1854, to Port Huron, Michigan, occupied a large colonial house standing in the middle of an old Government fort reservation of ten acres overlooking the wide expanse of the St. Clair River just after it leaves Lake Huron. It was in many ways an ideal homestead, toward which the family has always felt the strongest attachment, but the association with Milan has never wholly ceased. The old house in which Edison was born is still occupied (in 1910) by Mr. S. O. Edison, a half-brother of Edison's father, and a man of marked inventive ability. He was once prominent in the iron-furnace industry of Ohio, and was for a time associated in the iron trade with the father of the late President McKinley. Among his inventions may be mentioned a machine for making fuel from wheat straw, and a smoke-consuming device.

This birthplace of Edison remains the plain, substantial little brick house it was originally: one-storied, with rooms finished on the attic floor. Being built on the hillside, its basement opens into the rear yard. It was at first heated by means of open coal grates, which may not have been altogether adequate in severe winters, owing to the altitude and the north-eastern exposure, but a large furnace is one of the more modern changes. Milan itself is not materially unlike the smaller Ohio towns of its own time or those of later creation, but the venerable appearance of the big elm-trees that fringe the trim lawns tells of its age. It is, indeed, an extremely neat, snug little place, with well-kept homes, mostly of frame construction, and flagged streets crossing each other at right angles. There are no poor--at least, everybody is apparently well-to-do. While a leisurely atmosphere pervades the town, few idlers are seen. Some of the residents are engaged in local business; some are occupied in farming and grape culture; others are employed in the iron-works near-by, at Norwalk. The stores and places of public resort are gathered about the square, where there is plenty of room for hitching when the Saturday trading is done at that point, at which periods the fitful bustle recalls the old wheat days when young Edison ran with curiosity among the six and eight horse teams that had brought in grain. This square is still covered with fine primeval forest trees, and has at its centre a handsome soldiers' monument of the Civil War, to which four paved walks converge. It is an altogether pleasant and unpretentious town, which cherishes with no small amount of pride its association with the name of Thomas Alva Edison.

In view of Edison's Dutch descent, it is rather singular to find him with the name of Alva, for the Spanish Duke of Alva was notoriously the worst tyrant ever known to the Low Countries, and his evil deeds occupy many stirring pages in Motley's famous history. As a matter of fact, Edison was named after Capt. Alva Bradley, an old friend of his father, and a celebrated ship-owner on the Lakes. Captain Bradley died a few years ago in wealth, while his old associate, with equal ability for making money, was never able long to keep it (differing again from the Revolutionary New York banker from whom his son's other name, "Thomas," was taken).

CHAPTER III

BOYHOOD AT PORT HURON, MICHIGAN

THE new home found by the Edison family at Port Huron, where Alva spent his brief boyhood before he became a telegraph operator and roamed the whole middle West of that period, was unfortunately destroyed by fire just after the close of the Civil War. A smaller but perhaps more comfortable home was then built by Edison's father on some property he had bought at the near-by village of Gratiot, and there his mother spent the remainder of her life in confirmed invalidism, dying in 1871. Hence the pictures and postal cards sold largely to souvenir-hunters as the Port Huron home do not actually show that in or around which the events now referred to took place.

It has been a romance of popular biographers, based upon the fact that Edison began his career as a newsboy, to assume that these earlier years were spent in poverty and privation, as indeed they usually are by the "newsies" who swarm and shout their papers in our large cities. While it seems a pity to destroy this erroneous idea, suggestive of a heroic climb from the depths to the heights, nothing could be further from the truth. Socially the Edison family stood high in Port Huron at a time when there was relatively more wealth and general activity than to-day. The town in its pristine prime was a great lumber centre, and hummed with the industry of numerous sawmills. An incredible quantity of lumber was made there yearly until the forests near-by vanished and the industry with them. The wealth of the community, invested largely in this business and in allied transportation companies, was accumulated rapidly and as freely spent during those days of prosperity in St. Clair County, bringing with it a high standard of domestic comfort. In all this the Edisons shared on equal terms.

Thus, contrary to the stories that have been so widely published, the Edisons, while not rich by any means, were in comfortable circumstances, with a well-stocked farm and large orchard to draw upon also for sustenance. Samuel Edison, on moving to Port Huron, became a dealer in grain and feed, and gave attention to that business for many years. But he was also active in the lumber industry in the Saginaw district and several other things. It was difficult for a man of such mercurial, restless temperament to stay constant to any one occupation; in fact, had he been less visionary he would have been more prosperous, but might not have had a son so gifted with insight and imagination. One instance of the optimistic vagaries which led him incessantly to spend time and money on projects that would not have appealed to a man less sanguine was the construction on his property of a wooden observation tower over a hundred feet high, the top of which was reached toilsomely by winding stairs, after the payment of twenty-five cents. It is true that the tower commanded a pretty view by land and water, but Colonel Sellers himself might have projected this enterprise as a possible source of steady income. At first few visitors panted up the long flights of steps to the breezy platform. During the first two months Edison's father took in three dollars, and felt extremely blue over the prospect, and to young Edison and his relatives were left the lonely pleasures of the lookout and the enjoyment of the telescope with which it was equipped. But one fine day there came an excursion from an inland town to see the lake. They picnicked in the grove, and six hundred of them went up the tower. After that the railroad company began to advertise these excursions, and the receipts each year paid for the observatory.

It might be thought that, immersed in business and preoccupied with schemes of this character, Mr. Edison was to blame for the neglect of his son's education. But that was not the case. The conditions were peculiar. It was at the Port Huron public school that Edison received all the regular scholastic instruction he ever enjoyed--just three months. He might have spent the full term there, but, as already noted, his teacher had found him "addled." He was always, according to his own recollection, at the foot of the class, and had come almost to regard himself as a dunce, while his father entertained vague anxieties as to his stupidity. The truth of the matter seems to be that Mrs. Edison, a teacher of uncommon ability and force, held no very high opinion of the average public-school methods and results, and was both eager to undertake the instruction of her son and ambitious for the future of a boy whom she knew from pedagogic experience to be receptive and thoughtful to a very unusual degree. With her he found study easy and pleasant. The quality of culture in that simple but refined home, as well as the intellectual character of this youth without schooling, may be inferred from the fact that before he had reached the age of twelve he had read, with his mother's help, Gibbon's Decline and Fall of the Roman Empire, Hume's History of England, Sears' History of the World, Burton's Anatomy of Melancholy, and the Dictionary of Sciences; and had even attempted to struggle through Newton's Principia, whose mathematics were decidedly beyond both teacher and student. Besides, Edison, like Faraday, was never a mathematician, and has had little personal use for arithmetic beyond that which is called "mental." He said once to a friend: "I can always hire some mathematicians, but they can't hire me." His father, by-the-way, always encouraged these literary tastes, and paid him a small sum for each new book mastered. It will be noted that fiction makes no showing in the list; but it was not altogether excluded from the home library, and Edison has all his life enjoyed it, particularly the works of such writers as Victor Hugo, after whom, because of his enthusiastic admiration--possibly also because of his imagination--he was nicknamed by his fellow-operators, "Victor Hugo

Edison."

Electricity at that moment could have no allure for a youthful mind. Crude telegraphy represented what was known of it practically, and about that the books read by young Edison were not redundantly informational. Even had that not been so, the inclinations of the boy barely ten years old were toward chemistry, and fifty years later there is seen no change of predilection. It sounds like heresy to say that Edison became an electrician by chance, but it is the sober fact that to this pre-eminent and brilliant leader in electrical achievement escape into the chemical domain still has the aspect of a delightful truant holiday. One of the earliest stories about his boyhood relates to the incident when he induced a lad employed in the family to swallow a large quantity of Seidlitz powders in the belief that the gases generated would enable him to fly. The agonies of the victim attracted attention, and Edison's mother marked her displeasure by an application of the switch kept behind the old Seth Thomas "grandfather clock." The disastrous result of this experiment did not discourage Edison at all, as he attributed failure to the lad rather than to the motive power. In the cellar of the Edison homestead young Alva soon accumulated a chemical outfit, constituting the first in a long series of laboratories. The word "laboratory" had always been associated with alchemists in the past, but as with "filament" this untutored stripling applied an iconoclastic practicability to it long before he realized the significance of the new departure. Goethe, in his legend of Faust, shows the traditional or conventional philosopher in his laboratory, an aged, tottering, gray-bearded investigator, who only becomes youthful upon diabolical intervention, and would stay senile without it. In the Edison laboratory no such weird transformation has been necessary, for the philosopher had youth, fiery energy, and a grimly practical determination that would submit to no denial of the goal of something of real benefit to mankind. Edison and Faust are indeed the extremes of philosophic thought and accomplishment.

The home at Port Huron thus saw the first Edison laboratory. The boy began experimenting when he was about ten or eleven years of age. He got a copy of Parker's School Philosophy, an elementary book on physics, and about every experiment in it he tried. Young Alva, or "Al," as he was called, thus early displayed his great passion for chemistry, and in the cellar of the house he collected no fewer than two hundred bottles, gleaned in baskets from all parts of the town. These were arranged carefully on shelves and all labelled "Poison," so that no one else would handle or disturb them. They contained the chemicals with which he was constantly experimenting. To others this diversion was both mysterious and meaningless, but he had soon become familiar with all the chemicals obtainable at the local drug stores, and had tested to his satisfaction many of the statements encountered in his scientific reading. Edison has said that sometimes he has wondered how it was he did not become an analytical chemist instead of concentrating on electricity, for which he had at first no great inclination.

Deprived of the use of a large part of her cellar, tiring of the "mess" always to be found there, and somewhat fearful of results, his mother once told the boy to clear everything out and restore order. The thought of losing all his possessions was the cause of so much ardent distress that his mother relented, but insisted that he must get a lock and key, and keep the embryonic laboratory closed up all the time except when he was there. This was done. From such work came an early familiarity with the nature of electrical batteries and the production of current from them. Apparently the greater part of his spare time was spent in the cellar, for he did not share to any extent in the sports of the boys of the neighborhood, his chum and chief companion, Michael Oates, being a lad of Dutch origin, many years older, who did chores around the house, and who could be recruited as a general utility Friday for the experiments of this young explorer--such as that with the Seidlitz powders.

Such pursuits as these consumed the scant pocket-money of the boy very rapidly. He was not in regular attendance at school, and had read all the books within reach. It was thus he turned newsboy, overcoming the reluctance of his parents, particularly that of his mother, by pointing out that he could by this means earn all he wanted for his experiments and get fresh reading in the shape of papers and magazines free of charge. Besides, his leisure hours in Detroit he would be able to spend at the public library. He applied (in 1859) for the privilege of selling newspapers on the trains of the Grand Trunk Railroad, between Port Huron and Detroit, and obtained the concession after a short delay, during which he made an essay in his task of selling newspapers.

Edison had, as a fact, already had some commercial experience from the age of eleven. The ten acres of the reservation offered an excellent opportunity for truck-farming, and the versatile head of the family could not avoid trying his luck in this branch of work. A large "market garden" was laid out, in which Edison worked pretty steadily with the help of the Dutch boy, Michael Oates--he of the flying experiment. These boys had a horse and small wagon intrusted to them, and every morning in the season they would load up with onions, lettuce, peas, etc., and go through the town.

As much as $600 was turned over to Mrs. Edison in one year from this source. The boy was indefatigable but not altogether charmed with agriculture. "After a while I tired of this work, as hoeing corn in a hot sun is unattractive, and I did not wonder that it had built up cities. Soon the Grand Trunk Railroad was extended from Toronto to Port Huron, at the foot of Lake Huron, and thence to Detroit, at about the same time the War of the Rebellion broke out. By a great amount of persistence I got permission from my mother to go on the local train as a newsboy. The local train from Port Huron to Detroit, a distance of sixty-three miles, left at 7 A.M. and arrived again at 9.30 P.M. After being on the train for several months, I started two stores in Port Huron--one for periodicals, and the other for vegetables, butter, and berries in the season. These were attended by two boys who shared in the profits. The periodical store I soon closed, as the boy in charge could not be trusted. The vegetable store I kept up for nearly a year. After the railroad had been opened a short time, they put on an express which left Detroit in the morning and returned in the evening. I received permission to put a newsboy on this train. Connected with this train was a car, one part for baggage and the other part for U. S. mail, but for a long time it was not used. Every morning I had two large baskets of vegetables from the Detroit market loaded in the mail-car and sent to Port Huron, where the boy would take them to the store. They were much better than those grown locally, and sold readily. I never was asked to pay freight, and to this day cannot explain why, except that I was so small and industrious, and the nerve to appropriate a U. S. mail-car to do a free freight business was so monumental. However, I kept this up for a long time, and in addition bought butter from the farmers along the line, and an immense amount of blackberries in the season. I bought wholesale and at a low price, and permitted the wives of the engineers and trainmen to have the benefit of the discount. After a while there was a daily immigrant train put on. This train generally had from seven to ten coaches filled always with Norwegians, all bound for Iowa and Minnesota. On these trains I employed a boy who sold bread, tobacco, and stick candy. As the war progressed the daily newspaper sales became very profitable, and I gave up the vegetable store."

The hours of this occupation were long, but the work was not particularly heavy, and Edison soon found opportunity for his favorite avocation--chemical experimentation. His train left Port Huron at 7 A.M., and made its southward trip to Detroit in about three hours. This gave a stay in that city from 10 A.M. until the late afternoon, when the train left, arriving at Port Huron about 9.30 P.M. The train was made up of three coaches--baggage, smoking, and ordinary passenger or "ladies." The baggage-car was divided into three compartments--one for trunks and packages, one for the mail, and one for smoking. In those days no use was made of the smoking-compartment, as there was no ventilation, and it was turned over to young Edison, who not only kept papers there and his stock of goods as a "candy butcher," but soon had it equipped with an extraordinary variety of apparatus. There was plenty of leisure on the two daily runs, even for an industrious boy, and thus he found time to transfer his laboratory from the cellar and re-establish it on the train.

His earnings were also excellent--so good, in fact, that eight or ten dollars a day were often taken in, and one dollar went every day to his mother. Thus supporting himself, he felt entitled to spend any other profit left over on chemicals and apparatus. And spent it was, for with access to Detroit and its large stores, where he bought his supplies, and to the public library, where he could quench his thirst for technical information, Edison gave up all his spare time and money to chemistry. Surely the country could have presented at that moment no more striking example of the passionate pursuit of knowledge under difficulties than this newsboy, barely fourteen years of age, with his jars and test-tubes installed on a railway baggage-car.

Nor did this amazing equipment stop at batteries and bottles. The same little space a few feet square was soon converted by this precocious youth into a newspaper office. The outbreak of the Civil War gave a great stimulus to the demand for all newspapers, noticing which he became ambitious to publish a local journal of his own, devoted to the news of that section of the Grand Trunk road. A small printing-press that had been used for hotel bills of fare was picked up in Detroit, and type was also bought, some of it being placed on the train so that composition could go on in spells of leisure. To one so mechanical in his tastes as Edison, it was quite easy to learn the rudiments of the printing art, and thus the Weekly Herald came into existence, of which he was compositor, pressman, editor, publisher, and newsdealer. Only one or two copies of this journal are now discoverable, but its appearance can be judged from the reduced facsimile here shown. The thing was indeed well done as the work of a youth shown by the date to be less than fifteen years old. The literary style is good, there are only a few trivial slips in spelling, and the appreciation is keen of what would be interesting news and gossip. The price was three cents a copy, or eight cents a month for regular subscribers, and the circulation ran up to over four hundred copies an issue. This was by no means the result of mere public curiosity, but attested the value of the sheet as a genuine newspaper, to which many persons in the railroad service along the line were willing contributors. Indeed, with the aid of the railway telegraph, Edison was often able to print late news of importance, of local origin, that the distant regular papers like those of Detroit, which he handled as a newsboy, could not get. It is no wonder that this clever little sheet received the approval and patronage of the English engineer Stephenson when inspecting the Grand Trunk system, and was noted by no less distinguished a contemporary than the London Times as the first newspaper in the world to be printed on a train in motion. The youthful proprietor sometimes cleared as much as twenty to thirty dollars a month from this unique journalistic enterprise.

But all this extra work required attention, and Edison solved the difficulty of attending also to the newsboy business by the employment of a young friend, whom he trained and treated liberally as an understudy. There was often plenty of work for both in the early days of the war, when the news of battle caused intense excitement and large sales of papers. Edison, with native shrewdness already so strikingly displayed, would telegraph the station agents and get them to bulletin the event of the day at the front, so that when each station was reached there were eager purchasers waiting. He recalls in particular the sensation caused by the great battle of Shiloh, or Pittsburg Landing, in April, 1862, in which both Grant and Sherman were engaged, in which Johnston died, and in which there was a ghastly total of 25,000 killed and wounded.

In describing his enterprising action that day, Edison says that when he reached Detroit the bulletin-boards of the newspaper offices were surrounded with dense crowds, which read awestricken the news that there were 60,000 killed and wounded, and that the result was uncertain. "I knew that if the same excitement was attained at the various small towns along the road, and especially at Port Huron, the sale of papers would be great. I then conceived the idea of telegraphing the news ahead, went to the operator in the depot, and by giving him Harper's Weekly and some other papers for three months, he agreed to telegraph to all the stations the matter on the bulletin-board. I hurriedly copied it, and he sent it, requesting the agents to display it on the blackboards used for stating the arrival and departure of trains. I decided that instead of the usual one hundred papers I could sell one thousand; but not having sufficient money to purchase that number, I determined in my desperation to see the editor himself and get credit. The great paper at that time was the Detroit Free Press. I walked into the office marked 'Editorial' and told a young man that I wanted to see the editor on important business--important to me, anyway, I was taken into an office where there were two men, and I stated what I had done about telegraphing, and that I wanted a thousand papers, but only had money for three hundred, and I wanted credit. One of the men refused it, but the other told the first spokesman to let me have them. This man, I afterward learned, was Wilbur F. Storey, who subsequently founded the Chicago Times, and became celebrated in the newspaper world. By the aid of another boy I lugged the papers to the train and started folding them. The first station, called Utica, was a small one where I generally sold two papers. I saw a crowd ahead on the platform, and thought it some excursion, but the moment I landed there was a rush for me; then I realized that the telegraph was a great invention. I sold thirty-five papers there. The next station was Mount Clemens, now a watering-place, but then a town of about one thousand. I usually sold six to eight papers there. I decided that if I found a corresponding crowd there, the only thing to do to correct my lack of judgment in not getting more papers was to raise the price from five cents to ten. The crowd was there, and I raised the price. At the various towns there were corresponding crowds. It had been my practice at Port Huron to jump from the train at a point about one-fourth of a mile from the station, where the train generally slackened speed. I had drawn several loads of sand to this point to jump on, and had become quite expert. The little Dutch boy with the horse met me at this point. When the wagon approached the outskirts of the town I was met by a large crowd. I then yelled: 'Twenty-five cents apiece, gentlemen! I haven't enough to go around!' I sold all out, and made what to me then was an immense sum of money."

Such episodes as this added materially to his income, but did not necessarily increase his savings, for he was then, as now, an utter spendthrift so long as some new apparatus or supplies for experiment could be had. In fact, the laboratory on wheels soon became crowded with such equipment, most costly chemicals were bought on the instalment plan, and Fresenius' Qualitative Analysis served as a basis for ceaseless testing and study. George Pullman, who then had a small shop at Detroit and was working on his sleeping-car, made Edison a lot of wooden apparatus for his chemicals, to the boy's delight. Unfortunately a sudden change came, fraught with disaster. The train, running one day at thirty miles an hour over a piece of poorly laid track, was thrown suddenly out of the perpendicular with a violent lurch, and, before Edison could catch it, a stick of phosphorus was jarred from its shelf, fell to the floor, and burst into flame. The car took fire, and the boy, in dismay, was still trying to quench the blaze when the conductor, a quick-tempered Scotchman, who acted also as baggage-master, hastened to the scene with water and saved his car. On the arrival at Mount Clemens station, its next stop, Edison and his entire outfit, laboratory, printing-plant, and all, were promptly ejected by the enraged conductor, and the train then moved off, leaving him on the platform, tearful and indignant in the midst of his beloved but ruined possessions. It was lynch law of a kind; but in view of the responsibility, this action of the conductor lay well within his rights and duties.

It was through this incident that Edison acquired the deafness that has persisted all through his life, a severe box on the ears from the scorched and angry conductor being the direct cause of the infirmity. Although this deafness would be regarded as a great affliction by most people, and has brought in its train other serious baubles, Mr. Edison has always regarded it philosophically, and said about it recently: "This deafness has been of great advantage to me in various ways. When in a telegraph office, I could only hear the instrument directly on the table at which I sat, and unlike the other operators, I was not bothered by the other instruments. Again, in experimenting on the telephone, I had to improve the transmitter so I could hear it. This made the telephone commercial, as the magneto telephone receiver of Bell was too weak to be used as a transmitter commercially. It was the same with the phonograph. The great defect of that instrument was the rendering of the overtones in music, and the hissing consonants in speech. I worked over one year, twenty hours a day, Sundays and all, to get the word 'specie' perfectly recorded and reproduced on the phonograph. When this was done I knew that everything else could be done which was a fact. Again, my nerves have been preserved intact. Broadway is as quiet to me as a country village is to a person with normal hearing."

Saddened but not wholly discouraged, Edison soon reconstituted his laboratory and printing-office at home, although on the part of the family there was some fear and objection after this episode, on the score of fire. But Edison promised not to bring in anything of a dangerous nature. He did not cease the publication of the Weekly Herald. On the contrary, he prospered in both his enterprises until persuaded by the "printer's devil" in the office of the Port Huron Commercial to change the character of his journal, enlarge it, and issue it under the name of Paul Pry, a happy designation for this or kindred ventures in the domain of society journalism. No copies of Paul Pry can now be found, but it is known that its style was distinctly personal, that gossip was its specialty, and that no small offence was given to the people whose peculiarities or peccadilloes were discussed in a frank and breezy style by the two boys. In one instance the resentment of the victim of such unsought publicity was so intense he laid hands on Edison and pitched the startled young editor into the St. Clair River. The name of this violator of the freedom of the press was thereafter excluded studiously from the columns of Paul Pry, and the incident may have been one of those which soon caused the abandonment of the paper. Edison had great zest in this work, and but for the strong influences in other directions would probably have continued in the newspaper field, in which he was, beyond question, the youngest publisher and editor of the day.

Before leaving this period of his career, it is to be noted that it gave Edison many favorable opportunities. In Detroit he could spend frequent hours in the public library, and it is matter of record that he began his liberal acquaintance with its contents by grappling bravely with a certain section and trying to read it through consecutively, shelf by shelf, regardless of subject. In a way this is curiously suggestive of the earnest, energetic method of "frontal attack" with which the inventor has since addressed himself to so many problems in the arts and sciences.

The Grand Trunk Railroad machine-shops at Port Huron were a great attraction to the boy, who appears to have spent a good deal of his time there. He who was to have much to do with the evolution of the modern electric locomotive was fascinated by the mechanism of the steam locomotive; and whenever he could get the chance Edison rode in the cab with the engineer of his train. He became thoroughly familiar with the intricacies of fire-box, boiler, valves, levers, and gears, and liked nothing better than to handle the locomotive himself during the run. On one trip, when the engineer lay asleep while his eager substitute piloted the train, the boiler "primed," and a deluge overwhelmed the young driver, who stuck to his post till the run and the ordeal were ended. Possibly this helped to spoil a locomotive engineer, but went to make a great master of the new motive power. "Steam is half an Englishman," said Emerson. The temptation is strong to say that workaday electricity is half an American. Edison's own account of the incident is very laughable: "The engine was one of a number leased to the Grand Trunk by the Chicago, Burlington & Quincy. It had bright brass bands all over, the woodwork beautifully painted, and everything highly polished, which was the custom up to the time old Commodore Vanderbilt stopped it on his roads. After running about fifteen miles the fireman couldn't keep his eyes open (this event followed an all-night dance of the trainmen's fraternal organization), and he agreed to permit me to run the engine. I took charge, reducing the speed to about twelve miles an hour, and brought the train of seven cars to her destination at the Grand Trunk junction safely. But something occurred which was very much out of the ordinary. I was very much worried about the water, and I knew that if it got low the boiler was likely to explode. I hadn't gone twenty miles before black damp mud blew out of the stack and covered every part of the engine, including myself. I was about to awaken the fireman to find out the cause of this when it stopped. Then I approached a station where the fireman always went out to the cowcatcher, opened the oil-cup on the steam-chest, and poured oil in. I started to carry out the procedure when, upon opening the oil-cup, the steam rushed out with a tremendous noise, nearly knocking me off the engine. I succeeded in closing the oil-cup and got back in the cab, and made up my mind that she would pull through without oil. I learned afterward that the engineer always shut off steam when the fireman went out to oil. This point I failed to notice. My powers of observation were very much improved after this occurrence. Just before I reached the junction another outpour of black mud occurred, and the whole engine was a sight--so much so that when I pulled into the yard everybody turned to see it, laughing immoderately. I found the reason of the mud was that I carried so much water it passed over into the stack, and this washed out all the accumulated soot."

One afternoon about a week before Christmas Edison's train jumped the track near Utica, a station on the line. Four old Michigan Central cars with rotten sills collapsed in the ditch and went all to pieces, distributing figs, raisins, dates, and candies all over the track and the vicinity. Hating to see so much waste, Edison tried to save all he could by eating it on the spot, but as a result "our family doctor had the time of his life with me in this connection."

An absurd incident described by Edison throws a vivid light on the free-and-easy condition of early railroad travel and on the Southern extravagance of the time. "In 1860, just before the war broke out there came to the train one afternoon, in Detroit, two fine-looking young men accompanied by a colored servant. They bought tickets for Port Huron, the terminal point for the train. After leaving the junction just outside of Detroit, I brought in the evening papers. When I came opposite the two young men, one of them said: 'Boy, what have you got?' I said: 'Papers.' 'All right.' He took them and threw them out of the window, and, turning to the colored man, said: 'Nicodemus, pay this boy.' I told Nicodemus the amount, and he opened a satchel and paid me. The passengers didn't know what to make of the transaction. I returned with the illustrated papers and magazines. These were seized and thrown out of the window, and I was told to get my money of Nicodemus. I then returned with all the old magazines and novels I had not been able to sell, thinking perhaps this would be too much for them. I was small and thin, and the layer reached above my head, and was all I could possibly carry. I had prepared a list, and knew the amount in case they bit again. When I opened the door, all the passengers roared with laughter. I walked right up to the young men. One asked me what I had. I said 'Magazines and novels.' He promptly threw them out of the window, and Nicodemus settled. Then I came in with cracked hickory nuts, then pop-corn balls, and, finally, molasses candy. All went out of the window. I felt like Alexander the Great!--I had no more chance! I had sold all I had. Finally I put a rope to my trunk, which was about the size of a carpenter's chest, and started to pull this from the baggage-car to the passenger-car. It was almost too much for my strength, but at last I got it in front of those men. I pulled off my coat, shoes, and hat, and laid them on the chest. Then he asked: 'What have you got, boy?' I said: 'Everything, sir, that I can spare that is for sale.' The passengers fairly jumped with laughter. Nicodemus paid me $27 for this last sale, and threw the whole out of the door in the rear of the car. These men were from the South, and I have always retained a soft spot in my heart for a Southern gentleman."

While Edison was a newsboy on the train a request came to him one day to go to the office of E. B. Ward & Company, at that time the largest owners of steamboats on the Great Lakes. The captain of their largest boat had died suddenly, and they wanted a message taken to another captain who lived about fourteen miles from Ridgeway station on the railroad. This captain had retired, taken up some lumber land, and had cleared part of it. Edison was offered $15 by Mr. Ward to go and fetch him, but as it was a wild country and would be dark, Edison stood out for $25, so that he could get the companionship of another lad. The terms were agreed to. Edison arrived at Ridgeway at 8.30 P.M., when it was raining and as dark as ink. Getting another boy with difficulty to volunteer, he launched out on his errand in the pitch-black night. The two boys carried lanterns, but the road was a rough path through dense forest. The country was wild, and it was a usual occurrence to see deer, bear, and coon skins nailed up on the sides of houses to dry. Edison had read about bears, but couldn't remember whether they were day or night prowlers. The farther they went the more apprehensive they became, and every stump in the ravished forest looked like a bear. The other lad proposed seeking safety up a tree, but Edison demurred on the plea that bears could climb, and that the message must be delivered that night to enable the captain to catch the morning train. First one lantern went out, then the other. "We leaned up against a tree and cried. I thought if I ever got out of that scrape alive I would know more about the habits of animals and everything else, and be prepared for all kinds of mischance when I undertook an enterprise. However, the intense darkness dilated the pupils of our eyes so as to make them very sensitive, and we could just see at times the outlines of the road. Finally, just as a faint gleam of daylight arrived, we entered the captain's yard and delivered the message. In my whole life I never spent such a night of horror as this, but I got a good lesson."

An amusing incident of this period is told by Edison. "When I was a boy," he says, "the Prince of Wales, the late King Edward, came to Canada (1860). Great preparations were made at Sarnia, the Canadian town opposite Port Huron. About every boy, including myself, went over to see the affair. The town was draped in flags most profusely, and carpets were laid on the cross-walks for the prince to walk on. There were arches, etc. A stand was built raised above the general level, where the prince was to be received by the mayor. Seeing all these preparations, my idea of a prince was very high; but when he did arrive I mistook the Duke of Newcastle for him, the duke being a fine-looking man. I soon saw that I was mistaken: that the prince was a young stripling, and did not meet expectations. Several of us expressed our belief that a prince wasn't much, after all, and said that we were thoroughly disappointed. For this one boy was whipped. Soon the Canuck boys attacked the Yankee boys, and we were all badly licked. I, myself, got a black eye. That has always prejudiced me against that kind of ceremonial and folly." It is certainly interesting to note that in later years the prince for whom Edison endured the ignominy of a black eye made generous compensation in a graceful letter accompanying the gold Albert Medal awarded by the Royal Society of Arts.

Another incident of the period is as follows: "After selling papers in Port Huron, which was often not reached until about 9.30 at night, I seldom got home before 11.00 or 11.30. About half-way home from the station and the town, and within twenty-five feet of the road in a dense wood, was a soldiers' graveyard where three hundred soldiers were buried, due to a cholera epidemic which took place at Fort Gratiot, near by, many years previously. At first we used to shut our eyes and run the horse past this graveyard, and if the horse stepped on a twig my heart would give a violent movement, and it is a wonder that I haven't some valvular disease of that organ. But soon this running of the horse became monotonous, and after a while all fears of graveyards absolutely disappeared from my system. I was in the condition of Sam Houston, the pioneer and founder of Texas, who, it was said, knew no fear. Houston lived some distance from the town and generally went home late at night, having to pass through a dark cypress swamp over a corduroy road. One night, to test his alleged fearlessness, a man stationed himself behind a tree and enveloped himself in a sheet. He confronted Houston suddenly, and Sam stopped and said: 'If you are a man, you can't hurt me. If you are a ghost, you don't want to hurt me. And if you are the devil, come home with me; I married your sister!'"

It is not to be inferred, however, from some of the preceding statements that the boy was of an exclusively studious bent of mind. He had then, as now, the keen enjoyment of a joke, and no particular aversion to the practical form. An incident of the time is in point. "After the breaking out of the war there was a regiment of volunteer soldiers quartered at Fort Gratiot, the reservation extending to the boundary line of our house. Nearly every night we would hear a call, such as 'Corporal of the Guard, No. 1.' This would be repeated from sentry to sentry until it reached the barracks, when Corporal of the Guard, No. 1, would come and see what was wanted. I and the little Dutch boy, after returning from the town after selling our papers, thought we would take a hand at military affairs. So one night, when it was very dark, I shouted for Corporal of the Guard, No. 1. The second sentry, thinking it was the terminal sentry who shouted, repeated it to the third, and so on. This brought the corporal along the half mile, only to find that he was fooled. We tried him three nights; but the third night they were watching, and caught the little Dutch boy, took him to the lock-up at the fort, and shut him up. They chased me to the house. I rushed for the cellar. In one small apartment there were two barrels of potatoes and a third one nearly empty. I poured these remnants into the other barrels, sat down, and pulled the barrel over my head, bottom up. The soldiers had awakened my father, and they were searching for me with candles and lanterns. The corporal was absolutely certain I came into the cellar, and couldn't see how I could have gotten out, and wanted to know from my father if there was no secret hiding-place. On assurance of my father, who said that there was not, he said it was most extraordinary. I was glad when they left, as I was cramped, and the potatoes were rotten that had been in the barrel and violently offensive. The next morning I was found in bed, and received a good switching on the legs from my father, the first and only one I ever received from him, although my mother kept a switch behind the old Seth Thomas clock that had the bark worn off. My mother's ideas and mine differed at times, especially when I got experimenting and mussed up things. The Dutch boy was released next morning."

CHAPTER IV

THE YOUNG TELEGRAPH OPERATOR

"WHILE a newsboy on the railroad," says Edison, "I got very much interested in electricity, probably from visiting telegraph offices with a chum who had tastes similar to mine." It will also have been noted that he used the telegraph to get items for his little journal, and to bulletin his special news of the Civil War along the line. The next step was natural, and having with his knowledge of chemistry no trouble about "setting up" his batteries, the difficulties of securing apparatus were chiefly those connected with the circuits and the instruments. American youths to-day are given, if of a mechanical turn of mind, to amateur telegraphy or telephony, but seldom, if ever, have to make any part of the system constructed. In Edison's boyish days it was quite different, and telegraphic supplies were hard to obtain. But he and his "chum" had a line between their homes, built of common stove-pipe wire. The insulators were bottles set on nails driven into trees and short poles.

The magnet wire was wound with rags for insulation, and pieces of spring brass were used for keys. With an idea of securing current cheaply, Edison applied the little that he knew about static electricity, and actually experimented with cats, which he treated vigorously as frictional machines until the animals fled in dismay, and Edison had learned his first great lesson in the relative value of sources of electrical energy. The line was made to work, however, and additional to the messages that the boys interchanged, Edison secured practice in an ingenious manner. His father insisted on 11.30 as proper bedtime, which left but a short interval after the long day on the train. But each evening, when the boy went home with a bundle of papers that had not been sold in the town, his father would sit up reading the "returnables." Edison, therefore, on some excuse, left the papers with his friend, but suggested that he could get the news from him by telegraph, bit by bit. The scheme interested his father, and was put into effect, the messages being written down and handed over for perusal. This yielded good practice nightly, lasting until 12 and 1 o'clock, and was maintained for some time until Mr. Edison became willing that his son should stay up for a reasonable time. The papers were then brought home again, and the boys amused themselves to their hearts' content until the line was pulled down by a stray cow wandering through the orchard. Meantime better instruments had been secured, and the rudiments of telegraphy had been fairly mastered.

The mixed train on which Edison was employed as newsboy did the way-freight work and shunting at the Mount Clemens station, about half an hour being usually spent in the work. One August morning, in 1862, while the shunting was in progress, and a laden box-car had been pushed out of a siding, Edison, who was loitering about the platform, saw the little son of the station agent, Mr. J. U. Mackenzie, playing with the gravel on the main track along which the car without a brakeman was rapidly approaching. Edison dropped his papers and his glazed cap, and made a dash for the child, whom he picked up and lifted to safety without a second to spare, as the wheel of the car struck his heel; and both were cut about the face and hands by the gravel ballast on which they fell. The two boys were picked up by the train-hands and carried to the platform, and the grateful father at once offered to teach the rescuer, whom he knew and liked, the art of train telegraphy and to make an operator of him. It is needless to say that the proposal was eagerly accepted.

Edison found time for his new studies by letting one of his friends look after the newsboy work on the train for part of the trip, reserving to himself the run between Port Huron and Mount Clemens. That he was already well qualified as a beginner is evident from the fact that he had mastered the Morse code of the telegraphic alphabet, and was able to take to the station a neat little set of instruments he had just finished with his own hands at a gun-shop in Detroit. This was probably a unique achievement in itself among railway operators of that day or of later times. The drill of the student involved chiefly the acquisition of the special signals employed in railway work, including the numerals and abbreviations applied to save time. Some of these have passed into the slang of the day, "73" being well known as a telegrapher's expression of compliments or good wishes, while "23" is an accident or death message, and has been given broader popular significance as a general synonym for "hoodoo." All of this came easily to Edison, who had, moreover, as his Herald showed, an unusual familiarity with train movement along that portion of the Grand Trunk road.

Three or four months were spent pleasantly and profitably by the youth in this course of study, and Edison took to it enthusiastically, giving it no less than eighteen hours a day. He then put up a little telegraph line from the station to the village, a distance of about a mile, and opened an office in a drug store; but the business was naturally very small. The telegraph operator at Port Huron knowing of his proficiency, and wanting to get into the United States Military Telegraph Corps, where the pay in those days of the Civil War was high, succeeded in convincing his brother-in-law, Mr. M. Walker, that young Edison could fill the position. Edison was, of course, well acquainted with the operators along the road and at the southern terminal, and took up his new duties very easily. The office was located in a jewelry store, where newspapers and periodicals were also sold. Edison was to be found at the office both day and night, sleeping there. "I became quite valuable to Mr. Walker. After working all day I worked at the office nights as well, for the reason that 'press report' came over one of the wires until 3 A.M., and I would cut in and copy it as well as I could, to become more rapidly proficient. The goal of the rural telegraph operator was to be able to take press. Mr. Walker tried to get my father to apprentice me at $20 per month, but they could not agree. I then applied for a job on the Grand Trunk Railroad as a railway operator, and was given a place, nights, at Stratford Junction, Canada." Apparently his friend Mackenzie helped him in the matter. The position carried a salary of $25 per month. No serious objections were raised by his family, for the distance from Port Huron was not great, and Stratford was near Bayfield, the old home from which the Edisons had come, so that there were doubtless friends or even relatives in the vicinity. This was in 1863.

Mr. Walker was an observant man, who has since that time installed a number of waterworks systems and obtained several patents of his own. He describes the boy of sixteen as engrossed intensely in his experiments and scientific reading, and somewhat indifferent, for this reason, to his duties as operator. This office was not particularly busy, taking from $50 to $75 a month, but even the messages taken in would remain unsent on the hook while Edison was in the cellar below trying to solve some chemical problem. The manager would see him studying sometimes an article in such a paper as the Scientific American, and then disappearing to buy a few sundries for experiments. Returning from the drug store with his chemicals, he would not be seen again until required by his duties, or until he had found out for himself, if possible, in this offhand manner, whether what he had read was correct or not. When he had completed his experiment all interest in it was lost, and the jars and wires would be left to any fate that might befall them. In like manner Edison would make free use of the watchmaker's tools that lay on the little table in the front window, and would take the wire pliers there without much thought as to their value as distinguished from a lineman's tools. The one idea was to do quickly what he wanted to do; and the same swift, almost headlong trial of anything that comes to hand, while the fervor of a new experiment is felt, has been noted at all stages of the inventor's career. One is reminded of Palissy's recklessness, when in his efforts to make the enamel melt on his pottery he used the very furniture of his home for firewood.

Mr. Edison remarks the fact that there was very little difference between the telegraph of that time and of to-day, except the general use of the old Morse register with the dots and dashes recorded by indenting paper strips that could be read and checked later at leisure if necessary. He says: "The telegraph men couldn't explain how it worked, and I was always trying to get them to do so. I think they couldn't. I remember the best explanation I got was from an old Scotch line repairer employed by the Montreal Telegraph Company, which operated the railroad wires. He said that if you had a dog like a dachshund, long enough to reach from Edinburgh to London, if you pulled his tail in Edinburgh he would bark in London. I could understand that, but I never could get it through me what went through the dog or over the wire." To-day Mr. Edison is just as unable to solve the inner mystery of electrical transmission. Nor is he alone. At the banquet given to celebrate his jubilee in 1896 as professor at Glasgow University, Lord Kelvin, the greatest physicist of our time, admitted with tears in his eyes and the note of tragedy in his voice, that when it came to explaining the nature of electricity, he knew just as little as when he had begun as a student, and felt almost as though his life had been wasted while he tried to grapple with the great mystery of physics.

Another episode of this period is curious in its revelation of the tenacity with which Edison has always held to some of his oldest possessions with a sense of personal attachment. "While working at Stratford Junction," he says, "I was told by one of the freight conductors that in the freight-house at Goodrich there were several boxes of old broken-up batteries. I went there and found over eighty cells of the well-known Grove nitric-acid battery. The operator there, who was also agent, when asked by me if I could have the electrodes of each cell, made of sheet platinum, gave his permission readily, thinking they were of tin. I removed them all, amounting to several ounces. Platinum even in those days was very expensive, costing several dollars an ounce, and I owned only three small strips. I was overjoyed at this acquisition, and those very strips and the reworked scrap are used to this day in my laboratory over forty years later."

It was at Stratford that Edison's inventiveness was first displayed. The hours of work of a night operator are usually from 7 P.M. to 7 A.M., and to insure attention while on duty it is often provided that the operator every hour, from 9 P.M. until relieved by the day operator, shall send in the signal "6" to the train dispatcher's office. Edison revelled in the opportunity for study and experiment given him by his long hours of freedom in the daytime, but needed sleep, just as any healthy youth does. Confronted by the necessity of sending in this watchman's signal as evidence that he was awake and on duty, he constructed a small wheel with notches on the rim, and attached it to the clock in such a manner that the night-watchman could start it when the line was quiet, and at each hour the wheel revolved and sent in accurately the dots required for "sixing." The invention was a success, the device being, indeed, similar to that of the modern district messenger box; but it was soon noticed that, in spite of the regularity of the report, "Sf" could not be raised even if a train message were sent immediately after. Detection and a reprimand came in due course, but were not taken very seriously.

A serious occurrence that might have resulted in accident drove him soon after from Canada, although the youth could hardly be held to blame for it. Edison says: "This night job just suited me, as I could have the whole day to myself. I had the faculty of sleeping in a chair any time for a few minutes at a time. I taught the night-yardman my call, so I could get half an hour's sleep now and then between trains, and in case the station was called the watchman would awaken me. One night I got an order to hold a freight train, and I replied that I would. I rushed out to find the signalman, but before I could find him and get the signal set, the train ran past. I ran to the telegraph office, and reported that I could not hold her. The reply was: 'Hell!' The train dispatcher, on the strength of my message that I would hold the train, had permitted another to leave the last station in the opposite direction. There was a lower station near the junction where the day operator slept. I started for it on foot. The night was dark, and I fell into a culvert and was knocked senseless." Owing to the vigilance of the two engineers on the locomotives, who saw each other approaching on the straight single track, nothing more dreadful happened than a summons to the thoughtless operator to appear before the general manager at Toronto. On reaching the manager's office, his trial for neglect of duty was fortunately interrupted by the call of two Englishmen; and while their conversation proceeded, Edison slipped quietly out of the room, hurried to the Grand Trunk freight depot, found a conductor he knew taking out a freight train for Sarnia, and was not happy until the ferry-boat from Sarnia had landed him once more on the Michigan shore. The Grand Trunk still owes Mr. Edison the wages due him at the time he thus withdrew from its service, but the claim has never been pressed.

The same winter of 1863-64, while at Port Huron, Edison had a further opportunity of displaying his ingenuity. An ice-jam had broken the light telegraph cable laid in the bed of the river across to Sarnia, and thus communication was interrupted. The river is three-quarters of a mile wide, and could not be crossed on foot; nor could the cable be repaired. Edison at once suggested using the steam whistle of the locomotive, and by manipulating the valve conversed the short and long outbursts of shrill sound into the Morse code. An operator on the Sarnia shore was quick enough to catch the significance of the strange whistling, and messages were thus sent in wireless fashion across the ice-floes in the river. It is said that such signals were also interchanged by military telegraphers during the war, and possibly Edison may have heard of the practice; but be that as it may, he certainly showed ingenuity and resource in applying such a method to meet the necessity. It is interesting to note that at this point the Grand Trunk now has its St. Clair tunnel, through which the trains are hauled under the river-bed by electric locomotives.

Edison had now begun unconsciously the roaming and drifting that took him during the next five years all over the Middle States, and that might well have wrecked the career of any one less persistent and industrious. It was a period of his life corresponding to the

Wanderjahre of the German artisan, and was an easy way of gratifying a taste for travel without the risk of privation. To-day there is little temptation to the telegrapher to go to distant parts of the country on the chance that he may secure a livelihood at the key. The ranks are well filled everywhere, and of late years the telegraph as an art or industry has shown relatively slight expansion, owing chiefly to the development of telephony. Hence, if vacancies occur, there are plenty of operators available, and salaries have remained so low as to lead to one or two formidable and costly strikes that unfortunately took no account of the economic conditions of demand and supply. But in the days of the Civil War there was a great dearth of skilful manipulators of the key. About fifteen hundred of the best operators in the country were at the front on the Federal side alone, and several hundred more had enlisted. This created a serious scarcity, and a nomadic operator going to any telegraphic centre would be sure to find a place open waiting for him. At the close of the war a majority of those who had been with the two opposed armies remained at the key under more peaceful surroundings, but the rapid development of the commercial and railroad systems fostered a new demand, and then for a time it seemed almost impossible to train new operators fast enough. In a few years, however, the telephone sprang into vigorous existence, dating from 1876, drawing off some of the most adventurous spirits from the telegraph field; and the deterrent influence of the telephone on the telegraph had made itself felt by 1890. The expiration of the leading Bell telephone patents, five years later, accentuated even more sharply the check that had been put on telegraphy, as hundreds and thousands of "independent" telephone companies were then organized, throwing a vast network of toll lines over Ohio, Indiana, Illinois, Iowa, and other States, and affording cheap, instantaneous means of communication without any necessity for the intervention of an operator.

It will be seen that the times have changed radically since Edison became a telegrapher, and that in this respect a chapter of electrical history has been definitely closed. There was a day when the art offered a distinct career to all of its practitioners, and young men of ambition and good family were eager to begin even as messenger boys, and were ready to undergo a severe ordeal of apprenticeship with the belief that they could ultimately attain positions of responsibility and profit. At the same time operators have always been shrewd enough to regard the telegraph as a stepping-stone to other careers in life. A bright fellow entering the telegraph service to-day finds the experience he may gain therein valuable, but he soon realizes that there are not enough good-paying official positions to "go around," so as to give each worthy man a chance after he has mastered the essentials of the art. He feels, therefore, that to remain at the key involves either stagnation or deterioration, and that after, say, twenty-five years of practice he will have lost ground as compared with friends who started out in other occupations. The craft of an operator, learned without much difficulty, is very attractive to a youth, but a position at the key is no place for a man of mature years. His services, with rare exceptions, grow less valuable as he advances in age and nervous strain breaks him down. On the contrary, men engaged in other professions find, as a rule, that they improve and advance with experience, and that age brings larger rewards and opportunities.

The list of well-known Americans who have been graduates of the key is indeed an extraordinary one, and there is no department of our national life in which they have not distinguished themselves. The contrast, in this respect, between them and their European colleagues is highly significant. In Europe the telegraph systems are all under government management, the operators have strictly limited spheres of promotion, and at the best the transition from one kind of employment to another is not made so easily as in the New World. But in the United States we have seen Rufus Bullock become Governor of Georgia, and Ezra Cornell Governor of New York. Marshall Jewell was Postmaster-General of President Grant's Cabinet, and Daniel Lamont was Secretary of State in President Cleveland's. Gen. T. T. Eckert, past-President of the Western Union Telegraph Company, was Assistant Secretary of War under President Lincoln; and Robert J. Wynne, afterward a consul-general, served as Assistant Postmaster General. A very large proportion of the presidents and leading officials of the great railroad systems are old telegraphers, including Messrs. W. C. Brown, President of the New York Central Railroad, and Marvin Hughitt, President of the Chicago & North western Railroad. In industrial and financial life there have been Theodore N. Vail, President of the Bell telephone system; L. C. Weir, late President of the Adams Express; A. B. Chandler, President of the Postal Telegraph and Cable Company; Sir W. Van Home, identified with Canadian development; Robert C. Clowry, President of the Western Union Telegraph Company; D. H. Bates, Manager of the Baltimore & Ohio telegraph for Robert Garrett; and Andrew Carnegie, the greatest ironmaster the world has ever known, as well as its greatest philanthropist. In journalism there have been leaders like Edward Rosewater, founder of the Omaha Bee; W. J. Elverson, of the Philadelphia Press; and Frank A. Munsey, publisher of half a dozen big magazines. George Kennan has achieved fame in literature, and Guy Carleton and Harry de Souchet have been successful as dramatists. These are but typical of hundreds of men who could be named who have risen from work at the key to become recognized leaders in differing spheres of activity.

But roving has never been favorable to the formation of steady habits. The young men who thus floated about the country from one telegraph office to another were often brilliant operators, noted for speed in sending and receiving, but they were undisciplined, were without the restraining influences of home life, and were so highly paid for their work that they could indulge freely in dissipation if inclined that way. Subjected to nervous tension for hours together at the key, many of them unfortunately took to drink, and having ended one engagement in a city by a debauch that closed the doors of the office to them, would drift away to the nearest town, and there securing work, would repeat the performance. At one time, indeed, these men were so numerous and so much in evidence as to constitute a type that the public was disposed to accept as representative of the telegraphic fraternity; but as the conditions creating him ceased to exist, the "tramp operator" also passed into history. It was, however, among such characters that Edison was very largely thrown in these early days of aimless drifting, to learn something perhaps of their nonchalant philosophy of life, sharing bed and board with them under all kinds of adverse conditions, but always maintaining a stoic abstemiousness, and never feeling other than a keen regret at the waste of so much genuine ability and kindliness on the part of those knights errant of the key whose inevitable fate might so easily have been his own.

Such a class or group of men can always be presented by an individual type, and this is assuredly best embodied in Milton F. Adams, one of Edison's earliest and closest friends, to whom reference will be made in later chapters, and whose life has been so full of adventurous episodes that he might well be regarded as the modern Gil Blas. That career is certainly well worth the telling as "another story," to use the Kipling phrase. Of him Edison says: "Adams was one of a class of operators never satisfied to work at any place for any great length of time. He had the 'wanderlust.' After enjoying hospitality in Boston in 1868-69, on the floor of my hall-bedroom, which was a paradise for the entomologist, while the boarding-house itself was run on the banting system of flesh reduction, he came to me one day and said: 'Good-bye, Edison; I have got sixty cents, and I am going to San Francisco.' And he did go. How, I never knew personally. I learned afterward that he got a job there, and then within a week they had a telegraphers' strike. He got a big torch and sold patent medicine on the streets at night to support the strikers. Then he went to Peru as partner of a man who had a grizzly bear which they proposed entering against a bull in the bull-ring in that city. The grizzly was killed in five minutes, and so the scheme died. Then Adams crossed the Andes, and started a market-report bureau in Buenos Ayres. This didn't pay, so he started a restaurant in Pernambuco, Brazil. There he did very well, but something went wrong (as it always does to a nomad), so he went to the Transvaal, and ran a panorama called 'Paradise Lost' in the Kaffir kraals. This didn't pay, and he became the editor of a newspaper; then went to England to raise money for a railroad in Cape Colony. Next I heard of him in New York, having just arrived from Bogota, United States of Colombia, with a power of attorney and $2000 from a native of that republic, who had applied for a patent for tightening a belt to prevent it from slipping on a pulley--a device which he thought a new and great invention, but which was in use ever since machinery was invented. I gave Adams, then, a position as salesman for electrical apparatus. This he soon got tired of, and I lost sight of him." Adams, in speaking of this episode, says that when he asked for transportation expenses to St. Louis, Edison pulled out of his pocket a ferry ticket to Hoboken, and said to his associates: "I'll give him that, and he'll get there all right." This was in the early days of electric lighting; but down to the present moment the peregrinations of this versatile genius of the key have never ceased in one hemisphere or the other, so that as Mr. Adams himself remarked to the authors in April, 1908: "The life has been somewhat variegated, but never dull."

The fact remains also that throughout this period Edison, while himself a very Ishmael, never ceased to study, explore, experiment. Referring to this beginning of his career, he mentions a curious fact that throws light on his ceaseless application. "After I became a telegraph operator," he says, "I practiced for a long time to become a rapid reader of print, and got so expert I could sense the meaning of a whole line at once. This faculty, I believe, should be taught in schools, as it appears to be easily acquired. Then one can read two or three books in a day, whereas if each word at a time only is sensed, reading is laborious."

CHAPTER V

ARDUOUS YEARS IN THE CENTRAL WEST

IN 1903, when accepting the position of honorary electrician to the International Exposition held in St. Louis in 1904, to commemorate the centenary of the Louisiana Purchase, Mr. Edison spoke in his letter of the Central West as a "region where as a young telegraph operator I spent many arduous years before moving East." The term of probation thus referred to did not end until 1868, and while it lasted Edison's wanderings carried him from Detroit to New Orleans, and took him, among other cities, to Indianapolis, Cincinnati, Louisville, and Memphis, some of which he visited twice in his peregrinations to secure work. From Canada, after the episodes noted in the last chapter, he went to Adrian, Michigan, and of what happened there Edison tells a story typical of his wanderings for several years to come. "After leaving my first job at Stratford Junction, I got a position as operator on the Lake Shore & Michigan Southern at Adrian, Michigan, in the division superintendent's office. As usual, I took the 'night trick,' which most operators disliked, but which I preferred, as it gave me more leisure to experiment. I had obtained from the station agent a small room, and had established a little shop of my own. One day the day operator wanted to get off, and I was on duty. About 9 o'clock the superintendent handed me a despatch which he said was very important, and which I must get off at once. The wire at the time was very busy, and I asked if I should break in. I got orders to do so, and acting under those orders of the superintendent, I broke in and tried to send the despatch; but the other operator would not permit it, and the struggle continued for ten minutes. Finally I got possession of the wire and sent the message. The superintendent of telegraph, who then lived in Adrian and went to his office in Toledo every day, happened that day to be in the Western Union office up-town--and it was the superintendent I was really struggling with! In about twenty minutes he arrived livid with rage, and I was discharged on the spot. I informed him that the general superintendent had told me to break in and send the despatch, but the general superintendent then and there repudiated the whole thing. Their families were socially close, so I was sacrificed. My faith in human nature got a slight jar."

Edison then went to Toledo and secured a position at Fort Wayne, on the Pittsburg, Fort Wayne & Chicago Railroad, now leased to the Pennsylvania system. This was a "day job," and he did not like it. He drifted two months later to Indianapolis, arriving there in the fall of 1864, when he was at first assigned to duty at the Union Station at a salary of $75 a month for the Western Union Telegraph Company, whose service he now entered, and with which he has been destined to maintain highly important and close relationships throughout a large part of his life. Superintendent Wallick appears to have treated him generously and to have loaned him instruments, a kindness that was greatly appreciated, for twenty years later the inventor called on his old employer, and together they visited the scene where the borrowed apparatus had been mounted on a rough board in the depot. Edison did not stay long in Indianapolis, however, resigning in February, 1865, and proceeding to Cincinnati. The transfer was possibly due to trouble caused by one of his early inventions embodying what has been characterized by an expert as "probably the most simple and ingenious arrangement of connections for a repeater." His ambition was to take "press report," but finding, even after considerable practice, that he "broke" frequently, he adjusted two embossing Morse registers--one to receive the press matter, and the other to repeat the dots and dashes at a lower speed, so that the message could be copied leisurely. Hence he could not be rushed or "broken" in receiving, while he could turn out "copy" that was a marvel of neatness and clearness. All was well so long as ordinary conditions prevailed, but when an unusual pressure occurred the little system fell behind, and the newspapers complained of the slowness with which reports were delivered to them. It is easy to understand that with matter received at a rate of forty words per minute and worked off at twenty-five words per minute a serious congestion or delay would result, and the newspapers were more anxious for the news than they were for fine penmanship.

Of this device Mr. Edison remarks: "Together we took press for several nights, my companion keeping the apparatus in adjustment and I copying. The regular press operator would go to the theatre or take a nap, only finishing the report after 1 A.M. One of the newspapers complained of bad copy toward the end of the report--that, is from 1 to 3 A.M., and requested that the operator taking the report up to 1 A.M.--which was ourselves--take it all, as the copy then was perfectly unobjectionable. This led to an investigation by the manager, and the scheme was forbidden.

"This instrument, many years afterward, was applied by me for transferring messages from one wire to any other wire simultaneously, or after any interval of time. It consisted of a disk of paper, the indentations being formed in a volute spiral, exactly as in the disk phonograph to-day. It was this instrument which gave me the idea of the phonograph while working on the telephone."

Arrived in Cincinnati, where he got employment in the Western Union commercial telegraph department at a wage of $60 per month, Edison made the acquaintance of Milton F. Adams, already referred to as facile princeps the typical telegrapher in all his more sociable and brilliant aspects. Speaking of that time, Mr. Adams says: "I can well recall when Edison drifted in to take a job. He was a youth of about eighteen years, decidedly unprepossessing in dress and rather uncouth in manner. I was twenty-one, and very dudish. He was quite thin in those days, and his nose was very prominent, giving a Napoleonic look to his face, although the curious resemblance did not strike me at the time. The boys did not take to him cheerfully, and he was lonesome. I sympathized with him, and we became close companions. As an operator he had no superiors and very few equals. Most of the time he was monkeying with the batteries and circuits, and devising things to make the work of telegraphy less irksome. He also relieved the monotony of office-work by fitting up the battery circuits to play jokes on his fellow-operators, and to deal with the vermin that infested the premises. He arranged in the cellar what he called his 'rat paralyzer,' a very simple contrivance consisting of two plates insulated from each other and connected with the main battery. They were so placed that when a rat passed over them the fore feet on the one plate and the hind feet on the other completed the circuit and the rat departed this life, electrocuted."

Shortly after Edison's arrival at Cincinnati came the close of the Civil War and the assassination of President Lincoln. It was natural that telegraphers should take an intense interest in the general struggle, for not only did they handle all the news relating to it, but many of them were at one time or another personal participants. For example, one of the operators in the Cincinnati office was George Ellsworth, who was telegrapher for Morgan, the famous Southern Guerrilla, and was with him when he made his raid into Ohio and was captured near the Pennsylvania line. Ellsworth himself made a narrow escape by swimming the Ohio River with the aid of an army mule. Yet we can well appreciate the unimpressionable way in which some of the men did their work, from an anecdote that Mr. Edison tells of that awful night of Friday, April 14, 1865: "I noticed," he says, "an immense crowd gathering in the street outside a newspaper office. I called the attention of the other operators to the crowd, and we sent a messenger boy to find the cause of the excitement. He returned in a few minutes and shouted 'Lincoln's shot.' Instinctively the operators looked from one face to another to see which man had received the news. All the faces were blank, and every man said he had not taken a word about the shooting. 'Look over your files,' said the boss to the man handling the press stuff. For a few moments we waited in suspense, and then the man held up a sheet of paper containing a short account of the shooting of the President. The operator had worked so mechanically that he had handled the news without the slightest knowledge of its significance." Mr. Adams says that at the time the city was en fete on account of the close of the war, the name of the assassin was received by telegraph, and it was noted with a thrill of horror that it was that of a brother of Edwin Booth and of Junius Brutus Booth--the latter of whom was then playing at the old National Theatre. Booth was hurried away into seclusion, and the next morning the city that had been so gay over night with bunting was draped with mourning.

Edison's diversions in Cincinnati were chiefly those already observed. He read a great deal, but spent most of his leisure in experiment. Mr. Adams remarks: "Edison and I were very fond of tragedy. Forrest and John McCullough were playing at the National Theatre, and when our capital was sufficient we would go to see those eminent tragedians alternate in Othello and Iago. Edison always enjoyed Othello greatly. Aside from an occasional visit to the Loewen Garden 'over the Rhine,' with a glass of beer and a few pretzels, consumed while listening to the excellent music of a German band, the theatre was the sum and substance of our innocent dissipation."

The Cincinnati office, as a central point, appears to have been attractive to many of the clever young operators who graduated from it to positions of larger responsibility. Some of them were conspicuous for their skill and versatility. Mr. Adams tells this interesting story as an illustration: "L. C. Weir, or Charlie, as he was known, at that time agent for the Adams Express Company, had the remarkable ability of taking messages and copying them twenty-five words behind the sender. One day he came into the operating-room, and passing a table he heard Louisville calling Cincinnati. He reached over to the key and answered the call. My attention was arrested by the fact that he walked off after responding, and the sender happened to be a good one. Weir coolly asked for a pen, and when he sat down the sender was just one message ahead of him with date, address, and signature. Charlie started in, and in a beautiful, large, round hand copied that message. The sender went right along, and when he finished with six messages closed his key. When Weir had done with the last one the sender began to think that after all there had been no receiver, as Weir did not 'break,' but simply gave his O. K. He afterward became president of the Adams Express, and was certainly a wonderful operator." The operating-room referred to was on the fifth floor of the building with no elevators.

Those were the early days of trade unionism in telegraphy, and the movement will probably never quite die out in the craft which has always shown so much solidarity. While Edison was in Cincinnati a delegation of five union operators went over from Cleveland to form a local branch, and the occasion was one of great conviviality. Night came, but the unionists were conspicuous by their absence, although more circuits than one were intolerant of delay and clamorous for attention---eight local unionists being away. The Cleveland report wire was in special need, and Edison, almost alone in the office, devoted himself to it all through the night and until 3 o'clock the next morning, when he was relieved.

He had previously been getting $80 a month, and had eked this out by copying plays for the theatre. His rating was that of a "plug" or inferior operator; but he was determined to lift himself into the class of first-class operators, and had kept up the practice of going to the office at night to "copy press," acting willingly as a substitute for any operator who wanted to get off for a few hours--which often meant all night. Speaking of this special ordeal, for which he had thus been unconsciously preparing, Edison says: "My copy looked fine if viewed as a whole, as I could write a perfectly straight line across the wide sheet, which was not ruled. There were no flourishes, but the individual letters would not bear close inspection. When I missed understanding a word, there was no time to think what it was, so I made an illegible one to fill in, trusting to the printers to sense it. I knew they could read anything, although Mr. Bloss, an editor of the Inquirer, made such bad copy that one of his editorials was pasted up on the notice-board in the telegraph office with an offer of one dollar to any man who could 'read twenty consecutive words.' Nobody ever did it. When I got through I was too nervous to go home, so waited the rest of the night for the day manager, Mr. Stevens, to see what was to be the outcome of this Union formation and of my efforts. He was an austere man, and I was afraid of him. I got the morning papers, which came out at 4 A. M., and the press report read perfectly, which surprised me greatly. I went to work on my regular day wire to Portsmouth, Ohio, and there was considerable excitement, but nothing was said to me, neither did Mr. Stevens examine the copy on the office hook, which I was watching with great interest. However, about 3 P. M. he went to the hook, grabbed the bunch and looked at it as a whole without examining it in detail, for which I was thankful. Then he jabbed it back on the hook, and I knew I was all right. He walked over to me, and said: 'Young man, I want you to work the Louisville wire nights; your salary will be $125.' Thus I got from the plug classification to that of a 'first-class man.'"

But no sooner was this promotion secured than he started again on his wanderings southward, while his friend Adams went North, neither having any difficulty in making the trip. "The boys in those days had extraordinary facilities for travel. As a usual thing it was only necessary for them to board a train and tell the conductor they were operators. Then they would go as far as they liked. The number of operators was small, and they were in demand everywhere." It was in this way Edison made his way south as far as Memphis, Tennessee, where the telegraph service at that time was under military law, although the operators received $125 a month. Here again Edison began to invent and improve on existing apparatus, with the result of having once more to "move on." The story may be told in his own terse language: "I was not the inventor of the auto repeater, but while in Memphis I worked on one. Learning that the chief operator, who was a protege of the superintendent, was trying in some way to put New York and New Orleans together for the first time since the close of the war, I redoubled my efforts, and at 2 o'clock one morning I had them speaking to each other. The office of the Memphis Avalanche was in the same building. The paper got wind of it and sent messages. A column came out in the morning about it; but when I went to the office in the afternoon to report for duty I was discharged with out explanation. The superintendent would not even give me a pass to Nashville, so I had to pay my fare. I had so little money left that I nearly starved at Decatur, Alabama, and had to stay three days before going on north to Nashville. Arrived in that city, I went to the telegraph office, got money enough to buy a little solid food, and secured a pass to Louisville. I had a companion with me who was also out of a job. I arrived at Louisville on a bitterly cold day, with ice in the gutters. I was wearing a linen duster and was not much to look at, but got a position at once, working on a press wire. My travelling companion was less successful on account of his 'record.' They had a limit even in those days when the telegraph service was so demoralized."

Some reminiscences of Mr. Edison are of interest as bearing not only upon the "demoralized" telegraph service, but the conditions from which the New South had to emerge while working out its salvation. "The telegraph was still under military control, not having been turned over to the original owners, the Southern Telegraph Company. In addition to the regular force, there was an extra force of two or three operators, and some stranded ones, who were a burden to us, for board was high. One of these derelicts was a great source of worry to me, personally. He would come in at all hours and either throw ink around or make a lot of noise. One night he built a fire in the grate and started to throw pistol cartridges into the flames. These would explode, and I was twice hit by the bullets, which left a black-and-blue mark. Another night he came in and got from some part of the building a lot of stationery with

'Confederate States' printed at the head. He was a fine operator, and wrote a beautiful hand. He would take a sheet of this paper, write capital 'A', and then take another sheet and make the 'A' differently; and so on through the alphabet; each time crumpling the paper up in his hand and throwing it on the floor. He would keep this up until the room was filled nearly flush with the table. Then he would quit.

"Everything at that time was 'wide open.' Disorganization reigned supreme. There was no head to anything. At night myself and a companion would go over to a gorgeously furnished faro-bank and get our midnight lunch. Everything was free. There were over twenty keno-rooms running. One of them that I visited was in a Baptist church, the man with the wheel being in the pulpit, and the gamblers in the pews.

"While there the manager of the telegraph office was arrested for something I never understood, and incarcerated in a military prison about half a mile from the office. The building was in plain sight from the office, and four stories high. He was kept strictly incommunicado. One day, thinking he might be confined in a room facing the office, I put my arm out of the window and kept signalling dots and dashes by the movement of the arm. I tried this several times for two days. Finally he noticed it, and putting his arm through the bars of the window he established communication with me. He thus sent several messages to his friends, and was afterward set free."

Another curious story told by Edison concerns a fellow-operator on night duty at Chattanooga Junction, at the time he was at Memphis: "When it was reported that Hood was marching on Nashville, one night a Jew came into the office about 11 o'clock in great excitement, having heard the Hood rumor. He, being a large sutler, wanted to send a message to save his goods. The operator said it was impossible--that orders had been given to send no private messages. Then the Jew wanted to bribe my friend, who steadfastly refused for the reason, as he told the Jew, that he might be court-martialled and shot. Finally the Jew got up to $800. The operator swore him to secrecy and sent the message. Now there was no such order about private messages, and the Jew, finding it out, complained to Captain Van Duzer, chief of telegraphs, who investigated the matter, and while he would not discharge the operator, laid him off indefinitely. Van Duzer was so lenient that if an operator were discharged, all the operator had to do was to wait three days and then go and sit on the stoop of Van Duzer's office all day, and he would be taken back. But Van Duzer swore he would never give in in this case. He said that if the operator had taken $800 and sent the message at the regular rate, which was twenty-five cents, it would have been all right, as the Jew would be punished for trying to bribe a military operator; but when the operator took the $800 and then sent the message deadhead, he couldn't stand it, and he would never relent."

A third typical story of this period deals with a cipher message for Thomas. Mr. Edison narrates it as follows: "When I was an operator in Cincinnati working the Louisville wire nights for a time, one night a man over on the Pittsburg wire yelled out: 'D. I. cipher,' which meant that there was a cipher message from the War Department at Washington and that it was coming--and he yelled out 'Louisville.' I started immediately to call up that place. It was just at the change of shift in the office. I could not get Louisville, and the cipher message began to come. It was taken by the operator on the other table direct from the War Department. It was for General Thomas, at Nashville. I called for about twenty minutes and notified them that I could not get Louisville. I kept at it for about fifteen minutes longer, and notified them that there was still no answer from Louisville. They then notified the War Department that they could not get Louisville. Then we tried to get it by all kinds of roundabout ways, but in no case could anybody get them at that office. Soon a message came from the War Department to send immediately for the manager of the Cincinnati office. He was brought to the office and several messages were exchanged, the contents of which, of course, I did not know, but the matter appeared to be very serious, as they were afraid of General Hood, of the Confederate Army, who was then attempting to march on Nashville; and it was very important that this cipher of about twelve hundred words or so should be got through immediately to General Thomas. I kept on calling up to 12 or 1 o'clock, but no Louisville. About 1 o'clock the operator at the Indianapolis office got hold of an operator on a wire which ran from Indianapolis to Louisville along the railroad, who happened to come into his office. He arranged with this operator to get a relay of horses, and the message was sent through Indianapolis to this operator who had engaged horses to carry the despatches to Louisville and find out the trouble, and get the despatches through without delay to General Thomas. In those days the telegraph fraternity was rather demoralized, and the discipline was very lax. It was found out a couple of days afterward that there were three night operators at Louisville. One of them had gone over to Jeffersonville and had fallen off a horse and broken his leg, and was in a hospital. By a remarkable coincidence another of the men had been stabbed in a keno-room, and was also in hospital while the third operator had gone to Cynthiana to see a man hanged and had got left by the train."

I think the most important line of
investigation is the production of
Electricity direct from carbon.
Edison

Young Edison remained in Louisville for about two years, quite a long stay for one with such nomadic instincts. It was there that he perfected the peculiar vertical style of writing which, beginning with him in telegraphy, later became so much of a fad with teachers of penmanship and in the schools. He says of this form of writing, a current example of which is given above: "I developed this style in Louisville while taking press reports. My wire was connected to the 'blind' side of a repeater at Cincinnati, so that if I missed a word or sentence, or if the wire worked badly, I could not break in and get the last words, because the Cincinnati man had no instrument by which he could hear me. I had to take what came. When I got the job, the cable across the Ohio River at Covington, connecting with the line to Louisville, had a variable leak in it, which caused the strength of the signalling current to make violent fluctuations. I obviated this by using several relays, each with a different adjustment, working several sounders all connected with one sounding-plate. The clatter was bad, but I could read it with fair ease. When, in addition to this infernal leak, the wires north to Cleveland worked badly, it required a large amount of imagination to get the sense of what was being sent. An imagination requires an appreciable time for its exercise, and as the stuff was coming at the rate of thirty-five to forty words a minute, it was very difficult to write down what was coming and imagine what wasn't coming. Hence it was necessary to become a very rapid writer, so I started to find the fastest style. I found that the vertical style, with each letter separate and without any flourishes, was the most rapid, and that the smaller the letter the greater the rapidity. As I took on an average from eight to fifteen columns of news report every day, it did not take long to perfect this method." Mr. Edison has adhered to this characteristic style of penmanship down to the present time.

As a matter of fact, the conditions at Louisville at that time were not much better than they had been at Memphis. The telegraph operating-room was in a deplorable condition. It was on the second story of a dilapidated building on the principal street of the city, with the battery-room in the rear; behind which was the office of the agent of the Associated Press. The plastering was about one-third gone from the ceiling. A small stove, used occasionally in the winter, was connected to the chimney by a tortuous pipe. The office was never cleaned. The switchboard for manipulating the wires was about thirty-four inches square. The brass connections on it were black with age and with the arcing effects of lightning, which, to young Edison, seemed particularly partial to Louisville. "It would strike on the wires," he says, "with an explosion like a cannon-shot, making that office no place for an operator with heart-disease." Around the dingy walls were a dozen tables, the ends next to the wall. They were about the size of those seen in old-fashioned country hotels for holding the wash-bowl and pitcher. The copper wires connecting the instruments to the switchboard were small, crystallized, and rotten. The battery-room was filled with old record-books and message bundles, and one hundred cells of nitric-acid battery, arranged on a stand in the centre of the room. This stand, as well as the floor, was almost eaten through by the destructive action of the powerful acid. Grim and uncompromising as the description reads, it was typical of the equipment in those remote days of the telegraph at the close of the war.

Illustrative of the length to which telegraphers could go at a time when they were so much in demand, Edison tells the following story: "When I took the position there was a great shortage of operators. One night at 2 A.M. another operator and I were on duty. I was taking press report, and the other man was working the New York wire. We heard a heavy tramp, tramp, tramp on the rickety stairs. Suddenly the door was thrown open with great violence, dislodging it from one of the hinges. There appeared in the doorway one of the best operators we had, who worked daytime, and who was of a very quiet disposition except when intoxicated. He was a great friend of the manager of the office. His eyes were bloodshot and wild, and one sleeve had been torn away from his coat. Without noticing either of us he went up to the stove and kicked it over. The stove-pipe fell, dislocated at every joint. It was half full of exceedingly fine soot, which floated out and filled the room completely. This produced a momentary respite to his labors. When the atmosphere had cleared sufficiently to see, he went around and pulled every table away from the wall, piling them on top of the stove in the middle of the room. Then he proceeded to pull the switchboard away from the wall. It was held tightly by screws. He succeeded, finally, and when it gave way he fell with the board, and striking on a table cut himself so that he soon became covered with blood. He then went to the battery-room and knocked all the batteries off on the floor. The nitric acid soon began to combine with the plaster in the room below, which was the public receiving-room for messengers and bookkeepers. The excess acid poured through and ate up the account-books. After having finished everything to his satisfaction, he left. I told the other operator to do nothing. We would leave things just as they were, and wait until the manager came. In the mean time, as I knew all the wires coming through to the switchboard, I rigged up a temporary set of instruments so that the New York business could be cleared up, and we also got the remainder of the press matter. At 7 o'clock the day men began to appear. They were told to go down-stairs and wait the coming of the manager. At 8 o'clock he appeared, walked around, went into the battery-room, and then came to me, saying: 'Edison, who did this?' I told him that Billy L. had come in full of soda-water and invented the ruin before him. He walked backward and forward, about a minute, then coming up to my table put his fist down, and said: 'If Billy L. ever does that again, I will discharge him.' It was needless to say that there were other operators who took advantage of that kind of discipline, and I had many calls at night after that, but none with such destructive effects."

This was one aspect of life as it presented itself to the sensitive and observant young operator in Louisville. But there was another, more intellectual side, in the contact afforded with journalism and its leaders, and the information taken in almost unconsciously as to the political and social movements of the time. Mr. Edison looks back on this with great satisfaction. "I remember," he says, "the discussions between the celebrated poet and journalist George D. Prentice, then editor of the Courier-Journal, and Mr. Tyler, of the Associated Press. I believe Prentice was the father of the humorous paragraph of the American newspaper. He was poetic, highly educated, and a brilliant talker. He was very thin and small. I do not think he weighed over one hundred and twenty five pounds. Tyler was a graduate of Harvard, and had a very clear enunciation, and, in sharp contrast to Prentice, he was a large man. After the paper had gone to press, Prentice would generally come over to Tyler's office and start talking. Having while in Tyler's office heard them arguing on the immortality of the soul, etc., I asked permission of Mr. Tyler if, after finishing the press matter, I might come in and listen to the conversation, which I did many times after. One thing I never could comprehend was that Tyler had a sideboard with liquors and generally crackers. Prentice would pour out half a glass of what they call corn whiskey, and would dip the crackers in it and eat them. Tyler took it sans food. One teaspoonful of that stuff would put me to sleep."

Mr. Edison throws also a curious side-light on the origin of the comic column in the modern American newspaper, the telegraph giving to a new joke or a good story the ubiquity and instantaneity of an important historical event. "It was the practice of the press operators all over the country at that time, when a lull occurred, to start in and send jokes or stories the day men had collected; and these were copied and pasted up on the bulletin-board. Cleveland was the originating office for 'press,' which it received from New York, and sent it out simultaneously to Milwaukee, Chicago, Toledo, Detroit, Pittsburg, Columbus, Dayton, Cincinnati, Indianapolis, Vincennes, Terre Haute, St. Louis, and Louisville. Cleveland would call first on Milwaukee, if he had anything. If so, he would send it, and Cleveland would repeat it to all of us. Thus any joke or story originating anywhere in that area was known the next day all over. The press men would come in and copy anything which could be published, which was about three per cent. I collected, too, quite a large scrap-book of it, but unfortunately have lost it."

Edison tells an amusing story of his own pursuits at this time. Always an omnivorous reader, he had some difficulty in getting a sufficient quantity of literature for home consumption, and was in the habit of buying books at auctions and second-hand stores. One day at an auction-room he secured a stack of twenty unbound volumes of the North American Review for two dollars. These he had bound and delivered at the telegraph office. One morning, when he was free as usual at 3 o'clock, he started off at a rapid pace with ten volumes on his shoulder. He found himself very soon the subject of a fusillade. When he stopped, a breathless policeman grabbed him by the throat and ordered him to drop his parcel and explain matters, as a suspicious character. He opened the package showing the books, somewhat to the disgust of the officer, who imagined he had caught a burglar sneaking away in the dark alley with his booty. Edison explained that being deaf he had heard no challenge, and therefore had kept moving; and the policeman remarked apologetically that it was fortunate for Edison he was not a better shot.

The incident is curiously revelatory of the character of the man, for it must be admitted that while literary telegraphers are by no means scarce, there are very few who would spend scant savings on back numbers of a ponderous review at an age when tragedy, beer, and pretzels are far more enticing. Through all his travels Edison has preserved those books, and has them now in his library at Llewellyn Park, on Orange Mountain, New Jersey.

Drifting after a time from Louisville, Edison made his way as far north as Detroit, but, like the famous Duke of York, soon made his way back again. Possibly the severer discipline after the happy-go-lucky regime in the Southern city had something to do with this restlessness, which again manifested itself, however, on his return thither. The end of the war had left the South a scene of destruction and desolation, and many men who had fought bravely and well found it hard to reconcile themselves to the grim task of reconstruction. To them it seemed better to "let ill alone" and seek some other clime where conditions would be less onerous. At this moment a great deal of exaggerated talk was current as to the sunny life and easy wealth of Latin America, and under its influences many "unreconstructed" Southerners made their way to Mexico, Brazil, Peru, or the Argentine. Telegraph operators were naturally in touch with this movement, and Edison's fertile imagination was readily inflamed by the glowing idea of all these vague possibilities. Again he threw up his steady work and, with a couple of sanguine young friends, made his way to New Orleans. They had the notion of taking positions in the Brazilian Government telegraphs, as an advertisement had been inserted in some paper stating that operators were wanted. They had timed their departure from Louisville so as to catch a specially chartered steamer, which was to leave New Orleans for Brazil on a certain day, to convey a large number of Confederates and their families, who were disgusted with the United States and were going to settle in Brazil, where slavery still prevailed. Edison and his friends arrived in New Orleans just at the time of the great riot, when several hundred negroes were killed, and the city was in the hands of a mob. The Government had seized the steamer chartered for Brazil, in order to bring troops from the Yazoo River to New Orleans to stop the rioting. The young operators therefore visited another shipping-office to make inquiries as to vessels for Brazil, and encountered an old Spaniard who sat in a chair near the steamer agent's desk, and to whom they explained their intentions. He had lived and worked in South America, and was very emphatic in his assertion, as he shook his yellow, bony finger at them, that the worst mistake they could possibly make would be to leave the United States. He would not leave on any account, and they as young Americans would always regret it if they forsook their native land, whose freedom, climate, and opportunities could not be equalled anywhere on the face of the globe. Such sincere advice as this could not be disdained, and Edison made his way North again. One cannot resist speculation as to what might have happened to Edison himself and to the development of electricity had he made this proposed plunge into the enervating tropics. It will be remembered that at a somewhat similar crisis in life young Robert Burns entertained seriously the idea of forsaking Scotland for the West Indies. That he did not go was certainly better for Scottish verse, to which he contributed later so many immortal lines; and it was probably better for himself, even if he died a gauger. It is simply impossible to imagine Edison working out the phonograph, telephone, and incandescent lamp under the tropical climes he sought. Some years later he was informed that both his companions had gone to Vera Cruz, Mexico, and had died there of yellow fever.

Work was soon resumed at Louisville, where the dilapidated old office occupied at the close of the war had been exchanged for one much more comfortable and luxurious in its equipment. As before, Edison was allotted to press report, and remembers very distinctly taking the Presidential message and veto of the District of Columbia bill by President Johnson. As the matter was received over the wire he paragraphed it so that each printer had exactly three lines, thus enabling the matter to be set up very expeditiously in the newspaper offices. This earned him the gratitude of the editors, a dinner, and all the newspaper "exchanges" he wanted. Edison's accounts of the sprees and debauches of other night operators in the loosely managed offices enable one to understand how even a little steady application to the work in hand would be appreciated. On one occasion Edison acted as treasurer for his bibulous companions, holding the stakes, so to speak, in order that the supply of liquor might last longer. One of the mildest mannered of the party took umbrage at the parsimony of the treasurer and knocked him down, whereupon the others in the party set upon the assailant and mauled him so badly that he had to spend three weeks in hospital. At another time two of his companions sharing the temporary hospitality of his room smashed most of the furniture, and went to bed with their boots on. Then his kindly good-nature rebelled. "I felt that this was running hospitality into the ground, so I pulled them out and left them on the floor to cool off from their alcoholic trance."

Edison seems on the whole to have been fairly comfortable and happy in Louisville, surrounding himself with books and experimental apparatus, and even inditing a treatise on electricity. But his very thirst for knowledge and new facts again proved his undoing. The instruments in the handsome new offices were fastened in their proper places, and operators were strictly forbidden to remove them, or to use the batteries except on regular work. This prohibition meant little to Edison, who had access to no other instruments except those of the company. "I went one night," he says, "into the battery-room to obtain some sulphuric acid for experimenting. The carboy tipped over, the acid ran out, went through to the manager's room below, and ate up his desk and all the carpet. The next morning I was summoned before him, and told that what the company wanted was operators, not experimenters. I was at liberty to take my pay and get out."

The fact that Edison is a very studious man, an insatiate lover and reader of books, is well known to his associates; but surprise is often expressed at his fund of miscellaneous information. This, it will be seen, is partly explained by his work for years as a "press" reporter. He says of this: "The second time I was in Louisville, they had moved into a new office, and the discipline was now good. I took the press job. In fact, I was a very poor sender, and therefore made the taking of press report a specialty. The newspaper men allowed me to come over after going to press at 3 A.M. and get all the exchanges I wanted. These I would take home and lay at the foot of my bed. I never slept more than four or five hours' so that I would awake at nine or ten and read these papers until dinner-time. I thus kept posted, and knew from their activity every member of Congress, and what committees they were on; and all about the topical doings, as well as the prices of breadstuffs in all the primary markets. I was in a much better position than most operators to call on my imagination to supply missing words or sentences, which were frequent in those days of old, rotten wires, badly insulated, especially on stormy nights. Upon such occasions I had to supply in some cases one-fifth of the whole matter--pure guessing--but I got caught only once. There had been some kind of convention in Virginia, in which John Minor Botts was the leading figure. There was great excitement about it, and two votes had been taken in the convention on the two days. There was no doubt that the vote the next day would go a certain way. A very bad storm came up about 10 o'clock, and my wire worked very badly. Then there was a cessation of all signals; then I made out the words 'Minor Botts.' The next was a New York item. I filled in a paragraph about the convention and how the vote had gone, as I was sure it would. But next day I learned that instead of there being a vote the convention had adjourned without action until the day after." In like manner, it was at Louisville that Mr. Edison got an insight into the manner in which great political speeches are more frequently reported than the public suspects. "The Associated Press had a shorthand man travelling with President Johnson when he made his celebrated swing around the circle in a private train delivering hot speeches in defence of his conduct. The man engaged me to write out the notes from his reading. He came in loaded and on the verge of incoherence. We started in, but about every two minutes I would have to scratch out whole paragraphs and insert the same things said in another and better way. He would frequently change words, always to the betterment of the speech. I couldn't understand this, and when he got through, and I had copied about three columns, I asked him why those changes, if he read from notes. 'Sonny,' he said, 'if these politicians had their speeches published as they deliver them, a great many shorthand writers would be out of a job. The best shorthanders and the holders of good positions are those who can take a lot of rambling, incoherent stuff and make a rattling good speech out of it.'"

Going back to Cincinnati and beginning his second term there as an operator, Edison found the office in new quarters and with greatly improved management. He was again put on night duty, much to his satisfaction. He rented a room in the top floor of an office building, bought a cot and an oil-stove, a foot lathe, and some tools. He cultivated the acquaintance of Mr. Sommers, superintendent of telegraph of the Cincinnati & Indianapolis Railroad, who gave him permission to take such scrap apparatus as he might desire, that was of no use to the company. With Sommers on one occasion he had an opportunity to indulge his always strong sense of humor. "Sommers was a very witty man," he says, "and fond of experimenting. We worked on a self-adjusting telegraph relay, which would have been very valuable if we could have got it. I soon became the possessor of a second-hand Ruhmkorff induction coil, which, although it would only give a small spark, would twist the arms and clutch the hands of a man so that he could not let go of the apparatus. One day we went down to the round-house of the Cincinnati & Indianapolis Railroad and connected up the long wash-tank in the room with the coil, one electrode being connected to earth. Above this wash-room was a flat roof. We bored a hole through the roof, and could see the men as they came in. The first man as he entered dipped his hands in the water. The floor being wet he formed a circuit, and up went his hands. He tried it the second time, with the same result. He then stood against the wall with a puzzled expression. We surmised that he was waiting for somebody else to come in, which occurred shortly after--with the same result. Then they went out, and the place was soon crowded, and there was considerable excitement. Various theories were broached to explain the curious phenomenon. We enjoyed the sport immensely." It must be remembered that this was over forty years ago, when there was no popular instruction in electricity, and when its possibilities for practical joking were known to very few. To-day such a crowd of working-men would be sure to include at least one student of a night school or correspondence course who would explain the mystery offhand.

Note has been made of the presence of Ellsworth in the Cincinnati office, and his service with the Confederate guerrilla Morgan, for whom he tapped Federal wires, read military messages, sent false ones, and did serious mischief generally. It is well known that one operator can recognize another by the way in which he makes his signals--it is his style of handwriting. Ellsworth possessed in a remarkable degree the skill of imitating these peculiarities, and thus he deceived the Union operators easily. Edison says that while apparently a quiet man in bearing, Ellsworth, after the excitement of fighting, found the tameness of a telegraph office obnoxious, and that he became a bad "gun man" in the Panhandle of Texas, where he was killed. "We soon became acquainted," says Edison of this period in Cincinnati, "and he wanted me to invent a secret method of sending despatches so that an intermediate operator could not tap the wire and understand it. He said that if it could be accomplished, he could sell it to the Government for a large sum of money. This suited me, and I started in and succeeded in making such an instrument, which had in it the germ of my quadruplex now used throughout the world, permitting the despatch of four messages over one wire simultaneously. By the time I had succeeded in getting the apparatus to work, Ellsworth suddenly disappeared. Many years afterward I used this little device again for the same purpose. At Menlo Park, New Jersey, I had my laboratory. There were several Western Union wires cut into the laboratory, and used by me in experimenting at night. One day I sat near an instrument which I had left connected during the night. I soon found it was a private wire between New York and Philadelphia, and I heard among a lot of stuff a message that surprised me. A week after that I had occasion to go to New York, and, visiting the office of the lessee of the wire, I asked him if he hadn't sent such and such a message. The expression that came over his face was a sight. He asked me how I knew of any message. I told him the circumstances, and suggested that he had better cipher such communications, or put on a secret sounder. The result of the interview was that I installed for him my old Cincinnati apparatus, which was used thereafter for many years."

Edison did not make a very long stay in Cincinnati this time, but went home after a while to Port Huron. Soon tiring of idleness and isolation he sent "a cry from Macedonia" to his old friend "Milt" Adams, who was in Boston, and whom he wished to rejoin if he could get work promptly in the East.

Edison himself gives the details of this eventful move, when he went East to grow up with the new art of electricity. "I had left Louisville the second time, and went home to see my parents. After stopping at home for some time, I got restless, and thought I would like to work in the East. Knowing that a former operator named Adams, who had worked with me in the Cincinnati office, was in Boston, I wrote him that I wanted a job there. He wrote back that if I came on immediately he could get me in the Western Union office. I had helped out the Grand Trunk Railroad telegraph people by a new device when they lost one of the two submarine cables they had across the river, making the remaining cable act just as well for their purpose, as if they had two. I thought I was entitled to a pass, which they conceded; and I started for Boston. After leaving Toronto a terrific blizzard came up and the train got snowed under in a cut. After staying there twenty-four hours, the trainmen made snowshoes of fence-rail splints and started out to find food, which they did about a half mile away. They found a roadside inn, and by means of snowshoes all the passengers were taken to the inn. The train reached Montreal four days late. A number of the passengers and myself went to the military headquarters to testify in favor of a soldier who was on furlough, and was two days late, which was a serious matter with military people, I learned. We willingly did this, for this soldier was a great story-teller, and made the time pass quickly. I met here a telegraph operator named Stanton, who took me to his boarding-house, the most cheerless I have ever been in. Nobody got enough to eat; the bedclothes were too short and too thin; it was 28 degrees below zero, and the wash-water was frozen solid. The board was cheap, being only $1.50 per week.

"Stanton said that the usual live-stock accompaniment of operators' boarding-houses was absent; he thought the intense cold had caused them to hibernate. Stanton, when I was working in Cincinnati, left his position and went out on the Union Pacific to work at Julesburg, which was a cattle town at that time and very tough. I remember seeing him off on the train, never expecting to see him again. Six months afterward, while working press wire in Cincinnati, about 2 A.M., there was flung into the middle of the operating-room a large tin box. It made a report like a pistol, and we all jumped up startled. In walked Stanton. 'Gentlemen,' he said 'I have just returned from a pleasure trip to the land beyond the Mississippi. All my wealth is contained in my metallic travelling case and you are welcome to it.' The case contained one paper collar. He sat down, and I noticed that he had a woollen comforter around his neck with his coat buttoned closely. The night was intensely warm. He then opened his coat and revealed the fact that he had nothing but the bare skin. 'Gentlemen,' said he, 'you see before you an operator who has reached the limit of impecuniosity.'" Not far from the limit of impecuniosity was Edison himself, as he landed in Boston in 1868 after this wintry ordeal.

This chapter has run to undue length, but it must not close without one citation from high authority as to the service of the military telegraph corps so often referred to in it. General Grant in his Memoirs, describing the movements of the Army of the Potomac, lays stress on the service of his telegraph operators, and says: "Nothing could be more complete than the organization and discipline of this body of brave and intelligent men. Insulated wires were wound upon reels, two men and a mule detailed to each reel. The pack-saddle was provided with a rack like a sawbuck, placed crosswise, so that the wheel would revolve freely; there was a wagon provided with a telegraph operator, battery, and instruments for each division corps and army, and for my headquarters. Wagons were also loaded with light poles supplied with an iron spike at each end to hold the wires up. The moment troops were in position to go into camp, the men would put up their wires. Thus in a few minutes' longer time than it took a mule to walk the length of its coil, telegraphic communication would be effected between all the headquarters of the army. No orders ever had to be given to establish the telegraph."

CHAPTER VI

WORK AND INVENTION IN BOSTON

MILTON ADAMS was working in the office of the Franklin Telegraph Company in Boston when he received Edison's appeal from Port Huron, and with characteristic impetuosity at once made it his business to secure a position for his friend. There was no opening in the Franklin office, so Adams went over to the Western Union office, and asked the manager, Mr. George F. Milliken, if he did not want an operator who, like young Lochinvar, came out of the West. "What kind of copy does he make?" was the cautious response. "I passed Edison's letter through the window for his inspection. Milliken read it, and a look of surprise came over his countenance as he asked me if he could take it off the line like that. I said he certainly could, and that there was nobody who could stick him. Milliken said that if he was that kind of an operator I could send for him, and I wrote to Edison to come on, as I had a job for him in the main office of the Western Union." Meantime Edison had secured his pass over the Grand Trunk Railroad, and spent four days and nights on the journey, suffering extremes of cold and hunger. Franklin's arrival in Philadelphia finds its parallel in the very modest debut of Adams's friend in Boston.

It took only five minutes for Edison to get the "job," for Superintendent Milliken, a fine type of telegraph official, saw quickly through the superficialities, and realized that it was no ordinary young operator he was engaging. Edison himself tells the story of what happened. "The manager asked me when I was ready to go to work. 'Now,' I replied I was then told to return at 5.30 P.M., and punctually at that hour I entered the main operating-room and was introduced to the night manager. The weather being cold, and being clothed poorly, my peculiar appearance caused much mirth, and, as I afterward learned, the night operators had consulted together how they might 'put up a job on the jay from the woolly West.' I was given a pen and assigned to the New York No. 1 wire. After waiting an hour, I was told to come over to a special table and take a special report for the Boston Herald, the conspirators having arranged to have one of the fastest senders in New York send the despatch and 'salt' the new man. I sat down unsuspiciously at the table, and the New York man started slowly. Soon he increased his speed, to which I easily adapted my pace. This put my rival on his mettle, and he put on his best powers, which, however, were soon reached. At this point I happened to look up, and saw the operators all looking over my shoulder, with their faces shining with fun and excitement. I knew then that they were trying to put up a job on me, but kept my own counsel. The New York man then commenced to slur over his words, running them together and sticking the signals; but I had been used to this style of telegraphy in taking report, and was not in the least discomfited. Finally, when I thought the fun had gone far enough, and having about completed the special, I quietly opened the key and remarked, telegraphically, to my New York friend: 'Say, young man, change off and send with your other foot.' This broke the New York man all up, and he turned the job over to another man to finish."

Edison had a distaste for taking press report, due to the fact that it was steady, continuous work, and interfered with the studies and investigations that could be carried on in the intervals of ordinary commercial telegraphy. He was not lazy in any sense. While he had no very lively interest in the mere routine work of a telegraph office, he had the profoundest curiosity as to the underlying principles of electricity that made telegraphy possible, and he had an unflagging desire and belief in his own ability to improve the apparatus he handled daily. The whole intellectual atmosphere of Boston was favorable to the development of the brooding genius in this shy, awkward, studious youth, utterly indifferent to clothes and personal appearance, but ready to spend his last dollar on books and scientific paraphernalia. It is matter of record that he did once buy a new suit for thirty dollars in Boston, but the following Sunday, while experimenting with acids in his little workshop, the suit was spoiled. "That is what I get for putting so much money in a new suit," was the laconic remark of the youth, who was more than delighted to pick up a complete set of Faraday's works about the same time. Adams says that when Edison brought home these books at 4 A.M. he read steadily until breakfast-time, and then he remarked, enthusiastically: "Adams, I have got so much to do and life is so short, I am going to hustle." And thereupon he started on a run for breakfast. Edison himself says: "It was in Boston I bought Faraday's works. I think I must have tried about everything in those books. His explanations were simple. He used no mathematics. He was the Master Experimenter. I don't think there were many copies of Faraday's works sold in those days. The only people who did anything in electricity were the telegraphers and the opticians making simple school apparatus to demonstrate the principles." One of these firms was Palmer & Hall, whose catalogue of 1850 showed a miniature electric locomotive made by Mr. Thomas Hall, and exhibited in operation the following year at the Charitable Mechanics' Fair in Boston. In 1852 Mr. Hall made for a Dr. A. L. Henderson, of Buffalo, New York, a model line of railroad with electric-motor engine, telegraph line, and electric railroad signals, together with a figure operating the signals at each end of the line automatically. This was in reality the first example of railroad trains moved by telegraph signals, a practice now so common and universal as to attract no comment. To show how little some fundamental methods can change in fifty years, it may be noted that Hall conveyed the current to his tiny car through forty feet of rail, using the rail as conductor, just as Edison did more than thirty years later in his historic experiments for Villard at Menlo Park; and just as a large proportion of American trolley systems do at this present moment.

It was among such practical, investigating folk as these that Edison was very much at home. Another notable man of this stamp, with whom Edison was thrown in contact, was the late Mr. Charles Williams, who, beginning his career in the electrical field in the forties, was at the height of activity as a maker of apparatus when Edison arrived in the city; and who afterward, as an associate of Alexander Graham Bell, enjoyed the distinction of being the first manufacturer in the world of telephones. At his Court Street workshop Edison was a frequent visitor. Telegraph repairs and experiments were going on constantly, especially on the early fire-alarm telegraphs [1] of Farmer and Gamewell, and with the aid of one of the men there--probably George Anders--Edison worked out into an operative model his first invention, a vote-recorder, the first Edison patent, for which papers were executed on October 11, 1868, and which was taken out June 1, 1869, No. 90,646. The purpose of this particular device was to permit a vote in the National House of Representatives to be taken in a minute or so, complete lists being furnished of all members voting on the two sides of any question Mr.

Edison, in recalling the circumstances, says: "Roberts was the telegraph operator who was the financial backer to the extent of $100. The invention when completed was taken to Washington. I think it was exhibited before a committee that had something to do with the Capitol. The chairman of the committee, after seeing how quickly and perfectly it worked, said: 'Young man, if there is any invention on earth that we don't want down here, it is this. One of the greatest weapons in the hands of a minority to prevent bad legislation is filibustering on votes, and this instrument would prevent it.' I saw the truth of this, because as press operator I had taken miles of Congressional proceedings, and to this day an enormous amount of time is wasted during each session of the House in foolishly calling the members' names and recording and then adding their votes, when the whole operation could be done in almost a moment by merely pressing a particular button at each desk. For filibustering purposes, however, the present methods are most admirable." Edison determined from that time forth to devote his inventive faculties only to things for which there was a real, genuine demand, something that subserved the actual necessities of humanity. This first patent was taken out for him by the late Hon. Carroll D. Wright, afterward U. S. Commissioner of Labor, and a well-known publicist, then practicing patent law in Boston. He describes Edison as uncouth in manner, a chewer rather than a smoker of tobacco, but full of intelligence and ideas.

[Footnote 1: The general scheme of a fire-alarm telegraph system embodies a central office to which notice can be sent from any number of signal boxes of the outbreak of a fire in the district covered by the box, the central office in turn calling out the nearest fire engines, and warning the fire department in general of the occurrence. Such fire alarms can be exchanged automatically, or by operators, and are sometimes associated with a large fire-alarm bell or whistle. Some boxes can be operated by the passing public; others need special keys. The box mechanism is usually of the ratchet, step-by-step movement, familiar in district messenger call-boxes.]

Edison's curiously practical, though imaginative, mind demanded realities to work upon, things that belong to "human nature's daily food," and he soon harked back to telegraphy, a domain in which he was destined to succeed, and over which he was to reign supreme as an inventor. He did not, however, neglect chemistry, but indulged his tastes in that direction freely, although we have no record that this work was anything more, at that time, than the carrying out of experiments outlined in the books. The foundations were being laid for the remarkable chemical knowledge that later on grappled successfully with so many knotty problems in the realm of chemistry; notably with the incandescent lamp and the storage battery. Of one incident in his chemical experiments he tells the following story: "I had read in a scientific paper the method of making nitroglycerine, and was so fired by the wonderful properties it was said to possess, that I determined to make some of the compound. We tested what we considered a very small quantity, but this produced such terrible and unexpected results that we became alarmed, the fact dawning upon us that we had a very large white elephant in our possession. At 6 A.M. I put the explosive into a sarsaparilla bottle, tied a string to it, wrapped it in a paper, and gently let it down into the sewer, corner of State and Washington Streets." The associate in this was a man whom he had found endeavoring to make electrical apparatus for sleight-of-hand performances.

In the Boston telegraph office at that time, as perhaps at others, there were operators studying to enter college; possibly some were already in attendance at Harvard University. This condition was not unusual at one time; the first electrical engineer graduated from Columbia University, New York, followed up his studies while a night operator, and came out brilliantly at the head of his class. Edison says of these scholars that they paraded their knowledge rather freely, and that it was his delight to go to the second-hand book stores on Cornhill and study up questions which he could spring upon them when he got an occasion. With those engaged on night duty he got midnight lunch from an old Irishman called "the Cake Man," who appeared regularly with his wares at 12 midnight. "The office was on the ground floor, and had been a restaurant previous to its occupation by the Western Union Telegraph Company. It was literally loaded with cockroaches, which lived between the wall and the board running around the room at the floor, and which came after the lunch. These were such a bother on my table that I pasted two strips of tinfoil on the wall at my desk, connecting one piece to the positive pole of the big battery supplying current to the wires and the negative pole to the other strip. The cockroaches moving up on the wall would pass over the strips. The moment they got their legs across both strips there was a flash of light and the cockroaches went into gas. This automatic electrocuting device attracted so much attention, and got half a column in an evening paper, that the manager made me stop it." The reader will remember that a similar plan of campaign against rats was carried out by Edison while in the West.

About this time Edison had a narrow escape from injury that might easily have shortened his career, and he seems to have provoked the trouble more or less innocently by using a little elementary chemistry. "After being in Boston several months," he says, "working New York wire No. 1, I was requested to work the press wire, called the 'milk route,' as there were so many towns on it taking press simultaneously. New York office had reported great delays on the wire, due to operators constantly interrupting, or 'breaking,' as it was called, to have words repeated which they had failed to get; and New York claimed that Boston was one of the worst offenders. It was a rather hard position for me, for if I took the report without breaking, it would prove the previous Boston operator incompetent. The results made the operator have some hard feelings against me. He was put back on the wire, and did much better after that. It seems that the office boy was down on this man. One night he asked me if I could tell him how to fix a key so that it would not 'break,' even if the circuit-breaker was open, and also so that it could not be easily detected. I told him to jab a penful of ink on the platinum points, as there was sugar enough to make it sufficiently thick to hold up when the operator tried to break--the current still going through the ink so that he could not break.

"The next night about 1 A.M. this operator, on the press wire, while

I was standing near a House printer studying it, pulled out a glass insulator, then used upside down as a substitute for an ink-bottle, and threw it with great violence at me, just missing my head. It would certainly have killed me if it had not missed. The cause of the trouble was that this operator was doing the best he could not to break, but being compelled to, opened his key and found he couldn't. The press matter came right along, and he could not stop it. The office boy had put the ink in a few minutes before, when the operator had turned his head during a lull. He blamed me instinctively as the cause of the trouble. Later on we became good friends. He took his meals at the same emaciator that I did. His main object in life seemed to be acquiring the art of throwing up wash-pitchers and catching them without breaking them. About one-third of his salary was used up in paying for pitchers."

One day a request reached the Western Union Telegraph office in Boston, from the principal of a select school for young ladies, to the effect that she would like some one to be sent up to the school to exhibit and describe the Morse telegraph to her "children." There has always been a warm interest in Boston in the life and work of Morse, who was born there, at Charlestown, barely a mile from the birthplace of Franklin, and this request for a little lecture on Morse's telegraph was quite natural. Edison, who was always ready to earn some extra money for his experiments, and was already known as the best-informed operator in the office, accepted the invitation. What happened is described by Adams as follows: "We gathered up a couple of sounders, a battery, and sonic wire, and at the appointed time called on her to do the stunt. Her school-room was about twenty by twenty feet, not including a small platform. We rigged up the line between the two ends of the room, Edison taking the stage while I was at the other end of the room. All being in readiness, the principal was told to bring in her children. The door opened and in came about twenty young ladies elegantly gowned, not one of whom was under seventeen. When Edison saw them I thought he would faint. He called me on the line and asked me to come to the stage and explain the mysteries of the Morse system. I replied that I thought he was in the right place, and told him to get busy with his talk on dots and dashes. Always modest, Edison was so overcome he could hardly speak, but he managed to say, finally, that as his friend Mr. Adams was better equipped with cheek than he was, we would change places, and he would do the demonstrating while I explained the whole thing. This caused the bevy to turn to see where the lecturer was. I went on the stage, said something, and we did some telegraphing over the line. I guess it was satisfactory; we got the money, which was the main point to us." Edison tells the story in a similar manner, but insists that it was he who saved the situation. "I managed to say that I would work the apparatus, and Mr. Adams would make the explanations. Adams was so embarrassed that he fell over an ottoman. The girls tittered, and this increased his embarrassment until he couldn't say a word. The situation was so desperate that for a reason I never could explain I started in myself and talked and explained better than I ever did before or since. I can talk to two or three persons; but when there are more they radiate some unknown form of influence which paralyzes my vocal cords. However, I got out of this scrape, and many times afterward when I chanced with other operators to meet some of the young ladies on their way home from school, they would smile and nod, much to the mystification of the operators, who were ignorant of this episode."

Another amusing story of this period of impecuniosity and financial strain is told thus by Edison: "My friend Adams was working in the Franklin Telegraph Company, which competed with the Western Union. Adams was laid off, and as his financial resources had reached absolute zero centigrade, I undertook to let him sleep in my hall bedroom. I generally had hall bedrooms, because they were cheap and I needed money to buy apparatus. I also had the pleasure of his genial company at the boarding-house about a mile distant, but at the sacrifice of some apparatus. One morning, as we were hastening to breakfast, we came into Tremont Row, and saw a large crowd in front of two small 'gents' furnishing goods stores. We stopped to ascertain the cause of the excitement. One store put up a paper sign in the display window which said: 'Three-hundred pairs of stockings received this day, five cents a pair--no connection with the store next door.' Presently the other store put up a sign stating they had received three hundred pairs, price three cents per pair, and stated that they had no connection with the store next door. Nobody went in. The crowd kept increasing. Finally, when the price had reached three pairs for one cent, Adams said to me: 'I can't stand this any longer; give me a cent.' I gave him a nickel, and he elbowed his way in; and throwing the money on the counter, the store being filled with women clerks, he said: 'Give me three pairs.' The crowd was breathless, and the girl took down a box and drew out three pairs of baby socks. 'Oh!' said Adams, 'I want men's size.' 'Well, sir, we do not permit one to pick sizes for that amount of money.' And the crowd roared; and this broke up the sales."

It has generally been supposed that Edison did not take up work on the stock ticker until after his arrival a little later in New York; but he says: "After the vote-recorder I invented a stock ticker, and started a ticker service in Boston; had thirty or forty subscribers, and operated from a room over the Gold Exchange. This was about a year after Callahan started in New York." To say the least, this evidenced great ability and enterprise on the part of the youth. The dealings in gold during the Civil War and after its close had brought gold indicators into use, and these had soon been followed by "stock tickers," the first of which was introduced in New York in 1867. The success of this new but still primitively crude class of apparatus was immediate. Four manufacturers were soon busy trying to keep pace with the demands for it from brokers; and the Gold & Stock Telegraph Company formed to exploit the system soon increased its capital from $200,000 to $300,000, paying 12 per cent. dividends on the latter amount. Within its first year the capital was again increased to $1,000,000, and dividends of 10 per cent. were paid easily on that sum also. It is needless to say that such facts became quickly known among the operators, from whose ranks, of course, the new employees were enlisted; and it was a common ambition among the more ingenious to produce a new ticker. From the beginning, each phase of electrical development--indeed, each step in mechanics--has been accompanied by the well-known phenomenon of invention; namely, the attempt of the many to perfect and refine and even re-invent where one or two daring spirits have led the way. The figures of capitalization and profit just mentioned were relatively much larger in the sixties than they are to-day; and to impressionable young operators they spelled illimitable wealth. Edison was, however, about the only one in Boston of whom history makes record as achieving any tangible result in this new art; and he soon longed for the larger telegraphic opportunity of New York. His friend, Milt Adams, went West with quenchless zest for that kind of roving life and aimless adventure of which the serious minded Edison had already had more than enough. Realizing that to New York he must look for further support in his efforts, Edison, deep in debt for his embryonic inventions, but with high hope and courage, now made the next momentous step in his career. He was far riper in experience and practice of his art than any other telegrapher of his age, and had acquired, moreover, no little knowledge of the practical business of life. Note has been made above of his invention of a stock ticker in Boston, and of his establishing a stock-quotation circuit. This was by no means all, and as a fitting close to this chapter he may be quoted as to some other work and its perils in experimentation: "I also engaged in putting up private lines, upon which I used an alphabetical dial instrument for telegraphing between business establishments, a forerunner of modern telephony. This instrument was very simple and practical, and any one could work it after a few minutes' explanation. I had these instruments made at Mr. Hamblet's, who had a little shop where he was engaged in experimenting with electric clocks. Mr. Hamblet was the father and introducer in after years of the Western Union Telegraph system of time distribution. My laboratory was the headquarters for the men, and also of tools and supplies for those private lines. They were put up cheaply, as I used the roofs of houses, just as the Western Union did. It never occurred to me to ask permission from the owners; all we did was to go to the store, etc., say we were telegraph men, and wanted to go up to the wires on the roof; and permission was always granted.

"In this laboratory I had a large induction coil which I had borrowed to make some experiments with. One day I got hold of both electrodes of the coil, and it clinched my hand on them so that I couldn't let go. The battery was on a shelf. The only way I could get free was to back off and pull the coil, so that the battery wires would pull the cells off the shelf and thus break the circuit. I shut my eyes and pulled, but the nitric acid splashed all over my face and ran down my back. I rushed to a sink, which was only half big enough, and got in as well as I could and wiggled around for several minutes to permit the water to dilute the acid and stop the pain. My face and back were streaked with yellow; the skin was thoroughly oxidized. I did not go on the street by daylight for two weeks, as the appearance of my face was dreadful. The skin, however, peeled off, and new skin replaced it without any damage."

CHAPTER VII

THE STOCK TICKER

"THE letters and figures used in the language of the tape," said a well-known Boston stock speculator, "are very few, but they spell ruin in ninety-nine million ways." It is not to be inferred, however, that the modern stock ticker has anything to do with the making or losing of fortunes. There were regular daily stock-market reports in London newspapers in 1825, and New York soon followed the example. As far back as 1692, Houghton issued in London a weekly review of financial and commercial transactions, upon which Macaulay based the lively narrative of stock speculation in the seventeenth century, given in his famous history. That which the ubiquitous stock ticker has done is to give instantaneity to the news of what the stock market is doing, so that at every minute, thousands of miles apart, brokers, investors, and gamblers may learn the exact conditions. The existence of such facilities is to be admired rather than deplored. News is vital to Wall Street, and there is no living man on whom the doings in Wall Street are without effect. The financial history of the United States and of the world, as shown by the prices of government bonds and general securities, has been told daily for forty years on these narrow strips of paper tape, of which thousands of miles are run yearly through the "tickers" of New York alone. It is true that the record of the chattering little machine, made in cabalistic abbreviations on the tape, can drive a man suddenly to the very verge of insanity with joy or despair; but if there be blame for that, it attaches to the American spirit of speculation and not to the ingenious mechanism which reads and registers the beating of the financial pulse.

Edison came first to New York in 1868, with his early stock printer, which he tried unsuccessfully to sell. He went back to Boston, and quite undismayed got up a duplex telegraph. "Toward the end of my stay in Boston," he says, "I obtained a loan of money, amounting to $800, to build a peculiar kind of duplex telegraph for sending two messages over a single wire simultaneously. The apparatus was built, and I left the Western Union employ and went to Rochester, New York, to test the apparatus on the lines of the Atlantic & Pacific Telegraph between that city and New York. But the assistant at the other end could not be made to understand anything, notwithstanding I had written out a very minute description of just what to do. After trying for a week I gave it up and returned to New York with but a few cents in my pocket." Thus he who has never speculated in a stock in his life was destined to make the beginnings of his own fortune by providing for others the apparatus that should bring to the eye, all over a great city, the momentary fluctuations of stocks and bonds. No one could have been in direr poverty than he when the steamboat landed him in New York in 1869. He was in debt, and his few belongings in books and instruments had to be left behind. He was not far from starving. Mr. W. S. Mallory, an associate of many years, quotes directly from him on this point: "Some years ago we had a business negotiation in New York which made it necessary for Mr. Edison and me to visit the city five or six times within a comparatively short period. It was our custom to leave Orange about 11 A.M., and on arrival in New York to get our lunch before keeping the appointments, which were usually made for two o'clock. Several of these lunches were had at Delmonico's, Sherry's, and other places of similar character, but one day, while en route, Mr. Edison said: 'I have been to lunch with you several times; now to-day I am going to take you to lunch with me, and give you the finest lunch you ever had.' When we arrived in Hoboken, we took the downtown ferry across the Hudson, and when we arrived on the Manhattan side Mr. Edison led the way to Smith & McNell's, opposite Washington Market, and well known to old New Yorkers. We went inside and as soon as the waiter appeared Mr. Edison ordered apple dumplings and a cup of coffee for himself. He consumed his share of the lunch with the greatest possible pleasure. Then, as soon as he had finished, he went to the cigar counter and purchased cigars. As we walked to keep the appointment he gave me the following reminiscence: When he left Boston and decided to come to New York he had only money enough for the trip. After leaving the boat his first thought was of breakfast; but he was without money to obtain it. However, in passing a wholesale tea-house he saw a man tasting tea, so he went in and asked the 'taster' if he might have some of the tea. This the man gave him, and thus he obtained his first breakfast in New York. He knew a telegraph operator here, and on him he depended for a loan to tide him over until such time as he should secure a position. During the day he succeeded in locating this operator, but found that he also was out of a job, and that the best he could do was to loan him one dollar, which he did. This small sum of money represented both food and lodging until such time as work could be obtained. Edison said that as the result of the time consumed and the exercise in walking while he found his friend, he was extremely hungry, and that he gave most serious consideration as to what he should buy in the way of food, and what particular kind of food would be most satisfying and filling. The result was that at Smith & McNell's he decided on apple dumplings and a cup of coffee, than which he never ate anything more appetizing. It was not long before he was at work and was able to live in a normal manner."

During the Civil War, with its enormous increase in the national debt and the volume of paper money, gold had gone to a high premium; and, as ever, by its fluctuations in price the value of all other commodities was determined. This led to the creation of a "Gold Room" in Wall Street, where the precious metal could be dealt in; while for dealings in stocks there also existed the "Regular Board," the "Open Board," and the "Long Room." Devoted to one, but the leading object of speculation, the "Gold Room" was the very focus of all the financial and gambling activity of the time, and its quotations governed trade and commerce. At first notations in chalk on a blackboard sufficed, but seeing their inadequacy, Dr. S. S. Laws, vice-president and actual presiding officer of the Gold Exchange, devised and introduced what was popularly known as the "gold indicator." This exhibited merely the prevailing price of gold; but as its quotations changed from instant to instant, it was in a most literal sense "the cynosure of neighboring eyes." One indicator looked upon the Gold Room; the other opened toward the street. Within the exchange the face could easily be seen high up on the west wall of the room, and the machine was operated by Mr. Mersereau, the official registrar of the Gold Board.

Doctor Laws, who afterward became President of the State University of Missouri, was an inventor of unusual ability and attainments. In his early youth he had earned his livelihood in a tool factory; and, apparently with his savings, he went to Princeton, where he studied electricity under no less a teacher than the famous Joseph Henry. At the outbreak of the war in 1861 he was president of one of the Presbyterian synodical colleges in the South, whose buildings passed into the hands of the Government. Going to Europe, he returned to New York in 1863, and, becoming interested with a relative in financial matters, his connection with the Gold Exchange soon followed, when it was organized. The indicating mechanism he now devised was electrical, controlled at central by two circuit-closing keys, and was a prototype of all the later and modern step-by-step printing telegraphs, upon which the distribution of financial news depends. The "fraction" drum of the indicator could be driven in either direction, known as the advance and retrograde movements, and was divided and marked in eighths. It geared into a "unit" drum, just as do speed-indicators and cyclometers. Four electrical pulsations were required to move the drum the distance between the fractions. The general operation was simple, and in normally active times the mechanism and the registrar were equal to all emergencies. But it is obvious that the record had to be carried away to the brokers' offices and other places by messengers; and the delay, confusion, and mistakes soon suggested to Doctor Laws the desirability of having a number of indicators at such scattered points, operated by a master transmitter, and dispensing with the regiments of noisy boys. He secured this privilege of distribution, and, resigning from the exchange, devoted his exclusive attention to the "Gold Reporting Telegraph," which he patented, and for which, at the end of 1866, he had secured fifty subscribers. His indicators were small oblong boxes, in the front of which was a long slot, allowing the dials as they travelled past, inside, to show the numerals constituting the quotation; the dials or wheels being arranged in a row horizontally, overlapping each other, as in modern fare registers which are now seen on most trolley cars. It was not long before there were three hundred subscribers; but the very success of this device brought competition and improvement. Mr. E. A. Callahan, an ingenious printing-telegraph operator, saw that there were unexhausted possibilities in the idea, and his foresight and inventiveness made him the father of the "ticker," in connection with which he was thus, like Laws, one of the first to grasp and exploit the underlying principle of the "central station" as a universal source of supply. The genesis of his invention Mr. Callahan has told in an interesting way: "In 1867, on the site of the present Mills Building on Broad Street, opposite the Stock Exchange of today, was an old building which had been cut up to subserve the necessities of its occupants, all engaged in dealing in gold and stocks. It had one main entrance from the street to a hallway, from which entrance to the offices of two prominent broker firms was obtained. Each firm had its own army of boys, numbering from twelve to fifteen, whose duties were to ascertain the latest quotations from the different exchanges. Each boy devoted his attention to some particularly active stock. Pushing each other to get into these narrow quarters, yelling out the prices at the door, and pushing back for later ones, the hustle made this doorway to me a most undesirable refuge from an April shower. I was simply whirled into the street. I naturally thought that much of this noise and confusion might be dispensed with, and that the prices might be furnished through some system of telegraphy which would not require the employment of skilled operators. The conception of the stock ticker dates from this incident."

Mr. Callahan's first idea was to distribute gold quotations, and to this end he devised an "indicator." It consisted of two dials mounted separately, each revolved by an electromagnet, so that the desired figures were brought to an aperture in the case enclosing the apparatus, as in the Laws system. Each shaft with its dial was provided with two ratchet wheels, one the reverse of the other. One was used in connection with the propelling lever, which was provided with a pawl to fit into the teeth of the reversed ratchet wheel on its forward movement. It was thus made impossible for either dial to go by momentum beyond its limit. Learning that Doctor Laws, with the skilful aid of F. L. Pope, was already active in the same direction, Mr. Callahan, with ready wit, transformed his indicator into a "ticker" that would make a printed record. The name of the "ticker" came through the casual remark of an observer to whom the noise was the most striking feature of the mechanism. Mr. Callahan removed the two dials, and, substituting type wheels, turned the movements face to face, so that each type wheel could imprint its characters upon a paper tape in two lines. Three wires stranded together ran from the central office to each instrument. Of these one furnished the current for the alphabet wheel, one for the figure wheel, and one for the mechanism that took care of the inking and printing on the tape. Callahan made the further innovation of insulating his circuit wires, although the cost was then forty times as great as that of bare wire. It will be understood that electromagnets were the ticker's actuating agency. The ticker apparatus was placed under a neat glass shade and mounted on a shelf. Twenty-five instruments were energized from one circuit, and the quotations were supplied from a "central" at 18 New Street. The Gold & Stock Telegraph Company was promptly organized to supply to brokers the system, which was very rapidly adopted throughout the financial district of New York, at the southern tip of Manhattan Island. Quotations were transmitted by the Morse telegraph from the floor of the Stock Exchange to the "central," and thence distributed to the subscribers. Success with the "stock" news system was instantaneous.

It was at this juncture that Edison reached New York, and according to his own statement found shelter at night in the battery-room of the Gold Indicator Company, having meantime applied for a position as operator with the Western Union. He had to wait a few days, and during this time he seized the opportunity to study the indicators and the complicated general transmitter in the office, controlled from the keyboard of the operator on the floor of the Gold Exchange. What happened next has been the basis of many inaccurate stories, but is dramatic enough as told in Mr. Edison's own version: "On the third day of my arrival and while sitting in the office, the complicated general instrument for sending on all the lines, and which made a very great noise, suddenly came to a stop with a crash. Within two minutes over three hundred boys--a boy from every broker in the street--rushed up-stairs and crowded the long aisle and office, that hardly had room for one hundred, all yelling that such and such a broker's wire was out of order and to fix it at once. It was pandemonium, and the man in charge became so excited that he lost control of all the knowledge he ever had. I went to the indicator, and, having studied it thoroughly, knew where the trouble ought to be, and found it. One of the innumerable contact springs had broken off and had fallen down between the two gear wheels and stopped the instrument; but it was not very noticeable. As I went out to tell the man in charge what the matter was, Doctor Laws appeared on the scene, the most excited person I had seen. He demanded of the man the cause of the trouble, but the man was speechless. I ventured to say that I knew what the trouble was, and he said, 'Fix it! Fix it! Be quick!' I removed the spring and set the contact wheels at zero; and the line, battery, and inspecting men all scattered through the financial district to set the instruments. In about two hours things were working again. Doctor Laws came in to ask my name and what I was doing. I told him, and he asked me to come to his private office the following day. His office was filled with stacks of books all relating to metaphysics and kindred matters. He asked me a great many questions about the instruments and his system, and I showed him how he could simplify things generally. He then requested that I should call next day. On arrival, he stated at once that he had decided to put me in charge of the whole plant, and that my salary would be $300 per month! This was such a violent jump from anything I had ever seen before, that it rather paralyzed me for a while, I thought it was too much to be lasting, but I determined to try and live up to that salary if twenty hours a day of hard work would do it. I kept this position, made many improvements, devised several stock tickers, until the Gold & Stock Telegraph Company consolidated with the Gold Indicator Company." Certainly few changes in fortune have been more sudden and dramatic in any notable career than this which thus placed an ill-clad, unkempt, half-starved, eager lad in a position of such responsibility in days when the fluctuations in the price of gold at every instant meant fortune or ruin to thousands.

Edison, barely twenty-one years old, was a keen observer of the stirring events around him. "Wall Street" is at any time an interesting study, but it was never at a more agitated and sensational period of its history than at this time. Edison's arrival in New York coincided with an active speculation in gold which may, indeed, be said to have provided him with occupation; and was soon followed by the attempt of Mr. Jay Gould and his associates to corner the gold market, precipitating the panic of Black Friday, September 24, 1869. Securing its import duties in the precious metal and thus assisting to create an artificial stringency in the gold market, the Government had made it a practice to relieve the situation by selling a million of gold each month. The metal was thus restored to circulation. In some manner, President Grant was persuaded that general conditions and the movement of the crops would be helped if the sale of gold were suspended for a time; and, this put into effect, he went to visit an old friend in Pennsylvania remote from railroads and telegraphs. The Gould pool had acquired control of $10,000,000 in gold, and drove the price upward rapidly from 144 toward their goal of 200. On Black Friday they purchased another $28,000,000 at 160, and still the price went up. The financial and commercial interests of the country were in panic; but the pool persevered in its effort to corner gold, with a profit of many millions contingent on success. Yielding to frantic requests, President Grant, who returned to Washington, caused Secretary Boutwell, of the Treasury, to throw $4,000,000 of gold into the market. Relief was instantaneous, the corner was broken, but the harm had been done. Edison's remarks shed a vivid side-light on this extraordinary episode: "On Black Friday," he says, "we had a very exciting time with the indicators. The Gould and Fisk crowd had cornered gold, and had run the quotations up faster than the indicator could follow. The indicator was composed of several wheels; on the circumference of each wheel were the numerals; and one wheel had fractions. It worked in the same way as an ordinary counter; one wheel made ten revolutions, and at the tenth it advanced the adjacent wheel; and this in its turn having gone ten revolutions, advanced the next wheel, and so on. On the morning of Black Friday the indicator was quoting 150 premium, whereas the bids by Gould's agents in the Gold Room were 165 for five millions or any part. We had a paper-weight at the transmitter (to speed it up), and by one o'clock reached the right quotation. The excitement was prodigious. New Street, as well as Broad Street, was jammed with excited people. I sat on the top of the Western Union telegraph booth to watch the surging, crazy crowd. One man came to the booth, grabbed a pencil, and attempted to write a message to Boston. The first stroke went clear off the blank; he was so excited that he had the operator write the message for him. Amid great excitement Speyer, the banker, went crazy and it took five men to hold him; and everybody lost their head. The Western Union operator came to me and said: 'Shake, Edison, we are O. K. We haven't got a cent.' I felt very happy because we were poor. These occasions are very enjoyable to a poor man; but they occur rarely."

There is a calm sense of detachment about this description that has been possessed by the narrator even in the most anxious moments of his career. He was determined to see all that could be seen, and, quitting his perch on the telegraph booth, sought the more secluded headquarters of the pool forces. "A friend of mine was an operator who worked in the office of Belden & Company, 60 Broadway, which were headquarters for Fisk. Mr. Gould was up-town in the Erie offices in the Grand Opera House. The firm on Broad Street, Smith, Gould & Martin, was the other branch. All were connected with wires. Gould seemed to be in charge, Fisk being the executive down-town. Fisk wore a velvet corduroy coat and a very peculiar vest. He was very chipper, and seemed to be light-hearted and happy. Sitting around the room were about a dozen fine-looking men. All had the complexion of cadavers. There was a basket of champagne. Hundreds of boys were rushing in paying checks, all checks being payable to Belden & Company. When James Brown, of Brown Brothers & Company, broke the corner by selling five million gold, all payments were repudiated by Smith, Gould & Martin; but they continued to receive checks at Belden & Company's for some time, until the Street got wind of the game. There was some kind of conspiracy with the Government people which I could not make out, but I heard messages that opened my eyes as to the ramifications of Wall Street. Gold fell to 132, and it took us all night to get the indicator back to that quotation. All night long the streets were full of people. Every broker's office was brilliantly lighted all night, and all hands were at work. The clearing-house for gold had been swamped, and all was mixed up. No one knew if he was bankrupt or not."

Edison in those days rather liked the modest coffee-shops, and mentions visiting one. "When on the New York No. 1 wire, that I worked in Boston, there was an operator named Jerry Borst at the other end. He was a first-class receiver and rapid sender. We made up a scheme to hold this wire, so he changed one letter of the alphabet and I soon got used to it; and finally we changed three letters. If any operator tried to receive from Borst, he couldn't do it, so Borst and I always worked together. Borst did less talking than any operator I ever knew. Never having seen him, I went while in New York to call upon him. I did all the talking. He would listen, stroke his beard, and say nothing. In the evening I went over to an all-night lunch-house in Printing House Square in a basement--Oliver's. Night editors, including Horace Greeley, and Henry Raymond, of the New York Times, took their midnight lunch there. When I went with Borst and another operator, they pointed out two or three men who were then celebrated in the newspaper world. The night was intensely hot and close. After getting our lunch and upon reaching the sidewalk, Borst opened his mouth, and said: 'That's a great place; a plate of cakes, a cup of coffee, and a Russian bath, for ten cents.' This was about fifty per cent. of his conversation for two days."

The work of Edison on the gold-indicator had thrown him into close relationship with Mr. Franklin L. Pope, the young telegraph engineer then associated with Doctor Laws, and afterward a distinguished expert and technical writer, who became President of the American Institute of Electrical Engineers in 1886. Each recognized the special ability of the other, and barely a week after the famous events of Black Friday the announcement of their partnership appeared in the Telegrapher of October 1, 1869. This was the first "professional card," if it may be so described, ever issued in America by a firm of electrical engineers, and is here reproduced. It is probable that the advertisement, one of the largest in the Telegrapher, and appearing frequently, was not paid for at full rates, as the publisher, Mr. J. N. Ashley, became a partner in the firm, and not altogether a "sleeping one" when it came to a division of profits, which at times were considerable. In order to be nearer his new friend Edison boarded with Pope at Elizabeth, New Jersey, for some time, living "the strenuous life" in the performance of his duties. Associated with Pope and Ashley, he followed up his work on telegraph printers with marked success. "While with them I devised a printer to print gold quotations instead of indicating them. The lines were started, and the whole was sold out to the Gold & Stock Telegraph Company. My experimenting was all done in the small shop of a Doctor Bradley, located near the station of the Pennsylvania Railroad in Jersey City. Every night I left for Elizabeth on the 1 A.M. train, then walked half a mile to Mr. Pope's house and up at 6 A.M. for breakfast to catch the 7 A.M. train. This continued all winter, and many were the occasions when I was nearly frozen in the Elizabeth walk." This Doctor Bradley appears to have been the first in this country to make electrical measurements of precision with the galvanometer, but was an old-school experimenter who would work for years on an instrument without commercial value. He was also extremely irascible, and when on one occasion the connecting wire would not come out of one of the binding posts of a new and costly galvanometer, he jerked the instrument to the floor and then jumped on it. He must have been, however, a man of originality, as evidenced by his attempt to age whiskey by electricity, an attempt that has often since been made. "The hobby he had at the time I was there," says Edison, "was the aging of raw whiskey by passing strong electric currents through it. He had arranged twenty jars with platinum electrodes held in place by hard rubber. When all was ready, he filled the cells with whiskey, connected the battery, locked the door of the small room in which they were placed, and gave positive orders that no one should enter. He then disappeared for three days. On the second day we noticed a terrible smell in the shop, as if from some dead animal. The next day the doctor arrived and, noticing the smell, asked what was dead. We all thought something had got into his whiskey-room and died. He opened it and was nearly overcome. The hard rubber he used was, of course, full of sulphur, and this being attacked by the nascent hydrogen, had produced sulphuretted hydrogen gas in torrents, displacing all of the air in the room. Sulphuretted hydrogen is, as is well known, the gas given off by rotten eggs."

Another glimpse of this period of development is afforded by an interesting article on the stock-reporting telegraph in the Electrical World of March 4, 1899, by Mr. Ralph W. Pope, the well-known Secretary of the American Institute of Electrical Engineers, who had as a youth an active and intimate connection with that branch of electrical industry. In the course of his article he mentions the curious fact that Doctor Laws at first, in receiving quotations from the Exchanges, was so distrustful of the Morse system that he installed long lines of speaking-tube as a more satisfactory and safe device than a telegraph wire. As to the relations of that time Mr. Pope remarks: "The rivalry between the two concerns resulted in consolidation, Doctor Laws's enterprise being absorbed by the Gold & Stock Telegraph Company, while the Laws stock printer was relegated to the scrap-heap and the museum. Competition in the field did not, however, cease. Messrs. Pope and Edison invented a one-wire printer, and started a system of 'gold printers' devoted to the recording of gold quotations and sterling exchange only. It was intended more especially for importers and exchange brokers, and was furnished at a lower price than the indicator service.... The building and equipment of private telegraph lines was also entered upon. This business was also subsequently absorbed by the Gold & Stock Telegraph Company, which was probably at this time at the height of its prosperity. The financial organization of the company was peculiar and worthy of attention. Each subscriber for a machine paid in $100 for the privilege of securing an instrument. For the service he paid $25 weekly. In case he retired or failed, he could transfer his 'right,' and employees were constantly on the alert for purchasable rights, which could be disposed of at a profit. It was occasionally worth the profit to convince a man that he did not actually own the machine which had been placed in his office.... The Western Union Telegraph Company secured a majority of its stock, and Gen. Marshall Lefferts was elected president. A private-line department was established, and the business taken over from Pope, Edison, and Ashley was rapidly enlarged."

At this juncture General Lefferts, as President of the Gold & Stock Telegraph Company, requested Edison to go to work on improving the stock ticker, furnishing the money; and the well-known "Universal" ticker, in wide-spread use in its day, was one result. Mr. Edison gives a graphic picture of the startling effect on his fortunes: "I made a great many inventions; one was the special ticker used for many years outside of New York in the large cities. This was made exceedingly simple, as they did not have the experts we had in New York to handle anything complicated. The same ticker was used on the London Stock Exchange. After I had made a great number of inventions and obtained patents, the General seemed anxious that the matter should be closed up. One day I exhibited and worked a successful device whereby if a ticker should get out of unison in a broker's office and commence to print wild figures, it could be brought to unison from the central station, which saved the labor of many men and much trouble to the broker. He called me into his office, and said: 'Now, young man, I want to close up the matter of your inventions. How much do you think you should receive?' I had made up my mind that, taking into consideration the time and killing pace I was working at, I should be entitled to $5000, but could get along with $3000. When the psychological moment arrived, I hadn't the nerve to name such a large sum, so I said: 'Well, General, suppose you make me an offer.' Then he said: 'How would $40,000 strike you?' This caused me to come as near fainting as I ever got. I was afraid he would hear my heart beat. I managed to say that I thought it was fair. 'All right, I will have a contract drawn; come around in three days and sign it, and I will give you the money.' I arrived on time, but had been doing some considerable thinking on the subject. The sum seemed to be very large for the amount of work, for at that time I determined the value by the time and trouble, and not by what the invention was worth to others. I thought there was something unreal about it. However, the contract was handed to me. I signed without reading it." Edison was then handed the first check he had ever received, one for $40,000 drawn on the Bank of New York, at the corner of William and Wall Streets. On going to the bank and passing in the check at the wicket of the paying teller, some brief remarks were made to him, which in his deafness he did not understand. The check was handed back to him, and Edison, fancying for a moment that in some way he had been cheated, went outside "to the large steps to let the cold sweat evaporate." He then went back to the General, who, with his secretary, had a good laugh over the matter, told him the check must be endorsed, and sent with him a young man to identify him. The ceremony of identification performed with the paying teller, who was quite merry over the incident, Edison was given the amount in bundles of small bills "until there certainly seemed to be one cubic foot." Unaware that he was the victim of a practical joke, Edison proceeded gravely to stow away the money in his overcoat pockets and all his other pockets. He then went to Newark and sat up all night with the money for fear it might be stolen. Once more he sought help next morning, when the General laughed heartily, and, telling the clerk that the joke must not be carried any further, enabled him to deposit the currency in the bank and open an account.

Thus in an inconceivably brief time had Edison passed from poverty to independence; made a deep impression as to his originality and ability on important people, and brought out valuable inventions; lifting himself at one bound out of the ruck of mediocrity, and away from the deadening drudgery of the key. Best of all he was enterprising, one of the leaders and pioneers for whom the world is always looking; and, to use his own criticism of himself, he had "too sanguine a temperament to keep money in solitary confinement." With quiet self-possession he seized his opportunity, began to buy machinery, rented a shop and got work for it. Moving quickly into a larger shop, Nos. 10 and 12 Ward Street, Newark, New Jersey, he secured large orders from General Lefferts to build stock tickers, and employed fifty men. As business increased he put on a night force, and was his own foreman on both shifts. Half an hour of sleep three or four times in the twenty-four hours was all he needed in those days, when one invention succeeded another with dazzling rapidity, and when he worked with the fierce, eruptive energy of a great volcano, throwing out new ideas incessantly with spectacular effect on the arts to which they related. It has always been a theory with Edison that we sleep altogether too much; but on the other hand he never, until long past fifty, knew or practiced the slightest moderation in work or in the use of strong coffee and black cigars. He has, moreover, while of tender and kindly disposition, never hesitated to use men up as freely as a Napoleon or Grant; seeing only the goal of a complete invention or perfected device, to attain which all else must become subsidiary. He gives a graphic picture of his first methods as a manufacturer: "Nearly all my men were on piece work, and I allowed them to make good wages, and never cut until the pay became absurdly high as they got more expert. I kept no books. I had two hooks. All the bills and accounts I owed I jabbed on one hook; and memoranda of all owed to myself I put on the other. When some of the bills fell due, and I couldn't deliver tickers to get a supply of money, I gave a note. When the notes were due, a messenger came around from the bank with the note and a protest pinned to it for $1.25. Then I would go to New York and get an advance, or pay the note if I had the money. This method of giving notes for my accounts and having all notes protested I kept up over two years, yet my credit was fine. Every store I traded with was always glad to furnish goods, perhaps in amazed admiration of my system of doing business, which was certainly new." After a while Edison got a bookkeeper, whose vagaries made him look back with regret on the earlier, primitive method. "The first three months I had him go over the books to find out how much we had made. He reported $3000. I gave a supper to some of my men to celebrate this, only to be told two days afterward that he had made a mistake, and that we had lost $500; and then a few days after that he came to me again and said he was all mixed up, and now found that we had made over $7000." Edison changed bookkeepers, but never thereafter counted anything real profit until he had paid all his debts and had the profits in the bank.

The factory work at this time related chiefly to stock tickers, principally the "Universal," of which at one time twelve hundred were in use. Edison's connection with this particular device was very close while it lasted. In a review of the ticker art, Mr. Callahan stated, with rather grudging praise, that "a ticker at the present time (1901) would be considered as impracticable and unsalable if it were not provided with a unison device," and he goes on to remark: "The first unison on stock tickers was one used on the Laws printer. [2] It was a crude and unsatisfactory piece of mechanism and necessitated doubling of the battery in order to bring it into action. It was short-lived. The Edison unison comprised a lever with a free end travelling in a spiral or worm on the type-wheel shaft until it met a pin at the end of the worm, thus obstructing the shaft and leaving the type-wheels at the zero-point until released by the printing lever. This device is too well known to require a further description. It is not applicable to any instrument using two independently moving type-wheels; but on nearly if not all other instruments will be found in use." The stock ticker has enjoyed the devotion of many brilliant inventors--G. M. Phelps, H. Van Hoevenbergh, A. A. Knudson, G. B. Scott, S. D. Field, John Burry--and remains in extensive use as an appliance for which no substitute or competitor has been found. In New York the two great stock exchanges have deemed it necessary to own and operate a stock-ticker service for the sole benefit of their members; and down to the present moment the process of improvement has gone on, impelled by the increasing volume of business to be reported. It is significant of Edison's work, now dimmed and overlaid by later advances, that at the very outset he recognized the vital importance of interchangeability in the construction of this delicate and sensitive apparatus. But the difficulties of these early days were almost insurmountable. Mr. R. W. Pope says of the "Universal" machines that they were simple and substantial and generally satisfactory, but adds: "These instruments were supposed to have been made with interchangeable parts; but as a matter of fact the instances in which these parts would fit were very few. The instruction-book prepared for the use of inspectors stated that 'The parts should not be tinkered nor bent, as they are accurately made and interchangeable.' The difficulties encountered in fitting them properly doubtless gave rise to a story that Mr. Edison had stated that there were three degrees of interchangeability. This was interpreted to mean: First, the parts will fit; second, they will almost fit; third, they do not fit, and can't be made to fit."

[Footnote 2: This I invented as well.--T. A. E.]

This early shop affords an illustration of the manner in which Edison has made a deep impression on the personnel of the electrical arts. At a single bench there worked three men since rich or prominent. One was Sigmund Bergmann, for a time partner with Edison in his lighting developments in the United States, and now head and principal owner of electrical works in Berlin employing ten thousand men. The next man adjacent was John Kruesi, afterward engineer of the great General Electric Works at Schenectady. A third was Schuckert, who left the bench to settle up his father's little estate at Nuremberg, stayed there and founded electrical factories, which became the third largest in Germany, their proprietor dying very wealthy. "I gave them a good training as to working hours and hustling," says their quondam master; and this is equally true as applied to many scores of others working in companies bearing the Edison name or organized under Edison patents. It is curiously significant in this connection that of the twenty-one presidents of the national society, the American Institute of Electrical Engineers, founded in 1884, eight have been intimately associated with Edison--namely, Norvin Green and F. L. Pope, as business colleagues of the days of which we now write; while Messrs. Frank J. Sprague, T. C. Martin, A. E. Kennelly, S. S. Wheeler, John W. Lieb, Jr., and Louis A. Ferguson have all been at one time or another in the Edison employ. The remark was once made that if a famous American teacher sat at one end of a log and a student at the other end, the elements of a successful university were present. It is equally true that in Edison and the many men who have graduated from his stern school of endeavor, America has had its foremost seat of electrical engineering.

CHAPTER VIII

AUTOMATIC, DUPLEX, AND QUADRUPLEX TELEGRAPHY

WORK of various kinds poured in upon the young manufacturer, busy also with his own schemes and inventions, which soon began to follow so many distinct lines of inquiry that it ceases to be easy or necessary for the historian to treat them all in chronological sequence. Some notion of his ceaseless activity may be formed from the fact that he started no fewer than three shops in Newark during 1870-71, and while directing these was also engaged by the men who controlled the Automatic Telegraph Company of New York, which had a circuit to Washington, to help it out of its difficulties. "Soon after starting the large shop (10 and 12 Ward Street, Newark), I rented shop-room to the inventor of a new rifle. I think it was the Berdan. In any event, it was a rifle which was subsequently adopted by the British Army. The inventor employed a tool-maker who was the finest and best tool-maker I had ever seen. I noticed that he worked pretty near the whole of the twenty-four hours. This kind of application I was looking for. He was getting $21.50 per week, and was also paid for overtime. I asked him if he could run the shop. 'I don't know; try me!' he said. 'All right, I will give you $60 per week to run both shifts.' He went at it. His executive ability was greater than that of any other man I have yet seen. His memory was prodigious, conversation laconic, and movements rapid. He doubled the production inside three months, without materially increasing the pay-roll, by increasing the cutting speeds of tools, and by the use of various devices. When in need of rest he would lie down on a work-bench, sleep twenty or thirty minutes, and wake up fresh. As this was just what I could do, I naturally conceived a great pride in having such a man in charge of my work. But almost everything has trouble connected with it. He disappeared one day, and although I sent men everywhere that it was likely he could be found, he was not discovered. After two weeks he came into the factory in a terrible condition as to clothes and face. He sat down and, turning to me, said: 'Edison, it's no use, this is the third time; I can't stand prosperity. Put my salary back and give me a job.' I was very sorry to learn that it was whiskey that spoiled such a career. I gave him an inferior job and kept him for a long time."

Edison had now entered definitely upon that career as an inventor which has left so deep an imprint on the records of the United States Patent Office, where from his first patent in 1869 up to the summer of 1910 no fewer than 1328 separate patents have been applied for in his name, averaging thirty-two every year, and one about every eleven days; with a substantially corresponding number issued. The height of this inventive activity was attained about 1882, in which year no fewer than 141 patents were applied for, and seventy-five granted to him, or nearly nine times as many as in 1876, when invention as a profession may be said to have been adopted by this prolific genius. It will be understood, of course, that even these figures do not represent the full measure of actual invention, as in every process and at every step there were many discoveries that were not brought to patent registration, but remained "trade secrets." And furthermore, that in practically every case the actual patented invention followed from one to a dozen or more gradually developing forms of the same idea.

An Englishman named George Little had brought over a system of automatic telegraphy which worked well on a short line, but was a failure when put upon the longer circuits for which automatic methods are best adapted.

The general principle involved in automatic or rapid telegraphs, except the photographic ones, is that of preparing the message in advance, for dispatch, by perforating narrow strips of paper with holes--work which can be done either by hand-punches or by typewriter apparatus. A certain group of perforations corresponds to a Morse group of dots and dashes for a letter of the alphabet. When the tape thus made ready is run rapidly through a transmitting machine, electrical contact occurs wherever there is a perforation, permitting the current from the battery to flow into the line and thus transmit signals correspondingly. At the distant end these signals are received sometimes on an ink-writing recorder as dots and dashes, or even as typewriting letters; but in many of the earlier systems, like that of Bain, the record at the higher rates of speed was effected by chemical means, a tell-tale stain being made on the travelling strip of paper by every spurt of incoming current. Solutions of potassium iodide were frequently used for this purpose, giving a sharp, blue record, but fading away too rapidly.

The Little system had perforating apparatus operated by electromagnets; its transmitting machine was driven by a small electromagnetic motor; and the record was made by electrochemical decomposition, the writing member being a minute platinum roller instead of the more familiar iron stylus. Moreover, a special type of wire had been put up for the single circuit of two hundred and eighty miles between New York and Washington. This is believed to have been the first "compound" wire made for telegraphic or other signalling purposes, the object being to secure greater lightness with textile strength and high conductivity. It had a steel core, with a copper ribbon wound spirally around it, and tinned to the core wire. But the results obtained were poor, and in their necessity the parties in interest turned to Edison.

Mr. E. H. Johnson tells of the conditions: "Gen. W. J. Palmer and some New York associates had taken up the Little automatic system and had expended quite a sum in its development, when, thinking they had reduced it to practice, they got Tom Scott, of the Pennsylvania Railroad to send his superintendent of telegraph over to look into and report upon it. Of course he turned it down. The syndicate was appalled at this report, and in this extremity General Palmer thought of the man who had impressed him as knowing it all by the telling of telegraphic tales as a means of whiling away lonesome hours on the plains of Colorado, where they were associated in railroad-building. So this man--it was I--was sent for to come to New York and assuage their grief if possible. My report was that the system was sound fundamentally, that it contained the germ of a good thing, but needed working out. Associated with General Palmer was one Col. Josiah C. Reiff, then Eastern bond agent for the Kansas Pacific Railroad. The Colonel was always resourceful, and didn't fail in this case. He knew of a young fellow who was doing some good work for Marshall Lefferts, and who it was said was a genius at invention, and a very fiend for work. His name was Edison, and he had a shop out at Newark, New Jersey. He came and was put in my care for the purpose of a mutual exchange of ideas and for a report by me as to his competency in the matter. This was my introduction to Edison. He confirmed my views of the automatic system. He saw its possibilities, as well as the chief obstacles to be overcome--viz., the sluggishness of the wire, together with the need of mechanical betterment of the apparatus; and he agreed to take the job on one condition--namely, that Johnson would stay and help, as 'he was a man with ideas.' Mr. Johnson was accordingly given three months' leave from Colorado railroad-building, and has never seen Colorado since."

Applying himself to the difficulties with wonted energy, Edison devised new apparatus, and solved the problem to such an extent that he and his assistants succeeded in transmitting and recording one thousand words per minute between New York and Washington, and thirty-five hundred words per minute to Philadelphia. Ordinary manual transmission by key is not in excess of forty to fifty words a minute. Stated very briefly, Edison's principal contribution to the commercial development of the automatic was based on the observation that in a line of considerable length electrical impulses become enormously extended, or sluggish, due to a phenomenon known as self-induction, which with ordinary Morse work is in a measure corrected by condensers. But in the automatic the aim was to deal with impulses following each other from twenty-five to one hundred times as rapidly as in Morse lines, and to attempt to receive and record intelligibly such a lightning-like succession of signals would have seemed impossible. But Edison discovered that by utilizing a shunt around the receiving instrument, with a soft iron core, the self-induction would produce a momentary and instantaneous reversal of the current at the end of each impulse, and thereby give an absolutely sharp definition to each signal. This discovery did away entirely with sluggishness, and made it possible to secure high speeds over lines of comparatively great lengths. But Edison's work on the automatic did not stop with this basic suggestion, for he took up and perfected the mechanical construction of the instruments, as well as the perforators, and also suggested numerous electrosensitive chemicals for the receivers, so that the automatic telegraph, almost entirely by reason of his individual work, was placed on a plane of commercial practicability. The long line of patents secured by him in this art is an interesting exhibit of the development of a germ to a completed system, not, as is usually the case, by numerous inventors working over considerable periods of time, but by one man evolving the successive steps at a white heat of activity.

This system was put in commercial operation, but the company, now encouraged, was quite willing to allow Edison to work out his idea of an automatic that would print the message in bold Roman letters instead of in dots and dashes; with consequent gain in speed in delivery of the message after its receipt in the operating-room, it being obviously necessary in the case of any message received in Morse characters to copy it in script before delivery to the recipient. A large shop was rented in Newark, equipped with $25,000 worth of machinery, and Edison was given full charge. Here he built their original type of apparatus, as improved, and also pushed his experiments on the letter system so far that at a test, between New York and Philadelphia, three thousand words were sent in one minute and recorded in Roman type. Mr. D. N. Craig, one of the early organizers of the Associated Press, became interested in this company, whose president was Mr. George Harrington, formerly Assistant Secretary of the United States Treasury.

Mr. Craig brought with him at this time--the early seventies--from

Milwaukee a Mr. Sholes, who had a wooden model of a machine to which had been given the then new and unfamiliar name of "typewriter." Craig was interested in the machine, and put the model in Edison's hands to perfect. "This typewriter proved a difficult thing," says Edison, "to make commercial. The alignment of the letters was awful. One letter would be one-sixteenth of an inch above the others; and all the letters wanted to wander out of line. I worked on it till the machine gave fair results. [3] Some were made and used in the office of the Automatic company. Craig was very sanguine that some day all business letters would be written on a typewriter. He died before that took place; but it gradually made its way. The typewriter I got into commercial shape is now known as the Remington. About this time I got an idea I could devise an apparatus by which four messages could simultaneously be sent over a single wire without interfering with each other. I now had five shops, and with experimenting on this new scheme I was pretty busy; at least I did not have ennui."

[Footnote 3: See illustration on opposite page, showing reproduction of the work done with this machine.]

A very interesting picture of Mr. Edison at this time is furnished by Mr. Patrick B. Delany, a well-known inventor in the field of automatic and multiplex telegraphy, who at that time was a chief operator of the Franklin Telegraph Company at Philadelphia. His remark about Edison that "his ingenuity inspired confidence, and wavering financiers stiffened up when it became known that he was to develop the automatic" is a noteworthy evidence of the manner in which the young inventor had already gained a firm footing. He continues: "Edward H. Johnson was brought on from the Denver & Rio Grande Railway to assist in the practical introduction of automatic telegraphy on a commercial basis, and about this time, in 1872, I joined the enterprise. Fairly good results were obtained between New York and Washington, and Edison, indifferent to theoretical difficulties, set out to prove high speeds between New York and Charleston, South Carolina, the compound wire being hitched up to one of the Southern & Atlantic wires from Washington to Charleston for the purpose of experimentation. Johnson and I went to the Charleston end to carry out Edison's plans, which were rapidly unfolded by telegraph every night from a loft on lower Broadway, New York. We could only get the wire after all business was cleared, usually about midnight, and for months, in the quiet hours, that wire was subjected to more electrical acrobatics than any other wire ever experienced. When the experiments ended, Edison's system was put into regular commercial operation between New York and Washington; and did fine work. If the single wire had not broken about every other day, the venture would have been a financial success; but moisture got in between the copper ribbon and the steel core, setting up galvanic action which made short work of the steel. The demonstration was, however, sufficiently successful to impel Jay Gould to contract to pay about $4,000,000 in stock for the patents. The contract was never completed so far as the $4,000,000 were concerned, but Gould made good use of it in getting control of the Western Union."

One of the most important persons connected with the automatic enterprise was Mr. George Harrington, to whom we have above referred, and with whom Mr. Edison entered into close confidential relations, so that the inventions made were held jointly, under a partnership deed covering "any inventions or improvements that may be useful or desired in automatic telegraphy." Mr. Harrington was assured at the outset by Edison that while the Little perforator would give on the average only seven or eight words per minute, which was not enough for commercial purposes, he could devise one giving fifty or sixty words, and that while the Little solution for the receiving tape cost $15 to $17 per gallon, he could furnish a ferric solution costing only five or six cents per gallon. In every respect Edison "made good," and in a short time the system was a success, "Mr. Little having withdrawn his obsolete perforator, his ineffective resistance, his costly chemical solution, to give place to Edison's perforator, Edison's resistance and devices, and Edison's solution costing a few cents per gallon. But," continues Mr. Harrington, in a memorable affidavit, "the inventive efforts of Mr. Edison were not confined to automatic telegraphy, nor did they cease with the opening of that line to Washington." They all led up to the quadruplex.

Flattered by their success, Messrs. Harrington and Reiff, who owned with Edison the foreign patents for the new automatic system, entered into an arrangement with the British postal telegraph authorities for a trial of the system in England, involving its probable adoption if successful. Edison was sent to England to make the demonstration, in 1873, reporting there to Col. George E. Gouraud, who had been an associate in the United States Treasury with Mr. Harrington, and was now connected with the new enterprise. With one small satchel of clothes, three large boxes of instruments, and a bright fellow-telegrapher named Jack Wright, he took voyage on the Jumping Java, as she was humorously known, of the Cunard line. The voyage was rough and the little Java justified her reputation by jumping all over the ocean. "At the table," says Edison, "there were never more than ten or twelve people. I wondered at the time how it could pay to run an ocean steamer with so few people; but when we got into calm water and could see the green fields, I was astounded to see the number of people who appeared. There were certainly two or three hundred. I learned afterward that they were mostly going to the Vienna Exposition. Only two days could I get on deck, and on one of these a gentleman had a bad scalp wound from being thrown against the iron wall of a small smoking-room erected over a freight hatch."

Arrived in London, Edison set up his apparatus at the Telegraph Street headquarters, and sent his companion to Liverpool with the instruments for that end. The condition of the test was that he was to send from Liverpool and receive in London, and to record at the rate of one thousand words per minute, five hundred words to be sent every half hour for six hours. Edison was given a wire and batteries to operate with, but a preliminary test soon showed that he was going to fail. Both wire and batteries were poor, and one of the men detailed by the authorities to watch the test remarked quietly, in a friendly way: "You are not going to have much show. They are going to give you an old Bridgewater Canal wire that is so poor we don't work it, and a lot of 'sand batteries' at Liverpool." [4] The situation was rather depressing to the young American thus encountering, for the first time, the stolid conservatism and opposition to change that characterizes so much of official life and methods in Europe. "I thanked him," says Edison, "and hoped to reciprocate somehow. I knew I was in a hole. I had been staying at a little hotel in Covent Garden called the Hummums! and got nothing but roast beef and flounders, and my imagination was getting into a coma. What I needed was pastry. That night I found a French pastry shop in High Holborn Street and filled up. My imagination got all right. Early in the morning I saw Gouraud, stated my case, and asked if he would stand for the purchase of a powerful battery to send to Liverpool. He said 'Yes.' I went immediately to Apps on the Strand and asked if he had a powerful battery. He said he hadn't; that all that he had was Tyndall's Royal Institution battery, which he supposed would not serve. I saw it--one hundred cells--and getting the price--one hundred guineas--hurried to Gouraud. He said 'Go ahead.' I telegraphed to the man in Liverpool. He came on, got the battery to Liverpool, set up and ready, just two hours before the test commenced. One of the principal things that made the system a success was that the line was put to earth at the sending end through a magnet, and the extra current from this, passed to the line, served to sharpen the recording waves. This new battery was strong enough to pass a powerful current through the magnet without materially diminishing the strength of the line current."

[Footnote 4: The sand battery is now obsolete. In this type, the cell containing the elements was filled with sand, which was kept moist with an electrolyte.]

The test under these more favorable circumstances was a success. "The record was as perfect as copper plate, and not a single remark was made in the 'time lost' column." Edison was now asked if he thought he could get a greater speed through submarine cables with this system than with the regular methods, and replied that he would like a chance to try it. For this purpose, twenty-two hundred miles of Brazilian cable then stored under water in tanks at the Greenwich works of the Telegraph Construction & Maintenance Company, near London, was placed at his disposal from 8 P.M. until 6 A.M. "This just suited me, as I preferred night-work. I got my apparatus down and set up, and then to get a preliminary idea of what the distortion of the signal would be, I sent a single dot, which should have been recorded upon my automatic paper by a mark about one-thirty-second of an inch long. Instead of that it was twenty-seven feet long! If I ever had any conceit, it vanished from my boots up. I worked on this cable more than two weeks, and the best I could do was two words per minute, which was only one-seventh of what the guaranteed speed of the cable should be when laid. What I did not know at the time was that a coiled cable, owing to induction, was infinitely worse than when laid out straight, and that my speed was as good as, if not better than, with the regular system; but no one told me this." While he was engaged on these tests Colonel Gouraud came down one night to visit him at the lonely works, spent a vigil with him, and toward morning wanted coffee. There was only one little inn near by, frequented by longshoremen and employees from the soap-works and cement-factories--a rough lot--and there at daybreak they went as soon as the other customers had left for work. "The place had a bar and six bare tables, and was simply infested with roaches. The only things that I ever could get were coffee made from burnt bread, with brown molasses-cake. I ordered these for Gouraud. The taste of the coffee, the insects, etc., were too much. He fainted. I gave him a big dose of gin, and this revived him. He went back to the works and waited until six when the day men came, and telegraphed for a carriage. He lost all interest in the experiments after that, and I was ordered back to America." Edison states, however, that the automatic was finally adopted in England and used for many years; indeed, is still in use there. But they took whatever was needed from his system, and he "has never had a cent from them."

Arduous work was at once resumed at home on duplex and quadruplex telegraphy, just as though there had been no intermission or discouragement over dots twenty-seven feet long. A clue to his activity is furnished in the fact that in 1872 he had applied for thirty-eight patents in the class of telegraphy, and twenty-five in 1873; several of these being for duplex methods, on which he had experimented. The earlier apparatus had been built several years prior to this, as shown by a curious little item of news that appeared in the Telegrapher of January 30, 1869: "T. A. Edison has resigned his situation in the Western Union office, Boston, and will devote his time to bringing out his inventions." Oh, the supreme, splendid confidence of youth! Six months later, as we have seen, he had already made his mark, and the same journal, in October, 1869, could say: "Mr. Edison is a young man of the highest order of mechanical talent, combined with good scientific electrical knowledge and experience. He has already invented and patented a number of valuable and useful inventions, among which may be mentioned the best instrument for double transmission yet brought out." Not bad for a novice of twenty-two. It is natural, therefore, after his intervening work on indicators, stock tickers, automatic telegraphs, and typewriters, to find him harking back to duplex telegraphy, if, indeed, he can be said to have dropped it in the interval. It has always been one of the characteristic features of Edison's method of inventing that work in several lines has gone forward at the same time. No one line of investigation has ever been enough to occupy his thoughts fully; or to express it otherwise, he has found rest in turning from one field of work to another, having absolutely no recreations or hobbies, and not needing them. It may also be said that, once entering it, Mr. Edison has never abandoned any field of work. He may change the line of attack; he may drop the subject for a time; but sooner or later the note-books or the Patent Office will bear testimony to the reminiscent outcropping of latent thought on the matter. His attention has shifted chronologically, and by process of evolution, from one problem to another, and some results are found to be final; but the interest of the man in the thing never dies out. No one sees more vividly than he the fact that in the interplay of the arts one industry shapes and helps another, and that no invention lives to itself alone.

The path to the quadruplex lay through work on the duplex, which, suggested first by Moses G. Farmer in 1852, had been elaborated by many ingenious inventors, notably in this country by Stearns, before Edison once again applied his mind to it. The different methods of such multiple transmission--namely, the simultaneous dispatch of the two communications in opposite directions over the same wire, or the dispatch of both at once in the same direction--gave plenty of play to ingenuity. Prescott's Elements of the Electric Telegraph, a standard work in its day, described "a method of simultaneous transmission invented by T. A. Edison, of New Jersey, in 1873," and says of it: "Its peculiarity consists in the fact that the signals are transmitted in one direction by reversing the polarity of a constant current, and in the opposite direction by increasing or decreasing the strength of the same current." Herein lay the germ of the Edison quadruplex. It is also noted that "In 1874 Edison invented a method of simultaneous transmission by induced currents, which has given very satisfactory results in experimental trials." Interest in the duplex as a field of invention dwindled, however, as the quadruplex loomed up, for while the one doubled the capacity of a circuit, the latter created three "phantom wires," and thus quadruplexed the working capacity of any line to which it was applied. As will have been gathered from the above, the principle embodied in the quadruplex is that of working over the line with two currents from each end that differ from each other in strength or nature, so that they will affect only instruments adapted to respond to just such currents and no others; and by so arranging the receiving apparatus as not to be affected by the currents transmitted from its own end of the line. Thus by combining instruments that respond only to variation in the strength of current from the distant station, with instruments that respond only to the change in the direction of current from the distant station, and by grouping a pair of these at each end of the line, the quadruplex is the result. Four sending and four receiving operators are kept busy at each end, or eight in all. Aside from other material advantages, it is estimated that at least from $15,000,000 to $20,000,000 has been saved by the Edison quadruplex merely in the cost of line construction in America.

The quadruplex has not as a rule the same working efficiency that four separate wires have. This is due to the fact that when one of the receiving operators is compelled to "break" the sending operator for any reason, the "break" causes the interruption of the work of eight operators, instead of two, as would be the case on a single wire. The working efficiency of the quadruplex, therefore, with the apparatus in good working condition, depends entirely upon the skill of the operators employed to operate it. But this does not reflect upon or diminish the ingenuity required for its invention. Speaking of the problem involved, Edison said some years later to Mr. Upton, his mathematical assistant, that "he always considered he was only working from one room to another. Thus he was not confused by the amount of wire and the thought of distance."

The immense difficulties of reducing such a system to practice may be readily conceived, especially when it is remembered that the "line" itself, running across hundreds of miles of country, is subject to all manner of atmospheric conditions, and varies from moment to moment in its ability to carry current, and also when it is borne in mind that the quadruplex requires at each end of the line a so-called "artificial line," which must have the exact resistance of the working line and must be varied with the variations in resistance of the working line. At this juncture other schemes were fermenting in his brain; but the quadruplex engrossed him. "This problem was of most difficult and complicated kind, and I bent all my energies toward its solution. It required a peculiar effort of the mind, such as the imagining of eight different things moving simultaneously on a mental plane, without anything to demonstrate their efficiency." It is perhaps hardly to be wondered at that when notified he would have to pay 12 1/2 per cent. extra if his taxes in Newark were not at once paid, he actually forgot his own name when asked for it suddenly at the City Hall, lost his place in the line, and, the fatal hour striking, had to pay the surcharge after all!

So important an invention as the quadruplex could not long go begging, but there were many difficulties connected with its introduction, some of which are best described in Mr. Edison's own words: "Around 1873 the owners of the Automatic Telegraph Company commenced negotiations with Jay Gould for the purchase of the wires between New York and Washington, and the patents for the system, then in successful operation. Jay Gould at that time controlled the Atlantic & Pacific Telegraph Company, and was competing with the Western Union and endeavoring to depress Western Union stock on the Exchange. About this time I invented the quadruplex. I wanted to interest the Western Union Telegraph Company in it, with a view of selling it, but was unsuccessful until I made an arrangement with the chief electrician of the company, so that he could be known as a joint inventor and receive a portion of the money. At that time I was very short of money, and needed it more than glory. This electrician appeared to want glory more than money, so it was an easy trade. I brought my apparatus over and was given a separate room with a marble-tiled floor, which, by-the-way, was a very hard kind of floor to sleep on, and started in putting on the finishing touches.

"After two months of very hard work, I got a detail at regular times of eight operators, and we got it working nicely from one room to another over a wire which ran to Albany and back. Under certain conditions of weather, one side of the quadruplex would work very shakily, and I had not succeeded in ascertaining the cause of the trouble. On a certain day, when there was a board meeting of the company, I was to make an exhibition test. The day arrived. I had picked the best operators in New York, and they were familiar with the apparatus. I arranged that if a storm occurred, and the bad side got shaky, they should do the best they could and draw freely on their imaginations. They were sending old messages. About 1, o'clock everything went wrong, as there was a storm somewhere near Albany, and the bad side got shaky. Mr. Orton, the president, and Wm. H. Vanderbilt and the other directors came in. I had my heart trying to climb up around my oesophagus. I was paying a sheriff five dollars a day to withhold judgment which had been entered against me in a case which I had paid no attention to; and if the quadruplex had not worked before the president, I knew I was to have trouble and might lose my machinery. The New York Times came out next day with a full account. I was given $5000 as part payment for the invention, which made me easy, and I expected the whole thing would be closed up. But Mr. Orton went on an extended tour just about that time. I had paid for all the experiments on the quadruplex and exhausted the money, and I was again in straits. In the mean time I had introduced the apparatus on the lines of the company, where it was very successful.

"At that time the general superintendent of the Western Union was Gen. T. T. Eckert (who had been Assistant Secretary of War with Stanton). Eckert was secretly negotiating with Gould to leave the Western Union and take charge of the Atlantic & Pacific--Gould's company. One day Eckert called me into his office and made inquiries about money matters. I told him Mr. Orton had gone off and left me without means, and I was in straits. He told me I would never get another cent, but that he knew a man who would buy it. I told him of my arrangement with the electrician, and said I could not sell it as a whole to anybody; but if I got enough for it, I would sell all my interest in any SHARE I might have. He seemed to think his party would agree to this. I had a set of quadruplex over in my shop, 10 and 12 Ward Street, Newark, and he arranged to bring him over next evening to see the apparatus. So the next morning Eckert came over with Jay Gould and introduced him to me. This was the first time I had ever seen him. I exhibited and explained the apparatus, and they departed. The next day Eckert sent for me, and I was taken up to Gould's house, which was near the Windsor Hotel, Fifth Avenue. In the basement he had an office. It was in the evening, and we went in by the servants' entrance, as Eckert probably feared that he was watched. Gould started in at once and asked me how much I wanted. I said: 'Make me an offer.' Then he said: 'I will give you $30,000.' I said: 'I will sell any interest I may have for that money,' which was something more than I thought I could get. The next morning I went with Gould to the office of his lawyers, Sherman & Sterling, and received a check for $30,000, with a remark by Gould that I had got the steamboat Plymouth Rock, as he had sold her for $30,000 and had just received the check. There was a big fight on between Gould's company and the Western Union, and this caused more litigation. The electrician, on account of the testimony involved, lost his glory. The judge never decided the case, but went crazy a few months afterward." It was obviously a characteristically shrewd move on the part of Mr. Gould to secure an interest in the quadruplex, as a factor in his campaign against the Western Union, and as a decisive step toward his control of that system, by the subsequent merger that included not only the Atlantic & Pacific Telegraph Company, but the American Union Telegraph Company.

Nor was Mr. Gould less appreciative of the value of Edison's automatic system. Referring to matters that will be taken up later in the narrative, Edison says: "After this Gould wanted me to help install the automatic system in the Atlantic & Pacific company, of which General Eckert had been elected president, the company having bought the Automatic Telegraph Company. I did a lot of work for this company making automatic apparatus in my shop at Newark. About this time I invented a district messenger call-box system, and organized a company called the Domestic Telegraph Company, and started in to install the system in New York. I had great difficulty in getting subscribers, having tried several canvassers, who, one after the other, failed to get subscribers. When I was about to give it up, a test operator named Brown, who was on the Automatic Telegraph wire between New York and Washington, which passed through my Newark shop, asked permission to let him try and see if he couldn't get subscribers. I had very little faith in his ability to get any, but I thought I would give him a chance, as he felt certain of his ability to succeed. He started in, and the results were surprising. Within a month he had procured two hundred subscribers, and the company was a success. I have never quite understood why six men should fail absolutely, while the seventh man should succeed. Perhaps hypnotism would account for it. This company was sold out to the

Atlantic & Pacific company." As far back as 1872, Edison had applied for a patent on district messenger signal boxes, but it was not issued until January, 1874, another patent being granted in September of the same year. In this field of telegraph application, as in others, Edison was a very early comer, his only predecessor being the fertile and ingenious Callahan, of stock-ticker fame. The first president of the Gold & Stock Telegraph Company, Elisha W. Andrews, had resigned in 1870 in order to go to England to introduce the stock ticker in London. He lived in Englewood, New Jersey, and the very night he had packed his trunk the house was burglarized. Calling on his nearest friend the next morning for even a pair of suspenders, Mr. Andrews was met with regrets of inability, because the burglars had also been there. A third and fourth friend in the vicinity was appealed to with the same disheartening reply of a story of wholesale spoliation. Mr. Callahan began immediately to devise a system of protection for Englewood; but at that juncture a servant-girl who had been for many years with a family on the Heights in Brooklyn went mad suddenly and held an aged widow and her daughter as helpless prisoners for twenty-four hours without food or water. This incident led to an extension of the protective idea, and very soon a system was installed in Brooklyn with one hundred subscribers. Out of this grew in turn the district messenger system, for it was just as easy to call a messenger as to sound a fire-alarm or summon the police. To-day no large city in America is without a service of this character, but its function was sharply limited by the introduction of the telephone.

Returning to the automatic telegraph it is interesting to note that so long as Edison was associated with it as a supervising providence it did splendid work, which renders the later neglect of automatic or "rapid telegraphy" the more remarkable. Reid's standard Telegraph in America bears astonishing testimony on this point in 1880, as follows: "The Atlantic & Pacific Telegraph Company had twenty-two automatic stations. These included the chief cities on the seaboard, Buffalo, Chicago, and Omaha. The through business during nearly two years was largely transmitted in this way. Between New York and Boston two thousand words a minute have been sent. The perforated paper was prepared at the rate of twenty words per minute. Whatever its demerits this system enabled the Atlantic & Pacific company to handle a much larger business during 1875 and 1876 than it could otherwise have done with its limited number of wires in their then condition." Mr. Reid also notes as a very thorough test of the perfect practicability of the system, that it handled the President's message, December 3, 1876, of 12,600 words with complete success. This long message was filed at Washington at 1.05 and delivered in New York at 2.07. The first 9000 words were transmitted in forty-five minutes. The perforated strips were prepared in thirty minutes by ten persons, and duplicated by nine copyists. But to-day, nearly thirty-five years later, telegraphy in America is still practically on a basis of hand transmission!

Of this period and his association with Jay Gould, some very interesting glimpses are given by Edison. "While engaged in putting in the automatic system, I saw a great deal of Gould, and frequently went uptown to his office to give information. Gould had no sense of humor. I tried several times to get off what seemed to me a funny story, but he failed to see any humor in them. I was very fond of stories, and had a choice lot, always kept fresh, with which I could usually throw a man into convulsions. One afternoon Gould started in to explain the great future of the Union Pacific Railroad, which he then controlled. He got a map, and had an immense amount of statistics. He kept at it for over four hours, and got very enthusiastic. Why he should explain to me, a mere inventor, with no capital or standing, I couldn't make out. He had a peculiar eye, and I made up my mind that there was a strain of insanity somewhere. This idea was strengthened shortly afterward when the Western Union raised the monthly rental of the stock tickers. Gould had one in his house office, which he watched constantly. This he had removed, to his great inconvenience, because the price had been advanced a few dollars! He railed over it. This struck me as abnormal. I think Gould's success was due to abnormal development. He certainly had one trait that all men must have who want to succeed. He collected every kind of information and statistics about his schemes, and had all the data. His connection with men prominent in official life, of which I was aware, was surprising to me. His conscience seemed to be atrophied, but that may be due to the fact that he was contending with men who never had any to be atrophied. He worked incessantly until 12 or 1 o'clock at night. He took no pride in building up an enterprise. He was after money, and money only. Whether the company was a success or a failure mattered not to him. After he had hammered the Western Union through his opposition company and had tired out Mr. Vanderbilt, the latter retired from control, and Gould went in and consolidated his company and controlled the Western Union. He then repudiated the contract with the Automatic Telegraph people, and they never received a cent for their wires or patents, and I lost three years of very hard labor. But I never had any grudge against him, because he was so able in his line, and as long as my part was successful the money with me was a secondary consideration. When Gould got the Western Union I knew no further progress in telegraphy was possible, and I went into other lines." The truth is that General Eckert was a conservative--even a reactionary--and being prejudiced like many other American telegraph managers against "machine telegraphy," threw out all such improvements.

The course of electrical history has been variegated by some very remarkable litigation; but none was ever more extraordinary than that referred to here as arising from the transfer of the Automatic Telegraph Company to Mr. Jay Gould and the Atlantic & Pacific Telegraph Company. The terms accepted by Colonel Reiff from Mr. Gould, on December 30, 1874, provided that the purchasing telegraph company should increase its capital to $15,000,000, of which the Automatic interests were to receive $4,000,000 for their patents, contracts, etc. The stock was then selling at about 25, and in the later consolidation with the Western Union "went in" at about 60; so that the real purchase price was not less than $1,000,000 in cash. There was a private arrangement in writing with Mr. Gould that he was to receive one-tenth of the "result" to the Automatic group, and a tenth of the further results secured at home and abroad. Mr. Gould personally bought up and gave money and bonds for one or two individual interests on the above basis, including that of Harrington, who in his representative capacity executed assignments to Mr. Gould. But payments were then stopped, and the other owners were left without any compensation, although all that belonged to them in the shape of property and patents was taken over bodily into Atlantic & Pacific hands, and never again left them. Attempts at settlement were made in their behalf, and dragged wearily, due apparently to the fact that the plans were blocked by General Eckert, who had in some manner taken offence at a transaction effected without his active participation in all the details. Edison, who became under the agreement the electrician of the Atlantic & Pacific Telegraph Company, has testified to the unfriendly attitude assumed toward him by General Eckert, as president. In a graphic letter from Menlo Park to Mr. Gould, dated February 2, 1877, Edison makes a most vigorous and impassioned complaint of his treatment, "which, acting cumulatively, was a long, unbroken disappointment to me"; and he reminds Mr. Gould of promises made to him the day the transfer had been effected of Edison's interest in the quadruplex. The situation was galling to the busy, high-spirited young inventor, who, moreover, "had to live"; and it led to his resumption of work for the Western Union Telegraph Company, which was only too glad to get him back. Meantime, the saddened and perplexed Automatic group was left unpaid, and it was not until 1906, on a bill filed nearly thirty years before, that Judge Hazel, in the United States Circuit Court for the Southern District of New York, found strongly in favor of the claimants and ordered an accounting. The court held that there had been a most wrongful appropriation of the patents, including alike those relating to the automatic, the duplex, and the quadruplex, all being included in the general arrangement under which Mr. Gould had held put his tempting bait of $4,000,000. In the end, however, the complainant had nothing to show for all his struggle, as the master who made the accounting set the damages at one dollar!

Aside from the great value of the quadruplex, saving millions of dollars, for a share in which Edison received $30,000, the automatic itself is described as of considerable utility by Sir William Thomson in his juror report at the Centennial Exposition of 1876, recommending it for award. This leading physicist of his age, afterward Lord Kelvin, was an adept in telegraphy, having made the ocean cable talk, and he saw in Edison's "American Automatic," as exhibited by the Atlantic & Pacific company, a most meritorious and useful system. With the aid of Mr. E. H. Johnson he made exhaustive tests, carrying away with him to Glasgow University the surprising records that he obtained. His official report closes thus: "The electromagnetic shunt with soft iron core, invented by Mr. Edison, utilizing Professor Henry's discovery of electromagnetic induction in a single circuit to produce a momentary reversal of the line current at the instant when the battery is thrown off and so cut off the chemical marks sharply at the proper instant, is the electrical secret of the great speed he has achieved. The main peculiarities of Mr. Edison's automatic telegraph shortly stated in conclusion are: (1) the perforator; (2) the contact-maker; (3) the electromagnetic shunt; and (4) the ferric cyanide of iron solution. It deserves award as a very important step in land telegraphy." The attitude thus disclosed toward Mr. Edison's work was never changed, except that admiration grew as fresh inventions were brought forward. To the day of his death Lord Kelvin remained on terms of warmest friendship with his American co-laborer, with whose genius he thus first became acquainted at Philadelphia in the environment of Franklin.

It is difficult to give any complete idea of the activity maintained at the Newark shops during these anxious, harassed years, but the statement that at one time no fewer than forty-five different inventions were being worked upon, will furnish some notion of the incandescent activity of the inventor and his assistants. The hours were literally endless; and upon one occasion, when the order was in hand for a large quantity of stock tickers, Edison locked his men in until the job had been finished of making the machine perfect, and "all the bugs taken out," which meant sixty hours of unintermitted struggle with the difficulties. Nor were the problems and inventions all connected with telegraphy. On the contrary, Edison's mind welcomed almost any new suggestion as a relief from the regular work in hand. Thus: "Toward the latter part of 1875, in the Newark shop, I invented a device for multiplying copies of letters, which I sold to Mr. A. B. Dick, of Chicago, and in the years since it has been universally introduced throughout the world. It is called the 'Mimeograph.' I also invented devices for and introduced paraffin paper, now used universally for wrapping up candy, etc." The mimeograph employs a pointed stylus, used as in writing with a lead-pencil, which is moved over a kind of tough prepared paper placed on a finely grooved steel plate. The writing is thus traced by means of a series of minute perforations in the sheet, from which, as a stencil, hundreds of copies can be made. Such stencils can be prepared on typewriters. Edison elaborated this principle in two other forms--one pneumatic and one electric--the latter being in essence a reciprocating motor. Inside the barrel of the electric pen a little plunger, carrying the stylus, travels to and fro at a very high rate of speed, due to the attraction and repulsion of the solenoid coils of wire surrounding it; and as the hand of the writer guides it the pen thus makes its record in a series of very minute perforations in the paper. The current from a small battery suffices to energize the pen, and with the stencil thus made hundreds of copies of the document can be furnished. As a matter of fact, as many as three thousand copies have been made from a single mimeographic stencil of this character.

CHAPTER IX

THE TELEPHONE, MOTOGRAPH, AND MICROPHONE

A VERY great invention has its own dramatic history. Episodes full of human interest attend its development. The periods of weary struggle, the daring adventure along unknown paths, the clash of rival claimants, are closely similar to those which mark the revelation and subjugation of a new continent. At the close of the epoch of discovery it is seen that mankind as a whole has made one more great advance; but in the earlier stages one watched chiefly the confused vicissitudes of fortune of the individual pioneers. The great modern art of telephony has had thus in its beginnings, its evolution, and its present status as a universal medium of intercourse, all the elements of surprise, mystery, swift creation of wealth, tragic interludes, and colossal battle that can appeal to the imagination and hold public attention. And in this new electrical industry, in laying its essential foundations, Edison has again been one of the dominant figures.

As far back as 1837, the American, Page, discovered the curious fact that an iron bar, when magnetized and demagnetized at short intervals of time, emitted sounds due to the molecular disturbances in the mass. Philipp Reis, a simple professor in Germany, utilized this principle in the construction of apparatus for the transmission of sound; but in the grasp of the idea he was preceded by Charles Bourseul, a young French soldier in Algeria, who in 1854, under the title of "Electrical Telephony," in a Parisian illustrated paper, gave a brief and lucid description as follows:

"We know that sounds are made by vibrations, and are made sensible to the ear by the same vibrations, which are reproduced by the intervening medium. But the intensity of the vibrations diminishes very rapidly with the distance; so that even with the aid of speaking-tubes and trumpets it is impossible to exceed somewhat narrow limits. Suppose a man speaks near a movable disk sufficiently flexible to lose none of the vibrations of the voice; that this disk alternately makes and breaks the connection with a battery; you may have at a distance another disk which will simultaneously execute the same vibrations.... Any one who is not deaf and dumb may use this mode of transmission, which would require no apparatus except an electric battery, two vibrating disks, and a wire."

This would serve admirably for a portrayal of the Bell telephone, except that it mentions distinctly the use of the make-and-break method (i. e., where the circuit is necessarily opened and closed as in telegraphy, although, of course, at an enormously higher rate), which has never proved practical.

So far as is known Bourseul was not practical enough to try his own suggestion, and never made a telephone. About 1860, Reis built several forms of electrical telephonic apparatus, all imitating in some degree the human ear, with its auditory tube, tympanum, etc., and examples of the apparatus were exhibited in public not only in Germany, but in England. There is a variety of testimony to the effect that not only musical sounds, but stray words and phrases, were actually transmitted with mediocre, casual success. It was impossible, however, to maintain the devices in adjustment for more than a few seconds, since the invention depended upon the make-and-break principle, the circuit being made and broken every time an impulse-creating sound went through it, causing the movement of the diaphragm on which the sound-waves impinged. Reis himself does not appear to have been sufficiently interested in the marvellous possibilities of the idea to follow it up--remarking to the man who bought his telephonic instruments and tools that he had shown the world the way. In reality it was not the way, although a monument erected to his memory at Frankfort styles him the inventor of the telephone. As one of the American judges said, in deciding an early litigation over the invention of the telephone, a hundred years of Reis would not have given the world the telephonic art for public use. Many others after Reis tried to devise practical make-and-break telephones, and all failed; although their success would have rendered them very valuable as a means of fighting the Bell patent. But the method was a good starting-point, even if it did not indicate the real path. If Reis had been willing to experiment with his apparatus so that it did not make-and-break, he would probably have been the true father of the telephone, besides giving it the name by which it is known. It was not necessary to slam the gate open and shut. All that was required was to keep the gate closed, and rattle the latch softly. Incidentally it may be noted that Edison in experimenting with the Reis transmitter recognized at once the defect caused by the make-and-break action, and sought to keep the gap closed by the use, first, of one drop of water, and later of several drops. But the water decomposed, and the incurable defect was still there.

The Reis telephone was brought to America by Dr. P. H. Van der Weyde, a well-known physicist in his day, and was exhibited by him before a technical audience at Cooper Union, New York, in 1868, and described shortly after in the technical press. The apparatus attracted attention, and a set was secured by Prof. Joseph Henry for the Smithsonian Institution. There the famous philosopher showed and explained it to Alexander Graham Bell, when that young and persevering Scotch genius went to get help and data as to harmonic telegraphy, upon which he was working, and as to transmitting vocal sounds. Bell took up immediately and energetically the idea that his two predecessors had dropped--and reached the goal. In 1875 Bell, who as a student and teacher of vocal physiology had unusual qualifications for determining feasible methods of speech transmission, constructed his first pair of magneto telephones for such a purpose. In February of 1876 his first telephone patent was applied for, and in March it was issued. The first published account of the modern speaking telephone was a paper read by Bell before the American Academy of Arts and Sciences in Boston in May of that year; while at the Centennial Exposition at Philadelphia the public first gained any familiarity with it. It was greeted at once with scientific acclaim and enthusiasm as a distinctly new and great invention, although at first it was regarded more as a scientific toy than as a commercially valuable device.

By an extraordinary coincidence, the very day that Bell's application for a patent went into the United States Patent Office, a caveat was filed there by Elisha Gray, of Chicago, covering the specific idea of transmitting speech and reproducing it in a telegraphic circuit "through an instrument capable of vibrating responsively to all the tones of the human voice, and by which they are rendered audible." Out of this incident arose a struggle and a controversy whose echoes are yet heard as to the legal and moral rights of the two inventors, the assertion even being made that one of the most important claims of Gray, that on a liquid battery transmitter, was surreptitiously "lifted" into the Bell application, then covering only the magneto telephone. It was also asserted that the filing of the Gray caveat antedated by a few hours the filing of the Bell application. All such issues when brought to the American courts were brushed aside, the Bell patent being broadly maintained in all its remarkable breadth and fullness, embracing an entire art; but Gray was embittered and chagrined, and to the last expressed his belief that the honor and glory should have been his. The path of Gray to the telephone was a natural one. A Quaker carpenter who studied five years at Oberlin College, he took up electrical invention, and brought out many ingenious devices in rapid succession in the telegraphic field, including the now universal needle annunciator for hotels, etc., the useful telautograph, automatic self-adjusting relays, private-line printers--leading up to his famous "harmonic" system. This was based upon the principle that a sound produced in the presence of a reed or tuning-fork responding to the sound, and acting as the armature of a magnet in a closed circuit, would, by induction, set up electric impulses in the circuit and cause a distant magnet having a similarly tuned armature to produce the same tone or note. He also found that over the same wire at the same time another series of impulses corresponding to another note could be sent through the agency of a second set of magnets without in any way interfering with the first series of impulses. Building the principle into apparatus, with a keyboard and vibrating "reeds" before his magnets, Doctor Gray was able not only to transmit music by his harmonic telegraph, but went so far as to send nine different telegraph messages at the same instant, each set of instruments depending on its selective note, while any intermediate office could pick up the message for itself by simply tuning its relays to the keynote required. Theoretically the system could be split up into any number of notes and semi-tones. Practically it served as the basis of some real telegraphic work, but is not now in use. Any one can realize, however, that it did not take so acute and ingenious a mind very long to push forward to the telephone, as a dangerous competitor with Bell, who had also, like Edison, been working assiduously in the field of acoustic and multiple telegraphs. Seen in the retrospect, the struggle for the goal at this moment was one of the memorable incidents in electrical history.

Among the interesting papers filed at the Orange Laboratory is a lithograph, the size of an ordinary patent drawing, headed "First Telephone on Record." The claim thus made goes back to the period when all was war, and when dispute was hot and rife as to the actual invention of the telephone. The device shown, made by Edison in 1875, was actually included in a caveat filed January 14, 1876, a month before Bell or Gray. It shows a little solenoid arrangement, with one end of the plunger attached to the diaphragm of a speaking or resonating chamber. Edison states that while the device is crudely capable of use as a magneto telephone, he did not invent it for transmitting speech, but as an apparatus for analyzing the complex waves arising from various sounds. It was made in pursuance of his investigations into the subject of harmonic telegraphs. He did not try the effect of sound-waves produced by the human voice until Bell came forward a few months later; but he found then that this device, made in 1875, was capable of use as a telephone. In his testimony and public utterances Edison has always given Bell credit for the discovery of the transmission of articulate speech by talking against a diaphragm placed in front of an electromagnet; but it is only proper here to note, in passing, the curious fact that he had actually produced a device that COULD talk, prior to 1876, and was therefore very close to Bell, who took the one great step further. A strong characterization of the value and importance of the work done by Edison in the development of the carbon transmitter will be found in the decision of Judge Brown in the United States Circuit Court of Appeals, sitting in Boston, on February 27, 1901, declaring void the famous Berliner patent of the Bell telephone system. [5]

[Footnote 5: See Federal Reporter, vol. 109, p. 976 et seq.]

Bell's patent of 1876 was of an all-embracing character, which only the make-and-break principle, if practical, could have escaped. It was pointed out in the patent that Bell discovered the great principle that electrical undulations induced by the vibrations of a current produced by sound-waves can be represented graphically by the same sinusoidal curve that expresses the original sound vibrations themselves; or, in other words, that a curve representing sound vibrations will correspond precisely to a curve representing electric impulses produced or generated by those identical sound vibrations--as, for example, when the latter impinge upon a diaphragm acting as an armature of an electromagnet, and which by movement to and fro sets up the electric impulses by induction. To speak plainly, the electric impulses correspond in form and character to the sound vibration which they represent. This reduced to a patent "claim" governed the art as firmly as a papal bull for centuries enabled Spain to hold the Western world. The language of the claim is: "The method of and apparatus for transmitting vocal or other sounds telegraphically as herein described, by causing electrical undulations similar in form to the vibrations of the air accompanying the said vocal or other sounds substantially as set forth." It was a long time, however, before the inclusive nature of this grant over every possible telephone was understood or recognized, and litigation for and against the patent lasted during its entire life. At the outset, the commercial value of the telephone was little appreciated by the public, and Bell had the greatest difficulty in securing capital; but among far-sighted inventors there was an immediate "rush to the gold fields." Bell's first apparatus was poor, the results being described by himself as "unsatisfactory and discouraging," which was almost as true of the devices he exhibited at the Philadelphia Centennial. The new-comers, like Edison, Berliner, Blake, Hughes, Gray, Dolbear, and others, brought a wealth of ideas, a fund of mechanical ingenuity, and an inventive ability which soon made the telephone one of the most notable gains of the century, and one of the most valuable additions to human resources. The work that Edison did was, as usual, marked by infinite variety of method as well as by the power to seize on the one needed element of practical success. Every one of the six million telephones in use in the United States, and of the other millions in use through out the world, bears the imprint of his genius, as at one time the instruments bore his stamped name. For years his name was branded on every Bell telephone set, and his patents were a mainstay of what has been popularly called the "Bell monopoly." Speaking of his own efforts in this field, Mr. Edison says:

"In 1876 I started again to experiment for the Western Union and Mr. Orton. This time it was the telephone. Bell invented the first telephone, which consisted of the present receiver, used both as a transmitter and a receiver (the magneto type). It was attempted to introduce it commercially, but it failed on account of its faintness and the extraneous sounds which came in on its wires from various causes. Mr. Orton wanted me to take hold of it and make it commercial. As I had also been working on a telegraph system employing tuning-forks, simultaneously with both Bell and Gray, I was pretty familiar with the subject. I started in, and soon produced the carbon transmitter, which is now universally used.

"Tests were made between New York and Philadelphia, also between New York and Washington, using regular Western Union wires. The noises were so great that not a word could be heard with the Bell receiver when used as a transmitter between New York and Newark, New Jersey. Mr. Orton and W. K. Vanderbilt and the board of directors witnessed and took part in the tests. The Western Union then put them on private lines. Mr. Theodore Puskas, of Budapest, Hungary, was the first man to suggest a telephone exchange, and soon after exchanges were established. The telephone department was put in the hands of Hamilton McK. Twombly, Vanderbilt's ablest son-in-law, who made a success of it. The Bell company, of Boston, also started an exchange, and the fight was on, the Western Union pirating the Bell receiver, and the Boston company pirating the Western Union transmitter. About this time I wanted to be taken care of. I threw out hints of this desire. Then Mr. Orton sent for me. He had learned that inventors didn't do business by the regular process, and concluded he would close it right up. He asked me how much I wanted. I had made up my mind it was certainly worth $25,000, if it ever amounted to anything for central-station work, so that was the sum I had in mind to stick to and get--obstinately. Still it had been an easy job, and only required a few months, and I felt a little shaky and uncertain. So I asked him to make me an offer. He promptly said he would give me $100,000. 'All right,' I said. 'It is yours on one condition, and that is that you do not pay it all at once, but pay me at the rate of $6000 per year for seventeen years'--the life of the patent. He seemed only too pleased to do this, and it was closed. My ambition was about four times too large for my business capacity, and I knew that I would soon spend this money experimenting if I got it all at once, so I fixed it that I couldn't. I saved seventeen years of worry by this stroke."

Thus modestly is told the debut of Edison in the telephone art, to which with his carbon transmitter he gave the valuable principle of varying the resistance of the transmitting circuit with changes in the pressure, as well as the vital practice of using the induction coil as a means of increasing the effective length of the talking circuit. Without these, modern telephony would not and could not exist. [6] But Edison, in telephonic work, as in other directions, was remarkably fertile and prolific. His first inventions in the art, made in 1875-76, continue through many later years, including all kinds of carbon instruments --the water telephone, electrostatic telephone, condenser telephone, chemical telephone, various magneto telephones, inertia telephone, mercury telephone, voltaic pile telephone, musical transmitter, and the electromotograph. All were actually made and tested.

[Footnote 6: Briefly stated, the essential difference between Bell's telephone and Edison's is this: With the former the sound vibrations impinge upon a steel diaphragm arranged adjacent to the pole of a bar electromagnet, whereby the diaphragm acts as an armature, and by its vibrations induces very weak electric impulses in the magnetic coil. These impulses, according to Bell's theory, correspond in form to the sound-waves, and passing over the line energize the magnet coil at the receiving end, and by varying the magnetism cause the receiving diaphragm to be similarly vibrated to reproduce the sounds. A single apparatus is therefore used at each end, performing the double function of transmitter and receiver. With Edison's telephone a closed circuit is used on which is constantly flowing a battery current, and included in that circuit is a pair of electrodes, one or both of which is of carbon. These electrodes are always in contact with a certain initial pressure, so that current will be always flowing over the circuit. One of the electrodes is connected with the diaphragm on which the sound-waves impinge, and the vibration of this diaphragm causes the pressure between the electrodes to be correspondingly varied, and thereby effects a variation in the current, resulting in the production of impulses which actuate the receiving magnet. In other words, with Bell's telephone the sound-waves themselves generate the electric impulses, which are hence extremely faint. With the Edison telephone, the sound-waves actuate an electric valve, so to speak, and permit variations in a current of any desired strength.

A second distinction between the two telephones is this: With the Bell apparatus the very weak electric impulses generated by the vibration of the transmitting diaphragm pass over the entire line to the receiving end, and in consequence the permissible length of line is limited to a few miles under ideal conditions. With Edison's telephone the battery current does not flow on the main line, but passes through the primary circuit of an induction coil, by which corresponding impulses of enormously higher potential are sent out on the main line to the receiving end. In consequence, the line may be hundreds of miles in length. No modern telephone system in use to-day lacks these characteristic features--the varying resistance and the induction coil.]

The principle of the electromotograph was utilized by Edison in more ways than one, first of all in telegraphy at this juncture. The well-known Page patent, which had lingered in the Patent Office for years, had just been issued, and was considered a formidable weapon. It related to the use of a retractile spring to withdraw the armature lever from the magnet of a telegraph or other relay or sounder, and thus controlled the art of telegraphy, except in simple circuits. "There was no known way," remarks Edison, "whereby this patent could be evaded, and its possessor would eventually control the use of what is known as the relay and sounder, and this was vital to telegraphy. Gould was pounding the Western Union on the Stock Exchange, disturbing its railroad contracts, and, being advised by his lawyers that this patent was of great value, bought it. The moment Mr. Orton heard this he sent for me and explained the situation, and wanted me to go to work immediately and see if I couldn't evade it or discover some other means that could be used in case Gould sustained the patent. It seemed a pretty hard job, because there was no known means of moving a lever at the other end of a telegraph wire except by the use of a magnet. I said I would go at it that night. In experimenting some years previously, I had discovered a very peculiar phenomenon, and that was that if a piece of metal connected to a battery was rubbed over a moistened piece of chalk resting on a metal connected to the other pole, when the current passed the friction was greatly diminished. When the current was reversed the friction was greatly increased over what it was when no current was passing. Remembering this, I substituted a piece of chalk rotated by a small electric motor for the magnet, and connecting a sounder to a metallic finger resting on the chalk, the combination claim of Page was made worthless. A hitherto unknown means was introduced in the electric art. Two or three of the devices were made and tested by the company's expert. Mr. Orton, after he had me sign the patent application and got it in the Patent Office, wanted to settle for it at once. He asked my price. Again I said: 'Make me an offer.' Again he named $100,000. I accepted, providing he would pay it at the rate of $6000 a year for seventeen years. This was done, and thus, with the telephone money, I received $12,000 yearly for that period from the Western Union Telegraph Company."

A year or two later the motograph cropped up again in Edison's work in a curious manner. The telephone was being developed in England, and Edison had made arrangements with Colonel Gouraud, his old associate in the automatic telegraph, to represent his interests. A company was formed, a large number of instruments were made and sent to Gouraud in London, and prospects were bright. Then there came a threat of litigation from the owners of the Bell patent, and Gouraud found he could not push the enterprise unless he could avoid using what was asserted to be an infringement of the Bell receiver. He cabled for help to Edison, who sent back word telling him to hold the fort. "I had recourse again," says Edison, "to the phenomenon discovered by me years previous, that the friction of a rubbing electrode passing over a moist chalk surface was varied by electricity. I devised a telephone receiver which was afterward known as the 'loud-speaking telephone,' or 'chalk receiver.' There was no magnet, simply a diaphragm and a cylinder of compressed chalk about the size of a thimble. A thin spring connected to the centre of the diaphragm extended outwardly and rested on the chalk cylinder, and was pressed against it with a pressure equal to that which would be due to a weight of about six pounds. The chalk was rotated by hand. The volume of sound was very great. A person talking into the carbon transmitter in New York had his voice so amplified that he could be heard one thousand feet away in an open field at Menlo Park. This great excess of power was due to the fact that the latter came from the person turning the handle. The voice, instead of furnishing all the power as with the present receiver, merely controlled the power, just as an engineer working a valve would control a powerful engine.

"I made six of these receivers and sent them in charge of an expert on the first steamer. They were welcomed and tested, and shortly afterward I shipped a hundred more. At the same time I was ordered to send twenty young men, after teaching them to become expert. I set up an exchange, around the laboratory, of ten instruments. I would then go out and get each one out of order in every conceivable way, cutting the wires of one, short-circuiting another, destroying the adjustment of a third, putting dirt between the electrodes of a fourth, and so on. A man would be sent to each to find out the trouble. When he could find the trouble ten consecutive times, using five minutes each, he was sent to London. About sixty men were sifted to get twenty. Before all had arrived, the Bell company there, seeing we could not be stopped, entered into negotiations for consolidation. One day I received a cable from Gouraud offering '30,000' for my interest. I cabled back I would accept. When the draft came I was astonished to find it was for L30,000. I had thought it was dollars."

In regard to this singular and happy conclusion, Edison makes some interesting comments as to the attitude of the courts toward inventors, and the difference between American and English courts. "The men I sent over were used to establish telephone exchanges all over the Continent, and some of them became wealthy. It was among this crowd in London that Bernard Shaw was employed before he became famous. The chalk telephone was finally discarded in favor of the Bell receiver--the latter being more simple and cheaper. Extensive litigation with new-comers followed. My carbon-transmitter patent was sustained, and preserved the monopoly of the telephone in England for many years. Bell's patent was not sustained by the courts. Sir Richard Webster, now Chief-Justice of England, was my counsel, and sustained all of my patents in England for many years. Webster has a marvellous capacity for understanding things scientific; and his address before the courts was lucidity itself. His brain is highly organized. My experience with the legal fraternity is that scientific subjects are distasteful to them, and it is rare in this country, on account of the system of trying patent suits, for a judge really to reach the meat of the controversy, and inventors scarcely ever get a decision squarely and entirely in their favor. The fault rests, in my judgment, almost wholly with the system under which testimony to the extent of thousands of pages bearing on all conceivable subjects, many of them having no possible connection with the invention in dispute, is presented to an over-worked judge in an hour or two of argument supported by several hundred pages of briefs; and the judge is supposed to extract some essence of justice from this mass of conflicting, blind, and misleading statements. It is a human impossibility, no matter how able and fair-minded the judge may be. In England the case is different. There the judges are face to face with the experts and other witnesses. They get the testimony first-hand and only so much as they need, and there are no long-winded briefs and arguments, and the case is decided then and there, a few months perhaps after suit is brought, instead of many years afterward, as in this country. And in England, when a case is once finally decided it is settled for the whole country, while here it is not so. Here a patent having once been sustained, say, in Boston, may have to be litigated all over again in New York, and again in Philadelphia, and so on for all the Federal circuits. Furthermore, it seems to me that scientific disputes should be decided by some court containing at least one or two scientific men--men capable of comprehending the significance of an invention and the difficulties of its accomplishment--if justice is ever to be given to an inventor. And I think, also, that this court should have the power to summon before it and examine any recognized expert in the special art, who might be able to testify to FACTS for or against the patent, instead of trying to gather the truth from the tedious essays of hired experts, whose depositions are really nothing but sworn arguments. The real gist of patent suits is generally very simple, and I have no doubt that any judge of fair intelligence, assisted by one or more scientific advisers, could in a couple of days at the most examine all the necessary witnesses; hear all the necessary arguments, and actually decide an ordinary patent suit in a way that would more nearly be just, than can now be done at an expenditure of a hundred times as much money and months and years of preparation. And I have no doubt that the time taken by the court would be enormously less, because if a judge attempts to read the bulky records and briefs, that work alone would require several days.

"Acting as judges, inventors would not be very apt to correctly decide a complicated law point; and on the other hand, it is hard to see how a lawyer can decide a complicated scientific point rightly. Some inventors complain of our Patent Office, but my own experience with the Patent Office is that the examiners are fair-minded and intelligent, and when they refuse a patent they are generally right; but I think the whole trouble lies with the system in vogue in the Federal courts for trying patent suits, and in the fact, which cannot be disputed, that the Federal judges, with but few exceptions, do not comprehend complicated scientific questions. To secure uniformity in the several Federal circuits and correct errors, it has been proposed to establish a central court of patent appeals in Washington. This I believe in; but this court should also contain at least two scientific men, who would not be blind to the sophistry of paid experts. [7] Men whose inventions would have created wealth of millions have been ruined and prevented from making any money whereby they could continue their careers as creators of wealth for the general good, just because the experts befuddled the judge by their misleading statements."

[Footnote 7: As an illustration of the perplexing nature of expert evidence in patent cases, the reader will probably be interested in perusing the following extracts from the opinion of Judge Dayton, in the suit of Bryce Bros. Co. vs. Seneca Glass Co., tried in the United States Circuit Court, Northern District of West Virginia, reported in The Federal Reporter, 140, page 161:

"On this subject of the validity of this patent, a vast amount of conflicting, technical, perplexing, and almost hypercritical discussion and opinion has been indulged, both in the testimony and in the able and exhaustive arguments and briefs of counsel. Expert Osborn for defendant, after setting forth minutely his superior qualifications mechanical education, and great experience, takes up in detail the patent claims, and shows to his own entire satisfaction that none of them are new; that all of them have been applied, under one form or another, in some twenty-two previous patents, and in two other machines, not

patented, to-wit, the Central Glass and Kuny Kahbel ones;
that the whole machine is only 'an aggregation of well-known
mechanical elements that any skilled designer would bring to
his use in the construction of such a machine.' This
certainly, under ordinary conditions, would settle the
matter beyond peradventure; for this witness is a very wise
and learned man in these things, and very positive. But
expert Clarke appears for the plaintiff, and after setting
forth just as minutely his superior qualifications,
mechanical education, and great experience, which appear
fully equal in all respects to those of expert Osborn,
proceeds to take up in detail the patent claims, and shows
to his entire satisfaction that all, with possibly one
exception, are new, show inventive genius, and distinct
advances upon the prior art. In the most lucid, and even
fascinating, way he discusses all the parts of this machine,
compares it with the others, draws distinctions, points out
the merits of the one in controversy and the defects of all
the others, considers the twenty-odd patents referred to by
Osborn, and in the politest, but neatest, manner imaginable
shows that expert Osborn did not know what he was talking
about, and sums the whole matter up by declaring this
'invention of Mr. Schrader's, as embodied in the patent in
suit, a radical and wide departure, from the Kahbel machine'
(admitted on all sides to be nearest prior approach to it),
'a distinct and important advance in the art of engraving
glassware, and generally a machine for this purpose which
has involved the exercise of the inventive faculty in the
highest degree.'

"Thus a more radical and irreconcilable disagreement between
experts touching the same thing could hardly be found. So it
is with the testimony. If we take that for the defendant,
the Central Glass Company machine, and especially the Kuny
Kahbel machine, built and operated years before this patent
issued, and not patented, are just as good, just as
effective and practical, as this one, and capable of turning
out just as perfect work and as great a variety of it. On
the other hand, if we take that produced by the plaintiff,
we are driven to the conclusion that these prior machines,
the product of the same mind, were only progressive steps
forward from utter darkness, so to speak, into full
inventive sunlight, which made clear to him the solution of
the problem in this patented machine. The shortcomings of
the earlier machines are minutely set forth, and the
witnesses for the plaintiff are clear that they are neither
practical nor profitable.

"But this is not all of the trouble that confronts us in
this case. Counsel of both sides, with an indomitable
courage that must command admiration, a courage that has led
them to a vast amount of study, investigation, and thought,
that in fact has made them all experts, have dissected this
record of 356 closely printed pages, applied all mechanical

principles and laws to the facts as they see them, and, besides, have ransacked the law-books and cited an enormous number of cases, more or less in point, as illustration of their respective contentions. The courts find nothing more difficult than to apply an abstract principle to all classes of cases that may arise. The facts in each case so frequently create an exception to the general rule that such rule must be honored rather in its breach than in its observance. Therefore, after a careful examination of these cases, it is no criticism of the courts to say that both sides have found abundant and about an equal amount of authority to sustain their respective contentions, and, as a result, counsel have submitted, in briefs, a sum total of 225 closely printed pages, in which they have clearly, yet, almost to a mathematical certainty, demonstrated on the one side that this Schrader machine is new and patentable, and on the other that it is old and not so. Under these circumstances, it would be unnecessary labor and a fruitless task for me to enter into any further technical discussion of the mechanical problems involved, for the purpose of seeking to convince either side of its error. In cases of such perplexity as this generally some incidents appear that speak more unerringly than do the tongues of the witnesses, and to some of these I purpose to now refer."]

Mr. Bernard Shaw, the distinguished English author, has given a most vivid and amusing picture of this introduction of Edison's telephone into England, describing the apparatus as "a much too ingenious invention, being nothing less than a telephone of such stentorian efficiency that it bellowed your most private communications all over the house, instead of whispering them with some sort of discretion." Shaw, as a young man, was employed by the Edison Telephone Company, and was very much alive to his surroundings, often assisting in public demonstrations of the apparatus "in a manner which I am persuaded laid the foundation of Mr. Edison's reputation." The sketch of the men sent over from America is graphic: "Whilst the Edison Telephone Company lasted it crowded the basement of a high pile of offices in Queen Victoria Street with American artificers. These deluded and romantic men gave me a glimpse of the skilled proletariat of the United States. They sang obsolete sentimental songs with genuine emotion; and their language was frightful even to an Irishman. They worked with a ferocious energy which was out of all proportion to the actual result achieved. Indomitably resolved to assert their republican manhood by taking no orders from a tall-hatted Englishman whose stiff politeness covered his conviction that they were relatively to himself inferior and common persons, they insisted on being slave-driven with genuine American oaths by a genuine free and equal American foreman. They utterly despised the artfully slow British workman, who did as little for his wages as he possibly could; never hurried himself; and had a deep reverence for one whose pocket could be tapped by respectful behavior. Need I add that they were contemptuously wondered at by this same British workman as a parcel of outlandish adult boys who sweated themselves for their employer's benefit instead of looking after their own interest? They adored Mr. Edison as the greatest man of all time in every possible department of science, art, and philosophy, and execrated Mr. Graham Bell, the inventor of the rival telephone, as his Satanic adversary; but each of them had (or intended to have) on the brink of completion an improvement on the telephone, usually a new transmitter. They were free-souled creatures, excellent company, sensitive, cheerful, and profane; liars, braggarts, and hustlers, with an air of making slow old England hum, which never left them even when, as often happened, they were wrestling with difficulties of their own making, or struggling in no-thoroughfares, from which they had to be retrieved like stray sheep by Englishmen without imagination enough to go wrong."

Mr. Samuel Insull, who afterward became private secretary to Mr. Edison, and a leader in the development of American electrical manufacturing and the central-station art, was also in close touch with the London situation thus depicted, being at the time private secretary to Colonel Gouraud, and acting for the first half hour as the amateur telephone operator in the first experimental exchange erected in Europe. He took notes of an early meeting where the affairs of the company were discussed by leading men like Sir John Lubbock (Lord Avebury) and the Right Hon. E. P. Bouverie (then a cabinet minister), none of whom could see in the telephone much more than an auxiliary for getting out promptly in the next morning's papers the midnight debates in Parliament. "I remember another incident," says Mr. Insull. "It was at some celebration of one of the Royal Societies at the Burlington House, Piccadilly. We had a telephone line running across the roofs to the basement of the building. I think it was to Tyndall's laboratory in Burlington Street. As the ladies and gentlemen came through, they naturally wanted to look at the great curiosity, the loud-speaking telephone: in fact, any telephone was a curiosity then. Mr. and Mrs. Gladstone came through. I was handling the telephone at the Burlington House end. Mrs. Gladstone asked the man over the telephone whether he knew if a man or woman was speaking; and the reply came in quite loud tones that it was a man!"

With Mr. E. H. Johnson, who represented Edison, there went to England for the furtherance of this telephone enterprise, Mr. Charles Edison, a nephew of the inventor. He died in Paris, October, 1879, not twenty years of age. Stimulated by the example of his uncle, this brilliant youth had already made a mark for himself as a student and inventor, and when only eighteen he secured in open competition the contract to install a complete fire-alarm telegraph system for Port Huron. A few months later he was eagerly welcomed by his uncle at Menlo Park, and after working on the telephone was sent to London to aid in its introduction. There he made the acquaintance of Professor Tyndall, exhibited the telephone to the late King of England; and also won the friendship of the late King of the Belgians, with whom he took up the project of establishing telephonic communication between Belgium and England. At the time of his premature death he was engaged in installing the Edison quadruplex between Brussels and Paris, being one of the very few persons then in Europe familiar with the working of that invention.

Meantime, the telephonic art in America was undergoing very rapid development. In March, 1878, addressing "the capitalists of the Electric Telephone Company" on the future of his invention, Bell outlined with prophetic foresight and remarkable clearness the coming of the modern telephone exchange. Comparing with gas and water distribution, he said: "In a similar manner, it is conceivable that cables of telephone wires could be laid underground or suspended overhead communicating by branch wires with private dwellings, country houses, shops, manufactories, etc., uniting them through the main cable with a central office, where the wire could be connected as desired, establishing direct communication between any two places in the city.... Not only so, but I believe, in the future, wires will unite the head offices of telephone companies in different cities; and a man in one part of the country may communicate by word of mouth with another in a distant place."

All of which has come to pass. Professor Bell also suggested how this could be done by "the employ of a man in each central office for the purpose of connecting the wires as directed." He also indicated the two methods of telephonic tariff--a fixed rental and a toll; and mentioned the practice, now in use on long-distance lines, of a time charge. As a matter of fact, this "centralizing" was attempted in May, 1877, in Boston, with the circuits of the Holmes burglar-alarm system, four banking-houses being thus interconnected; while in January of 1878 the Bell telephone central-office system at New Haven, Connecticut, was opened for business, "the first fully equipped commercial telephone exchange ever established for public or general service."

All through this formative period Bell had adhered to and introduced the magneto form of telephone, now used only as a receiver, and very poorly adapted for the vital function of a speech-transmitter. From August, 1877, the Western Union Telegraph Company worked along the other line, and in 1878, with its allied Gold & Stock Telegraph Company, it brought into existence the American Speaking Telephone Company to introduce the Edison apparatus, and to create telephone exchanges all over the country. In this warfare, the possession of a good battery transmitter counted very heavily in favor of the Western Union, for upon that the real expansion of the whole industry depended; but in a few months the Bell system had its battery transmitter, too, tending to equalize matters. Late in the same year patent litigation was begun which brought out clearly the merits of Bell, through his patent, as the original and first inventor of the electric speaking telephone; and the Western Union Telegraph Company made terms with its rival. A famous contract bearing date of November 10, 1879, showed that under the Edison and other controlling patents the Western Union Company had already set going some eighty-five exchanges, and was making large quantities of telephonic apparatus. In return for its voluntary retirement from the telephonic field, the Western Union Telegraph Company, under this contract, received a royalty of 20 per cent. of all the telephone earnings of the Bell system while the Bell patents ran; and thus came to enjoy an annual income of several hundred thousand dollars for some years, based chiefly on its modest investment in Edison's work. It was also paid several thousand dollars in cash for the Edison, Phelps, Gray, and other apparatus on hand. It secured further 40 per cent. of the stock of the local telephone systems of New York and Chicago; and last, but by no means least, it exacted from the Bell interests an agreement to stay out of the telegraph field.

By March, 1881, there were in the United States only nine cities of more than ten thousand inhabitants, and only one of more than fifteen thousand, without a telephone exchange. The industry thrived under competition, and the absence of it now had a decided effect in checking growth; for when the Bell patent expired in 1893, the total of telephone sets in operation in the United States was only 291,253. To quote from an official Bell statement:

"The brief but vigorous Western Union competition was a kind of blessing in disguise. The very fact that two distinct interests were actively engaged in the work of organizing and establishing competing telephone exchanges all over the country, greatly facilitated the spread of the idea and the growth of the business, and familiarized the people with the use of the telephone as a business agency; while the keenness of the competition, extending to the agents and employees of both companies, brought about a swift but quite unforeseen and unlooked-for expansion in the individual exchanges of the larger cities, and a corresponding advance in their importance, value, and usefulness."

The truth of this was immediately shown in 1894, after the Bell patents had expired, by the tremendous outburst of new competitive activity, in "independent" country systems and toll lines through sparsely settled districts--work for which the Edison apparatus and methods were peculiarly adapted, yet against which the influence of the Edison patent was invoked. The data secured by the United States Census Office in 1902 showed that the whole industry had made gigantic leaps in eight years, and had 2,371,044 telephone stations in service, of which 1,053,866 were wholly or nominally independent of the Bell. By 1907 an even more notable increase was shown, and the Census figures for that year included no fewer than 6,118,578 stations, of which 1,986,575 were "independent." These six million instruments every single set employing the principle of the carbon transmitter--were grouped into 15,527 public exchanges, in the very manner predicted by Bell thirty years before, and they gave service in the shape of over eleven billions of talks. The outstanding capitalized value of the plant was $814,616,004, the income for the year was nearly $185,000,000, and the people employed were 140,000. If Edison had done nothing else, his share in the creation of such an industry would have entitled him to a high place among inventors.

This chapter is of necessity brief in its reference to many extremely interesting points and details; and to some readers it may seem incomplete in its references to the work of other men than Edison, whose influence on telephony as an art has also been considerable. In reply to this pertinent criticism, it may be pointed out that this is a life of Edison, and not of any one else; and that even the discussion of his achievements alone in these various fields requires more space than the authors have at their disposal. The attempt has been made, however, to indicate the course of events and deal fairly with the facts. The controversy that once waged with great excitement over the invention of the microphone, but has long since died away, is suggestive of the difficulties involved in trying to do justice to everybody. A standard history describes the microphone thus:

"A form of apparatus produced during the early days of the telephone by Professor Hughes, of England, for the purpose of rendering faint, indistinct sounds distinctly audible, depended for its operation on the changes that result in the resistance of loose contacts. This apparatus was called the microphone, and was in reality but one of the many forms that it is possible to give to the telephone transmitter. For example, the Edison granular transmitter was a variety of microphone, as was also Edison's transmitter, in which the solid button of carbon was employed. Indeed, even the platinum point, which in the early form of the Reis transmitter pressed against the platinum contact cemented to the centre of the diaphragm, was a microphone."

At a time when most people were amazed at the idea of hearing, with the aid of a "microphone," a fly walk at a distance of many miles, the priority of invention of such a device was hotly disputed. Yet without desiring to take anything from the credit of the brilliant American, Hughes, whose telegraphic apparatus is still in use all over Europe, it may be pointed out that this passage gives Edison the attribution of at least two original forms of which those suggested by Hughes were mere variations and modifications. With regard to this matter, Mr. Edison himself remarks: "After I sent one of my men over to London especially, to show Preece the carbon transmitter, and where Hughes first saw it, and heard it--then within a month he came out with the microphone, without any acknowledgment whatever. Published dates will show that Hughes came along after me."

There have been other ways also in which Edison has utilized the peculiar property that carbon possesses of altering its resistance to the passage of current, according to the pressure to which it is subjected, whether at the surface, or through closer union of the mass. A loose road with a few inches of dust or pebbles on it offers appreciable resistance to the wheels of vehicles travelling over it; but if the surface is kept hard and smooth the effect is quite different. In the same way carbon, whether solid or in the shape of finely divided powder, offers a high resistance to the passage of electricity; but if the carbon is squeezed together the conditions change, with less resistance to electricity in the circuit. For his quadruplex system, Mr. Edison utilized this fact in the construction of a rheostat or resistance box. It consists of a series of silk disks saturated with a sizing of plumbago and well dried. The disks are compressed by means of an adjustable screw; and in this manner the resistance of a circuit can be varied over a wide range.

In like manner Edison developed a "pressure" or carbon relay, adapted to the transference of signals of variable strength from one circuit to another. An ordinary relay consists of an electromagnet inserted in the main line for telegraphing, which brings a local battery and sounder circuit into play, reproducing in the local circuit the signals sent over the main line. The relay is adjusted to the weaker currents likely to be received, but the signals reproduced on the sounder by the agency of the relay are, of course, all of equal strength, as they depend upon the local battery, which has only this steady work to perform. In cases where it is desirable to reproduce the signals in the local circuit with the same variations in strength as they are received by the relay, the Edison carbon pressure relay does the work. The poles of the electromagnet in the local circuit are hollowed out and filled up with carbon disks or powdered plumbago. The armature and the carbon-tipped poles of the electromagnet form part of the local circuit; and if the relay is actuated by a weak current the armature will be attracted but feebly. The carbon being only slightly compressed will offer considerable resistance to the flow of current from the local battery, and therefore the signal on the local sounder will be weak. If, on the contrary, the incoming current on the main line be strong, the armature will be strongly attracted, the carbon will be sharply compressed, the resistance in the local circuit will be proportionately lowered, and the signal heard on the local sounder will be a loud one. Thus it will be seen, by another clever juggle with the willing agent, carbon, for which he has found so many duties, Edison is able to transfer or transmit exactly, to the local circuit, the main-line current in all its minutest variations.

In his researches to determine the nature of the motograph phenomena, and to open up other sources of electrical current generation, Edison has worked out a very ingenious and somewhat perplexing piece of apparatus known as the "chalk battery." It consists of a series of chalk cylinders mounted on a shaft revolved by hand. Resting against each of these cylinders is a palladium-faced spring, and similar springs make contact with the shaft between each cylinder. By connecting all these springs in circuit with a galvanometer and revolving the shaft rapidly, a notable deflection is obtained of the galvanometer needle, indicating the production of electrical energy. The reason for this does not appear to have been determined.

Last but not least, in this beautiful and ingenious series, comes the "tasimeter," an instrument of most delicate sensibility in the presence of heat. The name is derived from the Greek, the use of the apparatus being primarily to measure extremely minute differences of pressure. A strip of hard rubber with pointed ends rests perpendicularly on a platinum plate, beneath which is a carbon button, under which again lies another platinum plate. The two plates and the carbon button form part of an electric circuit containing a battery and a galvanometer. The hard-rubber strip is exceedingly sensitive to heat. The slightest degree of heat imparted to it causes it to expand invisibly, thus increasing the pressure contact on the carbon button and producing a variation in the resistance of the circuit, registered immediately by the little swinging needle of the galvanometer. The instrument is so sensitive that with a delicate galvanometer it will show the impingement of the heat from a person's hand thirty feet away. The suggestion to employ such an apparatus in astronomical observations occurs at once, and it may be noted that in one instance the heat of rays of light from the remote star Arcturus gave results.

CHAPTER X

THE PHONOGRAPH

AT the opening of the Electrical Show in New York City in October, 1908, to celebrate the jubilee of the Atlantic Cable and the first quarter century of lighting with the Edison service on Manhattan Island, the exercises were all conducted by means of the Edison phonograph. This included the dedicatory speech of Governor Hughes, of New York; the modest remarks of Mr. Edison, as president; the congratulations of the presidents of several national electric bodies, and a number of vocal and instrumental selections of operatic nature. All this was heard clearly by a very large audience, and was repeated on other evenings. The same speeches were used again phonographically at the Electrical Show in Chicago in 1909--and now the records are preserved for reproduction a hundred or a thousand years hence. This tour de force, never attempted before, was merely an exemplification of the value of the phonograph not only in establishing at first hand the facts of history, but in preserving the human voice. What would we not give to listen to the very accents and tones of the Sermon on the Mount, the orations of Demosthenes, the first Pitt's appeal for American liberty, the Farewell of Washington, or the Address at Gettysburg? Until Edison made his wonderful invention in 1877, the human race was entirely without means for preserving or passing on to posterity its own linguistic utterances or any other vocal sound. We have some idea how the ancients looked and felt and wrote; the abundant evidence takes us back to the cave-dwellers. But all the old languages are dead, and the literary form is their embalmment. We do not even know definitely how Shakespeare's and Goldsmith's plays were pronounced on the stage in the theatres of the time; while it is only a guess that perhaps Chaucer would sound much more modern than he scans.

The analysis of sound, which owes so much to Helmholtz, was one step toward recording; and the various means of illustrating the phenomena of sound to the eye and ear, prior to the phonograph, were all ingenious. One can watch the dancing little flames of Koenig, and see a voice expressed in tongues of fire; but the record can only be photographic. In like manner, the simple phonautograph of Leon Scott, invented about 1858, records on a revolving cylinder of blackened paper the sound vibrations transmitted through a membrane to which a tiny stylus is attached; so that a human mouth uses a pen and inscribes its sign vocal. Yet after all we are just as far away as ever from enabling the young actors at Harvard to give Aristophanes with all the true, subtle intonation and inflection of the Athens of 400 B.C. The instrument is dumb. Ingenuity has been shown also in the invention of "talking-machines," like Faber's, based on the reed organ pipe. These automata can be made by dexterous manipulation to jabber a little, like a doll with its monotonous "ma-ma," or a cuckoo clock; but they lack even the sterile utility of the imitative art of ventriloquism. The real great invention lies in creating devices that shall be able to evoke from tinfoil, wax, or composition at any time to-day or in the future the sound that once was as evanescent as the vibrations it made on the air.

Contrary to the general notion, very few of the great modern inventions have been the result of a sudden inspiration by which, Minerva-like, they have sprung full-fledged from their creators' brain; but, on the contrary, they have been evolved by slow and gradual steps, so that frequently the final advance has been often almost imperceptible. The Edison phonograph is an important exception to the general rule; not, of course, the phonograph of the present day with all of its mechanical perfection, but as an instrument capable of recording and reproducing sound. Its invention has been frequently attributed to the discovery that a point attached to a telephone diaphragm would, under the effect of sound-waves, vibrate with sufficient force to prick the finger. The story, though interesting, is not founded on fact; but, if true, it is difficult to see how the discovery in question could have contributed materially to the ultimate accomplishment. To a man of Edison's perception it is absurd to suppose that the effect of the so-called discovery would not have been made as a matter of deduction long before the physical sensation was experienced. As a matter of fact, the invention of the phonograph was the result of pure reason. Some time prior to 1877, Edison had been experimenting on an automatic telegraph in which the letters were formed by embossing strips of paper with the proper arrangement of dots and dashes. By drawing this strip beneath a contact lever, the latter was actuated so as to control the circuits and send the desired signals over the line. It was observed that when the strip was moved very rapidly the vibration of the lever resulted in the production of an audible note. With these facts before him, Edison reasoned that if the paper strip could be imprinted with elevations and depressions representative of sound-waves, they might be caused to actuate a diaphragm so as to reproduce the corresponding sounds. The next step in the line of development was to form the necessary undulations on the strip, and it was then reasoned that original sounds themselves might be utilized to form a graphic record by actuating a diaphragm and causing a cutting or indenting point carried thereby to vibrate in contact with a moving surface, so as to cut or indent the record therein. Strange as it may seem, therefore, and contrary to the general belief, the phonograph was developed backward, the production of the sounds being of prior development to the idea of actually recording them.

Mr. Edison's own account of the invention of the phonograph is intensely interesting. "I was experimenting," he says, "on an automatic method of recording telegraph messages on a disk of paper laid on a revolving platen, exactly the same as the disk talking-machine of to-day. The platen had a spiral groove on its surface, like the disk. Over this was placed a circular disk of paper; an electromagnet with the embossing point connected to an arm travelled over the disk; and any signals given through the magnets were embossed on the disk of paper. If this disk was removed from the machine and put on a similar machine provided with a contact point, the embossed record would cause the signals to be repeated into another wire. The ordinary speed of telegraphic signals is thirty-five to forty words a minute; but with this machine several hundred words were possible.

"From my experiments on the telephone I knew of the power of a diaphragm to take up sound vibrations, as I had made a little toy which, when you recited loudly in the funnel, would work a pawl connected to the diaphragm; and this engaging a ratchet-wheel served to give continuous rotation to a pulley. This pulley was connected by a cord to a little paper toy representing a man sawing wood. Hence, if one shouted: 'Mary had a little lamb,' etc., the paper man would start sawing wood. I reached the conclusion that if I could record the movements of the diaphragm properly, I could cause such record to reproduce the original movements imparted to the diaphragm by the voice, and thus succeed in recording and reproducing the human voice.

"Instead of using a disk I designed a little machine using a cylinder provided with grooves around the surface. Over this was to be placed tinfoil, which easily received and recorded the movements of the diaphragm. A sketch was made, and the piece-work price, $18, was marked on the sketch. I was in the habit of marking the price I would pay on each sketch. If the workman lost, I would pay his regular wages; if he made more than the wages, he kept it. The workman who got the sketch was John Kruesi. I didn't have much faith that it would work, expecting that I might possibly hear a word or so that would give hope of a future for the idea. Kruesi, when he had nearly finished it, asked what it was for. I told him I was going to record talking, and then have the machine talk back. He thought it absurd. However, it was finished, the foil was put on; I then shouted 'Mary had a little lamb,' etc. I adjusted the reproducer, and the machine reproduced it perfectly. I was never so taken aback in my life. Everybody was astonished. I was always afraid of things that worked the first time. Long experience proved that there were great drawbacks found generally before they could be got commercial; but here was something there was no doubt of."

No wonder that honest John Kruesi, as he stood and listened to the marvellous performance of the simple little machine he had himself just finished, ejaculated in an awe-stricken tone: "Mein Gott im Himmel!" And yet he had already seen Edison do a few clever things. No wonder they sat up all night fixing and adjusting it so as to get better and better results--reciting and singing, trying each other's voices, and then listening with involuntary awe as the words came back again and again, just as long as they were willing to revolve the little cylinder with its dotted spiral indentations in the tinfoil under the vibrating stylus of the reproducing diaphragm. It took a little time to acquire the knack of turning the crank steadily while leaning over the recorder to talk into the machine; and there was some deftness required also in fastening down the tinfoil on the cylinder where it was held by a pin running in a longitudinal slot. Paraffined paper appears also to have been experimented with as an impressible material. It is said that Carman, the foreman of the machine shop, had gone the length of wagering Edison a box of cigars that the device would not work. All the world knows that he lost.

The original Edison phonograph thus built by Kruesi is preserved in the South Kensington Museum, London. That repository can certainly have no greater treasure of its kind. But as to its immediate use, the inventor says: "That morning I took it over to New York and walked into the office of the Scientific American, went up to Mr. Beach's desk, and said I had something to show him. He asked what it was. I told him I had a machine that would record and reproduce the human voice. I opened the package, set up the machine and recited, 'Mary had a little lamb,' etc.

Then I reproduced it so that it could be heard all over the room. They kept me at it until the crowd got so great Mr. Beach was afraid the floor would collapse; and we were compelled to stop. The papers next morning contained columns. None of the writers seemed to understand how it was done. I tried to explain, it was so very simple, but the results were so surprising they made up their minds probably that they never would understand it--and they didn't.

"I started immediately making several larger and better machines, which I exhibited at Menlo Park to crowds. The Pennsylvania Railroad ran special trains. Washington people telegraphed me to come on. I took a phonograph to Washington and exhibited it in the room of James G. Blaine's niece (Gail Hamilton); and members of Congress and notable people of that city came all day long until late in the evening. I made one break. I recited 'Mary,' etc., and another ditty:

'There was a little girl, who had a little curl
Right in the middle of her forehead;
And when she was good she was very, very good,
But when she was bad she was horrid.'

"It will be remembered that Senator Roscoe Conkling, then very prominent, had a curl of hair on his forehead; and all the caricaturists developed it abnormally. He was very sensitive about the subject. When he came in he was introduced; but being rather deaf, I didn't catch his name, but sat down and started the curl ditty. Everybody tittered, and I was told that Mr. Conkling was displeased. About 11 o'clock at night word was received from President Hayes that he would be very much pleased if I would come up to the White House. I was taken there, and found Mr. Hayes and several others waiting. Among them I remember Carl Schurz, who was playing the piano when I entered the room. The exhibition continued till about 12.30 A.M., when Mrs. Hayes and several other ladies, who had been induced to get up and dress, appeared. I left at 3.30 A.M.

"For a long time some people thought there was trickery. One morning at Menlo Park a gentleman came to the laboratory and asked to see the phonograph. It was Bishop Vincent, who helped Lewis Miller found the Chautauqua I exhibited it, and then he asked if he could speak a few words. I put on a fresh foil and told him to go ahead. He commenced to recite Biblical names with immense rapidity. On reproducing it he said: 'I am satisfied, now. There isn't a man in the United States who could recite those names with the same rapidity.'"

The phonograph was now fairly launched as a world sensation, and a reference to the newspapers of 1878 will show the extent to which it and Edison were themes of universal discussion. Some of the press notices of the period were most amazing--and amusing. As though the real achievements of this young man, barely thirty, were not tangible and solid enough to justify admiration of his genius, the "yellow journalists" of the period began busily to create an "Edison myth," with gross absurdities of assertion and attribution from which the modest subject of it all has not yet ceased to suffer with unthinking people. A brilliantly vicious example of this method of treatment is to be found in the Paris Figaro of that year, which under the appropriate title of

"This Astounding Eddison" lay bare before the French public the most startling revelations as to the inventor's life and character. "It should be understood," said this journal, "that Mr. Eddison does not belong to himself. He is the property of the telegraph company which lodges him in New York at a superb hotel; keeps him on a luxurious footing, and pays him a formidable salary so as to be the one to know of and profit by his discoveries. The company has, in the dwelling of Eddison, men in its employ who do not quit him for a moment, at the table, on the street, in the laboratory. So that this wretched man, watched more closely than ever was any malefactor, cannot even give a moment's thought to his own private affairs without one of his guards asking him what he is thinking about." This foolish "blague" was accompanied by a description of Edison's new "aerophone," a steam machine which carried the voice a distance of one and a half miles. "You speak to a jet of vapor. A friend previously advised can answer you by the same method." Nor were American journals backward in this wild exaggeration.

The furor had its effect in stimulating a desire everywhere on the part of everybody to see and hear the phonograph. A small commercial organization was formed to build and exploit the apparatus, and the shops at Menlo Park laboratory were assisted by the little Bergmann shop in New York. Offices were taken for the new enterprise at 203 Broadway, where the Mail and Express building now stands, and where, in a general way, under the auspices of a talented dwarf, C. A. Cheever, the embryonic phonograph and the crude telephone shared rooms and expenses. Gardiner G. Hubbard, father-in-law of Alex. Graham Bell, was one of the stockholders in the Phonograph Company, which paid Edison $10,000 cash and a 20 per cent. royalty. This curious partnership was maintained for some time, even when the Bell Telephone offices were removed to Reade Street, New York, whither the phonograph went also; and was perhaps explained by the fact that just then the ability of the phonograph as a money-maker was much more easily demonstrated than was that of the telephone, still in its short range magneto stage and awaiting development with the aid of the carbon transmitter.

The earning capacity of the phonograph then, as largely now, lay in its exhibition qualities. The royalties from Boston, ever intellectually awake and ready for something new, ran as high as $1800 a week. In New York there was a ceaseless demand for it, and with the aid of Hilbourne L. Roosevelt, a famous organ builder, and uncle of ex-President Roosevelt, concerts were given at which the phonograph was "featured." To manage this novel show business the services of James Redpath were called into requisition with great success. Redpath, famous as a friend and biographer of John Brown, as a Civil War correspondent, and as founder of the celebrated Redpath Lyceum Bureau in Boston, divided the country into territories, each section being leased for exhibition purposes on a basis of a percentage of the "gate money." To 203 Broadway from all over the Union flocked a swarm of showmen, cranks, and particularly of old operators, who, the seedier they were in appearance, the more insistent they were that "Tom" should give them, for the sake of "Auld lang syne," this chance to make a fortune for him and for themselves. At the top of the building was a floor on which these novices were graduated in the use and care of the machine, and then, with an equipment of tinfoil and other supplies, they were sent out on the road. It was a diverting experience while it lasted. The excitement over the phonograph was maintained for many months, until a large proportion of the inhabitants of the country had seen it; and then the show receipts declined and dwindled away. Many of the old operators, taken on out of good-nature, were poor exhibitors and worse accountants, and at last they and the machines with which they had been intrusted faded from sight. But in the mean time Edison had learned many lessons as to this practical side of development that were not forgotten when the renascence of the phonograph began a few years later, leading up to the present enormous and steady demand for both machines and records.

It deserves to be pointed out that the phonograph has changed little in the intervening years from the first crude instruments of 1877-78. It has simply been refined and made more perfect in a mechanical sense. Edison was immensely impressed with its possibilities, and greatly inclined to work upon it, but the coming of the electric light compelled him to throw all his energies for a time into the vast new field awaiting conquest. The original phonograph, as briefly noted above, was rotated by hand, and the cylinder was fed slowly longitudinally by means of a nut engaging a screw thread on the cylinder shaft. Wrapped around the cylinder was a sheet of tinfoil, with which engaged a small chisel-like recording needle, connected adhesively with the centre of an iron diaphragm. Obviously, as the cylinder was turned, the needle followed a spiral path whose pitch depended upon that of the feed screw. Along this path a thread was cut in the cylinder so as to permit the needle to indent the foil readily as the diaphragm vibrated. By rotating the cylinder and by causing the diaphragm to vibrate under the effect of vocal or musical sounds, the needle-like point would form a series of indentations in the foil corresponding to and characteristic of the sound-waves. By now engaging the point with the beginning of the grooved record so formed, and by again rotating the cylinder, the undulations of the record would cause the needle and its attached diaphragm to vibrate so as to effect the reproduction. Such an apparatus was necessarily undeveloped, and was interesting only from a scientific point of view. It had many mechanical defects which prevented its use as a practical apparatus. Since the cylinder was rotated by hand, the speed at which the record was formed would vary considerably, even with the same manipulator, so that it would have been impossible to record and reproduce music satisfactorily; in doing which exact uniformity of speed is essential. The formation of the record in tinfoil was also objectionable from a practical standpoint, since such a record was faint and would be substantially obliterated after two or three reproductions. Furthermore, the foil could not be easily removed from and replaced upon the instrument, and consequently the reproduction had to follow the recording immediately, and the successive tinfoils were thrown away. The instrument was also heavy and bulky. Notwithstanding these objections the original phonograph created, as already remarked, an enormous popular excitement, and the exhibitions were considered by many sceptical persons as nothing more than clever ventriloquism. The possibilities of the instrument as a commercial apparatus were recognized from the very first, and some of the fields in which it was predicted that the phonograph would be used are now fully occupied. Some have not yet been realized. Writing in 1878 in the North

American-Review, Mr. Edison thus summed up his own ideas as to the future applications of the new invention:

"Among the many uses to which the phonograph will be applied are the following:

1. Letter writing and all kinds of dictation without the aid of a stenographer.

2. Phonographic books, which will speak to blind people without effort on their part.

3. The teaching of elocution.

4. Reproduction of music.

5. The 'Family Record'--a registry of sayings, reminiscences, etc., by members of a family in their own voices, and of the last words of dying persons.

6. Music-boxes and toys.

7. Clocks that should announce in articulate speech the time for going home, going to meals, etc.

8. The preservation of languages by exact reproduction of the manner of pronouncing.

9. Educational purposes; such as preserving the explanations made by a teacher, so that the pupil can refer to them at any moment, and spelling or other lessons placed upon the phonograph for convenience in committing to memory.

10. Connection with the telephone, so as to make that instrument an auxiliary in the transmission of permanent and invaluable records, instead of being the recipient of momentary and fleeting communication."

Of the above fields of usefulness in which it was expected that the phonograph might be applied, only three have been commercially realized--namely, the reproduction of musical, including vaudeville or talking selections, for which purpose a very large proportion of the phonographs now made is used; the employment of the machine as a mechanical stenographer, which field has been taken up actively only within the past few years; and the utilization of the device for the teaching of languages, for which purpose it has been successfully employed, for example, by the International Correspondence Schools of Scranton, Pennsylvania, for several years. The other uses, however, which were early predicted for the phonograph have not as yet been worked out practically, although the time seems not far distant when its general utility will be widely enlarged. Both dolls and clocks have been made, but thus far the world has not taken them seriously.

The original phonograph, as invented by Edison, remained in its crude and immature state for almost ten years--still the object of philosophical interest, and as a convenient text-book illustration of the effect of sound vibration. It continued to be a theme of curious interest to the imaginative, and the subject of much fiction, while its neglected commercial possibilities were still more or less vaguely referred to. During this period of arrested development, Edison was continuously working on the invention and commercial exploitation of the incandescent lamp. In 1887 his time was comparatively free, and the phonograph was then taken up with renewed energy, and the effort made to overcome its mechanical defects and to furnish a commercial instrument, so that its early promise might be realized. The important changes made from that time up to 1890 converted the phonograph from a scientific toy into a successful industrial apparatus. The idea of forming the record on tinfoil had been early abandoned, and in its stead was substituted a cylinder of wax-like material, in which the record was cut by a minute chisel-like gouging tool. Such a record or phonogram, as it was then called, could be removed from the machine or replaced at any time, many reproductions could be obtained without wearing out the record, and whenever desired the record could be shaved off by a turning-tool so as to present a fresh surface on which a new record could be formed, something like an ancient palimpsest. A wax cylinder having walls less than one-quarter of an inch in thickness could be used for receiving a large number of records, since the maximum depth of the record groove is hardly ever greater than one one-thousandth of an inch. Later on, and as the crowning achievement in the phonograph field, from a commercial point of view, came the duplication of records to the extent of many thousands from a single "master." This work was actively developed between the years 1890 and 1898, and its difficulties may be appreciated when the problem is stated; the copying from a single master of many millions of excessively minute sound-waves having a maximum width of one hundredth of an inch, and a maximum depth of one thousandth of an inch, or less than the thickness of a sheet of tissue-paper. Among the interesting developments of this process was the coating of the original or master record with a homogeneous film of gold so thin that three hundred thousand of these piled one on top of the other would present a thickness of only one inch!

Another important change was in the nature of a reversal of the original arrangement, the cylinder or mandrel carrying the record being mounted in fixed bearings, and the recording or reproducing device being fed lengthwise, like the cutting-tool of a lathe, as the blank or record was rotated. It was early recognized that a single needle for forming the record and the reproduction therefrom was an undesirable arrangement, since the formation of the record required a very sharp cutting-tool, while satisfactory and repeated reproduction suggested the use of a stylus which would result in the minimum wear. After many experiments and the production of a number of types of machines, the present recorders and reproducers were evolved, the former consisting of a very small cylindrical gouging tool having a diameter of about forty thousandths of an inch, and the latter a ball or button-shaped stylus with a diameter of about thirty-five thousandths of an inch. By using an incisor of this sort, the record is formed of a series of connected gouges with rounded sides, varying in depth and width, and with which the reproducer automatically engages and maintains its engagement. Another difficulty encountered in the commercial development of the phonograph was the adjustment of the recording stylus so as to enter the wax-like surface to a very slight depth, and of the reproducer so as to engage exactly the record when formed. The earlier types of machines were provided with separate screws for effecting these adjustments; but considerable skill was required to obtain good results, and great difficulty was experienced in meeting the variations in the wax-like cylinders, due to the warping under atmospheric changes. Consequently, with the early types of commercial phonographs, it was first necessary to shave off the blank accurately before a record was formed thereon, in order that an absolutely true surface might be presented. To overcome these troubles, the very ingenious suggestion was then made and adopted, of connecting the recording and reproducing styluses to their respective diaphragms through the instrumentality of a compensating weight, which acted practically as a fixed support under the very rapid sound vibrations, but which yielded readily to distortions or variations in the wax-like cylinders. By reason of this improvement, it became possible to do away with all adjustments, the mass of the compensating weight causing the recorder to engage the blank automatically to the required depth, and to maintain the reproducing stylus always with the desired pressure on the record when formed. These automatic adjustments were maintained even though the blank or record might be so much out of true as an eighth of an inch, equal to more than two hundred times the maximum depth of the record groove.

Another improvement that followed along the lines adopted by Edison for the commercial development of the phonograph was making the recording and reproducing styluses of sapphire, an extremely hard, non-oxidizable jewel, so that those tiny instruments would always retain their true form and effectively resist wear. Of course, in this work many other things were done that may still be found on the perfected phonograph as it stands to-day, and many other suggestions were made which were contemporaneously adopted, but which were later abandoned. For the curious-minded, reference is made to the records in the Patent Office, which will show that up to 1893 Edison had obtained upward of sixty-five patents in this art, from which his line of thought can be very closely traced. The phonograph of to-day, except for the perfection of its mechanical features, in its beauty of manufacture and design, and in small details, may be considered identical with the machine of 1889, with the exception that with the latter the rotation of the record cylinder was effected by an electric motor.

Its essential use as then contemplated was as a substitute for stenographers, and the most extravagant fancies were indulged in as to utility in that field. To exploit the device commercially, the patents were sold to Philadelphia capitalists, who organized the North American Phonograph Company, through which leases for limited periods were granted to local companies doing business in special territories, generally within the confines of a single State. Under that plan, resembling the methods of 1878, the machines and blank cylinders were manufactured by the Edison Phonograph Works, which still retains its factories at Orange, New Jersey. The marketing enterprise was early doomed to failure, principally because the instruments were not well understood, and did not possess the necessary refinements that would fit them for the special field in which they were to be used. At first the instruments were leased; but it was found that the leases were seldom renewed. Efforts were then made to sell them, but the prices were high--from $100 to $150. In the midst of these difficulties, the chief promoter of the enterprise, Mr. Lippincott, died; and it was soon found that the roseate dreams of success entertained by the sanguine promoters were not to be realized. The North American Phonograph Company failed, its principal creditor being Mr. Edison, who, having acquired the assets of the defunct concern, organized the National Phonograph Company, to which he turned over the patents; and with characteristic energy he attempted again to build up a business with which his favorite and, to him, most interesting invention might be successfully identified. The National Phonograph Company from the very start determined to retire at least temporarily from the field of stenographic use, and to exploit the phonograph for musical purposes as a competitor of the music-box. Hence it was necessary that for such work the relatively heavy and expensive electric motor should be discarded, and a simple spring motor constructed with a sufficiently sensitive governor to permit accurate musical reproduction. Such a motor was designed, and is now used on all phonographs except on such special instruments as may be made with electric motors, as well as on the successful apparatus that has more recently been designed and introduced for stenographic use. Improved factory facilities were introduced; new tools were made, and various types of machines were designed so that phonographs can now be bought at prices ranging from $10 to $200. Even with the changes which were thus made in the two machines, the work of developing the business was slow, as a demand had to be created; and the early prejudice of the public against the phonograph, due to its failure as a stenographic apparatus, had to be overcome. The story of the phonograph as an industrial enterprise, from this point of departure, is itself full of interest, but embraces so many details that it is necessarily given in a separate later chapter. We must return to the days of 1878, when Edison, with at least three first-class inventions to his credit--the quadruplex, the carbon telephone, and the phonograph--had become a man of mark and a "world character."

The invention of the phonograph was immediately followed, as usual, by the appearance of several other incidental and auxiliary devices, some patented, and others remaining simply the application of the principles of apparatus that had been worked out. One of these was the telephonograph, a combination of a telephone at a distant station with a phonograph. The diaphragm of the phonograph mouthpiece is actuated by an electromagnet in the same way as that of an ordinary telephone receiver, and in this manner a record of the message spoken from a distance can be obtained and turned into sound at will. Evidently such a process is reversible, and the phonograph can send a message to the distant receiver.

This idea was brilliantly demonstrated in practice in February, 1889, by Mr. W. J. Hammer, one of Edison's earliest and most capable associates, who carried on telephonographic communication between New York and an audience in Philadelphia. The record made in New York on the Edison phonograph was repeated into an Edison carbon transmitter, sent over one hundred and three miles of circuit, including six miles of underground cable; received by an Edison motograph; repeated by that on to a phonograph; transferred from the phonograph to an Edison carbon transmitter, and by that delivered to the Edison motograph receiver in the enthusiastic lecture-hall, where every one could hear each sound and syllable distinctly. In real practice this spectacular playing with sound vibrations, as if they were lacrosse balls to toss around between the goals, could be materially simplified.

The modern megaphone, now used universally in making announcements to large crowds, particularly at sporting events, is also due to this period as a perfection by Edison of many antecedent devices going back, perhaps, much further than the legendary funnels through which Alexander the Great is said to have sent commands to his outlying forces. The improved Edison megaphone for long-distance work comprised two horns of wood or metal about six feet long, tapering from a diameter of two feet six inches at the mouth to a small aperture provided with ear-tubes. These converging horns or funnels, with a large speaking-trumpet in between them, are mounted on a tripod, and the megaphone is complete. Conversation can be carried on with this megaphone at a distance of over two miles, as with a ship or the balloon. The modern megaphone now employs the receiver form thus introduced as its very effective transmitter, with which the old-fashioned speaking-trumpet cannot possibly compete; and the word "megaphone" is universally applied to the single, side-flaring horn.

A further step in this line brought Edison to the "aerophone," around which the Figaro weaved its fanciful description. In the construction of the aerophone the same kind of tympanum is used as in the phonograph, but the imitation of the human voice, or the transmission of sound, is effected by the quick opening and closing of valves placed within a steam-whistle or an organ-pipe. The vibrations of the diaphragm communicated to the valves cause them to operate in synchronism, so that the vibrations are thrown upon the escaping air or steam; and the result is an instrument with a capacity of magnifying the sounds two hundred times, and of hurling them to great distances intelligibly, like a huge fog-siren, but with immense clearness and penetration. All this study of sound transmission over long distances without wires led up to the consideration and invention of pioneer apparatus for wireless telegraphy--but that also is another chapter.

Yet one more ingenious device of this period must be noted--Edison's vocal engine, the patent application for which was executed in August, 1878, the patent being granted the following December. Reference to this by Edison himself has already been quoted. The "voice-engine," or "phonomotor," converts the vibrations of the voice or of music, acting on the diaphragm, into motion which is utilized to drive some secondary appliance, whether as a toy or for some useful purpose. Thus a man can actually talk a hole through a board.

Somewhat weary of all this work and excitement, and not having enjoyed any cessation from toil, or period of rest, for ten years, Edison jumped eagerly at the opportunity afforded him in the summer of 1878 of making a westward trip. Just thirty years later, on a similar trip over the same ground, he jotted down for this volume some of his reminiscences. The lure of 1878 was the opportunity to try the ability of his delicate tasimeter during the total eclipse of the sun, July 29. His admiring friend, Prof. George F. Barker, of the University of Pennsylvania, with whom he had now been on terms of intimacy for some years, suggested the holiday, and was himself a member of the excursion party that made its rendezvous at Rawlins, Wyoming Territory. Edison had tested his tasimeter, and was satisfied that it would measure down to the millionth part of a degree Fahrenheit. It was just ten years since he had left the West in poverty and obscurity, a penniless operator in search of a job; but now he was a great inventor and famous, a welcome addition to the band of astronomers and physicists assembled to observe the eclipse and the corona.

"There were astronomers from nearly every nation," says Mr. Edison. "We had a special car. The country at that time was rather new; game was in great abundance, and could be seen all day long from the car window, especially antelope. We arrived at Rawlins about 4 P.M. It had a small machine shop, and was the point where locomotives were changed for the next section. The hotel was a very small one, and by doubling up we were barely accommodated. My room-mate was Fox, the correspondent of the New York Herald. After we retired and were asleep a thundering knock on the door awakened us. Upon opening the door a tall, handsome man with flowing hair dressed in western style entered the room. His eyes were bloodshot, and he was somewhat inebriated. He introduced himself as 'Texas Jack'--Joe Chromondo--and said he wanted to see Edison, as he had read about me in the newspapers. Both Fox and I were rather scared, and didn't know what was to be the result of the interview. The landlord requested him not to make so much noise, and was thrown out into the hall. Jack explained that he had just come in with a party which had been hunting, and that he felt fine. He explained, also, that he was the boss pistol-shot of the West; that it was he who taught the celebrated Doctor Carver how to shoot. Then suddenly pointing to a weather-vane on the freight depot, he pulled out a Colt revolver and fired through the window, hitting the vane. The shot awakened all the people, and they rushed in to see who was killed. It was only after I told him I was tired and would see him in the morning that he left. Both Fox and I were so nervous we didn't sleep any that night.

"We were told in the morning that Jack was a pretty good fellow, and was not one of the 'bad men,' of whom they had a good supply. They had one in the jail, and Fox and I went over to see him. A few days before he had held up a Union Pacific train and robbed all the passengers. In the jail also was a half-breed horse-thief. We interviewed the bad man through bars as big as railroad rails. He looked like a 'bad man.' The rim of his ear all around came to a sharp edge and was serrated. His eyes were nearly white, and appeared as if made of glass and set in wrong, like the life-size figures of Indians in the Smithsonian Institution. His face was also extremely irregular. He wouldn't answer a single question. I learned afterward that he got seven years in prison, while the horse-thief was hanged. As horses ran wild, and there was no protection, it meant death to steal one."

This was one interlude among others. "The first thing the astronomers did was to determine with precision their exact locality upon the earth. A number of observations were made, and Watson, of Michigan University, with two others, worked all night computing, until they agreed. They said they were not in error more than one hundred feet, and that the station was twelve miles out of the position given on the maps. It seemed to take an immense amount of mathematics. I preserved one of the sheets, which looked like the time-table of a Chinese railroad. The instruments of the various parties were then set up in different parts of the little town, and got ready for the eclipse which was to occur in three or four days. Two days before the event we all got together, and obtaining an engine and car, went twelve miles farther west to visit the United States Government astronomers at a place called Separation, the apex of the Great Divide, where the waters run east to the Mississippi and west to the Pacific. Fox and I took our Winchester rifles with an idea of doing a little shooting. After calling on the Government people we started to interview the telegraph operator at this most lonely and desolate spot. After talking over old acquaintances I asked him if there was any game around. He said, 'Plenty of jack-rabbits.' These jack-rabbits are a very peculiar species. They have ears about six inches long and very slender legs, about three times as long as those of an ordinary rabbit, and travel at a great speed by a series of jumps, each about thirty feet long, as near as I could judge. The local people called them 'narrow-gauge mules.' Asking the operator the best direction, he pointed west, and noticing a rabbit in a clear space in the sage bushes, I said, 'There is one now.' I advanced cautiously to within one hundred feet and shot. The rabbit paid no attention. I then advanced to within ten feet and shot again--the rabbit was still immovable. On looking around, the whole crowd at the station were watching--and then I knew the rabbit was stuffed! However, we did shoot a number of live ones until Fox ran out of cartridges. On returning to the station I passed away the time shooting at cans set on a pile of tins. Finally the operator said to Fox: 'I have a fine Springfield musket, suppose you try it!' So Fox took the musket and fired. It knocked him nearly over. It seems that the musket had been run over by a handcar, which slightly bent the long barrel, but not sufficiently for an amateur like Fox to notice. After Fox had his shoulder treated with arnica at the Government hospital tent, we returned to Rawlins."

The eclipse was, however, the prime consideration, and Edison followed the example of his colleagues in making ready. The place which he secured for setting up his tasimeter was an enclosure hardly suitable for the purpose, and he describes the results as follows:

"I had my apparatus in a small yard enclosed by a board fence six feet high, at one end there was a house for hens. I noticed that they all went to roost just before totality. At the same time a slight wind arose, and at the moment of totality the atmosphere was filled with thistle-down and other light articles. I noticed one feather, whose weight was at least one hundred and fifty milligrams, rise perpendicularly to the top of the fence, where it floated away on the wind. My apparatus was entirely too sensitive, and I got no results." It was found that the heat from the corona of the sun was ten times the index capacity of the instrument; but this result did not leave the value of the device in doubt. The Scientific American remarked;

"Seeing that the tasimeter is affected by a wider range of etheric undulations than the eye can take cognizance of, and is withal far more acutely sensitive, the probabilities are that it will open up hitherto inaccessible regions of space, and possibly extend the range of aerial knowledge as far beyond the limit obtained by the telescope as that is beyond the narrow reach of unaided vision."

The eclipse over, Edison, with Professor Barker, Major Thornberg, several soldiers, and a number of railroad officials, went hunting about one hundred miles south of the railroad in the Ute country. A few months later the Major and thirty soldiers were ambushed near the spot at which the hunting-party had camped, and all were killed. Through an introduction from Mr. Jay Gould, who then controlled the Union Pacific, Edison was allowed to ride on the cow-catchers of the locomotives. "The different engineers gave me a small cushion, and every day I rode in this manner, from Omaha to the Sacramento Valley, except through the snow-shed on the summit of the Sierras, without dust or anything else to obstruct the view. Only once was I in danger when the locomotive struck an animal about the size of a small cub bear--which I think was a badger. This animal struck the front of the locomotive just under the headlight with great violence, and was then thrown off by the rebound. I was sitting to one side grasping the angle brace, so no harm was done."

This welcome vacation lasted nearly two months; but Edison was back in his laboratory and hard at work before the end of August, gathering up many loose ends, and trying out many thoughts and ideas that had accumulated on the trip. One hot afternoon--August 30th, as shown by the document in the case--Mr. Edison was found by one of the authors of this biography employed most busily in making a mysterious series of tests on paper, using for ink acids that corrugated and blistered the paper where written upon. When interrogated as to his object, he stated that the plan was to afford blind people the means of writing directly to each other, especially if they were also deaf and could not hear a message on the phonograph. The characters which he was thus forming on the paper were high enough in relief to be legible to the delicate touch of a blind man's fingers, and with simple apparatus letters could be thus written, sent, and read. There was certainly no question as to the result obtained at the moment, which was all that was asked; but the Edison autograph thus and then written now shows the paper eaten out by the acid used, although covered with glass for many years. Mr. Edison does not remember that he ever recurred to this very interesting test.

He was, however, ready for anything new or novel, and no record can ever be made or presented that would do justice to a tithe of the thoughts and fancies daily and hourly put upon the rack. The famous note-books, to which reference will be made later, were not begun as a regular series, as it was only the profusion of these ideas that suggested the vital value of such systematic registration. Then as now, the propositions brought to Edison ranged over every conceivable subject, but the years have taught him caution in grappling with them. He tells an amusing story of one dilemma into which his good-nature led him at this period: "At Menlo Park one day, a farmer came in and asked if I knew any way to kill potato-bugs. He had twenty acres of potatoes, and the vines were being destroyed. I sent men out and culled two quarts of bugs, and tried every chemical I had to destroy them. Bisulphide of carbon was found to do it instantly. I got a drum and went over to the potato farm and sprinkled it on the vines with a pot. Every bug dropped dead. The next morning the farmer came in very excited and reported that the stuff had killed the vines as well. I had to pay $300 for not experimenting properly."

During this year, 1878, the phonograph made its way also to Europe, and various sums of money were paid there to secure the rights to its manufacture and exploitation. In England, for example, the Microscopic Company paid $7500 down and agreed to a royalty, while arrangements were effected also in France, Russia, and other countries. In every instance, as in this country, the commercial development had to wait several years, for in the mean time another great art had been brought into existence, demanding exclusive attention and exhaustive toil. And when the work was done the reward was a new heaven and a new earth--in the art of illumination.

CHAPTER XI

THE INVENTION OF THE INCANDESCENT LAMP

IT is possible to imagine a time to come when the hours of work and rest will once more be regulated by the sun. But the course of civilization has been marked by an artificial lengthening of the day, and by a constant striving after more perfect means of illumination. Why mankind should sleep through several hours of sunlight in the morning, and stay awake through a needless time in the evening, can probably only be attributed to total depravity. It is certainly a most stupid, expensive, and harmful habit. In no one thing has man shown greater fertility of invention than in lighting; to nothing does he cling more tenaciously than to his devices for furnishing light. Electricity to-day reigns supreme in the field of illumination, but every other kind of artificial light that has ever been known is still in use somewhere. Toward its light-bringers the race has assumed an attitude of veneration, though it has forgotten, if it ever heard, the names of those who first brightened its gloom and dissipated its darkness. If the tallow candle, hitherto unknown, were now invented, its creator would be hailed as one of the greatest benefactors of the present age.

Up to the close of the eighteenth century, the means of house and street illumination were of two generic kinds--grease and oil; but then came a swift and revolutionary change in the adoption of gas. The ideas and methods of Murdoch and Lebon soon took definite shape, and "coal smoke" was piped from its place of origin to distant points of consumption. As early as 1804, the first company ever organized for gas lighting was formed in London, one side of Pall Mall being lit up by the enthusiastic pioneer, Winsor, in 1807. Equal activity was shown in America, and Baltimore began the practice of gas lighting in 1816. It is true that there were explosions, and distinguished men like Davy and Watt opined that the illuminant was too dangerous; but the "spirit of coal" had demonstrated its usefulness convincingly, and a commercial development began, which, for extent and rapidity, was not inferior to that marking the concurrent adoption of steam in industry and transportation.

Meantime the wax candle and the Argand oil lamp held their own bravely. The whaling fleets, long after gas came into use, were one of the greatest sources of our national wealth. To New Bedford, Massachusetts, alone, some three or four hundred ships brought their whale and sperm oil, spermaceti, and whalebone; and at one time that port was accounted the richest city in the United States in proportion to its population. The ship-owners and refiners of that whaling metropolis were slow to believe that their monopoly could ever be threatened by newer sources of illumination; but gas had become available in the cities, and coal-oil and petroleum were now added to the list of illuminating materials. The American whaling fleet, which at the time of Edison's birth mustered over seven hundred sail, had dwindled probably to a bare tenth when he took up the problem of illumination; and the competition of oil from the ground with oil from the sea, and with coal-gas, had made the artificial production of light cheaper than ever before, when up to the middle of the century it had remained one of the heaviest items of domestic expense. Moreover, just about the time that Edison took up incandescent lighting, water-gas was being introduced on a large scale as a commercial illuminant that could be produced at a much lower cost than coal-gas.

Throughout the first half of the nineteenth century the search for a practical electric light was almost wholly in the direction of employing methods analogous to those already familiar; in other words, obtaining the illumination from the actual consumption of the light-giving material. In the third quarter of the century these methods were brought to practicality, but all may be referred back to the brilliant demonstrations of Sir Humphry Davy at the Royal Institution, circa 1809-10, when, with the current from a battery of two thousand cells, he produced an intense voltaic arc between the points of consuming sticks of charcoal. For more than thirty years the arc light remained an expensive laboratory experiment; but the coming of the dynamo placed that illuminant on a commercial basis. The mere fact that electrical energy from the least expensive chemical battery using up zinc and acids costs twenty times as much as that from a dynamo--driven by steam-engine--is in itself enough to explain why so many of the electric arts lingered in embryo after their fundamental principles had been discovered. Here is seen also further proof of the great truth that one invention often waits for another.

From 1850 onward the improvements in both the arc lamp and the dynamo were rapid; and under the superintendence of the great Faraday, in 1858, protecting beams of intense electric light from the voltaic arc were shed over the waters of the Straits of Dover from the beacons of South Foreland and Dungeness. By 1878 the arc-lighting industry had sprung into existence in so promising a manner as to engender an extraordinary fever and furor of speculation. At the Philadelphia Centennial Exposition of 1876, Wallace-Farmer dynamos built at Ansonia, Connecticut, were shown, with the current from which arc lamps were there put in actual service. A year or two later the work of Charles F. Brush and Edward Weston laid the deep foundation of modern arc lighting in America, securing as well substantial recognition abroad.

Thus the new era had been ushered in, but it was based altogether on the consumption of some material--carbon--in a lamp open to the air. Every lamp the world had ever known did this, in one way or another. Edison himself began at that point, and his note-books show that he made various experiments with this type of lamp at a very early stage. Indeed, his experiments had led him so far as to anticipate in 1875 what are now known as "flaming arcs," the exceedingly bright and generally orange or rose-colored lights which have been introduced within the last few years, and are now so frequently seen in streets and public places. While the arcs with plain carbons are bluish-white, those with carbons containing calcium fluoride have a notable golden glow.

He was convinced, however, that the greatest field of lighting lay in the illumination of houses and other comparatively enclosed areas, to replace the ordinary gas light, rather than in the illumination of streets and other outdoor places by lights of great volume and brilliancy. Dismissing from his mind quickly the commercial impossibility of using arc lights for general indoor illumination, he arrived at the conclusion that an electric lamp giving light by incandescence was the solution of the problem.

Edison was familiar with the numerous but impracticable and commercially unsuccessful efforts that had been previously made by other inventors and investigators to produce electric light by incandescence, and at the time that he began his experiments, in 1877, almost the whole scientific world had pronounced such an idea as impossible of fulfilment. The leading electricians, physicists, and experts of the period had been studying the subject for more than a quarter of a century, and with but one known exception had proven mathematically and by close reasoning that the "Subdivision of the Electric Light," as it was then termed, was practically beyond attainment. Opinions of this nature have ever been but a stimulus to Edison when he has given deep thought to a subject, and has become impressed with strong convictions of possibility, and in this particular case he was satisfied that the subdivision of the electric light--or, more correctly, the subdivision of the electric current--was not only possible but entirely practicable.

It will have been perceived from the foregoing chapters that from the time of boyhood, when he first began to rub against the world, his commercial instincts were alert and predominated in almost all of the enterprises that he set in motion. This characteristic trait had grown stronger as he matured, having received, as it did, fresh impetus and strength from his one lapse in the case of his first patented invention, the vote-recorder. The lesson he then learned was to devote his inventive faculties only to things for which there was a real, genuine demand, and that would subserve the actual necessities of humanity; and it was probably a fortunate circumstance that this lesson was learned at the outset of his career as an inventor. He has never assumed to be a philosopher or "pure scientist."

In order that the reader may grasp an adequate idea of the magnitude and importance of Edison's invention of the incandescent lamp, it will be necessary to review briefly the "state of the art" at the time he began his experiments on that line. After the invention of the voltaic battery, early in the last century, experiments were made which determined that heat could be produced by the passage of the electric current through wires of platinum and other metals, and through pieces of carbon, as noted already, and it was, of course, also observed that if sufficient current were passed through these conductors they could be brought from the lower stage of redness up to the brilliant white heat of incandescence. As early as 1845 the results of these experiments were taken advantage of when Starr, a talented American who died at the early age of twenty-five, suggested, in his English patent of that year, two forms of small incandescent electric lamps, one having a burner made from platinum foil placed under a glass cover without excluding the air; and the other composed of a thin plate or pencil of carbon enclosed in a Torricellian vacuum. These suggestions of young Starr were followed by many other experimenters, whose improvements consisted principally in devices to increase the compactness and portability of the lamp, in the sealing of the lamp chamber to prevent the admission of air, and in means for renewing the carbon burner when it had been consumed. Thus Roberts, in 1852, proposed to cement the neck of the glass globe into a metallic cup, and to provide it with a tube or stop-cock for exhaustion by means of a hand-pump. Lodyguine, Konn, Kosloff, and Khotinsky, between 1872 and 1877, proposed various ingenious devices for perfecting the joint between the metal base and the glass globe, and also provided their lamps with several short carbon pencils, which were automatically brought into circuit successively as the pencils were consumed. In 1876 or 1877, Bouliguine proposed the employment of a long carbon pencil, a short section only of which was in circuit at any one time and formed the burner, the lamp being provided with a mechanism for automatically pushing other sections of the pencil into position between the contacts to renew the burner. Sawyer and Man proposed, in 1878, to make the bottom plate of glass instead of metal, and provided ingenious arrangements for charging the lamp chamber with an atmosphere of pure nitrogen gas which does not support combustion.

These lamps and many others of similar character, ingenious as they were, failed to become of any commercial value, due, among other things, to the brief life of the carbon burner. Even under the best conditions it was found that the carbon members were subject to a rapid disintegration or evaporation, which experimenters assumed was due to the disrupting action of the electric current; and hence the conclusion that carbon contained in itself the elements of its own destruction, and was not a suitable material for the burner of an incandescent lamp. On the other hand, platinum, although found to be the best of all materials for the purpose, aside from its great expense, and not combining with oxygen at high temperatures as does carbon, required to be brought so near the melting-point in order to give light, that a very slight increase in the temperature resulted in its destruction. It was assumed that the difficulty lay in the material of the burner itself, and not in its environment.

It was not realized up to such a comparatively recent date as 1879 that the solution of the great problem of subdivision of the electric current would not, however, be found merely in the production of a durable incandescent electric lamp--even if any of the lamps above referred to had fulfilled that requirement. The other principal features necessary to subdivide the electric current successfully were: the burning of an indefinite number of lights on the same circuit; each light to give a useful and economical degree of illumination; and each light to be independent of all the others in regard to its operation and extinguishment.

The opinions of scientific men of the period on the subject are well represented by the two following extracts--the first, from a lecture at the Royal United Service Institution, about February, 1879, by Mr. (Sir) W. H. Preece, one of the most eminent electricians in England, who, after discussing the question mathematically, said: "Hence the sub-division of the light is an absolute ignis fatuus." The other extract is from a book written by Paget Higgs, LL.D., D.Sc., published in London in 1879, in which he says: "Much nonsense has been talked in relation to this subject. Some inventors have claimed the power to 'indefinitely divide' the electric current, not knowing or forgetting that such a statement is incompatible with the well-proven law of conservation of energy."

"Some inventors," in the last sentence just quoted, probably--indeed, we think undoubtedly--refers to Edison, whose earlier work in electric lighting (1878) had been announced in this country and abroad, and who had then stated boldly his conviction of the practicability of the subdivision of the electrical current. The above extracts are good illustrations, however, of scientific opinions up to the end of 1879, when Mr. Edison's epoch-making invention rendered them entirely untenable. The eminent scientist, John Tyndall, while not sharing these precise views, at least as late as January 17, 1879, delivered a lecture before the Royal Institution on "The Electric Light," when, after pointing out the development of the art up to Edison's work, and showing the apparent hopelessness of the problem, he said: "Knowing something of the intricacy of the practical problem, I should certainly prefer seeing it in Edison's hands to having it in mine."

The reader may have deemed this sketch of the state of the art to be a considerable digression; but it is certainly due to the subject to present the facts in such a manner as to show that this great invention was neither the result of improving some process or device that was known or existing at the time, nor due to any unforeseen lucky chance, nor the accidental result of other experiments. On the contrary, it was the legitimate outcome of a series of exhaustive experiments founded upon logical and original reasoning in a mind that had the courage and hardihood to set at naught the confirmed opinions of the world, voiced by those generally acknowledged to be the best exponents of the art--experiments carried on amid a storm of jeers and derision, almost as contemptuous as if the search were for the discovery of perpetual motion. In this we see the man foreshadowed by the boy who, when he obtained his books on chemistry or physics, did not accept any statement of fact or experiment therein, but worked out every one of them himself to ascertain whether or not they were true.

Although this brings the reader up to the year 1879, one must turn back two years and accompany Edison in his first attack on the electric-light problem. In 1877 he sold his telephone invention (the carbon transmitter) to the Western Union Telegraph Company, which had previously come into possession also of his quadruplex inventions, as already related. He was still busily engaged on the telephone, on acoustic electrical transmission, sextuplex telegraphs, duplex telegraphs, miscellaneous carbon articles, and other inventions of a minor nature. During the whole of the previous year and until late in the summer of 1877, he had been working with characteristic energy and enthusiasm on the telephone; and, in developing this invention to a successful issue, had preferred the use of carbon and had employed it in numerous forms, especially in the form of carbonized paper.

Eighteen hundred and seventy-seven in Edison's laboratory was a veritable carbon year, for it was carbon in some shape or form for interpolation in electric circuits of various kinds that occupied the thoughts of the whole force from morning to night. It is not surprising, therefore, that in September of that year, when Edison turned his thoughts actively toward electric lighting by incandescence, his early experiments should be in the line of carbon as an illuminant. His originality of method was displayed at the very outset, for one of the first experiments was the bringing to incandescence of a strip of carbon in the open air to ascertain merely how much current was required. This conductor was a strip of carbonized paper about an inch long, one-sixteenth of an inch broad, and six or seven one-thousandths of an inch thick, the ends of which were secured to clamps that formed the poles of a battery. The carbon was lighted up to incandescence, and, of course, oxidized and disintegrated immediately. Within a few days this was followed by experiments with the same kind of carbon, but in vacuo by means of a hand-worked air-pump. This time the carbon strip burned at incandescence for about eight minutes. Various expedients to prevent oxidization were tried, such, for instance, as coating the carbon with powdered glass, which in melting would protect the carbon from the atmosphere, but without successful results.

Edison was inclined to concur in the prevailing opinion as to the easy destructibility of carbon, but, without actually settling the point in his mind, he laid aside temporarily this line of experiment and entered a new field. He had made previously some trials of platinum wire as an incandescent burner for a lamp, but left it for a time in favor of carbon. He now turned to the use of almost infusible metals--such as boron, ruthenium, chromium, etc.--as separators or tiny bridges between two carbon points, the current acting so as to bring these separators to a high degree of incandescence, at which point they would emit a brilliant light. He also placed some of these refractory metals directly in the circuit, bringing them to incandescence, and used silicon in powdered form in glass tubes placed in the electric circuit. His notes include the use of powdered silicon mixed with lime or other very infusible non-conductors or semi-conductors. Edison's conclusions on these substances were that, while in some respects they were within the bounds of possibility for the subdivision of the electric current, they did not reach the ideal that he had in mind for commercial results.

Edison's systematized attacks on the problem were two in number, the first of which we have just related, which began in September, 1877, and continued until about January, 1878. Contemporaneously, he and his force of men were very busily engaged day and night on other important enterprises and inventions. Among the latter, the phonograph may be specially mentioned, as it was invented in the late fall of 1877. From that time until July, 1878, his time and attention day and night were almost completely absorbed by the excitement caused by the invention and exhibition of the machine. In July, feeling entitled to a brief vacation after several years of continuous labor, Edison went with the expedition to Wyoming to observe an eclipse of the sun, and incidentally to test his tasimeter, a delicate instrument devised by him for measuring heat transmitted through immense distances of space. His trip has been already described. He was absent about two months. Coming home rested and refreshed, Mr. Edison says: "After my return from the trip to observe the eclipse of the sun, I went with Professor Barker, Professor of Physics in the University of Pennsylvania, and Doctor Chandler, Professor of Chemistry in Columbia College, to see Mr. Wallace, a large manufacturer of brass in Ansonia, Connecticut. Wallace at this time was experimenting on series arc lighting. Just at that time I wanted to take up something new, and Professor Barker suggested that I go to work and see if I could subdivide the electric light so it could be got in small units like gas. This was not a new suggestion, because I had made a number of experiments on electric lighting a year before this. They had been laid aside for the phonograph. I determined to take up the search again and continue it. On my return home I started my usual course of collecting every kind of data about gas; bought all the transactions of the gas-engineering societies, etc., all the back volumes of gas journals, etc. Having obtained all the data, and investigated gas-jet distribution in New York by actual observations, I made up my mind that the problem of the subdivision of the electric current could be solved and made commercial." About the end of August, 1878, he began his second organized attack on the subdivision of the current, which was steadily maintained until he achieved signal victory a year and two months later.

The date of this interesting visit to Ansonia is fixed by an inscription made by Edison on a glass goblet which he used. The legend in diamond scratches runs: "Thomas A. Edison, September 8, 1878, made under the electric light." Other members of the party left similar memorials, which under the circumstances have come to be greatly prized. A number of experiments were witnessed in arc lighting, and Edison secured a small Wallace-Farmer dynamo for his own work, as well as a set of Wallace arc lamps for lighting the Menlo Park laboratory. Before leaving Ansonia, Edison remarked, significantly: "Wallace, I believe I can beat you making electric lights. I don't think you are working in the right direction." Another date which shows how promptly the work was resumed is October 14, 1878, when Edison filed an application for his first lighting patent: "Improvement in Electric Lights." In after years, discussing the work of Wallace, who was not only a great pioneer electrical manufacturer, but one of the founders of the wire-drawing and brass-working industry, Edison said: "Wallace was one of the earliest pioneers in electrical matters in this country. He has done a great deal of good work, for which others have received the credit; and the work which he did in the early days of electric lighting others have benefited by largely, and he has been crowded to one side and forgotten." Associated in all this work with Wallace at Ansonia was Prof. Moses G. Farmer, famous for the introduction of the fire-alarm system; as the discoverer of the self-exciting principle of the modern dynamo; as a pioneer experimenter in the electric-railway field; as a telegraph engineer, and as a lecturer on mines and explosives to naval classes at Newport. During 1858, Farmer, who, like Edison, was a ceaseless investigator, had made a series of studies upon the production of light by electricity, and had even invented an automatic regulator by which a number of platinum lamps in multiple arc could be kept at uniform voltage for any length of time. In July, 1859, he lit up one of the rooms of his house at Salem, Massachusetts, every evening with such lamps, using in them small pieces of platinum and iridium wire, which were made to incandesce by means of current from primary batteries. Farmer was not one of the party that memorable day in September, but his work was known through his intimate connection with Wallace, and there is no doubt that reference was made to it. Such work had not led very far, the "lamps" were hopelessly short-lived, and everything was obviously experimental; but it was all helpful and suggestive to one whose open mind refused no hint from any quarter.

At the commencement of his new attempts, Edison returned to his experiments with carbon as an incandescent burner for a lamp, and made a very large number of trials, all in vacuo. Not only were the ordinary strip paper carbons tried again, but tissue-paper coated with tar and lampblack was rolled into thin sticks, like knitting-needles, carbonized and raised to incandescence in vacuo. Edison also tried hard carbon, wood carbons, and almost every conceivable variety of paper carbon in like manner. With the best vacuum that he could then get by means of the ordinary air-pump, the carbons would last, at the most, only from ten to fifteen minutes in a state of incandescence. Such results were evidently not of commercial value.

Edison then turned his attention in other directions. In his earliest consideration of the problem of subdividing the electric current, he had decided that the only possible solution lay in the employment of a lamp whose incandescing body should have a high resistance combined with a small radiating surface, and be capable of being used in what is called "multiple arc," so that each unit, or lamp, could be turned on or off without interfering with any other unit or lamp. No other arrangement could possibly be considered as commercially practicable.

The full significance of the three last preceding sentences will not be obvious to laymen, as undoubtedly many of the readers of this book may be; and now being on the threshold of the series of Edison's experiments that led up to the basic invention, we interpolate a brief explanation, in order that the reader may comprehend the logical reasoning and work that in this case produced such far-reaching results.

If we consider a simple circuit in which a current is flowing, and include in the circuit a carbon horseshoe-like conductor which it is desired to bring to incandescence by the heat generated by the current passing through it, it is first evident that the resistance offered to the current by the wires themselves must be less than that offered by the burner, because, otherwise current would be wasted as heat in the conducting wires. At the very foundation of the electric-lighting art is the essentially commercial consideration that one cannot spend very much for conductors, and Edison determined that, in order to use wires of a practicable size, the voltage of the current (i.e., its pressure or the characteristic that overcomes resistance to its flow) should be one hundred and ten volts, which since its adoption has been the standard. To use a lower voltage or pressure, while making the solution of the lighting problem a simple one as we shall see, would make it necessary to increase the size of the conducting wires to a prohibitive extent. To increase the voltage or pressure materially, while permitting some saving in the cost of conductors, would enormously increase the difficulties of making a sufficiently high resistance conductor to secure light by incandescence. This apparently remote consideration --weight of copper used--was really the commercial key to the problem, just as the incandescent burner was the scientific key to that problem. Before Edison's invention incandescent lamps had been suggested as a possibility, but they were provided with carbon rods or strips of relatively low resistance, and to bring these to incandescence required a current of low pressure, because a current of high voltage would pass through them so readily as not to generate heat; and to carry a current of low pressure through wires without loss would require wires of enormous size. [8] Having a current of relatively high pressure to contend with, it was necessary to provide a carbon burner which, as compared with what had previously been suggested, should have a very great resistance. Carbon as a material, determined after patient search, apparently offered the greatest hope, but even with this substance the necessary high resistance could be obtained only by making the burner of extremely small cross-section, thereby also reducing its radiating surface. Therefore, the crucial point was the production of a hair-like carbon filament, with a relatively great resistance and small radiating surface, capable of withstanding mechanical shock, and susceptible of being maintained at a temperature of over two thousand degrees for a thousand hours or more before breaking. And this filamentary conductor required to be supported in a vacuum chamber so perfectly formed and constructed that during all those hours, and subjected as it is to varying temperatures, not a particle of air should enter to disintegrate the filament. And not only so, but the lamp after its design must not be a mere laboratory possibility, but a practical commercial article capable of being manufactured at low cost and in large quantities. A statement of what had to be done in those days of actual as well as scientific electrical darkness is quite sufficient to explain Tyndall's attitude of mind in preferring that the problem should be in Edison's hands rather than in his own. To say that the solution of the problem lay merely in reducing the size of the carbon burner to a mere hair, is to state a half-truth only; but who, we ask, would have had the temerity even to suggest that such an attenuated body could be maintained at a white heat, without disintegration, for a thousand hours? The solution consisted not only in that, but in the enormous mass of patiently worked-out details--the manufacture of the filaments, their uniform carbonization, making the globes, producing a perfect vacuum, and countless other factors, the omission of any one of which would probably have resulted eventually in failure.

[Footnote 8: As a practical illustration of these facts it was calculated by Professor Barker, of the University of Pennsylvania (after Edison had invented the incandescent lamp), that if it should cost $100,000 for copper conductors to supply current to Edison lamps in a given area, it would cost about $200,000,000 for copper conductors for lighting the same area by lamps of the earlier experimenters--such, for instance, as the lamp invented by Konn in 1875. This enormous difference would be accounted for by the fact that Edison's lamp was one having a high resistance and relatively small radiating surface, while Konn's lamp was one having a very low resistance and large radiating surface.]

Continuing the digression one step farther in order to explain the term "multiple arc," it may be stated that there are two principal systems of distributing electric current, one termed "series," and the other "multiple arc." The two are illustrated, diagrammatically, side by side, the arrows indicating flow of current. The series system, it will be seen, presents one continuous path for the current. The current for the last lamp must pass through the first and all the intermediate lamps. Hence, if any one light goes out, the continuity of the path is broken, current cannot flow, and all the lamps are extinguished unless a loop or by-path is provided. It is quite obvious that such a system would be commercially impracticable where small units, similar to gas jets, were employed. On the other hand, in the multiple-arc system, current may be considered as flowing in two parallel conductors like the vertical sides of a ladder, the ends of which never come together. Each lamp is placed in a separate circuit across these two conductors, like a rung in the ladder, thus making a separate and independent path for the current in each case. Hence, if a lamp goes out, only that individual subdivision, or ladder step, is affected; just that one particular path for the current is interrupted, but none of the other lamps is interfered with. They remain lighted, each one independent of the other. The reader will quite readily understand, therefore, that a multiple-arc system is the only one practically commercial where electric light is to be used in small units like those of gas or oil.

Such was the nature of the problem that confronted Edison at the outset. There was nothing in the whole world that in any way approximated a solution, although the most brilliant minds in the electrical art had been assiduously working on the subject for a quarter of a century preceding. As already seen, he came early to the conclusion that the only solution lay in the use of a lamp of high resistance and small radiating surface, and, with characteristic fervor and energy, he attacked the problem from this standpoint, having absolute faith in a successful outcome. The mere fact that even with the successful production of the electric lamp the assault on the complete problem of commercial lighting would hardly be begun did not deter him in the slightest. To one of Edison's enthusiastic self-confidence the long vista of difficulties ahead--we say it in all sincerity--must have been alluring.

After having devoted several months to experimental trials of carbon, at the end of 1878, as already detailed, he turned his attention to the platinum group of metals and began a series of experiments in which he used chiefly platinum wire and iridium wire, and alloys of refractory metals in the form of wire burners for incandescent lamps. These metals have very high fusing-points, and were found to last longer than the carbon strips previously used when heated up to incandescence by the electric current, although under such conditions as were then possible they were melted by excess of current after they had been lighted a comparatively short time, either in the open air or in such a vacuum as could be obtained by means of the ordinary air-pump.

Nevertheless, Edison continued along this line of experiment with unremitting vigor, making improvement after improvement, until about April, 1879, he devised a means whereby platinum wire of a given length, which would melt in the open air when giving a light equal to four candles, would emit a light of twenty-five candle-power without fusion. This was accomplished by introducing the platinum wire into an all-glass globe, completely sealed and highly exhausted of air, and passing a current through the platinum wire while the vacuum was being made. In this, which was a new and radical invention, we see the first step toward the modern incandescent lamp. The knowledge thus obtained that current passing through the platinum during exhaustion would drive out occluded gases (i.e., gases mechanically held in or upon the metal), and increase the infusibility of the platinum, led him to aim at securing greater perfection in the vacuum, on the theory that the higher the vacuum obtained, the higher would be the infusibility of the platinum burner. And this fact also was of the greatest importance in making successful the final use of carbon, because without the subjection of the carbon to the heating effect of current during the formation of the vacuum, the presence of occluded gases would have been a fatal obstacle.

Continuing these experiments with most fervent zeal, taking no account of the passage of time, with an utter disregard for meals, and but scanty hours of sleep snatched reluctantly at odd periods of the day or night, Edison kept his laboratory going without cessation. A great variety of lamps was made of the platinum-iridium type, mostly with thermal devices to regulate the temperature of the burner and prevent its being melted by an excess of current. The study of apparatus for obtaining more perfect vacua was unceasingly carried on, for Edison realized that in this there lay a potent factor of ultimate success. About August he had obtained a pump that would produce a vacuum up to about the one-hundred-thousandth part of an atmosphere, and some time during the next month, or beginning of October, had obtained one that would produce a vacuum up to the one-millionth part of an atmosphere. It must be remembered that the conditions necessary for MAINTAINING this high vacuum were only made possible by his invention of the one-piece all-glass globe, in which all the joints were hermetically sealed during its manufacture into a lamp, whereby a high vacuum could be retained continuously for any length of time.

In obtaining this perfection of vacuum apparatus, Edison realized that he was approaching much nearer to a solution of the problem. In his experiments with the platinum-iridium lamps, he had been working all the time toward the proposition of high resistance and small radiating surface, until he had made a lamp having thirty feet of fine platinum wire wound upon a small bobbin of infusible material; but the desired economy, simplicity, and durability were not obtained in this manner, although at all times the burner was maintained at a critically high temperature. After attaining a high degree of perfection with these lamps, he recognized their impracticable character, and his mind reverted to the opinion he had formed in his early experiments two years before--viz., that carbon had the requisite resistance to permit a very simple conductor to accomplish the object if it could be used in the form of a hair-like "filament," provided the filament itself could be made sufficiently homogeneous. As we have already seen, he could not use carbon successfully in his earlier experiments, for the strips of carbon he then employed, although they were much larger than "filaments," would not stand, but were consumed in a few minutes under the imperfect conditions then at his command.

Now, however, that he had found means for obtaining and maintaining high vacua, Edison immediately went back to carbon, which from the first he had conceived of as the ideal substance for a burner. His next step proved conclusively the correctness of his old deductions. On October 21, 1879, after many patient trials, he carbonized a piece of cotton sewing-thread bent into a loop or horseshoe form, and had it sealed into a glass globe from which he exhausted the air until a vacuum up to one-millionth of an atmosphere was produced. This lamp, when put on the circuit, lighted up brightly to incandescence and maintained its integrity for over forty hours, and lo! the practical incandescent lamp was born. The impossible, so called, had been attained; subdivision of the electric-light current was made practicable; the goal had been reached; and one of the greatest inventions of the century was completed. Up to this time Edison had spent over $40,000 in his electric-light experiments, but the results far more than justified the expenditure, for with this lamp he made the discovery that the FILAMENT of carbon, under the conditions of high vacuum, was commercially stable and would stand high temperatures without the disintegration and oxidation that took place in all previous attempts that he knew of for making an incandescent burner out of carbon. Besides, this lamp possessed the characteristics of high resistance and small radiating surface, permitting economy in the outlay for conductors, and requiring only a small current for each unit of light--conditions that were absolutely necessary of fulfilment in order to accomplish commercially the subdivision of the electric-light current.

This slender, fragile, tenuous thread of brittle carbon, glowing steadily and continuously with a soft light agreeable to the eyes, was the tiny key that opened the door to a world revolutionized in its interior illumination. It was a triumphant vindication of Edison's reasoning powers, his clear perceptions, his insight into possibilities, and his inventive faculty, all of which had already been productive of so many startling, practical, and epoch-making inventions. And now he had stepped over the threshold of a new art which has since become so world-wide in its application as to be an integral part of modern human experience. [9]

[Footnote 9: The following extract from Walker on Patents (4th edition) will probably be of interest to the reader:

"Sec. 31a. A meritorious exception, to the rule of the last section, is involved in the adjudicated validity of the Edison incandescent-light patent. The carbon filament, which constitutes the only new part of the combination of the second claim of that patent, differs from the earlier carbon burners of Sawyer and Man, only in having a diameter of one-sixty-fourth of an inch or less, whereas the burners of Sawyer and Man had a diameter of one-thirty-second of an inch or more. But that reduction of one-half in diameter increased the resistance of the burner FOURFOLD, and reduced its radiating surface TWOFOLD, and thus increased eightfold, its ratio of resistance to radiating surface. That eightfold increase of proportion enabled the resistance of the conductor of electricity from the generator to the burner to be increased eightfold, without any increase of percentage of loss of energy in that conductor, or decrease of percentage of development of heat in the burner; and thus enabled the area of the cross-section of that conductor to be reduced eightfold, and thus to be made with one-eighth of the amount of copper or other metal, which would be required if the reduction of diameter of the burner from one-thirty-second to one-sixty-fourth of an inch had not been made. And that great reduction in the size and cost of conductors, involved also a great difference in the composition of the electric energy employed in the system; that difference consisting in generating the necessary amount of electrical energy with comparatively high electromotive force, and comparatively low current, instead of contrariwise. For this reason, the use of carbon filaments, one-sixty-fourth of an inch in diameter or less, instead of carbon burners one-thirty-second of an inch in diameter or more, not only worked an enormous economy in conductors, but also necessitated a great change in generators, and did both according to a philosophy, which Edison was the first to know, and which is stated in this paragraph in its simplest form and aspect, and which lies at the foundation of the incandescent electric lighting of the world."]

No sooner had the truth of this new principle been established than the work to establish it firmly and commercially was carried on more assiduously than ever. The next immediate step was a further investigation of the possibilities of improving the quality of the carbon filament. Edison had previously made a vast number of experiments with carbonized paper for various electrical purposes, with such good results that he once more turned to it and now made fine filament-like loops of this material which were put into other lamps. These proved even more successful (commercially considered) than the carbonized thread--so much so that after a number of such lamps had been made and put through severe tests, the manufacture of lamps from these paper carbons was begun and carried on continuously. This necessitated first the devising and making of a large number of special tools for cutting the carbon filaments and for making and putting together the various parts of the lamps. Meantime, great excitement had been caused in this country and in Europe by the announcement of Edison's success. In the Old World, scientists generally still declared the impossibility of subdividing the electric-light current, and in the public press Mr. Edison was denounced as a dreamer. Other names of a less complimentary nature were applied to him, even though his lamp were actually in use, and the principle of commercial incandescent lighting had been established.

Between October 21, 1879, and December 21, 1879, some hundreds of these paper-carbon lamps had been made and put into actual use, not only in the laboratory, but in the streets and several residences at Menlo Park, New Jersey, causing great excitement and bringing many visitors from far and near. On the latter date a full-page article appeared in the New York Herald which so intensified the excited feeling that Mr. Edison deemed it advisable to make a public exhibition. On New Year's Eve, 1879, special trains were run to Menlo Park by the Pennsylvania Railroad, and over three thousand persons took advantage of the opportunity to go out there and witness this demonstration for themselves. In this great crowd were many public officials and men of prominence in all walks of life, who were enthusiastic in their praises.

In the mean time, the mind that conceived and made practical this invention could not rest content with anything less than perfection, so far as it could be realized. Edison was not satisfied with paper carbons. They were not fully up to the ideal that he had in mind. What he sought was a perfectly uniform and homogeneous carbon, one like the "One-Hoss Shay," that had no weak spots to break down at inopportune times. He began to carbonize everything in nature that he could lay hands on. In his laboratory note-books are innumerable jottings of the things that were carbonized and tried, such as tissue-paper, soft paper, all kinds of cardboards, drawing-paper of all grades, paper saturated with tar, all kinds of threads, fish-line, threads rubbed with tarred lampblack, fine threads plaited together in strands, cotton soaked in boiling tar, lamp-wick, twine, tar and lampblack mixed with a proportion of lime, vulcanized fibre, celluloid, boxwood, cocoanut hair and shell, spruce, hickory, baywood, cedar and maple shavings, rosewood, punk, cork, bagging, flax, and a host of other things. He also extended his searches far into the realms of nature in the line of grasses, plants, canes, and similar products, and in these experiments at that time and later he carbonized, made into lamps, and tested no fewer than six thousand different species of vegetable growths.

The reasons for such prodigious research are not apparent on the face of the subject, nor is this the occasion to enter into an explanation, as that alone would be sufficient to fill a fair-sized book. Suffice it to say that Edison's omnivorous reading, keen observation, power of assimilating facts and natural phenomena, and skill in applying the knowledge thus attained to whatever was in hand, now came into full play in determining that the results he desired could only be obtained in certain directions.

At this time he was investigating everything with a microscope, and one day in the early part of 1880 he noticed upon a table in the laboratory an ordinary palm-leaf fan. He picked it up and, looking it over, observed that it had a binding rim made of bamboo, cut from the outer edge of the cane; a very long strip. He examined this, and then gave it to one of his assistants, telling him to cut it up and get out of it all the filaments he could, carbonize them, put them into lamps, and try them. The results of this trial were exceedingly successful, far better than with anything else thus far used; indeed, so much so, that after further experiments and microscopic examinations Edison was convinced that he was now on the right track for making a thoroughly stable, commercial lamp; and shortly afterward he sent a man to Japan to procure further supplies of bamboo. The fascinating story of the bamboo hunt will be told later; but even this bamboo lamp was only one item of a complete system to be devised--a system that has since completely revolutionized the art of interior illumination.

Reference has been made in this chapter to the preliminary study that Edison brought to bear on the development of the gas art and industry. This study was so exhaustive that one can only compare it to the careful investigation made in advance by any competent war staff of the elements of strength and weakness, on both sides, in a possible campaign. A popular idea of Edison that dies hard, pictures a breezy, slap-dash, energetic inventor arriving at new results by luck and intuition, making boastful assertions and then winning out by mere chance. The native simplicity of the man, the absence of pose and ceremony, do much to strengthen this notion; but the real truth is that while gifted with unusual imagination, Edison's march to the goal of a new invention is positively humdrum and monotonous in its steady progress. No one ever saw Edison in a hurry; no one ever saw him lazy; and that which he did with slow, careful scrutiny six months ago, he will be doing with just as much calm deliberation of research six months hence--and six years hence if necessary. If, for instance, he were asked to find the most perfect pebble on the Atlantic shore of New Jersey, instead of hunting here, there, and everywhere for the desired object, we would no doubt find him patiently screening the entire beach, sifting out the most perfect stones and eventually, by gradual exclusion, reaching the long-sought-for pebble; and the mere fact that in this search years might be taken, would not lessen his enthusiasm to the slightest extent.

In the "prospectus book" among the series of famous note-books, all the references and data apply to gas. The book is numbered 184, falls into the period now dealt with, and runs along casually with items spread out over two or three years. All these notes refer specifically to "Electricity vs. Gas as General Illuminants," and cover an astounding range of inquiry and comment. One of the very first notes tells the whole story: "Object, Edison to effect exact imitation of all done by gas, so as to replace lighting by gas by lighting by electricity. To improve the illumination to such an extent as to meet all requirements of natural, artificial, and commercial conditions." A large programme, but fully executed! The notes, it will be understood, are all in Edison's handwriting. They go on to observe that "a general system of distribution is the only possible means of economical illumination," and they dismiss isolated-plant lighting as in mills and factories as of so little importance to the public--"we shall leave the consideration of this out of this book." The shrewd prophecy is made that gas will be manufactured less for lighting, as the result of electrical competition, and more and more for heating, etc., thus enlarging its market and increasing its income. Comment is made on kerosene and its cost, and all kinds of general statistics are jotted down as desirable. Data are to be obtained on lamp and dynamo efficiency, and "Another review of the whole thing as worked out upon pure science principles by Rowland, Young, Trowbridge; also Rowland on the possibilities and probabilities of cheaper production by better manufacture--higher incandescence without decrease of life of lamps." Notes are also made on meters and motors. "It doesn't matter if electricity is used for light or for power"; while small motors, it is observed, can be used night or day, and small steam-engines are inconvenient. Again the shrewd comment: "Generally poorest district for light, best for power, thus evening up whole city--the effect of this on investment."

It is pointed out that "Previous inventions failed--necessities for commercial success and accomplishment by Edison. Edison's great effort--not to make a large light or a blinding light, but a small light having the mildness of gas." Curves are then called for for iron and copper investment--also energy line--curves of candle-power and electromotive force; curves on motors; graphic representation of the consumption of gas January to December; tables and formulae; representations graphically of what one dollar will buy in different kinds of light; "table, weight of copper required different distance, 100-ohm lamp, 16 candles"; table with curves showing increased economy by larger engine, higher power, etc. There is not much that is dilettante about all this. Note is made of an article in April, 1879, putting the total amount of gas investment in the whole world at that time at $1,500,000,000; which is now (1910) about the amount of the electric-lighting investment in the United States. Incidentally a note remarks: "So unpleasant is the effect of the products of gas that in the new Madison Square Theatre every gas jet is ventilated by special tubes to carry away the products of combustion." In short, there is no aspect of the new problem to which Edison failed to apply his acutest powers; and the speed with which the new system was worked out and introduced was simply due to his initial mastery of all the factors in the older art. Luther Stieringer, an expert gas engineer and inventor, whose services were early enlisted, once said that Edison knew more about gas than any other man he had ever met. The remark is an evidence of the kind of preparation Edison gave himself for his new task.

CHAPTER XII

MEMORIES OF MENLO PARK

FROM the spring of 1876 to 1886 Edison lived and did his work at Menlo Park; and at this stage of the narrative, midway in that interesting and eventful period, it is appropriate to offer a few notes and jottings on the place itself, around which tradition is already weaving its fancies, just as at the time the outpouring of new inventions from it invested the name with sudden prominence and with the glamour of romance. "In 1876 I moved," says Edison, "to Menlo Park, New Jersey, on the Pennsylvania Railroad, several miles below Elizabeth. The move was due to trouble I had about rent. I had rented a small shop in Newark, on the top floor of a padlock factory, by the month. I gave notice that I would give it up at the end of the month, paid the rent, moved out, and delivered the keys. Shortly afterward I was served with a paper, probably a judgment, wherein I was to pay nine months' rent. There was some law, it seems, that made a monthly renter liable for a year. This seemed so unjust that I determined to get out of a place that permitted such injustice." For several Sundays he walked through different parts of New Jersey with two of his assistants before he decided on Menlo Park. The change was a fortunate one, for the inventor had married Miss Mary E. Stillwell, and was now able to establish himself comfortably with his wife and family while enjoying immediate access to the new laboratory. Every moment thus saved was valuable.

To-day the place and region have gone back to the insignificance from which Edison's genius lifted them so startlingly. A glance from the car windows reveals only a gently rolling landscape dotted with modest residences and unpretentious barns; and there is nothing in sight by way of memorial to suggest that for nearly a decade this spot was the scene of the most concentrated and fruitful inventive activity the world has ever known. Close to the Menlo Park railway station is a group of gaunt and deserted buildings, shelter of the casual tramp, and slowly crumbling away when not destroyed by the carelessness of some ragged smoker. This silent group of buildings comprises the famous old laboratory and workshops of Mr. Edison, historic as being the birthplace of the carbon transmitter, the phonograph, the incandescent lamp, and the spot where Edison also worked out his systems of electrical distribution, his commercial dynamo, his electric railway, his megaphone, his tasimeter, and many other inventions of greater or lesser degree. Here he continued, moreover, his earlier work on the quadruplex, sextuplex, multiplex, and automatic telegraphs, and did his notable pioneer work in wireless telegraphy. As the reader knows, it had been a master passion with Edison from boyhood up to possess a laboratory, in which with free use of his own time and powers, and with command of abundant material resources, he could wrestle with Nature and probe her closest secrets. Thus, from the little cellar at Port Huron, from the scant shelves in a baggage car, from the nooks and corners of dingy telegraph offices, and the grimy little shops in New York and Newark, he had now come to the proud ownership of an establishment to which his favorite word "laboratory" might justly be applied. Here he could experiment to his heart's content and invent on a larger, bolder scale than ever--and he did!

Menlo Park was the merest hamlet. Omitting the laboratory structures, it had only about seven houses, the best looking of which Edison lived in, a place that had a windmill pumping water into a reservoir. One of the stories of the day was that Edison had his front gate so connected with the pumping plant that every visitor as he opened or closed the gate added involuntarily to the supply in the reservoir. Two or three of the houses were occupied by the families of members of the staff; in the others boarders were taken, the laboratory, of course, furnishing all the patrons. Near the railway station was a small saloon kept by an old Scotchman named Davis, where billiards were played in idle moments, and where in the long winter evenings the hot stove was a centre of attraction to loungers and story-tellers. The truth is that there was very little social life of any kind possible under the strenuous conditions prevailing at the laboratory, where, if anywhere, relaxation was enjoyed at odd intervals of fatigue and waiting.

The main laboratory was a spacious wooden building of two floors. The office was in this building at first, until removed to the brick library when that was finished. There S. L. Griffin, an old telegraph friend of Edison, acted as his secretary and had charge of a voluminous and amazing correspondence. The office employees were the Carman brothers and the late John F. Randolph, afterwards secretary. According to Mr. Francis Jehl, of Budapest, then one of the staff, to whom the writers are indebted for a great deal of valuable data on this period: "It was on the upper story of this laboratory that the most important experiments were executed, and where the incandescent lamp was born. This floor consisted of a large hall containing several long tables, upon which could be found all the various instruments, scientific and chemical apparatus that the arts at that time could produce. Books lay promiscuously about, while here and there long lines of bichromate-of-potash cells could be seen, together with experimental models of ideas that Edison or his assistants were engaged upon. The side walls of this hall were lined with shelves filled with bottles, phials, and other receptacles containing every imaginable chemical and other material that could be obtained, while at the end of this hall, and near the organ which stood in the rear, was a large glass case containing the world's most precious metals in sheet and wire form, together with very rare and costly chemicals. When evening came on, and the last rays of the setting sun penetrated through the side windows, this hall looked like a veritable Faust laboratory.

"On the ground floor we had our testing-table, which stood on two large pillars of brick built deep into the earth in order to get rid of all vibrations on account of the sensitive instruments that were upon it. There was the Thomson reflecting mirror galvanometer and electrometer, while nearby were the standard cells by which the galvanometers were adjusted and standardized. This testing-table was connected by means of wires with all parts of the laboratory and machine-shop, so that measurements could be conveniently made from a distance, as in those days we had no portable and direct-reading instruments, such as now exist. Opposite this table we installed, later on, our photometrical chamber, which was constructed on the Bunsen principle. A little way from this table, and separated by a partition, we had the chemical laboratory with its furnaces and stink-chambers. Later on another chemical laboratory was installed near the photometer-room, and this Dr. A. Haid had charge of."

Next to the laboratory in importance was the machine-shop, a large and well-lighted building of brick, at one end of which there was the boiler and engine-room. This shop contained light and heavy lathes, boring and drilling machines, all kinds of planing machines; in fact, tools of all descriptions, so that any apparatus, however delicate or heavy, could be made and built as might be required by Edison in experimenting. Mr. John Kruesi had charge of this shop, and was assisted by a number of skilled mechanics, notably John Ott, whose deft fingers and quick intuitive grasp of the master's ideas are still in demand under the more recent conditions at the Llewellyn Park laboratory in Orange.

Between the machine-shop and the laboratory was a small building of wood used as a carpenter-shop, where Tom Logan plied his art. Nearby was the gasoline plant. Before the incandescent lamp was perfected, the only illumination was from gasoline gas; and that was used later for incandescent-lamp glass-blowing, which was done in another small building on one side of the laboratory. Apparently little or no lighting service was obtained from the Wallace-Farmer arc lamps secured from Ansonia, Connecticut. The dynamo was probably needed for Edison's own experiments.

On the outskirts of the property was a small building in which lampblack was crudely but carefully manufactured and pressed into very small cakes, for use in the Edison carbon transmitters of that time. The night-watchman, Alfred Swanson, took care of this curious plant, which consisted of a battery of petroleum lamps that were forced to burn to the sooting point. During his rounds in the night Swanson would find time to collect from the chimneys the soot that the lamps gave. It was then weighed out into very small portions, which were pressed into cakes or buttons by means of a hand-press. These little cakes were delicately packed away between layers of cotton in small, light boxes and shipped to Bergmann in New York, by whom the telephone transmitters were being made. A little later the Edison electric railway was built on the confines of the property out through the woods, at first only a third of a mile in length, but reaching ultimately to Pumptown, almost three miles away.

Mr. Edison's own words may be quoted as to the men with whom he surrounded himself here and upon whose services he depended principally for help in the accomplishment of his aims. In an autobiographical article in the Electrical World of March 5, 1904, he says: "It is interesting to note that in addition to those mentioned above (Charles Batchelor and Frank Upton), I had around me other men who ever since have remained active in the field, such as Messrs. Francis Jehl, William J. Hammer, Martin Force, Ludwig K. Boehm, not forgetting that good friend and co-worker, the late John Kruesi. They found plenty to do in the various developments of the art, and as I now look back I sometimes wonder how we did so much in so short a time." Mr. Jehl in his reminiscences adds another name to the above--namely, that of John W. Lawson, and then goes on to say: "These are the names of the pioneers of incandescent lighting, who were continuously at the side of Edison day and night for some years, and who, under his guidance, worked upon the carbon-filament lamp from its birth to ripe maturity. These men all had complete faith in his ability and stood by him as on a rock, guarding their work with the secretiveness of a burglar-proof safe. Whenever it leaked out in the world that Edison was succeeding in his work on the electric light, spies and others came to the Park; so it was of the utmost importance that the experiments and their results should be kept a secret until Edison had secured the protection of the Patent Office." With this staff was associated from the first Mr. E. H. Johnson, whose work with Mr. Edison lay chiefly, however, outside the laboratory, taking him to all parts of the country and to Europe. There were also to be regarded as detached members of it the Bergmann brothers, manufacturing for Mr. Edison in New York, and incessantly experimenting for him. In addition there must be included Mr. Samuel Insull, whose activities for many years as private secretary and financial manager were devoted solely to Mr. Edison's interests, with Menlo Park as a centre and main source of anxiety as to pay-rolls and other constantly recurring obligations. The names of yet other associates occur from time to time in this narrative--"Edison men" who have been very proud of their close relationship to the inventor and his work at old Menlo. "There was also Mr. Charles L. Clarke, who devoted himself mainly to engineering matters, and later on acted as chief engineer of the Edison Electric Light Company for some years. Then there were William Holzer and James Hipple, both of whom took an active part in the practical development of the glass-blowing department of the laboratory, and, subsequently, at the first Edison lamp factory at Menlo Park. Later on Messrs. Jehl, Hipple, and Force assisted Mr. Batchelor to install the lamp-works of the French Edison Company at Ivry-sur-Seine. Then there were Messrs. Charles T. Hughes, Samuel D. Mott, and Charles T. Mott, who devoted their time chiefly to commercial affairs. Mr. Hughes conducted most of this work, and later on took a prominent part in Edison's electric-railway experiments. His business ability was on a high level, while his personal character endeared him to us all."

Among other now well-known men who came to us and assisted in various kinds of work were Messrs. Acheson, Worth, Crosby, Herrick, and Hill, while Doctor Haid was placed by Mr. Edison in charge of a special chemical laboratory. Dr. E. L. Nichols was also with us for a short time conducting a special series of experiments. There was also Mr. Isaacs, who did a great deal of photographic work, and to whom we must be thankful for the pictures of Menlo Park in connection with Edison's work.

"Among others who were added to Mr. Kruesi's staff in the machine-shop were Messrs. J. H. Vail and W. S. Andrews. Mr. Vail had charge of the dynamo-room. He had a good general knowledge of machinery, and very soon acquired such familiarity with the dynamos that he could skip about among them with astonishing agility to regulate their brushes or to throw rosin on the belts when they began to squeal. Later on he took an active part in the affairs and installations of the Edison Light Company. Mr. Andrews stayed on Mr. Kruesi's staff as long as the laboratory machine-shop was kept open, after which he went into the employ of the Edison Electric Light Company and became actively engaged in the commercial and technical exploitation of the system. Another man who was with us at Menlo Park was Mr. Herman Claudius, an Austrian, who at one time was employed in connection with the State Telegraphs of his country. To him Mr. Edison assigned the task of making a complete model of the network of conductors for the contemplated first station in New York."

Mr. Francis R. Upton, who was early employed by Mr. Edison as his mathematician, furnishes a pleasant, vivid picture of his chief associates engaged on the memorable work at Menlo Park. He says: "Mr. Charles Batchelor was Mr. Edison's principal assistant at that time. He was an Englishman, and came to this country to set up the thread-weaving machinery for the Clark thread-works. He was a most intelligent, patient, competent, and loyal assistant to Mr. Edison. I remember distinctly seeing him work many hours to mount a small filament; and his hand would be as steady and his patience as unyielding at the end of those many hours as it was at the beginning, in spite of repeated failures. He was a wonderful mechanic; the control that he had of his fingers was marvellous, and his eyesight was sharp. Mr. Batchelor's judgment and good sense were always in evidence.

"Mr. Kruesi was the superintendent, a Swiss trained in the best Swiss ideas of accuracy. He was a splendid mechanic with a vigorous temper, and wonderful ability to work continuously and to get work out of men. It was an ideal combination, that of Edison, Batchelor, and Kruesi. Mr. Edison with his wonderful flow of ideas which were sharply defined in his mind, as can be seen by any of the sketches that he made, as he evidently always thinks in three dimensions; Mr. Kruesi, willing to take the ideas, and capable of comprehending them, would distribute the work so as to get it done with marvellous quickness and great accuracy. Mr. Batchelor was always ready for any special fine experimenting or observation, and could hold to whatever he was at as long as Mr. Edison wished; and always brought to bear on what he was at the greatest skill."

While Edison depended upon Upton for his mathematical work, he was wont to check it up in a very practical manner, as evidenced by the following incident described by Mr. Jehl: "I was once with Mr. Upton calculating some tables which he had put me on, when Mr. Edison appeared with a glass bulb having a pear-shaped appearance in his hand. It was the kind that we were going to use for our lamp experiments; and Mr. Edison asked Mr. Upton to please calculate for him its cubic contents in centimetres. Now Mr. Upton was a very able mathematician, who, after he finished his studies at Princeton, went to Germany and got his final gloss under that great master, Helmholtz. Whatever he did and worked on was executed in a pure mathematical manner, and any wrangler at Oxford would have been delighted to see him juggle with integral and differential equations, with a dexterity that was surprising. He drew the shape of the bulb exactly on paper, and got the equation of its lines with which he was going to calculate its contents, when Mr. Edison again appeared and asked him what it was. He showed Edison the work he had already done on the subject, and told him that he would very soon finish calculating it. 'Why,' said Edison, 'I would simply take that bulb and fill it with mercury and weigh it; and from the weight of the mercury and its specific gravity I'll get it in five minutes, and use less mental energy than is necessary in such a fatiguing operation.'"

Menlo Park became ultimately the centre of Edison's business life as it was of his inventing. After the short distasteful period during the introduction of his lighting system, when he spent a large part of his time at the offices at 65 Fifth Avenue, New York, or on the actual work connected with the New York Edison installation, he settled back again in Menlo Park altogether. Mr. Samuel Insull describes the business methods which prevailed throughout the earlier Menlo Park days of "storm and stress," and the curious conditions with which he had to deal as private secretary: "I never attempted to systematize Edison's business life. Edison's whole method of work would upset the system of any office. He was just as likely to be at work in his laboratory at midnight as midday. He cared not for the hours of the day or the days of the week. If he was exhausted he might more likely be asleep in the middle of the day than in the middle of the night, as most of his work in the way of inventions was done at night. I used to run his office on as close business methods as my experience admitted; and I would get at him whenever it suited his convenience. Sometimes he would not go over his mail for days at a time; but other times he would go regularly to his office in the morning. At other times my engagements used to be with him to go over his business affairs at Menlo Park at night, if I was occupied in New York during the day. In fact, as a matter of convenience I used more often to get at him at night, as it left my days free to transact his affairs, and enabled me, probably at a midnight luncheon, to get a few minutes of his time to look over his correspondence and get his directions as to what I should do in some particular negotiation or matter of finance. While it was a matter of suiting Edison's convenience as to when I should transact business with him, it also suited my own ideas, as it enabled me after getting through my business with him to enjoy the privilege of watching him at his work, and to learn something about the technical side of matters. Whatever knowledge I may have of the electric light and power industry I feel I owe it to the tuition of Edison. He was about the most willing tutor, and I must confess that he had to be a patient one."

Here again occurs the reference to the incessant night-work at Menlo Park, a note that is struck in every reminiscence and in every record of the time. But it is not to be inferred that the atmosphere of grim determination and persistent pursuit of the new invention characteristic of this period made life a burden to the small family of laborers associated with Edison. Many a time during the long, weary nights of experimenting Edison would call a halt for refreshments, which he had ordered always to be sent in when night-work was in progress. Everything would be dropped, all present would join in the meal, and the last good story or joke would pass around. In his notes Mr. Jehl says: "Our lunch always ended with a cigar, and I may mention here that although Edison was never fastidious in eating, he always relished a good cigar, and seemed to find in it consolation and solace.... It often happened that while we were enjoying the cigars after our midnight repast, one of the boys would start up a tune on the organ and we would all sing together, or one of the others would give a solo. Another of the boys had a voice that sounded like something between the ring of an old tomato can and a pewter jug. He had one song that he would sing while we roared with laughter. He was also great in imitating the tin-foil phonograph.... When Boehm was in good-humor he would play his zither now and then, and amuse us by singing pretty German songs. On many of these occasions the laboratory was the rendezvous of jolly and convivial visitors, mostly old friends and acquaintances of Mr. Edison. Some of the office employees would also drop in once in a while, and as everybody present was always welcome to partake of the midnight meal, we all enjoyed these gatherings. After a while, when we were ready to resume work, our visitors would intimate that they were going home to bed, but we fellows could stay up and work, and they would depart, generally singing some song like Good-night, ladies! . . . It often happened that when Edison had been working up to three or four o'clock in the morning, he would lie down on one of the laboratory tables, and with nothing but a couple of books for a pillow, would fall into a sound sleep. He said it did him more good than being in a soft bed, which spoils a man. Some of the laboratory assistants could be seen now and then sleeping on a table in the early morning hours. If their snoring became objectionable to those still at work, the 'calmer' was applied. This machine consisted of a Babbitt's soap box without a cover. Upon it was mounted a broad ratchet-wheel with a crank, while into the teeth of the wheel there played a stout, elastic slab of wood. The box would be placed on the table where the snorer was sleeping and the crank turned rapidly. The racket thus produced was something terrible, and the sleeper would jump up as though a typhoon had struck the laboratory. The irrepressible spirit of humor in the old days, although somewhat strenuous at times, caused many a moment of hilarity which seemed to refresh the boys, and enabled them to work with renewed vigor after its manifestation." Mr. Upton remarks that often during the period of the invention of the incandescent lamp, when under great strain and fatigue, Edison would go to the organ and play tunes in a primitive way, and come back to crack jokes with the staff. "But I have often felt that Mr. Edison never could comprehend the limitations of the strength of other men, as his own physical and mental strength have always seemed to be without limit. He could work continuously as long as he wished, and had sleep at his command. His sleep was always instant, profound, and restful. He has told me that he never dreamed. I have known Mr. Edison now for thirty-one years, and feel that he has always kept his mind direct and simple, going straight to the root of troubles. One of the peculiarities I have noticed is that I have never known him to break into a conversation going on around him, and ask what people were talking about. The nearest he would ever come to it was when there had evidently been some story told, and his face would express a desire to join in the laugh, which would immediately invite telling the story to him."

Next to those who worked with Edison at the laboratory and were with him constantly at Menlo Park were the visitors, some of whom were his business associates, some of them scientific men, and some of them hero-worshippers and curiosity-hunters. Foremost in the first category was Mr. E. H. Johnson, who was in reality Edison's most intimate friend, and was required for constant consultation; but whose intense activity, remarkable grasp of electrical principles, and unusual powers of exposition, led to his frequent detachment for long trips, including those which resulted in the introduction of the telephone, phonograph, and electric light in England and on the Continent. A less frequent visitor was Mr. S. Bergmann, who had all he needed to occupy his time in experimenting and manufacturing, and whose contemporaneous Wooster Street letter-heads advertised Edison's inventions as being made there. Among the scientists were Prof. George F. Barker, of Philadelphia, a big, good-natured philosopher, whose valuable advice Edison esteemed highly. In sharp contrast to him was the earnest, serious Rowland, of

Johns Hopkins University, afterward the leading American physicist of his day. Profs. C. F. Brackett and C. F. Young, of Princeton University, were often received, always interested in what Edison was doing, and proud that one of their own students, Mr. Upton, was taking such a prominent part in the development of the work.

Soon after the success of the lighting experiments and the installation at Menlo Park became known, Edison was besieged by persons from all parts of the world anxious to secure rights and concessions for their respective countries. Among these was Mr. Louis Rau, of Paris, who organized the French Edison Company, the pioneer Edison lighting corporation in Europe, and who, with the aid of Mr. Batchelor, established lamp-works and a machine-shop at Ivry sur-Seine, near Paris, in 1882. It was there that Mr. Nikola Tesla made his entree into the field of light and power, and began his own career as an inventor; and there also Mr. Etienne Fodor, general manager of the Hungarian General Electric Company at Budapest, received his early training. It was he who erected at Athens the first European Edison station on the now universal three-wire system. Another visitor from Europe, a little later, was Mr. Emil Rathenau, the present director of the great Allgemeine Elektricitaets Gesellschaft of Germany. He secured the rights for the empire, and organized the Berlin Edison system, now one of the largest in the world. Through his extraordinary energy and enterprise the business made enormous strides, and Mr. Rathenau has become one of the most conspicuous industrial figures in his native country. From Italy came Professor Colombo, later a cabinet minister, with his friend Signor Buzzi, of Milan. The rights were secured for the peninsula; Colombo and his friends organized the Italian Edison Company, and erected at Milan the first central station in that country. Mr. John W. Lieb, Jr., now a vice-president of the New York Edison Company, was sent over by Mr. Edison to steer the enterprise technically, and spent ten years in building it up, with such brilliant success that he was later decorated as Commander of the Order of the Crown of Italy by King Victor. Another young American enlisted into European service was Mr. E. G. Acheson, the inventor of carborundum, who built a number of plants in Italy and France before he returned home. Mr. Lieb has since become President of the American Institute of Electrical Engineers and the Association of Edison Illuminating Companies, while Doctor Acheson has been President of the American Electrochemical Society.

Switzerland sent Messrs. Turrettini, Biedermann, and Thury, all distinguished engineers, to negotiate for rights in the republic; and so it went with regard to all the other countries of Europe, as well as those of South America. It was a question of keeping such visitors away rather than of inviting them to take up the exploitation of the Edison system; for what time was not spent in personal interviews was required for the masses of letters from every country under the sun, all making inquiries, offering suggestions, proposing terms. Nor were the visitors merely those on business bent. There were the lion-hunters and celebrities, of whom Sarah Bernhardt may serve as a type. One visit of note was that paid by Lieut. G. W. De Long, who had an earnest and protracted conversation with Edison over the Arctic expedition he was undertaking with the aid of Mr. James Gordon Bennett, of the New York Herald. The Jeannette was being fitted out, and Edison told De Long that he would make and present him with a small dynamo machine, some incandescent lamps, and an arc lamp. While the little dynamo was being built all the men in the laboratory wrote their names on the paper insulation that was wound upon the iron core of the armature. As the Jeannette had no steam-engine on board that could be used for the purpose, Edison designed the dynamo so that it could be worked by man power and told Lieutenant De Long "it would keep the boys warm up in the Arctic," when they generated current with it. The ill-fated ship never returned from her voyage, but went down in the icy waters of the North, there to remain until some future cataclysm of nature, ten thousand years hence, shall reveal the ship and the first marine dynamo as curious relics of a remote civilization.

Edison also furnished De Long with a set of telephones provided with extensible circuits, so that parties on the ice-floes could go long distances from the ship and still keep in communication with her. So far as the writers can ascertain this is the first example of "field telephony." Another nautical experiment that he made at this time, suggested probably by the requirements of the Arctic expedition, was a buoy that was floated in New York harbor, and which contained a small Edison dynamo and two or three incandescent lamps. The dynamo was driven by the wave or tide motion through intermediate mechanism, and thus the lamps were lit up from time to time, serving as signals. These were the prototypes of the lighted buoys which have since become familiar, as in the channel off Sandy Hook.

One notable afternoon was that on which the New York board of aldermen took a special train out to Menlo Park to see the lighting system with its conductors underground in operation. The Edison Electric Illuminating Company was applying for a franchise, and the aldermen, for lack of scientific training and specific practical information, were very sceptical on the subject--as indeed they might well be. "Mr. Edison demonstrated personally the details and merits of the system to them. The voltage was increased to a higher pressure than usual, and all the incandescent lamps at Menlo Park did their best to win the approbation of the New York City fathers. After Edison had finished exhibiting all the good points of his system, he conducted his guests upstairs in the laboratory, where a long table was spread with the best things that one of the most prominent New York caterers could furnish. The laboratory witnessed high times that night, for all were in the best of humor, and many a bottle was drained in toasting the health of Edison and the aldermen." This was one of the extremely rare occasions on which Edison has addressed an audience; but the stake was worth the effort. The representatives of New York could with justice drink the health of the young inventor, whose system is one of the greatest boons the city has ever had conferred upon it.

Among other frequent visitors was Mr, Edison's father, "one of those amiable, patriarchal characters with a Horace Greeley beard, typical Americans of the old school," who would sometimes come into the laboratory with his two grandchildren, a little boy and girl called "Dash" and "Dot." He preferred to sit and watch his brilliant son at work "with an expression of satisfaction on his face that indicated a sense of happiness and content that his boy, born in that distant, humble home in Ohio, had risen to fame and brought such honor upon the name. It was, indeed, a pathetic sight to see a father venerate his son as the elder Edison did." Not less at home was Mr. Mackenzie, the Mt. Clemens station agent, the life of whose child Edison had saved when a train newsboy. The old Scotchman was one of the innocent, chartered libertines of the place, with an unlimited stock of good jokes and stories, but seldom of any practical use. On one occasion, however, when everything possible and impossible under the sun was being carbonized for lamp filaments, he allowed a handful of his bushy red beard to be taken for the purpose; and his laugh was the loudest when the Edison-Mackenzie hair lamps were brought up to incandescence--their richness in red rays being slyly attributed to the nature of the filamentary material! Oddly enough, a few years later, some inventor actually took out a patent for making incandescent lamps with carbonized hair for filaments!

Yet other visitors again haunted the place, and with the following reminiscence of one of them, from Mr. Edison himself, this part of the chapter must close: "At Menlo Park one cold winter night there came into the laboratory a strange man in a most pitiful condition. He was nearly frozen, and he asked if he might sit by the stove. In a few moments he asked for the head man, and I was brought forward. He had a head of abnormal size, with highly intellectual features and a very small and emaciated body. He said he was suffering very much, and asked if I had any morphine. As I had about everything in chemistry that could be bought, I told him I had. He requested that I give him some, so I got the morphine sulphate. He poured out enough to kill two men, when I told him that we didn't keep a hotel for suicides, and he had better cut the quantity down. He then bared his legs and arms, and they were literally pitted with scars, due to the use of hypodermic syringes. He said he had taken it for years, and it required a big dose to have any effect. I let him go ahead. In a short while he seemed like another man and began to tell stories, and there were about fifty of us who sat around listening until morning. He was a man of great intelligence and education. He said he was a Jew, but there was no distinctive feature to verify this assertion. He continued to stay around until he finished every combination of morphine with an acid that I had, probably ten ounces all told. Then he asked if he could have strychnine. I had an ounce of the sulphate. He took enough to kill a horse, and asserted it had as good an effect as morphine. When this was gone, the only thing I had left was a chunk of crude opium, perhaps two or three pounds. He chewed this up and disappeared. I was greatly disappointed, because I would have laid in another stock of morphine to keep him at the laboratory. About a week afterward he was found dead in a barn at Perth Amboy."

Returning to the work itself, note of which has already been made in this and preceding chapters, we find an interesting and unique reminiscence in Mr. Jehl's notes of the reversion to carbon as a filament in the lamps, following an exhibition of metallic-filament lamps given in the spring of 1879 to the men in the syndicate advancing the funds for these experiments: "They came to Menlo Park on a late afternoon train from New York. It was already dark when they were conducted into the machine-shop, where we had several platinum lamps installed in series. When Edison had finished explaining the principles and details of the lamp, he asked Kruesi to let the dynamo machine run. It was of the Gramme type, as our first dynamo of the Edison design was not yet finished. Edison then ordered the 'juice' to be turned on slowly. To-day I can see those lamps rising to a cherry red, like glowbugs, and hear Mr. Edison saying 'a little more juice,' and the lamps began to glow. 'A little more' is the command again, and then one of the lamps emits for an instant a light like a star in the distance, after which there is an eruption and a puff; and the machine-shop is in total darkness. We knew instantly which lamp had failed, and Batchelor replaced that by a good one, having a few in reserve near by. The operation was repeated two or three times with about the same results, after which the party went into the library until it was time to catch the train for New York."

Such an exhibition was decidedly discouraging, and it was not a jubilant party that returned to New York, but: "That night Edison remained in the laboratory meditating upon the results that the platinum lamp had given so far. I was engaged reading a book near a table in the front, while Edison was seated in a chair by a table near the organ. With his head turned downward, and that conspicuous lock of hair hanging loosely on one side, he looked like Napoleon in the celebrated picture, On the Eve of a Great Battle. Those days were heroic ones, for he then battled against mighty odds, and the prospects were dim and not very encouraging. In cases of emergency Edison always possessed a keen faculty of deciding immediately and correctly what to do; and the decision he then arrived at was predestined to be the turning-point that led him on to ultimate success.... After that exhibition we had a house-cleaning at the laboratory, and the metallic-filament lamps were stored away, while preparations were made for our experiments on carbon lamps."

Thus the work went on. Menlo Park has hitherto been associated in the public thought with the telephone, phonograph, and incandescent lamp; but it was there, equally, that the Edison dynamo and system of distribution were created and applied to their specific purposes. While all this study of a possible lamp was going on, Mr. Upton was busy calculating the economy of the "multiple arc" system, and making a great many tables to determine what resistance a lamp should have for the best results, and at what point the proposed general system would fall off in economy when the lamps were of the lower resistance that was then generally assumed to be necessary. The world at that time had not the shadow of an idea as to what the principles of a multiple arc system should be, enabling millions of lamps to be lighted off distributing circuits, each lamp independent of every other; but at Menlo Park at that remote period in the seventies Mr. Edison's mathematician was formulating the inventor's conception in clear, instructive figures; "and the work then executed has held its own ever since." From the beginning of his experiments on electric light, Mr. Edison had a well-defined idea of producing not only a practicable lamp, but also a SYSTEM of commercial electric lighting. Such a scheme involved the creation of an entirely new art, for there was nothing on the face of the earth from which to draw assistance or precedent, unless we except the elementary forms of dynamos then in existence. It is true, there were several types of machines in use for the then very limited field of arc lighting, but they were regarded as valueless as a part of a great comprehensive scheme which could supply everybody with light. Such machines were confessedly inefficient, although representing the farthest reach of a young art. A commission appointed at that time by the Franklin Institute, and including Prof. Elihu Thomson, investigated the merits of existing dynamos and reported as to the best of them: "The Gramme machine is the most economical as a means of converting motive force into electricity; it utilizes in the arc from 38 to 41 per cent. of the motive work produced, after deduction is made for friction and the resistance of the air." They reported also that the Brush arc lighting machine "produces in the luminous arc useful work equivalent to 31 per cent. of the motive power employed, or to 38 1/2 per cent. after the friction has been deducted." Commercial possibilities could not exist in the face of such low economy as this, and Mr. Edison realized that he would have to improve the dynamo himself if he wanted a better machine. The scientific world at that time was engaged in a controversy regarding the external and internal resistance of a circuit in which a generator was situated. Discussing the subject Mr. Jehl, in his biographical notes, says: "While this controversy raged in the scientific papers, and criticism and confusion seemed at its height, Edison and Upton discussed this question very thoroughly, and Edison declared he did not intend to build up a system of distribution in which the external resistance would be equal to the internal resistance. He said he was just about going to do the opposite; he wanted a large external resistance and a low internal one. He said he wanted to sell the energy outside of the station and not waste it in the dynamo and conductors, where it brought no profits.... In these later days, when these ideas of Edison are used as common property, and are applied in every modern system of distribution, it is astonishing to remember that when they were propounded they met with most vehement antagonism from the world at large." Edison, familiar with batteries in telegraphy, could not bring himself to believe that any substitute generator of electrical energy could be efficient that used up half its own possible output before doing an equal amount of outside work.

Undaunted by the dicta of contemporaneous science, Mr. Edison attacked the dynamo problem with his accustomed vigor and thoroughness. He chose the drum form for his armature, and experimented with different kinds of iron. Cores were made of cast iron, others of forged iron; and still others of sheets of iron of various thicknesses separated from each other by paper or paint. These cores were then allowed to run in an excited field, and after a given time their temperature was measured and noted. By such practical methods Edison found that the thin, laminated cores of sheet iron gave the least heat, and had the least amount of wasteful eddy currents. His experiments and ideas on magnetism at that period were far in advance of the time. His work and tests regarding magnetism were repeated later on by Hopkinson and Kapp, who then elucidated the whole theory mathematically by means of formulae and constants. Before this, however, Edison had attained these results by pioneer work, founded on his original reasoning, and utilized them in the construction of his dynamo, thus revolutionizing the art of building such machines.

After thorough investigation of the magnetic qualities of different kinds of iron, Edison began to make a study of winding the cores, first determining the electromotive force generated per turn of wire at various speeds in fields of different intensities. He also considered various forms and shapes for the armature, and by methodical and systematic research obtained the data and best conditions upon which he could build his generator. In the field magnets of his dynamo he constructed the cores and yoke of forged iron having a very large cross-section, which was a new thing in those days. Great attention was also paid to all the joints, which were smoothed down so as to make a perfect magnetic contact. The Edison dynamo, with its large masses of iron, was a vivid contrast to the then existing types with their meagre quantities of the ferric element. Edison also made tests on his field magnets by slowly raising the strength of the exciting current, so that he obtained figures similar to those shown by a magnetic curve, and in this way found where saturation commenced, and where it was useless to expend more current on the field. If he had asked Upton at the time to formulate the results of his work in this direction, for publication, he would have anticipated the historic work on magnetism that was executed by the two other investigators; Hopkinson and Kapp, later on.

The laboratory note-books of the period bear abundant evidence of the systematic and searching nature of these experiments and investigations, in the hundreds of pages of notes, sketches, calculations, and tables made at the time by Edison, Upton, Batchelor, Jehl, and by others who from time to time were intrusted with special experiments to elucidate some particular point. Mr. Jehl says: "The experiments on armature-winding were also very interesting. Edison had a number of small wooden cores made, at both ends of which we inserted little brass nails, and we wound the wooden cores with twine as if it were wire on an armature. In this way we studied armature-winding, and had matches where each of us had a core, while bets were made as to who would be the first to finish properly and correctly a certain kind of winding. Care had to be taken that the wound core corresponded to the direction of the current, supposing it were placed in a field and revolved. After Edison had decided this question, Upton made drawings and tables from which the real armatures were wound and connected to the commutator. To a student of to-day all this seems simple, but in those days the art of constructing dynamos was about as dark as air navigation is at present.... Edison also improved the armature by dividing it and the commutator into a far greater number of sections than up to that time had been the practice. He was also the first to use mica in insulating the commutator sections from each other."

In the mean time, during the progress of the investigations on the dynamo, word had gone out to the world that Edison expected to invent a generator of greater efficiency than any that existed at the time. Again he was assailed and ridiculed by the technical press, for had not the foremost electricians and physicists of Europe and America worked for years on the production of dynamos and arc lamps as they then existed? Even though this young man at Menlo Park had done some wonderful things for telegraphy and telephony; even if he had recorded and reproduced human speech, he had his limitations, and could not upset the settled dictum of science that the internal resistance must equal the external resistance.

Such was the trend of public opinion at the time, but "after Mr. Kruesi had finished the first practical dynamo, and after Mr. Upton had tested it thoroughly and verified his figures and results several times--for he also was surprised--Edison was able to tell the world that he had made a generator giving an efficiency of 90 per cent." Ninety per cent. as against 40 per cent. was a mighty hit, and the world would not believe it. Criticism and argument were again at their height, while Upton, as Edison's duellist, was kept busy replying to private and public challenges of the fact.... "The tremendous progress of the world in the last quarter of a century, owing to the revolution caused by the all-conquering march of 'Heavy Current Engineering,' is the outcome of Edison's work at Menlo Park that raised the efficiency of the dynamo from 40 per cent. to 90 per cent."

Mr. Upton sums it all up very precisely in his remarks upon this period: "What has now been made clear by accurate nomenclature was then very foggy in the text-books. Mr. Edison had completely grasped the effect of subdivision of circuits, and the influence of wires leading to such subdivisions, when it was most difficult to express what he knew in technical language. I remember distinctly when Mr. Edison gave me the problem of placing a motor in circuit in multiple arc with a fixed resistance; and I had to work out the problem entirely, as I could find no prior solution. There was nothing I could find bearing upon the counter electromotive force of the armature, and the effect of the resistance of the armature on the work given out by the armature. It was a wonderful experience to have problems given me out of the intuitions of a great mind, based on enormous experience in practical work, and applying to new lines of progress. One of the main impressions left upon me after knowing Mr. Edison for many years is the marvellous accuracy of his guesses. He will see the general nature of a result long before it can be reached by mathematical calculation. His greatness was always to be clearly seen when difficulties arose. They always made him cheerful, and started him thinking; and very soon would come a line of suggestions which would not end until the difficulty was met and overcome, or found insurmountable. I have often felt that Mr. Edison got himself purposely into trouble by premature publications and otherwise, so that he would have a full incentive to get himself out of the trouble."

This chapter may well end with a statement from Mr. Jehl, shrewd and observant, as a participator in all the early work of the development of the Edison lighting system: "Those who were gathered around him in the old Menlo Park laboratory enjoyed his confidence, and he theirs. Nor was this confidence ever abused. He was respected with a respect which only great men can obtain, and he never showed by any word or act that he was their employer in a sense that would hurt the feelings, as is often the case in the ordinary course of business life. He conversed, argued, and disputed with us all as if he were a colleague on the same footing. It was his winning ways and manners that attached us all so loyally to his side, and made us ever ready with a boundless devotion to execute any request or desire." Thus does a great magnet, run through a heap of sand and filings, exert its lines of force and attract irresistibly to itself the iron and steel particles that are its affinity, and having sifted them out, leaving the useless dust behind, hold them to itself with responsive tenacity.

CHAPTER XIII

A WORLD-HUNT FOR FILAMENT MATERIAL

IN writing about the old experimenting days at Menlo Park, Mr. F. R. Upton says: "Edison's day is twenty-four hours long, for he has always worked whenever there was anything to do, whether day or night, and carried a force of night workers, so that his experiments could go on continually. If he wanted material, he always made it a principle to have it at once, and never hesitated to use special messengers to get it. I remember in the early days of the electric light he wanted a mercury pump for exhausting the lamps. He sent me to Princeton to get it. I got back to Metuchen late in the day, and had to carry the pump over to the laboratory on my back that evening, set it up, and work all night and the next day getting results."

This characteristic principle of obtaining desired material in the quickest and most positive way manifested itself in the search that Edison instituted for the best kind of bamboo for lamp filaments, immediately after the discovery related in a preceding chapter. It is doubtful whether, in the annals of scientific research and experiment, there is anything quite analogous to the story of this search and the various expeditions that went out from the Edison laboratory in 1880 and subsequent years, to scour the earth for a material so apparently simple as a homogeneous strip of bamboo, or other similar fibre. Prolonged and exhaustive experiment, microscopic examination, and an intimate knowledge of the nature of wood and plant fibres, however, had led Edison to the conclusion that bamboo or similar fibrous filaments were more suitable than anything else then known for commercial incandescent lamps, and he wanted the most perfect for that purpose. Hence, the quickest way was to search the tropics until the proper material was found.

The first emissary chosen for this purpose was the late William H. Moore, of Rahway, New Jersey, who left New York in the summer of 1880, bound for China and Japan, these being the countries preeminently noted for the production of abundant species of bamboo. On arrival in the East he quickly left the cities behind and proceeded into the interior, extending his search far into the more remote country districts, collecting specimens on his way, and devoting much time to the study of the bamboo, and in roughly testing the relative value of its fibre in canes of one, two, three, four, and five year growths. Great bales of samples were sent to Edison, and after careful tests a certain variety and growth of Japanese bamboo was determined to be the most satisfactory material for filaments that had been found. Mr. Moore, who was continuing his searches in that country, was instructed to arrange for the cultivation and shipment of regular supplies of this particular species. Arrangements to this end were accordingly made with a Japanese farmer, who began to make immediate shipments, and who subsequently displayed so much ingenuity in fertilizing and cross-fertilizing that the homogeneity of the product was constantly improved. The use of this bamboo for Edison lamp filaments was continued for many years.

Although Mr. Moore did not meet with the exciting adventures of some subsequent explorers, he encountered numerous difficulties and novel experiences in his many months of travel through the hinterland of Japan and China. The attitude toward foreigners thirty years ago was not as friendly as it has since become, but Edison, as usual, had made a happy choice of messengers, as Mr. Moore's good nature and diplomacy attested. These qualities, together with his persistence and perseverance and faculty of intelligent discrimination in the matter of fibres, helped to make his mission successful, and gave to him the honor of being the one who found the bamboo which was adopted for use as filaments in commercial Edison lamps.

Although Edison had satisfied himself that bamboo furnished the most desirable material thus far discovered for incandescent-lamp filaments, he felt that in some part of the world there might be found a natural product of the same general character that would furnish a still more perfect and homogeneous material. In his study of this subject, and during the prosecution of vigorous and searching inquiries in various directions, he learned that Mr. John C. Brauner, then residing in Brooklyn, New York, had an expert knowledge of indigenous plants of the particular kind desired. During the course of a geological survey which he had made for the Brazilian Government, Mr. Brauner had examined closely the various species of palms which grow plentifully in that country, and of them there was one whose fibres he thought would be just what Edison wanted.

Accordingly, Mr. Brauner was sent for and dispatched to Brazil in December, 1880, to search for and send samples of this and such other palms, fibres, grasses, and canes as, in his judgment, would be suitable for the experiments then being carried on at Menlo Park. Landing at Para, he crossed over into the Amazonian province, and thence proceeded through the heart of the country, making his way by canoe on the rivers and their tributaries, and by foot into the forests and marshes of a vast and almost untrodden wilderness. In this manner Mr. Brauner traversed about two thousand miles of the comparatively unknown interior of Southern Brazil, and procured a large variety of fibrous specimens, which he shipped to Edison a few months later. When these fibres arrived in the United States they were carefully tested and a few of them found suitable but not superior to the Japanese bamboo, which was then being exclusively used in the manufacture of commercial Edison lamps.

Later on Edison sent out an expedition to explore the wilds of Cuba and Jamaica. A two months' investigation of the latter island revealed a variety of bamboo growths, of which a great number of specimens were obtained and shipped to Menlo Park; but on careful test they were found inferior to the Japanese bamboo, and hence rejected. The exploration of the glades and swamps of Florida by three men extended over a period of five months in a minute search for fibrous woods of the palmetto species. A great variety was found, and over five hundred boxes of specimens were shipped to the laboratory from time to time, but none of them tested out with entirely satisfactory results.

The use of Japanese bamboo for carbon filaments was therefore continued in the manufacture of lamps, although an incessant search was maintained for a still more perfect material. The spirit of progress, so pervasive in Edison's character, led him, however, to renew his investigations further afield by sending out two other men to examine the bamboo and similar growths of those parts of South America not covered by Mr. Brauner. These two men were Frank McGowan and C. F. Hanington, both of whom had been for nearly seven years in the employ of the Edison Electric Light Company in New York. The former was a stocky, rugged Irishman, possessing the native shrewdness and buoyancy of his race, coupled with undaunted courage and determination; and the latter was a veteran of the Civil War, with some knowledge of forest and field, acquired as a sportsman. They left New York in September, 1887, arriving in due time at Para, proceeding thence twenty-three hundred miles up the Amazon River to Iquitos. Nothing of an eventful nature occurred during this trip, but on arrival at Iquitos the two men separated; Mr. McGowan to explore on foot and by canoe in Peru, Ecuador, and Colombia, while Mr. Hanington returned by the Amazon River to Para. Thence Hanington went by steamer to Montevideo, and by similar conveyance up the River de la Plata and through Uruguay, Argentine, and Paraguay to the southernmost part of Brazil, collecting a large number of specimens of palms and grasses.

The adventures of Mr. McGowan, after leaving Iquitos, would fill a book if related in detail. The object of the present narrative and the space at the authors' disposal, however, do not permit of more than a brief mention of his experiences. His first objective point was Quito, about five hundred miles away, which he proposed to reach on foot and by means of canoeing on the Napo River through a wild and comparatively unknown country teeming with tribes of hostile natives. The dangers of the expedition were pictured to him in glowing colors, but spurning prophecies of dire disaster, he engaged some native Indians and a canoe and started on his explorations, reaching Quito in eighty-seven days, after a thorough search of the country on both sides of the Napo River. From Quito he went to Guayaquil, from there by steamer to Buenaventura, and thence by rail, twelve miles, to Cordova. From this point he set out on foot to explore the Cauca Valley and the Cordilleras.

Mr. McGowan found in these regions a great variety of bamboo, small and large, some species growing seventy-five to one hundred feet in height, and from six to nine inches in diameter. He collected a large number of specimens, which were subsequently sent to Orange for Edison's examination. After about fifteen months of exploration attended by much hardship and privation, deserted sometimes by treacherous guides, twice laid low by fevers, occasionally in peril from Indian attacks, wild animals and poisonous serpents, tormented by insect pests, endangered by floods, one hundred and nineteen days without meat, ninety-eight days without taking off his clothes, Mr. McGowan returned to America, broken in health but having faithfully fulfilled the commission intrusted to him. The Evening Sun, New York, obtained an interview with him at that time, and in its issue of May 2, 1889, gave more than a page to a brief story of his interesting adventures, and then commented editorially upon them, as follows:

"A ROMANCE OF SCIENCE"

"The narrative given elsewhere in the Evening Sun of the wanderings of
Edison's missionary of science, Mr. Frank McGowan, furnishes a new proof
that the romances of real life surpass any that the imagination can
frame.

"In pursuit of a substance that should meet the requirements of the
Edison incandescent lamp, Mr. McGowan penetrated the wilderness of the
Amazon, and for a year defied its fevers, beasts, reptiles, and deadly
insects in his quest of a material so precious that jealous Nature has
hidden it in her most secret fastnesses.

"No hero of mythology or fable ever dared such dragons to rescue some
captive goddess as did this dauntless champion of civilization. Theseus,
or Siegfried, or any knight of the fairy books might envy the victories
of Edison's irresistible lieutenant.

"As a sample story of adventure, Mr. McGowan's narrative is a marvel fit
to be classed with the historic journeyings of the greatest travellers.
But it gains immensely in interest when we consider that it succeeded in
its scientific purpose. The mysterious bamboo was discovered, and large
quantities of it were procured and brought to the Wizard's laboratory,
there to suffer another wondrous change and then to light up our
pleasure-haunts and our homes with a gentle radiance."

A further, though rather sad, interest attaches to the McGowan story,
for only a short time had elapsed after his return to America when he
disappeared suddenly and mysteriously, and in spite of long-continued
and strenuous efforts to obtain some light on the subject, no clew
or trace of him was ever found. He was a favorite among the Edison
"oldtimers," and his memory is still cherished, for when some of the
"boys" happen to get together, as they occasionally do, some one is
almost sure to "wonder what became of poor 'Mac.'" He was last seen at
Mouquin's famous old French restaurant on Fulton Street, New York, where
he lunched with one of the authors of this book and the late Luther
Stieringer. He sat with them for two or three hours discussing his
wonderful trip, and telling some fascinating stories of adventure. Then
the party separated at the Ann Street door of the restaurant, after
making plans to secure the narrative in more detailed form for
subsequent use--and McGowan has not been seen from that hour to this.
The trail of the explorer was more instantly lost in New York than in
the vast recesses of the Amazon swamps.

The next and last explorer whom Edison sent out in search of
natural fibres was Mr. James Ricalton, of Maplewood, New Jersey, a
school-principal, a well-known traveller, and an ardent student of
natural science. Mr. Ricalton's own story of his memorable expedition is
so interesting as to be worthy of repetition here:

"A village schoolmaster is not unaccustomed to door-rappings; for the steps of belligerent mothers are often thitherward bent seeking redress for conjured wrongs to their darling boobies.

"It was a bewildering moment, therefore, to the Maplewood teacher when, in answering a rap at the door one afternoon, he found, instead of an irate mother, a messenger from the laboratory of the world's greatest inventor bearing a letter requesting an audience a few hours later.

"Being the teacher to whom reference is made, I am now quite willing to confess that for the remainder of that afternoon, less than a problem in Euclid would have been sufficient to disqualify me for the remaining scholastic duties of the hour. I felt it, of course, to be no small honor for a humble teacher to be called to the sanctum of Thomas A. Edison. The letter, however, gave no intimation of the nature of the object for which I had been invited to appear before Mr. Edison....

"When I was presented to Mr. Edison his way of setting forth the mission he had designated for me was characteristic of how a great mind conceives vast undertakings and commands great things in few words. At this time Mr. Edison had discovered that the fibre of a certain bamboo afforded a very desirable carbon for the electric lamp, and the variety of bamboo used was a product of Japan. It was his belief that in other parts of the world other and superior varieties might be found, and to that end he had dispatched explorers to bamboo regions in the valleys of the great South American rivers, where specimens were found of extraordinary quality; but the locality in which these specimens were found was lost in the limitless reaches of those great river-bottoms. The great necessity for more durable carbons became a desideratum so urgent that the tireless inventor decided to commission another explorer to search the tropical jungles of the Orient.

"This brings me then to the first meeting of Edison, when he set forth substantially as follows, as I remember it twenty years ago, the purpose for which he had called me from my scholastic duties. With a quizzical gleam in his eye, he said: 'I want a man to ransack all the tropical jungles of the East to find a better fibre for my lamp; I expect it to be found in the palm or bamboo family. How would you like that job?' Suiting my reply to his love of brevity and dispatch, I said, 'That would suit me.' 'Can you go to-morrow?' was his next question. 'Well, Mr. Edison, I must first of all get a leave of absence from my Board of Education, and assist the board to secure a substitute for the time of my absence. How long will it take, Mr. Edison?' 'How can I tell? Maybe six months, and maybe five years; no matter how long, find it.' He continued: 'I sent a man to South America to find what I want; he found it; but lost the place where he found it, so he might as well never have found it at all.' Hereat I was enjoined to proceed forthwith to court the Board of Education for a leave of absence, which I did successfully, the board considering that a call so important and honorary was entitled to their unqualified favor, which they generously granted.

"I reported to Mr. Edison on the following day, when he instructed me to come to the laboratory at once to learn all the details of drawing and carbonizing fibres, which it would be necessary to do in the Oriental

jungles. This I did, and, in the mean time, a set of suitable tools for
this purpose had been ordered to be made in the laboratory. As soon as
I learned my new trade, which I accomplished in a few days, Mr. Edison
directed me to the library of the laboratory to occupy a few days in
studying the geography of the Orient and, particularly, in drawing maps
of the tributaries of the Ganges, the Irrawaddy, and the Brahmaputra
rivers, and other regions which I expected to explore.

"It was while thus engaged that Mr. Edison came to me one day and said:
'If you will go up to the house' (his palatial home not far away) 'and
look behind the sofa in the library you will find a joint of bamboo, a
specimen of that found in South America; bring it down and make a study
of it; if you find something equal to that I will be satisfied.' At the
home I was guided to the library by an Irish servant-woman, to whom I
communicated my knowledge of the definite locality of the sample joint.
She plunged her arm, bare and herculean, behind the aforementioned sofa,
and holding aloft a section of wood, called out in a mood of discovery:
'Is that it?' Replying in the affirmative, she added, under an impulse
of innocent divination that whatever her wizard master laid hands upon
could result in nothing short of an invention, 'Sure, sor, and what's he
going to invint out o' that?'

"My kit of tools made, my maps drawn, my Oriental geography reviewed, I
come to the point when matters of immediate departure are discussed; and
when I took occasion to mention to my chief that, on the subject of life
insurance, underwriters refuse to take any risks on an enterprise so
hazardous, Mr. Edison said that, if I did not place too high a valuation
on my person, he would take the risk himself. I replied that I was born
and bred in New York State, but now that I had become a Jersey man I did
not value myself at above fifteen hundred dollars. Edison laughed and
said that he would assume the risk, and another point was settled. The
next matter was the financing of the trip, about which Mr. Edison asked
in a tentative way about the rates to the East. I told him the expense
of such a trip could not be determined beforehand in detail, but that I
had established somewhat of a reputation for economic travel, and that
I did not believe any traveller could surpass me in that respect. He
desired no further assurance in that direction, and thereupon ordered a
letter of credit made out with authorization to order a second when the
first was exhausted. Herein then are set forth in briefest space the
preliminaries of a circuit of the globe in quest of fibre.

"It so happened that the day on which I set out fell on Washington's
Birthday, and I suggested to my boys and girls at school that they make
a line across the station platform near the school at Maplewood,
and from this line I would start eastward around the world, and if
good-fortune should bring me back I would meet them from the westward at
the same line. As I had often made them 'toe the scratch,' for once they
were only too well pleased to have me toe the line for them.

"This was done, and I sailed via England and the Suez Canal to Ceylon,
that fair isle to which Sindbad the Sailor made his sixth voyage,
picturesquely referred to in history as the 'brightest gem in the
British Colonial Crown.' I knew Ceylon to be eminently tropical; I knew
it to be rich in many varieties of the bamboo family, which has been

called the king of the grasses; and in this family had I most hope of finding the desired fibre. Weeks were spent in this paradisiacal isle. Every part was visited. Native wood craftsmen were offered a premium on every new species brought in, and in this way nearly a hundred species were tested, a greater number than was found in any other country. One of the best specimens tested during the entire trip around the world was found first in Ceylon, although later in Burmah, it being indigenous to the latter country. It is a gigantic tree-grass or reed growing in clumps of from one to two hundred, often twelve inches in diameter, and one hundred and fifty feet high, and known as the giant bamboo (Bambusa gigantia). This giant grass stood the highest test as a carbon, and on account of its extraordinary size and qualities I extend it this special mention. With others who have given much attention to this remarkable reed, I believe that in its manifold uses the bamboo is the world's greatest dendral benefactor.

"From Ceylon I proceeded to India, touching the great peninsula first at Cape Comorin, and continuing northward by way of Pondicherry, Madura, and Madras; and thence to the tableland of Bangalore and the Western Ghauts, testing many kinds of wood at every point, but particularly the palm and bamboo families. From the range of the Western Ghauts I went to Bombay and then north by the way of Delhi to Simla, the summer capital of the Himalayas; thence again northward to the headwaters of the Sutlej River, testing everywhere on my way everything likely to afford the desired carbon.

"On returning from the mountains I followed the valleys of the Jumna and the Ganges to Calcutta, whence I again ascended the Sub-Himalayas to Darjeeling, where the numerous river-bottoms were sprinkled plentifully with many varieties of bamboo, from the larger sizes to dwarfed species covering the mountain slopes, and not longer than the grass of meadows. Again descending to the plains I passed eastward to the Brahmaputra River, which I ascended to the foot-hills in Assam; but finding nothing of superior quality in all this northern region I returned to Calcutta and sailed thence to Rangoon, in Burmah; and there, finding no samples giving more excellent tests in the lower reaches of the Irrawaddy, I ascended that river to Mandalay, where, through Burmese bamboo wiseacres, I gathered in from round about and tested all that the unusually rich Burmese flora could furnish. In Burmah the giant bamboo, as already mentioned, is found indigenous; but beside it no superior varieties were found. Samples tested at several points on the Malay Peninsula showed no new species, except at a point north of Singapore, where I found a species large and heavy which gave a test nearly equal to that of the giant bamboo in Ceylon.

"After completing the Malay Peninsula I had planned to visit Java and Borneo; but having found in the Malay Peninsula and in Ceylon a bamboo fibre which averaged a test from one to two hundred per cent. better than that in use at the lamp factory, I decided it was unnecessary to visit these countries or New Guinea, as my 'Eureka' had already been established, and that I would therefore set forth over the return hemisphere, searching China and Japan on the way. The rivers in Southern China brought down to Canton bamboos of many species, where this wondrously utilitarian reed enters very largely into the industrial life of that people, and not merely into the industrial life, but even into the culinary arts, for bamboo sprouts are a universal vegetable in China; but among all the bamboos of China I found none of superexcellence in carbonizing qualities. Japan came next in the succession of countries to be explored, but there the work was much simplified, from the fact that the Tokio Museum contains a complete classified collection of all the different species in the empire, and there samples could be obtained and tested.

"Now the last of the important bamboo-producing countries in the globe circuit had been done, and the 'home-lap' was in order; the broad Pacific was spanned in fourteen days; my natal continent in six; and on the 22d of February, on the same day, at the same hour, at the same minute, one year to a second, 'little Maude,' a sweet maid of the school, led me across the line which completed the circuit of the globe, and where I was greeted by the cheers of my boys and girls. I at once reported to Mr. Edison, whose manner of greeting my return was as characteristic of the man as his summary and matter-of-fact manner of my dispatch. His little catechism of curious inquiry was embraced in four small and intensely Anglo-Saxon words--with his usual pleasant smile he extended his hand and said: 'Did you get it?' This was surely a summing of a year's exploration not less laconic than Caesar's review of his Gallic campaign. When I replied that I had, but that he must be the final judge of what I had found, he said that during my absence he had succeeded in making an artificial carbon which was meeting the requirements satisfactorily; so well, indeed, that I believe no practical use was ever made of the bamboo fibres thereafter.

"I have herein given a very brief resume of my search for fibre through the Orient; and during my connection with that mission I was at all times not less astonished at Mr. Edison's quick perception of conditions and his instant decision and his bigness of conceptions, than I had always been with his prodigious industry and his inventive genius.

"Thinking persons know that blatant men never accomplish much, and Edison's marvellous brevity of speech along with his miraculous achievements should do much to put bores and garrulity out of fashion."

Although Edison had instituted such a costly and exhaustive search throughout the world for the most perfect of natural fibres, he did not necessarily feel committed for all time to the exclusive use of that material for his lamp filaments. While these explorations were in progress, as indeed long before, he had given much thought to the production of some artificial compound that would embrace not only the required homogeneity, but also many other qualifications necessary for the manufacture of an improved type of lamp which had become desirable by reason of the rapid adoption of his lighting system.

At the very time Mr. McGowan was making his explorations deep in South America, and Mr. Ricalton his swift trip around the world, Edison, after much investigation and experiment, had produced a compound which promised better results than bamboo fibres. After some changes dictated by experience, this artificial filament was adopted in the manufacture of lamps. No radical change was immediately made, however, but the product of the lamp factory was gradually changed over, during the course of a few years, from the use of bamboo to the "squirted" filament, as the new material was called. An artificial compound of one kind or another has indeed been universally adopted for the purpose by all manufacturers; hence the incandescing conductors in all carbon-filament lamps of the present day are made in that way. The fact remains, however, that for nearly nine years all Edison lamps (many millions in the aggregate) were made with bamboo filaments, and many of them for several years after that, until bamboo was finally abandoned in the early nineties, except for use in a few special types which were so made until about the end of 1908. The last few years have witnessed a remarkable advance in the manufacture of incandescent lamps in the substitution of metallic filaments for those of carbon. It will be remembered that many of the earlier experiments were based on the use of strips of platinum; while other rare metals were the subject of casual trial. No real success was attained in that direction, and for many years the carbon-filament lamp reigned supreme. During the last four or five years lamps with filaments made from tantalum and tungsten have been produced and placed on the market with great success, and are now largely used. Their price is still very high, however, as compared with that of the carbon lamp, which has been vastly improved in methods of construction, and whose average price of fifteen cents is only one-tenth of what it was when Edison first brought it out.

With the close of Mr. McGowan's and Mr. Ricalton's expeditions, there ended the historic world-hunt for natural fibres. From start to finish the investigations and searches made by Edison himself, and carried on by others under his direction, are remarkable not only from the fact that they entailed a total expenditure of about $100,000, (disbursed under his supervision by Mr. Upton), but also because of their unique inception and thoroughness they illustrate one of the strongest traits of his character--an invincible determination to leave no stone unturned to acquire that which he believes to be in existence, and which, when found, will answer the purpose that he has in mind.

CHAPTER XIV

INVENTING A COMPLETE SYSTEM OF LIGHTING

IN Berlin, on December 11, 1908, with notable eclat, the seventieth birthday was celebrated of Emil Rathenau, the founder of the great Allgemein Elektricitaets Gesellschaft. This distinguished German, creator of a splendid industry, then received the congratulations of his fellow-countrymen, headed by Emperor William, who spoke enthusiastically of his services to electro-technics and to Germany. In his interesting acknowledgment, Mr. Rathenau told how he went to Paris in 1881, and at the electrical exhibition there saw the display of Edison's inventions in electric lighting "which have met with as little proper appreciation as his countless innovations in connection with telegraphy, telephony, and the entire electrical industry." He saw the Edison dynamo, and he saw the incandescent lamp, "of which millions have been manufactured since that day without the great master being paid the tribute to his invention." But what impressed the observant, thoroughgoing German was the breadth with which the whole lighting art had been elaborated and perfected, even at that early day. "The Edison system of lighting was as beautifully conceived down to the very details, and as thoroughly worked out as if it had been tested for decades in various towns. Neither sockets, switches, fuses, lamp-holders, nor any of the other accessories necessary to complete the installation were wanting; and the generating of the current, the regulation, the wiring with distributing boxes, house connections, meters, etc., all showed signs of astonishing skill and incomparable genius."

Such praise on such an occasion from the man who introduced incandescent electric lighting into Germany is significant as to the continued appreciation abroad of Mr. Edison's work. If there is one thing modern Germany is proud and jealous of, it is her leadership in electrical engineering and investigation. But with characteristic insight, Mr. Rathenau here placed his finger on the great merit that has often been forgotten. Edison was not simply the inventor of a new lamp and a new dynamo. They were invaluable elements, but far from all that was necessary. His was the mighty achievement of conceiving and executing in all its details an art and an industry absolutely new to the world. Within two years this man completed and made that art available in its essential, fundamental facts, which remain unchanged after thirty years of rapid improvement and widening application.

Such a stupendous feat, whose equal is far to seek anywhere in the history of invention, is worth studying, especially as the task will take us over much new ground and over very little of the territory already covered. Notwithstanding the enormous amount of thought and labor expended on the incandescent lamp problem from the autumn of 1878 to the winter of 1879, it must not be supposed for one moment that Edison's whole endeavor and entire inventive skill had been given to the lamp alone, or the dynamo alone. We have sat through the long watches of the night while Edison brooded on the real solution of the swarming problems. We have gazed anxiously at the steady fingers of the deft and cautious Batchelor, as one fragile filament after another refused to stay intact until it could be sealed into its crystal prison and there glow with light that never was before on land or sea. We have calculated armatures and field coils for the new dynamo with Upton, and held the stakes for Jehl and his fellows at their winding bees. We have seen the mineral and vegetable kingdoms rifled and ransacked for substances that would yield the best "filament." We have had the vague consciousness of assisting at a great development whose evidences to-day on every hand attest its magnitude. We have felt the fierce play of volcanic effort, lifting new continents of opportunity from the infertile sea, without any devastation of pre-existing fields of human toil and harvest. But it still remains to elucidate the actual thing done; to reduce it to concrete data, and in reducing, to unfold its colossal dimensions.

The lighting system that Edison contemplated in this entirely new departure from antecedent methods included the generation of electrical energy, or current, on a very large scale; its distribution throughout extended areas, and its division and subdivision into small units converted into light at innumerable points in every direction from the source of supply, each unit to be independent of every other and susceptible to immediate control by the user.

This was truly an altogether prodigious undertaking. We need not wonder that Professor Tyndall, in words implying grave doubt as to the possibility of any solution of the various problems, said publicly that he would much rather have the matter in Edison's hands than in his own. There were no precedents, nothing upon which to build or improve. The problems could only be answered by the creation of new devices and methods expressly worked out for their solution. An electric lamp answering certain specific requirements would, indeed, be the key to the situation, but its commercial adaptation required a multifarious variety of apparatus and devices. The word "system" is much abused in invention, and during the early days of electric lighting its use applied to a mere freakish lamp or dynamo was often ludicrous. But, after all, nothing short of a complete system could give real value to the lamp as an invention; nothing short of a system could body forth the new art to the public. Let us therefore set down briefly a few of the leading items needed for perfect illumination by electricity, all of which were part of the Edison programme:

First--To conceive a broad and fundamentally correct method of distributing the current, satisfactory in a scientific sense and practical commercially in its efficiency and economy. This meant, ready made, a comprehensive plan analogous to illumination by gas, with a network of conductors all connected together, so that in any given city area the lights could be fed with electricity from several directions, thus eliminating any interruption due to the disturbance on any particular section.

Second--To devise an electric lamp that would give about the same amount of light as a gas jet, which custom had proven to be a suitable and useful unit. This lamp must possess the quality of requiring only a small investment in the copper conductors reaching it. Each lamp must be independent of every other lamp. Each and all the lights must be produced and operated with sufficient economy to compete on a commercial basis with gas. The lamp must be durable, capable of being easily and safely handled by the public, and one that would remain capable of burning at full incandescence and candle-power a great length of time.

Third--To devise means whereby the amount of electrical energy furnished to each and every customer could be determined, as in the case of gas, and so that this could be done cheaply and reliably by a meter at the customer's premises.

Fourth--To elaborate a system or network of conductors capable of being placed underground or overhead, which would allow of being tapped at any intervals, so that service wires could be run from the main conductors in the street into each building. Where these mains went below the surface of the thoroughfare, as in large cities, there must be protective conduit or pipe for the copper conductors, and these pipes must allow of being tapped wherever necessary. With these conductors and pipes must also be furnished manholes, junction-boxes, connections, and a host of varied paraphernalia insuring perfect general distribution.

Fifth--To devise means for maintaining at all points in an extended area of distribution a practically even pressure of current, so that all the lamps, wherever located, near or far away from the central station, should give an equal light at all times, independent of the number that might be turned on; and safeguarding the lamps against rupture by sudden and violent fluctuations of current. There must also be means for thus regulating at the point where the current was generated the quality or pressure of the current throughout the whole lighting area, with devices for indicating what such pressure might actually be at various points in the area.

Sixth--To design efficient dynamos, such not being in existence at the time, that would convert economically the steam-power of high-speed engines into electrical energy, together with means for connecting and disconnecting them with the exterior consumption circuits; means for regulating, equalizing their loads, and adjusting the number of dynamos to be used according to the fluctuating demands on the central station. Also the arrangement of complete stations with steam and electric apparatus and auxiliary devices for insuring their efficient and continuous operation.

Seventh--To invent devices that would prevent the current from becoming excessive upon any conductors, causing fire or other injury; also switches for turning the current on and off; lamp-holders, fixtures, and the like; also means and methods for establishing the interior circuits that were to carry current to chandeliers and fixtures in buildings.

Here was the outline of the programme laid down in the autumn of 1878, and pursued through all its difficulties to definite accomplishment in about eighteen months, some of the steps being made immediately, others being taken as the art evolved. It is not to be imagined for one moment that Edison performed all the experiments with his own hands. The method of working at Menlo Park has already been described in these pages by those who participated. It would not only have been physically impossible for one man to have done all this work himself, in view of the time and labor required, and the endless detail; but most of the apparatus and devices invented or suggested by him as the art took shape required the handiwork of skilled mechanics and artisans of a high order of ability. Toward the end of 1879 the laboratory force thus numbered at least one hundred earnest men. In this respect of collaboration, Edison has always adopted a policy that must in part be taken to explain his many successes. Some inventors of the greatest ability, dealing with ideas and conceptions of importance, have found it impossible to organize or even to tolerate a staff of co-workers, preferring solitary and secret toil, incapable of team work, or jealous of any intrusion that could possibly bar them from a full and complete claim to the result when obtained. Edison always stood shoulder to shoulder with his associates, but no one ever questioned the leadership, nor was it ever in doubt where the inspiration originated. The real truth is that Edison has always been so ceaselessly fertile of ideas himself, he has had more than his whole staff could ever do to try them all out; he has sought co-operation, but no exterior suggestion. As a matter of fact a great many of the "Edison men" have made notable inventions of their own, with which their names are imperishably associated; but while they were with Edison it was with his work that they were and must be busied.

It was during this period of "inventing a system" that so much systematic and continuous work with good results was done by Edison in the design and perfection of dynamos. The value of his contributions to the art of lighting comprised in this work has never been fully understood or appreciated, having been so greatly overshadowed by his invention of the incandescent lamp, and of a complete system of distribution. It is a fact, however, that the principal improvements he made in dynamo-electric generators were of a radical nature and remain in the art. Thirty years bring about great changes, especially in a field so notably progressive as that of the generation of electricity; but different as are the dynamos of to-day from those of the earlier period, they embody essential principles and elements that Edison then marked out and elaborated as the conditions of success. There was indeed prompt appreciation in some well-informed quarters of what Edison was doing, evidenced by the sensation caused in the summer of 1881, when he designed, built, and shipped to Paris for the first Electrical Exposition ever held, the largest dynamo that had been built up to that time. It was capable of lighting twelve hundred incandescent lamps, and weighed with its engine twenty-seven tons, the armature alone weighing six tons. It was then, and for a long time after, the eighth wonder of the scientific world, and its arrival and installation in Paris were eagerly watched by the most famous physicists and electricians of Europe.

Edison's amusing description of his experience in shipping the dynamo to Paris when built may appropriately be given here: "I built a very large dynamo with the engine directly connected, which I intended for the Paris Exposition of 1881. It was one or two sizes larger than those I had previously built. I had only a very short period in which to get it ready and put it on a steamer to reach the Exposition in time. After the machine was completed we found the voltage was too low. I had to devise a way of raising the voltage without changing the machine, which I did by adding extra magnets. After this was done, we tested the machine, and the crank-shaft of the engine broke and flew clear across the shop. By working night and day a new crank-shaft was put in, and we only had three days left from that time to get it on board the steamer; and had also to run a test. So we made arrangements with the Tammany leader, and through him with the police, to clear the street--one of the New York crosstown streets--and line it with policemen, as we proposed to make a quick passage, and didn't know how much time it would take. About four hours before the steamer had to get it, the machine was shut down after the test, and a schedule was made out in advance of what each man had to do. Sixty men were put on top of the dynamo to get it ready, and each man had written orders as to what he was to perform. We got it all taken apart and put on trucks and started off. They drove the horses with a fire-bell in front of them to the French pier, the policemen lining the streets. Fifty men were ready to help the stevedores get it on the steamer--and we were one hour ahead of time."

This Exposition brings us, indeed, to a dramatic and rather pathetic parting of the ways. The hour had come for the old laboratory force that had done such brilliant and memorable work to disband, never again to assemble under like conditions for like effort, although its members all remained active in the field, and many have ever since been associated prominently with some department of electrical enterprise. The fact was they had done their work so well they must now disperse to show the world what it was, and assist in its industrial exploitation. In reality, they were too few for the demands that reached Edison from all parts of the world for the introduction of his system; and in the emergency the men nearest to him and most trusted were those upon whom he could best depend for such missionary work as was now required. The disciples full of fire and enthusiasm, as well as of knowledge and experience, were soon scattered to the four winds, and the rapidity with which the Edison system was everywhere successfully introduced is testimony to the good judgment with which their leader had originally selected them as his colleagues. No one can say exactly just how this process of disintegration began, but Mr. E. H. Johnson had already been sent to England in the Edison interests, and now the question arose as to what should be done with the French demands and the Paris Electrical Exposition, whose importance as a point of new departure in electrical industry was speedily recognized on both sides of the Atlantic. It is very interesting to note that as the earlier staff broke up, Edison became the centre of another large body, equally devoted, but more particularly concerned with the commercial development of his ideas. Mr. E. G. Acheson mentions in his personal notes on work at the laboratory, that in December of 1880, while on some experimental work, he was called to the new lamp factory started recently at Menlo Park, and there found Edison, Johnson, Batchelor, and Upton in conference, and "Edison informed me that Mr. Batchelor, who was in charge of the construction, development, and operation of the lamp factory, was soon to sail for Europe to prepare for the exhibit to be made at the Electrical Exposition to be held in Paris during the coming summer." These preparations overlap the reinforcement of the staff with some notable additions, chief among them being Mr. Samuel Insull, whose interesting narrative of events fits admirably into the story at this stage, and gives a vivid idea of the intense activity and excitement with which the whole atmosphere around Edison was then surcharged: "I first met Edison on March 1, 1881. I arrived in New York on the City of Chester about five or six in the evening, and went direct to 65 Fifth Avenue. I had come over to act as Edison's private secretary, the position having been obtained for me through the good offices of Mr. E. H. Johnson, whom I had known in London, and who wrote to Mr. U. H. Painter, of Washington, about me in the fall of 1880. Mr. Painter sent the letter on to Mr. Batchelor, who turned it over to Edison. Johnson returned to America late in the fall of 1880, and in January, 1881, cabled to me to come to this country. At the time he cabled for me Edison was still at Menlo Park, but when I arrived in New York the famous offices of the Edison Electric Light Company had been opened at '65' Fifth Avenue, and Edison had moved into New York with the idea of assisting in the exploitation of the Light Company's business.

"I was taken by Johnson direct from the Inman Steamship pier to 65 Fifth Avenue, and met Edison for the first time. There were three rooms on the ground floor at that time. The front one was used as a kind of reception-room; the room immediately behind it was used as the office of the president of the Edison Electric Light Company, Major S. B. Eaton. The rear room, which was directly back of the front entrance hall, was Edison's office, and there I first saw him. There was very little in the room except a couple of walnut roller-top desks--which were very generally used in American offices at that time. Edison received me with great cordiality. I think he was possibly disappointed at my being so young a man; I had only just turned twenty-one, and had a very boyish appearance. The picture of Edison is as vivid to me now as if the incident occurred yesterday, although it is now more than twenty-nine years since that first meeting. I had been connected with Edison's affairs in England as private secretary to his London agent for about two years; and had been taught by Johnson to look on Edison as the greatest electrical inventor of the day--a view of him, by-the-way, which has been greatly strengthened as the years have rolled by. Owing to this, and to the fact that I felt highly flattered at the appointment as his private secretary, I was naturally prepared to accept him as a hero. With my strict English ideas as to the class of clothes to be worn by a prominent man, there was nothing in Edison's dress to impress me. He wore a rather seedy black diagonal Prince Albert coat and waistcoat, with trousers of a dark material, and a white silk handkerchief around his neck, tied in a careless knot falling over the stiff bosom of a white shirt somewhat the worse for wear. He had a large wide-awake hat of the sombrero pattern then generally used in this country, and a rough, brown overcoat, cut somewhat similarly to his Prince Albert coat. His hair was worn quite long, and hanging carelessly over his fine forehead. His face was at that time, as it is now, clean shaven. He was full in face and figure, although by no means as stout as he has grown in recent years. What struck me above everything else was the wonderful intelligence and magnetism of his expression, and the extreme brightness of his eyes. He was far more modest than in my youthful picture of him. I had expected to find a man of distinction. His appearance, as a whole, was not what you would call 'slovenly,' it is best expressed by the word 'careless.'"

Mr. Insull supplements this pen-picture by another, bearing upon the hustle and bustle of the moment: "After a short conversation Johnson hurried me off to meet his family, and later in the evening, about eight o'clock, he and I returned to Edison's office; and I found myself launched without further ceremony into Edison's business affairs. Johnson had already explained to me that he was sailing the next morning, March 2d, on the S.S. Arizona, and that Mr. Edison wanted to spend the evening discussing matters in connection with his European affairs. It was assumed, inasmuch as I had just arrived from London, that I would be able to give more or less information on this subject. As Johnson was to sail the next morning at five o'clock, Edison explained that it would be necessary for him to have an understanding of European matters. Edison started out by drawing from his desk a check-book and stating how much money he had in the bank; and he wanted to know what European telephone securities were most salable, as he wished to raise the necessary funds to put on their feet the incandescent lamp factory, the Electric Tube works, and the necessary shops to build dynamos. All through the interview I was tremendously impressed with Edison's wonderful resourcefulness and grasp, and his immediate appreciation of any suggestion of consequence bearing on the subject under discussion.

"He spoke with very great enthusiasm of the work before him--namely, the development of his electric-lighting system; and his one idea seemed to be to raise all the money he could with the object of pouring it into the manufacturing side of the lighting business. I remember how extraordinarily I was impressed with him on this account, as I had just come from a circle of people in London who not only questioned the possibility of the success of Edison's invention, but often expressed doubt as to whether the work he had done could be called an invention at all. After discussing affairs with Johnson--who was receiving his final instructions from Edison--far into the night, and going down to the steamer to see Johnson aboard, I finished my first night's business with Edison somewhere between four and five in the morning, feeling thoroughly imbued with the idea that I had met one of the great master minds of the world. You must allow for my youthful enthusiasm, but you must also bear in mind Edison's peculiar gift of magnetism, which has enabled him during his career to attach so many men to him. I fell a victim to the spell at the first interview."

Events moved rapidly in those days. The next morning, Tuesday, Edison took his new fidus Achates with him to a conference with John Roach, the famous old ship-builder, and at it agreed to take the AEtna Iron works, where Roach had laid the foundations of his fame and fortune. These works were not in use at the time. They were situated on Goerck Street, New York, north of Grand Street, on the east side of the city, and there, very soon after, was established the first Edison dynamo-manufacturing establishment, known for many years as the Edison Machine Works. The same night Insull made his first visit to Menlo Park. Up to that time he had seen very little incandescent lighting, for the simple reason that there was very little to see. Johnson had had a few Edison lamps in London, lit up from primary batteries, as a demonstration; and in the summer of 1880 Swan had had a few series lamps burning in London. In New York a small gas-engine plant was being started at the Edison offices on Fifth Avenue. But out at Menlo Park there was the first actual electric-lighting central station, supplying distributed incandescent lamps and some electric motors by means of underground conductors imbedded in asphaltum and surrounded by a wooden box. Mr. Insull says: "The system employed was naturally the two-wire, as at that time the three-wire had not been thought of. The lamps were partly of the horseshoe filament paper-carbon type, and partly bamboo-filament lamps, and were of an efficiency of 95 to 100 watts per 16 c.p. I can never forget the impression that this first view of the electric-lighting industry produced on me. Menlo Park must always be looked upon as the birthplace of the electric light and power industry. At that time it was the only place where could be seen an electric light and power multiple arc distribution system, the operation of which seemed as successful to my youthful mind as the operation of one of the large metropolitan systems to-day. I well remember about ten o'clock that night going down to the Menlo Park depot and getting the station agent, who was also the telegraph operator, to send some cable messages for me to my London friends, announcing that I had seen Edison's incandescent lighting system in actual operation, and that so far as I could tell it was an accomplished fact. A few weeks afterward I received a letter from one of my London friends, who was a doubting Thomas, upbraiding me for coming so soon under the spell of the 'Yankee inventor.'"

It was to confront and deal with just this element of doubt in London and in Europe generally, that the dispatch of Johnson to England and of Batchelor to France was intended. Throughout the Edison staff there was a mingled feeling of pride in the work, resentment at the doubts expressed about it, and keen desire to show how excellent it was. Batchelor left for Paris in July, 1881--on his second trip to Europe that year--and the exhibit was made which brought such an instantaneous recognition of the incalculable value of Edison's lighting inventions, as evidenced by the awards and rewards immediately bestowed upon him. He was made an officer of the Legion of Honor, and Prof. George F. Barker cabled as follows from Paris, announcing the decision of the expert jury which passed upon the exhibits: "Accept my congratulations. You have distanced all competitors and obtained a diploma of honor, the highest award given in the Exposition. No person in any class in which you were an exhibitor received a like reward."

Nor was this all. Eminent men in science who had previously expressed their disbelief in the statements made as to the Edison system were now foremost in generous praise of his notable achievements, and accorded him full credit for its completion. A typical instance was M. Du Moncel, a distinguished electrician, who had written cynically about Edison's work and denied its practicability. He now recanted publicly in this language, which in itself shows the state of the art when Edison came to the front: "All these experiments achieved but moderate success, and when, in 1879, the new Edison incandescent carbon lamp was announced, many of the scientists, and I, particularly, doubted the accuracy of the reports which came from America. This horseshoe of carbonized paper seemed incapable to resist mechanical shocks and to maintain incandescence for any considerable length of time. Nevertheless, Mr. Edison was not discouraged, and despite the active opposition made to his lamp, despite the polemic acerbity of which he was the object, he did not cease to perfect it; and he succeeded in producing the lamps which we now behold exhibited at the Exposition, and are admired by all for their perfect steadiness."

The competitive lamps exhibited and tested at this time comprised those of Edison, Maxim, Swan, and Lane-Fox. The demonstration of Edison's success stimulated the faith of his French supporters, and rendered easier the completion of plans for the Societe Edison Continental, of Paris, formed to operate the Edison patents on the Continent of Europe. Mr. Batchelor, with Messrs. Acheson and Hipple, and one or two other assistants, at the close of the Exposition transferred their energies to the construction and equipment of machine-shops and lamp factories at Ivry-sur-Seine for the company, and in a very short time the installation of plants began in various countries--France, Italy, Holland, Belgium, etc.

All through 1881 Johnson was very busy, for his part, in England. The first "Jumbo" Edison dynamo had gone to Paris; the second and third went to London, where they were installed in 1881 by Mr. Johnson and his assistant, Mr. W. J. Hammer, in the three-thousand-light central station on Holborn Viaduct, the plant going into operation on January 12, 1882. Outside of Menlo Park this was the first regular station for incandescent lighting in the world, as the Pearl Street station in New York did not go into operation until September of the same year. This historic plant was hurriedly thrown together on Crown land, and would doubtless have been the nucleus of a great system but for the passage of the English electric lighting act of 1882, which at once throttled the industry by its absurd restrictive provisions, and which, though greatly modified, has left England ever since in a condition of serious inferiority as to development in electric light and power. The streets and bridges of Holborn Viaduct were lighted by lamps turned on and off from the station, as well as the famous City Temple of Dr. Joseph Parker, the first church in the world to be lighted by incandescent lamps--indeed, so far as can be ascertained, the first church to be illuminated by electricity in any form. Mr. W. J. Hammer, who supplies some very interesting notes on the installation, says: "I well remember the astonishment of Doctor Parker and his associates when they noted the difference of temperature as compared with gas. I was informed that the people would not go in the gallery in warm weather, owing to the great heat caused by the many gas jets, whereas on the introduction of the incandescent lamp there was no complaint." The telegraph operating-room of the General Post-Office, at St. Martin's-Le Grand and Newgate Street nearby, was supplied with four hundred lamps through the instrumentality of Mr. (Sir) W. H. Preece, who, having been seriously sceptical as to Mr. Edison's results, became one of his most ardent advocates, and did much to facilitate the introduction of the light. This station supplied its customers by a network of feeders and mains of the standard underground two-wire Edison tubing-conductors in sections of iron pipe--such as was used subsequently in New York, Milan, and other cities. It also had a measuring system for the current, employing the Edison electrolytic meter. Arc lamps were operated from its circuits, and one of the first sets of practicable storage batteries was used experimentally at the station. In connection with these batteries Mr. Hammer tells a characteristic anecdote of Edison: "A careless boy passing through the station whistling a tune and swinging carelessly a hammer in his hand, rapped a carboy of sulphuric acid which happened to be on the floor above a 'Jumbo' dynamo. The blow broke the glass carboy, and the acid ran down upon the field magnets of the dynamo, destroying the windings of one of the twelve magnets. This accident happened while I was taking a vacation in Germany, and a prominent scientific man connected with the company cabled Mr. Edison to know whether the machine would work if the coil was cut out. Mr. Edison sent the laconic reply: 'Why doesn't he try it and see?' Mr. E. H. Johnson was kept busy not only with the cares and responsibilities of this pioneer English plant, but by negotiations as to company formations, hearings before Parliamentary committees, and particularly by distinguished visitors, including all the foremost scientific men in England, and a great many well-known members of the peerage. Edison was fortunate in being represented by a man with so much address, intimate knowledge of the subject, and powers of explanation. As one of the leading English papers said at the time, with equal humor and truth: 'There is but one Edison, and Johnson is his prophet.'"

As the plant continued in operation, various details and ideas of improvement emerged, and Mr. Hammer says: "Up to the time of the construction of this plant it had been customary to place a single-pole switch on one wire and a safety fuse on the other; and the practice of putting fuses on both sides of a lighting circuit was first used here. Some of the first, if not the very first, of the insulated fixtures were used in this plant, and many of the fixtures were equipped with ball insulating joints, enabling the chandeliers--or 'electroliers'--to be turned around, as was common with the gas chandeliers. This particular device was invented by Mr. John B. Verity, whose firm built many of the fixtures for the Edison Company, and constructed the notable electroliers shown at the Crystal Palace Exposition of 1882."

We have made a swift survey of developments from the time when the system of lighting was ready for use, and when the staff scattered to introduce it. It will be readily understood that Edison did not sit with folded hands or drop into complacent satisfaction the moment he had reached the practical stage of commercial exploitation. He was not willing to say "Let us rest and be thankful," as was one of England's great Liberal leaders after a long period of reform. On the contrary, he was never more active than immediately after the work we have summed up at the beginning of this chapter. While he had been pursuing his investigations of the generator in conjunction with the experiments on the incandescent lamp, he gave much thought to the question of distribution of the current over large areas, revolving in his mind various plans for the accomplishment of this purpose, and keeping his mathematicians very busy working on the various schemes that suggested themselves from time to time. The idea of a complete system had been in his mind in broad outline for a long time, but did not crystallize into commercial form until the incandescent lamp was an accomplished fact. Thus in January, 1880, his first patent application for a "System of Electrical Distribution" was signed. It was filed in the Patent Office a few days later, but was not issued as a patent until August 30, 1887. It covered, fundamentally, multiple arc distribution, how broadly will be understood from the following extracts from the New York Electrical Review of September 10, 1887: "It would appear as if the entire field of multiple distribution were now in the hands of the owners of this patent.... The patent is about as broad as a patent can be, being regardless of specific devices, and laying a powerful grasp on the fundamental idea of multiple distribution from a number of generators throughout a metallic circuit."

Mr. Edison made a number of other applications for patents on electrical distribution during the year 1880. Among these was the one covering the celebrated "Feeder" invention, which has been of very great commercial importance in the art, its object being to obviate the "drop" in pressure, rendering lights dim in those portions of an electric-light system that were remote from the central station. [10]

[Footnote 10: For further explanation of "Feeder" patent, see Appendix.]

From these two patents alone, which were absolutely basic and fundamental in effect, and both of which were, and still are, put into actual use wherever central-station lighting is practiced, the reader will see that Mr. Edison's patient and thorough study, aided by his keen foresight and unerring judgment, had enabled him to grasp in advance with a master hand the chief and underlying principles of a true system--that system which has since been put into practical use all over the world, and whose elements do not need the touch or change of more modern scientific knowledge.

These patents were not by any means all that he applied for in the year 1880, which it will be remembered was the year in which he was perfecting the incandescent electric lamp and methods, to put into the market for competition with gas. It was an extraordinarily busy year for Mr. Edison and his whole force, which from time to time was increased in number. Improvement upon improvement was the order of the day. That which was considered good to-day was superseded by something better and more serviceable to-morrow. Device after device, relating to some part of the entire system, was designed, built, and tried, only to be rejected ruthlessly as being unsuitable; but the pursuit was not abandoned. It was renewed over and over again in innumerable ways until success had been attained.

During the year 1880 Edison had made application for sixty patents, of which thirty-two were in relation to incandescent lamps; seven covered inventions relating to distributing systems (including the two above particularized); five had reference to inventions of parts, such as motors, sockets, etc.; six covered inventions relating to dynamo-electric machines; three related to electric railways, and seven to miscellaneous apparatus, such as telegraph relays, magnetic ore separators, magneto signalling apparatus, etc.

The list of Mr. Edison's patents (see Appendices) is not only a monument to his life's work, but serves to show what subjects he has worked on from year to year since 1868. The reader will see from an examination of this list that the years 1880, 1881, 1882, and 1883 were the most prolific periods of invention. It is worth while to scrutinize this list closely to appreciate the wide range of his activities. Not that his patents cover his entire range of work by any means, for his note-books reveal a great number of major and minor inventions for which he has not seen fit to take out patents. Moreover, at the period now described Edison was the victim of a dishonest patent solicitor, who deprived him of a number of patents in the following manner:

"Around 1881-82 I had several solicitors attending to different classes of work. One of these did me a most serious injury. It was during the time that I was developing my electric-lighting system, and I was working and thinking very hard in order to cover all the numerous parts, in order that it would be complete in every detail. I filed a great many applications for patents at that time, but there were seventy-eight of the inventions I made in that period that were entirely lost to me and my company by reason of the dishonesty of this patent solicitor. Specifications had been drawn, and I had signed and sworn to the application for patents for these seventy-eight inventions, and naturally I supposed they had been filed in the regular way.

"As time passed I was looking for some action of the Patent Office, as usual, but none came. I thought it very strange, but had no suspicions until I began to see my inventions recorded in the Patent Office Gazette as being patented by others. Of course I ordered an investigation, and found that the patent solicitor had drawn from the company the fees for filing all these applications, but had never filed them. All the papers had disappeared, however, and what he had evidently done was to sell them to others, who had signed new applications and proceeded to take out patents themselves on my inventions. I afterward found that he had been previously mixed up with a somewhat similar crooked job in connection with telephone patents.

"I am free to confess that the loss of these seventy-eight inventions has left a sore spot in me that has never healed. They were important, useful, and valuable, and represented a whole lot of tremendous work and mental effort, and I had had a feeling of pride in having overcome through them a great many serious obstacles, One of these inventions covered the multipolar dynamo. It was an elaborated form of the type covered by my patent No. 219,393 which had a ring armature. I modified and improved on this form and had a number of pole pieces placed all around the ring, with a modified form of armature winding. I built one of these machines and ran it successfully in our early days at the Goerck Street shop.

"It is of no practical use to mention the man's name. I believe he is dead, but he may have left a family. The occurrence is a matter of the old Edison Company's records."

It will be seen from an examination of the list of patents in the Appendix that Mr. Edison has continued year after year adding to his contributions to the art of electric lighting, and in the last twenty-eight years--1880-1908--has taken out no fewer than three hundred and seventy-five patents in this branch of industry alone. These patents may be roughly tabulated as follows:

    Incandescent lamps and their manufacture....................149
    Distributing systems and their control and regulation....... 77
    Dynamo-electric machines and accessories....................106
    Minor parts, such as sockets, switches, safety catches,
    meters, underground conductors and parts, etc.............. 43

Quite naturally most of these patents cover inventions that are in the nature of improvements or based upon devices which he had already created; but there are a number that relate to inventions absolutely fundamental and original in their nature. Some of these have already been alluded to; but among the others there is one which is worthy of special mention in connection with the present consideration of a complete system. This is patent No. 274,290, applied for November 27, 1882, and is known as the "Three-wire" patent. It is described more fully in the Appendix.

The great importance of the "Feeder" and "Three-wire" inventions will be apparent when it is realized that without them it is a question whether electric light could be sold to compete with low-priced gas, on account of the large investment in conductors that would be necessary. If a large city area were to be lighted from a central station by means of copper conductors running directly therefrom to all parts of the district, it would be necessary to install large conductors, or suffer such a drop of pressure at the ends most remote from the station as to cause the lights there to burn with a noticeable diminution of candle-power. The Feeder invention overcame this trouble, and made it possible to use conductors ONLY ONE-EIGHTH THE SIZE that would otherwise have been necessary to produce the same results.

A still further economy in cost of conductors was effected by the "Three-wire" invention, by the use of which the already diminished conductors could be still further reduced TO ONE-THIRD of this smaller size, and at the same time allow of the successful operation of the station with far better results than if it were operated exactly as at first conceived. The Feeder and Three-wire systems are at this day used in all parts of the world, not only in central-station work, but in the installation and operation of isolated electric-light plants in large buildings. No sensible or efficient station manager or electric contractor would ever think of an installation made upon any other plan. Thus Mr. Edison's early conceptions of the necessities of a complete system, one of them made even in advance of practice, have stood firm, unimproved, and unchanged during the past twenty-eight years, a period of time which has witnessed more wonderful and rapid progress in electrical science and art than has been known during any similar art or period of time since the world began.

It must be remembered that the complete system in all its parts is not comprised in the few of Mr. Edison's patents, of which specific mention is here made. In order to comprehend the magnitude and extent of his work and the quality of his genius, it is necessary to examine minutely the list of patents issued for the various elements which go to make up such a system. To attempt any relation in detail of the conception and working-out of each part or element; to enter into any description of the almost innumerable experiments and investigations that were made would entail the writing of several volumes, for Mr. Edison's close-written note-books covering these subjects number nearly two hundred.

It is believed that enough evidence has been given in this chapter to lead to an appreciation of the assiduous work and practical skill involved in "inventing a system" of lighting that would surpass, and to a great extent, in one single quarter of a century, supersede all the other methods of illumination developed during long centuries. But it will be appropriate before passing on to note that on January 17, 1908, while this biography was being written, Mr. Edison became the fourth recipient of the John Fritz gold medal for achievement in industrial progress. This medal was founded in 1902 by the professional friends and associates of the veteran American ironmaster and metallurgical inventor, in honor of his eightieth birthday. Awards are made by a board of sixteen engineers appointed in equal numbers from the four great national engineering societies--the American Society of Civil Engineers, the American Institute of Mining Engineers, the American Society of Mechanical Engineers, and the American Institute of

Electrical Engineers, whose membership embraces the very pick and flower of professional engineering talent in America. Up to the time of the Edison award, three others had been made. The first was to Lord Kelvin, the Nestor of physics in Europe, for his work in submarine-cable telegraphy and other scientific achievement. The second was to George Westinghouse for the air-brake. The third was to Alexander Graham Bell for the invention and introduction of the telephone. The award to Edison was not only for his inventions in duplex and quadruplex telegraphy, and for the phonograph, but for the development of a commercially practical incandescent lamp, and the development of a complete system of electric lighting, including dynamos, regulating devices, underground system, protective devices, and meters. Great as has been the genius brought to bear on electrical development, there is no other man to whom such a comprehensive tribute could be paid.

CHAPTER XV

INTRODUCTION OF THE EDISON ELECTRIC LIGHT

IN the previous chapter on the invention of a system, the narrative has been carried along for several years of activity up to the verge of the successful and commercial application of Edison's ideas and devices for incandescent electric lighting. The story of any one year in this period, if treated chronologically, would branch off in a great many different directions, some going back to earlier work, others forward to arts not yet within the general survey; and the effect of such treatment would be confusing. In like manner the development of the Edison lighting system followed several concurrent, simultaneous lines of advance; and an effort was therefore made in the last chapter to give a rapid glance over the whole movement, embracing a term of nearly five years, and including in its scope both the Old World and the New. What is necessary to the completeness of the story at this stage is not to recapitulate, but to take up some of the loose ends of threads woven in and follow them through until the clear and comprehensive picture of events can be seen.

Some things it would be difficult to reproduce in any picture of the art and the times. One of the greatest delusions of the public in regard to any notable invention is the belief that the world is waiting for it with open arms and an eager welcome. The exact contrary is the truth. There is not a single new art or device the world has ever enjoyed of which it can be said that it was given an immediate and enthusiastic reception. The way of the inventor is hard. He can sometimes raise capital to help him in working out his crude conceptions, but even then it is frequently done at a distressful cost of personal surrender. When the result is achieved the invention makes its appeal on the score of economy of material or of effort; and then "labor" often awaits with crushing and tyrannical spirit to smash the apparatus or forbid its very use. Where both capital and labor are agreed that the object is worthy of encouragement, there is the supreme indifference of the public to overcome, and the stubborn resistance of pre-existing devices to combat. The years of hardship and struggle are thus prolonged, the chagrin of poverty and neglect too frequently embitters the inventor's scanty bread; and one great spirit after another has succumbed to the defeat beyond which lay the procrastinated triumph so dearly earned. Even in America, where the adoption of improvements and innovations is regarded as so prompt and sure, and where the huge tolls of the Patent Office and the courts bear witness to the ceaseless efforts of the inventor, it is impossible to deny the sad truth that unconsciously society discourages invention rather than invites it. Possibly our national optimism as revealed in invention--the seeking a higher good--needs some check. Possibly the leaders would travel too fast and too far on the road to perfection if conservatism did not also play its salutary part in insisting that the procession move forward as a whole.

Edison and his electric light were happily more fortunate than other men and inventions, in the relative cordiality of the reception given them. The merit was too obvious to remain unrecognized. Nevertheless, it was through intense hostility and opposition that the young art made its way, pushed forward by Edison's own strong personality and by his unbounded, unwavering faith in the ultimate success of his system. It may seem strange that great effort was required to introduce a light so manifestly convenient, safe, agreeable, and advantageous, but the facts are matter of record; and to-day the recollection of some of the episodes brings a fierce glitter into the eye and keen indignation into the voice of the man who has come so victoriously through it all.

It was not a fact at any time that the public was opposed to the idea of the electric light. On the contrary, the conditions for its acceptance had been ripening fast. Yet the very vogue of the electric arc light made harder the arrival of the incandescent. As a new illuminant for the streets, the arc had become familiar, either as a direct substitute for the low gas lamp along the sidewalk curb, or as a novel form of moonlight, raised in groups at the top of lofty towers often a hundred and fifty feet high. Some of these lights were already in use for large indoor spaces, although the size of the unit, the deadly pressure of the current, and the sputtering sparks from the carbons made them highly objectionable for such purposes. A number of parent arc-lighting companies were in existence, and a great many local companies had been called into being under franchises for commercial business and to execute regular city contracts for street lighting. In this manner a good deal of capital and the energies of many prominent men in politics and business had been rallied distinctively to the support of arc lighting. Under the inventive leadership of such brilliant men as Brush, Thomson, Weston, and Van Depoele--there were scores of others--the industry had made considerable progress and the art had been firmly established. Here lurked, however, very vigorous elements of opposition, for Edison predicted from the start the superiority of the small electric unit of light, and devoted himself exclusively to its perfection and introduction. It can be readily seen that this situation made it all the more difficult for the Edison system to secure the large sums of money needed for its exploitation, and to obtain new franchises or city ordinances as a public utility. Thus in a curious manner the modern art of electric lighting was in a very true sense divided against itself, with intense rivalries and jealousies which were none the less real because they were but temporary and occurred in a field where ultimate union of forces was inevitable. For a long period the arc was dominant and supreme in the lighting branch of the electrical industries, in all respects, whether as to investment, employees, income, and profits, or in respect to the manufacturing side. When the great National Electric Light Association was formed in 1885, its organizers were the captains of arc lighting, and not a single Edison company or licensee could be found in its ranks, or dared to solicit membership. The Edison companies, soon numbering about three hundred, formed their own association--still maintained as a separate and useful body--and the lines were tensely drawn in a way that made it none too easy for the Edison service to advance, or for an impartial man to remain friendly with both sides. But the growing popularity of incandescent lighting, the flexibility and safety of the system, the ease with which other electric devices for heat, power, etc., could be put indiscriminately on the same circuits with the lamps, in due course rendered the old attitude of opposition obviously foolish and untenable. The United States Census Office statistics of 1902 show that the income from incandescent lighting by central stations had by that time become over 52 per cent. of the total, while that from arc lighting was less than 29; and electric-power service due to the ease with which motors could be introduced on incandescent circuits brought in 15 per cent. more. Hence twenty years after the first Edison stations were established the methods they involved could be fairly credited with no less than 67 per cent. of all central-station income in the country, and the proportion has grown since then. It will be readily understood that under these conditions the modern lighting company supplies to its customers both incandescent and arc lighting, frequently from the same dynamo-electric machinery as a source of current; and that the old feud as between the rival systems has died out. In fact, for some years past the presidents of the National Electric Light Association have been chosen almost exclusively from among the managers of the great Edison lighting companies in the leading cities.

The other strong opposition to the incandescent light came from the gas industry. There also the most bitter feeling was shown. The gas manager did not like the arc light, but it interfered only with his street service, which was not his largest source of income by any means. What did arouse his ire and indignation was to find this new opponent, the little incandescent lamp, pushing boldly into the field of interior lighting, claiming it on a great variety of grounds of superiority, and calmly ignoring the question of price, because it was so much better. Newspaper records and the pages of the technical papers of the day show to what an extent prejudice and passion were stirred up and the astounding degree to which the opposition to the new light was carried.

Here again was given a most convincing demonstration of the truth that such an addition to the resources of mankind always carries with it unsuspected benefits even for its enemies. In two distinct directions the gas art was immediately helped by Edison's work. The competition was most salutary in the stimulus it gave to improvements in processes for making, distributing, and using gas, so that while vast economies have been effected at the gas works, the customer has had an infinitely better light for less money. In the second place, the coming of the incandescent light raised the standard of illumination in such a manner that more gas than ever was wanted in order to satisfy the popular demand for brightness and brilliancy both indoors and on the street. The result of the operation of these two forces acting upon it wholly from without, and from a rival it was desired to crush, has been to increase enormously the production and use of gas in the last twenty-five years. It is true that the income of the central stations is now over $300,000,000 a year, and that isolated-plant lighting represents also a large amount of diverted business; but as just shown, it would obviously be unfair to regard all this as a loss from the standpoint of gas. It is in great measure due to new sources of income developed by electricity for itself.

A retrospective survey shows that had the men in control of the American gas-lighting art, in 1880, been sufficiently far-sighted, and had they taken a broader view of the situation, they might easily have remained dominant in the whole field of artificial lighting by securing the ownership of the patents and devices of the new industry. Apparently not a single step of that kind was undertaken, nor probably was there a gas manager who would have agreed with Edison in the opinion written down by him at the time in little note-book No. 184, that gas properties were having conferred on them an enhanced earning capacity. It was doubtless fortunate and providential for the electric-lighting art that in its state of immature development it did not fall into the hands of men who were opposed to its growth, and would not have sought its technical perfection. It was allowed to carve out its own career, and thus escaped the fate that is supposed to have attended other great inventions--of being bought up merely for purposes of suppression. There is a vague popular notion that this happens to the public loss; but the truth is that no discovery of any real value is ever entirely lost. It may be retarded; but that is all. In the case of the gas companies and the incandescent light, many of them to whom it was in the early days as great an irritant as a red flag to a bull, emulated the performance of that animal and spent a great deal of money and energy in bellowing and throwing up dirt in the effort to destroy the hated enemy. This was not long nor universally the spirit shown; and to-day in hundreds of cities the electric and gas properties are united under the one management, which does not find it impossible to push in a friendly and progressive way the use of both illuminants. The most conspicuous example of this identity of interest is given in New York itself.

So much for the early opposition, of which there was plenty. But it may be questioned whether inertia is not equally to be dreaded with active ill-will. Nothing is more difficult in the world than to get a good many hundreds of thousands or millions of people to do something they have never done before. A very real difficulty in the introduction of his lamp and lighting system by Edison lay in the absolute ignorance of the public at large, not only as to whom it was in the merits, but as to the very appearance of the light, Some few thousand people had gone out to Menlo Park, and had there seen the lamps in operation at the laboratory or on the hillsides, but they were an insignificant proportion of the inhabitants of the United States. Of course, a great many accounts were written and read, but while genuine interest was aroused it was necessarily apathetic. A newspaper description or a magazine article may be admirably complete in itself, with illustrations, but until some personal experience is had of the thing described it does not convey a perfect mental picture, nor can it always make the desire active and insistent. Generally, people wait to have the new thing brought to them; and hence, as in the case of the Edison light, an educational campaign of a practical nature is a fundamental condition of success.

Another serious difficulty confronting Edison and his associates was that nowhere in the world were there to be purchased any of the appliances necessary for the use of the lighting system. Edison had resolved from the very first that the initial central station embodying his various ideas should be installed in New York City, where he could superintend the installation personally, and then watch the operation. Plans to that end were now rapidly maturing; but there would be needed among many other things--every one of them new and novel--dynamos, switchboards, regulators, pressure and current indicators, fixtures in great variety, incandescent lamps, meters, sockets, small switches, underground conductors, junction-boxes, service-boxes, manhole-boxes, connectors, and even specially made wire. Now, not one of these miscellaneous things was in existence; not an outsider was sufficiently informed about such devices to make them on order, except perhaps the special wire. Edison therefore started first of all a lamp factory in one of the buildings at Menlo Park, equipped it with novel machinery and apparatus, and began to instruct men, boys, and girls, as they could be enlisted, in the absolutely new art, putting Mr. Upton in charge.

With regard to the conditions attendant upon the manufacture of the lamps, Edison says: "When we first started the electric light we had to have a factory for manufacturing lamps. As the Edison Light Company did not seem disposed to go into manufacturing, we started a small lamp factory at Menlo Park with what money I could raise from my other inventions and royalties, and some assistance. The lamps at that time were costing about $1.25 each to make, so I said to the company: 'If you will give me a contract during the life of the patents, I will make all the lamps required by the company and deliver them for forty cents.' The company jumped at the chance of this offer, and a contract was drawn up. We then bought at a receiver's sale at Harrison, New Jersey, a very large brick factory building which had been used as an oil-cloth works. We got it at a great bargain, and only paid a small sum down, and the balance on mortgage. We moved the lamp works from Menlo Park to Harrison. The first year the lamps cost us about $1.10 each. We sold them for forty cents; but there were only about twenty or thirty thousand of them. The next year they cost us about seventy cents, and we sold them for forty. There were a good many, and we lost more money the second year than the first. The third year I succeeded in getting up machinery and in changing the processes, until it got down so that they cost somewhere around fifty cents. I still sold them for forty cents, and lost more money that year than any other, because the sales were increasing rapidly. The fourth year I got it down to thirty-seven cents, and I made all the money up in one year that I had lost previously. I finally got it down to twenty-two cents, and sold them for forty cents; and they were made by the million. Whereupon the Wall Street people thought it was a very lucrative business, so they concluded they would like to have it, and bought us out.

"One of the incidents which caused a very great cheapening was that, when we started, one of the important processes had to be done by experts. This was the sealing on of the part carrying the filament into the globe, which was rather a delicate operation in those days, and required several months of training before any one could seal in a fair number of parts in a day. When we got to the point where we employed eighty of these experts they formed a union; and knowing it was impossible to manufacture lamps without them, they became very insolent. One instance was that the son of one of these experts was employed in the office, and when he was told to do anything would not do it, or would give an insolent reply. He was discharged, whereupon the union notified us that unless the boy was taken back the whole body would go out. It got so bad that the manager came to me and said he could not stand it any longer; something had got to be done. They were not only more surly; they were diminishing the output, and it became impossible to manage the works. He got me enthused on the subject, so I started in to see if it were not possible to do that operation by machinery. After feeling around for some days I got a clew how to do it. I then put men on it I could trust, and made the preliminary machinery. That seemed to work pretty well. I then made another machine which did the work nicely. I then made a third machine, and would bring in yard men, ordinary laborers, etc., and when I could get these men to put the parts together as well as the trained experts, in an hour, I considered the machine complete. I then went secretly to work and made thirty of the machines. Up in the top loft of the factory we stored those machines, and at night we put up the benches and got everything all ready. Then we discharged the office-boy. Then the union went out. It has been out ever since.

"When we formed the works at Harrison we divided the interests into one hundred shares or parts at $100 par. One of the boys was hard up after a time, and sold two shares to Bob Cutting. Up to that time we had never paid anything; but we got around to the point where the board declared a dividend every Saturday night. We had never declared a dividend when Cutting bought his shares, and after getting his dividends for three weeks in succession, he called up on the telephone and wanted to know what kind of a concern this was that paid a weekly dividend. The works sold for $1,085,000."

Incidentally it may be noted, as illustrative of the problems brought to Edison, that while he had the factory at Harrison an importer in the Chinese trade went to him and wanted a dynamo to be run by hand power. The importer explained that in China human labor was cheaper than steam power. Edison devised a machine to answer the purpose, and put long spokes on it, fitted it up, and shipped it to China. He has not, however, heard of it since.

For making the dynamos Edison secured, as noted in the preceding chapter, the Roach Iron Works on Goerck Street, New York, and this was also equipped. A building was rented on Washington Street, where machinery and tools were put in specially designed for making the underground tube conductors and their various paraphernalia; and the faithful John Kruesi was given charge of that branch of production. To Sigmund Bergmann, who had worked previously with Edison on telephone apparatus and phonographs, and was already making Edison specialties in a small way in a loft on Wooster Street, New York, was assigned the task of constructing sockets, fixtures, meters, safety fuses, and numerous other details.

Thus, broadly, the manufacturing end of the problem of introduction was cared for. In the early part of 1881 the Edison Electric Light Company leased the old Bishop mansion at 65 Fifth Avenue, close to Fourteenth Street, for its headquarters and show-rooms. This was one of the finest homes in the city of that period, and its acquisition was a premonitory sign of the surrender of the famous residential avenue to commerce. The company needed not only offices, but, even more, such an interior as would display to advantage the new light in everyday use; and this house with its liberal lines, spacious halls, lofty ceilings, wide parlors, and graceful, winding stairway was ideal for the purpose. In fact, in undergoing this violent change, it did not cease to be a home in the real sense, for to this day many an Edison veteran's pulse is quickened by some chance reference to "65," where through many years the work of development by a loyal and devoted band of workers was centred. Here Edison and a few of his assistants from Menlo Park installed immediately in the basement a small generating plant, at first with a gas-engine which was not successful, and then with a Hampson high-speed engine and boiler, constituting a complete isolated plant. The building was wired from top to bottom, and equipped with all the appliances of the art. The experience with the little gas-engine was rather startling. "At an early period at '65' we decided," says Edison, "to light it up with the Edison system, and put a gas-engine in the cellar, using city gas. One day it was not going very well, and I went down to the man in charge and got exploring around. Finally I opened the pedestal--a storehouse for tools, etc. We had an open lamp, and when we opened the pedestal, it blew the doors off, and blew out the windows, and knocked me down, and the other man."

For the next four or five years "65" was a veritable beehive, day and night. The routine was very much the same as that at the laboratory, in its utter neglect of the clock. The evenings were not only devoted to the continuance of regular business, but the house was thrown open to the public until late at night, never closing before ten o'clock, so as to give everybody who wished an opportunity to see that great novelty of the time--the incandescent light--whose fame had meanwhile been spreading all over the globe. The first year, 1881, was naturally that which witnessed the greatest rush of visitors; and the building hardly ever closed its doors till midnight. During the day business was carried on under great stress, and Mr. Insull has described how Edison was to be found there trying to lead the life of a man of affairs in the conventional garb of polite society, instead of pursuing inventions and researches in his laboratory. But the disagreeable ordeal could not be dodged. After the experience Edison could never again be tempted to quit his laboratory and work for any length of time; but in this instance there were some advantages attached to the sacrifice, for the crowds of lion-hunters and people seeking business arrangements would only have gone out to Menlo Park; while, on the other hand, the great plans for lighting New York demanded very close personal attention on the spot.

As it was, not only Edison, but all the company's directors, officers, and employees, were kept busy exhibiting and explaining the light. To the public of that day, when the highest known form of house illuminant was gas, the incandescent lamp, with its ability to burn in any position, its lack of heat so that you could put your hand on the brilliant glass globe; the absence of any vitiating effect on the atmosphere, the obvious safety from fire; the curious fact that you needed no matches to light it, and that it was under absolute control from a distance--these and many other features came as a distinct revelation and marvel, while promising so much additional comfort, convenience, and beauty in the home, that inspection was almost invariably followed by a request for installation.

The camaraderie that existed at this time was very democratic, for all were workers in a common cause; all were enthusiastic believers in the doctrine they proclaimed, and hoped to profit by the opening up of the new art. Often at night, in the small hours, all would adjourn for refreshments to a famous resort nearby, to discuss the events of to-day and to-morrow, full of incident and excitement. The easy relationship of the time is neatly sketched by Edison in a humorous complaint as to his inability to keep his own cigars: "When at '65' I used to have in my desk a box of cigars. I would go to the box four or five times to get a cigar, but after it got circulated about the building, everybody would come to get my cigars, so that the box would only last about a day and a half. I was telling a gentleman one day that I could not keep a cigar. Even if I locked them up in my desk they would break it open. He suggested to me that he had a friend over on Eighth Avenue who made a superior grade of cigars, and who would show them a trick. He said he would have some of them made up with hair and old paper, and I could put them in without a word and see the result. I thought no more about the matter. He came in two or three months after, and said: 'How did that cigar business work?' I didn't remember anything about it. On coming to investigate, it appeared that the box of cigars had been delivered and had been put in my desk, and I had smoked them all! I was too busy on other things to notice."

It was no uncommon sight to see in the parlors in the evening John Pierpont Morgan, Norvin Green, Grosvenor P. Lowrey, Henry Villard, Robert L. Cutting, Edward D. Adams, J. Hood Wright, E. G. Fabbri, R. M. Galloway, and other men prominent in city life, many of them stock-holders and directors; all interested in doing this educational work. Thousands of persons thus came--bankers, brokers, lawyers, editors, and reporters, prominent business men, electricians, insurance experts, under whose searching and intelligent inquiries the facts were elicited, and general admiration was soon won for the system, which in advance had solved so many new problems. Edison himself was in universal request and the subject of much adulation, but altogether too busy and modest to be spoiled by it. Once in a while he felt it his duty to go over the ground with scientific visitors, many of whom were from abroad, and discuss questions which were not simply those of technique, but related to newer phenomena, such as the action of carbon, the nature and effects of high vacua; the principles of electrical subdivision; the value of insulation, and many others which, unfortunate to say, remain as esoteric now as they were then, ever fruitful themes of controversy.

Speaking of those days or nights, Edison says: "Years ago one of the great violinists was Remenyi. After his performances were over he used to come down to '65' and talk economics, philosophy, moral science, and everything else. He was highly educated and had great mental capacity. He would talk with me, but I never asked him to bring his violin. One night he came with his violin, about twelve o'clock. I had a library at the top of the house, and Remenyi came up there. He was in a genial humor, and played the violin for me for about two hours--$2000 worth. The front doors were closed, and he walked up and down the room as he played. After that, every time he came to New York he used to call at '65' late at night with his violin. If we were not there, he could come down to the slums at Goerck Street, and would play for an hour or two and talk philosophy. I would talk for the benefit of his music. Henry E. Dixey, then at the height of his 'Adonis' popularity, would come in in those days, after theatre hours, and would entertain us with stories--1882-84. Another visitor who used to give us a good deal of amusement and pleasure was Captain Shaw, the head of the London Fire Brigade. He was good company. He would go out among the fire-laddies and have a great time. One time Robert Lincoln and Anson Stager, of the Western Union, interested in the electric light, came on to make some arrangement with Major Eaton, President of the Edison Electric Light Company. They came to '65' in the afternoon, and Lincoln commenced telling stories--like his father. They told stories all the afternoon, and that night they left for Chicago. When they got to Cleveland, it dawned upon them that they had not done any business, so they had to come back on the next train to New York to transact it. They were interested in the Chicago Edison Company, now one of the largest of the systems in the world. Speaking of telling stories, I once got telling a man stories at the Harrison lamp factory, in the yard, as he was leaving. It was winter, and he was all in furs. I had nothing on to protect me against the cold. I told him one story after the other--six of them. Then I got pleurisy, and had to be shipped to Florida for cure."

The organization of the Edison Electric Light Company went back to 1878; but up to the time of leasing 65 Fifth Avenue it had not been engaged in actual business. It had merely enjoyed the delights of anxious anticipation, and the perilous pleasure of backing Edison's experiments. Now active exploitation was required. Dr. Norvin Green, the well-known President of the Western Union Telegraph Company, was president also of the Edison Company, but the pressing nature of his regular duties left him no leisure for such close responsible management as was now required. Early in 1881 Mr. Grosvenor P. Lowrey, after consultation with Mr. Edison, prevailed upon Major S. B. Eaton, the leading member of a very prominent law firm in New York, to accept the position of vice-president and general manager of the company, in which, as also in some of the subsidiary Edison companies, and as president, he continued actively and energetically for nearly four years, a critical, formative period in which the solidity of the foundation laid is attested by the magnitude and splendor of the superstructure.

The fact that Edison conferred at this point with Mr. Lowrey should, perhaps, be explained in justice to the distinguished lawyer, who for so many years was the close friend of the inventor, and the chief counsel in all the tremendous litigation that followed the effort to enforce and validate the Edison patents. As in England Mr. Edison was fortunate in securing the legal assistance of Sir Richard Webster, afterward Lord Chief Justice of England, so in America it counted greatly in his favor to enjoy the advocacy of such a man as Lowrey, prominent among the famous leaders of the New York bar. Born in Massachusetts, Mr. Lowrey, in his earlier days of straitened circumstances, was accustomed to defray some portion of his educational expenses by teaching music in the Berkshire villages, and by a curious coincidence one of his pupils was F. L. Pope, later Edison's partner for a time. Lowrey went West to "Bleeding Kansas" with the first Governor, Reeder, and both were active participants in the exciting scenes of the "Free State" war until driven away in 1856, like many other free-soilers, by the acts of the "Border Ruffian" legislature. Returning East, Mr. Lowrey took up practice in New York, soon becoming eminent in his profession, and upon the accession of William Orton to the presidency of the Western Union Telegraph Company in 1866, he was appointed its general counsel, the duties of which post he discharged for fifteen years. One of the great cases in which he thus took a leading and distinguished part was that of the quadruplex telegraph; and later he acted as legal adviser to Henry Villard in his numerous grandiose enterprises. Lowrey thus came to know Edison, to conceive an intense admiration for him, and to believe in his ability at a time when others could not detect the fire of genius smouldering beneath the modest exterior of a gaunt young operator slowly "finding himself." It will be seen that Mr Lowrey was in a peculiarly advantageous position to make his convictions about Edison felt, so that it was he and his friends who rallied quickly to the new banner of discovery, and lent to the inventor the aid that came at a critical period. In this connection it may be well to quote an article that appeared at the time of Mr. Lowrey's death, in 1893: "One of the most important services which Mr. Lowrey has ever performed was in furnishing and procuring the necessary financial backing for Thomas A. Edison in bringing out and perfecting his system of incandescent lighting. With characteristic pertinacity, Mr. Lowrey stood by the inventor through thick and thin, in spite of doubt, discouragement, and ridicule, until at last success crowned his efforts. In all the litigation which has resulted from the wide-spread infringements of the Edison patents, Mr. Lowrey has ever borne the burden and heat of the day, and perhaps in no other field has he so personally distinguished himself as in the successful advocacy of the claims of Edison to the invention of the incandescent lamp and everything 'hereunto pertaining.'"

This was the man of whom Edison had necessarily to make a confidant and adviser, and who supplied other things besides the legal direction and financial alliance, by his knowledge of the world and of affairs. There were many vital things to be done in the exploitation of the system that Edison simply could not and would not do; but in Lowrey's savoir faire, ready wit and humor, chivalry of devotion, graceful eloquence, and admirable equipoise of judgment were all the qualities that the occasion demanded and that met the exigencies.

We are indebted to Mr. Insull for a graphic sketch of Edison at this period, and of the conditions under which work was done and progress was made: "I do not think I had any understanding with Edison when I first went with him as to my duties. I did whatever he told me, and looked after all kinds of affairs, from buying his clothes to financing his business. I used to open the correspondence and answer it all, sometimes signing Edison's name with my initial, and sometimes signing my own name. If the latter course was pursued, and I was addressing a stranger, I would sign as Edison's private secretary. I held his power of attorney, and signed his checks. It was seldom that Edison signed a letter or check at this time. If he wanted personally to send a communication to anybody, if it was one of his close associates, it would probably be a pencil memorandum signed 'Edison.' I was a shorthand writer, but seldom took down from Edison's dictation, unless it was on some technical subject that I did not understand. I would go over the correspondence with Edison, sometimes making a marginal note in shorthand, and sometimes Edison would make his own notes on letters, and I would be expected to clean up the correspondence with Edison's laconic comments as a guide as to the character of answer to make. It was a very common thing for Edison to write the words 'Yes' or 'No,' and this would be all I had on which to base my answer. Edison marginalized documents extensively. He had a wonderful ability in pointing out the weak points of an agreement or a balance-sheet, all the while protesting he was no lawyer or accountant; and his views were expressed in very few words, but in a characteristic and emphatic manner.

"The first few months I was with Edison he spent most of the time in the office at 65 Fifth Avenue. Then there was a great deal of trouble with the life of the lamps there, and he disappeared from the office and spent his time largely at Menlo Park. At another time there was a great deal of trouble with some of the details of construction of the dynamos, and Edison spent a lot of time at Goerck Street, which had been rapidly equipped with the idea of turning out bi-polar dynamo-electric machines, direct-connected to the engine, the first of which went to Paris and London, while the next were installed in the old Pearl Street station of the Edison Electric Illuminating Company of New York, just south of Fulton Street, on the west side of the street. Edison devoted a great deal of his time to the engineering work in connection with the laying out of the first incandescent electric-lighting system in New York. Apparently at that time--between the end of 1881 and spring of 1882--the most serious work was the manufacture and installation of underground conductors in this territory. These conductors were manufactured by the Electric Tube Company, which Edison controlled in a shop at 65 Washington Street, run by John Kruesi. Half-round copper conductors were used, kept in place relatively to each other and in the tube, first of all by a heavy piece of cardboard, and later on by a rope; and then put in a twenty-foot iron pipe; and a combination of asphaltum and linseed oil was forced into the pipe for the insulation. I remember as a coincidence that the building was only twenty feet wide. These lengths of conductors were twenty feet six inches long, as the half-round coppers extended three inches beyond the drag-ends of the lengths of pipe; and in one of the operations we used to take the length of tubing out of the window in order to turn it around. I was elected secretary of the Electric Tube Company, and was expected to look after its finance; and it was in this position that my long intimacy with John Kruesi started."

At this juncture a large part of the correspondence referred very naturally to electric lighting, embodying requests for all kinds of information, catalogues, prices, terms, etc.; and all these letters were turned over to the lighting company by Edison for attention. The company was soon swamped with propositions for sale of territorial rights and with other negotiations, and some of these were accompanied by the offer of very large sums of money. It was the beginning of the electric-light furor which soon rose to sensational heights. Had the company accepted the cash offers from various localities, it could have gathered several millions of dollars at once into its treasury; but this was not at all in accord with Mr. Edison's idea, which was to prove by actual experience the commercial value of the system, and then to license central-station companies in large cities and towns, the parent company taking a percentage of their capital for the license under the Edison patents, and contracting also for the supply of apparatus, lamps, etc. This left the remainder of the country open for the cash sale of plants wherever requested. His counsels prevailed, and the wisdom of the policy adopted was seen in the swift establishment of Edison companies in centres of population both great and small, whose business has ever been a constant and growing source of income for the parent manufacturing interests.

From first to last Edison has been an exponent and advocate of the central-station idea of distribution now so familiar to the public mind, but still very far from being carried out to its logical conclusion. In this instance, demands for isolated plants for lighting factories, mills, mines, hotels, etc., began to pour in, and something had to be done with them. This was a class of plant which the inquirers desired to purchase outright and operate themselves, usually because of remoteness from any possible source of general supply of current. It had not been Edison's intention to cater to this class of customer until his broad central-station plan had been worked out, and he has always discouraged the isolated plant within the limits of urban circuits; but this demand was so insistent it could not be denied, and it was deemed desirable to comply with it at once, especially as it was seen that the steady call for supplies and renewals would benefit the new Edison manufacturing plants. After a very short trial, it was found necessary to create a separate organization for this branch of the industry, leaving the Edison Electric Light Company to continue under the original plan of operation as a parent, patent-holding and licensing company. Accordingly a new and distinct corporation was formed called the Edison Company for Isolated Lighting, to which was issued a special license to sell and operate plants of a self-contained character. As a matter of fact such work began in advance of almost every other kind. A small plant using the paper-carbon filament lamps was furnished by Edison at the earnest solicitation of Mr. Henry Villard for the steamship Columbia, in 1879, and it is amusing to note that Mr. Upton carried the lamps himself to the ship, very tenderly and jealously, like fresh eggs, in a market-garden basket. The installation was most successful. Another pioneer plant was that equipped and started in January, 1881, for Hinds & Ketcham, a New York firm of lithographers and color printers, who had previously been able to work only by day, owing to difficulties in color-printing by artificial light. A year later they said: "It is the best substitute for daylight we have ever known, and almost as cheap."

Mr. Edison himself describes various instances in which the demand for isolated plants had to be met: "One night at '65,'" he says, "James Gordon Bennett came in. We were very anxious to get into a printing establishment. I had caused a printer's composing case to be set up with the idea that if we could get editors and publishers in to see it, we should show them the advantages of the electric light. So ultimately Mr. Bennett came, and after seeing the whole operation of everything, he ordered Mr. Howland, general manager of the Herald, to light the newspaper offices up at once with electricity."

Another instance of the same kind deals with the introduction of the light for purely social purposes: "While at 65 Fifth Avenue," remarks Mr. Edison, "I got to know Christian Herter, then the largest decorator in the United States. He was a highly intellectual man, and I loved to talk to him. He was always railing against the rich people, for whom he did work, for their poor taste. One day Mr. W. H. Vanderbilt came to '65,' saw the light, and decided that he would have his new house lighted with it. This was one of the big 'box houses' on upper Fifth Avenue. He put the whole matter in the hands of his son-in-law, Mr. H. McK. Twombly, who was then in charge of the telephone department of the Western Union. Twombly closed the contract with us for a plant. Mr. Herter was doing the decoration, and it was extraordinarily fine. After a while we got the engines and boilers and wires all done, and the lights in position, before the house was quite finished, and thought we would have an exhibit of the light. About eight o'clock in the evening we lit up, and it was very good. Mr. Vanderbilt and his wife and some of his daughters came in, and were there a few minutes when a fire occurred. The large picture-gallery was lined with silk cloth interwoven with fine metallic thread. In some manner two wires had got crossed with this tinsel, which became red-hot, and the whole mass was soon afire. I knew what was the matter, and ordered them to run down and shut off. It had not burst into flame, and died out immediately. Mrs. Vanderbilt became hysterical, and wanted to know where it came from. We told her we had the plant in the cellar, and when she learned we had a boiler there she said she would not occupy the house. She would not live over a boiler. We had to take the whole installation out. The houses afterward went onto the New York Edison system."

The art was, however, very crude and raw, and as there were no artisans in existence as mechanics or electricians who had any knowledge of the practice, there was inconceivable difficulty in getting such isolated plants installed, as well as wiring the buildings in the district to be covered by the first central station in New York. A night school was, therefore, founded at Fifth Avenue, and was put in charge of Mr. E. H. Johnson, fresh from his successes in England. The most available men for the purpose were, of course, those who had been accustomed to wiring for the simpler electrical systems then in vogue--telephones, district-messenger calls, burglar alarms, house annunciators, etc., and a number of these "wiremen" were engaged and instructed patiently in the rudiments of the new art by means of a blackboard and oral lessons. Students from the technical schools and colleges were also eager recruits, for here was something that promised a career, and one that was especially alluring to youth because of its novelty. These beginners

were also instructed in general engineering problems under the guidance
of Mr. C. L. Clarke, who was brought in from the Menlo Park laboratory
to assume charge of the engineering part of the company's affairs.
Many of these pioneer students and workmen became afterward large and
successful contractors, or have filled positions of distinction
as managers and superintendents of central stations. Possibly the
electrical industry may not now attract as much adventurous genius as it
did then, for automobiles, aeronautics, and other new arts have come
to the front in a quarter of a century to enlist the enthusiasm of a
younger generation of mercurial spirits; but it is certain that at the
period of which we write, Edison himself, still under thirty-five, was
the centre of an extraordinary group of men, full of effervescing and
aspiring talent, to which he gave glorious opportunity.

A very novel literary feature of the work was the issuance of a bulletin
devoted entirely to the Edison lighting propaganda. Nowadays the
"house organ," as it is called, has become a very hackneyed feature
of industrial development, confusing in its variety and volume, and
a somewhat doubtful adjunct to a highly perfected, widely circulating
periodical technical press. But at that time, 1882, the Bulletin of
the Edison Electric Light Company, published in ordinary 12mo form, was
distinctly new in advertising and possibly unique, as it is difficult
to find anything that compared with it. The Bulletin was carried on for
some years, until its necessity was removed by the development of other
opportunities for reaching the public; and its pages serve now as a
vivid and lively picture of the period to which its record applies. The
first issue, of January 12, 1882, was only four pages, but it dealt
with the question of insurance; plants at Santiago, Chili, and Rio de
Janeiro; the European Company with 3,500,000 francs subscribed; the work
in Paris, London, Strasburg, and Moscow; the laying of over six miles of
street mains in New York; a patent decision in favor of Edison; and the
size of safety catch wire. By April of 1882, the Bulletin had attained
the respectable size of sixteen pages; and in December it was a portly
magazine of forty-eight. Every item bears testimony to the rapid
progress being made; and by the end of 1882 it is seen that no fewer
than 153 isolated Edison plants had been installed in the United States
alone, with a capacity of 29,192 lamps. Moreover, the New York central
station had gone into operation, starting at 3 P.M. on September 4, and
at the close of 1882 it was lighting 225 houses wired for about 5000
lamps. This epochal story will be told in the next chapter. Most
interesting are the Bulletin notes from England, especially in regard
to the brilliant exhibition given by Mr. E. H. Johnson at the Crystal
Palace, Sydenham, visited by the Duke and Duchess of Edinburgh, twice by
the Dukes of Westminster and Sutherland, by three hundred members of
the Gas Institute, and by innumerable delegations from cities, boroughs,
etc. Describing this before the Royal Society of Arts, Sir W. H. Preece,
F.R.S., remarked: "Many unkind things have been said of Mr. Edison and
his promises; perhaps no one has been severer in this direction than
myself. It is some gratification for me to announce my belief that he
has at last solved the problem he set himself to solve, and to be able
to describe to the Society the way in which he has solved it." Before
the exhibition closed it was visited by the Prince and Princess of
Wales--now the deceased Edward VII. and the Dowager Queen Alexandra--and
the Princess received from Mr. Johnson as a souvenir a tiny electric

chandelier fashioned like a bouquet of fern leaves and flowers, the buds being some of the first miniature incandescent lamps ever made.

The first item in the first Bulletin dealt with the "Fire Question," and all through the successive issues runs a series of significant items on the same subject. Many of them are aimed at gas, and there are several grim summaries of death and fires due to gas-leaks or explosions. A tendency existed at the time to assume that electricity was altogether safe, while its opponents, predicating their attacks on arc-lighting casualties, insisted it was most dangerous. Edison's problem in educating the public was rather difficult, for while his low-pressure, direct-current system has always been absolutely without danger to life, there has also been the undeniable fact that escaping electricity might cause a fire just as a leaky water-pipe can flood a house. The important question had arisen, therefore, of satisfying the fire underwriters as to the safety of the system. He had foreseen that there would be an absolute necessity for special devices to prevent fires from occurring by reason of any excess of current flowing in any circuit; and several of his earliest detail lighting inventions deal with this subject. The insurance underwriters of New York and other parts of the country gave a great deal of time and study to the question through their most expert representatives, with the aid of Edison and his associates, other electric-light companies cooperating; and the knowledge thus gained was embodied in insurance rules to govern wiring for electric lights, formulated during the latter part of 1881, adopted by the New York Board of Fire Underwriters, January 12, 1882, and subsequently endorsed by other boards in the various insurance districts. Under temporary rulings, however, a vast amount of work had already been done, but it was obvious that as the industry grew there would be less and less possibility of supervision except through such regulations, insisting upon the use of the best devices and methods. Indeed, the direct superintendence soon became unnecessary, owing to the increasing knowledge and greater skill acquired by the installing staff; and this system of education was notably improved by a manual written by Mr. Edison himself. Copies of this brochure are as scarce to-day as First Folio Shakespeares, and command prices equal to those of other American first editions. The little book is the only known incursion of its author into literature, if we except the brief articles he has written for technical papers and for the magazines. It contained what was at once a full, elaborate, and terse explanation of a complete isolated plant, with diagrams of various methods of connection and operation, and a carefully detailed description of every individual part, its functions and its characteristics. The remarkable success of those early years was indeed only achieved by following up with Chinese exactness the minute and intimate methods insisted upon by Edison as to the use of the apparatus and devices employed. It was a curious example of establishing standard practice while changing with kaleidoscopic rapidity all the elements involved. He was true to an ideal as to the pole-star, but was incessantly making improvements in every direction. With an iconoclasm that has often seemed ruthless and brutal he did not hesitate to sacrifice older devices the moment a new one came in sight that embodied a real advance in securing effective results. The process is heroic but costly. Nobody ever had a bigger scrap-heap than Edison; but who dare proclaim the process intrinsically wasteful if the losses occur in the initial stages, and the economies in all the later ones?

With Edison in this introduction of his lighting system the method was ruthless, but not reckless. At an early stage of the commercial development a standardizing committee was formed, consisting of the heads of all the departments, and to this body was intrusted the task of testing and criticising all existing and proposed devices, as well as of considering the suggestions and complaints of workmen offered from time to time. This procedure was fruitful in two principal results--the education of the whole executive force in the technical details of the system; and a constant improvement in the quality of the Edison installations; both contributing to the rapid growth of the industry.

For many years Goerck Street played an important part in Edison's affairs, being the centre of all his manufacture of heavy machinery. But it was not in a desirable neighborhood, and owing to the rapid growth of the business soon became disadvantageous for other reasons. Edison tells of his frequent visits to the shops at night, with the escort of "Jim" Russell, a well-known detective, who knew all the denizens of the place: "We used to go out at night to a little, low place, an all-night house--eight feet wide and twenty-two feet long--where we got a lunch at two or three o'clock in the morning. It was the toughest kind of restaurant ever seen. For the clam chowder they used the same four clams during the whole season, and the average number of flies per pie was seven. This was by actual count."

As to the shops and the locality: "The street was lined with rather old buildings and poor tenements. We had not much frontage. As our business increased enormously, our quarters became too small, so we saw the district Tammany leader and asked him if we could not store castings and other things on the sidewalk. He gave us permission--told us to go ahead, and he would see it was all right. The only thing he required for this was that when a man was sent with a note from him asking us to give him a job, he was to be put on. We had a hand-laborer foreman--'Big Jim'--a very powerful Irishman, who could lift above half a ton. When one of the Tammany aspirants appeared, he was told to go right to work at $1.50 per day. The next day he was told off to lift a certain piece, and if the man could not lift it he was discharged. That made the Tammany man all safe. Jim could pick the piece up easily. The other man could not, and so we let him out. Finally the Tammany leader called a halt, as we were running big engine lathes out on the sidewalk, and he was afraid we were carrying it a little too far. The lathes were worked right out in the street, and belted through the windows of the shop."

At last it became necessary to move from Goerck Street, and Mr. Edison gives a very interesting account of the incidents in connection with the transfer of the plant to Schenectady, New York: "After our works at Goerck Street got too small, we had labor troubles also. It seems I had rather a socialistic strain in me, and I raised the pay of the workmen twenty-five cents an hour above the prevailing rate of wages, whereupon Hoe & Company, our near neighbors, complained at our doing this. I said I thought it was all right. But the men, having got a little more wages, thought they would try coercion and get a little more, as we were considered soft marks. Whereupon they struck at a time that was critical. However, we were short of money for pay-rolls; and we concluded it might not be so bad after all, as it would give us a couple of weeks to catch up. So when the men went out they appointed a committee to meet us; but for two weeks they could not find us, so they became somewhat more anxious than we were. Finally they said they would like to go back. We said all right, and back they went. It was quite a novelty to the men not to be able to find us when they wanted to; and they didn't relish it at all.

"What with these troubles and the lack of room, we decided to find a factory elsewhere, and decided to try the locomotive works up at Schenectady. It seems that the people there had had a falling out among themselves, and one of the directors had started opposition works; but before he had completed all the buildings and put in machinery some compromise was made, and the works were for sale. We bought them very reasonably and moved everything there. These works were owned by me and my assistants until sold to the Edison General Electric Company. At one time we employed several thousand men; and since then the works have been greatly expanded.

"At these new works our orders were far in excess of our capital to handle the business, and both Mr. Insull and I were afraid we might get into trouble for lack of money. Mr. Insull was then my business manager, running the whole thing; and, therefore, when Mr. Henry Villard and his syndicate offered to buy us out, we concluded it was better to be sure than be sorry; so we sold out for a large sum. Villard was a very aggressive man with big ideas, but I could never quite understand him. He had no sense of humor. I remember one time we were going up on the Hudson River boat to inspect the works, and with us was Mr. Henderson, our chief engineer, who was certainly the best raconteur of funny stories I ever knew. We sat at the tail-end of the boat, and he started in to tell funny stories. Villard could not see a single point, and scarcely laughed at all; and Henderson became so disconcerted he had to give it up. It was the same way with Gould. In the early telegraph days I remember going with him to see Mackay in 'The Impecunious Country Editor.' It was very funny, full of amusing and absurd situations; but Gould never smiled once."

The formation of the Edison General Electric Company involved the consolidation of the immediate Edison manufacturing interests in electric light and power, with a capitalization of $12,000,000, now a relatively modest sum; but in those days the amount was large, and the combination caused a great deal of newspaper comment as to such a coinage of brain power. The next step came with the creation of the great General Electric Company of to-day, a combination of the Edison, Thomson-Houston, and Brush lighting interests in manufacture, which to this day maintains the ever-growing plants at Harrison, Lynn, and Schenectady, and there employs from twenty to twenty-five thousand people.

CHAPTER XVI

THE FIRST EDISON CENTRAL STATION

A NOTED inventor once said at the end of a lifetime of fighting to defend his rights, that he found there were three stages in all great inventions: the first, in which people said the thing could not be done; the second, in which they said anybody could do it; and the third, in which they said it had always been done by everybody. In his central-station work Edison has had very much this kind of experience; for while many of his opponents came to acknowledge the novelty and utility of his plans, and gave him unstinted praise, there are doubtless others who to this day profess to look upon him merely as an adapter. How different the view of so eminent a scientist as Lord Kelvin was, may be appreciated from his remark when in later years, in reply to the question why some one else did not invent so obvious and simple a thing as the Feeder System, he said: "The only answer I can think of is that no one else was Edison."

Undaunted by the attitude of doubt and the predictions of impossibility, Edison had pushed on until he was now able to realize all his ideas as to the establishment of a central station in the work that culminated in New York City in 1882. After he had conceived the broad plan, his ambition was to create the initial plant on Manhattan Island, where it would be convenient of access for watching its operation, and where the demonstration of its practicability would have influence in financial circles. The first intention was to cover a district extending from Canal Street on the north to Wall Street on the south; but Edison soon realized that this territory was too extensive for the initial experiment, and he decided finally upon the district included between Wall, Nassau, Spruce, and Ferry streets, Peck Slip and the East River, an area nearly a square mile in extent. One of the preliminary steps taken to enable him to figure on such a station and system was to have men go through this district on various days and note the number of gas jets burning at each hour up to two or three o'clock in the morning. The next step was to divide the region into a number of sub-districts and institute a house-to-house canvass to ascertain precisely the data and conditions pertinent to the project. When the canvass was over, Edison knew exactly how many gas jets there were in every building in the entire district, the average hours of burning, and the cost of light; also every consumer of power, and the quantity used; every hoistway to which an electric motor could be applied; and other details too numerous to mention, such as related to the gas itself, the satisfaction of the customers, and the limitations of day and night demand. All this information was embodied graphically in large maps of the district, by annotations in colored inks; and Edison thus could study the question with every detail before him. Such a reconnaissance, like that of a coming field of battle, was invaluable, and may help give a further idea of the man's inveterate care for the minutiae of things.

The laboratory note-books of this period--1878-80, more particularly--show an immense amount of calculation by Edison and his chief mathematician, Mr. Upton, on conductors for the distribution of current over large areas, and then later in the district described. With the results of this canvass before them, the sizes of the main conductors to be laid throughout the streets of this entire territory were figured, block by block; and the results were then placed on the map. These data revealed the fact that the quantity of copper required for the main conductors would be exceedingly large and costly; and, if ever, Edison was somewhat dismayed. But as usual this apparently insurmountable difficulty only spurred him on to further effort. It was but a short time thereafter that he solved the knotty problem by an invention mentioned in a previous chapter. This is known as the "feeder and main" system, for which he signed the application for a patent on August 4, 1880. As this invention effected a saving of seven-eighths of the cost of the chief conductors in a straight multiple arc system, the mains for the first district were refigured, and enormous new maps were made, which became the final basis of actual installation, as they were subsequently enlarged by the addition of every proposed junction-box, bridge safety-catch box, and street-intersection box in the whole area.

When this patent, after protracted fighting, was sustained by Judge Green in 1893, the Electrical Engineer remarked that the General Electric Company "must certainly feel elated" because of its importance; and the journal expressed its fear that although the specifications and claims related only to the maintenance of uniform pressure of current on lighting circuits, the owners might naturally seek to apply it also to feeders used in the electric-railway work already so extensive. At this time, however, the patent had only about a year of life left, owing to the expiration of the corresponding English patent. The fact that thirteen years had elapsed gives a vivid idea of the ordeal involved in sustaining a patent and the injustice to the inventor, while there is obviously hardship to those who cannot tell from any decision of the court whether they are infringing or not. It is interesting to note that the preparation for hearing this case in New Jersey was accompanied by models to show the court exactly the method and its economy, as worked out in comparison with what is known as the "tree system" of circuits--the older alternative way of doing it. As a basis of comparison, a district of thirty-six city blocks in the form of a square was assumed. The power station was placed at the centre of the square; each block had sixteen consumers using fifteen lights each. Conductors were run from the station to supply each of the four quarters of the district with light. In one example the "feeder" system was used; in the other the "tree." With these models were shown two cubes which represented one one-hundredth of the actual quantity of copper required for each quarter of the district by the two-wire tree system as compared with the feeder system under like conditions. The total weight of copper for the four quarter districts by the tree system was 803,250 pounds, but when the feeder system was used it was only 128,739 pounds! This was a reduction from $23.24 per lamp for copper to $3.72 per lamp. Other models emphasized this extraordinary contrast. At the time Edison was doing this work on economizing in conductors, much of the criticism against him was based on the assumed extravagant use of copper implied in the obvious "tree" system, and it was very naturally said that there was not enough copper in the world to supply his demands. It is true that the modern electrical arts have been a great stimulator of copper production, now taking a quarter of all made; yet evidently but for such inventions as this such arts could not have come into existence at all, or else in growing up they would have forced copper to starvation prices. [11]

[Footnote 11: For description of feeder patent see Appendix.]

It should be borne in mind that from the outset Edison had determined upon installing underground conductors as the only permanent and satisfactory method for the distribution of current from central stations in cities; and that at Menlo Park he laid out and operated such a system with about four hundred and twenty-five lamps. The underground system there was limited to the immediate vicinity of the laboratory and was somewhat crude, as well as much less complicated than would be the network of over eighty thousand lineal feet, which he calculated to be required for the underground circuits in the first district of New York City. At Menlo Park no effort was made for permanency; no provision was needed in regard to occasional openings of the street for various purposes; no new customers were to be connected from time to time to the mains, and no repairs were within contemplation. In New York the question of permanency was of paramount importance, and the other contingencies were sure to arise as well as conditions more easy to imagine than to forestall. These problems were all attacked in a resolute, thoroughgoing manner, and one by one solved by the invention of new and unprecedented devices that were adequate for the purposes of the time, and which are embodied in apparatus of slight modification in use up to the present day.

Just what all this means it is hard for the present generation to imagine. New York and all the other great cities in 1882, and for some years thereafter, were burdened and darkened by hideous masses of overhead wires carried on ugly wooden poles along all the main thoroughfares. One after another rival telegraph and telephone, stock ticker, burglar-alarm, and other companies had strung their circuits without any supervision or restriction; and these wires in all conditions of sag or decay ramified and crisscrossed in every direction, often hanging broken and loose-ended for months, there being no official compulsion to remove any dead wire. None of these circuits carried dangerous currents; but the introduction of the arc light brought an entirely new menace in the use of pressures that were even worse than the bully of the West who "kills on sight," because this kindred peril was invisible, and might lurk anywhere. New poles were put up, and the lighting circuits on them, with but a slight insulation of cotton impregnated with some "weather-proof" compound, straggled all over the city exposed to wind and rain and accidental contact with other wires, or with the metal of buildings. So many fatalities occurred that the insulated wire used, called "underwriters," because approved by the insurance bodies, became jocularly known as "undertakers," and efforts were made to improve its protective qualities. Then came the overhead circuits for distributing electrical energy to motors for operating elevators, driving machinery, etc., and these, while using a lower, safer potential, were proportionately larger. There were no wires underground. Morse had tried that at the very beginning of electrical application, in telegraphy, and all agreed that renewals of the experiment were at once costly and foolish. At last, in cities like New York, what may be styled generically the "overhead system" of wires broke down under its own weight; and various methods of underground conductors were tried, hastened in many places by the chopping down of poles and wires as the result of some accident that stirred the public indignation. One typical tragic scene was that in New York, where, within sight of the City Hall, a lineman was killed at his work on the arc light pole, and his body slowly roasted before the gaze of the excited populace, which for days afterward dropped its silver and copper coin into the alms-box nailed to the fatal pole for the benefit of his family. Out of all this in New York came a board of electrical control, a conduit system, and in the final analysis the Public Service Commission, that is credited to Governor Hughes as the furthest development of utility corporation control.

The "road to yesterday" back to Edison and his insistence on underground wires is a long one, but the preceding paragraph traces it. Even admitting that the size and weight of his low-tension conductors necessitated putting them underground, this argues nothing against the propriety and sanity of his methods. He believed deeply and firmly in the analogy between electrical supply and that for water and gas, and pointed to the trite fact that nobody hoisted the water and gas mains into the air on stilts, and that none of the pressures were inimical to human safety. The arc-lighting methods were unconsciously and unwittingly prophetic of the latter-day long-distance transmissions at high pressure that, electrically, have placed the energy of Niagara at the command of Syracuse and Utica, and have put the power of the falling waters of the Sierras at the disposal of San Francisco, two hundred miles away. But within city limits overhead wires, with such space-consuming potentials, are as fraught with mischievous peril to the public as the dynamite stored by a nonchalant contractor in the cellar of a schoolhouse. As an offset, then, to any tendency to depreciate the intrinsic value of Edison's lighting work, let the claim be here set forth modestly and subject to interference, that he was the father of underground wires in America, and by his example outlined the policy now dominant in every city of the first rank. Even the comment of a cynic in regard to electrical development may be accepted: "Some electrical companies wanted all the air; others apparently had use for all the water; Edison only asked for the earth."

The late Jacob Hess, a famous New York Republican politician, was a member of the commission appointed to put the wires underground in New York City, in the "eighties." He stated that when the commission was struggling with the problem, and examining all kinds of devices and plans, patented and unpatented, for which fabulous sums were often asked, the body turned to Edison in its perplexity and asked for advice. Edison said: "All you have to do, gentlemen, is to insulate your wires, draw them through the cheapest thing on earth--iron pipe--run your pipes through channels or galleries under the street, and you've got the whole thing done." This was practically the system adopted and in use to this day. What puzzled the old politician was that Edison would accept nothing for his advice.

Another story may also be interpolated here as to the underground work done in New York for the first Edison station. It refers to the "man higher up," although the phrase had not been coined in those days of lower public morality. That a corporation should be "held up" was

Page 181

accepted philosophically by the corporation as one of the unavoidable incidents of its business; and if the corporation "got back" by securing some privilege without paying for it, the public was ready to condone if not applaud. Public utilities were in the making, and no one in particular had a keen sense of what was right or what was wrong, in the hard, practical details of their development. Edison tells this illuminating story: "When I was laying tubes in the streets of New York, the office received notice from the Commissioner of Public Works to appear at his office at a certain hour. I went up there with a gentleman to see the Commissioner, H. O. Thompson. On arrival he said to me: 'You are putting down these tubes. The Department of Public Works requires that you should have five inspectors to look after this work, and that their salary shall be $5 per day, payable at the end of each week. Good-morning.' I went out very much crestfallen, thinking I would be delayed and harassed in the work which I was anxious to finish, and was doing night and day. We watched patiently for those inspectors to appear. The only appearance they made was to draw their pay Saturday afternoon."

Just before Christmas in 1880--December 17--as an item for the silk stocking of Father Knickerbocker--the Edison Electric Illuminating Company of New York was organized. In pursuance of the policy adhered to by Edison, a license was issued to it for the exclusive use of the system in that territory--Manhattan Island--in consideration of a certain sum of money and a fixed percentage of its capital in stock for the patent rights. Early in 1881 it was altogether a paper enterprise, but events moved swiftly as narrated already, and on June 25, 1881, the first "Jumbo" prototype of the dynamo-electric machines to generate current at the Pearl Street station was put through its paces before being shipped to Paris to furnish new sensations to the flaneur of the boulevards. A number of the Edison officers and employees assembled at Goerck Street to see this "gigantic" machine go into action, and watched its performance with due reverence all through the night until five o'clock on Sunday morning, when it respected the conventionalities by breaking a shaft and suspending further tests. After this dynamo was shipped to France, and its successors to England for the Holborn Viaduct plant, Edison made still further improvements in design, increasing capacity and economy, and then proceeded vigorously with six machines for Pearl Street.

An ideal location for any central station is at the very centre of the district served. It may be questioned whether it often goes there. In the New York first district the nearest property available was a double building at Nos. 255 and 257 Pearl Street, occupying a lot so by 100 feet. It was four stories high, with a fire-wall dividing it into two equal parts. One of these parts was converted for the uses of the station proper, and the other was used as a tube-shop by the underground construction department, as well as for repair-shops, storage, etc. Those were the days when no one built a new edifice for station purposes; that would have been deemed a fantastic extravagance. One early station in New York for arc lighting was an old soap-works whose well-soaked floors did not need much additional grease to render them choice fuel for the inevitable flames. In this Pearl Street instance, the building, erected originally for commercial uses, was quite incapable of sustaining the weight of the heavy dynamos and steam-engines to be installed on the second floor; so the old flooring was torn out and a new one of heavy girders supported by stiff columns was substituted. This heavy construction, more familiar nowadays, and not unlike the supporting metal structure of the Manhattan Elevated road, was erected independent of the enclosing walls, and occupied the full width of 257 Pearl Street, and about three-quarters of its depth. This change in the internal arrangements did not at all affect the ugly external appearance, which did little to suggest the stately and ornate stations since put up by the New York Edison Company, the latest occupying whole city blocks.

Of this episode Edison gives the following account: "While planning for my first New York station--Pearl Street--of course, I had no real estate, and from lack of experience had very little knowledge of its cost in New York; so I assumed a rather large, liberal amount of it to plan my station on. It occurred to me one day that before I went too far with my plans I had better find out what real estate was worth. In my original plan I had 200 by 200 feet. I thought that by going down on a slum street near the water-front I would get some pretty cheap property. So I picked out the worst dilapidated street there was, and found I could only get two buildings, each 25 feet front, one 100 feet deep and the other 85 feet deep. I thought about $10,000 each would cover it; but when I got the price I found that they wanted $75,000 for one and $80,000 for the other. Then I was compelled to change my plans and go upward in the air where real estate was cheap. I cleared out the building entirely to the walls and built my station of structural ironwork, running it up high."

Into this converted structure was put the most complete steam plant obtainable, together with all the mechanical and engineering adjuncts bearing upon economical and successful operation. Being in a narrow street and a congested district, the plant needed special facilities for the handling of coal and ashes, as well as for ventilation and forced draught. All of these details received Mr. Edison's personal care and consideration on the spot, in addition to the multitude of other affairs demanding his thought. Although not a steam or mechanical engineer, his quick grasp of principles and omnivorous reading had soon supplied the lack of training; nor had he forgotten the practical experience picked up as a boy on the locomotives of the Grand Trunk road. It is to be noticed as a feature of the plant, in common with many of later construction, that it was placed well away from the water's edge, and equipped with non-condensing engines; whereas the modern plant invariably seeks the bank of a river or lake for the purpose of a generous supply of water for its condensing engines or steam-turbines. These are among the refinements of practice coincidental with the advance of the art.

At the award of the John Fritz gold medal in April, 1909, to Charles T. Porter for his work in advancing the knowledge of steam-engineering, and for improvements in engine construction, Mr. Frank J. Sprague spoke on behalf of the American Institute of Electrical Engineers of the debt of electricity to the high-speed steam-engine. He recalled the fact that at the French Exposition of 1867 Mr. Porter installed two Porter-Allen engines to drive electric alternating-current generators for supplying current to primitive lighthouse apparatus. While the engines were not directly coupled to the dynamos, it was a curious fact that the piston speeds and number of revolutions were what is common to-day in isolated direct-coupled plants. In the dozen years following Mr. Porter built many engines with certain common characteristics--i.e., high piston speed and revolutions, solid engine bed, and babbitt-metal bearings; but there was no electric driving until 1880, when Mr. Porter installed a high-speed engine for Edison at his laboratory in Menlo Park. Shortly after this he was invited to construct for the Edison Pearl Street station the first of a series of engines for so-called "steam-dynamos," each independently driven by a direct-coupled engine. Mr. Sprague compared the relations thus established between electricity and the high-speed engine not to those of debtor and creditor, but rather to those of partners--an industrial marriage--one of the most important in the engineering world. Here were two machines destined to be joined together, economizing space, enhancing economy, augmenting capacity, reducing investment, and increasing dividends.

While rapid progress was being made in this and other directions, the wheels of industry were humming merrily at the Edison Tube Works, for over fifteen miles of tube conductors were required for the district, besides the boxes to connect the network at the street intersections, and the hundreds of junction boxes for taking the service conductors into each of the hundreds of buildings. In addition to the immense amount of money involved, this specialized industry required an enormous amount of experiment, as it called for the development of an entirely new art. But with Edison's inventive fertility--if ever there was a cross-fertilizer of mechanical ideas it is he--and with Mr. Kruesi's never-failing patience and perseverance applied to experiment and evolution, rapid progress was made. A franchise having been obtained from the city, the work of laying the underground conductors began in the late fall of 1881, and was pushed with almost frantic energy. It is not to be supposed, however, that the Edison tube system had then reached a finality of perfection in the eyes of its inventor. In his correspondence with Kruesi, as late as 1887, we find Edison bewailing the inadequacy of the insulation of the conductors under twelve hundred volts pressure, as for example: "Dear Kruesi,--There is nothing wrong with your present compound. It is splendid. The whole trouble is air-bubbles. The hotter it is poured the greater the amount of air-bubbles. At 212 it can be put on rods and there is no bubble. I have a man experimenting and testing all the time. Until I get at the proper method of pouring and getting rid of the air-bubbles, it will be waste of time to experiment with other asphalts. Resin oil distils off easily. It may answer, but paraffine or other similar substances must be put in to prevent brittleness, One thing is certain, and that is, everything must be poured in layers, not only the boxes, but the tubes. The tube itself should have a thin coating. The rope should also have a coating. The rods also. The whole lot, rods and rope, when ready for tube, should have another coat, and then be placed in tube and filled. This will do the business." Broad and large as a continent in his ideas, if ever there was a man of finical fussiness in attention to detail, it is Edison. A letter of seven pages of about the same date in 1887 expatiates on the vicious troubles caused by the air-bubble, and remarks with fine insight into the problems of insulation and the idea of layers of it: "Thus you have three separate coatings, and it is impossible an air-hole in one should match the other."

To a man less thorough and empirical in method than Edison, it would have been sufficient to have made his plans clear to associates or subordinates and hold them responsible for accurate results. No such vicarious treatment would suit him, ready as he has always been to share the work where he could give his trust. In fact he realized, as no one else did at this stage, the tremendous import of this novel and comprehensive scheme for giving the world light; and he would not let go, even if busy to the breaking-point. Though plunged in a veritable maelstrom of new and important business interests, and though applying for no fewer than eighty-nine patents in 1881, all of which were granted, he superintended on the spot all this laying of underground conductors for the first district. Nor did he merely stand around and give orders. Day and night he actually worked in the trenches with the laborers, amid the dirt and paving-stones and hurry-burly of traffic, helping to lay the tubes, filling up junction-boxes, and taking part in all the infinite detail. He wanted to know for himself how things went, why for some occult reason a little change was necessary, what improvement could be made in the material. His hours of work were not regulated by the clock, but lasted until he felt the need of a little rest. Then he would go off to the station building in Pearl Street, throw an overcoat on a pile of tubes, lie down and sleep for a few hours, rising to resume work with the first gang. There was a small bedroom on the third floor of the station available for him, but going to bed meant delay and consumed time. It is no wonder that such impatience, such an enthusiasm, drove the work forward at a headlong pace.

Edison says of this period: "When we put down the tubes in the lower part of New York, in the streets, we kept a big stock of them in the cellar of the station at Pearl Street. As I was on all the time, I would take a nap of an hour or so in the daytime--any time--and I used to sleep on those tubes in the cellar. I had two Germans who were testing there, and both of them died of diphtheria, caught in the cellar, which was cold and damp. It never affected me."

It is worth pausing just a moment to glance at this man taking a fitful rest on a pile of iron pipe in a dingy building. His name is on the tip of the world's tongue. Distinguished scientists from every part of Europe seek him eagerly. He has just been decorated and awarded high honors by the French Government. He is the inventor of wonderful new apparatus, and the exploiter of novel and successful arts. The magic of his achievements and the rumors of what is being done have caused a wild drop in gas securities, and a sensational rise in his own electric-light stock from $100 to $3500 a share. Yet these things do not at all affect his slumber or his democratic simplicity, for in that, as in everything else, he is attending strictly to business, "doing the thing that is next to him."

Part of the rush and feverish haste was due to the approach of frost, which, as usual in New York, suspended operations in the earth; but the laying of the conductors was resumed promptly in the spring of 1882; and meantime other work had been advanced. During the fall and winter months two more "Jumbo" dynamos were built and sent to London, after which the construction of six for New York was swiftly taken in hand. In the month of May three of these machines, each with a capacity of twelve hundred incandescent lamps, were delivered at Pearl Street and assembled on the second floor. On July 5th--owing to the better opportunity for ceaseless toil given by a public holiday--the construction of the operative part of the station was so far completed that the first of the dynamos was operated under steam; so that three days later the satisfactory experiment was made of throwing its flood of electrical energy into a bank of one thousand lamps on an upper floor. Other tests followed in due course. All was excitement. The field-regulating apparatus and the electrical-pressure indicator--first of its kind--were also tested, and in turn found satisfactory. Another vital test was made at this time--namely, of the strength of the iron structure itself on which the plant was erected. This was done by two structural experts; and not till he got their report as to ample factors of safety was Edison reassured as to this detail.

A remark of Edison, familiar to all who have worked with him, when it is reported to him that something new goes all right and is satisfactory from all points of view, is: "Well, boys, now let's find the bugs," and the hunt for the phylloxera begins with fiendish, remorseless zest. Before starting the plant for regular commercial service, he began personally a series of practical experiments and tests to ascertain in advance what difficulties would actually arise in practice, so that he could provide remedies or preventives. He had several cots placed in the adjoining building, and he and a few of his most strenuous assistants worked day and night, leaving the work only for hurried meals and a snatch of sleep. These crucial tests, aiming virtually to break the plant down if possible within predetermined conditions, lasted several weeks, and while most valuable in the information they afforded, did not hinder anything, for meantime customers' premises throughout the district were being wired and supplied with lamps and meters.

On Monday, September 4, 1882, at 3 o'clock, P.M., Edison realized the consummation of his broad and original scheme. The Pearl Street station was officially started by admitting steam to the engine of one of the "Jumbos," current was generated, turned into the network of underground conductors, and was transformed into light by the incandescent lamps that had thus far been installed. This date and event may properly be regarded as historical, for they mark the practical beginning of a new art, which in the intervening years has grown prodigiously, and is still increasing by leaps and bounds.

Everything worked satisfactorily in the main. There were a few mechanical and engineering annoyances that might naturally be expected to arise in a new and unprecedented enterprise; but nothing of sufficient moment to interfere with the steady and continuous supply of current to customers at all hours of the day and night. Indeed, once started, this station was operated uninterruptedly for eight years with only insignificant stoppage.

It will have been noted by the reader that there was nothing to indicate rashness in starting up the station, as only one dynamo was put in operation. Within a short time, however, it was deemed desirable to supply the underground network with more current, as many additional customers had been connected and the demand for the new light was increasing very rapidly. Although Edison had successfully operated several dynamos in multiple arc two years before--i.e., all feeding current together into the same circuits--there was not, at this early period of experience, any absolute certainty as to what particular results might occur upon the throwing of the current from two or more such massive dynamos into a great distributing system. The sequel showed the value of Edison's cautious method in starting the station by operating only a single unit at first.

He decided that it would be wise to make the trial operation of a second "Jumbo" on a Sunday, when business houses were closed in the district, thus obviating any danger of false impressions in the public mind in the event of any extraordinary manifestations. The circumstances attending the adding of a second dynamo are thus humorously described by Edison: "My heart was in my mouth at first, but everything worked all right.... Then we started another engine and threw them in parallel. Of all the circuses since Adam was born, we had the worst then! One engine would stop, and the other would run up to about a thousand revolutions, and then they would see-saw. The trouble was with the governors. When the circus commenced, the gang that was standing around ran out precipitately, and I guess some of them kept running for a block or two. I grabbed the throttle of one engine, and E. H. Johnson, who was the only one present to keep his wits, caught hold of the other, and we shut them off." One of the "gang" that ran, but, in this case, only to the end of the room, afterward said: "At the time it was a terrifying experience, as I didn't know what was going to happen. The engines and dynamos made a horrible racket, from loud and deep groans to a hideous shriek, and the place seemed to be filled with sparks and flames of all colors. It was as if the gates of the infernal regions had been suddenly opened."

This trouble was at once attacked by Edison in his characteristic and strenuous way. The above experiment took place between three and four o'clock on a Sunday afternoon, and within a few hours he had gathered his superintendent and men of the machine-works and had them at work on a shafting device that he thought would remedy the trouble. He says: "Of course, I discovered that what had happened was that one set was running the other as a motor. I then put up a long shaft, connecting all the governors together, and thought this would certainly cure the trouble; but it didn't. The torsion of the shaft was so great that one governor still managed to get ahead of the others. Well, it was a serious state of things, and I worried over it a lot. Finally I went down to Goerck Street and got a piece of shafting and a tube in which it fitted. I twisted the shafting one way and the tube the other as far as I could, and pinned them together. In this way, by straining the whole outfit up to its elastic limit in opposite directions, the torsion was practically eliminated, and after that the governors ran together all right."

Edison realized, however, that in commercial practice this was only a temporary expedient, and that a satisfactory permanence of results could only be attained with more perfect engines that could be depended upon for close and simple regulation. The engines that were made part of the first three "Jumbos" placed in the station were the very best that could be obtained at the time, and even then had been specially designed and built for the purpose. Once more quoting Edison on this subject: "About that time" (when he was trying to run several dynamos in parallel in the Pearl Street station) "I got hold of Gardiner C. Sims, and he undertook to build an engine to run at three hundred and fifty revolutions and give one hundred and seventy-five horse-power. He went back to Providence and set to work, and brought the engine back with him to the shop. It worked only a few minutes when it busted. That man sat around that shop and slept in it for three weeks, until he got his engine right and made it work the way he wanted it to. When he reached this period I gave orders for the engine-works to run night and day until we got enough engines, and when all was ready we started the engines. Then everything worked all right.... One of these engines that Sims built ran twenty-four hours a day, three hundred and sixty-five days in the year, for over a year before it stopped." [12]

[Footnote 12: We quote the following interesting notes of Mr. Charles L. Clarke on the question of see-sawing, or "hunting," as it was afterward termed:

"In the Holborn Viaduct station the difficulty of 'hunting' was not experienced. At the time the 'Jumbos' were first operated in multiple arc, April 8, 1882, one machine was driven by a Porter-Allen engine, and the other by an Armington & Sims engine, and both machines were on a solid foundation. At the station at Milan, Italy, the first 'Jumbos' operated in multiple arc were driven by Porter-Allen engines, and dash-pots were applied to the governors. These machines were also upon a solid foundation, and no trouble was experienced.

"At the Pearl Street station, however, the machines were supported upon long iron floor-beams, and at the high speed of 350 revolutions per minute, considerable vertical vibration was given to the engines. And the writer is inclined to the opinion that this vibration, acting in the same direction as the action of gravitation, which was one of the two controlling forces in the operation of the Porter-Allen governor, was the primary cause of the 'hunting.' In the Armington & Sims engine the controlling forces in the operation of the governor were the centrifugal force of revolving weights, and the opposing force of compressed springs, and neither the action of gravitation nor the vertical vibrations of the engine could have any sensible effect upon the governor."]

The Pearl Street station, as this first large plant was called, made rapid and continuous growth in its output of electric current. It started, as we have said, on September 4, 1882, supplying about four hundred lights to a comparatively small number of customers. Among those first supplied was the banking firm of Drexel, Morgan & Company, corner of Broad and Wall streets, at the outermost limits of the system. Before the end of December of the same year the light had so grown in favor that it was being supplied to over two hundred and forty customers whose buildings were wired for over five thousand lamps. By this time three more "Jumbos" had been added to the plant. The output from this time forward increased steadily up to the spring of 1884, when the demands of the station necessitated the installation of two additional "Jumbos" in the adjoining building, which, with the venous improvements that had been made in the mean time, gave the station a capacity of over eleven thousand lamps actually in service at any one time.

During the first three months of operating the Pearl Street station light was supplied to customers without charge. Edison had perfect confidence in his meters, and also in the ultimate judgment of the public as to the superiority of the incandescent electric light as against other illuminants. He realized, however, that in the beginning of the operation of an entirely novel plant there was ample opportunity for unexpected contingencies, although the greatest care had been exercised to make everything as perfect as possible. Mechanical defects or other unforeseen troubles in any part of the plant or underground system might arise and cause temporary stoppages of operation, thus giving grounds for uncertainty which would create a feeling of public distrust in the permanence of the supply of light.

As to the kind of mishap that was wont to occur, Edison tells the following story: "One afternoon, after our Pearl Street station started, a policeman rushed in and told us to send an electrician at once up to the corner of Ann and Nassau streets--some trouble. Another man and I went up. We found an immense crowd of men and boys there and in the adjoining streets--a perfect jam. There was a leak in one of our junction-boxes, and on account of the cellars extending under the street, the top soil had become insulated. Hence, by means of this leak powerful currents were passing through this thin layer of moist earth. When a horse went to pass over it he would get a very severe shock. When I arrived I saw coming along the street a ragman with a dilapidated old horse, and one of the boys told him to go over on the other side of the road--which was the place where the current leaked. When the ragman heard this he took that side at once. The moment the horse struck the electrified soil he stood straight up in the air, and then reared again; and the crowd yelled, the policeman yelled; and the horse started to run away. This continued until the crowd got so serious that the policeman had to clear it out; and we were notified to cut the current off. We got a gang of men, cut the current off for several junction-boxes, and fixed the leak. One man who had seen it came to me next day and wanted me to put in apparatus for him at a place where they sold horses. He said he could make a fortune with it, because he could get old nags in there and make them act like thoroughbreds."

So well had the work been planned and executed, however, that nothing happened to hinder the continuous working of the station and the supply of light to customers. Hence it was decided in December, 1882, to begin charging a price for the service, and, accordingly, Edison electrolytic meters were installed on the premises of each customer then connected. The first bill for lighting, based upon the reading of one of these meters, amounted to $50.40, and was collected on January 18, 1883, from the Ansonia Brass and Copper Company, 17 and 19 Cliff Street. Generally speaking, customers found that their bills compared fairly with gas bills for corresponding months where the same amount of light was used, and they paid promptly and cheerfully, with emphatic encomiums of the new light. During November, 1883, a little over one year after the station was started, bills for lighting amounting to over $9000 were collected.

An interesting story of meter experience in the first few months of operation of the Pearl Street station is told by one of the "boys" who was then in position to know the facts; "Mr. J. P. Morgan, whose firm was one of the first customers, expressed to Mr. Edison some doubt as to the accuracy of the meter. The latter, firmly convinced of its correctness, suggested a strict test by having some cards printed and hung on each fixture at Mr. Morgan's place. On these cards was to be noted the number of lamps in the fixture, and the time they were turned on and off each day for a month. At the end of that time the lamp-hours were to be added together by one of the clerks and figured on a basis of a definite amount per lamp-hour, and compared with the bill that would be rendered by the station for the corresponding period. The results of the first month's test showed an apparent overcharge by the Edison company. Mr. Morgan was exultant, while Mr. Edison was still confident and suggested a continuation of the test. Another month's trial showed somewhat similar results. Mr. Edison was a little disturbed, but insisted that there was a mistake somewhere. He went down to Drexel, Morgan & Company's office to investigate, and, after looking around, asked when the office was cleaned out. He was told it was done at night by the janitor, who was sent for, and upon being interrogated as to what light he used, said that he turned on a central fixture containing about ten lights. It came out that he had made no record of the time these lights were in use. He was told to do so in future, and another month's test was made. On comparison with the company's bill, rendered on the meter-reading, the meter came within a few cents of the amount computed from the card records, and Mr. Morgan was completely satisfied of the accuracy of the meter."

It is a strange but not extraordinary commentary on the perversity of human nature and the lack of correct observation, to note that even after the Pearl Street station had been in actual operation twenty-four hours a day for nearly three months, there should still remain an attitude of "can't be done." That such a scepticism still obtained is evidenced by the public prints of the period. Edison's electric-light system and his broad claims were freely discussed and animadverted upon at the very time he was demonstrating their successful application. To show some of the feeling at the time, we reproduce the following letter, which appeared November 29, 1882:

"To the Editor of the Sun:

"SIR,--In reading the discussions relative to the Pearl Street station of the Edison light, I have noted that while it is claimed that there is scarcely any loss from leakage of current, nothing is said about the loss due to the resistance of the long circuits. I am informed that this is the secret of the failure to produce with the power in position a sufficient amount of current to run all the lamps that have been put up, and that while six, and even seven, lights to the horse-power may be produced from an isolated plant, the resistance of the long underground wires reduces this result in the above case to less than three lights to the horse-power, thus making the cost of production greatly in excess of gas. Can the Edison company explain this? 'INVESTIGATOR'."

This was one of the many anonymous letters that had been written to the newspapers on the subject, and the following reply by the Edison company was printed December 3, 1882:

"To the Editor of the Sun:

"SIR,--'Investigator' in Wednesday's Sun, says that the Edison company is troubled at its Pearl Street station with a 'loss of current, due to the resistance of the long circuits'; also that, whereas Edison gets 'six or even seven lights to the horse-power in isolated plants, the resistance of the long underground wires reduces that result in the Pearl Street station to less than three lights to the horse-power.' Both of these statements are false. As regards loss due to resistance, there is a well-known law for determining it, based on Ohm's law. By use of that law we knew in advance, that is to say, when the original plans for the station were drawn, just what this loss would be, precisely the same as a mechanical engineer when constructing a mill with long lines of shafting can forecast the loss of power due to friction. The practical result in the Pearl Street station has fully demonstrated the correctness of our estimate thus made in advance. As regards our getting only three lights per horse-power, our station has now been running three months, without stopping a moment, day or night, and we invariably get over six lamps per horse-power, or substantially the same as we do in our isolated plants. We are now lighting one hundred and ninety-three buildings, wired for forty-four hundred lamps, of which about two-thirds are in constant use, and we are adding additional houses and lamps daily. These figures can be verified at the office of the Board of Underwriters, where certificates with full details permitting the use of our light are filed by their own inspector. To light these lamps we run from one to three dynamos, according to the lamps in use at any given time, and we shall start additional dynamos as fast as we can connect more buildings. Neither as regards the loss due to resistance, nor as regards the number of lamps per horse-power, is there the slightest trouble or disappointment on the part of our company, and your correspondent is entirely in error is assuming that there is. Let me suggest that if 'Investigator' really wishes to investigate, and is competent and willing to learn the exact facts, he can do so at this office, where there is no mystery of concealment, but, on the contrary, a strong desire to communicate facts to intelligent inquirers. Such a method of investigating must certainly be more satisfactory to one honestly seeking knowledge than that of first assuming an error as the basis of a question, and then demanding an explanation.

"Yours very truly,

"S. B. EATON, President."

Viewed from the standpoint of over twenty-seven years later, the wisdom and necessity of answering anonymous newspaper letters of this kind might be deemed questionable, but it must be remembered that, although the Pearl Street station was working successfully, and Edison's comprehensive plans were abundantly vindicated, the enterprise was absolutely new and only just stepping on the very threshold of commercial exploitation. To enter in and possess the land required the confidence of capital and the general public. Hence it was necessary to maintain a constant vigilance to defeat the insidious attacks of carping critics and others who would attempt to injure the Edison system by misleading statements.

It will be interesting to the modern electrician to note that when this pioneer station was started, and in fact for some little time afterward, there was not a single electrical instrument in the whole station--not a voltmeter or an ammeter! Nor was there a central switchboard! Each dynamo had its own individual control switch. The feeder connections were all at the front of the building, and the general voltage control apparatus was on the floor above. An automatic pressure indicator had been devised and put in connection with the main circuits. It consisted, generally speaking, of an electromagnet with relays connecting with a red and a blue lamp. When the electrical pressure was normal, neither lamp was lighted; but if the electromotive force rose above a predetermined amount by one or two volts, the red lamp lighted up, and the attendant at the hand-wheel of the field regulator inserted resistance in the field circuit, whereas, if the blue lamp lighted, resistance was cut out until the pressure was raised to normal. Later on this primitive indicator was supplanted by the "Bradley Bridge," a crude form of the "Howell" pressure indicators, which were subsequently used for many years in the Edison stations.

Much could be added to make a complete pictorial description of the historic Pearl Street station, but it is not within the scope of this narrative to enter into diffuse technical details, interesting as they may be to many persons. We cannot close this chapter, however, without mention of the fate of the Pearl Street station, which continued in successful commercial operation until January 2, 1890, when it was partially destroyed by fire. All the "Jumbos" were ruined, excepting No. 9, which is still a venerated relic in the possession of the New York Edison Company. Luckily, the boilers were unharmed. Belt-driven generators and engines were speedily installed, and the station was again in operation in a few days. The uninjured "Jumbo," No. 9, again continued to perform its duty. But in the words of Mr. Charles L. Clarke, "the glory of the old Pearl Street station, unique in bearing the impress of Mr. Edison's personality, and, as it were, constructed with his own hands, disappeared in the flame and smoke of that Thursday morning fire."

The few days' interruption of the service was the only serious one that has taken place in the history of the New York Edison Company from September 4, 1882, to the present date. The Pearl Street station was operated for some time subsequent to the fire, but increasing demands in the mean time having led to the construction of other stations, the mains of the First District were soon afterward connected to another plant, the Pearl Street station was dismantled, and the building was sold in 1895.

The prophetic insight into the magnitude of central-station lighting that Edison had when he was still experimenting on the incandescent lamp over thirty years ago is a little less than astounding, when it is so amply verified in the operations of the New York Edison Company (the successor of the Edison Electric Illuminating Company of New York) and many others. At the end of 1909 the New York Edison Company alone was operating twenty-eight stations and substations, having a total capacity of 159,500 kilowatts. Connected with its lines were approximately 85,000 customers wired for 3,813,899 incandescent lamps and nearly 225,000 horse-power through industrial electric motors connected with the underground service. A large quantity of electrical energy is also supplied for heating and cooking, charging automobiles, chemical and plating work, and various other uses.

CHAPTER XVII

OTHER EARLY STATIONS--THE METER

WE have now seen the Edison lighting system given a complete, convincing demonstration in Paris, London, and New York; and have noted steps taken for its introduction elsewhere on both sides of the Atlantic. The Paris plant, like that at the Crystal Palace, was a temporary exhibit. The London plant was less temporary, but not permanent, supplying before it was torn out no fewer than three thousand lamps in hotels, churches, stores, and dwellings in the vicinity of Holborn Viaduct. There Messrs. Johnson and Hammer put into practice many of the ideas now standard in the art, and secured much useful data for the work in New York, of which the story has just been told.

As a matter of fact the first Edison commercial station to be operated in this country was that at Appleton, Wisconsin, but its only serious claim to notice is that it was the initial one of the system driven by water-power. It went into service August 15, 1882, about three weeks before the Pearl Street station. It consisted of one small dynamo of a capacity of two hundred and eighty lights of 10 c.p. each, and was housed in an unpretentious wooden shed. The dynamo-electric machine, though small, was robust, for under all the varying speeds of water-power, and the vicissitudes of the plant to which it, belonged, it continued in active use until 1899--seventeen years.

Edison was from the first deeply impressed with the possibilities of water-power, and, as this incident shows, was prompt to seize such a very early opportunity. But his attention was in reality concentrated closely on the supply of great centres of population, a task which he then felt might well occupy his lifetime; and except in regard to furnishing isolated plants he did not pursue further the development of hydro-electric stations. That was left to others, and to the application of the alternating current, which has enabled engineers to harness remote powers, and, within thoroughly economical limits, transmit thousands of horse-power as much as two hundred miles at pressures of 80,000 and 100,000 volts. Owing to his insistence on low pressure, direct current for use in densely populated districts, as the only safe and truly universal, profitable way of delivering electrical energy to the consumers, Edison has been frequently spoken of as an opponent of the alternating current. This does him an injustice. At the time a measure was before the Virginia legislature, in 1890, to limit the permissible pressures of current so as to render it safe, he said: "You want to allow high pressure wherever the conditions are such that by no possible accident could that pressure get into the houses of the consumers; you want to give them all the latitude you can." In explaining this he added: "Suppose you want to take the falls down at Richmond, and want to put up a water-power? Why, if we erect a station at the falls, it is a great economy to get it up to the city. By digging a cheap trench and putting in an insulated cable, and connecting such station with the central part of Richmond, having the end of the cable come up into the station from the earth and there connected with motors, the power of the falls would be transmitted to these motors. If now the motors were made to run dynamos conveying low-pressure currents to the public, there is no possible way whereby this high-pressure current could get to the public." In other words, Edison made the sharp fundamental distinction between high pressure alternating current for transmission and low pressure direct current for distribution; and this is exactly the practice that has been adopted in all the great cities of the country to-day. There seems no good reason for believing that it will change. It might perhaps have been altogether better for Edison, from the financial standpoint, if he had not identified himself so completely with one kind of current, but that made no difference to him, as it was a matter of conviction; and Edison's convictions are granitic. Moreover, this controversy over the two currents, alternating and direct, which has become historical in the field of electricity--and is something like the "irrepressible conflict" we heard of years ago in national affairs--illustrates another aspect of Edison's character. Broad as the prairies and free in thought as the winds that sweep them, he is idiosyncratically opposed to loose and wasteful methods, to plans of empire that neglect the poor at the gate. Everything he has done has been aimed at the conservation of energy, the contraction of space, the intensification of culture. Burbank and his tribe represent in the vegetable world, Edison in the mechanical. Not only has he developed distinctly new species, but he has elucidated the intensive art of getting $1200 out of an electrical acre instead of $12--a manured market-garden inside London and a ten-bushel exhausted wheat farm outside Lawrence, Kansas, being the antipodes of productivity--yet very far short of exemplifying the difference of electrical yield between an acre of territory in Edison's "first New York district" and an acre in some small town.

Edison's lighting work furnished an excellent basis--in fact, the only one--for the development of the alternating current now so generally employed in central-station work in America; and in the McGraw Electrical Directory of April, 1909, no fewer than 4164 stations out of 5780 reported its use. When the alternating current was introduced for practical purposes it was not needed for arc lighting, the circuit for which, from a single dynamo, would often be twenty or thirty miles in length, its current having a pressure of not less than five or six thousand volts. For some years it was not found feasible to operate motors on alternating-current circuits, and that reason was often urged against it seriously. It could not be used for electroplating or deposition, nor could it charge storage batteries, all of which are easily within the ability of the direct current. But when it came to be a question of lighting a scattered suburb, a group of dwellings on the outskirts, a remote country residence or a farm-house, the alternating current, in all elements save its danger, was and is ideal. Its thin wires can be carried cheaply over vast areas, and at each local point of consumption the transformer of size exactly proportioned to its local task takes the high-voltage transmission current and lowers its potential at a ratio of 20 or 40 to 1, for use in distribution and consumption circuits. This evolution has been quite distinct, with its own inventors like Gaulard and Gibbs and Stanley, but came subsequent to the work of supplying small, dense areas of population; the art thus growing from within, and using each new gain as a means for further achievement.

Nor was the effect of such great advances as those made by Edison limited to the electrical field. Every department of mechanics was stimulated and benefited to an extraordinary degree. Copper for the circuits was more highly refined than ever before to secure the best conductivity, and purity was insisted on in every kind of insulation. Edison was intolerant of sham and shoddy, and nothing would satisfy him that could not stand cross-examination by microscope, test-tube, and galvanometer. It was, perhaps, the steam-engine on which the deepest imprint for good was made, referred to already in the remarks of Mr. F. J. Sprague in the preceding chapter, but best illustrated in the perfection of the modern high-speed engine of the Armington & Sims type. Unless he could secure an engine of smoother running and more exactly governed and regulated than those available for his dynamo and lamp, Edison realized that he would find it almost impossible to give a steady light. He did not want his customers to count the heart-beats of the engine in the flicker of the lamp. Not a single engine was even within gunshot of the standard thus set up, but the emergency called forth its man in Gardiner C. Sims, a talented draughtsman and designer who had been engaged in locomotive construction and in the engineering department of the United States Navy. He may be quoted as to what happened: "The deep interest, financial and moral, and friendly backing I received from Mr. Edison, together with valuable suggestions, enabled me to bring out the engine; as I was quite alone in the world--poor--I had found a friend who knew what he wanted and explained it clearly. Mr. Edison was a leader far ahead of the time. He compelled the design of the successful engine.

"Our first engine compelled the inventing and making of a suitable engine indicator to indicate it--the Tabor. He obtained the desired speed and load with a friction brake; also regulator of speed; but waited for an indicator to verify it. Then again there was no known way to lubricate an engine for continuous running, and Mr. Edison informed me that as a marine engine started before the ship left New York and continued running until it reached its home port, so an engine for his purposes must produce light at all times. That was a poser to me, for a five-hours' run was about all that had been required up to that time.

"A day or two later Mr. Edison inquired: 'How far is it from here to Lawrence; it is a long walk, isn't it?' 'Yes, rather.' He said: 'Of course you will understand I meant without oil.' To say I was deeply perplexed does not express my feelings. We were at the machine works, Goerck Street. I started for the oil-room, when, about entering, I saw a small funnel lying on the floor. It had been stepped on and flattened. I took it up, and it had solved the engine-oiling problem--and my walk to Lawrence like a tramp actor's was off! The eccentric strap had a round glass oil-cup with a brass base that screwed into the strap. I took it off, and making a sketch, went to Dave Cunningham, having the funnel in my hand to illustrate what I wanted made. I requested him to make a sheet-brass oil-cup and solder it to the base I had. He did so. I then had a standard made to hold another oil-cup, so as to see and regulate the drop-feed. On this combination I obtained a patent which is now universally used."

It is needless to say that in due course the engine builders of the United States developed a variety of excellent prime movers for electric-light and power plants, and were grateful to the art from which such a stimulus came to their industry; but for many years one never saw an Edison installation without expecting to find one or more Armington & Sims high-speed engines part of it. Though the type has gone out of existence, like so many other things that are useful in their day and generation, it was once a very vital part of the art, and one more illustration of that intimate manner in which the advances in different fields of progress interact and co-operate.

Edison had installed his historic first great central-station system in New York on the multiple arc system covered by his feeder and main invention, which resulted in a notable saving in the cost of conductors as against a straight two-wire system throughout of the "tree" kind. He soon foresaw that still greater economy would be necessary for commercial success not alone for the larger territory opening, but for the compact districts of large cities. Being firmly convinced that there was a way out, he pushed aside a mass of other work, and settled down to this problem, with the result that on November 20, 1882, only two months after current had been sent out from Pearl Street, he executed an application for a patent covering what is now known as the "three-wire system." It has been universally recognized as one of the most valuable inventions in the history of the lighting art. [13] Its use resulted in a saving of over 60 per cent. of copper in conductors, figured on the most favorable basis previously known, inclusive of those calculated under his own feeder and main system. Such economy of outlay being effected in one of the heaviest items of expense in central-station construction, it was now made possible to establish plants in towns where the large investment would otherwise have been quite prohibitive. The invention is in universal use today, alike for direct and for alternating current, and as well in the equipment of large buildings as in the distribution system of the most extensive central-station networks. One cannot imagine the art without it.

[Footnote 13: For technical description and illustration of

this invention, see Appendix.]

The strong position held by the Edison system, under the strenuous competition that was already springing up, was enormously improved by the introduction of the three-wire system; and it gave an immediate impetus to incandescent lighting. Desiring to put this new system into practical use promptly, and receiving applications for licenses from all over the country, Edison selected Brockton, Massachusetts, and Sunbury, Pennsylvania, as the two towns for the trial. Of these two Brockton required the larger plant, but with the conductors placed underground. It was the first to complete its arrangements and close its contract. Mr. Henry Villard, it will be remembered, had married the daughter of Garrison, the famous abolitionist, and it was through his relationship with the Garrison family that Brockton came to have the honor of exemplifying so soon the principles of an entirely new art. Sunbury, however, was a much smaller installation, employed overhead conductors, and hence was the first to "cross the tape." It was specially suited for a trial plant also, in the early days when a yield of six or eight lamps to the horse-power was considered subject for congratulation. The town being situated in the coal region of Pennsylvania, good coal could then be obtained there at seventy-five cents a ton.

The Sunbury generating plant consisted of an Armington & Sims engine driving two small Edison dynamos having a total capacity of about four hundred lamps of 16 c.p. The indicating instruments were of the crudest construction, consisting of two voltmeters connected by "pressure wires" to the centre of electrical distribution. One ammeter, for measuring the quantity of current output, was interpolated in the "neutral bus" or third-wire return circuit to indicate when the load on the two machines was out of balance. The circuits were opened and closed by means of about half a dozen roughly made plug-switches. [14] The "bus-bars" to receive the current from the dynamos were made of No. 000 copper line wire, straightened out and fastened to the wooden sheathing of the station by iron staples without any presence to insulation. Commenting upon this Mr. W. S. Andrews, detailed from the central staff, says: "The interior winding of the Sunbury station, including the running of two three-wire feeders the entire length of the building from back to front, the wiring up of the dynamos and switchboard and all instruments, together with bus-bars, etc.--in fact, all labor and material used in the electrical wiring installation--amounted to the sum of $90. I received a rather sharp letter from the New York office expostulating for this EXTRAVAGANT EXPENDITURE, and stating that great economy must be observed in future!" The street conductors were of the overhead pole-line construction, and were installed by the construction company that had been organized by Edison to build and equip central stations. A special type of street pole had been devised by him for the three-wire system.

[Footnote 14: By reason of the experience gained at this station through the use of these crude plug-switches, Mr. Edison started a competition among a few of his assistants to devise something better. The result was the invention of a "breakdown" switch by Mr. W. S. Andrews, which was accepted by Mr. Edison as the best of the devices suggested, and was developed and used for a great many years afterward.]

Supplementing the story of Mr. Andrews is that of Lieut. F. J. Sprague, who also gives a curious glimpse of the glorious uncertainties and vicissitudes of that formative period. Mr. Sprague served on the jury at the Crystal Palace Exhibition with Darwin's son--the present Sir Horace--and after the tests were ended left the Navy and entered Edison's service at the suggestion of Mr. E. H. Johnson, who was Edison's shrewd recruiting sergeant in those days: "I resigned sooner than Johnson expected, and he had me on his hands. Meanwhile he had called upon me to make a report of the three-wire system, known in England as the Hopkinson, both Dr. John Hopkinson and Mr. Edison being independent inventors at practically the same time. I reported on that, left London, and landed in New York on the day of the opening of the Brooklyn Bridge in 1883--May 24--with a year's leave of absence.

"I reported at the office of Mr. Edison on Fifth Avenue and told him I had seen Johnson. He looked me over and said: 'What did he promise you?' I replied: 'Twenty-five hundred dollars a year.' He did not say much, but looked it. About that time Mr. Andrews and I came together. On July 2d of that year we were ordered to Sunbury, and to be ready to start the station on the fourth. The electrical work had to be done in forty-eight hours! Having travelled around the world, I had cultivated an indifference to any special difficulties of that kind. Mr. Andrews and I worked in collaboration until the night of the third. I think he was perhaps more appreciative than I was of the discipline of the Edison Construction Department, and thought it would be well for us to wait until the morning of the fourth before we started up. I said we were sent over to get going, and insisted on starting up on the night of the third. We had an Armington & Sims engine with sight-feed oiler. I had never seen one, and did not know how it worked, with the result that we soon burned up the babbitt metal in the bearings and spent a good part of the night getting them in order. The next day Mr. Edison, Mr. Insull, and the chief engineer of the construction department appeared on the scene and wanted to know what had happened. They found an engine somewhat loose in the bearings, and there followed remarks which would not look well in print. Andrews skipped from under; he obeyed orders; I did not. But the plant ran, and it was the first three-wire station in this country."

Seen from yet another angle, the worries of this early work were not merely those of the men on the "firing line." Mr. Insull, in speaking of this period, says: "When it was found difficult to push the central-station business owing to the lack of confidence in its financial success, Edison decided to go into the business of promoting and constructing central-station plants, and he formed what was known as the Thomas A. Edison Construction Department, which he put me in charge of. The organization was crude, the steam-engineering talent poor, and owing to the impossibility of getting any considerable capital subscribed, the plants were put in as cheaply as possible. I believe that this construction department was unkindly named the 'Destruction

Department.' It served its purpose; never made any money; and I had the unpleasant task of presiding at its obsequies."

On July 4th the Sunbury plant was put into commercial operation by Edison, and he remained a week studying its conditions and watching for any unforeseen difficulty that might arise. Nothing happened, however, to interfere with the successful running of the station, and for twenty years thereafter the same two dynamos continued to furnish light in Sunbury. They were later used as reserve machines, and finally, with the engine, retired from service as part of the "Collection of Edisonia"; but they remain in practically as good condition as when installed in 1883.

Sunbury was also provided with the first electro-chemical meters used in the United States outside New York City, so that it served also to accentuate electrical practice in a most vital respect--namely, the measurement of the electrical energy supplied to customers. At this time and long after, all arc lighting was done on a "flat rate" basis. The arc lamp installed outside a customer's premises, or in a circuit for public street lighting, burned so many hours nightly, so many nights in the month; and was paid for at that rate, subject to rebate for hours when the lamp might be out through accident. The early arc lamps were rated to require 9 to 10 amperes of current, at 45 volts pressure each, receiving which they were estimated to give 2000 c.p., which was arrived at by adding together the light found at four different positions, so that in reality the actual light was about 500 c.p. Few of these data were ever actually used, however; and it was all more or less a matter of guesswork, although the central-station manager, aiming to give good service, would naturally see that the dynamos were so operated as to maintain as steadily as possible the normal potential and current. The same loose methods applied to the early attempts to use electric motors on arc-lighting circuits, and contracts were made based on the size of the motor, the width of the connecting belt, or the amount of power the customer thought he used--never on the measurement of the electrical energy furnished him.

Here again Edison laid the foundation of standard practice. It is true that even down to the present time the flat rate is applied to a great deal of incandescent lighting, each lamp being charged for individually according to its probable consumption during each month. This may answer, perhaps, in a small place where the manager can gauge pretty closely from actual observation what each customer does; but even then there are elements of risk and waste; and obviously in a large city such a method would soon be likely to result in financial disaster to the plant. Edison held that the electricity sold must be measured just like gas or water, and he proceeded to develop a meter. There was infinite scepticism around him on the subject, and while other inventors were also giving the subject their thought, the public took it for granted that anything so utterly intangible as electricity, that could not be seen or weighed, and only gave secondary evidence of itself at the exact point of use, could not be brought to accurate registration. The general attitude of doubt was exemplified by the incident in Mr. J. P. Morgan's office, noted in the last chapter. Edison, however, had satisfied himself that there were various ways of accomplishing the task, and had determined that the current should be measured on the premises of every consumer. His electrolytic meter was very successful, and was of widespread use in America and in Europe until the perfection of mechanical meters by Elihu Thomson and others brought that type into general acceptance. Hence the Edison electrolytic meter is no longer used, despite its excellent qualities. Houston & Kennelly in their Electricity in Everyday Life sum the matter up as follows: "The Edison chemical meter is capable of giving fair measurements of the amount of current passing. By reason, however, of dissatisfaction caused from the inability of customers to read the indications of the meter, it has in later years, to a great extent, been replaced by registering meters that can be read by the customer."

The principle employed in the Edison electrolytic meter is that which exemplifies the power of electricity to decompose a chemical substance. In other words it is a deposition bath, consisting of a glass cell in which two plates of chemically pure zinc are dipped in a solution of zinc sulphate. When the lights or motors in the circuit are turned on, and a certain definite small portion of the current is diverted to flow through the meter, from the positive plate to the negative plate, the latter increases in weight by receiving a deposit of metallic zinc; the positive plate meantime losing in weight by the metal thus carried away from it. This difference in weight is a very exact measure of the quantity of electricity, or number of ampere-hours, that have, so to speak, passed through the cell, and hence of the whole consumption in the circuit. The amount thus due from the customer is ascertained by removing the cell, washing and drying the plates, and weighing them in a chemical balance. Associated with this simple form of apparatus were various ingenious details and refinements to secure regularity of operation, freedom from inaccuracy, and immunity from such tampering as would permit theft of current or damage. As the freezing of the zinc sulphate solution in cold weather would check its operation, Edison introduced, for example, into the meter an incandescent lamp and a thermostat so arranged that when the temperature fell to a certain point, or rose above another point, it was cut in or out; and in this manner the meter could be kept from freezing. The standard Edison meter practice was to remove the cells once a month to the meter-room of the central-station company for examination, another set being substituted. The meter was cheap to manufacture and install, and not at all liable to get out of order.

In December, 1888, Mr. W. J. Jenks read an interesting paper before the American Institute of Electrical Engineers on the six years of practical experience had up to that time with the meter, then more generally in use than any other. It appears from the paper that twenty-three Edison stations were then equipped with 5187 meters, which were relied upon for billing the monthly current consumption of 87,856 lamps and 350 motors of 1000 horse-power total. This represented about 75 per cent. of the entire lamp capacity of the stations. There was an average cost per lamp for meter operation of twenty-two cents a year, and each meter took care of an average of seventeen lamps. It is worthy of note, as to the promptness with which the Edison stations became paying properties, that four of the metered stations were earning upward of 15 per cent. on their capital stock; three others between 8 and 10 per cent.; eight between 5 and 8 per cent.; the others having been in operation too short a time to show definite results, although they also went quickly to a dividend basis. Reports made in the discussion at the meeting by engineers showed the simplicity and success of the meter. Mr. C. L. Edgar, of the Boston Edison system, stated that he had 800 of the meters in service cared for by two men and three boys, the latter employed in collecting the meter cells; the total cost being perhaps $2500 a year. Mr. J. W. Lieb wrote from Milan, Italy, that he had in use on the Edison system there 360 meters ranging from 350 ampere-hours per month up to 30,000.

In this connection it should be mentioned that the Association of Edison Illuminating Companies in the same year adopted resolutions unanimously to the effect that the Edison meter was accurate, and that its use was not expensive for stations above one thousand lights; and that the best financial results were invariably secured in a station selling current by meter. Before the same association, at its meeting in September, 1898, at Sault Ste. Marie, Mr. C. S. Shepard read a paper on the meter practice of the New York Edison Company, giving data as to the large number of Edison meters in use and the transition to other types, of which to-day the company has several on its circuits: "Until October, 1896, the New York Edison Company metered its current in consumer's premises exclusively by the old-style chemical meters, of which there were connected on that date 8109. It was then determined to purchase no more." Mr. Shepard went on to state that the chemical meters were gradually displaced, and that on September 1, 1898, there were on the system 5619 mechanical and 4874 chemical. The meter continued in general service during 1899, and probably up to the close of the century.

Mr. Andrews relates a rather humorous meter story of those early days: "The meter man at Sunbury was a firm and enthusiastic believer in the correctness of the Edison meter, having personally verified its reading many times by actual comparison of lamp-hours. One day, on making out a customer's bill, his confidence received a severe shock, for the meter reading showed a consumption calling for a charge of over $200, whereas he knew that the light actually used should not cost more than one-quarter of that amount. He weighed and reweighed the meter plates, and pursued every line of investigation imaginable, but all in vain. He felt he was up against it, and that perhaps another kind of a job would suit him better. Once again he went to the customer's meter to look around, when a small piece of thick wire on the floor caught his eye. The problem was solved. He suddenly remembered that after weighing the plates he went and put them in the customer's meter; but the wire attached to one of the plates was too long to go in the meter, and he had cut it off. He picked up the piece of wire, took it to the station, weighed it carefully, and found that it accounted for about $150 worth of electricity, which was the amount of the difference."

Edison himself is, however, the best repertory of stories when it comes to the difficulties of that early period, in connection with metering the current and charging for it. He may be quoted at length as follows: "When we started the station at Pearl Street, in September, 1882, we were not very commercial. We put many customers on, but did not make out many bills. We were more interested in the technical condition of the station than in the commercial part. We had meters in which there were two bottles of liquid. To prevent these electrolytes from freezing we had in each meter a strip of metal. When it got very cold the metal would contract and close a circuit, and throw a lamp into circuit inside the meter. The heat from this lamp would prevent the liquid from freezing, so that the meter could go on doing its duty. The first cold day after starting the station, people began to come in from their offices, especially down in Front Street and Water Street, saying the meter was on fire. We received numerous telephone messages about it. Some had poured water on it, and others said: 'Send a man right up to put it out.'

"After the station had been running several months and was technically a success, we began to look after the financial part. We started to collect some bills; but we found that our books were kept badly, and that the person in charge, who was no business man, had neglected that part of it. In fact, he did not know anything about the station, anyway. So I got the directors to permit me to hire a man to run the station. This was Mr. Chinnock, who was then superintendent of the Metropolitan Telephone Company of New York. I knew Chinnock to be square and of good business ability, and induced him to leave his job. I made him a personal guarantee, that if he would take hold of the station and put it on a commercial basis, and pay 5 per cent. on $600,000, I would give him $10,000 out of my own pocket. He took hold, performed the feat, and I paid him the $10,000. I might remark in this connection that years afterward I applied to the Edison Electric Light Company asking them if they would not like to pay me this money, as it was spent when I was very hard up and made the company a success, and was the foundation of their present prosperity. They said they 'were sorry'--that is, 'Wall Street sorry'--and refused to pay it. This shows what a nice, genial, generous lot of people they have over in Wall Street.

"Chinnock had a great deal of trouble getting the customers straightened out. I remember one man who had a saloon on Nassau Street. He had had his lights burning for two or three months. It was in June, and Chinnock put in a bill for $20; July for $20; August about $28; September about $35. Of course the nights were getting longer. October about $40; November about $45. Then the man called Chinnock up. He said: 'I want to see you about my electric-light bill.' Chinnock went up to see him. He said: 'Are you the manager of this electric-light plant?' Chinnock said: 'I have the honor.' 'Well,' he said, my bill has gone from $20 up to $28, $35, $45. I want you to understand, young fellow, that my limit is $60.'

"After Chinnock had had all this trouble due to the incompetency of the previous superintendent, a man came in and said to him: 'Did Mr. Blank have charge of this station?' 'Yes.' 'Did he know anything about running a station like this?' Chinnock said: 'Does he KNOW anything about running a station like this? No, sir. He doesn't even suspect anything.'

"One day Chinnock came to me and said: 'I have a new customer.' I said: 'What is it?' He said: 'I have a fellow who is going to take two hundred and fifty lights.' I said: 'What for?' 'He has a place down here in a top loft, and has got two hundred and fifty barrels of "rotgut" whiskey.

He puts a light down in the barrel and lights it up, and it ages the whiskey.' I met Chinnock several weeks after, and said: 'How is the whiskey man getting along?' 'It's all right; he is paying his bill. It fixes the whiskey and takes the shudder right out of it.' Somebody went and took out a patent on this idea later.

"In the second year we put the Stock Exchange on the circuits of the station, but were very fearful that there would be a combination of heavy demand and a dark day, and that there would be an overloaded station. We had an index like a steam-gauge, called an ampere-meter, to indicate the amount of current going out. I was up at 65 Fifth Avenue one afternoon. A sudden black cloud came up, and I telephoned to Chinnock and asked him about the load. He said: 'We are up to the muzzle, and everything is running all right.' By-and-by it became so thick we could not see across the street. I telephoned again, and felt something would happen, but fortunately it did not. I said to Chinnock: 'How is it now?' He replied: 'Everything is red-hot, and the ampere-meter has made seventeen revolutions.'"

In 1883 no such fittings as "fixture insulators" were known. It was the common practice to twine the electric wires around the disused gas-fixtures, fasten them with tape or string, and connect them to lamp-sockets screwed into attachments under the gas-burners--elaborated later into what was known as the "combination fixture." As a result it was no uncommon thing to see bright sparks snapping between the chandelier and the lighting wires during a sharp thunder-storm. A startling manifestation of this kind happened at Sunbury, when the vivid display drove nervous guests of the hotel out into the street, and the providential storm led Mr. Luther Stieringer to invent the "insulating joint." This separated the two lighting systems thoroughly, went into immediate service, and is universally used to-day.

Returning to the more specific subject of pioneer plants of importance, that at Brockton must be considered for a moment, chiefly for the reason that the city was the first in the world to possess an Edison station distributing current through an underground three-wire network of conductors--the essentially modern contemporaneous practice, standard twenty-five years later. It was proposed to employ pole-line construction with overhead wires, and a party of Edison engineers drove about the town in an open barouche with a blue-print of the circuits and streets spread out on their knees, to determine how much tree-trimming would be necessary. When they came to some heavily shaded spots, the fine trees were marked "T" to indicate that the work in getting through them would be "tough." Where the trees were sparse and the foliage was thin, the same cheerful band of vandals marked the spots "E" to indicate that there it would be "easy" to run the wires. In those days public opinion was not so alive as now to the desirability of preserving shade-trees, and of enhancing the beauty of a city instead of destroying it. Brockton had a good deal of pride in its fine trees, and a strong sentiment was very soon aroused against the mutilation proposed so thoughtlessly. The investors in the enterprise were ready and anxious to meet the extra cost of putting the wires underground. Edison's own wishes were altogether for the use of the methods he had so carefully devised; and hence that bustling home of shoe manufacture was spared this infliction of more overhead wires.

The station equipment at Brockton consisted at first of three dynamos, one of which was so arranged as to supply both sides of the system during light loads by a breakdown switch connection. This arrangement interfered with correct meter registration, as the meters on one side of the system registered backward during the hours in which the combination was employed. Hence, after supplying an all-night customer whose lamps were on one side of the circuits, the company might be found to owe him some thing substantial in the morning. Soon after the station went into operation this ingenious plan was changed, and the third dynamo was replaced by two others. The Edison construction department took entire charge of the installation of the plant, and the formal opening was attended on October 1, 1883, by Mr. Edison, who then remained a week in ceaseless study and consultation over the conditions developed by this initial three-wire underground plant. Some idea of the confidence inspired by the fame of Edison at this period is shown by the fact that the first theatre ever lighted from a central station by incandescent lamps was designed this year, and opened in 1884 at Brockton with an equipment of three hundred lamps. The theatre was never piped for gas! It was also from the Brockton central station that current was first supplied to a fire-engine house--another display of remarkably early belief in the trustworthiness of the service, under conditions where continuity of lighting was vital. The building was equipped in such a manner that the striking of the fire-alarm would light every lamp in the house automatically and liberate the horses. It was at this central station that Lieutenant Sprague began his historic work on the electric motor; and here that another distinguished engineer and inventor, Mr. H. Ward Leonard, installed the meters and became meter man, in order that he might study in every intimate detail the improvements and refinements necessary in that branch of the industry.

The authors are indebted for these facts and some other data embodied in this book to Mr. W. J. Jenks, who as manager of this plant here made his debut in the Edison ranks. He had been connected with local telephone interests, but resigned to take active charge of this plant, imbibing quickly the traditional Edison spirit, working hard all day and sleeping in the station at night on a cot brought there for that purpose. It was a time of uninterrupted watchfulness. The difficulty of obtaining engineers in those days to run the high-speed engines (three hundred and fifty revolutions per minute) is well illustrated by an amusing incident in the very early history of the station. A locomotive engineer had been engaged, as it was supposed he would not be afraid of anything. One evening there came a sudden flash of fire and a spluttering, sizzling noise. There had been a short-circuit on the copper mains in the station. The fireman hid behind the boiler and the engineer jumped out of the window. Mr. Sprague realized the trouble, quickly threw off the current and stopped the engine.

Mr. Jenks relates another humorous incident in connection with this plant: "One night I heard a knock at the office door, and on opening it saw two well-dressed ladies, who asked if they might be shown through. I invited them in, taking them first to the boiler-room, where I showed them the coal-pile, explaining that this was used to generate steam in the boiler. We then went to the dynamo-room, where I pointed out the machines converting the steam-power into electricity, appearing later in the form of light in the lamps. After that they were shown the meters by which the consumption of current was measured. They appeared to be interested, and I proceeded to enter upon a comparison of coal made into gas or burned under a boiler to be converted into electricity. The ladies thanked me effusively and brought their visit to a close. As they were about to go through the door, one of them turned to me and said: 'We have enjoyed this visit very much, but there is one question we would like to ask: What is it that you make here?'"

The Brockton station was for a long time a show plant of the Edison company, and had many distinguished visitors, among them being Prof. Elihu Thomson, who was present at the opening, and Sir W. H. Preece, of London. The engineering methods pursued formed the basis of similar installations in Lawrence, Massachusetts, in November, 1883; in Fall River, Massachusetts, in December, 1883; and in Newburgh, New York, the following spring.

Another important plant of this period deserves special mention, as it was the pioneer in the lighting of large spaces by incandescent lamps. This installation of five thousand lamps on the three-wire system was made to illuminate the buildings at the Louisville, Kentucky, Exposition in 1883, and, owing to the careful surveys, calculations, and preparations of H. M. Byllesby and the late Luther Stieringer, was completed and in operation within six weeks after the placing of the order. The Jury of Awards, in presenting four medals to the Edison company, took occasion to pay a high compliment to the efficiency of the system. It has been thought by many that the magnificent success of this plant did more to stimulate the growth of the incandescent lighting business than any other event in the history of the Edison company. It was literally the beginning of the electrical illumination of American Expositions, carried later to such splendid displays as those of the Chicago World's Fair in 1893, Buffalo in 1901, and St. Louis in 1904.

Thus the art was set going in the United States under many difficulties, but with every sign of coming triumph. Reference has already been made to the work abroad in Paris and London. The first permanent Edison station in Europe was that at Milan, Italy, for which the order was given as early as May, 1882, by an enterprising syndicate. Less than a year later, March 3, 1883, the installation was ready and was put in operation, the Theatre Santa Radegonda having been pulled down and a new central-station building erected in its place--probably the first edifice constructed in Europe for the specific purpose of incandescent lighting. Here "Jumbos" were installed from time to time, until at last there were no fewer than ten of them; and current was furnished to customers with a total of nearly ten thousand lamps connected to the mains. This pioneer system was operated continuously until February 9, 1900, or for a period of about seventeen years, when the sturdy old machines, still in excellent condition, were put out of service, so that a larger plant could be installed to meet the demand. This new plant takes high-tension polyphase current from a water-power thirty or forty miles away at Paderno, on the river Adda, flowing from the Apennines; but delivers low-tension direct current for distribution to the regular

Edison three-wire system throughout Milan.

About the same time that southern Europe was thus opened up to the new system, South America came into line, and the first Edison central station there was installed at Santiago, Chile, in the summer of 1883, under the supervision of Mr. W. N. Stewart. This was the result of the success obtained with small isolated plants, leading to the formation of an Edison company. It can readily be conceived that at such an extreme distance from the source of supply of apparatus the plant was subject to many peculiar difficulties from the outset, of which Mr. Stewart speaks as follows: "I made an exhibition of the 'Jumbo' in the theatre at Santiago, and on the first evening, when it was filled with the aristocracy of the city, I discovered to my horror that the binding wire around the armature was slowly stripping off and going to pieces. We had no means of boring out the field magnets, and we cut grooves in them. I think the machine is still running (1907). The station went into operation soon after with an equipment of eight Edison 'K' dynamos with certain conditions inimical to efficiency, but which have not hindered the splendid expansion of the local system. With those eight dynamos we had four belts between each engine and the dynamo. The steam pressure was limited to seventy-five pounds per square inch. We had two-wire underground feeders, sent without any plans or specifications for their installation. The station had neither voltmeter nor ammeter. The current pressure was regulated by a galvanometer. We were using coal costing $12 a ton, and were paid for our light in currency worth fifty cents on the dollar. The only thing I can be proud of in connection with the plant is the fact that I did not design it, that once in a while we made out to pay its operating expenses, and that occasionally we could run it for three months without a total breakdown."

It was not until 1885 that the first Edison station in Germany was established; but the art was still very young, and the plant represented pioneer lighting practice in the Empire. The station at Berlin comprised five boilers, and six vertical steam-engines driving by belts twelve Edison dynamos, each of about fifty-five horse-power capacity. A model of this station is preserved in the Deutschen Museum at Munich. In the bulletin of the Berlin Electricity Works for May, 1908, it is said with regard to the events that led up to the creation of the system, as noted already at the Rathenau celebration: "The year 1881 was a mile-stone in the history of the Allgemeine Elektricitaets Gesellschaft. The International Electrical Exposition at Paris was intended to place before the eyes of the civilized world the achievements of the century. Among the exhibits of that Exposition was the Edison system of incandescent lighting. IT BECAME THE BASIS OF MODERN HEAVY CURRENT TECHNICS." The last phrase is italicized as being a happy and authoritative description, as well as a tribute.

This chapter would not be complete if it failed to include some reference to a few of the earlier isolated plants of a historic character. Note has already been made of the first Edison plants afloat on the Jeannette and Columbia, and the first commercial plant in the New York lithographic establishment. The first mill plant was placed in the woollen factory of James Harrison at Newburgh, New York, about September 15, 1881. A year later, Mr. Harrison wrote with some pride: "I believe my mill was the first lighted with your electric light, and therefore may be called No. 1. Besides being job No. 1 it is a No. 1 job, and a No. 1 light, being better and cheaper than gas and absolutely safe as to fire." The first steam-yacht lighted by incandescent lamps was James Gordon Bennett's Namouna, equipped early in 1882 with a plant for one hundred and twenty lamps of eight candlepower, which remained in use there many years afterward.

The first Edison plant in a hotel was started in October, 1881, at the Blue Mountain House in the Adirondacks, and consisted of two "Z" dynamos with a complement of eight and sixteen candle lamps. The hotel is situated at an elevation of thirty-five hundred feet above the sea, and was at that time forty miles from the railroad. The machinery was taken up in pieces on the backs of mules from the foot of the mountain. The boilers were fired by wood, as the economical transportation of coal was a physical impossibility. For a six-hour run of the plant one-quarter of a cord of wood was required, at a cost of twenty-five cents per cord.

The first theatre in the United States to be lighted by an Edison isolated plant was the Bijou Theatre, Boston. The installation of boilers, engines, dynamos, wiring, switches, fixtures, three stage regulators, and six hundred and fifty lamps, was completed in eleven days after receipt of the order, and the plant was successfully operated at the opening of the theatre, on December 12, 1882.

The first plant to be placed on a United States steamship was the one consisting of an Edison "Z" dynamo and one hundred and twenty eight-candle lamps installed on the Fish Commission's steamer Albatross in 1883. The most interesting feature of this installation was the employment of special deep-sea lamps, supplied with current through a cable nine hundred and forty feet in length, for the purpose of alluring fish. By means of the brilliancy of the lamps marine animals in the lower depths were attracted and then easily ensnared.

CHAPTER XVIII

THE ELECTRIC RAILWAY

EDISON had no sooner designed his dynamo in 1879 than he adopted the same form of machine for use as a motor. The two are shown in the Scientific American of October 18, 1879, and are alike, except that the dynamo is vertical and the motor lies in a horizontal position, the article remarking: "Its construction differs but slightly from the electric generator." This was but an evidence of his early appreciation of the importance of electricity as a motive power; but it will probably surprise many people to know that he was the inventor of an electric motor before he perfected his incandescent lamp. His interest in the subject went back to his connection with General Lefferts in the days of the evolution of the stock ticker. While Edison was carrying on his shop at Newark, New Jersey, there was considerable excitement in electrical circles over the Payne motor, in regard to the alleged performance of which Governor Cornell of New York and other wealthy capitalists were quite enthusiastic. Payne had a shop in Newark, and in one small room was the motor, weighing perhaps six hundred pounds. It was of circular form, incased in iron, with the ends of several small magnets sticking through the floor. A pulley and belt, connected to a circular saw larger than the motor, permitted large logs of oak timber to be sawed with ease with the use of two small cells of battery. Edison's friend, General Lefferts, had become excited and was determined to invest a large sum of money in the motor company, but knowing Edison's intimate familiarity with all electrical subjects he was wise enough to ask his young expert to go and see the motor with him. At an appointed hour Edison went to the office of the motor company and found there the venerable Professor Morse, Governor Cornell, General Lefferts, and many others who had been invited to witness a performance of the motor. They all proceeded to the room where the motor was at work. Payne put a wire in the binding-post of the battery, the motor started, and an assistant began sawing a heavy oak log. It worked beautifully, and so great was the power developed, apparently, from the small battery, that Morse exclaimed: "I am thankful that I have lived to see this day." But Edison kept a close watch on the motor. The results were so foreign to his experience that he knew there was a trick in it. He soon discovered it. While holding his hand on the frame of the motor he noticed a tremble coincident with the exhaust of an engine across the alleyway, and he then knew that the power came from the engine by a belt under the floor, shifted on and off by a magnet, the other magnets being a blind. He whispered to the General to put his hand on the frame of the motor, watch the exhaust, and note the coincident tremor. The General did so, and in about fifteen seconds he said: "Well, Edison, I must go now. This thing is a fraud." And thus he saved his money, although others not so shrewdly advised were easily persuaded to invest by such a demonstration.

A few years later, in 1878, Edison went to Wyoming with a group of astronomers, to test his tasimeter during an eclipse of the sun, and saw the land white to harvest. He noticed the long hauls to market or elevator that the farmers had to make with their loads of grain at great expense, and conceived the idea that as ordinary steam-railroad service was too costly, light electric railways might be constructed that could be operated automatically over simple tracks, the propelling motors being controlled at various points. Cheap to build and cheap to maintain, such roads would be a great boon to the newer farming regions of the West, where the highways were still of the crudest character, and where transportation was the gravest difficulty with which the settlers had to contend. The plan seems to have haunted him, and he had no sooner worked out a generator and motor that owing to their low internal resistance could be operated efficiently, than he turned his hand to the practical trial of such a railroad, applicable to both the haulage of freight and the transportation of passengers. Early in 1880, when the tremendous rush of work involved in the invention of the incandescent lamp intermitted a little, he began the construction of a stretch of track close to the Menlo Park laboratory, and at the same time built an electric locomotive to operate over it.

This is a fitting stage at which to review briefly what had been done in electric traction up to that date. There was absolutely no art, but there had been a number of sporadic and very interesting experiments made. The honor of the first attempt of any kind appears to rest with this country and with Thomas Davenport, a self-trained blacksmith, of Brandon, Vermont, who made a small model of a circular electric railway and cars in 1834, and exhibited it the following year in Springfield, Boston, and other cities. Of course he depended upon batteries for current, but the fundamental idea was embodied of using the track for the circuit, one rail being positive and the other negative, and the motor being placed across or between them in multiple arc to receive the current. Such are also practically the methods of to-day. The little model was in good preservation up to the year 1900, when, being shipped to the Paris Exposition, it was lost, the steamer that carried it foundering in mid-ocean. The very broad patent taken out by this simple mechanic, so far ahead of his times, was the first one issued in America for an electric motor. Davenport was also the first man to apply electric power to the printing-press, in 1840. In his traction work he had a close second in Robert Davidson, of Aberdeen, Scotland, who in 1839 operated both a lathe and a small locomotive with the motor he had invented. His was the credit of first actually carrying passengers--two at a time, over a rough plank road--while it is said that his was the first motor to be tried on real tracks, those of the Edinburgh-Glasgow road, making a speed of four miles an hour.

The curse of this work and of all that succeeded it for a score of years was the necessity of depending upon chemical batteries for current, the machine usually being self-contained and hauling the batteries along with itself, as in the case of the famous Page experiments in April, 1851, when a speed of nineteen miles an hour was attained on the line of the Washington & Baltimore road. To this unfruitful period belonged, however, the crude idea of taking the current from a stationary source of power by means of an overhead contact, which has found its practical evolution in the modern ubiquitous trolley; although the patent for this, based on his caveat of 1879, was granted several years later than that to Stephen D. Field, for the combination of an electric motor operated by means of a current from a stationary dynamo or source of electricity conducted through the rails. As a matter of fact, in 1856 and again in 1875, George F. Green, a jobbing machinist, of Kalamazoo, Michigan, built small cars and tracks to which current was fed from a distant battery, enough energy being utilized to haul one hundred pounds of freight or one passenger up and down a "road" two hundred feet long. All the work prior to the development of the dynamo as a source of current was sporadic and spasmodic, and cannot be said to have left any trace on the art, though it offered many suggestions as to operative methods.

The close of the same decade of the nineteenth century that saw the electric light brought to perfection, saw also the realization in practice of all the hopes of fifty years as to electric traction. Both utilizations depended upon the supply of current now cheaply obtainable from the dynamo. These arts were indeed twins, feeding at inexhaustible breasts. In 1879, at the Berlin Exhibition, the distinguished firm of Siemens, to whose ingenuity and enterprise electrical development owes so much, installed a road about one-third of a mile in length, over which the locomotive hauled a train of three small cars at a speed of about eight miles an hour, carrying some twenty persons every trip.

Current was fed from a dynamo to the motor through a central third rail, the two outer rails being joined together as the negative or return circuit. Primitive but essentially successful, this little road made a profound impression on the minds of many inventors and engineers, and marked the real beginning of the great new era, which has already seen electricity applied to the operation of main lines of trunk railways. But it is not to be supposed that on the part of the public there was any great amount of faith then discernible; and for some years the pioneers had great difficulty, especially in this country, in raising money for their early modest experiments. Of the general conditions at this moment Frank J. Sprague says in an article in the Century Magazine of July, 1905, on the creation of the new art: "Edison was perhaps nearer the verge of great electric-railway possibilities than any other American. In the face of much adverse criticism he had developed the essentials of the low-internal-resistance dynamo with high-resistance field, and many of the essential features of multiple-arc distribution, and in 1880 he built a small road at his laboratory at Menlo Park."

On May 13th of the year named this interesting road went into operation as the result of hard and hurried work of preparation during the spring months. The first track was about a third of a mile in length, starting from the shops, following a country road, passing around a hill at the rear and curving home, in the general form of the letter "U." The rails were very light. Charles T. Hughes, who went with Edison in 1879, and was in charge of much of the work, states that they were "second" street-car rails, insulated with tar canvas paper and things of that sort--"asphalt." They were spiked down on ordinary sleepers laid upon the natural grade, and the gauge was about three feet six inches. At one point the grade dropped some sixty feet in a distance of three hundred, and the curves were of recklessly short radius. The dynamos supplying current to the road were originally two of the standard size "Z" machines then being made at the laboratory, popularly known throughout the Edison ranks as "Longwaisted Mary Anns," and the circuits from these were carried out to the rails by underground conductors. They were not large--about twelve horse-power each--generating seventy-five amperes of current at one hundred and ten volts, so that not quite twenty-five horse-power of electrical energy was available for propulsion.

The locomotive built while the roadbed was getting ready was a four-wheeled iron truck, an ordinary flat dump-car about six feet long and four feet wide, upon which was mounted a "Z" dynamo used as a motor, so that it had a capacity of about twelve horsepower. This machine was laid on its side, with the armature end coming out at the front of the locomotive, and the motive power was applied to the driving-axle by a cumbersome series of friction pulleys. Each wheel of the locomotive had a metal rim and a centre web of wood or papier-mache, and the current picked up by one set of wheels was carried through contact brushes and a brass hub to the motor; the circuit back to the track, or other rail, being closed through the other wheels in a similar manner. The motor had its field-magnet circuit in permanent connection as a shunt across the rails, protected by a crude bare copper-wire safety-catch. A switch in the armature circuit enabled the motorman to reverse the direction of travel by reversing the current flow through the armature coils.

Things went fairly well for a time on that memorable Thursday afternoon, when all the laboratory force made high holiday and scrambled for foothold on the locomotive for a trip; but the friction gearing was not equal to the sudden strain put upon it during one run and went to pieces. Some years later, also, Daft again tried friction gear in his historical experiments on the Manhattan Elevated road, but the results were attended with no greater success. The next resort of Edison was to belts, the armature shafting belted to a countershaft on the locomotive frame, and the countershaft belted to a pulley on the car-axle. The lever which threw the former friction gear into adjustment was made to operate an idler pulley for tightening the axle-belt. When the motor was started, the armature was brought up to full revolution and then the belt was tightened on the car-axle, compelling motion of the locomotive. But the belts were liable to slip a great deal in the process, and the chafing of the belts charred them badly. If that did not happen, and if the belt was made taut suddenly, the armature burned out--which it did with disconcerting frequency. The next step was to use a number of resistance-boxes in series with the armature, so that the locomotive could start with those in circuit, and then the motorman could bring it up to speed gradually by cutting one box out after the other. To stop the locomotive, the armature circuit was opened by the main switch, stopping the flow of current, and then brakes were applied by long levers. Matters generally and the motors in particular went much better, even if the locomotive was so freely festooned with resistance-boxes all of perceptible weight and occupying much of the limited space. These details show forcibly and typically the painful steps of advance that every inventor in this new field had to make in the effort to reach not alone commercial practicability, but mechanical feasibility. It was all empirical enough; but that was the only way open even to the highest talent.

Smugglers landing laces and silks have been known to wind them around their bodies, as being less ostentatious than carrying them in a trunk. Edison thought his resistance-boxes an equally superfluous display, and therefore ingeniously wound some copper resistance wire around one of the legs of the motor field magnet, where it was out of the way, served as a useful extra field coil in starting up the motor, and dismissed most of the boxes back to the laboratory--a few being retained under the seat for chance emergencies. Like the boxes, this coil was in series with the armature, and subject to plugging in and out at will by the motorman. Thus equipped, the locomotive was found quite satisfactory, and long did yeoman service. It was given three cars to pull, one an open awning-car with two park benches placed back to back; one a flat freight-car, and one box-car dubbed the "Pullman," with which Edison illustrated a system of electric braking. Although work had been begun so early in the year, and the road had been operating since May, it was not until July that Edison executed any application for patents on his "electromagnetic railway engine," or his ingenious braking system. Every inventor knows how largely his fate lies in the hands of a competent and alert patent attorney, in both the preparation and the prosecution of his case; and Mr. Sprague is justified in observing in his Century article: "The paucity of controlling claims obtained in these early patents is remarkable." It is notorious that Edison did not then enjoy the skilful aid in safeguarding his ideas that he commanded later.

The daily newspapers and technical journals lost no time in bringing the road to public attention, and the New York Herald of June 25th was swift to suggest that here was the locomotive that would be "most pleasing to the average New Yorker, whose head has ached with noise, whose eyes have been filled with dust, or whose clothes have been ruined with oil." A couple of days later, the Daily Graphic illustrated and described the road and published a sketch of a one-hundred-horse-power electric locomotive for the use of the Pennsylvania Railroad between Perth Amboy and Rahway. Visitors, of course, were numerous, including many curious, sceptical railroad managers, few if any of whom except Villard could see the slightest use for the new motive power. There is, perhaps, some excuse for such indifference. No men in the world have more new inventions brought to them than railroad managers, and this was the rankest kind of novelty. It was not, indeed, until a year later, in May, 1881, that the first regular road collecting fares was put in operation--a little stretch of one and a half miles from Berlin to Lichterfelde, with one miniature motorcar. Edison was in reality doing some heavy electric-railway engineering, his apparatus full of ideas, suggestions, prophecies; but to the operators of long trunk lines it must have seemed utterly insignificant and "excellent fooling."

Speaking of this situation, Mr. Edison says: "One day Frank Thomson, the President of the Pennsylvania Railroad, came out to see the electric light and the electric railway in operation. The latter was then about a mile long. He rode on it. At that time I was getting out plans to make an electric locomotive of three hundred horse-power with six-foot drivers, with the idea of showing people that they could dispense with their steam locomotives. Mr. Thomson made the objection that it was impracticable, and that it would be impossible to supplant steam. His great experience and standing threw a wet blanket on my hopes. But I thought he might perhaps be mistaken, as there had been many such instances on record. I continued to work on the plans, and about three years later I started to build the locomotive at the works at Goerck Street, and had it about finished when I was switched off on some other work. One of the reasons why I felt the electric railway to be eminently practical was that Henry Villard, the President of the Northern Pacific, said that one of the greatest things that could be done would be to build right-angle feeders into the wheat-fields of Dakota and bring in the wheat to the main lines, as the farmers then had to draw it from forty to eighty miles. There was a point where it would not pay to raise it at all; and large areas of the country were thus of no value. I conceived the idea of building a very light railroad of narrow gauge, and had got all the data as to the winds on the plains, and found that it would be possible with very large windmills to supply enough power to drive those wheat trains."

Among others who visited the little road at this juncture were persons interested in the Manhattan Elevated system of New York, on which experiments were repeatedly tried later, but which was not destined to adopt a method so obviously well suited to all the conditions until after many successful demonstrations had been made on elevated roads elsewhere. It must be admitted that Mr. Edison was not very profoundly impressed with the desire entertained in that quarter to utilize any improvement, for he remarks: "When the Elevated Railroad in New York, up Sixth Avenue, was started there was a great clamor about the noise, and injunctions were threatened. The management engaged me to make a report on the cause of the noise. I constructed an instrument that would record the sound, and set out to make a preliminary report, but I found that they never intended to do anything but let the people complain."

It was upon the co-operation of Villard that Edison fell back, and an agreement was entered into between them on September 14, 1881, which provided that the latter would "build two and a half miles of electric railway at Menlo Park, equipped with three cars, two locomotives, one for freight, and one for passengers, capacity of latter sixty miles an hour. Capacity freight engine, ten tons net freight; cost of handling a ton of freight per mile per horse-power to be less than ordinary locomotive.... If experiments are successful, Villard to pay actual outlay in experiments, and to treat with the Light Company for the installation of at least fifty miles of electric railroad in the wheat regions." Mr. Edison is authority for the statement that Mr. Villard advanced between $35,000 and $40,000, and that the work done was very satisfactory; but it did not end at that time in any practical results, as the Northern Pacific went into the hands of a receiver, and Mr. Villard's ability to help was hopelessly crippled. The directors of the Edison Electric Light Company could not be induced to have anything to do with the electric railway, and Mr. Insull states that the money advanced was treated by Mr. Edison as a personal loan and repaid to Mr. Villard, for whom he had a high admiration and a strong feeling of attachment. Mr. Insull says: "Among the financial men whose close personal friendship Edison enjoyed, I would mention Henry Villard, who, I think, had a higher appreciation of the possibilities of the Edison system than probably any other man of his time in Wall Street. He dropped out of the business at the time of the consolidation of the Thomson-Houston Company with the Edison General Electric Company; but from the earliest days of the business, when it was in its experimental period, when the Edison light and power system was but an idea, down to the day of his death, Henry Villard continued a strong supporter not only with his influence, but with his money. He was the first capitalist to back individually Edison's experiments in electric railways."

In speaking of his relationships with Mr. Villard at this time, Edison says: "When Villard was all broken down, and in a stupor caused by his disasters in connection with the Northern Pacific, Mrs. Villard sent for me to come and cheer him up. It was very difficult to rouse him from his despair and apathy, but I talked about the electric light to him, and its development, and told him that it would help him win it all back and put him in his former position. Villard made his great rally; he made money out of the electric light; and he got back control of the Northern Pacific. Under no circumstances can a hustler be kept down. If he is only square, he is bound to get back on his feet. Villard has often been blamed and severely criticised, but he was not the only one to blame. His engineers had spent $20,000,000 too much in building the road, and it was not his fault if he found himself short of money, and at that time unable to raise any more."

Villard maintained his intelligent interest in electric-railway development, with regard to which Edison remarks: "At one time Mr. Villard got the idea that he would run the mountain division of the Northern Pacific Railroad by electricity. He asked me if it could be done. I said: 'Certainly, it is too easy for me to undertake; let some one else do it.' He said: 'I want you to tackle the problem,' and he insisted on it. So I got up a scheme of a third rail and shoe and erected it in my yard here in Orange. When I got it all ready, he had all his division engineers come on to New York, and they came over here. I showed them my plans, and the unanimous decision of the engineers was that it was absolutely and utterly impracticable. That system is on the New York Central now, and was also used on the New Haven road in its first work with electricity."

At this point it may be well to cite some other statements of Edison as to kindred work, with which he has not usually been associated in the public mind. "In the same manner I had worked out for the Manhattan Elevated Railroad a system of electric trains, and had the control of each car centred at one place--multiple control. This was afterward worked out and made practical by Frank Sprague. I got up a slot contact for street railways, and have a patent on it--a sliding contact in a slot. Edward Lauterbach was connected with the Third Avenue Railroad in New York--as counsel--and I told him he was making a horrible mistake putting in the cable. I told him to let the cable stand still and send electricity through it, and he would not have to move hundreds of tons of metal all the time. He would rue the day when he put the cable in." It cannot be denied that the prophecy was fulfilled, for the cable was the beginning of the frightful financial collapse of the system, and was torn out in a few years to make way for the triumphant "trolley in the slot."

Incidental glimpses of this work are both amusing and interesting. Hughes, who was working on the experimental road with Mr. Edison, tells the following story: "Villard sent J. C. Henderson, one of his mechanical engineers, to see the road when it was in operation, and we went down one day--Edison, Henderson, and I--and went on the locomotive. Edison ran it, and just after we started there was a trestle sixty feet long and seven feet deep, and Edison put on all the power. When we went over it we must have been going forty miles an hour, and I could see the perspiration come out on Henderson. After we got over the trestle and started on down the track, Henderson said: 'When we go back I will walk. If there is any more of that kind of running I won't be in it myself.'" To the correspondence of Grosvenor P. Lowrey we are indebted for a similar reminiscence, under date of June 5, 1880: "Goddard and I have spent a part of the day at Menlo, and all is glorious. I have ridden at forty miles an hour on Mr. Edison's electric railway--and we ran off the track. I protested at the rate of speed over the sharp curves, designed to show the power of the engine, but Edison said they had done it often. Finally, when the last trip was to be taken, I said I did not like it, but would go along. The train jumped the track on a short curve, throwing Kruesi, who was driving the engine, with his face down in the dirt, and another man in a comical somersault through some underbrush. Edison was off in a minute, jumping and laughing, and declaring it a most beautiful accident. Kruesi got up, his face bleeding and a good deal shaken; and I shall never forget the expression of voice and face in which he said, with some foreign accent: 'Oh! yes, pairfeckly safe.' Fortunately no other hurts were suffered, and in a few minutes we had the train on the track and running again."

All this rough-and-ready dealing with grades and curves was not mere horse-play, but had a serious purpose underlying it, every trip having its record as to some feature of defect or improvement. One particular set of experiments relating to such work was made on behalf of visitors from South America, and were doubtless the first tests of the kind made for that continent, where now many fine electric street and interurban railway systems are in operation. Mr. Edison himself supplies the following data: "During the electric-railway experiments at Menlo Park, we had a short spur of track up one of the steep gullies. The experiment came about in this way. Bogota, the capital of Columbia, is reached on muleback--or was--from Honda on the headwaters of the Magdalena River. There were parties who wanted to know if transportation over the mule route could not be done by electricity. They said the grades were excessive, and it would cost too much to do it with steam locomotives, even if they could climb the grades. I said: 'Well, it can't be much more than 45 per cent.; we will try that first. If it will do that it will do anything else.' I started at 45 per cent. I got up an electric locomotive with a grip on the rail by which it went up the 45 per cent. grade. Then they said the curves were very short. I put the curves in. We started the locomotive with nobody on it, and got up to twenty miles an hour, taking those curves of very short radius; but it was weeks before we could prevent it from running off. We had to bank the tracks up to an angle of thirty degrees before we could turn the curve and stay on. These Spanish parties were perfectly satisfied we could put in an electric railway from Honda to Bogota successfully, and then they disappeared. I have never seen them since. As usual, I paid for the experiment."

In the spring of 1883 the Electric Railway Company of America was incorporated in the State of New York with a capital of $2,000,000 to develop the patents and inventions of Edison and Stephen D. Field, to the latter of whom the practical work of active development was confided, and in June of the same year an exhibit was made at the Chicago Railway Exposition, which attracted attention throughout the country, and did much to stimulate the growing interest in electric-railway work. With the aid of Messrs. F. B. Rae, C. L. Healy, and C. O. Mailloux a track and locomotive were constructed for the company by Mr. Field and put in service in the gallery of the main exhibition building. The track curved sharply at either end on a radius of fifty-six feet, and the length was about one-third of a mile. The locomotive named "The Judge," after Justice Field, an uncle of Stephen D. Field, took current from a central rail between the two outer rails, that were the return circuit, the contact being a rubbing wire brush on each side of the "third rail," answering the same purpose as the contact shoe of later date. The locomotive weighed three tons, was twelve feet long, five feet wide, and made a speed of nine miles an hour with a trailer car for passengers. Starting on June 5th, when the exhibition closed on June 23d this tiny but typical road had operated for over 118 hours, had made over 446 miles, and had carried 26,805 passengers. After the exposition closed the outfit was taken during the same year to the exposition at Louisville, Kentucky, where it was also successful, carrying a large number of passengers. It deserves note that at Chicago regular railway tickets were issued to paying passengers, the first ever employed on American electric railways.

With this modest but brilliant demonstration, to which the illustrious names of Edison and Field were attached, began the outburst of excitement over electric railways, very much like the eras of speculation and exploitation that attended only a few years earlier the introduction of the telephone and the electric light, but with such significant results that the capitalization of electric roads in America is now over $4,000,000,000, or twice as much as that of the other two arts combined. There was a tremendous rush into the electric-railway field after 1883, and an outburst of inventive activity that has rarely, if ever, been equalled. It is remarkable that, except Siemens, no European achieved fame in this early work, while from America the ideas and appliances of Edison, Van Depoele, Sprague, Field, Daft, and Short have been carried and adopted all over the world.

Mr. Edison was consulting electrician for the Electric Railway Company, but neither a director nor an executive officer. Just what the trouble was as to the internal management of the corporation it is hard to determine a quarter of a century later; but it was equipped with all essential elements to dominate an art in which after its first efforts it remained practically supine and useless, while other interests forged ahead and reaped both the profit and the glory. Dissensions arose between the representatives of the Field and Edison interests, and in April, 1890, the Railway Company assigned its rights to the Edison patents to the Edison General Electric Company, recently formed by the consolidation of all the branches of the Edison light, power, and manufacturing industry under one management. The only patent rights remaining to the Railway Company were those under three Field patents, one of which, with controlling claims, was put in suit June, 1890, against the Jamaica & Brooklyn Road Company, a customer of the Edison General Electric Company. This was, to say the least, a curious and anomalous situation. Voluminous records were made by both parties to the suit, and in the spring of 1894 the case was argued before the late Judge Townsend, who wrote a long opinion dismissing the bill of complaint. [15] The student will find therein a very complete and careful study of the early electric-railway art. After this decision was rendered, the Electric Railway Company remained for several years in a moribund condition, and on the last day of 1896 its property was placed in the hands of a receiver. In February of 1897 the receiver sold the three Field patents to their original owner, and he in turn sold them to the Westinghouse Electric and Manufacturing Company. The Railway Company then went into voluntary dissolution, a sad example of failure to seize the opportunity at the psychological moment, and on the part of the inventor to secure any adequate return for years of effort and struggle in founding one of the great arts. Neither of these men was squelched by such a calamitous result, but if there were not something of bitterness in their feelings as they survey what has come of their work, they would not be human.

As a matter of fact, Edison retained a very lively interest in electric-railway progress long after the pregnant days at Menlo Park, one of the best evidences of which is an article in the New York Electrical Engineer of November 18, 1891, which describes some important and original experiments in the direction of adapting electrical conditions to the larger cities. The overhead trolley had by that time begun its victorious career, but there was intense hostility displayed toward it in many places because of the inevitable increase in the number of overhead wires, which, carrying, as they did, a current of high voltage and large quantity, were regarded as a menace to life and property. Edison has always manifested a strong objection to overhead wires in cities, and urged placing them underground; and the outcry against the overhead "deadly" trolley met with his instant sympathy. His study of the problem brought him to the development of the modern "substation," although the twists that later evolutions have given the idea have left it scarcely recognizable.

[Footnote 15: See 61 Fed. Rep. 655.]

Mr. Villard, as President of the Edison General Electric Company, requested Mr. Edison, as electrician of the company, to devise a street-railway system which should be applicable to the largest cities where the use of the trolley would not be permitted, where the slot conduit system would not be used, and where, in general, the details of construction should be reduced to the simplest form. The limits imposed practically were such as to require that the system should not cost more than a cable road to install. Edison reverted to his ingenious lighting plan of years earlier, and thus settled on a method by which current should be conveyed from the power plant at high potential to motor-generators placed below the ground in close proximity to the rails. These substations would convert the current received at a pressure of, say, one thousand volts to one of twenty volts available between rail and rail, with a corresponding increase in the volume of the current. With the utilization of heavy currents at low voltage it became necessary, of course, to devise apparatus which should be able to pick up with absolute certainty one thousand amperes of current at this pressure through two inches of mud, if necessary. With his wonted activity and fertility Edison set about devising such a contact, and experimented with metal wheels under all conditions of speed and track conditions. It was several months before he could convey one hundred amperes by means of such contacts, but he worked out at last a satisfactory device which was equal to the task. The next point was to secure a joint between contiguous rails such as would permit of the passage of several thousand amperes without introducing undue resistance. This was also accomplished.

Objections were naturally made to rails out in the open on the street surface carrying large currents at a potential of twenty volts. It was said that vehicles with iron wheels passing over the tracks and spanning the two rails would short-circuit the current, "chew" themselves up, and destroy the dynamos generating the current by choking all that tremendous amount of energy back into them. Edison tackled the objection squarely and short-circuited his track with such a vehicle, but succeeded in getting only about two hundred amperes through the wheels, the low voltage and the insulating properties of the axle-grease being sufficient to account for such a result. An iron bar was also used, polished, and with a man standing on it to insure solid contact; but only one thousand amperes passed through it--i.e., the amount required by a single car, and, of course, much less than the capacity of the generators able to operate a system of several hundred cars.

Further interesting experiments showed that the expected large leakage of current from the rails in wet weather did not materialize. Edison found that under the worst conditions with a wet and salted track, at a potential difference of twenty volts between the two rails, the extreme loss was only two and one-half horse-power. In this respect the phenomenon followed the same rule as that to which telegraph wires are subject--namely, that the loss of insulation is greater in damp, murky weather when the insulators are covered with wet dust than during heavy rains when the insulators are thoroughly washed by the action of the water. In like manner a heavy rain-storm cleaned the tracks from the accumulations due chiefly to the droppings of the horses, which otherwise served largely to increase the conductivity. Of course, in dry weather the loss of current was practically nothing, and, under ordinary conditions, Edison held, his system was in respect to leakage and the problems of electrolytic attack of the current on adjacent pipes, etc., as fully insulated as the standard trolley network of the day. The cost of his system Mr. Edison placed at from $30,000 to $100,000 per mile of double track, in accordance with local conditions, and in this respect comparing very favorably with the cable systems then so much in favor for heavy traffic. All the arguments that could be urged in support of this ingenious system are tenable and logical at the present moment; but the trolley had its way except on a few lines where the conduit-and-shoe method was adopted; and in the intervening years the volume of traffic created and handled by electricity in centres of dense population has brought into existence the modern subway.

But down to the moment of the preparation of this biography, Edison has retained an active interest in transportation problems, and his latest work has been that of reviving the use of the storage battery for street-car purposes. At one time there were a number of storage-battery lines and cars in operation in such cities as Washington, New York, Chicago, and Boston; but the costs of operation and maintenance were found to be inordinately high as compared with those of the direct-supply methods, and the battery cars all disappeared. The need for them under many conditions remained, as, for example, in places in Greater New York where the overhead trolley wires are forbidden as objectionable, and where the ground is too wet or too often submerged to permit of the conduit with the slot. Some of the roads in Greater New York have been anxious to secure such cars, and, as usual, the most resourceful electrical engineer and inventor of his times has made the effort. A special experimental track has been laid at the Orange laboratory, and a car equipped with the Edison storage battery and other devices has been put under severe and extended trial there and in New York.

Menlo Park, in ruin and decay, affords no traces of the early Edison electric-railway work, but the crude little locomotive built by Charles T. Hughes was rescued from destruction, and has become the property of the Pratt Institute, of Brooklyn, to whose thousands of technical students it is a constant example and incentive. It was loaned in 1904 to the Association of Edison Illuminating Companies, and by it exhibited as part of the historical Edison collection at the St. Louis Exposition.

CHAPTER XIX

MAGNETIC ORE MILLING WORK

DURING the Hudson-Fulton celebration of October, 1909, Burgomaster Van Leeuwen, of Amsterdam, member of the delegation sent officially from Holland to escort the Half Moon and participate in the functions of the anniversary, paid a visit to the Edison laboratory at Orange to see the inventor, who may be regarded as pre-eminent among those of Dutch descent in this country. Found, as usual, hard at work--this time on his cement house, of which he showed the iron molds--Edison took occasion to remark that if he had achieved anything worth while, it was due to the obstinacy and pertinacity he had inherited from his forefathers. To which it may be added that not less equally have the nature of inheritance and the quality of atavism been exhibited in his extraordinary predilection for the miller's art. While those Batavian ancestors on the low shores of the Zuyder Zee devoted their energies to grinding grain, he has been not less assiduous than they in reducing the rocks of the earth itself to flour.

Although this phase of Mr. Edison's diverse activities is not as generally known to the world as many others of a more popular character, the milling of low-grade auriferous ores and the magnetic separation of iron ores have been subjects of engrossing interest and study to him for many years. Indeed, his comparatively unknown enterprise of separating magnetically and putting into commercial form low-grade iron ore, as carried on at Edison, New Jersey, proved to be the most colossal experiment that he has ever made.

If a person qualified to judge were asked to answer categorically as to whether or not that enterprise was a failure, he could truthfully answer both yes and no. Yes, in that circumstances over which Mr. Edison had no control compelled the shutting down of the plant at the very moment of success; and no, in that the mechanically successful and commercially practical results obtained, after the exercise of stupendous efforts and the expenditure of a fortune, are so conclusive that they must inevitably be the reliance of many future iron-masters. In other words, Mr. Edison was at least a quarter of a century ahead of the times in the work now to be considered.

Before proceeding to a specific description of this remarkable enterprise, however, let us glance at an early experiment in separating magnetic iron sands on the Atlantic sea-shore: "Some years ago I heard one day that down at Quogue, Long Island, there were immense deposits of black magnetic sand. This would be very valuable if the iron could be separated from the sand. So I went down to Quogue with one of my assistants and saw there for miles large beds of black sand on the beach in layers from one to six inches thick--hundreds of thousands of tons. My first thought was that it would be a very easy matter to concentrate this, and I found I could sell the stuff at a good price. I put up a small plant, but just as I got it started a tremendous storm came up, and every bit of that black sand went out to sea. During the twenty-eight years that have intervened it has never come back." This incident was really the prelude to the development set forth in this chapter.

In the early eighties Edison became familiar with the fact that the Eastern steel trade was suffering a disastrous change, and that business was slowly drifting westward, chiefly by reason of the discovery and opening up of enormous deposits of high-grade iron ore in the upper peninsula of Michigan. This ore could be excavated very cheaply by means of improved mining facilities, and transported at low cost to lake ports. Hence the iron and steel mills east of the Alleghanies--compelled to rely on limited local deposits of Bessemer ore, and upon foreign ores which were constantly rising in value--began to sustain a serious competition with Western mills, even in Eastern markets.

Long before this situation arose, it had been recognized by Eastern iron-masters that sooner or later the deposits of high-grade ore would be exhausted, and, in consequence, there would ensue a compelling necessity to fall back on the low-grade magnetic ores. For many years it had been a much-discussed question how to make these ores available for transportation to distant furnaces. To pay railroad charges on ores carrying perhaps 80 to 90 per cent. of useless material would be prohibitive. Hence the elimination of the worthless "gangue" by concentration of the iron particles associated with it, seemed to be the only solution of the problem.

Many attempts had been made in by-gone days to concentrate the iron in such ores by water processes, but with only a partial degree of success. The impossibility of obtaining a uniform concentrate was a most serious objection, had there not indeed been other difficulties which rendered this method commercially impracticable. It is quite natural, therefore, that the idea of magnetic separation should have occurred to many inventors. Thus we find numerous instances throughout the last century of experiments along this line; and particularly in the last forty or fifty years, during which various attempts have been made by others than Edison to perfect magnetic separation and bring it up to something like commercial practice. At the time he took up the matter, however, no one seems to have realized the full meaning of the tremendous problems involved.

From 1880 to 1885, while still very busy in the development of his electric-light system, Edison found opportunity to plan crushing and separating machinery. His first patent on the subject was applied for and issued early in 1880. He decided, after mature deliberation, that the magnetic separation of low-grade ores on a colossal scale at a low cost was the only practical way of supplying the furnace-man with a high quality of iron ore. It was his opinion that it was cheaper to quarry and concentrate lean ore in a big way than to attempt to mine, under adverse circumstances, limited bodies of high-grade ore. He appreciated fully the serious nature of the gigantic questions involved; and his plans were laid with a view to exercising the utmost economy in the design and operation of the plant in which he contemplated the automatic handling of many thousands of tons of material daily. It may be stated as broadly true that Edison engineered to handle immense masses of stuff automatically, while his predecessors aimed chiefly at close separation.

Reduced to its barest, crudest terms, the proposition of magnetic separation is simplicity itself. A piece of the ore (magnetite) may be reduced to powder and the ore particles separated therefrom by the help of a simple hand magnet. To elucidate the basic principle of Edison's method, let the crushed ore fall in a thin stream past such a magnet. The magnetic particles are attracted out of the straight line of the falling stream, and being heavy, gravitate inwardly and fall to one side of a partition placed below. The non-magnetic gangue descends in a straight line to the other side of the partition. Thus a complete separation is effected.

Simple though the principle appears, it was in its application to vast masses of material and in the solving of great engineering problems connected therewith that Edison's originality made itself manifest in the concentrating works that he established in New Jersey, early in the nineties. Not only did he develop thoroughly the refining of the crushed ore, so that after it had passed the four hundred and eighty magnets in the mill, the concentrates came out finally containing 91 to 93 per cent. of iron oxide, but he also devised collateral machinery, methods and processes all fundamental in their nature. These are too numerous to specify in detail, as they extended throughout the various ramifications of the plant, but the principal ones are worthy of mention, such as:

The giant rolls (for crushing).
Intermediate rolls.
Three-high rolls.
Giant cranes (215 feet long span).
Vertical dryer.
Belt conveyors.
Air separation.
Mechanical separation of phosphorus.
Briquetting.

That Mr. Edison's work was appreciated at the time is made evident by the following extract from an article describing the Edison plant, published in The Iron Age of October 28, 1897; in which, after mentioning his struggle with adverse conditions, it says: "There is very little that is showy, from the popular point of view, in the gigantic work which Mr. Edison has done during these years, but to those who are capable of grasping the difficulties encountered, Mr. Edison appears in the new light of a brilliant constructing engineer grappling with technical and commercial problems of the highest order. His genius as an inventor is revealed in many details of the great concentrating plant.... But to our mind, originality of the highest type as a constructor and designer appears in the bold way in which he sweeps aside accepted practice in this particular field and attains results not hitherto approached. He pursues methods in ore-dressing at which those who are trained in the usual practice may well stand aghast. But considering the special features of the problems to be solved, his methods will be accepted as those economically wise and expedient."

A cursory glance at these problems will reveal their import. Mountains must be reduced to dust; all this dust must be handled in detail, so to speak, and from it must be separated the fine particles of iron constituting only one-fourth or one-fifth of its mass; and then this iron-ore dust must be put into such shape that it could be commercially shipped and used. One of the most interesting and striking investigations made by Edison in this connection is worthy of note, and may be related in his own words: "I felt certain that there must be large bodies of magnetite in the East, which if crushed and concentrated would satisfy the wants of the Eastern furnaces for steel-making. Having determined to investigate the mountain regions of New Jersey, I constructed a very sensitive magnetic needle, which would dip toward the earth if brought over any considerable body of magnetic iron ore. One of my laboratory assistants went out with me and we visited many of the mines of New Jersey, but did not find deposits of any magnitude. One day, however, as we drove over a mountain range, not known as iron-bearing land, I was astonished to find that the needle was strongly attracted and remained so; thus indicating that the whole mountain was underlaid with vast bodies of magnetic ore.

"I knew it was a commercial problem to produce high-grade Bessemer ore from these deposits, and took steps to acquire a large amount of the property. I also planned a great magnetic survey of the East, and I believe it remains the most comprehensive of its kind yet performed. I had a number of men survey a strip reaching from Lower Canada to North Carolina. The only instrument we used was the special magnetic needle. We started in Lower Canada and travelled across the line of march twenty-five miles; then advanced south one thousand feet; then back across the line of march again twenty-five miles; then south another thousand feet, across again, and so on. Thus we advanced all the way to North Carolina, varying our cross-country march from two to twenty-five miles, according to geological formation. Our magnetic needle indicated the presence and richness of the invisible deposits of magnetic ore. We kept minute records of these indications, and when the survey was finished we had exact information of the deposits in every part of each State we had passed through. We also knew the width, length, and approximate depth of every one of these deposits, which were enormous.

"The amount of ore disclosed by this survey was simply fabulous. How much so may be judged from the fact that in the three thousand acres immediately surrounding the mills that I afterward established at Edison there were over 200,000,000 tons of low-grade ore. I also secured sixteen thousand acres in which the deposit was proportionately as large. These few acres alone contained sufficient ore to supply the whole United States iron trade, including exports, for seventy years."

Given a mountain of rock containing only one-fifth to one-fourth magnetic iron, the broad problem confronting Edison resolved itself into three distinct parts--first, to tear down the mountain bodily and grind it to powder; second, to extract from this powder the particles of iron mingled in its mass; and, third, to accomplish these results at a cost sufficiently low to give the product a commercial value.

Edison realized from the start that the true solution of this problem lay in the continuous treatment of the material, with the maximum employment of natural forces and the minimum of manual labor and generated power. Hence, all his conceptions followed this general principle so faithfully and completely that we find in the plant embodying his ideas the forces of momentum and gravity steadily in harness and keeping the traces taut; while there was no touch of the human hand upon the material from the beginning of the treatment to its finish--the staff being employed mainly to keep watch on the correct working of the various processes.

It is hardly necessary to devote space to the beginnings of the enterprise, although they are full of interest. They served, however, to convince Edison that if he ever expected to carry out his scheme on the extensive scale planned, he could not depend upon the market to supply suitable machinery for important operations, but would be obliged to devise and build it himself. Thus, outside the steam-shovel and such staple items as engines, boilers, dynamos, and motors, all of the diverse and complex machinery of the entire concentrating plant, as subsequently completed, was devised by him especially for the purpose. The necessity for this was due to the many radical variations made from accepted methods.

No such departure was as radical as that of the method of crushing the ore. Existing machinery for this purpose had been designed on the basis of mining methods then in vogue, by which the rock was thoroughly shattered by means of high explosives and reduced to pieces of one hundred pounds or less. These pieces were then crushed by power directly applied. If a concentrating mill, planned to treat five or six thousand tons per day, were to be operated on this basis the investment in crushers and the supply of power would be enormous, to say nothing of the risk of frequent breakdowns by reason of multiplicity of machinery and parts. From a consideration of these facts, and with his usual tendency to upset traditional observances, Edison conceived the bold idea of constructing gigantic rolls which, by the force of momentum, would be capable of crushing individual rocks of vastly greater size than ever before attempted. He reasoned that the advantages thus obtained would be fourfold: a minimum of machinery and parts; greater compactness; a saving of power; and greater economy in mining. As this last-named operation precedes the crushing, let us first consider it as it was projected and carried on by him.

Perhaps quarrying would be a better term than mining in this case, as Edison's plan was to approach the rock and tear it down bodily. The faith that "moves mountains" had a new opportunity. In work of this nature it had been customary, as above stated, to depend upon a high explosive, such as dynamite, to shatter and break the ore to lumps of one hundred pounds or less. This, however, he deemed to be a most uneconomical process, for energy stored as heat units in dynamite at $260 per ton was much more expensive than that of calories in a ton of coal at $3 per ton. Hence, he believed that only the minimum of work should be done with the costly explosive; and, therefore, planned to use dynamite merely to dislodge great masses of rock, and depended upon the steam-shovel, operated by coal under the boiler, to displace, handle, and remove the rock in detail. This was the plan that was subsequently put into practice in the great works at Edison, New Jersey. A series of three-inch holes twenty feet deep were drilled eight feet apart, about twelve feet back of the ore-bank, and into these were inserted dynamite cartridges. The blast would dislodge thirty to thirty-five thousand tons of rock, which was scooped up by great steam-shovels and loaded on to skips carried by a line of cars on a narrow-gauge railroad running to and from the crushing mill. Here the material was automatically delivered to the giant rolls. The problem included handling and crushing the "run of the mine," without selection. The steam-shovel did not discriminate, but picked up handily single pieces weighing five or six tons and loaded them on the skips with quantities of smaller lumps. When the skips arrived at the giant rolls, their contents were dumped automatically into a superimposed hopper. The rolls were well named, for with ear-splitting noise they broke up in a few seconds the great pieces of rock tossed in from the skips.

It is not easy to appreciate to the full the daring exemplified in these great crushing rolls, or rather "rock-crackers," without having watched them in operation delivering their "solar-plexus" blows. It was only as one might stand in their vicinity and hear the thunderous roar accompanying the smashing and rending of the massive rocks as they disappeared from view that the mind was overwhelmed with a sense of the magnificent proportions of this operation. The enormous force exerted during this process may be illustrated from the fact that during its development, in running one of the early forms of rolls, pieces of rock weighing more than half a ton would be shot up in the air to a height of twenty or twenty-five feet.

The giant rolls were two solid cylinders, six feet in diameter and five feet long, made of cast iron. To the faces of these rolls were bolted a series of heavy, chilled-iron plates containing a number of projecting knobs two inches high. Each roll had also two rows of four-inch knobs, intended to strike a series of hammer-like blows. The rolls were set face to face fourteen inches apart, in a heavy frame, and the total weight was one hundred and thirty tons, of which seventy tons were in moving parts. The space between these two rolls allowed pieces of rock measuring less than fourteen inches to descend to other smaller rolls placed below. The giant rolls were belt-driven, in opposite directions, through friction clutches, although the belt was not depended upon for the actual crushing. Previous to the dumping of a skip, the rolls were speeded up to a circumferential velocity of nearly a mile a minute, thus imparting to them the terrific momentum that would break up easily in a few seconds boulders weighing five or six tons each. It was as though a rock of this size had got in the way of two express trains travelling in opposite directions at nearly sixty miles an hour. In other words, it was the kinetic energy of the rolls that crumbled up the rocks with pile-driver effect. This sudden strain might have tended to stop the engine driving the rolls; but by an ingenious clutch arrangement the belt was released at the moment of resistance in the rolls by reason of the rocks falling between them. The act of breaking and crushing would naturally decrease the tremendous momentum, but after the rock was reduced and the pieces had passed through, the belt would again come into play, and once more speed up the rolls for a repetition of their regular prize-fighter duty.

On leaving the giant rolls the rocks, having been reduced to pieces not larger than fourteen inches, passed into the series of "Intermediate Rolls" of similar construction and operation, by which they were still further reduced, and again passed on to three other sets of rolls of smaller dimensions. These latter rolls were also face-lined with chilled-iron plates; but, unlike the larger ones, were positively driven, reducing the rock to pieces of about one-half-inch size, or smaller. The whole crushing operation of reduction from massive boulders to small pebbly pieces having been done in less time than the telling has occupied, the product was conveyed to the "Dryer," a tower nine feet square and fifty feet high, heated from below by great open furnace fires. All down the inside walls of this tower were placed cast-iron plates, nine feet long and seven inches wide, arranged alternately in "fish-ladder" fashion. The crushed rock, being delivered at the top, would fall down from plate to plate, constantly exposing different surfaces to the heat, until it landed completely dried in the lower portion of the tower, where it fell into conveyors which took it up to the stock-house.

This method of drying was original with Edison. At the time this adjunct to the plant was required, the best dryer on the market was of a rotary type, which had a capacity of only twenty tons per hour, with the expenditure of considerable power. As Edison had determined upon treating two hundred and fifty tons or more per hour, he decided to devise an entirely new type of great capacity, requiring a minimum of power (for elevating the material), and depending upon the force of gravity for handling it during the drying process. A long series of experiments resulted in the invention of the tower dryer with a capacity of three hundred tons per hour.

The rock, broken up into pieces about the size of marbles, having been dried and conveyed to the stock-house, the surplusage was automatically carried out from the other end of the stock-house by conveyors, to pass through the next process, by which it was reduced to a powder. The machinery for accomplishing this result represents another interesting and radical departure of Edison from accepted usage. He had investigated all the crushing-machines on the market, and tried all he could get. He found them all greatly lacking in economy of operation; indeed, the highest results obtainable from the best were 18 per cent. of actual work, involving a loss of 82 per cent. by friction. His nature revolted at such an immense loss of power, especially as he proposed the crushing of vast quantities of ore. Thus, he was obliged to begin again at the foundation, and he devised a crushing-machine which was subsequently named the "Three-High Rolls," and which practically reversed the above figures, as it developed 84 per cent. of work done with only 16 per cent. loss in friction.

A brief description of this remarkable machine will probably interest the reader. In the two end pieces of a heavy iron frame were set three rolls, or cylinders--one in the centre, another below, and the other above--all three being in a vertical line. These rolls were of cast iron three feet in diameter, having chilled-iron smooth face-plates of considerable thickness. The lowest roll was set in a fixed bearing at the bottom of the frame, and, therefore, could only turn around on its axis. The middle and top rolls were free to move up or down from and toward the lower roll, and the shafts of the middle and upper rolls were set in a loose bearing which could slip up and down in the iron frame. It will be apparent, therefore, that any material which passed in between the top and the middle rolls, and the middle and bottom rolls, could be ground as fine as might be desired, depending entirely upon the amount of pressure applied to the loose rolls. In operation the material passed first through the upper and middle rolls, and then between the middle and lowest rolls.

This pressure was applied in a most ingenious manner. On the ends of the shafts of the bottom and top rolls there were cylindrical sleeves, or bearings, having seven sheaves, in which was run a half-inch endless wire rope. This rope was wound seven times over the sheaves as above, and led upward and over a single-groove sheave which was operated by the piston of an air cylinder, and in this manner the pressure was applied to the rolls. It will be seen, therefore, that the system consisted in a single rope passed over sheaves and so arranged that it could be varied in length, thus providing for elasticity in exerting pressure and regulating it as desired. The efficiency of this system was incomparably greater than that of any other known crusher or grinder, for while a pressure of one hundred and twenty-five thousand pounds could be exerted by these rolls, friction was almost entirely eliminated because the upper and lower roll bearings turned with the rolls and revolved in the wire rope, which constituted the bearing proper.

The same cautious foresight exercised by Edison in providing a safety device--the fuse--to prevent fires in his electric-light system, was again displayed in this concentrating plant, where, to save possible injury to its expensive operating parts, he devised an analogous factor, providing all the crushing machinery with closely calculated "safety pins," which, on being overloaded, would shear off and thus stop the machine at once.

The rocks having thus been reduced to fine powder, the mass was ready for screening on its way to the magnetic separators. Here again Edison reversed prior practice by discarding rotary screens and devising a form of tower screen, which, besides having a very large working capacity by gravity, eliminated all power except that required to elevate the material. The screening process allowed the finest part of the crushed rock to pass on, by conveyor belts, to the magnetic separators, while the coarser particles were in like manner automatically returned to the rolls for further reduction.

In a narrative not intended to be strictly technical, it would probably tire the reader to follow this material in detail through the numerous steps attending the magnetic separation. These may be seen in a diagram reproduced from the above-named article in the Iron Age, and supplemented by the following extract from the Electrical Engineer, New York, October 28, 1897: "At the start the weakest magnet at the top frees the purest particles, and the second takes care of others; but the third catches those to which rock adheres, and will extract particles of which only one-eighth is iron. This batch of material goes back for another crushing, so that everything is subjected to an equality of refining. We are now in sight of the real 'concentrates,' which are conveyed to dryer No. 2 for drying again, and are then delivered to the fifty-mesh screens. Whatever is fine enough goes through to the eight-inch magnets, and the remainder goes back for recrushing. Below the eight-inch magnets the dust is blown out of the particles mechanically, and they then go to the four-inch magnets for final cleansing and separation.... Obviously, at each step the percentage of felspar and phosphorus is less and less until in the final concentrates the percentage of iron oxide is 91 to 93 per cent. As intimated at the outset, the tailings will be 75 per cent. of the rock taken from the veins of ore, so that every four tons of crude, raw, low-grade ore will have yielded roughly one ton of high-grade concentrate and three tons of sand, the latter also having its value in various ways."

This sand was transported automatically by belt conveyors to the rear of the works to be stored and sold. Being sharp, crystalline, and even in quality, it was a valuable by-product, finding a ready sale for building purposes, railway sand-boxes, and various industrial uses. The concentrate, in fine powdery form, was delivered in similar manner to a stock-house.

As to the next step in the process, we may now quote again from the article in the Iron Age: "While Mr. Edison and his associates were working on the problem of cheap concentration of iron ore, an added difficulty faced them in the preparation of the concentrates for the market. Furnacemen object to more than a very small proportion of fine ore in their mixtures, particularly when the ore is magnetic, not easily reduced. The problem to be solved was to market an agglomerated material so as to avoid the drawbacks of fine ore. The agglomerated product must be porous so as to afford access of the furnace-reducing gases to the ore. It must be hard enough to bear transportation, and to carry the furnace burden without crumbling to pieces. It must be waterproof, to a certain extent, because considerations connected with securing low rates of freight make it necessary to be able to ship the concentrates to market in open coal cars, exposed to snow and rain. In many respects the attainment of these somewhat conflicting ends was the most perplexing of the problems which confronted Mr. Edison. The agglomeration of the concentrates having been decided upon, two other considerations, not mentioned above, were of primary importance--first, to find a suitable cheap binding material; and, second, its nature must be such that very little would be necessary per ton of concentrates. These severe requirements were staggering, but Mr. Edison's courage did not falter. Although it seemed a well-nigh hopeless task, he entered upon the investigation with his usual optimism and vim. After many months of unremitting toil and research, and the trial of thousands of experiments, the goal was reached in the completion of a successful formula for agglomerating the fine ore and pressing it into briquettes by special machinery."

This was the final process requisite for the making of a completed commercial product. Its practice, of course, necessitated the addition of an entirely new department of the works, which was carried into effect by the construction and installation of the novel mixing and briquetting machinery, together with extensions of the conveyors, with which the plant had already been liberally provided.

Briefly described, the process consisted in mixing the concentrates with the special binding material in machines of an entirely new type, and in passing the resultant pasty mass into the briquetting machines, where it was pressed into cylindrical cakes three inches in diameter and one and a half inches thick, under successive pressures of 7800, 14,000, and 60,000 pounds. Each machine made these briquettes at the rate of sixty per minute, and dropped them into bucket conveyors by which they were carried into drying furnaces, through which they made five loops, and were then delivered to cross-conveyors which carried them into the stock-house. At the end of this process the briquettes were so hard that they would not break or crumble in loading on the cars or in transportation by rail, while they were so porous as to be capable of absorbing 26 per cent. of their own volume in alcohol, but repelling water absolutely--perfect "old soaks."

Thus, with never-failing persistence and patience, coupled with intense thought and hard work, Edison met and conquered, one by one, the complex difficulties that confronted him. He succeeded in what he had set out to do, and it is now to be noted that the product he had striven so sedulously to obtain was a highly commercial one, for not only did the briquettes of concentrated ore fulfil the purpose of their creation, but in use actually tended to increase the working capacity of the furnace, as the following test, quoted from the Iron Age, October 28, 1897, will attest: "The only trial of any magnitude of the briquettes in the blast-furnace was carried through early this year at the Crane Iron Works, Catasauqua, Pennsylvania, by Leonard Peckitt.

"The furnace at which the test was made produces from one hundred to one hundred and ten tons per day when running on the ordinary mixture. The charging of briquettes was begun with a percentage of 25 per cent., and was carried up to 100 per cent. The following is the record of the results:

RESULTS OF WORKING BRIQUETTES AT THE CRANE FURNACE

Briquette	Quantity of Tons Working Per Cent.	Silica	Phos-phorus	Sulphur	Man-ganese
January 5th	25	104	2.770	0.830	0.018	0.500
January 6th	37 1/2	4 1/2	2.620	0 740	0.018	0.350
January 7th	50	138 1/2	2.572	0.580	0.015	0.200
January 8th	75	119	1.844	0.264	0.022	0.200
January 9th	100	138 1/2	1.712	0.147	0.038	0.185

"On the 9th, at 5 P.M., the briquettes having been nearly exhausted, the percentage was dropped to 25 per cent., and on the 10th the output dropped to 120 tons, and on the 11th the furnace had resumed the usual work on the regular standard ores.

"These figures prove that the yield of the furnace is considerably increased. The Crane trial was too short to settle the question to what extent the increase in product may be carried. This increase in output, of course, means a reduction in the cost of labor and of general expenses.

"The richness of the ore and its purity of course affect the limestone consumption. In the case of the Crane trial there was a reduction from 30 per cent. to 12 per cent. of the ore charge.

"Finally, the fuel consumption is reduced, which in the case of the Eastern plants, with their relatively costly coke, is a very important consideration. It is regarded as possible that Eastern furnaces will be able to use a smaller proportion of the costlier coke and correspondingly increase in anthracite coal, which is a cheaper fuel in that section. So far as foundry iron is concerned, the experience at Catasauqua, Pennsylvania, brief as it has been, shows that a stronger and tougher metal is made."

Edison himself tells an interesting little story in this connection, when he enjoyed the active help of that noble character, John Fritz, the distinguished inventor and pioneer of the modern steel industry in America. He says: "When I was struggling along with the iron-ore concentration, I went to see several blast-furnace men to sell the ore at the market price. They saw I was very anxious to sell it, and they would take advantage of my necessity. But I happened to go to Mr. John Fritz, of the Bethlehem Steel Company, and told him what I was doing. 'Well,' he said to me, 'Edison, you are doing a good thing for the Eastern furnaces. They ought to help you, for it will help us out. I am willing to help you. I mix a little sentiment with business, and I will give you an order for one hundred thousand tons.' And he sat right down and gave me the order."

The Edison concentrating plant has been sketched in the briefest outline with a view of affording merely a bare idea of the great work of its projector. To tell the whole story in detail and show its logical sequence, step by step, would take little less than a volume in itself, for Edison's methods, always iconoclastic when progress is in sight, were particularly so at the period in question. It has been said that "Edison's scrap-heap contains the elements of a liberal education," and this was essentially true of the "discard" during the ore-milling experience. Interesting as it might be to follow at length the numerous phases of ingenious and resourceful development that took place during those busy years, the limit of present space forbids their relation. It would, however, be denying the justice that is Edison's due to omit all mention of two hitherto unnamed items in particular that have added to the world's store of useful devices. We refer first to the great travelling hoisting-crane having a span of two hundred and fifteen feet, and used for hoisting loads equal to ten tons, this being the largest of the kind made up to that time, and afterward used as a model by many others. The second item was the ingenious and varied forms of conveyor belt, devised and used by Edison at the concentrating works, and subsequently developed into a separate and extensive business by an engineer to whom he gave permission to use his plans and patterns.

Edison's native shrewdness and knowledge of human nature was put to practical use in the busy days of plant construction. It was found impossible to keep mechanics on account of indifferent residential accommodations afforded by the tiny village, remote from civilization, among the central mountains of New Jersey. This puzzling question was much discussed between him and his associate, Mr. W. S. Mallory, until finally he said to the latter: "If we want to keep the men here we must make it attractive for the women--so let us build some houses that will have running water and electric lights, and rent at a low rate." He set to work, and in a day finished a design for a type of house. Fifty were quickly built and fully described in advertising for mechanics. Three days' advertisements brought in over six hundred and fifty applications, and afterward Edison had no trouble in obtaining all the first-class men he required, as settlers in the artificial Yosemite he was creating.

We owe to Mr. Mallory a characteristic story of this period as to an incidental unbending from toil, which in itself illustrates the ever-present determination to conquer what is undertaken: "Along in the latter part of the nineties, when the work on the problem of concentrating iron ore was in progress, it became necessary when leaving the plant at Edison to wait over at Lake Hopatcong one hour for a connecting train. During some of these waits Mr. Edison had seen me play billiards. At the particular time this incident happened, Mrs. Edison and her family were away for the summer, and I was staying at the Glenmont home on the Orange Mountains.

"One hot Saturday night, after Mr. Edison had looked over the evening papers, he said to me: 'Do you want to play a game of billiards?' Naturally this astonished me very much, as he is a man who cares little or nothing for the ordinary games, with the single exception of parcheesi, of which he is very fond. I said I would like to play, so we went up into the billiard-room of the house. I took off the cloth, got out the balls, picked out a cue for Mr. Edison, and when we banked for the first shot I won and started the game. After making two or three shots I missed, and a long carom shot was left for Mr. Edison, the cue ball and object ball being within about twelve inches of each other, and the other ball a distance of nearly the length of the table. Mr. Edison attempted to make the shot, but missed it and said 'Put the balls back.' So I put them back in the same position and he missed it the second time. I continued at his request to put the balls back in the same position for the next fifteen minutes, until he could make the shot every time--then he said: 'I don't want to play any more.'"

Having taken a somewhat superficial survey of the great enterprise under consideration; having had a cursory glance at the technical development of the plant up to the point of its successful culmination in the making of a marketable, commercial product as exemplified in the test at the Crane Furnace, let us revert to that demonstration and note the events that followed. The facts of this actual test are far more eloquent than volumes of argument would be as a justification of Edison's assiduous labors for over eight years, and of the expenditure of a fortune in bringing his broad conception to a concrete possibility. In the patient solving of tremendous problems he had toiled up the mountain-side of success--scaling its topmost peak and obtaining a view of the boundless prospect. But, alas! "The best laid plans o' mice and men gang aft agley." The discovery of great deposits of rich Bessemer ore in the Mesaba range of mountains in Minnesota a year or two previous to the completion of his work had been followed by the opening up of those deposits and the marketing of the ore. It was of such rich character that, being cheaply mined by greatly improved and inexpensive methods, the market price of crude ore of like iron units fell from about $6.50 to $3.50 per ton at the time when Edison was ready to supply his concentrated product. At the former price he could have supplied the market and earned a liberal profit on his investment, but at $3.50 per ton he was left without a reasonable chance of competition. Thus was swept away the possibility of reaping the reward so richly earned by years of incessant thought, labor, and care. This great and notable plant, representing a very large outlay of money, brought to completion, ready for business, and embracing some of the most brilliant and remarkable of Edison's inventions and methods, must be abandoned by force of circumstances over which he had no control, and with it must die the high hopes that his progressive, conquering march to success had legitimately engendered.

The financial aspect of these enterprises is often overlooked and forgotten. In this instance it was of more than usual import and seriousness, as Edison was virtually his own "backer," putting into the company almost the whole of all the fortune his inventions had brought him. There is a tendency to deny to the capital that thus takes desperate chances its full reward if things go right, and to insist that it shall have barely the legal rate of interest and far less than the return of over-the-counter retail trade. It is an absolute fact that the great electrical inventors and the men who stood behind them have had little return for their foresight and courage. In this instance, when the inventor was largely his own financier, the difficulties and perils were redoubled. Let Mr. Mallory give an instance: "During the latter part of the panic of 1893 there came a period when we were very hard up for ready cash, due largely to the panicky conditions; and a large pay-roll had been raised with considerable difficulty. A short time before pay-day our treasurer called me up by telephone, and said: 'I have just received the paid checks from the bank, and I am fearful that my assistant, who has forged my name to some of the checks, has absconded with about $3000.' I went immediately to Mr. Edison and told him of the forgery and the amount of money taken, and in what an embarrassing position we were for the next pay-roll. When I had finished he said: 'It is too bad the money is gone, but I will tell you what to do. Go and see the president of the bank which paid the forged checks. Get him to admit the bank's liability, and then say to him that Mr. Edison does not think the bank should suffer because he happened to have a dishonest clerk in his employ. Also say to him that I shall not ask them to make the amount good.' This was done; the bank admitting its liability and being much pleased with this action. When I reported to

Mr. Edison he said: 'That's all right. We have made a friend of the bank, and we may need friends later on.' And so it happened that some time afterward, when we greatly needed help in the way of loans, the bank willingly gave us the accommodations we required to tide us over a critical period."

This iron-ore concentrating project had lain close to Edison's heart and ambition--indeed, it had permeated his whole being to the exclusion of almost all other investigations or inventions for a while. For five years he had lived and worked steadily at Edison, leaving there only on Saturday night to spend Sunday at his home in Orange, and returning to the plant by an early train on Monday morning. Life at Edison was of the simple kind--work, meals, and a few hours' sleep--day by day. The little village, called into existence by the concentrating works, was of the most primitive nature and offered nothing in the way of frivolity or amusement. Even the scenery is austere. Hence Edison was enabled to follow his natural bent in being surrounded day and night by his responsible chosen associates, with whom he worked uninterrupted by outsiders from early morning away into the late hours of the evening. Those who were laboring with him, inspired by his unflagging enthusiasm, followed his example and devoted all their long waking hours to the furtherance of his plans with a zeal that ultimately bore fruit in the practical success here recorded.

In view of its present status, this colossal enterprise at Edison may well be likened to the prologue of a play that is to be subsequently enacted for the benefit of future generations, but before ringing down the curtain it is desirable to preserve the unities by quoting the words of one of the principal actors, Mr. Mallory, who says: "The Concentrating Works had been in operation, and we had produced a considerable quantity of the briquettes, and had been able to sell only a portion of them, the iron market being in such condition that blast-furnaces were not making any new purchases of iron ore, and were having difficulty to receive and consume the ores which had been previously contracted for, so what sales we were able to make were at extremely low prices, my recollection being that they were between $3.50 and $3.80 per ton, whereas when the works had started we had hoped to obtain $6.00 to $6.50 per ton for the briquettes. We had also thoroughly investigated the wonderful deposit at Mesaba, and it was with the greatest possible reluctance that Mr. Edison was able to come finally to the conclusion that, under existing conditions, the concentrating plant could not then be made a commercial success. This decision was reached only after the most careful investigations and calculations, as Mr. Edison was just as full of fight and ambition to make it a success as when he first started.

"When this decision was reached Mr. Edison and I took the Jersey Central train from Edison, bound for Orange, and I did not look forward to the immediate future with any degree of confidence, as the concentrating plant was heavily in debt, without any early prospect of being able to pay off its indebtedness. On the train the matter of the future was discussed, and Mr. Edison said that, inasmuch as we had the knowledge gained from our experience in the concentrating problem, we must, if possible, apply it to some practical use, and at the same time we must work out some other plans by which we could make enough money to pay off the Concentrating Company's indebtedness, Mr. Edison stating most positively that no company with which he had personally been actively connected had ever failed to pay its debts, and he did not propose to have the Concentrating Company any exception.

"In the discussion that followed he suggested several kinds of work which he had in his mind, and which might prove profitable. We figured carefully over the probabilities of financial returns from the Phonograph Works and other enterprises, and after discussing many plans, it was finally decided that we would apply the knowledge we had gained in the concentrating plant by building a plant for manufacturing Portland cement, and that Mr. Edison would devote his attention to the developing of a storage battery which did not use lead and sulphuric acid. So these two lines of work were taken up by Mr. Edison with just as much enthusiasm and energy as is usual with him, the commercial failure of the concentrating plant seeming not to affect his spirits in any way. In fact, I have often been impressed strongly with the fact that, during the dark days of the concentrating problem, Mr. Edison's desire was very strong that the creditors of the Concentrating Works should be paid in full; and only once did I hear him make any reference to the financial loss which he himself made, and he then said: 'As far as I am concerned, I can any time get a job at $75 per month as a telegrapher, and that will amply take care of all my personal requirements.' As already stated, however, he started in with the maximum amount of enthusiasm and ambition, and in the course of about three years we succeeded in paying off all the indebtedness of the Concentrating Works, which amounted to several hundred thousand dollars.

"As to the state of Mr. Edison's mind when the final decision was reached to close down, if he was specially disappointed, there was nothing in his manner to indicate it, his every thought being for the future, and as to what could be done to pull us out of the financial situation in which we found ourselves, and to take advantage of the knowledge which we had acquired at so great a cost."

It will have been gathered that the funds for this great experiment were furnished largely by Edison. In fact, over two million dollars were spent in the attempt. Edison's philosophic view of affairs is given in the following anecdote from Mr. Mallory: "During the boom times of 1902, when the old General Electric stock sold at its high-water mark of about $330, Mr. Edison and I were on our way from the cement plant at New Village, New Jersey, to his home at Orange. When we arrived at Dover, New Jersey, we got a New York newspaper, and I called his attention to the quotation of that day on General Electric. Mr. Edison then asked: 'If I hadn't sold any of mine, what would it be worth to-day?' and after some figuring I replied: 'Over four million dollars.' When Mr. Edison is thinking seriously over a problem he is in the habit of pulling his right eyebrow, which he did now for fifteen or twenty seconds. Then his face lighted up, and he said: 'Well, it's all gone, but we had a hell of a good time spending it.'" With which revelation of an attitude worthy of Mark Tapley himself, this chapter may well conclude.

CHAPTER XX

EDISON PORTLAND CEMENT

NEW developments in recent years have been more striking than the general adoption of cement for structural purposes of all kinds in the United States; or than the increase in its manufacture here. As a material for the construction of office buildings, factories, and dwellings, it has lately enjoyed an extraordinary vogue; yet every indication is confirmatory of the belief that such use has barely begun. Various reasons may be cited, such as the growing scarcity of wood, once the favorite building material in many parts of the country, and the increasing dearness of brick and stone. The fact remains, indisputable, and demonstrated flatly by the statistics of production. In 1902 the American output of cement was placed at about 21,000,000 barrels, valued at over $17,000,000. In 1907 the production is given as nearly 49,000,000 barrels. Here then is an industry that doubled in five years. The average rate of industrial growth in the United States is 10 per cent. a year, or doubling every ten years. It is a singular fact that electricity also so far exceeds the normal rate as to double in value and quantity of output and investment every five years. There is perhaps more than ordinary coincidence in the association of Edison with two such active departments of progress.

As a purely manufacturing business the general cement industry is one of even remote antiquity, and if Edison had entered into it merely as a commercial enterprise by following paths already so well trodden, the fact would hardly have been worthy of even passing notice. It is not in his nature, however, to follow a beaten track except in regard to the recognition of basic principles; so that while the manufacture of Edison Portland cement embraces the main essentials and familiar processes of cement-making, such as crushing, drying, mixing, roasting, and grinding, his versatility and originality, as exemplified in the conception and introduction of some bold and revolutionary methods and devices, have resulted in raising his plant from the position of an outsider to the rank of the fifth largest producer in the United States, in the short space of five years after starting to manufacture.

Long before his advent in cement production, Edison had held very pronounced views on the value of that material as the one which would obtain largely for future building purposes on account of its stability. More than twenty-five years ago one of the writers of this narrative heard him remark during a discussion on ancient buildings: "Wood will rot, stone will chip and crumble, bricks disintegrate, but a cement and iron structure is apparently indestructible. Look at some of the old Roman baths. They are as solid as when they were built." With such convictions, and the vast fund of practical knowledge and experience he had gained at Edison in the crushing and manipulation of large masses of magnetic iron ore during the preceding nine years, it is not surprising that on that homeward railway journey, mentioned at the close of the preceding chapter, he should have decided to go into the manufacture of cement, especially in view of the enormous growth of its use for structural purposes during recent times.

The field being a new one to him, Edison followed his usual course of reading up every page of authoritative literature on the subject, and seeking information from all quarters. In the mean time, while he was busy also with his new storage battery, Mr. Mallory, who had been hard at work on the cement plan, announced that he had completed arrangements for organizing a company with sufficient financial backing to carry on the business; concluding with the remark that it was now time to engage engineers to lay out the plant. Edison replied that he intended to do that himself, and invited Mr. Mallory to go with him to one of the draughting-rooms on an upper floor of the laboratory.

Here he placed a large sheet of paper on a draughting-table, and immediately began to draw out a plan of the proposed works, continuing all day and away into the evening, when he finished; thus completing within the twenty-four hours the full lay-out of the entire plant as it was subsequently installed, and as it has substantially remained in practical use to this time. It will be granted that this was a remarkable engineering feat, especially in view of the fact that Edison was then a new-comer in the cement business, and also that if the plant were to be rebuilt to-day, no vital change would be desirable or necessary. In that one day's planning every part was considered and provided for, from the crusher to the packing-house. From one end to the other, the distance over which the plant stretches in length is about half a mile, and through the various buildings spread over this space there passes, automatically, in course of treatment, a vast quantity of material resulting in the production of upward of two and a quarter million pounds of finished cement every twenty-four hours, seven days in the week.

In that one day's designing provision was made not only for all important parts, but minor details, such, for instance, as the carrying of all steam, water, and air pipes, and electrical conductors in a large subway running from one end of the plant to the other; and, an oiling system for the entire works. This latter deserves special mention, not only because of its arrangement for thorough lubrication, but also on account of the resultant economy affecting the cost of manufacture.

Edison has strong convictions on the liberal use of lubricants, but argued that in the ordinary oiling of machinery there is great waste, while much dirt is conveyed into the bearings. He therefore planned a system by which the ten thousand bearings in the plant are oiled automatically; requiring the services of only two men for the entire work. This is accomplished by a central pumping and filtering plant and the return of the oil from all parts of the works by gravity. Every bearing is made dust-proof, and is provided with two interior pipes. One is above and the other below the bearing. The oil flows in through the upper pipe, and, after lubricating the shaft, flows out through the lower pipe back to the pumping station, where any dirt is filtered out and the oil returned to circulation. While this system of oiling is not unique, it was the first instance of its adaptation on so large and complete a scale, and illustrates the far-sightedness of his plans.

In connection with the adoption of this lubricating system there occurred another instance of his knowledge of materials and intuitive insight into the nature of things. He thought that too frequent circulation of a comparatively small quantity of oil would, to some extent, impair its lubricating qualities, and requested his assistants to verify this opinion by consultation with competent authorities. On making inquiry of the engineers of the Standard Oil Company, his theory was fully sustained. Hence, provision was made for carrying a large stock of oil, and for giving a certain period of rest to that already used.

A keen appreciation of ultimate success in the production of a fine quality of cement led Edison to provide very carefully in his original scheme for those details that he foresaw would become requisite--such, for instance, as ample stock capacity for raw materials and their automatic delivery in the various stages of manufacture, as well as mixing, weighing, and frequent sampling and analyzing during the progress through the mills. This provision even included the details of the packing-house, and his perspicacity in this case is well sustained from the fact that nine years afterward, in anticipation of building an additional packing-house, the company sent a representative to different parts of the country to examine the systems used by manufacturers in the packing of large quantities of various staple commodities involving somewhat similar problems, and found that there was none better than that devised before the cement plant was started. Hence, the order was given to build the new packing-house on lines similar to those of the old one.

Among the many innovations appearing in this plant are two that stand out in bold relief as indicating the large scale by which Edison measures his ideas. One of these consists of the crushing and grinding machinery, and the other of the long kilns. In the preceding chapter there has been given a description of the giant rolls, by means of which great masses of rock, of which individual pieces may weigh eight or more tons, are broken and reduced to about a fourteen-inch size. The economy of this is apparent when it is considered that in other cement plants the limit of crushing ability is "one-man size"--that is, pieces not too large for one man to lift.

The story of the kiln, as told by Mr. Mallory, is illustrative of Edison's tendency to upset tradition and make a radical departure from generally accepted ideas. "When Mr. Edison first decided to go into the cement business, it was on the basis of his crushing-rolls and air separation, and he had every expectation of installing duplicates of the kilns which were then in common use for burning cement. These kilns were usually made of boiler iron, riveted, and were about sixty feet long and six feet in diameter, and had a capacity of about two hundred barrels of cement clinker in twenty-four hours.

"When the detail plans for our plant were being drawn, Mr. Edison and I figured over the coal capacity and coal economy of the sixty-foot kiln, and each time thought that both could he materially bettered. After having gone over this matter several times, he said: 'I believe I can make a kiln which will give an output of one thousand barrels in twenty-four hours.' Although I had then been closely associated with him for ten years and was accustomed to see him accomplish great things, I could not help feeling the improbability of his being able to jump into an old-established industry--as a novice--and start by improving the 'heart' of the production so as to increase its capacity 400 per cent. When I pressed him for an explanation, he was unable to give any definite reasons, except that he felt positive it could be done. In this connection let me say that very many times I have heard Mr. Edison make predictions as to what a certain mechanical device ought to do in the way of output and costs, when his statements did not seem to be even among the possibilities. Subsequently, after more or less experience, these predictions have been verified, and I cannot help coming to the conclusion that he has a faculty, not possessed by the average mortal, of intuitively and correctly sizing up mechanical and commercial possibilities.

"But, returning to the kiln, Mr. Edison went to work immediately and very soon completed the design of a new type which was to be one hundred and fifty feet long and nine feet in diameter, made up in ten-foot sections of cast iron bolted together and arranged to be revolved on fifteen bearings. He had a wooden model made and studied it very carefully, through a series of experiments. These resulted so satisfactorily that this form was finally decided upon, and ultimately installed as part of the plant.

"Well, for a year or so the kiln problem was a nightmare to me. When we started up the plant experimentally, and the long kiln was first put in operation, an output of about four hundred barrels in twenty-four hours was obtained. Mr. Edison was more than disappointed at this result. His terse comment on my report was: 'Rotten. Try it again.' When we became a little more familiar with the operation of the kiln we were able to get the output up to about five hundred and fifty barrels, and a little later to six hundred and fifty barrels per day. I would go down to Orange and report with a great deal of satisfaction the increase in output, but Mr. Edison would apparently be very much disappointed, and often said to me that the trouble was not with the kiln, but with our method of operating it; and he would reiterate his first statement that it would make one thousand barrels in twenty-four hours.

"Each time I would return to the plant with the determination to increase the output if possible, and we did increase it to seven hundred and fifty, then to eight hundred and fifty barrels. Every time I reported these increases Mr. Edison would still be disappointed. I said to him several times that if he was so sure the kiln could turn out one thousand barrels in twenty-four hours we would be very glad to have him tell us how to do it, and that we would run it in any way he directed. He replied that he did not know what it was that kept the output down, but he was just as confident as ever that the kiln would make one thousand barrels per day, and that if he had time to work with and watch the kiln it would not take him long to find out the reasons why. He had made a number of suggestions throughout these various trials, however, and, as we continued to operate, we learned additional points in handling, and were able to get the output up to nine hundred barrels, then one thousand, and finally to over eleven hundred barrels per day, thus more than realizing the prediction made by Mr. Edison before even the plans were drawn. It is only fair to say, however, that prolonged experience has led us to the conclusion that the maximum economy in continuous operation of these kilns is obtained by working them at a little less than their maximum capacity.

"It is interesting to note, in connection with the Edison type of kiln, that when the older cement manufacturers first learned of it, they ridiculed the idea universally, and were not slow to predict our early 'finish' as cement manufacturers. The ultimate success of the kiln, however, proved their criticisms to be unwarranted. Once aware of its possibility, some of the cement manufacturers proceeded to avail themselves of the innovation (at first without Mr. Edison's consent), and to-day more than one-half of the Portland cement produced in this country is made in kilns of the Edison type. Old plants are lengthening their kilns wherever practicable, and no wide-awake manufacturer building a modern plant could afford to install other than these long kilns. This invention of Mr. Edison has been recognized by the larger cement manufacturers, and there is every prospect now that the entire trade will take licenses under his kiln patents."

When he decided to go into the cement business, Edison was thoroughly awake to the fact that he was proposing to "butt into" an old-established industry, in which the principal manufacturers were concerns of long standing. He appreciated fully its inherent difficulties, not only in manufacture, but also in the marketing of the product. These considerations, together with his long-settled principle of striving always to make the best, induced him at the outset to study methods of producing the highest quality of product. Thus he was led to originate innovations in processes, some of which have been preserved as trade secrets; but of the others there are two deserving special notice--namely, the accuracy of mixing and the fineness of grinding.

In cement-making, generally speaking, cement rock and limestone in the rough are mixed together in such relative quantities as may be determined upon in advance by chemical analysis. In many plants this mixture is made by barrow or load units, and may be more or less accurate. Rule-of-thumb methods are never acceptable to Edison, and he devised therefore a system of weighing each part of the mixture, so that it would be correct to a pound, and, even at that, made the device "fool-proof," for as he observed to one of his associates: "The man at the scales might get to thinking of the other fellow's best girl, so fifty or a hundred pounds of rock, more or less, wouldn't make much difference to him." The Edison checking plan embraces two hoppers suspended above two platform scales whose beams are electrically connected with a hopper-closing device by means of needles dipping into mercury cups. The scales are set according to the chemist's weighing orders, and the material is fed into the scales from the hoppers. The instant the beam tips, the connection is broken and the feed stops instantly, thus rendering it impossible to introduce any more material until the charge has been unloaded.

The fine grinding of cement clinker is distinctively Edisonian in both origin and application. As has been already intimated, its author followed a thorough course of reading on the subject long before reaching the actual projection or installation of a plant, and he had found all authorities to agree on one important point--namely, that the value of cement depends upon the fineness to which it is ground. [16] He also ascertained that in the trade the standard of fineness was that 75 per cent. of the whole mass would pass through a 200-mesh screen. Having made some improvements in his grinding and screening apparatus, and believing that in the future engineers, builders, and contractors would eventually require a higher degree of fineness, he determined, in advance of manufacturing, to raise the standard ten points, so that at least 85 per cent. of his product should pass through a 200-mesh screen. This was a bold step to be taken by a new-comer, but his judgment, backed by a full confidence in ability to live up to this standard, has been fully justified in its continued maintenance, despite the early incredulity of older manufacturers as to the possibility of attaining such a high degree of fineness.

[Footnote 16: For a proper understanding and full appreciation of the importance of fine grinding, it may be explained that Portland cement (as manufactured in the Lehigh Valley) is made from what is commonly spoken of as "cement rock," with the addition of sufficient limestone to give the necessary amount of lime. The rock is broken down and then ground to a fineness of 80 to 90 per cent. through a 200-mesh screen. This ground material passes through kilns and comes out in "clinker." This is ground and that part of this finely ground clinker that will pass a 200-mesh screen is cement; the residue is still clinker. These coarse particles, or clinkers, absorb water very slowly, are practically inert, and have very feeble cementing properties. The residue on a 200-mesh screen is useless.]

If Edison measured his happiness, as men often do, by merely commercial or pecuniary rewards of success, it would seem almost redundant to state that he has continued to manifest an intense interest in the cement plant. Ordinarily, his interest as an inventor wanes in proportion to the approach to mere commercialism--in other words, the keenness of his pleasure is in overcoming difficulties rather than the mere piling up of a bank account. He is entirely sensible of the advantages arising from a good balance at the banker's, but that has not been the goal of his ambition. Hence, although his cement enterprise reached the commercial stage a long time ago, he has been firmly convinced of his own ability to devise still further improvements and economical processes of greater or less fundamental importance, and has, therefore, made a constant study of the problem as a whole and in all its parts. By means of frequent reports, aided by his remarkable memory, he keeps in as close touch with the plant as if he were there in person every day, and is thus enabled to suggest improvement in any particular detail. The engineering force has a great respect for the accuracy of his knowledge of every part of the plant, for he remembers the dimensions and details of each item of machinery, sometimes to the discomfiture of those who are around it every day.

A noteworthy instance of Edison's memory occurred in connection with this cement plant. Some years ago, as its installation was nearing completion, he went up to look it over and satisfy himself as to what needed to be done. On the arrival of the train at 10.40 in the morning, he went to the mill, and, with Mr. Mason, the general superintendent, started at the crusher at one end, and examined every detail all the way through to the packing-house at the other end. He made neither notes nor memoranda, but the examination required all the day, which happened to be a Saturday. He took a train for home at 5.30 in the afternoon, and on arriving at his residence at Orange, got out some note-books and began to write entirely from memory each item consecutively. He continued at this task all through Saturday night, and worked steadily on until Sunday afternoon, when he completed a list of nearly six hundred items. The nature of this feat is more appreciable from the fact that a large number of changes included all the figures of new dimensions he had decided upon for some of the machinery throughout the plant.

As the reader may have a natural curiosity to learn whether or not the list so made was practical, it may be stated that it was copied and sent up to the general superintendent with instructions to make the modifications suggested, and report by numbers as they were attended to. This was faithfully done, all the changes being made before the plant was put into operation. Subsequent experience has amply proven the value of Edison's prescience at this time.

Although Edison's achievements in the way of improved processes and machinery have already made a deep impression in the cement industry, it is probable that this impression will become still more profoundly stamped upon it in the near future with the exploitation of his "Poured Cement House." The broad problem which he set himself was to provide handsome and practically indestructible detached houses, which could be taken by wage-earners at very moderate monthly rentals. He turned this question over in his mind for several years, and arrived at the conclusion that a house cast in one piece would be the answer. To produce such a house involved the overcoming of many engineering and other technical difficulties. These he attacked vigorously and disposed of patiently one by one.

In this connection a short anecdote may be quoted from Edison as indicative of one of the influences turning his thoughts in this direction. In the story of the ore-milling work, it has been noted that the plant was shut down owing to the competition of the cheap ore from the Mesaba Range. Edison says: "When I shut down, the insurance companies cancelled my insurance. I asked the reason why. 'Oh,' they said, 'this thing is a failure. The moral risk is too great.' 'All right; I am glad to hear it. I will now construct buildings that won't have any moral risk.' I determined to go into the Portland cement business. I organized a company and started cement-works which have now been running successfully for several years. I had so perfected the machinery in trying to get my ore costs down that the making of cheap cement was an easy matter to me. I built these works entirely of concrete and steel, so that there is not a wagon-load of lumber in them; and so that the insurance companies would not have any possibility of having any 'moral risk.' Since that time I have put up numerous factory buildings all of steel and concrete, without any combustible whatever about them--to avoid this 'moral risk.' I am carrying further the application of this idea in building private houses for poor people, in which there will be no 'moral risk' at all--nothing whatever to burn, not even by lightning."

As a casting necessitates a mold, together with a mixture sufficiently fluid in its nature to fill all the interstices completely, Edison devoted much attention to an extensive series of experiments for producing a free-flowing combination of necessary materials. His proposition was against all precedent. All expert testimony pointed to the fact that a mixture of concrete (cement, sand, crushed stone, and water) could not be made to flow freely to the smallest parts of an intricate set of molds; that the heavy parts of the mixture could not be held in suspension, but would separate out by gravity and make an unevenly balanced structure; that the surface would be full of imperfections, etc.

Undeterred by the unanimity of adverse opinions, however, he pursued his investigations with the thorough minuteness that characterizes all his laboratory work, and in due time produced a mixture which on elaborate test overcame all objections and answered the complex requirements perfectly, including the making of a surface smooth, even, and entirely waterproof. All the other engineering problems have received study in like manner, and have been overcome, until at the present writing the whole question is practically solved and has been reduced to actual practice. The Edison poured or cast cement house may be reckoned as a reality.

The general scheme, briefly outlined, is to prepare a model and plans of the house to be cast, and then to design a set of molds in sections of convenient size. When all is ready, these molds, which are of cast iron with smooth interior surfaces, are taken to the place where the house is to be erected. Here there has been provided a solid concrete cellar floor, technically called "footing." The molds are then locked together so that they rest on this footing. Hundreds of pieces are necessary for the complete set. When they have been completely assembled, there will be a hollow space in the interior, representing the shape of the house. Reinforcing rods are also placed in the molds, to be left behind in the finished house.

Next comes the pouring of the concrete mixture into this form. Large mechanical mixers are used, and, as it is made, the mixture is dumped into tanks, from which it is conveyed to a distributing tank on the top, or roof, of the form. From this tank a large number of open troughs or pipes lead the mixture to various openings in the roof, whence it flows down and fills all parts of the mold from the footing in the basement until it overflows at the tip of the roof.

The pouring of the entire house is accomplished in about six hours, and then the molds are left undisturbed for six days, in order that the concrete may set and harden. After that time the work of taking away the molds is begun. This requires three or four days. When the molds are taken away an entire house is disclosed, cast in one piece, from cellar to tip of roof, complete with floors, interior walls, stairways, bath and laundry tubs, electric-wire conduits, gas, water, and heating pipes.

No plaster is used anywhere; but the exterior and interior walls are smooth and may be painted or tinted, if desired. All that is now necessary is to put in the windows, doors, heater, and lighting fixtures, and to connect up the plumbing and heating arrangements, thus making the house ready for occupancy.

As these iron molds are not ephemeral like the wooden framing now used in cement construction, but of practically illimitable life, it is obvious that they can be used a great number of times. A complete set of molds will cost approximately $25,000, while the necessary plant will cost about $15,000 more. It is proposed to work as a unit plant for successful operation at least six sets of molds, to keep the men busy and the machinery going. Any one, with a sheet of paper, can ascertain the yearly interest on the investment as a fixed charge to be assessed against each house, on the basis that one hundred and forty-four houses can be built in a year with the battery of six sets of molds. Putting the sum at $175,000, and the interest at 6 per cent. on the cost of the molds and 4 per cent. for breakage, together with 6 per cent. interest and 15 per cent. depreciation on machinery, the plant charge is approximately $140 per house. It does not require a particularly acute prophetic vision to see "Flower Towns" of "Poured Houses" going up in whole suburbs outside all our chief centres of population.

Edison's conception of the workingman's ideal house has been a broad one from the very start. He was not content merely to provide a roomy, moderately priced house that should be fireproof, waterproof, and vermin-proof, and practically indestructible, but has been solicitous to get away from the idea of a plain "packing-box" type. He has also provided for ornamentation of a high class in designing the details of the structure. As he expressed it: "We will give the workingman and his family ornamentation in their house. They deserve it, and besides, it costs no more after the pattern is made to give decorative effects than it would to make everything plain." The plans have provided for a type of house that would cost not far from $30,000 if built of cut stone. He gave to Messrs. Mann & McNaillie, architects, New York, his idea of the type of house he wanted. On receiving these plans he changed them considerably, and built a model. After making many more changes in this while in the pattern shop, he produced a house satisfactory to himself.

This one-family house has a floor plan twenty-five by thirty feet, and is three stories high. The first floor is divided off into two large rooms--parlor and living-room--and the upper floors contain four large bedrooms, a roomy bath-room, and wide halls. The front porch extends eight feet, and the back porch three feet. A cellar seven and a half feet high extends under the whole house, and will contain the boiler, wash-tubs, and coal-bunker. It is intended that the house shall be built on lots forty by sixty feet, giving a lawn and a small garden.

It is contemplated that these houses shall be built in industrial communities, where they can be put up in groups of several hundred. If erected in this manner, and by an operator buying his materials in large quantities, Edison believes that these houses can be erected complete, including heating apparatus and plumbing, for $1200 each. This figure would also rest on the basis of using in the mixture the gravel excavated on the site. Comment has been made by persons of artistic taste on the monotony of a cluster of houses exactly alike in appearance, but this criticism has been anticipated, and the molds are so made as to be capable of permutations of arrangement. Thus it will be possible to introduce almost endless changes in the style of house by variation of the same set of molds.

For more than forty years Edison was avowedly an inventor for purely commercial purposes; but within the last two years he decided to retire from that field so far as new inventions were concerned, and to devote himself to scientific research and experiment in the leisure hours that might remain after continuing to improve his existing devices. But although the poured cement house was planned during the commercial period, the spirit in which it was conceived arose out of an earnest desire to place within the reach of the wage-earner an opportunity to better his physical, pecuniary, and mental conditions in so far as that could be done through the medium of hygienic and beautiful homes at moderate rentals. From the first Edison has declared that it was not his intention to benefit pecuniarily through the exploitation of this project. Having actually demonstrated the practicability and feasibility of his plans, he will allow responsible concerns to carry them into practice under such limitations as may be necessary to sustain the basic object, but without any payment to him except for the actual expense incurred. The hypercritical may cavil and say that, as a manufacturer of cement, Edison will be benefited. True, but as ANY good Portland cement can be used, and no restrictions as to source of supply are enforced, he, or rather his company, will be merely one of many possible purveyors.

This invention is practically a gift to the workingmen of the world and their families. The net result will be that those who care to avail themselves of the privilege may, sooner or later, forsake the crowded apartment or tenement and be comfortably housed in sanitary, substantial, and roomy homes fitted with modern conveniences, and beautified by artistic decorations, with no outlay for insurance or repairs; no dread of fire, and all at a rental which Edison believes will be not more, but probably less than, $10 per month in any city of the United States. While his achievement in its present status will bring about substantial and immediate benefits to wage-earners, his thoughts have already travelled some years ahead in the formulation of a still further beneficial project looking toward the individual ownership of these houses on a basis startling in its practical possibilities.

CHAPTER XXI

MOTION PICTURES

THE preceding chapters have treated of Edison in various aspects as an inventor, some of which are familiar to the public, others of which are believed to be in the nature of a novel revelation, simply because no one had taken the trouble before to put the facts together. To those who have perhaps grown weary of seeing Edison's name in articles of a sensational character, it may sound strange to say that, after all, justice has not been done to his versatile and many-sided nature; and that the mere prosaic facts of his actual achievement outrun the wildest flights of irrelevant journalistic imagination. Edison hates nothing more than to be dubbed a genius or played up as a "wizard"; but this fate has dogged him until he has come at last to resign himself to it with a resentful indignation only to be appreciated when watching him read the latest full-page Sunday "spread" that develops a casual conversation into oracular verbosity, and gives to his shrewd surmise the cast of inspired prophecy.

In other words, Edison's real work has seldom been seriously discussed. Rather has it been taken as a point of departure into a realm of fancy and romance, where as a relief from drudgery he is sometimes quite willing to play the pipe if some one will dance to it. Indeed, the stories woven around his casual suggestions are tame and vapid alongside his own essays in fiction, probably never to be published, but which show what a real inventor can do when he cuts loose to create a new heaven and a new earth, unrestrained by any formal respect for existing conditions of servitude to three dimensions and the standard elements.

The present chapter, essentially technical in its subject-matter, is perhaps as significant as any in this biography, because it presents Edison as the Master Impresario of his age, and maybe of many following ages also. His phonographs and his motion pictures have more audiences in a week than all the theatres in America in a year. The "Nickelodeon" is the central fact in modern amusement, and Edison founded it. All that millions know of music and drama he furnishes; and the whole study of the theatrical managers thus reaching the masses is not to ascertain the limitations of the new art, but to discover its boundless possibilities. None of the exuberant versions of things Edison has not done could endure for a moment with the simple narrative of what he has really done as the world's new Purveyor of Pleasure. And yet it all depends on the toilful conquest of a subtle and intricate art. The story of the invention of the phonograph has been told. That of the evolution of motion pictures follows. It is all one piece of sober, careful analysis, and stubborn, successful attack on the problem.

The possibility of making a record of animate movement, and subsequently reproducing it, was predicted long before the actual accomplishment. This, as we have seen, was also the case with the phonograph, the telephone, and the electric light. As to the phonograph, the prediction went only so far as the RESULT; the apparent intricacy of the problem being so great that the MEANS for accomplishing the desired end were seemingly beyond the grasp of the imagination or the mastery of invention.

With the electric light and the telephone the prediction included not only the result to be accomplished, but, in a rough and general way, the mechanism itself; that is to say, long before a single sound was intelligibly transmitted it was recognized that such a thing might be done by causing a diaphragm, vibrated by original sounds, to communicate its movements to a distant diaphragm by a suitably controlled electric current. In the case of the electric light, the heating of a conductor to incandescence in a highly rarefied atmosphere was suggested as a scheme of illumination long before its actual accomplishment, and in fact before the production of a suitable generator for delivering electric current in a satisfactory and economical manner.

It is a curious fact that while the modern art of motion pictures depends essentially on the development of instantaneous photography, the suggestion of the possibility of securing a reproduction of animate motion, as well as, in a general way, of the mechanism for accomplishing the result, was made many years before the instantaneous photograph became possible. While the first motion picture was not actually produced until the summer of 1889, its real birth was almost a century earlier, when Plateau, in France, constructed an optical toy, to which the impressive name of "Phenakistoscope" was applied, for producing an illusion of motion. This toy in turn was the forerunner of the Zoetrope, or so-called "Wheel of Life," which was introduced into this country about the year 1845. These devices were essentially toys, depending for their successful operation (as is the case with motion pictures) upon a physiological phenomenon known as persistence of vision. If, for instance, a bright light is moved rapidly in front of the eye in a dark room, it appears not as an illuminated spark, but as a line of fire; a so-called shooting star, or a flash of lightning produces the same effect. This result is purely physiological, and is due to the fact that the retina of the eye may be considered as practically a sensitized plate of relatively slow speed, and an image impressed upon it remains, before being effaced, for a period of from one-tenth to one-seventh of a second, varying according to the idiosyncrasies of the individual and the intensity of the light. When, therefore, it is said that we should only believe things we actually see, we ought to remember that in almost every instance we never see things as they are.

Bearing in mind the fact that when an image is impressed on the human retina it persists for an appreciable period, varying as stated, with the individual, and depending also upon the intensity of the illumination, it will be seen that, if a number of pictures or photographs are successively presented to the eye, they will appear as a single, continuous photograph, provided the periods between them are short enough to prevent one of the photographs from being effaced before its successor is presented. If, for instance, a series of identical portraits were rapidly presented to the eye, a single picture would apparently be viewed, or if we presented to the eye the series of photographs of a moving object, each one representing a minute successive phase of the movement, the movements themselves would apparently again take place.

With the Zoetrope and similar toys rough drawings were used for depicting a few broadly outlined successive phases of movement, because in their day instantaneous photography was unknown, and in addition there were certain crudities of construction that seriously interfered with the illumination of the pictures, rendering it necessary to make them practically as silhouettes on a very conspicuous background. Hence it will be obvious that these toys produced merely an ILLUSION of THEORETICAL motion.

But with the knowledge of even an illusion of motion, and with the philosophy of persistence of vision fully understood, it would seem that, upon the development of instantaneous photography, the reproduction of ACTUAL motion by means of pictures would have followed, almost as a necessary consequence. Yet such was not the case, and success was ultimately accomplished by Edison only after persistent experimenting along lines that could not have been predicted, including the construction of apparatus for the purpose, which, if it had not been made, would undoubtedly be considered impossible. In fact, if it were not for Edison's peculiar mentality, that refuses to recognize anything as impossible until indubitably demonstrated to be so, the production of motion pictures would certainly have been delayed for years, if not for all time.

One of the earliest suggestions of the possibility of utilizing photography for exhibiting the illusion of actual movement was made by Ducos, who, as early as 1864, obtained a patent in France, in which he said: "My invention consists in substituting rapidly and without confusion to the eye not only of an individual, but when so desired of a whole assemblage, the enlarged images of a great number of pictures when taken instantaneously and successively at very short intervals.... The observer will believe that he sees only one image, which changes gradually by reason of the successive changes of form and position of the objects which occur from one picture to the other. Even supposing that there be a slight interval of time during which the same object was not shown, the persistence of the luminous impression upon the eye will fill this gap. There will be as it were a living representation of nature and . . . the same scene will be reproduced upon the screen with the same degree of animation.... By means of my apparatus I am enabled especially to reproduce the passing of a procession, a review of military manoeuvres, the movements of a battle, a public fete, a theatrical scene, the evolution or the dances of one or of several persons, the changing expression of countenance, or, if one desires, the grimaces of a human face; a marine view, the motion of waves, the passage of clouds in a stormy sky, particularly in a mountainous country, the eruption of a volcano," etc.

Other dreamers, contemporaries of Ducos, made similar suggestions; they recognized the scientific possibility of the problem, but they were irretrievably handicapped by the shortcomings of photography. Even when substantially instantaneous photographs were evolved at a somewhat later date they were limited to the use of wet plates, which have to be prepared by the photographer and used immediately, and were therefore quite out of the question for any practical commercial scheme. Besides this, the use of plates would have been impracticable, because the limitations of their weight and size would have prevented the taking of a large number of pictures at a high rate of speed, even if the sensitized surface had been sufficiently rapid.

Nothing ever came of Ducos' suggestions and those of the early dreamers in this essentially practical and commercial art, and their ideas have made no greater impress upon the final result than Jules Verne's Nautilus of our boyhood days has developed the modern submarine. From time to time further suggestions were made, some in patents, and others in photographic and scientific publications, all dealing with the fascinating thought of preserving and representing actual scenes and events. The first serious attempt to secure an illusion of motion by photography was made in 1878 by Edward Muybridge as a result of a wager with the late Senator Leland Stanford, the California pioneer and horse-lover, who had asserted, contrary to the usual belief, that a trotting-horse at one point in its gait left the ground entirely. At this time wet plates of very great rapidity were known, and by arranging a series of cameras along the line of a track and causing the horse in trotting past them, by striking wires or strings attached to the shutters, to actuate the cameras at the right instant, a series of very clear instantaneous photographs was obtained. From these negatives, when developed, positive prints were made, which were later mounted on a modified form of Zoetrope and projected upon a screen.

One of these early exhibitions is described in the Scientific American of June 5, 1880: "While the separate photographs had shown the successive positions of a trotting or running horse in making a single stride, the Zoogyroscope threw upon the screen apparently the living animal. Nothing was wanting but the clatter of hoofs upon the turf, and an occasional breath of steam from the nostrils, to make the spectator believe that he had before him genuine flesh-and-blood steeds. In the views of hurdle-leaping, the simulation was still more admirable, even to the motion of the tail as the animal gathered for the jump, the raising of his head, all were there. Views of an ox trotting, a wild bull on the charge, greyhounds and deer running and birds flying in mid-air were shown, also athletes in various positions." It must not be assumed from this statement that even as late as the work of Muybridge anything like a true illusion of movement had been obtained, because such was not the case. Muybridge secured only one cycle of movement, because a separate camera had to be used for each photograph and consequently each cycle was reproduced over and over again. To have made photographs of a trotting-horse for one minute at the moderate rate of twelve per second would have required, under the Muybridge scheme, seven hundred and twenty separate cameras, whereas with the modern art only a single camera is used. A further defect with the Muybridge pictures was that since each photograph was secured when the moving object was in the centre of the plate, the reproduction showed the object always centrally on the screen with its arms or legs in violent movement, but not making any progress, and with the scenery rushing wildly across the field of view!

In the early 80's the dry plate was first introduced into general use, and from that time onward its rapidity and quality were gradually improved; so much so that after 1882 Prof. E. J. Marey, of the French Academy, who in 1874 had published a well-known treatise on "Animal Movement," was able by the use of dry plates to carry forward the experiments of Muybridge on a greatly refined scale. Marey was, however, handicapped by reason of the fact that glass plates were still used, although he was able with a single camera to obtain twelve photographs on successive plates in the space of one second. Marey, like Muybridge, photographed only one cycle of the movements of a single object, which was subsequently reproduced over and over again, and the camera was in the form of a gun, which could follow the object so that the successive pictures would be always located in the centre of the plates.

The review above given, as briefly as possible, comprises substantially the sum of the world's knowledge at the time the problem of recording and reproducing animate movement was first undertaken by Edison. The most that could be said of the condition of the art when Edison entered the field was that it had been recognized that if a series of instantaneous photographs of a moving object could be secured at an enormously high rate many times per second--they might be passed before the eye either directly or by projection upon a screen, and thereby result in a reproduction of the movements. Two very serious difficulties lay in the way of actual accomplishment, however--first, the production of a sensitive surface in such form and weight as to be capable of being successively brought into position and exposed, at the necessarily high rate; and, second, the production of a camera capable of so taking the pictures. There were numerous other workers in the field, but they added nothing to what had already been proposed. Edison himself knew nothing of Ducos, or that the suggestions had advanced beyond the single centrally located photographs of Muybridge and Marey. As a matter of public policy, the law presumes that an inventor must be familiar with all that has gone before in the field within which he is working, and if a suggestion is limited to a patent granted in New South Wales, or is described in a single publication in Brazil, an inventor in America, engaged in the same field of thought, is by legal fiction presumed to have knowledge not only of the existence of that patent or publication, but of its contents. We say this not in the way of an apology for the extent of Edison's contribution to the motion-picture art, because there can be no question that he was as much the creator of that art as he was of the phonographic art; but to show that in a practical sense the suggestion of the art itself was original with him. He himself says: "In the year 1887 the idea occurred to me that it was possible to devise an instrument which should do for the eye what the phonograph does for the ear, and that by a combination of the two, all motion and sound could be recorded and reproduced simultaneously. This idea, the germ of which came from the little toy called the Zoetrope and the work of Muybridge, Marey, and others, has now been accomplished, so that every change of facial expression can be recorded and reproduced life-size. The kinetoscope is only a small model illustrating the present stage of the progress, but with each succeeding month new possibilities are brought into view. I believe that in coming years, by my own work and that of Dickson, Muybridge, Marey, and others who will doubtless enter the field, grand opera can be given at the Metropolitan Opera House at New York without any material change from the original, and with artists and musicians long since dead."

In the earliest experiments attempts were made to secure the photographs, reduced microscopically, arranged spirally on a cylinder about the size of a phonograph record, and coated with a highly sensitized surface, the cylinder being given an intermittent movement, so as to be at rest during each exposure. Reproductions were obtained in the same way, positive prints being observed through a magnifying glass. Various forms of apparatus following this general type were made, but they were all open to the serious objection that the very rapid emulsions employed were relatively coarse-grained and prevented the securing of sharp pictures of microscopic size. On the other hand, the enlarging of the apparatus to permit larger pictures to be obtained would present too much weight to be stopped and started with the requisite rapidity. In these early experiments, however, it was recognized that, to secure proper results, a single camera should be used, so that the objects might move across its field just as they move across the field of the human eye; and the important fact was also observed that the rate at which persistence of vision took place represented the minimum speed at which the pictures should be obtained. If, for instance, five pictures per second were taken (half of the time being occupied in exposure and the other half in moving the exposed portion of the film out of the field of the lens and bringing a new portion into its place), and the same ratio is observed in exhibiting the pictures, the interval of time between successive pictures would be one-tenth of a second; and for a normal eye such an exhibition would present a substantially continuous photograph. If the angular movement of the object across the field is very slow, as, for instance, a distant vessel, the successive positions of the object are so nearly coincident that when reproduced before the eye an impression of smooth, continuous movement is secured. If, however, the object is moving rapidly across the field of view, one picture will be separated from its successor to a marked extent, and the resulting impression will be jerky and unnatural. Recognizing this fact, Edison always sought for a very high speed, so as to give smooth and natural reproductions, and even with his experimental apparatus obtained upward of forty-eight pictures per second, whereas, in practice, at the present time, the accepted rate varies between twenty and thirty per second. In the efforts of the present day to economize space by using a minimum length of film, pictures are frequently taken at too slow a rate, and the reproductions are therefore often objectionable, by reason of more or less jerkiness.

During the experimental period and up to the early part of 1889, the kodak film was being slowly developed by the Eastman Kodak Company. Edison perceived in this product the solution of the problem on which he had been working, because the film presented a very light body of tough material on which relatively large photographs could be taken at rapid intervals. The surface, however, was not at first sufficiently sensitive to admit of sharply defined pictures being secured at the necessarily high rates. It seemed apparent, therefore, that in order to obtain the desired speed there would have to be sacrificed that fineness of emulsion necessary for the securing of sharp pictures. But as was subsequently seen, this sacrifice was in time rendered unnecessary. Much credit is due the Eastman experts--stimulated and encouraged by Edison, but independently of him--for the production at last of a highly sensitized, fine-grained emulsion presenting the highly sensitized surface that Edison sought.

Having at last obtained apparently the proper material upon which to secure the photographs, the problem then remained to devise an apparatus by means of which from twenty to forty pictures per second could be taken; the film being stationary during the exposure and, upon the closing of the shutter, being moved to present a fresh surface. In connection with this problem it is interesting to note that this question of high speed was apparently regarded by all Edison's predecessors as the crucial point. Ducos, for example, expended a great deal of useless ingenuity in devising a camera by means of which a tape-line film could receive the photographs while being in continuous movement, necessitating the use of a series of moving lenses. Another experimenter, Dumont, made use of a single large plate and a great number of lenses which were successively exposed. Muybridge, as we have seen, used a series of cameras, one for each plate. Marey was limited to a very few photographs, because the entire surface had to be stopped and started in connection with each exposure.

After the accomplishment of the fact, it would seem to be the obvious thing to use a single lens and move the sensitized film with respect to it, intermittently bringing the surface to rest, then exposing it, then cutting off the light and moving the surface to a fresh position; but who, other than Edison, would assume that such a device could be made to repeat these movements over and over again at the rate of twenty to forty per second? Users of kodaks and other forms of film cameras will appreciate perhaps better than others the difficulties of the problem, because in their work, after an exposure, they have to advance the film forward painfully to the extent of the next picture before another exposure can take place, these operations permitting of speeds of but a few pictures per minute at best. Edison's solution of the problem involved the production of a kodak in which from twenty to forty pictures should be taken IN EACH SECOND, and with such fineness of adjustment that each should exactly coincide with its predecessors even when subjected to the test of enlargement by projection. This, however, was finally accomplished, and in the summer of 1889 the first modern motion-picture camera was made. More than this, the mechanism for operating the film was so constructed that the movement of the film took place in one-tenth of the time required for the exposure, giving the film an opportunity to come to rest prior to the opening of the shutter. From that day to this the Edison camera has been the accepted standard for securing pictures of objects in motion, and such changes as have been made in it have been purely in the nature of detail mechanical refinements.

The earliest form of exhibiting apparatus, known as the Kinetoscope, was a machine in which a positive print from the negative obtained in the camera was exhibited directly to the eye through a peep-hole; but in 1895 the films were applied to modified forms of magic lanterns, by which the images are projected upon a screen. Since that date the industry has developed very rapidly, and at the present time (1910) all of the principal American manufacturers of motion pictures are paying a royalty to Edison under his basic patents.

From the early days of pictures representing simple movements, such as a man sneezing, or a skirt-dance, there has been a gradual evolution, until now the pictures represent not only actual events in all their palpitating instantaneity, but highly developed dramas and scenarios enacted in large, well-equipped glass studios, and the result of infinite pains and expense of production. These pictures are exhibited in upward of eight thousand places of amusement in the United States, and are witnessed by millions of people each year. They constitute a cheap, clean form of amusement for many persons who cannot spare the money to go to the ordinary theatres, or they may be exhibited in towns that are too small to support a theatre. More than this, they offer to the poor man an effective substitute for the saloon. Probably no invention ever made has afforded more pleasure and entertainment than the motion picture.

Aside from the development of the motion picture as a spectacle, there has gone on an evolution in its use for educational purposes of wide range, which must not be overlooked. In fact, this form of utilization has been carried further in Europe than in this country as a means of demonstration in the arts and sciences. One may study animal life, watch a surgical operation, follow the movement of machinery, take lessons in facial expression or in calisthenics. It seems a pity that in motion pictures should at last have been found the only competition that the ancient marionettes cannot withstand. But aside from the disappearance of those entertaining puppets, all else is gain in the creation of this new art.

The work at the Edison laboratory in the development of the motion picture was as usual intense and concentrated, and, as might be expected, many of the early experiments were quite primitive in their character until command had been secured of relatively perfect apparatus. The subjects registered jerkily by the films were crude and amusing, such as of Fred Ott's sneeze, Carmencita dancing, Italians and their performing bears, fencing, trapeze stunts, horsemanship, blacksmithing--just simple movements without any attempt to portray the silent drama. One curious incident of this early study occurred when "Jim" Corbett was asked to box a few rounds in front of the camera, with a "dark un" to be selected locally. This was agreed to, and a celebrated bruiser was brought over from Newark. When this "sparring partner" came to face Corbett in the imitation ring he was so paralyzed with terror he could hardly move. It was just after Corbett had won one of his big battles as a prize-fighter, and the dismay of his opponent was excusable. The "boys" at the laboratory still laugh consumedly when they tell about it.

The first motion-picture studio was dubbed by the staff the "Black Maria." It was an unpretentious oblong wooden structure erected in the laboratory yard, and had a movable roof in the central part. This roof could be raised or lowered at will. The building was covered with black roofing paper, and was also painted black inside. There was no scenery to render gay this lugubrious environment, but the black interior served as the common background for the performers, throwing all their actions into high relief. The whole structure was set on a pivot so that it could be swung around with the sun; and the movable roof was opened so that the accentuating sunlight could stream in upon the actor whose gesticulations were being caught by the camera. These beginnings and crudities are very remote from the elaborate and expensive paraphernalia and machinery with which the art is furnished to-day.

At the present time the studios in which motion pictures are taken are expensive and pretentious affairs. An immense building of glass, with all the properties and stage-settings of a regular theatre, is required. The Bronx Park studio of the Edison company cost at least one hundred thousand dollars, while the well-known house of Pathe Freres in France--one of Edison's licensees--makes use of no fewer than seven of these glass theatres. All of the larger producers of pictures in this country and abroad employ regular stock companies of actors, men and women selected especially for their skill in pantomime, although, as most observers have perhaps suspected, in the actual taking of the pictures the performers are required to carry on an animated and prepared dialogue with the same spirit and animation as on the regular stage. Before setting out on the preparation of a picture, the book is first written--known in the business as a scenario--giving a complete statement as to the scenery, drops and background, and the sequence of events, divided into scenes as in an ordinary play. These are placed in the hands of a "producer," corresponding to a stage-director, generally an actor or theatrical man of experience, with a highly developed dramatic instinct. The various actors are selected, parts are assigned, and the scene-painters are set to work on the production of the desired scenery. Before the photographing of a scene, a long series of rehearsals takes place, the incidents being gone over and over again until the actors are "letter perfect." So persistent are the producers in the matter of rehearsals and the refining and elaboration of details, that frequently a picture that may be actually photographed and reproduced in fifteen minutes, may require two or three weeks for its production. After the rehearsal of a scene has advanced sufficiently to suit the critical requirements of the producer, the camera man is in requisition, and he is consulted as to lighting so as to produce the required photographic effect. Preferably, of course, sunlight is used whenever possible, hence the glass studios; but on dark days, and when night-work is necessary, artificial light of enormous candle-power is used, either mercury arcs or ordinary arc lights of great size and number.

Under all conditions the light is properly screened and diffused to suit the critical eye of the camera man. All being in readiness, the actual picture is taken, the actors going through their rehearsed parts, the producer standing out of the range of the camera, and with a megaphone to his lips yelling out his instructions, imprecations, and approval, and the camera man grinding at the crank of the camera and securing the pictures at the rate of twenty or more per second, making a faithful and permanent record of every movement and every change of facial expression. At the end of the scene the negative is developed in the ordinary way, and is then ready for use in the printing of the positives for sale. When a further scene in the play takes place in the same setting, and without regard to its position in the plot, it is taken up, rehearsed, and photographed in the same way, and afterward all the scenes are cemented together in the proper sequence, and form the complete negative. Frequently, therefore, in the production of a motion-picture play, the first and the last scene may be taken successively, the only thing necessary being, of course, that after all is done the various scenes should be arranged in their proper order. The frames, having served their purpose, now go back to the scene-painter for further use. All pictures are not taken in studios, because when light and weather permit and proper surroundings can be secured outside, scenes can best be obtained with natural scenery--city streets, woods, and fields. The great drawback to the taking of pictures out-of-doors, however, is the inevitable crowd, attracted by the novelty of the proceedings, which makes the camera man's life a torment by getting into the field of his instrument. The crowds are patient, however, and in one Edison picture involving the blowing up of a bridge by the villain of the piece and the substitution of a pontoon bridge by a company of engineers just in time to allow the heroine to pass over in her automobile, more than a thousand people stood around for almost an entire day waiting for the tedious rehearsals to end and the actual performance to begin. Frequently large bodies of men are used in pictures, such as troops of soldiers, and it is an open secret that for weeks during the Boer War regularly equipped British and Boer armies confronted each other on the peaceful hills of Orange, New Jersey, ready to enact before the camera the stirring events told by the cable from the seat of hostilities. These conflicts were essentially harmless, except in one case during the battle of Spion Kopje, when "General Cronje," in his efforts to fire a wooden cannon, inadvertently dropped his fuse into a large glass bottle containing gunpowder. The effect was certainly most dramatic, and created great enthusiasm among the many audiences which viewed the completed production; but the unfortunate general, who is still an employee, was taken to the hospital, and even now, twelve years afterward, he says with a grin that whenever he has a moment of leisure he takes the time to pick a few pieces of glass from his person!

Edison's great contribution to the regular stage was the incandescent electric lamp, which enabled the production of scenic effects never before even dreamed of, but which we accept now with so much complacency. Yet with the motion picture, effects are secured that could not be reproduced to the slightest extent on the real stage. The villain, overcome by a remorseful conscience, sees on the wall of the room the very crime which he committed, with HIMSELF as the principal actor; one of the easy effects of double exposure. The substantial and ofttimes corpulent ghost or spirit of the real stage has been succeeded by an intangible wraith, as transparent and unsubstantial as may be demanded in the best book of fairy tales--more double exposure. A man emerges from the water with a splash, ascends feet foremost ten yards or more, makes a graceful curve and lands on a spring-board, runs down it to the bank, and his clothes fly gently up from the ground and enclose his person--all unthinkable in real life, but readily possible by running the motion-picture film backward! The fairy prince commands the princess to appear, consigns the bad brothers to instant annihilation, turns the witch into a cat, confers life on inanimate things; and many more startling and apparently incomprehensible effects are carried out with actual reality, by stop-work photography. In one case, when the command for the heroine to come forth is given, the camera is stopped, the young woman walks to the desired spot, and the camera is again started; the effect to the eye--not knowing of this little by-play--is as if she had instantly appeared from space. The other effects are perhaps obvious, and the field and opportunities are absolutely unlimited. Other curious effects are secured by taking the pictures at a different speed from that at which they are exhibited. If, for example, a scene occupying thirty seconds is reproduced in ten seconds, the movements will be three times as fast, and vice versa. Many scenes familiar to the reader, showing automobiles tearing along the road and rounding corners at an apparently reckless speed, are really pictures of slow and dignified movements reproduced at a high speed.

Brief reference has been made to motion pictures of educational subjects, and in this field there are very great opportunities for development. The study of geography, scenes and incidents in foreign countries, showing the lives and customs and surroundings of other peoples, is obviously more entertaining to the child when actively depicted on the screen than when merely described in words. The lives of great men, the enacting of important historical events, the reproduction of great works of literature, if visually presented to the child must necessarily impress his mind with greater force than if shown by mere words. We predict that the time is not far distant when, in many of our public schools, two or three hours a week will be devoted to this rational and effective form of education.

By applying microphotography to motion pictures an additional field is opened up, one phase of which may be the study of germ life and bacteria, so that our future medical students may become as familiar with the habits and customs of the Anthrax bacillus, for example, as of the domestic cat.

From whatever point of view the subject is approached, the fact remains that in the motion picture, perhaps more than with any other invention, Edison has created an art that must always make a special appeal to the mind and emotions of men, and although so far it has not advanced much beyond the field of amusement, it contains enormous possibilities for serious development in the future. Let us not think too lightly of the humble five-cent theatre with its gaping crowd following with breathless interest the vicissitudes of the beautiful heroine. Before us lies an undeveloped land of opportunity which is destined to play an important part in the growth and welfare of the human race.

CHAPTER XXII

THE DEVELOPMENT OF THE EDISON STORAGE BATTERY

IT is more than a hundred years since the elementary principle of the storage battery or "accumulator" was detected by a Frenchman named Gautherot; it is just fifty years since another Frenchman, named Plante, discovered that on taking two thin plates of sheet lead, immersing them in dilute sulphuric acid, and passing an electric current through the cell, the combination exhibited the ability to give back part of the original charging current, owing to the chemical changes and reactions set up. Plante coiled up his sheets into a very handy cell like a little roll of carpet or pastry; but the trouble was that the battery took a long time to "form." One sheet becoming coated with lead peroxide and the other with finely divided or spongy metallic lead, they would receive current, and then, even after a long period of inaction, furnish or return an electromotive force of from 1.85 to 2.2 volts. This ability to store up electrical energy produced by dynamos in hours otherwise idle, whether driven by steam, wind, or water, was a distinct advance in the art; but the sensational step was taken about 1880, when Faure in France and Brush in America broke away from the slow and weary process of "forming" the plates, and hit on clever methods of furnishing them "ready made," so to speak, by dabbing red lead onto lead-grid plates, just as butter is spread on a slice of home-made bread. This brought the storage battery at once into use as a practical, manufactured piece of apparatus; and the world was captivated with the idea. The great English scientist, Sir William Thomson, went wild with enthusiasm when a Faure "box of electricity" was brought over from Paris to him in 1881 containing a million foot-pounds of stored energy. His biographer, Dr. Sylvanus P. Thompson, describes him as lying ill in bed with a wounded leg, and watching results with an incandescent lamp fastened to his bed curtain by a safety-pin, and lit up by current from the little Faure cell. Said Sir William: "It is going to be a most valuable, practical affair--as valuable as water-cisterns to people whether they had or had not systems of water-pipes and water-supply." Indeed, in one outburst of panegyric the shrewd physicist remarked that he saw in it "a realization of the most ardently and increasingly felt scientific aspiration of his life--an aspiration which he hardly dared to expect or to see realized." A little later, however, Sir William, always cautious and canny, began to discover the inherent defects of the primitive battery, as to disintegration, inefficiency, costliness, etc., and though offered tempting inducements, declined to lend his name to its financial introduction. Nevertheless, he accepted the principle as valuable, and put the battery to actual use.

For many years after this episode, the modern lead-lead type of battery thus brought forward with so great a flourish of trumpets had a hard time of it. Edison's attitude toward it, even as a useful supplement to his lighting system, was always one of scepticism, and he remarked contemptuously that the best storage battery he knew was a ton of coal. The financial fortunes of the battery, on both sides of the Atlantic, were as varied and as disastrous as its industrial; but it did at last emerge, and "made good." By 1905, the production of lead-lead storage batteries in the United States alone had reached a value for the year of nearly $3,000,000, and it has increased greatly since that time. The storage battery is now regarded as an important and indispensable adjunct in nearly all modern electric-lighting and electric-railway systems of any magnitude; and in 1909, in spite of its weight, it had found adoption in over ten thousand automobiles of the truck, delivery wagon, pleasure carriage, and runabout types in America.

Edison watched closely all this earlier development for about fifteen years, not changing his mind as to what he regarded as the incurable defects of the lead-lead type, but coming gradually to the conclusion that if a storage battery of some other and better type could be brought forward, it would fulfil all the early hopes, however extravagant, of such men as Kelvin (Sir William Thomson), and would become as necessary and as universal as the incandescent lamp or the electric motor. The beginning of the present century found him at his point of new departure.

Generally speaking, non-technical and uninitiated persons have a tendency to regard an invention as being more or less the ultimate result of some happy inspiration. And, indeed, there is no doubt that such may be the fact in some instances; but in most cases the inventor has intentionally set out to accomplish a definite and desired result--mostly through the application of the known laws of the art in which he happens to be working. It is rarely, however, that a man will start out deliberately, as Edison did, to evolve a radically new type of such an intricate device as the storage battery, with only a meagre clew and a vague starting-point.

In view of the successful outcome of the problem which, in 1900, he undertook to solve, it will be interesting to review his mental attitude at that period. It has already been noted at the end of a previous chapter that on closing the magnetic iron-ore concentrating plant at Edison, New Jersey, he resolved to work on a new type of storage battery. It was about this time that, in the course of a conversation with Mr. R. H. Beach, then of the street-railway department of the General Electric Company, he said: "Beach, I don't think Nature would be so unkind as to withhold the secret of a GOOD storage battery if a real earnest hunt for it is made. I'm going to hunt."

Frequently Edison has been asked what he considers the secret of achievement. To this query he has invariably replied: "Hard work, based on hard thinking." The laboratory records bear the fullest witness that he has consistently followed out this prescription to the utmost. The perfection of all his great inventions has been signalized by patient, persistent, and incessant effort which, recognizing nothing short of success, has resulted in the ultimate accomplishment of his ideas. Optimistic and hopeful to a high degree, Edison has the happy faculty of beginning the day as open-minded as a child--yesterday's disappointments and failures discarded and discounted by the alluring possibilities of to-morrow.

Of all his inventions, it is doubtful whether any one of them has called forth more original thought, work, perseverance, ingenuity, and monumental patience than the one we are now dealing with. One of his associates who has been through the many years of the storage-battery drudgery with him said: "If Edison's experiments, investigations, and work on this storage battery were all that he had ever done, I should say that he was not only a notable inventor, but also a great man. It is almost impossible to appreciate the enormous difficulties that have been overcome."

From a beginning which was made practically in the dark, it was not until he had completed more than ten thousand experiments that he obtained any positive preliminary results whatever. Through all this vast amount of research there had been no previous signs of the electrical action he was looking for. These experiments had extended over many months of constant work by day and night, but there was no breakdown of Edison's faith in ultimate success--no diminution of his sanguine and confident expectations. The failure of an experiment simply meant to him that he had found something else that would not work, thus bringing the possible goal a little nearer by a process of painstaking elimination.

Now, however, after these many months of arduous toil, in which he had examined and tested practically all the known elements in numerous chemical combinations, the electric action he sought for had been obtained, thus affording him the first inkling of the secret that he had industriously tried to wrest from Nature. It should be borne in mind that from the very outset Edison had disdained any intention of following in the only tracks then known by employing lead and sulphuric acid as the components of a successful storage battery. Impressed with what he considered the serious inherent defects of batteries made of these materials, and the tremendously complex nature of the chemical reactions taking place in all types of such cells, he determined boldly at the start that he would devise a battery without lead, and one in which an alkaline solution could be used--a form which would, he firmly believed, be inherently less subject to decay and dissolution than the standard type, which after many setbacks had finally won its way to an annual production of many thousands of cells, worth millions of dollars.

Two or three thousand of the first experiments followed the line of his well-known primary battery in the attempted employment of copper oxide as an element in a new type of storage cell; but its use offered no advantages, and the hunt was continued in other directions and pursued until Edison satisfied himself by a vast number of experiments that nickel and iron possessed the desirable qualifications he was in search of.

This immense amount of investigation which had consumed so many months of time, and which had culminated in the discovery of a series of reactions between nickel and iron that bore great promise, brought Edison merely within sight of a strange and hitherto unexplored country. Slowly but surely the results of the last few thousands of his preliminary experiments had pointed inevitably to a new and fruitful region ahead. He had discovered the hidden passage and held the clew which he had so industriously sought. And now, having outlined a definite path, Edison was all afire to push ahead vigorously in order that he might enter in and possess the land.

It is a trite saying that "history repeats itself," and certainly no axiom carries more truth than this when applied to the history of each of Edison's important inventions. The development of the storage battery has been no exception; indeed, far from otherwise, for in the ten years that have elapsed since the time he set himself and his mechanics, chemists, machinists, and experimenters at work to develop a practical commercial cell, the old story of incessant and persistent efforts so manifest in the working out of other inventions was fully repeated.

Very soon after he had decided upon the use of nickel and iron as the elemental metals for his storage battery, Edison established a chemical plant at Silver Lake, New Jersey, a few miles from the Orange laboratory, on land purchased some time previously. This place was the scene of the further experiments to develop the various chemical forms of nickel and iron, and to determine by tests what would be best adapted for use in cells manufactured on a commercial scale. With a little handful of selected experimenters gathered about him, Edison settled down to one of his characteristic struggles for supremacy. To some extent it was a revival of the old Menlo Park days (or, rather, nights). Some of these who had worked on the preliminary experiments, with the addition of a few new-comers, toiled together regardless of passing time and often under most discouraging circumstances, but with that remarkable esprit de corps that has ever marked Edison's relations with his co-workers, and that has contributed so largely to the successful carrying out of his ideas.

The group that took part in these early years of Edison's arduous labors included his old-time assistant, Fred Ott, together with his chemist, J. W. Aylsworth, as well as E. J. Ross, Jr., W. E. Holland, and Ralph Arbogast, and a little later W. G. Bee, all of whom have grown up with the battery and still devote their energies to its commercial development. One of these workers, relating the strenuous experiences of these few years, says: "It was hard work and long hours, but still there were some things that made life pleasant. One of them was the supper-hour we enjoyed when we worked nights. Mr. Edison would have supper sent in about midnight, and we all sat down together, including himself. Work was forgotten for the time, and all hands were ready for fun. I have very pleasant recollections of Mr. Edison at these times. He would always relax and help to make a good time, and on some occasions I have seen him fairly overflow with animal spirits, just like a boy let out from school. After the supper-hour was over, however, he again became the serious, energetic inventor, deeply immersed in the work at hand.

"He was very fond of telling and hearing stories, and always appreciated a joke. I remember one that he liked to get off on us once in a while. Our lighting plant was in duplicate, and about 12.30 or 1 o'clock in the morning, at the close of the supper-hour, a change would be made from one plant to the other, involving the gradual extinction of the electric lights and their slowly coming up to candle-power again, the whole change requiring probably about thirty seconds. Sometimes, as this was taking place, Edison would fold his hands, compose himself as if he were in sound sleep, and when the lights were full again would apparently wake up, with the remark, 'Well, boys, we've had a fine rest; now let's pitch into work again.'"

Another interesting and amusing reminiscence of this period of activity has been gathered from another of the family of experimenters: "Sometimes, when Mr. Edison had been working long hours, he would want to have a short sleep. It was one of the funniest things I ever witnessed to see him crawl into an ordinary roll-top desk and curl up and take a nap. If there was a sight that was still more funny, it was to see him turn over on his other side, all the time remaining in the desk. He would use several volumes of Watts's Dictionary of Chemistry for a pillow, and we fellows used to say that he absorbed the contents during his sleep, judging from the flow of new ideas he had on waking."

Such incidents as these serve merely to illustrate the lighter moments that stand out in relief against the more sombre background of the strenuous years, for, of all the absorbingly busy periods of Edison's inventive life, the first five years of the storage-battery era was one of the very busiest of them all. It was not that there remained any basic principle to be discovered or simplified, for that had already been done; but it was in the effort to carry these principles into practice that there arose the numerous difficulties that at times seemed insurmountable. But, according to another co-worker, "Edison seemed pleased when he used to run up against a serious difficulty. It would seem to stiffen his backbone and make him more prolific of new ideas. For a time I thought I was foolish to imagine such a thing, but I could never get away from the impression that he really appeared happy when he ran up against a serious snag. That was in my green days, and I soon learned that the failure of an experiment never discourages him unless it is by reason of the carelessness of the man making it. Then Edison gets disgusted. If it fails on its merits, he doesn't worry or fret about it, but, on the contrary, regards it as a useful fact learned; remains cheerful and tries something else. I have known him to reverse an unsuccessful experiment and come out all right."

To follow Edison's trail in detail through the innumerable twists and turns of his experimentation and research on the storage battery, during the past ten years, would not be in keeping with the scope of this narrative, nor would it serve any useful purpose. Besides, such details would fill a big volume. The narrative, however, would not be complete without some mention of the general outline of his work, and reference may be made briefly to a few of the chief items. And lest the reader think that the word "innumerable" may have been carelessly or hastily used above, we would quote the reply of one of the laboratory assistants when asked how many experiments had been made on the Edison storage battery since the year 1900: "Goodness only knows! We used to number our experiments consecutively from 1 to 10,000, and when we got up to 10,000 we turned back to 1 and ran up to 10,000 again, and so on. We ran through several series--I don't know how many, and have lost track of them now, but it was not far from fifty thousand."

From the very first, Edison's broad idea of his storage battery was to make perforated metallic containers having the active materials packed therein; nickel hydrate for the positive and iron oxide for the negative plate. This plan has been adhered to throughout, and has found its consummation in the present form of the completed commercial cell, but in the middle ground which stands between the early crude beginnings and the perfected type of to-day there lies a world of original thought, patient plodding, and achievement.

The first necessity was naturally to obtain the best and purest compounds for active materials. Edison found that comparatively little was known by manufacturing chemists about nickel and iron oxides of the high grade and purity he required. Hence it became necessary for him to establish his own chemical works and put them in charge of men specially trained by himself, with whom he worked. This was the plant at Silver Lake, above referred to. Here, for several years, there was ceaseless activity in the preparation of these chemical compounds by every imaginable process and subsequent testing. Edison's chief chemist says: "We left no stone unturned to find a way of making those chemicals so that they would give the highest results. We carried on the experiments with the two chemicals together. Sometimes the nickel would be ahead in the tests, and then again it would fall behind. To stimulate us to greater improvement, Edison hung up a card which showed the results of tests in milliampere-hours given by the experimental elements as we tried them with the various grades of nickel and iron we had made. This stirred up a great deal of ambition among the boys to push the figures up. Some of our earliest tests showed around 300, but as we improved the material, they gradually crept up to over 500. Just about that time Edison made a trip to Canada, and when he came back we had made such good progress that the figures had crept up to about 1000. I well remember how greatly he was pleased."

In speaking of the development of the negative element of the battery, Mr. Aylsworth said: "In like manner the iron element had to be developed and improved; and finally the iron, which had generally enjoyed superiority in capacity over its companion, the nickel element, had to go in training in order to retain its lead, which was imperative, in order to produce a uniform and constant voltage curve. In talking with me one day about the difficulties under which we were working and contrasting them with the phonograph experimentation, Edison said: 'In phonographic work we can use our ears and our eyes, aided with powerful microscopes; but in the battery our difficulties cannot be seen or heard, but must be observed by our mind's eye!' And by reason of the employment of such vision in the past, Edison is now able to see quite clearly through the forest of difficulties after eliminating them one by one."

The size and shape of the containing pockets in the battery plates or elements and the degree of their perforation were matters that received many years of close study and experiment; indeed, there is still to-day constant work expended on their perfection, although their present general form was decided upon several years ago. The mechanical construction of the battery, as a whole, in its present form, compels instant admiration on account of its beauty and completeness. Mr. Edison has spared neither thought, ingenuity, labor, nor money in the effort to make it the most complete and efficient storage cell obtainable, and the results show that his skill, judgment, and foresight have lost nothing of the power that laid the foundation of, and built up, other great arts at each earlier stage of his career.

Among the complex and numerous problems that presented themselves in the evolution of the battery was the one concerning the internal conductivity of the positive unit. The nickel hydrate was a poor electrical conductor, and although a metallic nickel pocket might be filled with it, there would not be the desired electrical action unless a conducting substance were mixed with it, and so incorporated and packed that there would be good electrical contact throughout. This proved to be a most knotty and intricate puzzle--tricky and evasive--always leading on and promising something, and at the last slipping away leaving the work undone. Edison's remarkable patience and persistence in dealing with this trying problem and in finally solving it successfully won for him more than ordinary admiration from his associates. One of them, in speaking of the seemingly interminable experiments to overcome this trouble, said: "I guess that question of conductivity of the positive pocket brought lots of gray hairs to his head. I never dreamed a man could have such patience and perseverance.

Any other man than Edison would have given the whole thing up a thousand times, but not he! Things looked awfully blue to the whole bunch of us many a time, but he was always hopeful. I remember one time things looked so dark to me that I had just about made up my mind to throw up my job, but some good turn came just then and I didn't. Now I'm glad I held on, for we've got a great future."

The difficulty of obtaining good electrical contact in the positive element was indeed Edison's chief trouble for many years. After a great amount of work and experimentation he decided upon a certain form of graphite, which seemed to be suitable for the purpose, and then proceeded to the commercial manufacture of the battery at a special factory in Glen Ridge, New Jersey, installed for the purpose. There was no lack of buyers, but, on the contrary, the factory was unable to turn out batteries enough. The newspapers had previously published articles showing the unusual capacity and performance of the battery, and public interest had thus been greatly awakened.

Notwithstanding the establishment of a regular routine of manufacture and sale, Edison did not cease to experiment for improvement. Although the graphite apparently did the work desired of it, he was not altogether satisfied with its performance and made extended trials of other substances, but at that time found nothing that on the whole served the purpose better. Continuous tests of the commercial cells were carried on at the laboratory, as well as more practical and heavy tests in automobiles, which were constantly kept running around the adjoining country over all kinds of roads. All these tests were very closely watched by Edison, who demanded rigorously that the various trials of the battery should be carried on with all strenuousness so as to get the utmost results and develop any possible weakness. So insistent was he on this, that if any automobile should run several days without bursting a tire or breaking some part of the machine, he would accuse the chauffeur of picking out easy roads.

After these tests had been going on for some time, and some thousands of cells had been sold and were giving satisfactory results to the purchasers, the test sheets and experience gathered from various sources pointed to the fact that occasionally a cell here and there would show up as being short in capacity. Inasmuch as the factory processes were very exact and carefully guarded, and every cell was made as uniform as human skill and care could provide, there thus arose a serious problem. Edison concentrated his powers on the investigation of this trouble, and found that the chief cause lay in the graphite. Some other minor matters also attracted his attention. What to do, was the important question that confronted him. To shut down the factory meant great loss and apparent failure. He realized this fully, but he also knew that to go on would simply be to increase the number of defective batteries in circulation, which would ultimately result in a permanent closure and real failure. Hence he took the course which one would expect of Edison's common sense and directness of action. He was not satisfied that the battery was a complete success, so he shut down and went to experimenting once more.

"And then," says one of the laboratory men, "we started on another series of record-breaking experiments that lasted over five years. I might almost say heart-breaking, too, for of all the elusive, disappointing things one ever hunted for that was the worst. But secrets have to be long-winded and roost high if they want to get away when the 'Old Man' goes hunting for them. He doesn't get mad when he misses them, but just keeps on smiling and firing, and usually brings them into camp. That's what he did on the battery, for after a whole lot of work he perfected the nickel-flake idea and process, besides making the great improvement of using tubes instead of flat pockets for the positive. He also added a minor improvement here and there, and now we have a finer battery than we ever expected."

In the interim, while the experimentation of these last five years was in progress, many customers who had purchased batteries of the original type came knocking at the door with orders in their hands for additional outfits wherewith to equip more wagons and trucks. Edison expressed his regrets, but said he was not satisfied with the old cells and was engaged in improving them. To which the customers replied that THEY were entirely satisfied and ready and willing to pay for more batteries of the same kind; but Edison could not be moved from his determination, although considerable pressure was at times brought to bear to sway his decision.

Experiment was continued beyond the point of peradventure, and after some new machinery had been built, the manufacture of the new type of cell was begun in the early summer of 1909, and at the present writing is being extended as fast as the necessary additional machinery can be made. The product is shipped out as soon as it is completed.

The nickel flake, which is Edison's ingenious solution of the conductivity problem, is of itself a most interesting product, intensely practical in its application and fascinating in its manufacture. The flake of nickel is obtained by electroplating upon a metallic cylinder alternate layers of copper and nickel, one hundred of each, after which the combined sheet is stripped from the cylinder. So thin are the layers that this sheet is only about the thickness of a visiting-card, and yet it is composed of two hundred layers of metal. The sheet is cut into tiny squares, each about one-sixteenth of an inch, and these squares are put into a bath where the copper is dissolved out. This releases the layers of nickel, so that each of these small squares becomes one hundred tiny sheets, or flakes, of pure metallic nickel, so thin that when they are dried they will float in the air, like thistle-down.

In their application to the manufacture of batteries, the flakes are used through the medium of a special machine, so arranged that small charges of nickel hydrate and nickel flake are alternately fed into the pockets intended for positives, and tamped down with a pressure equal to about four tons per square inch. This insures complete and perfect contact and consequent electrical conductivity throughout the entire unit.

The development of the nickel flake contains in itself a history of patient investigation, labor, and achievement, but we have not space for it, nor for tracing the great work that has been done in developing and perfecting the numerous other parts and adjuncts of this remarkable battery. Suffice it to say that when Edison went boldly out into new territory, after something entirely unknown, he was quite prepared for hard work and exploration. He encountered both in unstinted measure, but kept on going forward until, after long travel, he had found all that he expected and accomplished something more beside. Nature DID respond to his whole-hearted appeal, and, by the time the hunt was ended, revealed a good storage battery of entirely new type. Edison not only recognized and took advantage of the principles he had discovered, but in adapting them for commercial use developed most ingenious processes and mechanical appliances for carrying his discoveries into practical effect. Indeed, it may be said that the invention of an enormous variety of new machines and mechanical appliances rendered necessary by each change during the various stages of development of the battery, from first to last, stands as a lasting tribute to the range and versatility of his powers.

It is not within the scope of this narrative to enter into any description of the relative merits of the Edison storage battery, that being the province of a commercial catalogue. It does, however, seem entirely allowable to say that while at the present writing the tests that have been made extend over a few years only, their results and the intrinsic value of this characteristic Edison invention are of such a substantial nature as to point to the inevitable growth of another great industry arising from its manufacture, and to its wide-spread application to many uses.

The principal use that Edison has had in mind for his battery is transportation of freight and passengers by truck, automobile, and street-car. The greatly increased capacity in proportion to weight of the Edison cell makes it particularly adaptable for this class of work on account of the much greater radius of travel that is possible by its use. The latter point of advantage is the one that appeals most to the automobilist, as he is thus enabled to travel, it is asserted, more than three times farther than ever before on a single charge of the battery.

Edison believes that there are important advantages possible in the employment of his storage battery for street-car propulsion. Under the present system of operation, a plant furnishing the electric power for street railways must be large enough to supply current for the maximum load during "rush hours," although much of the machinery may be lying idle and unproductive in the hours of minimum load. By the use of storage-battery cars, this immense and uneconomical maximum investment in plant can be cut down to proportions of true commercial economy, as the charging of the batteries can be conducted at a uniform rate with a reasonable expenditure for generating machinery. Not only this, but each car becomes an independently moving unit, not subject to delay by reason of a general breakdown of the power plant or of the line. In addition to these advantages, the streets would be freed from their burden of trolley wires or conduits. To put his ideas into practice, Edison built a short railway line at the Orange works in the winter of 1909-10, and, in co-operation with Mr. R. H. Beach, constructed a special type of street-car, and equipped it with motor, storage battery, and other necessary operating devices. This car was subsequently put upon the street-car lines in New York City, and demonstrated its efficiency so completely that it was purchased by one of the street-car companies, which has since ordered additional cars for its lines. The demonstration of this initial car has been watched with interest by many railroad officials, and its performance has been of so successful a nature that at the present writing (the summer of 1910) it has been necessary to organize and equip a preliminary factory in which to construct many other cars of a similar type that have been ordered by other street-railway companies. This enterprise will be conducted by a corporation which has been specially organized for the purpose. Thus, there has been initiated the development of a new and important industry whose possible ultimate proportions are beyond the range of present calculation. Extensive as this industry may become, however, Edison is firmly convinced that the greatest field for his storage battery lies in its adaptation to commercial trucking and hauling, and to pleasure vehicles, in comparison with which the street-car business even with its great possibilities--will not amount to more than 1 per cent.

Edison has pithily summed up his work and his views in an article on "The To-Morrows of Electricity and Invention" in Popular Electricity for June, 1910, in which he says: "For years past I have been trying to perfect a storage battery, and have now rendered it entirely suitable to automobile and other work. There is absolutely no reason why horses should be allowed within city limits; for between the gasoline and the electric car, no room is left for them. They are not needed. The cow and the pig have gone, and the horse is still more undesirable. A higher public ideal of health and cleanliness is working toward such banishment very swiftly; and then we shall have decent streets, instead of stables made out of strips of cobblestones bordered by sidewalks. The worst use of money is to make a fine thoroughfare, and then turn it over to horses. Besides that, the change will put the humane societies out of business. Many people now charge their own batteries because of lack of facilities; but I believe central stations will find in this work very soon the largest part of their load. The New York Edison Company, or the Chicago Edison Company, should have as much current going out for storage batteries as for power motors; and it will be so some near day."

CHAPTER XXIII

MISCELLANEOUS INVENTIONS

IT has been the endeavor in this narrative to group Edison's inventions and patents so that his work in the different fields can be studied independently and separately. The history of his career has therefore fallen naturally into a series of chapters, each aiming to describe some particular development or art; and, in a way, the plan has been helpful to the writers while probably useful to the readers. It happens, however, that the process has left a vast mass of discovery and invention wholly untouched, and relegates to a concluding brief chapter some of the most interesting episodes of a fruitful life. Any one who will turn to the list of Edison patents at the end of the book will find a large number of things of which not even casual mention has been made, but which at the time occupied no small amount of the inventor's time and attention, and many of which are now part and parcel of modern civilization. Edison has, indeed, touched nothing that he did not in some way improve. As Thoreau said: "The laws of the Universe are not indifferent, but are forever on the side of the most sensitive," and there never was any one more sensitive to the defects of every art and appliance, nor any one more active in applying the law of evolution. It is perhaps this many-sidedness of Edison that has impressed the multitude, and that in the "popular vote" taken a couple of years ago by the New York Herald placed his name at the head of the list of ten greatest living Americans. It is curious and pertinent to note that a similar plebiscite taken by a technical journal among its expert readers had exactly the same result. Evidently the public does not agree with the opinion expressed by the eccentric artist Blake in his "Marriage of Heaven and Hell," when he said: "Improvement makes strange roads; but the crooked roads without improvements are roads of Genius."

The product of Edison's brain may be divided into three classes. The first embraces such arts and industries, or such apparatus, as have already been treated. The second includes devices like the tasimeter, phonomotor, odoroscope, etc., and others now to be noted. The third embraces a number of projected inventions, partially completed investigations, inventions in use but not patented, and a great many caveats filed in the Patent Office at various times during the last forty years for the purpose of protecting his ideas pending their contemplated realization in practice. These caveats served their purpose thoroughly in many instances, but there have remained a great variety of projects upon which no definite action was ever taken. One ought to add the contents of an unfinished piece of extraordinary fiction based wholly on new inventions and devices utterly unknown to mankind. Some day the novel may be finished, but Edison has no inclination to go back to it, and says he cannot understand how any man is able to make a speech or write a book, for he simply can't do it.

After what has been said in previous chapters, it will not seem so strange that Edison should have hundreds of dormant inventions on his hands. There are human limitations even for such a tireless worker as he is. While the preparation of data for this chapter was going on, one of the writers in discussing with him the vast array of unexploited things said: "Don't you feel a sense of regret in being obliged to leave so many things uncompleted?" To which he replied: "What's the use? One lifetime is too short, and I am busy every day improving essential parts of my established industries." It must suffice to speak briefly of a few leading inventions that have been worked out, and to dismiss with scant mention all the rest, taking just a few items, as typical and suggestive, especially when Edison can himself be quoted as to them. Incidentally it may be noted that things, not words, are referred to; for Edison, in addition to inventing the apparatus, has often had to coin the word to describe it. A large number of the words and phrases in modern electrical parlance owe their origin to him. Even the "call-word" of the telephone, "Hello!" sent tingling over the wire a few million times daily was taken from Menlo Park by men installing telephones in different parts of the world, men who had just learned it at the laboratory, and thus made it a universal sesame for telephonic conversation.

It is hard to determine where to begin with Edison's miscellaneous inventions, but perhaps telegraphy has the "right of line," and Edison's work in that field puts him abreast of the latest wireless developments that fill the world with wonder. "I perfected a system of train telegraphy between stations and trains in motion whereby messages could be sent from the moving train to the central office; and this was the forerunner of wireless telegraphy. This system was used for a number of years on the Lehigh Valley Railroad on their construction trains. The electric wave passed from a piece of metal on top of the car across the air to the telegraph wires; and then proceeded to the despatcher's office. In my first experiments with this system I tried it on the Staten Island Railroad, and employed an operator named King to do the experimenting. He reported results every day, and received instructions by mail; but for some reason he could send messages all right when the train went in one direction, but could not make it go in the contrary direction. I made suggestions of every kind to get around this phenomenon. Finally I telegraphed King to find out if he had any suggestions himself; and I received a reply that the only way he could propose to get around the difficulty was to put the island on a pivot so it could be turned around! I found the trouble finally, and the practical introduction on the Lehigh Valley road was the result. The system was sold to a very wealthy man, and he would never sell any rights or answer letters. He became a spiritualist subsequently, which probably explains it." It is interesting to note that Edison became greatly interested in the later developments by Marconi, and is an admiring friend and adviser of that well-known inventor.

The earlier experiments with wireless telegraphy at Menlo Park were made at a time when Edison was greatly occupied with his electric-light interests, and it was not until the beginning of 1886 that he was able to spare the time to make a public demonstration of the system as applied to moving trains. Ezra T. Gilliland, of Boston, had become associated with him in his experiments, and they took out several joint patents subsequently. The first practical use of the system took place on a thirteen-mile stretch of the Staten Island Railroad with the results mentioned by Edison above.

A little later, Edison and Gilliland joined forces with Lucius J. Phelps, another investigator, who had been experimenting along the same lines and had taken out several patents. The various interests were combined in a corporation under whose auspices the system was installed on the Lehigh Valley Railroad, where it was used for several years. The official demonstration trip on this road took place on October 6, 1887, on a six-car train running to Easton, Pennsylvania, a distance of fifty-four miles. A great many telegrams were sent and received while the train was at full speed, including a despatch to the "cable king," John Pender. London, England, and a reply from him. [17]

[Footnote 17: Broadly described in outline, the system consisted of an induction circuit obtained by laying strips of tin along the top or roof of a railway car, and the installation of a special telegraph line running parallel with the track and strung on poles of only medium height. The train and also each signalling station were equipped with regulation telegraphic apparatus, such as battery, key, relay, and sounder, together with induction-coil and condenser. In addition, there was a transmitting device in the shape of a musical reed, or buzzer. In practice, this buzzer was continuously operated at high speed by a battery. Its vibrations were broken by means of a key into long and short periods, representing Morse characters, which were transmitted inductively from the train circuit to the pole line, or vice versa, and received by the operator at the other end through a high-resistance telephone receiver inserted in the secondary circuit of the induction-coil.]

Although the space between the cars and the pole line was probably not more than about fifty feet, it is interesting to note that in Edison's early experiments at Menlo Park he succeeded in transmitting messages through the air at a distance of 580 feet. Speaking of this and of his other experiments with induction telegraphy by means of kites, communicating from one to the other and thus from the kites to instruments on the earth, Edison said recently: "We only transmitted about two and one-half miles through the kites. What has always puzzled me since is that I did not think of using the results of my experiments on 'etheric force' that I made in 1875. I have never been able to understand how I came to overlook them. If I had made use of my own work I should have had long-distance wireless telegraphy."

In one of the appendices to this book is given a brief technical account of Edison's investigations of the phenomena which lie at the root of modern wireless or "space" telegraphy, and the attention of the reader is directed particularly to the description and quotations there from the famous note-books of Edison's experiments in regard to what he called "etheric force." It will be seen that as early as 1875 Edison detected and studied certain phenomena--i.e., the production of electrical effects in non-closed circuits, which for a time made him think he was on the trail of a new force, as there was no plausible explanation for them by the then known laws of electricity and magnetism. Later came the magnificent work of Hertz identifying the phenomena as "electromagnetic waves" in the ether, and developing a new world of theory and science based upon them and their production by disruptive discharges.

Edison's assertions were treated with scepticism by the scientific world, which was not then ready for the discovery and not sufficiently furnished with corroborative data. It is singular, to say the least, to note how Edison's experiments paralleled and proved in advance those that came later; and even his apparatus such as the "dark box" for making the tiny sparks visible (as the waves impinged on the receiver) bears close analogy with similar apparatus employed by Hertz. Indeed, as Edison sent the dark-box apparatus to the Paris Exposition in 1881, and let Batchelor repeat there the puzzling experiments, it seems by no means unlikely that, either directly or on the report of some friend, Hertz may thus have received from Edison a most valuable suggestion, the inventor aiding the physicist in opening up a wonderful new realm.

In this connection, indeed, it is very interesting to quote two great authorities. In May, 1889, at a meeting of the Institution of Electrical Engineers in London, Dr. (now Sir) Oliver Lodge remarked in a discussion on a paper of his own on lightning conductors, embracing the Hertzian waves in its treatment: "Many of the effects I have shown--sparks in unsuspected places and other things--have been observed before. Henry observed things of the kind and Edison noticed some curious phenomena, and said it was not electricity but 'etheric force' that caused these sparks; and the matter was rather pooh-poohed. It was a small part of THIS VERY THING; only the time was not ripe; theoretical knowledge was not ready for it." Again in his "Signalling without Wires," in giving the history of the coherer principle, Lodge remarks: "Sparks identical in all respects with those discovered by Hertz had been seen in recent times both by Edison and by Sylvanus Thompson, being styled 'etheric force' by the former; but their theoretic significance had not been perceived, and they were somewhat sceptically regarded." During the same discussion in London, in 1889, Sir William Thomson (Lord Kelvin), after citing some experiments by Faraday with his insulated cage at the Royal Institution, said: "His (Faraday's) attention was not directed to look for Hertz sparks, or probably he might have found them in the interior. Edison seems to have noticed something of the kind in what he called 'etheric force.' His name 'etheric' may thirteen years ago have seemed to many people absurd. But now we are all beginning to call these inductive phenomena 'etheric.'" With which testimony from the great Kelvin as to his priority in determining the vital fact, and with the evidence that as early as 1875 he built apparatus that demonstrated the fact, Edison is probably quite content.

It should perhaps be noted at this point that a curious effect observed at the laboratory was shown in connection with Edison lamps at the Philadelphia Exhibition of 1884. It became known in scientific parlance as the "Edison effect," showing a curious current condition or discharge in the vacuum of the bulb. It has since been employed by Fleming in England and De Forest in this country, and others, as the basis for wireless-telegraph apparatus. It is in reality a minute rectifier of alternating current, and analogous to those which have since been made on a large scale.

When Roentgen came forward with his discovery of the new "X"-ray in 1895, Edison was ready for it, and took up experimentation with it on a large scale; some of his work being recorded in an article in the Century Magazine of May, 1896, where a great deal of data may be found. Edison says with regard to this work: "When the X-ray came up, I made the first fluoroscope, using tungstate of calcium. I also found that this tungstate could be put into a vacuum chamber of glass and fused to the inner walls of the chamber; and if the X-ray electrodes were let into the glass chamber and a proper vacuum was attained, you could get a fluorescent lamp of several candle-power. I started in to make a number of these lamps, but I soon found that the X-ray had affected poisonously my assistant, Mr. Dally, so that his hair came out and his flesh commenced to ulcerate. I then concluded it would not do, and that it would not be a very popular kind of light; so I dropped it.

"At the time I selected tungstate of calcium because it was

so fluorescent, I set four men to making all kinds of chemical combinations, and thus collected upward of 8000 different crystals of various chemical combinations, discovering several hundred different substances which would fluoresce to the X-ray. So far little had come of X-ray work, but it added another letter to the scientific alphabet. I don't know any thing about radium, and I have lots of company." The Electrical Engineer of June 3, 1896, contains a photograph of Mr. Edison taken by the light of one of his fluorescent lamps. The same journal in its issue of April 1, 1896, shows an Edison fluoroscope in use by an observer, in the now familiar and universal form somewhat like a stereoscope. This apparatus as invented by Edison consists of a flaring box, curved at one end to fit closely over the forehead and eyes, while the other end of the box is closed by a paste-board cover. On the inside of this is spread a layer of tungstate of calcium. By placing the object to be observed, such as the hand, between the vacuum-tube and the fluorescent screen, the "shadow" is formed on the screen and can be observed at leisure. The apparatus has proved invaluable in surgery and has become an accepted part of the equipment of modern surgery. In 1896, at the Electrical Exhibition in the Grand Central Palace, New York City, given under the auspices of the National Electric Light Association, thousands and thousands of persons with the use of this apparatus in Edison's personal exhibit were enabled to see their own bones; and the resultant public sensation was great. Mr. Mallory tells a characteristic story of Edison's own share in the memorable exhibit: "The exhibit was announced for opening on Monday. On the preceding Friday all the apparatus, which included a large induction-coil, was shipped from Orange to New York, and on Saturday afternoon Edison, accompanied by Fred Ott, one of his assistants, and myself, went over to install it so as to have it ready for Monday morning. Had everything been normal, a few hours would have sufficed for completion of the work, but on coming to test the big coil, it was found to be absolutely out of commission, having been so seriously injured as to necessitate its entire rewinding. It being summer-time, all the machine shops were closed until Monday morning, and there were several miles of wire to be wound on the coil. Edison would not consider a postponement of the exhibition, so there was nothing to do but go to work and wind it by hand. We managed to find a lathe, but there was no power; so each of us, including Edison, took turns revolving the lathe by pulling on the belt, while the other two attended to the winding of the wire. We worked continuously all through that Saturday night and all day Sunday until evening, when we finished the job. I don't remember ever being conscious of more muscles in my life. I guess Edison was tired also, but he took it very philosophically." This was apparently the first public demonstration of the X-ray to the American public.

Edison's ore-separation work has been already fully described, but the story would hardly be complete without a reference to similar work in gold extraction, dating back to the Menlo Park days: "I got up a method," says Edison, "of separating placer gold by a dry process, in which I could work economically ore as lean as five cents of gold to the cubic yard. I had several car-loads of different placer sands sent to me and proved I could do it. Some parties hearing I had succeeded in doing such a thing went to work and got hold of what was known as the Ortiz mine grant, twelve miles from Santa Fe, New Mexico. This mine, according to the reports of several mining engineers made in the last forty years, was considered one of the richest placer deposits in the United States, and various schemes had been put forward to bring water from the mountains forty miles away to work those immense beds. The reports stated that the Mexicans had been panning gold for a hundred years out of these deposits.

"These parties now made arrangements with the stockholders or owners of the grant, and with me, to work the deposits by my process. As I had had some previous experience with the statements of mining men, I concluded I would just send down a small plant and prospect the field before putting up a large one. This I did, and I sent two of my assistants, whom I could trust, down to this place to erect the plant; and started to sink shafts fifty feet deep all over the area. We soon learned that the rich gravel, instead of being spread over an area of three by seven miles, and rich from the grass roots down, was spread over a space of about twenty-five acres, and that even this did not average more than ten cents to the cubic yard. The whole placer would not give more than one and one-quarter cents per cubic yard. As my business arrangements had not been very perfectly made, I lost the usual amount."

Going to another extreme, we find Edison grappling with one of the biggest problems known to the authorities of New York--the disposal of its heavy snows. It is needless to say that witnessing the ordinary slow and costly procedure would put Edison on his mettle. "One time when they had a snow blockade in New York I started to build a machine with Batchelor--a big truck with a steam-engine and compressor on it. We would run along the street, gather all the snow up in front of us, pass it into the compressor, and deliver little blocks of ice behind us in the gutter, taking one-tenth the room of the snow, and not inconveniencing anybody. We could thus take care of a snow-storm by diminishing the bulk of material to be handled. The preliminary experiment we made was dropped because we went into other things. The machine would go as fast as a horse could walk."

Edison has always taken a keen interest in aerial flight, and has also experimented with aeroplanes, his preference inclining to the helicopter type, as noted in the newspapers and periodicals from time to time. The following statement from him refers to a type of aeroplane of great novelty and ingenuity: "James Gordon Bennett came to me and asked that I try some primary experiments to see if aerial navigation was feasible with 'heavier-than-air' machines. I got up a motor and put it on the scales and tried a large number of different things and contrivances connected to the motor, to see how it would lighten itself on the scales. I got some data and made up my mind that what was needed was a very powerful engine for its weight, in small compass. So I conceived of an engine employing guncotton. I took a lot of ticker paper tape, turned it into guncotton and got up an engine with an arrangement whereby I could feed this gun-cotton strip into the cylinder and explode it inside electrically. The feed took place between two copper rolls. The copper kept the temperature down, so that it could only explode up to the point where it was in contact with the feed rolls. It worked pretty well; but once the feed roll didn't save it, and the flame went through and exploded the whole roll and kicked up such a bad explosion I abandoned it. But the idea might be made to work."

Turning from the air to the earth, it is interesting to note that the introduction of the underground Edison system in New York made an appeal to inventive ingenuity and that one of the difficulties was met as follows: "When we first put the Pearl Street station in operation, in New York, we had cast-iron junction-boxes at the intersections of all the streets. One night, or about two o'clock in the morning, a policeman came in and said that something had exploded at the corner of William and Nassau streets. I happened to be in the station, and went out to see what it was. I found that the cover of the manhole, weighing about 200 pounds, had entirely disappeared, but everything inside was intact. It had even stripped some of the threads of the bolts, and we could never find that cover. I concluded it was either leakage of gas into the manhole, or else the acid used in pickling the casting had given off hydrogen, and air had leaked in, making an explosive mixture. As this was a pretty serious problem, and as we had a good many of the manholes, it worried me very much for fear that it would be repeated and the company might have to pay a lot of damages, especially in districts like that around William and Nassau, where there are a good many people about. If an explosion took place in the daytime it might lift a few of them up. However, I got around the difficulty by putting a little bottle of chloroform in each box, corked up, with a slight hole in the cork. The chloroform being volatile and very heavy, settled in the box and displaced all the air. I have never heard of an explosion in a manhole where this chloroform had been used. Carbon tetrachloride, now made electrically at Niagara Falls, is very cheap and would be ideal for the purpose."

Edison has never paid much attention to warfare, and has in general disdained to develop inventions for the destruction of life and property. Some years ago, however, he became the joint inventor of the Edison-Sims torpedo, with Mr. W. Scott Sims, who sought his co-operation. This is a dirigible submarine torpedo operated by electricity. In the torpedo proper, which is suspended from a long float so as to be submerged a few feet under water, are placed the small electric motor for propulsion and steering, and the explosive charge. The torpedo is controlled from the shore or ship through an electric cable which it pays out as it goes along, and all operations of varying the speed, reversing, and steering are performed at the will of the distant operator by means of currents sent through the cable. During the Spanish-American War of 1898 Edison suggested to the Navy Department the adoption of a compound of calcium carbide and calcium phosphite, which when placed in a shell and fired from a gun would explode as soon as it struck water and ignite, producing a blaze that would continue several minutes and make the ships of the enemy visible for four or five miles at sea. Moreover, the blaze could not be extinguished.

Edison has always been deeply interested in "conservation," and much of his work has been directed toward the economy of fuel in obtaining electrical energy directly from the consumption of coal. Indeed, it will be noted that the example of his handwriting shown in these volumes deals with the importance of obtaining available energy direct from the combustible without the enormous loss in the intervening stages that makes our best modern methods of steam generation and utilization so barbarously extravagant and wasteful. Several years ago, experimenting in this field, Edison devised and operated some ingenious pyromagnetic motors and generators, based, as the name implies, on the direct application of heat to the machines. The motor is founded upon the principle discovered by the famous Dr. William Gilbert--court physician to Queen Elizabeth, and the Father of modern electricity--that the magnetic properties of iron diminish with heat. At a light-red heat, iron becomes non-magnetic, so that a strong magnet exerts no influence over it. Edison employed this peculiar property by constructing a small machine in which a pivoted bar is alternately heated and cooled. It is thus attracted toward an adjacent electromagnet when cold and is uninfluenced when hot, and as the result motion is produced.

The pyromagnetic generator is based on the same phenomenon; its aim being of course to generate electrical energy directly from the heat of the combustible. The armature, or moving part of the machine, consists in reality of eight separate armatures all constructed of corrugated sheet iron covered with asbestos and wound with wire. These armatures are held in place by two circular iron plates, through the centre of which runs a shaft, carrying at its lower extremity a semicircular shield of fire-clay, which covers the ends of four of the armatures. The heat, of whatever origin, is applied from below, and the shaft being revolved, four of the armatures lose their magnetism constantly, while the other four gain it, so to speak. As the moving part revolves, therefore, currents of electricity are set up in the wires of the armatures and are collected by a commutator, as in an ordinary dynamo, placed on the upper end of the central shaft.

A great variety of electrical instruments are included in Edison's inventions, many of these in fundamental or earlier forms being devised for his systems of light and power, as noted already. There are numerous others, and it might be said with truth that Edison is hardly ever without some new device of this kind in hand, as he is by no means satisfied with the present status of electrical measurements. He holds in general that the meters of to-day, whether for heavy or for feeble currents, are too expensive, and that cheaper instruments are a necessity of the times. These remarks apply more particularly to what may be termed, in general, circuit meters. In other classes Edison has devised an excellent form of magnetic bridge, being an ingenious application of the principles of the familiar Wheatstone bridge, used so extensively for measuring the electrical resistance of wires; the testing of iron for magnetic qualities being determined by it in the same way. Another special instrument is a "dead beat" galvanometer which differs from the ordinary form of galvanometer in having no coils or magnetic needle. It depends for its action upon the heating effect of the current, which causes a fine platinum-iridium wire enclosed in a glass tube to expand; thus allowing a coiled spring to act on a pivoted shaft carrying a tiny mirror. The mirror as it moves throws a beam of light upon a scale and the indications are read by the spot of light. Most novel of all the apparatus of this measuring kind is the odoroscope, which is like the tasimeter described in an earlier chapter, except that a strip of gelatine takes the place of hard rubber, as the sensitive member. Besides being affected by heat, this device is exceedingly sensitive to moisture. A few drops of water or perfume thrown on the floor of a room are sufficient to give a very decided indication on the galvanometer in circuit with the instrument. Barometers, hygrometers, and similar instruments of great delicacy can be constructed on the principle of the odoroscope; and it may also be used in determining the character or pressure of gases and vapors in which it has been placed.

In the list of Edison's patents at the end of this work may be noted many other of his miscellaneous inventions, covering items such as preserving fruit in vacuo, making plate-glass, drawing wire, and metallurgical processes for treatment of nickel, gold, and copper ores; but to mention these inventions separately would trespass too much on our limited space here. Hence, we shall leave the interested reader to examine that list for himself.

From first to last Edison has filed in the United States Patent Office--in addition to more than 1400 applications for patents--some 120 caveats embracing not less than 1500 inventions. A "caveat" is essentially a notice filed by an inventor, entitling him to receive warning from the Office of any application for a patent for an invention that would "interfere" with his own, during the year, while he is supposed to be perfecting his device. The old caveat system has now been abolished, but it served to elicit from Edison a most astounding record of ideas and possible inventions upon which he was working, and many of which he of course reduced to practice. As an example of Edison's fertility and the endless variety of subjects engaging his thoughts, the following list of matters covered by ONE caveat is given. It is needless to say that all the caveats are not quite so full of "plums," but this is certainly a wonder.

Forty-one distinct inventions relating to the phonograph, covering various forms of recorders, arrangement of parts, making of records, shaving tool, adjustments, etc.

Eight forms of electric lamps using infusible earthy oxides and brought to high incandescence in vacuo by high potential current of several thousand volts; same character as impingement of X-rays on object in bulb.

A loud-speaking telephone with quartz cylinder and beam of ultra-violet light.

Four forms of arc light with special carbons.

A thermostatic motor.

A device for sealing together the inside part and bulb of an incandescent lamp mechanically.

Regulators for dynamos and motors.

Three devices for utilizing vibrations beyond the ultra violet.

A great variety of methods for coating incandescent lamp filaments with silicon, titanium, chromium, osmium, boron, etc.

Several methods of making porous filaments.

Several methods of making squirted filaments of a variety of materials, of which about thirty are specified.

Seventeen different methods and devices for separating magnetic ores.

A continuously operative primary battery.

A musical instrument operating one of Helmholtz's artificial larynxes.

A siren worked by explosion of small quantities of oxygen and hydrogen mixed.

Three other sirens made to give vocal sounds or articulate speech.

A device for projecting sound-waves to a distance without spreading and in a straight line, on the principle of smoke rings.

A device for continuously indicating on a galvanometer the depths of the ocean.

A method of preventing in a great measure friction of water against the hull of a ship and incidentally preventing fouling by barnacles.

A telephone receiver whereby the vibrations of the diaphragm are considerably amplified.

Two methods of "space" telegraphy at sea.

An improved and extended string telephone.

Devices and method of talking through water for considerable distances.

An audiphone for deaf people.

Sound-bridge for measuring resistance of tubes and other materials for conveying sound.

A method of testing a magnet to ascertain the existence of flaws in the iron or steel composing the same.

Method of distilling liquids by incandescent conductor immersed in the liquid.

Method of obtaining electricity direct from coal.

An engine operated by steam produced by the hydration and dehydration of metallic salts.

Device and method for telegraphing photographically.

Carbon crucible kept brilliantly incandescent by current in vacuo, for obtaining reaction with refractory metals.

Device for examining combinations of odors and their changes by rotation at different speeds.

From one of the preceding items it will be noted that even in the eighties Edison perceived much advantage to be gained in the line of economy by the use of lamp filaments employing refractory metals in their construction. From another caveat, filed in 1889, we extract the following, which shows that he realized the value of tungsten also for this purpose. "Filaments of carbon placed in a combustion tube with a little chloride ammonium. Chloride tungsten or titanium passed through hot tube, depositing a film of metal on the carbon; or filaments of zirconia oxide, or alumina or magnesia, thoria or other infusible oxides mixed or separate, and obtained by moistening and squirting through a die, are thus coated with above metals and used for incandescent lamps. Osmium from a volatile compound of same thus deposited makes a filament as good as carbon when in vacuo."

In 1888, long before there arose the actual necessity of duplicating phonograph records so as to produce replicas in great numbers, Edison described in one of his caveats a method and process much similar to the one which was put into practice by him in later years. In the same caveat he describes an invention whereby the power to indent on a phonograph cylinder, instead of coming directly from the voice, is caused by power derived from the rotation or movement of the phonogram surface itself. He did not, however, follow up this invention and put it into practice. Some twenty years later it was independently invented and patented by another inventor. A further instance of this kind is a method of telegraphy at sea by means of a diaphragm in a closed port-hole flush with the side of the vessel, and actuated by a steam-whistle which is controlled by a lever, similarly to a Morse key. A receiving diaphragm is placed in another and near-by chamber, which is provided with very sensitive stethoscopic ear-pieces, by which the Morse characters sent from another vessel may be received. This was also invented later by another inventor, and is in use to-day, but will naturally be rivalled by wireless telegraphy. Still another instance is seen in one of Edison's caveats, where he describes a method of distilling liquids by means of internally applied heat through electric conductors. Although Edison did not follow up the idea and take out a patent, this system of distillation was later hit upon by others and is in use at the present time.

In the foregoing pages of this chapter the authors have endeavored to present very briefly a sketchy notion of the astounding range of Edison's practical ideas, but they feel a sense of impotence in being unable to deal adequately with the subject in the space that can be devoted to it. To those who, like the authors, have had the privilege of examining the voluminous records which show the flights of his imagination, there comes a feeling of utter inadequacy to convey to others the full extent of the story they reveal.

The few specific instances above related, although not representing a tithe of Edison's work, will probably be sufficient to enable the reader to appreciate to some extent his great wealth of ideas and fertility of imagination, and also to realize that this imagination is not only intensely practical, but that it works prophetically along lines of natural progress.

CHAPTER XXIV

EDISON'S METHOD IN INVENTING

WHILE the world's progress depends largely upon their ingenuity, inventors are not usually persons who have adopted invention as a distinct profession, but, generally speaking, are otherwise engaged in various walks of life. By reason of more or less inherent native genius they either make improvements along lines of present occupation, or else evolve new methods and means of accomplishing results in fields for which they may have personal predilections.

Now and then, however, there arises a man so greatly endowed with natural powers and originality that the creative faculty within him is too strong to endure the humdrum routine of affairs, and manifests itself in a life devoted entirely to the evolution of methods and devices calculated to further the world's welfare. In other words, he becomes an inventor by profession. Such a man is Edison. Notwithstanding the fact that nearly forty years ago (not a great while after he had emerged from the ranks of peripatetic telegraph operators) he was the owner of a large and profitable business as a manufacturer of the telegraphic apparatus invented by him, the call of his nature was too strong to allow of profits being laid away in the bank to accumulate. As he himself has said, he has "too sanguine a temperament to allow money to stay in solitary confinement." Hence, all superfluous cash was devoted to experimentation. In the course of years he grew more and more impatient of the shackles that bound him to business routine, and, realizing the powers within him, he drew away gradually from purely manufacturing occupations, determining deliberately to devote his life to inventive work, and to depend upon its results as a means of subsistence.

All persons who make inventions will necessarily be more or less original in character, but to the man who chooses to become an inventor by profession must be conceded a mind more than ordinarily replete with virility and originality. That these qualities in Edison are superabundant is well known to all who have worked with him, and, indeed, are apparent to every one from his multiplied achievements within the period of one generation.

If one were allowed only two words with which to describe Edison, it is doubtful whether a close examination of the entire dictionary would disclose any others more suitable than "experimenter--inventor." These would express the overruling characteristics of his eventful career. It is as an "inventor" that he sets himself down in the membership list of the American Institute of Electrical Engineers. To attempt the strict placing of these words in relation to each other (except alphabetically) would be equal to an endeavor to solve the old problem as to which came first, the egg or the chicken; for although all his inventions have been evolved through experiment, many of his notable experiments have called forth the exercise of highly inventive faculties in their very inception. Investigation and experiment have been a consuming passion, an impelling force from within, as it were, from his petticoat days when he collected goose-eggs and tried to hatch them out by sitting over them himself. One might be inclined to dismiss this trivial incident smilingly, as a mere childish, thoughtless prank, had not subsequent development as a child, boy, and man revealed a born investigator with original reasoning powers that, disdaining crooks and bends, always aimed at the centre, and, like the flight of the bee, were accurate and direct.

It is not surprising, therefore, that a man of this kind should exhibit a ceaseless, absorbing desire for knowledge, and an apparently uncontrollable tendency to experiment on every possible occasion, even though his last cent were spent in thus satisfying the insatiate cravings of an inquiring mind.

During Edison's immature years, when he was flitting about from place to place as a telegraph operator, his experimentation was of a desultory, hand-to-mouth character, although it was always notable for originality, as expressed in a number of minor useful devices produced during this period. Small wonder, then, that at the end of these wanderings, when he had found a place to "rest the sole of his foot," he established a laboratory in which to carry on his researches in a more methodical and practical manner. In this was the beginning of the work which has since made such a profound impression on contemporary life.

There is nothing of the helter-skelter, slap-dash style in Edison's experiments. Although all the laboratory experimenters agree in the opinion that he "tries everything," it is not merely the mixing of a little of this, some of that, and a few drops of the other, in the HOPE that SOMETHING will come of it. Nor is the spirit of the laboratory work represented in the following dialogue overheard between two alleged carpenters picked up at random to help on a hurry job.

"How near does she fit, Mike?"

"About an inch."

"Nail her!"

A most casual examination of any of the laboratory records will reveal evidence of the minutest exactitude insisted on in the conduct of experiments, irrespective of the length of time they occupied. Edison's instructions, always clear cut and direct, followed by his keen oversight, admit of nothing less than implicit observance in all details, no matter where they may lead, and impel to the utmost minuteness and accuracy.

To some extent there has been a popular notion that many of Edison's successes have been due to mere dumb fool luck--to blind, fortuitous "happenings." Nothing could be further from the truth, for, on the contrary, it is owing almost entirely to the comprehensive scope of his knowledge, the breadth of his conception, the daring originality of his methods, and minuteness and extent of experiment, combined with unwavering pertinacity, that new arts have been created and additions made to others already in existence. Indeed, without this tireless minutiae, and methodical, searching spirit, it would have been practically impossible to have produced many of the most important of these inventions.

Needless to say, mastery of its literature is regarded by him as a most important preliminary in taking up any line of investigation. What others may have done, bearing directly or collaterally on the subject, in print, is carefully considered and sifted to the point of exhaustion. Not that he takes it for granted that the conclusions are correct, for he frequently obtains vastly different results by repeating in his own way experiments made by others as detailed in books.

"Edison can travel along a well-used road and still find virgin soil," remarked recently one of his most practical experimenters, who had been working along a certain line without attaining the desired result. "He wanted to get a particular compound having definite qualities, and I had tried in all sorts of ways to produce it but with only partial success. He was confident that it could be done, and said he would try it himself. In doing so he followed the same path in which I had travelled, but, by making an undreamed-of change in one of the operations, succeeded in producing a compound that virtually came up to his specifications. It is not the only time I have known this sort of thing to happen."

In speaking of Edison's method of experimenting, another of his laboratory staff says: "He is never hindered by theory, but resorts to actual experiment for proof. For instance, when he conceived the idea of pouring a complete concrete house it was universally held that it would be impossible because the pieces of stone in the mixture would not rise to the level of the pouring-point, but would gravitate to a lower plane in the soft cement. This, however, did not hinder him from making a series of experiments which resulted in an invention that proved conclusively the contrary."

Having conceived some new idea and read everything obtainable relating to the subject in general, Edison's fertility of resource and originality come into play. Taking one of the laboratory note-books, he will write in it a memorandum of the experiments to be tried, illustrated, if necessary, by sketches. This book is then passed on to that member of the experimental staff whose special training and experience are best adapted to the work. Here strenuousness is expected; and an immediate commencement of investigation and prompt report are required. Sometimes the subject may be such as to call for a long line of frequent tests which necessitate patient and accurate attention to minute details. Results must be reported often--daily, or possibly with still greater frequency. Edison does not forget what is going on; but in his daily tours through the laboratory keeps in touch with all the work that is under the hands of his various assistants, showing by an instant grasp of the present conditions of any experiment that he has a full consciousness of its meaning and its reference to his original conception.

The year 1869 saw the beginning of Edison's career as an acknowledged inventor of commercial devices. From the outset, an innate recognition of system dictated the desirability and wisdom of preserving records of his experiments and inventions. The primitive records, covering the earliest years, were mainly jotted down on loose sheets of paper covered with sketches, notes, and data, pasted into large scrap-books, or preserved in packages; but with the passing of years and enlargement of his interests, it became the practice to make all original laboratory notes in large, uniform books. This course was pursued until the Menlo Park period, when he instituted a new regime that has been continued down to the present day. A standard form of note-book, about eight and a half by six inches, containing about two hundred pages, was adopted. A number of these books were (and are now) always to be found scattered around in the different sections of the laboratory, and in them have been noted by Edison all his ideas, sketches, and memoranda. Details of the various experiments concerning them have been set down by his assistants from time to time.

These later laboratory note-books, of which there are now over one thousand in the series, are eloquent in the history they reveal of the strenuous labors of Edison and his assistants and the vast fields of research he has covered during the last thirty years. They are overwhelmingly rich in biographic material, but analysis would be a prohibitive task for one person, and perhaps interesting only to technical readers. Their pages cover practically every department of science. The countless thousands of separate experiments recorded exhibit the operations of a master mind seeking to surprise Nature into a betrayal of her secrets by asking her the same question in a hundred different ways. For instance, when Edison was investigating a certain problem of importance many years ago, the note-books show that on this point alone about fifteen thousand experiments and tests were made by one of his assistants.

A most casual glance over these note-books will illustrate the following remark, which was made to one of the writers not long ago by a member of the laboratory staff who has been experimenting there for twenty years: "Edison can think of more ways of doing a thing than any man I ever saw or heard of. He tries everything and never lets up, even though failure is apparently staring him in the face. He only stops when he simply can't go any further on that particular line. When he decides on any mode of procedure he gives his notes to the experimenter and lets him alone, only stepping in from time to time to look at the operations and receive reports of progress."

The history of the development of the telephone transmitter, phonograph, incandescent lamp, dynamo, electrical distributing systems from central stations, electric railway, ore-milling, cement, motion pictures, and a host of minor inventions may be found embedded in the laboratory note-books. A passing glance at a few pages of these written records will serve to illustrate, though only to a limited extent, the thoroughness of Edison's method. It is to be observed that these references can be but of the most meagre kind, and must be regarded as merely throwing a side-light on the subject itself. For instance, the complex problem of a practical telephone transmitter gave rise to a series of most exhaustive experiments. Combinations in almost infinite variety, including gums, chemical compounds, oils, minerals, and metals were suggested by Edison; and his assistants were given long lists of materials to try with reference to predetermined standards of articulation, degrees of loudness, and perfection of hissing sounds. The note-books contain hundreds of pages showing that a great many thousands of experiments were tried and passed upon. Such remarks as "N. G."; "Pretty good"; "Whistling good, but no articulation"; "Rattly"; "Articulation, whispering, and whistling good"; "Best to-night so far"; and others are noted opposite the various combinations as they were tried. Thus, one may follow the investigation through a maze of experiments which led up to the successful invention of the carbon button transmitter, the vital device to give the telephone its needed articulation and perfection.

The two hundred and odd note-books, covering the strenuous period during which Edison was carrying on his electric-light experiments, tell on their forty thousand pages or more a fascinating story of the evolution of a new art in its entirety. From the crude beginnings, through all the varied phases of this evolution, the operations of a master mind are apparent from the contents of these pages, in which are recorded the innumerable experiments, calculations, and tests that ultimately brought light out of darkness.

The early work on a metallic conductor for lamps gave rise to some very thorough research on melting and alloying metals, the preparation of metallic oxides, the coating of fine wires by immersing them in a great variety of chemical solutions. Following his usual custom, Edison would indicate the lines of experiment to be followed, which were carried out and recorded in the note-books. He himself, in January, 1879, made personally a most minute and searching investigation into the properties and behavior of plating-iridium, boron, rutile, zircon, chromium, molybdenum, and nickel, under varying degrees of current strength, on which there may be found in the notes about forty pages of detailed experiments and deductions in his own handwriting, concluding with the remark (about nickel): "This is a great discovery for electric light in the way of economy."

This period of research on nickel, etc., was evidently a trying one, for after nearly a month's close application he writes, on January 27, 1879: "Owing to the enormous power of the light my eyes commenced to pain after seven hours' work, and I had to quit." On the next day appears the following entry: "Suffered the pains of hell with my eyes last night from 10 P.M. till 4 A.M., when got to sleep with a big dose of morphine. Eyes getting better, and do not pain much at 4 P.M.; but I lose to-day."

The "try everything" spirit of Edison's method is well illustrated in this early period by a series of about sixteen hundred resistance tests of various ores, minerals, earths, etc., occupying over fifty pages of one of the note-books relating to the metallic filament for his lamps.

But, as the reader has already learned, the metallic filament was soon laid aside in favor of carbon, and we find in the laboratory notes an amazing record of research and experiment conducted in the minute and searching manner peculiar to Edison's method. His inquiries were directed along all the various roads leading to the desired goal, for long before he had completed the invention of a practical lamp he realized broadly the fundamental requirements of a successful system of electrical distribution, and had given instructions for the making of a great variety of calculations which, although far in advance of the time, were clearly foreseen by him to be vitally important in the ultimate solution of the complicated problem. Thus we find many hundreds of pages of the note-books covered with computations and calculations by Mr. Upton, not only on the numerous ramifications of the projected system and comparisons with gas, but also on proposed forms of dynamos and the proposed station in New York. A mere recital by titles of the vast number of experiments and tests on carbons, lamps, dynamos, armatures, commutators, windings, systems, regulators, sockets, vacuum-pumps, and the thousand and one details relating to the subject in general, originated by Edison, and methodically and systematically carried on under his general direction, would fill a great many pages here, and even then would serve only to convey a confused impression of ceaseless probing.

It is possible only to a broad, comprehensive mind well stored with knowledge, and backed with resistless, boundless energy, that such a diversified series of experiments and investigations could be carried on simultaneously and assimilated, even though they should relate to a class of phenomena already understood and well defined. But if we pause to consider that the commercial subdivision of the electric current (which was virtually an invention made to order) involved the solution of problems so unprecedented that even they themselves had to be created, we cannot but conclude that the afflatus of innate genius played an important part in the unique methods of investigation instituted by Edison at that and other times.

The idea of attributing great successes to "genius" has always been repudiated by Edison, as evidenced by his historic remark that "Genius is 1 per cent. inspiration and 99 per cent. perspiration." Again, in a conversation many years ago at the laboratory between Edison, Batchelor, and E. H. Johnson, the latter made allusion to Edison's genius as evidenced by some of his achievements, when Edison replied:

"Stuff! I tell you genius is hard work, stick-to-it-iveness, and common sense."

"Yes," said Johnson, "I admit there is all that to it, but there's still more. Batch and I have those qualifications, but although we knew quite a lot about telephones, and worked hard, we couldn't invent a brand-new non-infringing telephone receiver as you did when Gouraud cabled for one. Then, how about the subdivision of the electric light?"

"Electric current," corrected Edison.

"True," continued Johnson; "you were the one to make that very distinction. The scientific world had been working hard on subdivision for years, using what appeared to be common sense. Results worse than nil. Then you come along, and about the first thing you do, after looking the ground over, is to start off in the opposite direction, which subsequently proves to be the only possible way to reach the goal. It seems to me that this is pretty close to the dictionary definition of genius."

It is said that Edison replied rather incoherently and changed the topic of conversation.

This innate modesty, however, does not prevent Edison from recognizing and classifying his own methods of investigation. In a conversation with two old associates recently (April, 1909), he remarked: "It has been said of me that my methods are empirical. That is true only so far as chemistry is concerned. Did you ever realize that practically all industrial chemistry is colloidal in its nature? Hard rubber, celluloid, glass, soap, paper, and lots of others, all have to deal with amorphous substances, as to which comparatively little has been really settled. My methods are similar to those followed by Luther Burbank. He plants an acre, and when this is in bloom he inspects it. He has a sharp eye, and can pick out of thousands a single plant that has promise of what he wants. From this he gets the seed, and uses his skill and knowledge in producing from it a number of new plants which, on development, furnish the means of propagating an improved variety in large quantity. So, when I am after a chemical result that I have in mind, I may make hundreds or thousands of experiments out of which there may be one that promises results in the right direction. This I follow up to its legitimate conclusion, discarding the others, and usually get what I am after. There is no doubt about this being empirical; but when it comes to problems of a mechanical nature, I want to tell you that all I've ever tackled and solved have been done by hard, logical thinking." The intense earnestness and emphasis with which this was said were very impressive to the auditors. This empirical method may perhaps be better illustrated by a specific example. During the latter part of the storage battery investigations, after the form of positive element had been determined upon, it became necessary to ascertain what definite proportions and what quality of nickel hydrate and nickel flake would give the best results. A series of positive tubes were filled with the two materials in different proportions--say, nine parts hydrate to one of flake; eight parts hydrate to two of flake; seven parts hydrate to three of flake, and so on through varying proportions. Three sets of each of these positives were made, and all put into separate test tubes with a uniform type of negative element. These were carried through a long series of charges and discharges under strict test conditions. From the tabulated results of hundreds of tests there were selected three that showed the best results. These, however, showed only the superiority of certain PROPORTIONS of the materials. The next step would be to find out the best QUALITY. Now, as there are several hundred variations in the quality of nickel flake, and perhaps a thousand ways to make the hydrate, it will be realized that Edison's methods led to stupendous detail, for these tests embraced a trial of all the qualities of both materials in the three proportions found to be most suitable. Among these many thousands of experiments any that showed extraordinary results were again elaborated by still further series of tests, until Edison was satisfied that he had obtained the best result in that particular line.

The laboratory note-books do not always tell the whole story or meaning of an experiment that may be briefly outlined on one of their pages. For example, the early filament made of a mixture of lampblack and tar is merely a suggestion in the notes, but its making afforded an example of Edison's pertinacity. These materials, when mixed, became a friable mass, which he had found could be brought into such a cohesive, putty-like state by manipulation, as to be capable of being rolled out into filaments as fine as seven-thousandths of an inch in cross-section. One of the laboratory assistants was told to make some of this mixture, knead it, and roll some filaments. After a time he brought the mass to Edison, and said:

"There's something wrong about this, for it crumbles even after manipulating it with my fingers."

"How long did you knead it?" said Edison.

"Oh! more than an hour," replied the assistant.

"Well, just keep on for a few hours more and it will come out all right," was the rejoinder. And this proved to be correct, for, after a prolonged kneading and rolling, the mass changed into a cohesive, stringy, homogeneous putty. It was from a mixture of this kind that spiral filaments were made and used in some of the earliest forms of successful incandescent lamps; indeed, they are described and illustrated in Edison's fundamental lamp patent (No. 223,898).

The present narrative would assume the proportions of a history of the incandescent lamp, should the authors attempt to follow Edison's investigations through the thousands of pages of note-books away back in the eighties and early nineties. Improvement of the lamp was constantly in his mind all those years, and besides the vast amount of detail experimental work he laid out for his assistants, he carried on a great deal of research personally. Sometimes whole books are filled in his own handwriting with records of experiments showing every conceivable variation of some particular line of inquiry; each trial bearing some terse comment expressive of results. In one book appear the details of one of these experiments on September 3, 1891, at 4.30 A.M., with the comment: "Brought up lamp higher than a 16-c.p. 240 was ever brought before--Hurrah!" Notwithstanding the late hour, he turns over to the next page and goes on to write his deductions from this result as compared with those previously obtained. Proceeding day by day, as appears by this same book, he follows up another line of investigation on lamps, apparently full of difficulty, for after one hundred and thirty-two other recorded experiments we find this note: "Saturday 3.30 went home disgusted with incandescent lamps." This feeling was evidently evanescent, for on the succeeding Monday the work was continued and carried on by him as keenly as before, as shown by the next batch of notes.

This is the only instance showing any indication of impatience that the authors have found in looking through the enormous mass of laboratory notes. All his assistants agree that Edison is the most patient, tireless experimenter that could be conceived of. Failures do not distress him; indeed, he regards them as always useful, as may be gathered from the following, related by Dr. E. G. Acheson, formerly one of his staff: "I once made an experiment in Edison's laboratory at Menlo Park during the latter part of 1880, and the results were not as looked for. I considered the experiment a perfect failure, and while bemoaning the results of this apparent failure Mr. Edison entered, and, after learning the facts of the case, cheerfully remarked that I should not look upon it as a failure, for he considered every experiment a success, as in all cases it cleared up the atmosphere, and even though it failed to accomplish the results sought for, it should prove a valuable lesson for guidance in future work. I believe that Mr. Edison's success as an experimenter was, to a large extent, due to this happy view of all experiments."

Edison has frequently remarked that out of a hundred experiments he does not expect more than one to be successful, and as to that one he is always suspicious until frequent repetition has verified the original results.

This patient, optimistic view of the outcome of experiments has remained part of his character down to this day, just as his painstaking, minute, incisive methods are still unchanged. But to the careless, stupid, or lazy person he is a terror for the short time they remain around him. Honest mistakes may be tolerated, but not carelessness, incompetence, or lack of attention to business. In such cases Edison is apt to express himself freely and forcibly, as when he was asked why he had parted with a certain man, he said: "Oh, he was so slow that it would take him half an hour to get out of the field of a microscope." Another instance will be illustrative. Soon after the Brockton (Massachusetts) central station was started in operation many years ago, he wrote a note to Mr. W. S. Andrews, containing suggestions as to future stations, part of which related to the various employees and their duties. After outlining the duties of the meter man, Edison says: "I should not take too young a man for this, say, a man from twenty-three to thirty years old, bright and businesslike. Don't want any one who yearns to enter a laboratory and experiment. We have a bad case of that at Brockton; he neglects business to potter. What we want is a good lamp average and no unprofitable customer. You should have these men on probation and subject to passing an examination by me. This will wake them up."

Edison's examinations are no joke, according to Mr. J. H. Vail, formerly one of the Menlo Park staff. "I wanted a job," he said, "and was ambitious to take charge of the dynamo-room. Mr. Edison led me to a heap of junk in a corner and said: 'Put that together and let me know when it's running.' I didn't know what it was, but received a liberal education in finding out. It proved to be a dynamo, which I finally succeeded in assembling and running. I got the job." Another man who succeeded in winning a place as assistant was Mr. John F. Ott, who has remained in his employ for over forty years. In 1869, when Edison was occupying his first manufacturing shop (the third floor of a small building in Newark), he wanted a first-class mechanician, and Mr. Ott was sent to him. "He was then an ordinary-looking young fellow," says Mr. Ott, "dirty as any of the other workmen, unkempt, and not much better dressed than a tramp, but I immediately felt that there was a great deal in him." This is the conversation that ensued, led by Mr. Edison's question:

"What do you want?"

"Work."

"Can you make this machine work?" (exhibiting it and explaining its details).

"Yes."

"Are you sure?"

"Well, you needn't pay me if I don't."

And thus Mr. Ott went to work and succeeded in accomplishing the results desired. Two weeks afterward Mr. Edison put him in charge of the shop.

Edison's life fairly teems with instances of unruffled patience in the pursuit of experiments. When he feels thoroughly impressed with the possibility of accomplishing a certain thing, he will settle down composedly to investigate it to the end.

This is well illustrated in a story relating to his invention of the type of storage battery bearing his name. Mr. W. S. Mallory, one of his closest associates for many years, is the authority for the following: "When Mr. Edison decided to shut down the ore-milling plant at Edison, New Jersey, in which I had been associated with him, it became a problem as to what he could profitably take up next, and we had several discussions about it. He finally thought that a good storage battery was a great requisite, and decided to try and devise a new type, for he declared emphatically he would make no battery requiring sulphuric acid. After a little thought he conceived the nickel-iron idea, and started to work at once with characteristic energy. About 7 or 7.30 A.M. he would go down to the laboratory and experiment, only stopping for a short time at noon to eat a lunch sent down from the house. About 6 o'clock the carriage would call to take him to dinner, from which he would return by 7.30 or 8 o'clock to resume work. The carriage came again at midnight to take him home, but frequently had to wait until 2 or 3 o'clock, and sometimes return without him, as he had decided to continue all night.

"This had been going on more than five months, seven days a week, when I was called down to the laboratory to see him. I found him at a bench about three feet wide and twelve to fifteen feet long, on which there were hundreds of little test cells that had been made up by his corps of chemists and experimenters. He was seated at this bench testing, figuring, and planning. I then learned that he had thus made over nine thousand experiments in trying to devise this new type of storage battery, but had not produced a single thing that promised to solve the question. In view of this immense amount of thought and labor, my sympathy got the better of my judgment, and I said: 'Isn't it a shame that with the tremendous amount of work you have done you haven't been able to get any results?' Edison turned on me like a flash, and with a smile replied: 'Results! Why, man, I have gotten a lot of results! I know several thousand things that won't work.'

"At that time he sent me out West on a special mission. On my return, a few weeks later, his experiments had run up to over ten thousand, but he had discovered the missing link in the combination sought for. Of course, we all remember how the battery was completed and put on the market. Then, because he was dissatisfied with it, he stopped the sales and commenced a new line of investigation, which has recently culminated successfully. I shouldn't wonder if his experiments on the battery ran up pretty near to fifty thousand, for they fill more than one hundred and fifty of the note-books, to say nothing of some thousands of tests in curve sheets."

Although Edison has an absolute disregard for the total outlay of money in investigation, he is particular to keep down the cost of individual experiments to a minimum, for, as he observed to one of his assistants: "A good many inventors try to develop things life-size, and thus spend all their money, instead of first experimenting more freely on a small scale." To Edison life is not only a grand opportunity to find out things by experiment, but, when found, to improve them by further experiment. One night, after receiving a satisfactory report of progress from Mr. Mason, superintendent of the cement plant, he said: "The only way to keep ahead of the procession is to experiment. If you don't, the other fellow will. When there's no experimenting there's no progress. Stop experimenting and you go backward. If anything goes wrong, experiment until you get to the very bottom of the trouble."

It is easy to realize, therefore, that a character so thoroughly permeated with these ideas is not apt to stop and figure out expense when in hot pursuit of some desired object. When that object has been attained, however, and it passes from the experimental to the commercial stage, Edison's monetary views again come into strong play, but they take a diametrically opposite position, for he then begins immediately to plan the extreme of economy in the production of the article. A thousand and one instances could be quoted in illustration; but as they would tend to change the form of this narrative into a history of economy in manufacture, it will suffice to mention but one, and that a recent occurrence, which serves to illustrate how closely he keeps in touch with everything, and also how the inventive faculty and instinct of commercial economy run close together. It was during Edison's winter stay in Florida, in March, 1909. He had reports sent to him daily from various places, and studied them carefully, for he would write frequently with comments, instructions, and suggestions; and in one case, commenting on the oiling system at the cement plant, he wrote: "Your oil losses are now getting lower, I see." Then, after suggesting some changes to reduce them still further, he went on to say: "Here is a chance to save a mill per barrel based on your regular daily output."

This thorough consideration of the smallest detail is essentially characteristic of Edison, not only in economy of manufacture, but in all his work, no matter of what kind, whether it be experimenting, investigating, testing, or engineering. To follow him through the labyrinthine paths of investigation contained in the great array of laboratory note-books is to become involved in a mass of minutely detailed searches which seek to penetrate the inmost recesses of nature by an ultimate analysis of an infinite variety of parts. As the reader will obtain a fuller comprehension of this idea, and of Edison's methods, by concrete illustration rather than by generalization, the authors have thought it well to select at random two typical instances of specific investigations out of the thousands that are scattered through the notebooks. These will be found in the following extracts from one of the note-books, and consist of Edison's instructions to be carried out in detail by his experimenters:

"Take, say, 25 lbs. hard Cuban asphalt and separate all the different hydrocarbons, etc., as far as possible by means of solvents. It will be necessary first to dissolve everything out by, say, hot turpentine, then successively treat the residue with bisulphide carbon, benzol, ether, chloroform, naphtha, toluol, alcohol, and other probable solvents. After you can go no further, distil off all the solvents so the asphalt material has a tar-like consistency. Be sure all the ash is out of the turpentine portion; now, after distilling the turpentine off, act on the residue with all the solvents that were used on the residue, using for the first the solvent which is least likely to dissolve a great part of it. By thus manipulating the various solvents you will be enabled probably to separate the crude asphalt into several distinct hydrocarbons. Put each in a bottle after it has been dried, and label the bottle with the process, etc., so we may be able to duplicate it; also give bottle a number and describe everything fully in note-book."

"Destructively distil the following substances down to a point just short of carbonization, so that the residuum can be taken out of the retort, powdered, and acted on by all the solvents just as the asphalt in previous page. The distillation should be carried to, say, 600 degrees or 700 degrees Fahr., but not continued long enough to wholly reduce mass to charcoal, but always run to blackness. Separate the residuum in as many definite parts as possible, bottle and label, and keep accurate records as to process, weights, etc., so a reproduction of the experiment can at any time be made: Gelatine, 4 lbs.; asphalt, hard Cuban, 10 lbs.; coal-tar or pitch, 10 lbs.; wood-pitch, 10 lbs.; Syrian asphalt, 10 lbs.; bituminous coal, 10 lbs.; cane-sugar, 10 lbs.; glucose, 10 lbs.; dextrine, 10 lbs.; glycerine, 10 lbs.; tartaric acid, 5 lbs.; gum guiac, 5 lbs.; gum amber, 3 lbs.; gum tragacanth, 3 Lbs.; aniline red, 1 lb.; aniline oil, 1 lb.; crude anthracene, 5 lbs.; petroleum pitch, 10 lbs.; albumen from eggs, 2 lbs.; tar from passing chlorine through aniline oil, 2 lbs.; citric acid, 5 lbs.; sawdust of boxwood, 3 lbs.; starch, 5 lbs.; shellac, 3 lbs.; gum Arabic, 5 lbs.; castor oil, 5 lbs."

The empirical nature of his method will be apparent from an examination of the above items; but in pursuing it he leaves all uncertainty behind and, trusting nothing to theory, he acquires absolute knowledge. Whatever may be the mental processes by which he arrives at the starting-point of any specific line of research, the final results almost invariably prove that he does not plunge in at random; indeed, as an old associate remarked: "When Edison takes up any proposition in natural science, his perceptions seem to be elementally broad and analytical, that is to say, in addition to the knowledge he has acquired from books and observation, he appears to have an intuitive apprehension of the general order of things, as they might be supposed to exist in natural relation to each other. It has always seemed to me that he goes to the core of things at once."

Although nothing less than results from actual experiments are acceptable to him as established facts, this view of Edison may also account for his peculiar and somewhat weird ability to "guess" correctly, a faculty which has frequently enabled him to take short cuts to lines of investigation whose outcome has verified in a most remarkable degree statements apparently made offhand and without calculation. Mr. Upton says: "One of the main impressions left upon me, after knowing Mr. Edison for many years, is the marvellous accuracy of his guesses. He will see the general nature of a result long before it can be reached by mathematical calculation." This was supplemented by one of his engineering staff, who remarked: "Mr. Edison can guess better than a good many men can figure, and so far as my experience goes, I have found that he is almost invariably correct. His guess is more than a mere starting-point, and often turns out to be the final solution of a problem. I can only account for it by his remarkable insight and wonderful natural sense of the proportion of things, in addition to which he seems to carry in his head determining factors of all kinds, and has the ability to apply them instantly in considering any mechanical problem."

While this mysterious intuitive power has been of the greatest advantage in connection with the vast number of technical problems that have entered into his life-work, there have been many remarkable instances in which it has seemed little less than prophecy, and it is deemed worth while to digress to the extent of relating two of them. One day in the summer of 1881, when the incandescent lamp-industry was still in swaddling clothes, Edison was seated in the room of Major Eaton, vice-president of the Edison Electric Light Company, talking over business matters, when Mr. Upton came in from the lamp factory at Menlo Park, and said: "Well, Mr. Edison, we completed a thousand lamps to-day." Edison looked up and said "Good," then relapsed into a thoughtful mood. In about two minutes he raised his head, and said: "Upton, in fifteen years you will be making forty thousand lamps a day." None of those present ventured to make any remark on this assertion, although all felt that it was merely a random guess, based on the sanguine dream of an inventor. The business had not then really made a start, and being entirely new was without precedent upon which to base any such statement, but, as a matter of fact, the records of the lamp factory show that in 1896 its daily output of lamps was actually about forty thousand.

The other instance referred to occurred shortly after the Edison Machine Works was moved up to Schenectady, in 1886. One day, when he was at the works, Edison sat down and wrote on a sheet of paper fifteen separate predictions of the growth and future of the electrical business. Notwithstanding the fact that the industry was then in an immature state, and that the great boom did not set in until a few years afterward, twelve of these predictions have been fully verified by the enormous growth and development in all branches of the art.

What the explanation of this gift, power, or intuition may be, is perhaps better left to the psychologist to speculate upon. If one were to ask Edison, he would probably say, "Hard work, not too much sleep, and free use of the imagination." Whether or not it would be possible for the average mortal to arrive at such perfection of "guessing" by faithfully following this formula, even reinforced by the Edison recipe for stimulating a slow imagination with pastry, is open for demonstration.

Somewhat allied to this curious faculty is another no less remarkable, and that is, the ability to point out instantly an error in a mass of reported experimental results. While many instances could be definitely named, a typical one, related by Mr. J. D. Flack, formerly master mechanic at the lamp factory, may be quoted: "During the many years of lamp experimentation, batches of lamps were sent to the photometer department for test, and Edison would examine the tabulated test sheets. He ran over every item of the tabulations rapidly, and, apparently without any calculation whatever, would check off errors as fast as he came to them, saying: 'You have made a mistake; try this one over.' In every case the second test proved that he was right. This wonderful aptitude for infallibly locating an error without an instant's hesitation for mental calculation, has always appealed to me very forcibly."

The ability to detect errors quickly in a series of experiments is one of the things that has enabled Edison to accomplish such a vast amount of work as the records show. Examples of the minuteness of detail into which his researches extend have already been mentioned, and as there are always a number of such investigations in progress at the laboratory, this ability stands Edison in good stead, for he is thus enabled to follow, and, if necessary, correct each one step by step. In this he is aided by the great powers of a mind that is able to free itself from absorbed concentration on the details of one problem, and instantly to shift over and become deeply and intelligently concentrated in another and entirely different one. For instance, he may have been busy for hours on chemical experiments, and be called upon suddenly to determine some mechanical questions. The complete and easy transition is the constant wonder of his associates, for there is no confusion of ideas resulting from these quick changes, no hesitation or apparent effort, but a plunge into the midst of the new subject, and an instant acquaintance with all its details, as if he had been studying it for hours.

A good stiff difficulty--one which may, perhaps, appear to be an unsurmountable obstacle--only serves to make Edison cheerful, and brings out variations of his methods in experimenting. Such an occurrence will start him thinking, which soon gives rise to a line of suggestions for approaching the trouble from various sides; or he will sit down and write out a series of eliminations, additions, or changes to be worked out and reported upon, with such variations as may suggest themselves during their progress. It is at such times as these that his unfailing patience and tremendous resourcefulness are in evidence. Ideas and expedients are poured forth in a torrent, and although some of them have temporarily appeared to the staff to be ridiculous or irrelevant, they have frequently turned out to be the ones leading to a correct solution of the trouble.

Edison's inexhaustible resourcefulness and fertility of ideas have contributed largely to his great success, and have ever been a cause of amazement to those around him. Frequently, when it would seem to others that the extreme end of an apparently blind alley had been reached, and that it was impossible to proceed further, he has shown that there were several ways out of it. Examples without number could be quoted, but one must suffice by way of illustration. During the progress of the ore-milling work at Edison, it became desirable to carry on a certain operation by some special machinery. He requested the proper person on his engineering staff to think this matter up and submit a few sketches of what he would propose to do. He brought three drawings to Edison, who examined them and said none of them would answer. The engineer remarked that it was too bad, for there was no other way to do it. Mr. Edison turned to him quickly, and said: "Do you mean to say that these drawings represent the only way to do this work?" To which he received the reply: "I certainly do." Edison said nothing. This happened on a Saturday. He followed his usual custom of spending Sunday at home in Orange. When he returned to the works on Monday morning, he took with him sketches he had made, showing FORTY-EIGHT other ways of accomplishing the desired operation, and laid them on the engineer's desk without a word. Subsequently one of these ideas, with modifications suggested by some of the others, was put into successful practice.

Difficulties seem to have a peculiar charm for Edison, whether they relate to large or small things; and although the larger matters have contributed most to the history of the arts, the same carefulness of thought has often been the means of leading to improvements of permanent advantage even in minor details. For instance, in the very earliest days of electric lighting, the safe insulation of two bare wires fastened together was a serious problem that was solved by him. An iron pot over a fire, some insulating material melted therein, and narrow strips of linen drawn through it by means of a wooden clamp, furnished a readily applied and adhesive insulation, which was just as perfect for the purpose as the regular and now well-known insulating tape, of which it was the forerunner.

Dubious results are not tolerated for a moment in Edison's experimental work. Rather than pass upon an uncertainty, the experiment will be dissected and checked minutely in order to obtain absolute knowledge, pro and con. This searching method is followed not only in chemical or other investigations, into which complexities might naturally enter, but also in more mechanical questions, where simplicity of construction might naturally seem to preclude possibilities of uncertainty. For instance, at the time when he was making strenuous endeavors to obtain copper wire of high conductivity, strict laboratory tests were made of samples sent by manufacturers. One of these samples tested out poorer than a previous lot furnished from the same factory. A report of this to Edison brought the following note: "Perhaps the ---- wire had a bad spot in it. Please cut it up into lengths and test each one and send results to me immediately." Possibly the electrical fraternity does not realize that this earnest work of Edison, twenty-eight years ago, resulted in the establishment of the high quality of copper wire that has been the recognized standard since that time. Says Edison on this point: "I furnished the expert and apparatus to the Ansonia Brass and Copper Company in 1883, and he is there yet. It was this expert and this company who pioneered high-conductivity copper for the electrical trade."

Nor is it generally appreciated in the industry that the adoption of what is now regarded as a most obvious proposition--the high-economy incandescent lamp--was the result of that characteristic foresight which there has been occasion to mention frequently in the course of this narrative, together with the courage and "horse-sense" which have always been displayed by the inventor in his persistent pushing out with far-reaching ideas, in the face of pessimistic opinions. As is well known, the lamps of the first ten or twelve years of incandescent lighting were of low economy, but had long life. Edison's study of the subject had led him to the conviction that the greatest growth of the electric-lighting industry would be favored by a lamp taking less current, but having shorter, though commercially economical life; and after gradually making improvements along this line he developed, finally, a type of high-economy lamp which would introduce a most radical change in existing conditions, and lead ultimately to highly advantageous results. His start on this lamp, and an expressed desire to have it manufactured for regular use, filled even some of his business associates with dismay, for they could see nothing but disaster ahead in forcing such a lamp on the market. His persistence and profound conviction of the ultimate results were so strong and his arguments so sound, however, that the campaign was entered upon. Although it took two or three years to convince the public of the correctness of his views, the idea gradually took strong root, and has now become an integral principle of the business.

In this connection it may be noted that with remarkable prescience Edison saw the coming of the modern lamps of to-day, which, by reason of their small consumption of energy to produce a given candle-power, have dismayed central-station managers. A few years ago a consumption of 3.1 watts per candle-power might safely be assumed as an excellent average, and many stations fixed their rates and business on such a basis. The results on income when the consumption, as in the new metallic-filament lamps, drops to 1.25 watts per candle can readily be imagined. Edison has insisted that central stations are selling light and not current; and he points to the predicament now confronting them as truth of his assertion that when selling light they share in all the benefits of improvement, but that when they sell current the consumer gets all those benefits without division. The dilemma is encountered by central stations in a bewildered way, as a novel and unexpected experience; but Edison foresaw the situation and warned against it long ago. It is one of the greatest gifts of statesmanship to see new social problems years before they arise and solve them in advance. It is one of the greatest attributes of invention to foresee and meet its own problems in exactly the same way.

CHAPTER XXV

THE LABORATORY AT ORANGE AND THE STAFF

A LIVING interrogation-point and a born investigator from childhood, Edison has never been without a laboratory of some kind for upward of half a century.

In youthful years, as already described in this book, he became ardently interested in chemistry, and even at the early age of twelve felt the necessity for a special nook of his own, where he could satisfy his unconvinced mind of the correctness or inaccuracy of statements and experiments contained in the few technical books then at his command.

Ordinarily he was like other normal lads of his age--full of boyish, hearty enjoyments--but withal possessed of an unquenchable spirit of inquiry and an insatiable desire for knowledge. Being blessed with a wise and discerning mother, his aspirations were encouraged; and he was allowed a corner in her cellar. It is fair to offer tribute here to her bravery as well as to her wisdom, for at times she was in mortal terror lest the precocious experimenter below should, in his inexperience, make some awful combination that would explode and bring down the house in ruins on himself and the rest of the family.

Fortunately no such catastrophe happened, but young Edison worked away in his embryonic laboratory, satisfying his soul and incidentally depleting his limited pocket-money to the vanishing-point. It was, indeed, owing to this latter circumstance that in a year or two his aspirations necessitated an increase of revenue; and a consequent determination to earn some money for himself led to his first real commercial enterprise as "candy butcher" on the Grand Trunk Railroad, already mentioned in a previous chapter. It has also been related how his precious laboratory was transferred to the train; how he and it were subsequently expelled; and how it was re-established in his home, where he continued studies and experiments until the beginning of his career as a telegraph operator.

The nomadic life of the next few years did not lessen his devotion to study; but it stood seriously in the way of satisfying the ever-present craving for a laboratory. The lack of such a place never prevented experimentation, however, as long as he had a dollar in his pocket and some available "hole in the wall." With the turning of the tide of fortune that suddenly carried him, in New York in 1869, from poverty to the opulence of $300 a month, he drew nearer to a realization of his cherished ambition in having money, place, and some time (stolen from sleep) for more serious experimenting. Thus matters continued until, at about the age of twenty-two, Edison's inventions had brought him a relatively large sum of money, and he became a very busy manufacturer, and lessee of a large shop in Newark, New Jersey.

Now, for the first time since leaving that boyish laboratory in the old home at Port Huron, Edison had a place of his own to work in, to think in; but no one in any way acquainted with Newark as a swarming centre of miscellaneous and multitudinous industries would recommend it as a cloistered retreat for brooding reverie and introspection, favorable to creative effort. Some people revel in surroundings of hustle and bustle, and find therein no hindrance to great accomplishment. The electrical genius of Newark is Edward Weston, who has thriven amid its turmoil and there has developed his beautiful instruments of precision; just as Brush worked out his arc-lighting system in Cleveland; or even as Faraday, surrounded by the din and roar of London, laid the intellectual foundations of the whole modern science of dynamic electricity. But Edison, though deaf, could not make too hurried a retreat from Newark to Menlo Park, where, as if to justify his change of base, vital inventions soon came thick and fast, year after year. The story of Menlo has been told in another chapter, but the point was not emphasized that Edison then, as later, tried hard to drop manufacturing. He would infinitely rather be philosopher than producer; but somehow the necessity of manufacturing is constantly thrust back upon him by a profound--perhaps finical--sense of dissatisfaction with what other people make for him. The world never saw a man more deeply and desperately convinced that nothing in it approaches perfection. Edison is the doctrine of evolution incarnate, applied to mechanics. As to the removal from Newark, he may be allowed to tell his own story: "I had a shop at Newark in which I manufactured stock tickers and such things. When I moved to Menlo Park I took out only the machinery that would be necessary for experimental purposes and left the manufacturing machinery in the place. It consisted of many milling machines and other tools for duplicating. I rented this to a man who had formerly been my bookkeeper, and who thought he could make money out of manufacturing. There was about $10,000 worth of machinery. He was to pay me $2000 a year for the rent of the machinery and keep it in good order. After I moved to Menlo Park, I was very busy with the telephone and phonograph, and I paid no attention to this little arrangement. About three years afterward, it occurred to me that I had not heard at all from the man who had rented this machinery, so I thought I would go over to Newark and see how things were going. When I got there, I found that instead of being a machine shop it was a hotel! I have since been utterly unable to find out what became of the man or the machinery." Such incidents tend to justify Edison in his rather cynical remark that he has always been able to improve machinery much quicker than men. All the way up he has had discouraging experiences. "One day while I was carrying on my work in Newark, a Wall Street broker came from the city and said he was tired of the 'Street,' and wanted to go into something real. He said he had plenty of money. He wanted some kind of a job to keep his mind off Wall Street. So we gave him a job as a 'mucker' in chemical experiments. The second night he was there he could not stand the long hours and fell asleep on a sofa. One of the boys took a bottle of bromine and opened it under the sofa. It floated up and produced a violent effect on the mucous membrane. The broker was taken with such a fit of coughing he burst a blood-vessel, and the man who let the bromine out got away and never came back. I suppose he thought there was going to be a death. But the broker lived, and left the next day; and I have never seen him since, either." Edison tells also of another foolhardy laboratory trick of the same kind: "Some of my assistants in those days were very green in the business, as I did not care whether they had had any experience or not. I generally tried to turn them loose. One day I got a new man, and told him to conduct a certain experiment. He got a quart of ether and started to boil it over a naked flame. Of course it caught fire. The flame was about four feet in diameter and eleven feet high. We had to call out the fire department; and they came down and put a stream through the window. That let all the fumes and chemicals out and overcame the firemen; and there was the devil to pay. Another time we experimented with a tub full of soapy water, and put hydrogen into it to make large bubbles. One of the boys, who was washing bottles in the place, had read in some book that hydrogen was explosive, so he proceeded to blow the tub up. There was about four inches of soap in the bottom of the tub, fourteen inches high; and he filled it with soap bubbles up to the brim. Then he took a bamboo fish-pole, put a piece of paper at the end, and touched it off. It blew every window out of the place."

Always a shrewd, observant, and kindly critic of character, Edison tells many anecdotes of the men who gathered around him in various capacities at that quiet corner of New Jersey--Menlo Park--and later at Orange, in the Llewellyn Park laboratory; and these serve to supplement the main narrative by throwing vivid side-lights on the whole scene. Here, for example, is a picture drawn by Edison of a laboratory interlude--just a bit Rabelaisian: "When experimenting at Menlo Park we had all the way from forty to fifty men. They worked all the time. Each man was allowed from four to six hours' sleep. We had a man who kept tally, and when the time came for one to sleep, he was notified. At midnight we had lunch brought in and served at a long table at which the experimenters sat down. I also had an organ which I procured from Hilbourne Roosevelt--uncle of the ex-President--and we had a man play this organ while we ate our lunch. During the summertime, after we had made something which was successful, I used to engage a brick-sloop at Perth Amboy and take the whole crowd down to the fishing-banks on the Atlantic for two days. On one occasion we got outside Sandy Hook on the banks and anchored. A breeze came up, the sea became rough, and a large number of the men were sick. There was straw in the bottom of the boat, which we all slept on. Most of the men adjourned to this straw very sick. Those who were not got a piece of rancid salt pork from the skipper, and cut a large, thick slice out of it. This was put on the end of a fish-hook and drawn across the men's faces. The smell was terrific, and the effect added to the hilarity of the excursion.

"I went down once with my father and two assistants for a little fishing inside Sandy Hook. For some reason or other the fishing was very poor. We anchored, and I started in to fish. After fishing for several hours there was not a single bite. The others wanted to pull up anchor, but I fished two days and two nights without a bite, until they pulled up anchor and went away. I would not give up. I was going to catch that fish if it took a week."

This is general. Let us quote one or two piquant personal observations of a more specific nature as to the odd characters Edison drew around him in his experimenting. "Down at Menlo Park a man came in one day and wanted a job. He was a sailor. I hadn't any particular work to give him, but I had a number of small induction coils, and to give him something to do I told him to fix them up and sell them among his sailor friends. They were fixed up, and he went over to New York and sold them all. He was an extraordinary fellow. His name was Adams. One day I asked him how long it was since he had been to sea, and he replied two or three years. I asked him how he had made a living in the mean time, before he came to Menlo Park. He said he made a pretty good living by going around to different clinics and getting $10 at each clinic, because of having the worst case of heart-disease on record. I told him if that was the case he would have to be very careful around the laboratory. I had him there to help in experimenting, and the heart-disease did not seem to bother him at all.

"It appeared that he had once been a slaver; and altogether he was a tough character. Having no other man I could spare at that time, I sent him over with my carbon transmitter telephone to exhibit it in England. It was exhibited before the Post-Office authorities. Professor Hughes spent an afternoon in examining the apparatus, and in about a month came out with his microphone, which was absolutely nothing more nor less than my exact invention. But no mention was made of the fact that, just previously, he had seen the whole of my apparatus. Adams stayed over in Europe connected with the telephone for several years, and finally died of too much whiskey--but not of heart-disease. This shows how whiskey is the more dangerous of the two.

"Adams said that at one time he was aboard a coffee-ship in the harbor of Santos, Brazil. He fell down a hatchway and broke his arm. They took him up to the hospital--a Portuguese one--where he could not speak the language, and they did not understand English. They treated him for two weeks for yellow fever! He was certainly the most profane man we ever had around the laboratory. He stood high in his class."

And there were others of a different stripe. "We had a man with us at Menlo called Segredor. He was a queer kind of fellow. The men got in the habit of plaguing him; and, finally, one day he said to the assembled experimenters in the top room of the laboratory: 'The next man that does it, I will kill him.' They paid no attention to this, and next day one of them made some sarcastic remark to him. Segredor made a start for his boarding-house, and when they saw him coming back up the hill with a gun, they knew there would be trouble, so they all made for the woods. One of the men went back and mollified him. He returned to his work; but he was not teased any more. At last, when I sent men out hunting for bamboo, I dispatched Segredor to Cuba. He arrived in Havana on Tuesday, and on the Friday following he was buried, having died of the black vomit. On the receipt of the news of his death, half a dozen of the men wanted his job, but my searcher in the Astor Library reported that the chances of finding the right kind of bamboo for lamps in Cuba were very small; so I did not send a substitute."

Another thumb-nail sketch made of one of his associates is this: "When experimenting with vacuum-pumps to exhaust the incandescent lamps, I required some very delicate and close manipulation of glass, and hired a German glass-blower who was said to be the most expert man of his kind in the United States. He was the only one who could make clinical thermometers. He was the most extraordinarily conceited man I have ever come across. His conceit was so enormous, life was made a burden to him by all the boys around the laboratory. He once said that he was educated in a university where all the students belonged to families of the aristocracy; and the highest class in the university all wore little red caps. He said HE wore one."

Of somewhat different caliber was "honest" John Kruesi, who first made his mark at Menlo Park, and of whom Edison says: "One of the workmen I had at Menlo Park was John Kruesi, who afterward became, from his experience, engineer of the lighting station, and subsequently engineer of the Edison General Electric Works at Schenectady. Kruesi was very exact in his expressions. At the time we were promoting and putting up electric-light stations in Pennsylvania, New York, and New England, there would be delegations of different people who proposed to pay for these stations. They would come to our office in New York, at '65,' to talk over the specifications, the cost, and other things. At first, Mr. Kruesi was brought in, but whenever a statement was made which he could not understand or did not believe could be substantiated, he would blurt right out among these prospects that he didn't believe it. Finally it disturbed these committees so much, and raised so many doubts in their minds, that one of my chief associates said: 'Here, Kruesi, we don't want you to come to these meetings any longer. You are too painfully honest.' I said to him: 'We always tell the truth. It may be deferred truth, but it is the truth.' He could not understand that."

Various reasons conspired to cause the departure from Menlo Park midway in the eighties. For Edison, in spite of the achievement with which its name will forever be connected, it had lost all its attractions and all its possibilities. It had been outgrown in many ways, and strange as the remark may seem, it was not until he had left it behind and had settled in Orange, New Jersey, that he can be said to have given definite shape to his life. He was only forty in 1887, and all that he had done up to that time, tremendous as much of it was, had worn a haphazard, Bohemian air, with all the inconsequential freedom and crudeness somehow attaching to pioneer life. The development of the new laboratory in West Orange, just at the foot of Llewellyn Park, on the Orange Mountains, not only marked the happy beginning of a period of perfect domestic and family life, but saw in the planning and equipment of a model laboratory plant the consummation of youthful dreams, and of the keen desire to enjoy resources adequate at any moment to whatever strain the fierce fervor of research might put upon them. Curiously enough, while hitherto Edison had sought to dissociate his experimenting from his manufacturing, here he determined to develop a large industry to which a thoroughly practical laboratory would be a central feature, and ever a source of suggestion and inspiration. Edison's standpoint to-day is that an evil to be dreaded in manufacture is that of over-standardization, and that as soon as an article is perfect that is the time to begin improving it. But he who would improve must experiment.

The Orange laboratory, as originally planned, consisted of a main building two hundred and fifty feet long and three stories in height, together with four other structures, each one hundred by twenty-five feet, and only one story in height. All these were substantially built of brick. The main building was divided into five chief divisions--the library, office, machine shops, experimental and chemical rooms, and stock-room. The use of the smaller buildings will be presently indicated.

Surrounding the whole was erected a high picket fence with a gate placed on Valley Road. At this point a gate-house was provided and put in charge of a keeper, for then, as at the present time, Edison was greatly sought after; and, in order to accomplish any work at all, he was obliged to deny himself to all but the most important callers. The keeper of the gate was usually chosen with reference to his capacity for stony-hearted implacability and adherence to instructions; and this choice was admirably made in one instance when a new gateman, not yet thoroughly initiated, refused admittance to Edison himself. It was of no use to try and explain. To the gateman EVERY ONE was persona non grata without proper credentials, and Edison had to wait outside until he could get some one to identify him.

On entering the main building the first doorway from the ample passage leads the visitor into a handsome library finished throughout in yellow pine, occupying the entire width of the building, and almost as broad as long. The centre of this spacious room is an open rectangular space about forty by twenty-five feet, rising clear about forty feet from the main floor to a panelled ceiling. Around the sides of the room, bounding this open space, run two tiers of gallery, divided, as is the main floor beneath them; into alcoves of liberal dimensions. These alcoves are formed by racks extending from floor to ceiling, fitted with shelves, except on two sides of both galleries, where they are formed by a series of glass-fronted cabinets containing extensive collections of curious and beautiful mineralogical and geological specimens, among which is the notable Tiffany-Kunz collection of minerals acquired by Edison some years ago. Here and there in these cabinets may also be found a few models which he has used at times in his studies of anatomy and physiology.

The shelves on the remainder of the upper gallery and part of those on the first gallery are filled with countless thousands of specimens of ores and minerals of every conceivable kind gathered from all parts of the world, and all tagged and numbered. The remaining shelves of the first gallery are filled with current numbers (and some back numbers) of the numerous periodicals to which Edison subscribes. Here may be found the popular magazines, together with those of a technical nature relating to electricity, chemistry, engineering, mechanics, building, cement, building materials, drugs, water and gas, power, automobiles, railroads, aeronautics, philosophy, hygiene, physics, telegraphy, mining, metallurgy, metals, music, and others; also theatrical weeklies, as well as the proceedings and transactions of various learned and technical societies.

The first impression received as one enters on the main floor of the library and looks around is that of noble proportions and symmetry as a whole. The open central space of liberal dimensions and height, flanked by the galleries and relieved by four handsome electric-lighting fixtures suspended from the ceiling by long chains, conveys an idea of lofty spaciousness; while the huge open fireplace, surmounted by a great clock built into the wall, at one end of the room, the large rugs, the arm-chairs scattered around, the tables and chairs in the alcoves, give a general air of comfort combined with utility. In one of the larger alcoves, at the sunny end of the main hall, is Edison's own desk, where he may usually be seen for a while in the early morning hours looking over his mail or otherwise busily working on matters requiring his attention.

At the opposite end of the room, not far from the open fireplace, is a long table surrounded by swivel desk-chairs. It is here that directors' meetings are sometimes held, and also where weighty matters are often discussed by Edison at conference with his closer associates. It has been the privilege of the writers to be present at some of these conferences, not only as participants, but in some cases as lookers-on while awaiting their turn. On such occasions an interesting opportunity is offered to study Edison in his intense and constructive moods. Apparently oblivious to everything else, he will listen with concentrated mind and close attention, and then pour forth a perfect torrent of ideas and plans, and, if the occasion calls for it, will turn around to the table, seize a writing-pad and make sketch after sketch with lightning-like rapidity, tearing off each sheet as filled and tossing it aside to the floor. It is an ordinary indication that there has been an interesting meeting when the caretaker about fills a waste-basket with these discarded sketches.

Directly opposite the main door is a beautiful marble statue purchased by Edison at the Paris Exposition in 1889, on the occasion of his visit there. The statue, mounted on a base three feet high, is an allegorical representation of the supremacy of electric light over all other forms of illumination, carried out by the life-size figure of a youth with half-spread wings seated upon the ruins of a street gas-lamp, holding triumphantly high above his head an electric incandescent lamp. Grouped about his feet are a gear-wheel, voltaic pile, telegraph key, and telephone. This work of art was executed by A. Bordiga, of Rome, held a prominent place in the department devoted to Italian art at the Paris Exposition, and naturally appealed to Edison as soon as he saw it.

In the middle distance, between the entrance door and this statue, has long stood a magnificent palm, but at the present writing it has been set aside to give place to a fine model of the first type of the Edison poured cement house, which stands in a miniature artificial lawn upon a special table prepared for it; while on the floor at the foot of the table are specimens of the full-size molds in which the house will be cast.

The balustrades of the galleries and all other available places are filled with portraits of great scientists and men of achievement, as well as with pictures of historic and scientific interest. Over the fireplace hangs a large photograph showing the Edison cement plant in its entire length, flanked on one end of the mantel by a bust of Humboldt, and on the other by a statuette of Sandow, the latter having been presented to Edison by the celebrated athlete after the visit he made to Orange to pose for the motion pictures in the earliest days of their development. On looking up under the second gallery at this end is seen a great roll resting in sockets placed on each side of the room. This is a huge screen or curtain which may be drawn down to the floor to provide a means of projection for lantern slides or motion pictures, for the entertainment or instruction of Edison and his guests. In one of the larger alcoves is a large terrestrial globe pivoted in its special stand, together with a relief map of the United States; and here and there are handsomely mounted specimens of underground conductors and electric welds that were made at the Edison Machine Works at Schenectady before it was merged into the General Electric Company. On two pedestals stand, respectively, two other mementoes of the works, one a fifteen-light dynamo of the Edison type, and the other an elaborate electric fan--both of them gifts from associates or employees.

In noting these various objects of interest one must not lose sight of the fact that this part of the building is primarily a library, if indeed that fact did not at once impress itself by a glance at the well-filled unglazed book-shelves in the alcoves of the main floor. Here Edison's catholic taste in reading becomes apparent as one scans the titles of thousands of volumes ranged upon the shelves, for they include astronomy, botany, chemistry, dynamics, electricity, engineering, forestry, geology, geography, mechanics, mining, medicine, metallurgy, magnetism, philosophy, psychology, physics, steam, steam-engines, telegraphy, telephony, and many others. Besides these there are the journals and proceedings of numerous technical societies; encyclopaedias of various kinds; bound series of important technical magazines; a collection of United States and foreign patents, embracing some hundreds of volumes, together with an extensive assortment of miscellaneous books of special and general interest. There is another big library up in the house on the hill--in fact, there are books upon books all over the home. And wherever they are, those books are read.

As one is about to pass out of the library attention is arrested by an incongruity in the form of a cot, which stands in an alcove near the door. Here Edison, throwing himself down, sometimes seeks a short rest during specially long working tours. Sleep is practically instantaneous and profound, and he awakes in immediate and full possession of his faculties, arising from the cot and going directly "back to the job" without a moment's hesitation, just as a person wide awake would arise from a chair and proceed to attend to something previously determined upon.

Immediately outside the library is the famous stock-room, about which much has been written and invented. Its fame arose from the fact that Edison planned it to be a repository of some quantity, great or small, of every known and possibly useful substance not readily perishable, together with the most complete assortment of chemicals and drugs that experience and knowledge could suggest. Always strenuous in his experimentation, and the living embodiment of the spirit of the song, I Want What I Want When I Want It, Edison had known for years what it was to be obliged to wait, and sometimes lack, for some substance or chemical that he thought necessary to the success of an experiment. Naturally impatient at any delay which interposed in his insistent and searching methods, and realizing the necessity of maintaining the inspiration attending his work at any time, he determined to have within his immediate reach the natural resources of the world.

Hence it is not surprising to find the stock-room not only a museum, but a sample-room of nature, as well as a supply department. To a casual visitor the first view of this heterogeneous collection is quite bewildering, but on more mature examination it resolves itself into a natural classification--as, for instance, objects pertaining to various animals, birds, and fishes, such as skins, hides, hair, fur, feathers, wool, quills, down, bristles, teeth, bones, hoofs, horns, tusks, shells; natural products, such as woods, barks, roots, leaves, nuts, seeds, herbs, gums, grains, flours, meals, bran; also minerals in great assortment; mineral and vegetable oils, clay, mica, ozokerite, etc. In the line of textiles, cotton and silk threads in great variety, with woven goods of all kinds from cheese-cloth to silk plush. As for paper, there is everything in white and colored, from thinnest tissue up to the heaviest asbestos, even a few newspapers being always on hand. Twines of all sizes, inks, waxes, cork, tar, resin, pitch, turpentine, asphalt, plumbago, glass in sheets and tubes; and a host of miscellaneous articles revealed on looking around the shelves, as well as an interminable collection of chemicals, including acids, alkalies, salts, reagents, every conceivable essential oil and all the thinkable extracts. It may be remarked that this collection includes the eighteen hundred or more fluorescent salts made by Edison during his experimental search for the best material for a fluoroscope in the initial X-ray period. All known metals in form of sheet, rod and tube, and of great variety in thickness, are here found also, together with a most complete assortment of tools and accessories for machine shop and laboratory work.

The list is confined to the merest general mention of the scope of this remarkable and interesting collection, as specific details would stretch out into a catalogue of no small proportions. When it is stated, however, that a stock clerk is kept exceedingly busy all day answering the numerous and various demands upon him, the reader will appreciate that this comprehensive assortment is not merely a fad of Edison's, but stands rather as a substantial tribute to his wide-angled view of possible requirements as his various investigations take him far afield. It has no counterpart in the world!

Beyond the stock-room, and occupying about half the building on the same floor, lie a machine shop, engine-room, and boiler-room. This machine shop is well equipped, and in it is constantly employed a large force of mechanics whose time is occupied in constructing the heavier class of models and mechanical devices called for by the varied experiments and inventions always going on.

Immediately above, on the second floor, is found another machine shop in which is maintained a corps of expert mechanics who are called upon to do work of greater precision and fineness, in the construction of tools and experimental models. This is the realm presided over lovingly by John F. Ott, who has been Edison's designer of mechanical devices for over forty years. He still continues to ply his craft with unabated skill and oversees the work of the mechanics as his productions are wrought into concrete shape.

In one of the many experimental-rooms lining the sides of the second floor may usually be seen his younger brother, Fred Ott, whose skill as a dexterous manipulator and ingenious mechanic has found ample scope for exercise during the thirty-two years of his service with Edison, not only at the regular laboratories, but also at that connected with the inventor's winter home in Florida. Still another of the Ott family, the son of John F., for some years past has been on the experimental staff of the Orange laboratory. Although possessing in no small degree the mechanical and manipulative skill of the family, he has chosen chemistry as his special domain, and may be found with the other chemists in one of the chemical-rooms.

On this same floor is the vacuum-pump room with a glass-blowers' room adjoining, both of them historic by reason of the strenuous work done on incandescent lamps and X-ray tubes within their walls. The tools and appliances are kept intact, for Edison calls occasionally for their use in some of his later experiments, and there is a suspicion among the laboratory staff that some day he may resume work on incandescent lamps. Adjacent to these rooms are several others devoted to physical and mechanical experiments, together with a draughting-room.

Last to be mentioned, but the first in order as one leaves the head of the stairs leading up to this floor, is No. 12, Edison's favorite room, where he will frequently be found. Plain of aspect, being merely a space boarded off with tongued-and-grooved planks--as all the other rooms are--without ornament or floor covering, and containing only a few articles of cheap furniture, this room seems to exercise a nameless charm for him. The door is always open, and often he can be seen seated at a plain table in the centre of the room, deeply intent on some of the numerous problems in which he is interested. The table is usually pretty well filled with specimens or data of experimental results which have been put there for his examination. At the time of this writing these specimens consist largely of sections of positive elements of the storage battery, together with many samples of nickel hydrate, to which Edison devotes deep study. Close at hand is a microscope which is in frequent use by him in these investigations. Around the room, on shelves, are hundreds of bottles each containing a small quantity of nickel hydrate made in as many different ways, each labelled correspondingly. Always at hand will be found one or two of the laboratory note-books, with frequent entries or comments in the handwriting which once seen is never forgotten.

No. 12 is at times a chemical, a physical, or a mechanical room--occasionally a combination of all, while sometimes it might be called a consultation-room or clinic--for often Edison may be seen there in animated conference with a group of his assistants; but its chief distinction lies in its being one of his favorite haunts, and in the fact that within its walls have been settled many of the perplexing problems and momentous questions that have brought about great changes in electrical and engineering arts during the twenty-odd years that have elapsed since the Orange laboratory was built.

Passing now to the top floor the visitor finds himself at the head of a broad hall running almost the entire length of the building, and lined mostly with glass-fronted cabinets containing a multitude of experimental incandescent lamps and an immense variety of models of phonographs, motors, telegraph and telephone apparatus, meters, and a host of other inventions upon which Edison's energies have at one time and another been bent. Here also are other cabinets containing old papers and records, while further along the wall are piled up boxes of historical models and instruments. In fact, this hallway, with its conglomerate contents, may well be considered a scientific attic. It is to be hoped that at no distant day these Edisoniana will be assembled and arranged in a fireproof museum for the benefit of posterity.

In the front end of the building, and extending over the library, is a large room intended originally and used for a time as the phonograph music-hall for record-making, but now used only as an experimental-room for phonograph work, as the growth of the industry has necessitated a very much larger and more central place where records can be made on a commercial scale. Even the experimental work imposes no slight burden on it. On each side of the hallway above mentioned, rooms are partitioned off and used for experimental work of various kinds, mostly phonographic, although on this floor are also located the storage-battery testing-room, a chemical and physical room and Edison's private office, where all his personal correspondence and business affairs are conducted by his personal secretary, Mr. H. F. Miller. A visitor to this upper floor of the laboratory building cannot but be impressed with a consciousness of the incessant efforts that are being made to improve the reproducing qualities of the phonograph, as he hears from all sides the sounds of vocal and instrumental music constantly varying in volume and timbre, due to changes in the experimental devices under trial.

The traditions of the laboratory include cots placed in many of the rooms of these upper floors, but that was in the earlier years when the strenuous scenes of Menlo Park were repeated in the new quarters. Edison and his closest associates were accustomed to carry their labors far into the wee sma' hours, and when physical nature demanded a respite from work, a short rest would be obtained by going to bed on a cot. One would naturally think that the wear and tear of this intense application, day after day and night after night, would have tended to induce a heaviness and gravity of demeanor in these busy men; but on the contrary, the old spirit of good-humor and prankishness was ever present, as its frequent outbursts manifested from time to time. One instance will serve as an illustration. One morning, about 2.30, the late Charles Batchelor announced that he was tired and would go to bed. Leaving Edison and the others busily working, he went out and returned quietly in slippered feet, with his nightgown on, the handle of a feather duster stuck down his back with the feathers waving over his head, and his face marked. With unearthly howls and shrieks, a l'Indien, he pranced about the room, incidentally giving Edison a scare that made him jump up from his work. He saw the joke quickly, however, and joined in the general merriment caused by this prank.

Leaving the main building with its corps of busy experimenters, and coming out into the spacious yard, one notes the four long single-story brick structures mentioned above. The one nearest the Valley Road is called the galvanometer-room, and was originally intended by Edison to be used for the most delicate and minute electrical measurements. In order to provide rigid resting-places for the numerous and elaborate instruments he had purchased for this purpose, the building was equipped along three-quarters of its length with solid pillars, or tables, of brick set deep in the earth. These were built up to a height of about two and a half feet, and each was surmounted with a single heavy slab of black marble. A cement floor was laid, and every precaution was taken to render the building free from all magnetic influences, so that it would be suitable for electrical work of the utmost accuracy and precision. Hence, iron and steel were entirely eliminated in its construction, copper being used for fixtures for steam and water piping, and, indeed, for all other purposes where metal was employed.

This room was for many years the headquarters of Edison's able assistant, Dr. A. E. Kennelly, now professor of electrical engineering in Harvard University to whose energetic and capable management were intrusted many scientific investigations during his long sojourn at the laboratory. Unfortunately, however, for the continued success of Edison's elaborate plans, he had not been many years established in the laboratory before a trolley road through West Orange was projected and built, the line passing in front of the plant and within seventy-five feet of the galvanometer-room, thus making it practically impossible to use it for the delicate purposes for which it was originally intended.

For some time past it has been used for photography and some special experiments on motion pictures as well as for demonstrations connected with physical research; but some reminders of its old-time glory still remain in evidence. In lofty and capacious glass-enclosed cabinets, in company with numerous models of Edison's inventions, repose many of the costly and elaborate instruments rendered useless by the ubiquitous trolley. Instruments are all about, on walls, tables, and shelves, the photometer is covered up; induction coils of various capacities, with other electrical paraphernalia, lie around, almost as if the experimenter were absent for a few days but would soon return and resume his work.

In numbering the group of buildings, the galvanometer-room is No. 1, while the other single-story structures are numbered respectively 2, 3, and 4. On passing out of No. 1 and proceeding to the succeeding building is noticed, between the two, a garage of ample dimensions and a smaller structure, at the door of which stands a concrete-mixer. In this small building Edison has made some of his most important experiments in the process of working out his plans for the poured house. It is in this little place that there was developed the remarkable mixture which is to play so vital a part in the successful construction of these everlasting homes for living millions.

Drawing near to building No. 2, olfactory evidence presents itself of the immediate vicinity of a chemical laboratory. This is confirmed as one enters the door and finds that the entire building is devoted to chemistry. Long rows of shelves and cabinets filled with chemicals line the room; a profusion of retorts, alembics, filters, and other chemical apparatus on numerous tables and stands, greet the eye, while a corps of experimenters may be seen busy in the preparation of various combinations, some of which are boiling or otherwise cooking under their dexterous manipulation.

It would not require many visits to discover that in this room, also, Edison has a favorite nook. Down at the far end in a corner are a plain little table and chair, and here he is often to be found deeply immersed in a study of the many experiments that are being conducted. Not infrequently he is actively engaged in the manipulation of some compound of special intricacy, whose results might be illuminative of obscure facts not patent to others than himself. Here, too, is a select little library of chemical literature.

The next building, No. 3, has a double mission--the farther half being partitioned off for a pattern-making shop, while the other half is used as a store-room for chemicals in quantity and for chemical apparatus and utensils. A grimly humorous incident, as related by one of the laboratory staff, attaches to No. 3. It seems that some time ago one of the helpers in the chemical department, an excitable foreigner, became dissatisfied with his wages, and after making an unsuccessful application for an increase, rushed in desperation to Edison, and said "Eef I not get more money I go to take ze cyanide potassia." Edison gave him one quick, searching glance and, detecting a bluff, replied in an offhand manner: "There's a five-pound bottle in No. 3," and turned to his work again. The foreigner did not go to get the cyanide, but gave up his job.

The last of these original buildings, No. 4, was used for many years in Edison's ore-concentrating experiments, and also for rough-and-ready operations of other kinds, such as furnace work and the like. At the present writing it is used as a general stock-room.

In the foregoing details, the reader has been afforded but a passing glance at the great practical working equipment which constitutes the theatre of Edison's activities, for, in taking a general view of such a unique and comprehensive laboratory plant, its salient features only can be touched upon to advantage. It would be but repetition to enumerate here the practical results of the laboratory work during the past two decades, as they appear on other pages of this work. Nor can one assume for a moment that the history of Edison's laboratory is a closed book. On the contrary, its territorial boundaries have been increasing step by step with the enlargement of its labors, until now it has been obliged to go outside its own proper domains to occupy some space in and about the great Edison industrial buildings and space immediately adjacent. It must be borne in mind that the laboratory is only the core of a group of buildings devoted to production on a huge scale by hundreds of artisans.

Incidental mention has already been made of the laboratory at Edison's winter residence in Florida, where he goes annually to spend a month or six weeks. This is a miniature copy of the Orange laboratory, with its machine shop, chemical-room, and general experimental department. While it is only in use during his sojourn there, and carries no extensive corps of assistants, the work done in it is not of a perfunctory nature, but is a continuation of his regular activities, and serves to keep him in touch with the progress of experiments at Orange, and enables him to give instructions for their variation and continuance as their scope is expanded by his own investigations made while enjoying what he calls "vacation." What Edison in Florida speaks of as "loafing" would be for most of us extreme and healthy activity in the cooler Far North.

A word or two may be devoted to the visitors received at the laboratory, and to the correspondence. It might be injudicious to gauge the greatness of a man by the number of his callers or his letters; but they are at least an indication of the degree to which he interests the world. In both respects, for these forty years, Edison has been a striking example of the manner in which the sentiment of hero-worship can manifest itself, and of the deep desire of curiosity to get satisfaction by personal observation or contact. Edison's mail, like that of most well-known men, is extremely large, but composed in no small degree of letters--thousands of them yearly--that concern only the writers, and might well go to the waste-paper basket without prolonged consideration. The serious and important part of the mail, some personal and some business, occupies the attention of several men; all such letters finding their way promptly into the proper channels, often with a pithy endorsement by Edison scribbled on the margin. What to do with a host of others it is often difficult to decide, even when written by "cranks," who imagine themselves subject to strange electrical ailments from which Edison alone can relieve them. Many people write asking his opinion as to a certain invention, or offering him an interest in it if he will work it out. Other people abroad ask help in locating lost relatives; and many want advice as to what they shall do with their sons, frequently budding geniuses whose ability to wire a bell has demonstrated unusual qualities. A great many persons want autographs, and some would like photographs. The amazing thing about it all is that this flood of miscellaneous letters flows on in one steady, uninterrupted stream, year in and year out; always a curious psychological study in its variety and volume; and ever a proof of the fact that once a man has become established as a personality in the public eye and mind, nothing can stop the tide of correspondence that will deluge him.

It is generally, in the nature of things, easier to write a letter than to make a call; and the semi-retirement of Edison at a distance of an hour by train from New York stands as a means of protection to him against those who would certainly present their respects in person, if he could be got at without trouble. But it may be seriously questioned whether in the aggregate Edison's visitors are less numerous or less time-consuming than his epistolary besiegers. It is the common experience of any visitor to the laboratory that there are usually several persons ahead of him, no matter what the hour of the day, and some whose business has been sufficiently vital to get them inside the porter's gate, or even into the big library and lounging-room. Celebrities of all kinds and distinguished foreigners are numerous--princes, noblemen, ambassadors, artists, litterateurs, scientists, financiers, women. A very large part of the visiting is done by scientific bodies and societies; and then the whole place will be turned over to hundreds of eager, well-dressed men and women, anxious to see everything and to be photographed in the big courtyard around the central hero. Nor are these groups and delegations limited to this country, for even large parties of English, Dutch, Italian, or Japanese visitors come from time to time, and are greeted with the same ready hospitality, although Edison, it is easy to see, is torn between the conflicting emotions of a desire to be courteous, and an anxiety to guard the precious hours of work, or watch the critical stage of a new experiment.

One distinct group of visitors has always been constituted by the "newspaper men." Hardly a day goes by that the journals do not contain some reference to Edison's work or remarks; and the items are generally based on an interview. The reporters are never away from the laboratory very long; for if they have no actual mission of inquiry, there is always the chance of a good story being secured offhand; and the easy, inveterate good-nature of Edison toward reporters is proverbial in the craft. Indeed, it must be stated here that once in a while this confidence has been abused; that stories have been published utterly without foundation; that interviews have been printed which never took place; that articles with Edison's name as author have been widely circulated, although he never saw them; and that in such ways he has suffered directly. But such occasional incidents tend in no wise to lessen Edison's warm admiration of the press or his readiness to avail himself of it whenever a representative goes over to Orange to get the truth or the real facts in regard to any matter of public importance. As for the newspaper clippings containing such articles, or others in which Edison's name appears--they are literally like sands of the sea-shore for number; and the archives of the laboratory that preserve only a very minute percentage of them are a further demonstration of what publicity means, where a figure like Edison is concerned.

CHAPTER XXVI

EDISON IN COMMERCE AND MANUFACTURE

AN applicant for membership in the Engineers' Club of Philadelphia is required to give a brief statement of the professional work he has done. Some years ago a certain application was made, and contained the following terse and modest sentence:

"I have designed a concentrating plant and built a machine shop, etc., etc. THOMAS A. EDISON."

Although in the foregoing pages the reader has been made acquainted with the tremendous import of the actualities lying behind those "etc., etc.," the narrative up to this point has revealed Edison chiefly in the light of inventor, experimenter, and investigator. There have been some side glimpses of the industries he has set on foot, and of their financial aspects, and a later chapter will endeavor to sum up the intrinsic value of Edison's work to the world. But there are some other interesting points that may be touched on now in regard to a few of Edison's financial and commercial ventures not generally known or appreciated.

It is a popular idea founded on experience that an inventor is not usually a business man. One of the exceptions proving the rule may perhaps be met in Edison, though all depends on the point of view. All his life he has had a great deal to do with finance and commerce, and as one looks at the magnitude of the vast industries he has helped to create, it would not be at all unreasonable to expect him to be among the multi-millionaires. That he is not is due to the absence of certain qualities, the lack of which Edison is himself the first to admit. Those qualities may not be amiable, but great wealth is hardly ever accumulated without them. If he had not been so intent on inventing he would have made more of his great opportunities for getting rich. If this utter detachment from any love of money for its own sake has not already been illustrated in some of the incidents narrated, one or two stories are available to emphasize the point. They do not involve any want of the higher business acumen that goes to the proper conduct of affairs. It was said of Gladstone that he was the greatest Chancellor of the Exchequer England ever saw, but that as a retail merchant he would soon have ruined himself by his bookkeeping.

Edison confesses that he has never made a cent out of his patents in electric light and power--in fact, that they have been an expense to him, and thus a free gift to the world. [18] This was true of the European patents as well as the American. "I endeavored to sell my lighting patents in different countries of Europe, and made a contract with a couple of men. On account of their poor business capacity and lack of practicality, they conveyed under the patents all rights to different corporations but in such a way and with such confused wording of the contracts that I never got a cent. One of the companies started was the German Edison, now the great Allgemeine Elektricitaets Gesellschaft. The English company I never got anything for, because a lawyer had originally advised Drexel, Morgan & Co. as to the signing of a certain document, and said it was all right for me to sign. I signed, and I never got a cent because there was a clause in it which prevented me from ever getting anything." A certain easy-going belief in human nature, and even a certain carelessness of attitude toward business affairs, are here revealed. We have already pointed out two instances where in his dealings with the Western Union Company he stipulated that payments of $6000 per year for seventeen years were to be made instead of $100,000 in cash, evidently forgetful of the fact that the annual sum so received was nothing more than legal interest, which could have been earned indefinitely if the capital had been only insisted upon. In later life Edison has been more circumspect, but throughout his early career he was constantly getting into some kind of scrape. Of one experience he says:

[Footnote 18: Edison received some stock from the parent lighting company, but as the capital stock of that company was increased from time to time, his proportion grew smaller, and he ultimately used it to obtain ready money with which to create and finance the various "shops" in which were manufactured the various items of electric-lighting apparatus necessary to exploit his system. Besides, he was obliged to raise additional large sums of money from other sources for this purpose. He thus became a manufacturer with capital raised by himself, and the stock that he received later, on the formation of the General Electric Company, was not for his electric-light patents, but was in payment for his manufacturing establishments, which had then grown to be of great commercial importance.]

"In the early days I was experimenting with metallic filaments for the incandescent light, and sent a certain man out to California in search of platinum. He found a considerable quantity in the sluice-boxes of the Cherokee Valley Mining Company; but just then he found also that fruit-gardening was the thing, and dropped the subject. He then came to me and said that if he could raise $4000 he could go into some kind of orchard arrangement out there, and would give me half the profits. I was unwilling to do it, not having very much money just then, but his persistence was such that I raised the money and gave it to him. He went back to California, and got into mining claims and into fruit-growing, and became one of the politicians of the Coast, and, I believe, was on the staff of the Governor of the State. A couple of years ago he wounded his daughter and shot himself because he had become ruined financially. I never heard from him after he got the money."

Edison tells of another similar episode. "I had two men working for me--one a German, the other a Jew. They wanted me to put up a little money and start them in a shop in New York to make repairs, etc. I put up $800, and was to get half of the profits, and each of them one-quarter. I never got anything for it. A few years afterward I went to see them, and asked what they were doing, and said I would like to sell my interest. They said: 'Sell out what?' 'Why,' I said, 'my interest in the machinery.' They said: 'You don't own this machinery. This is our machinery. You have no papers to show anything. You had better get out.' I am inclined to think that the percentage of crooked people was smaller when I was young. It has been steadily rising, and has got up to a very respectable figure now. I hope it will never reach par." To which lugubrious episode so provocative of cynicism, Edison adds: "When I was a young fellow the first thing I did when I went to a town was to put something into the savings-bank and start an account. When I came to New York I put $30 into a savings-bank under the New York Sun office. After the money had been in about two weeks the bank busted. That was in 1870. In 1909 I got back $6.40, with a charge for $1.75 for law expenses. That shows the beauty of New York receiverships."

It is hardly to be wondered at that Edison is rather frank and unsparing in some of his criticisms of shady modern business methods, and the mention of the following incident always provokes him to a fine scorn. "I had an interview with one of the wealthiest men in New York. He wanted me to sell out my associates in the electric lighting business, and offered me all I was going to get and $100,000 besides. Of course I would not do it. I found out that the reason for this offer was that he had had trouble with Mr. Morgan, and wanted to get even with him." Wall Street is, in fact, a frequent object of rather sarcastic reference, applying even to its regular and probably correct methods of banking. "When I was running my ore-mine," he says, "and got up to the point of making shipments to John Fritz, I didn't have capital enough to carry the ore, so I went to J. P. Morgan & Co. and said I wanted them to give me a letter to the City Bank. I wanted to raise some money. I got a letter to Mr. Stillman; and went over and told him I wanted to open an account and get some loans and discounts. He turned me down, and would not do it. 'Well,' I said, 'isn't it banking to help a man in this way?' He said: 'What you want is a partner.' I felt very much crestfallen. I went over to a bank in Newark--the Merchants'--and told them what I wanted. They said: 'Certainly, you can have the money.' I made my deposit, and they pulled me through all right. My idea of Wall Street banking has been very poor since that time. Merchant banking seems to be different."

As a general thing, Edison has had no trouble in raising money when he needed it, the reason being that people have faith in him as soon as they come to know him. A little incident bears on this point. "In operating the Schenectady works Mr. Insull and I had a terrible burden. We had enormous orders and little money, and had great difficulty to meet our payrolls and buy supplies. At one time we had so many orders on hand we wanted $200,000 worth of copper, and didn't have a cent to buy it. We went down to the Ansonia Brass and Copper Company, and told Mr. Cowles just how we stood. He said: 'I will see what I can do. Will you let my bookkeeper look at your books?' We said: 'Come right up and look them over.' He sent his man up and found we had the orders and were all right, although we didn't have the money. He said: 'I will let you have the copper.' And for years he trusted us for all the copper we wanted, even if we didn't have the money to pay for it."

It is not generally known that Edison, in addition to being a newsboy and a contributor to the technical press, has also been a backer and an "angel" for various publications. This is perhaps the right place at which to refer to the matter, as it belongs in the list of his financial or commercial enterprises. Edison sums up this chapter of his life very pithily. "I was interested, as a telegrapher, in journalism, and started the Telegraph Journal, and got out about a dozen numbers when it was taken over by W. J. Johnston, who afterward founded the Electrical World on it as an offshoot from the Operator. I also started Science, and ran it for a year and a half. It cost me too much money to maintain, and I sold it to Gardiner Hubbard, the father-in-law of Alexander Graham Bell. He carried it along for years." Both these papers are still in prosperous existence, particularly the Electrical World, as the recognized exponent of electrical development in America, where now the public spends as much annually for electricity as it does for daily bread.

From all that has been said above it will be understood that Edison's real and remarkable capacity for business does not lie in ability to "take care of himself," nor in the direction of routine office practice, nor even in ordinary administrative affairs. In short, he would and does regard it as a foolish waste of his time to give attention to the mere occupancy of a desk.

His commercial strength manifests itself rather in the outlining of matters relating to organization and broad policy with a sagacity arising from a shrewd perception and appreciation of general business requirements and conditions, to which should be added his intensely comprehensive grasp of manufacturing possibilities and details, and an unceasing vigilance in devising means of improving the quality of products and increasing the economy of their manufacture.

Like other successful commanders, Edison also possesses the happy faculty of choosing suitable lieutenants to carry out his policies and to manage the industries he has created, such, for instance, as those with which this chapter has to deal--namely, the phonograph, motion picture, primary battery, and storage battery enterprises.

The Portland cement business has already been dealt with separately, and although the above remarks are appropriate to it also, Edison being its head and informing spirit, the following pages are intended to be devoted to those industries that are grouped around the laboratory at Orange, and that may be taken as typical of Edison's methods on the manufacturing side.

Within a few months after establishing himself at the present laboratory, in 1887, Edison entered upon one of those intensely active periods of work that have been so characteristic of his methods in commercializing his other inventions. In this case his labors were directed toward improving the phonograph so as to put it into thoroughly practicable form, capable of ordinary use by the public at large. The net result of this work was the general type of machine of which the well-known phonograph of today is a refinement evolved through many years of sustained experiment and improvement.

After a considerable period of strenuous activity in the eighties, the phonograph and its wax records were developed to a sufficient degree of perfection to warrant him in making arrangements for their manufacture and commercial introduction. At this time the surroundings of the Orange laboratory were distinctly rural in character. Immediately adjacent to the main building and the four smaller structures, constituting the laboratory plant, were grass meadows that stretched away for some considerable distance in all directions, and at its back door, so to speak, ducks paddled around and quacked in a pond undisturbed. Being now ready for manufacturing, but requiring more facilities, Edison increased his real-estate holdings by purchasing a large tract of land lying contiguous to what he already owned. At one end of the newly acquired land two unpretentious brick structures were erected, equipped with first-class machinery, and put into commission as shops for manufacturing phonographs and their record blanks; while the capacious hall forming the third story of the laboratory, over the library, was fitted up and used as a music-room where records were made.

Thus the modern Edison phonograph made its modest debut in 1888, in what was then called the "Improved" form to distinguish it from the original style of machine he invented in 1877, in which the record was made on a sheet of tin-foil held in place upon a metallic cylinder. The "Improved" form is the general type so well known for many years and sold at the present day--viz., the spring or electric motor-driven machine with the cylindrical wax record--in fact, the regulation Edison phonograph.

It did not take a long time to find a market for the products of the newly established factory, for a world-wide public interest in the machine had been created by the appearance of newspaper articles from time to time, announcing the approaching completion by Edison of his improved phonograph. The original (tin-foil) machine had been sufficient to illustrate the fact that the human voice and other sounds could be recorded and reproduced, but such a type of machine had sharp limitations in general use; hence the coming into being of a type that any ordinary person could handle was sufficient of itself to insure a market. Thus the demand for the new machines and wax records grew apace as the corporations organized to handle the business extended their lines. An examination of the newspaper files of the years 1888, 1889, and 1890 will reveal the great excitement caused by the bringing out of the new phonograph, and how frequently and successfully it was employed in public entertainments, either for the whole or part of an evening. In this and other ways it became popularized to a still further extent. This led to the demand for a nickel-in-the-slot machine, which, when established, became immensely popular over the whole country. In its earlier forms the "Improved" phonograph was not capable of such general non-expert handling as is the machine of the present day, and consequently there was a constant endeavor on Edison's part to simplify the construction of the machine and its manner of operation. Experimentation was incessantly going on with this in view, and in the processes of evolution changes were made here and there that resulted in a still greater measure of perfection.

In various ways there was a continual slow and steady growth of the industry thus created, necessitating the erection of many additional buildings as the years passed by. During part of the last decade there was a lull, caused mostly from the failure of corporate interests to carry out their contract relations with Edison, and he was thereby compelled to resort to legal proceedings, at the end of which he bought in the outstanding contracts and assumed command of the business personally.

Being thus freed from many irksome restrictions that had hung heavily upon him, Edison now proceeded to push the phonograph business under a broader policy than that which obtained under his previous contractual relations. With the ever-increasing simplification and efficiency of the machine and a broadening of its application, the results of this policy were manifested in a still more rapid growth of the business that necessitated further additions to the manufacturing plant. And thus matters went on until the early part of the present decade, when the factory facilities were becoming so rapidly outgrown as to render radical changes necessary. It was in these circumstances that Edison's sagacity and breadth of business capacity came to the front. With characteristic boldness and foresight he planned the erection of the series of magnificent concrete buildings that now stand adjacent to and around the laboratory, and in which the manufacturing plant is at present housed.

There was no narrowness in his views in designing these buildings, but, on the contrary, great faith in the future, for his plans included not only the phonograph industry, but provided also for the coming development of motion pictures and of the primary and storage battery enterprises.

In the aggregate there are twelve structures (including the administration building), of which six are of imposing dimensions, running from 200 feet long by 50 feet wide to 440 feet in length by 115 feet in width, all these larger buildings, except one, being five stories in height. They are constructed entirely of reinforced concrete with Edison cement, including walls, floors, and stairways, thus eliminating fire hazard to the utmost extent, and insuring a high degree of protection, cleanliness, and sanitation. As fully three-fourths of the area of their exterior framework consists of windows, an abundance of daylight is secured. These many advantages, combined with lofty ceilings on every floor, provide ideal conditions for the thousands of working people engaged in this immense plant.

In addition to these twelve concrete structures there are a few smaller brick and wooden buildings on the grounds, in which some special operations are conducted. These, however, are few in number, and at some future time will be concentrated in one or more additional concrete buildings. It will afford a clearer idea of the extent of the industries clustered immediately around the laboratory when it is stated that the combined floor space which is occupied by them in all these buildings is equivalent in the aggregate to over fourteen acres.

It would be instructive, but scarcely within the scope of the narrative, to conduct the reader through this extensive plant and see its many interesting operations in detail. It must suffice, however, to note its complete and ample equipment with modern machinery of every kind applicable to the work; its numerous (and some of them wonderfully ingenious) methods, processes, machines, and tools specially designed or invented for the manufacture of special parts and supplemental appliances for the phonograph or other Edison products; and also to note the interesting variety of trades represented in the different departments, in which are included chemists, electricians, electrical mechanicians, machinists, mechanics, pattern-makers, carpenters, cabinet-makers, varnishers, japanners, tool-makers, lapidaries, wax experts, photographic developers and printers, opticians, electroplaters, furnacemen, and others, together with factory experimenters and a host of general employees, who by careful training have become specialists and experts in numerous branches of these industries.

Edison's plans for this manufacturing plant were sufficiently well outlined to provide ample capacity for the natural growth of the business; and although that capacity (so far as phonographs is concerned) has actually reached an output of over 6000 complete phonographs PER WEEK, and upward of 130,000 molded records PER DAY--with a pay-roll embracing over 3500 employees, including office force--and amounting to about $45,000 per week--the limits of production have not yet been reached.

The constant outpouring of products in such large quantities bespeaks the unremitting activities of an extensive and busy selling organization to provide for their marketing and distribution. This important department (the National Phonograph Company), in all its branches, from president to office-boy, includes about two hundred employees on its office pay-roll, and makes its headquarters in the administration building, which is one of the large concrete structures above referred to. The policy of the company is to dispose of its wares through regular trade channels rather than to deal direct with the public, trusting to local activity as stimulated by a liberal policy of national advertising. Thus, there has been gradually built up a very extensive business until at the present time an enormous output of phonographs and records is distributed to retail customers in the United States and Canada through the medium of about one hundred and fifty jobbers and over thirteen thousand dealers. The Edison phonograph industry thus organized is helped by frequent conventions of this large commercial force.

Besides this, the National Phonograph Company maintains a special staff for carrying on the business with foreign countries. While the aggregate transactions of this department are not as extensive as those for the United States and Canada, they are of considerable volume, as the foreign office distributes in bulk a very large number of phonographs and records to selling companies and agencies in Europe, Asia, Australia, Japan, and, indeed, to all the countries of the civilized world. [19] Like England's drumbeat, the voice of the Edison phonograph is heard around the world in undying strains throughout the twenty-four hours.

[Footnote 19: It may be of interest to the reader to note some parts of the globe to which shipments of phonographs and records are made:

Samoan Islands Falkland Islands Siam Corea Crete Island Paraguay Chile Canary Islands Egypt British East Africa Cape Colony Portuguese East Africa Liberia Java Straits Settlements Madagascar Fanning Islands New Zealand French Indo-China Morocco Ecuador Brazil Madeira South Africa Azores Manchuria Ceylon Sierra Leone]

In addition to the main manufacturing plant at Orange, another important adjunct must not be forgotten, and that is, the Recording Department in New York City, where the master records are made under the superintendence of experts who have studied the intricacies of the art with Edison himself. This department occupies an upper story in a lofty building, and in its various rooms may be seen and heard many prominent musicians, vocalists, speakers, and vaudeville artists studiously and busily engaged in making the original records, which are afterward sent to Orange, and which, if approved by the expert committee, are passed on to the proper department for reproduction in large quantities.

When we consider the subject of motion pictures we find a similarity in general business methods, for while the projecting machines and copies of picture films are made in quantity at the Orange works (just as phonographs and duplicate records are so made), the original picture, or film, like the master record, is made elsewhere. There is this difference, however: that, from the particular nature of the work, practically ALL master records are made at one convenient place, while the essential interest in SOME motion pictures lies in the fact that they are taken in various parts of the world, often under exceptional circumstances. The "silent drama," however, calls also for many representations which employ conventional acting, staging, and the varied appliances of stagecraft. Hence, Edison saw early the necessity of providing a place especially devised and arranged for the production of dramatic performances in pantomime.

It is a far cry from the crude structure of early days--the "Black Maria" of 1891, swung around on its pivot in the Orange laboratory yard--to the well-appointed Edison theatres, or pantomime studios, in New York City. The largest of these is located in the suburban Borough of the Bronx, and consists of a three-story-and-basement building of reinforced concrete, in which are the offices, dressing-rooms, wardrobe and property-rooms, library and developing department. Contiguous to this building, and connected with it, is the theatre proper, a large and lofty structure whose sides and roof are of glass, and whose floor space is sufficiently ample for six different sets of scenery at one time, with plenty of room left for a profusion of accessories, such as tables, chairs, pianos, bunch-lights, search-lights, cameras, and a host of varied paraphernalia pertaining to stage effects.

The second Edison theatre, or studio, is located not far from the shopping district in New York City. In all essential features, except size and capacity, it is a duplicate of the one in the Bronx, of which it is a supplement.

To a visitor coming on the floor of such a theatre for the first time there is a sense of confusion in beholding the heterogeneous "sets" of scenery and the motley assemblage of characters represented in the various plays in the process of "taking," or rehearsal. While each set constitutes virtually a separate stage, they are all on the same floor, without wings or proscenium-arches, and separated only by a few feet. Thus, for instance, a Japanese house interior may be seen cheek by jowl with an ordinary prison cell, flanked by a mining-camp, which in turn stands next to a drawing-room set, and in each a set of appropriate characters in pantomimic motion. The action is incessant, for in any dramatic representation intended for the motion-picture film every second counts.

The production of several completed plays per week necessitates the employment of a considerable staff of people of miscellaneous trades and abilities. At each of these two studios there is employed a number of stage-directors, scene-painters, carpenters, property-men, photographers, costumers, electricians, clerks, and general assistants, besides a capable stock company of actors and actresses, whose generous numbers are frequently augmented by the addition of a special star, or by a number of extra performers, such as Rough Riders or other specialists. It may be, occasionally, that the exigencies of the occasion require the work of a performing horse, dog, or other animal. No matter what the object required may be, whether animate or inanimate, if it is necessary for the play it is found and pressed into service.

These two studios, while separated from the main plant, are under the same general management, and their original negative films are forwarded as made to the Orange works, where the large copying department is located in one of the concrete buildings. Here, after the film has been passed upon by a committee, a considerable number of positive copies are made by ingenious processes, and after each one is separately tested, or "run off," in one or other of the three motion-picture theatres in the building, they are shipped out to film exchanges in every part of the country. How extensive this business has become may be appreciated when it is stated that at the Orange plant there are produced at this time over eight million feet of motion-picture film per year. And Edison's company is only one of many producers.

Another of the industries at the Orange works is the manufacture of projecting kinetoscopes, by means of which the motion pictures are shown. While this of itself is also a business of considerable magnitude in its aggregate yearly transactions, it calls for no special comment in regard to commercial production, except to note that a corps of experimenters is constantly employed refining and perfecting details of the machine. Its basic features of operation as conceived by Edison remain unchanged.

On coming to consider the Edison battery enterprises, we must perforce extend the territorial view to include a special chemical-manufacturing plant, which is in reality a branch of the laboratory and the Orange works, although actually situated about three miles away.

Both the primary and the storage battery employ certain chemical products as essential parts of their elements, and indeed owe their very existence to the peculiar preparation and quality of such products, as exemplified by Edison's years of experimentation and research. Hence the establishment of his own chemical works at Silver Lake, where, under his personal supervision, the manufacture of these products is carried on in charge of specially trained experts. At the present writing the plant covers about seven acres of ground; but there is ample room for expansion, as Edison, with wise forethought, secured over forty acres of land, so as to be prepared for developments.

Not only is the Silver Lake works used for the manufacture of the chemical substances employed in the batteries, but it is the plant at which the Edison primary battery is wholly assembled and made up for distribution to customers. This in itself is a business of no small magnitude, having grown steadily on its merits year by year until it has now arrived at a point where its sales run into the hundreds of thousands of cells per annum, furnished largely to the steam railroads of the country for their signal service.

As to the storage battery, the plant at Silver Lake is responsible only for the production of the chemical compounds, nickel-hydrate and iron oxide, which enter into its construction. All the mechanical parts, the nickel plating, the manufacture of nickel flake, the assembling and testing, are carried on at the Orange works in two of the large concrete buildings above referred to. A visit to this part of the plant reveals an amazing fertility of resourcefulness and ingenuity in the devising of the special machines and appliances employed in constructing the mechanical parts of these cells, for it is practically impossible to fashion them by means of machinery and tools to be found in the open market, notwithstanding the immense variety that may be there obtained.

Since Edison completed his final series of investigations on his storage battery and brought it to its present state of perfection, the commercial values have increased by leaps and bounds. The battery, as it was originally put out some years ago, made for itself an enviable reputation; but with its improved form there has come a vast increase of business. Although the largest of the concrete buildings where its manufacture is carried on is over four hundred feet long and four stories in height, it has already become necessary to plan extensions and enlargements of the plant in order to provide for the production of batteries to fill the present demands. It was not until the summer of 1909 that Edison was willing to pronounce the final verdict of satisfaction with regard to this improved form of storage battery; but subsequent commercial results have justified his judgment, and it is not too much to predict that in all probability the business will assume gigantic proportions within a very few years. At the present time (1910) the Edison storage-battery enterprise is in its early stages of growth, and its status may be compared with that of the electric-light system about the year 1881.

There is one more industry, though of comparatively small extent, that is included in the activities of the Orange works, namely, the manufacture and sale of the Bates numbering machine. This is a well-known article of commerce, used in mercantile establishments for the stamping of consecutive, duplicate, and manifold numbers on checks and other documents. It is not an invention of Edison, but the organization owning it, together with the patent rights, were acquired by him some years ago, and he has since continued and enlarged the business both in scope and volume, besides, of course, improving and perfecting the apparatus itself. These machines are known everywhere throughout the country, and while the annual sales are of comparatively moderate amount in comparison with the totals of the other Edison industries at Orange, they represent in the aggregate a comfortable and encouraging business.

In this brief outline review of the flourishing and extensive commercial enterprises centred around the Orange laboratory, the facts, it is believed, contain a complete refutation of the idea that an inventor cannot be a business man. They also bear abundant evidence of the compatibility of these two widely divergent gifts existing, even to a high degree, in the same person. A striking example of the correctness of this proposition is afforded in the present case, when it is borne in mind that these various industries above described (whose annual sales run into many millions of dollars) owe not only their very creation (except the Bates machine) and existence to Edison's inventive originality and commercial initiative, but also their continued growth and prosperity to his incessant activities in dealing with their multifarious business problems. In publishing a portrait of Edison this year, one of the popular magazines placed under it this caption: "Were the Age called upon to pay Thomas A. Edison all it owes to him, the Age would have to make an assignment." The present chapter will have thrown some light on the idiosyncrasies of Edison as financier and as manufacturer, and will have shown that while the claim thus suggested may be quite good, it will certainly never be pressed or collected.

CHAPTER XXVII

THE VALUE OF EDISON'S INVENTIONS TO THE WORLD

IF the world were to take an account of stock, so to speak, and proceed in orderly fashion to marshal its tangible assets in relation to dollars and cents, the natural resources of our globe, from centre to circumference, would head the list. Next would come inventors, whose value to the world as an asset could be readily estimated from an increase of its wealth resulting from the actual transformations of these resources into items of convenience and comfort through the exercise of their inventive ingenuity.

Inventors of practical devices may be broadly divided into two classes--first, those who may be said to have made two blades of grass grow where only one grew before; and, second, great inventors, who have made grass grow plentifully on hitherto unproductive ground. The vast majority of practical inventors belong to and remain in the first of these divisions, but there have been, and probably always will be, a less number who, by reason of their greater achievements, are entitled to be included in both classes. Of these latter, Thomas Alva Edison is one, but in the pages of history he stands conspicuously pre-eminent--a commanding towering figure, even among giants.

The activities of Edison have been of such great range, and his conquests in the domains of practical arts so extensive and varied, that it is somewhat difficult to estimate with any satisfactory degree of accuracy the money value of his inventions to the world of to-day, even after making due allowance for the work of other great inventors and the propulsive effect of large amounts of capital thrown into the enterprises which took root, wholly or in part, through the productions of his genius and energies. This difficulty will be apparent, for instance, when we consider his telegraph and telephone inventions. These were absorbed in enterprises already existing, and were the means of assisting their rapid growth and expansion, particularly the telephone industry. Again, in considering the fact that Edison was one of the first in the field to design and perfect a practical and operative electric railway, the main features of which are used in all electric roads of to-day, we are confronted with the problem as to what proportion of their colossal investment and earnings should be ascribed to him.

Difficulties are multiplied when we pause for a moment to think of Edison's influence on collateral branches of business. In the public mind he is credited with the invention of the incandescent electric light, the phonograph, and other widely known devices; but how few realize his actual influence on other trades that are not generally thought of in connection with these things. For instance, let us note what a prominent engine builder, the late Gardiner C. Sims, has said: "Watt, Corliss, and Porter brought forward steam-engines to a high state of proficiency, yet it remained for Mr. Edison to force better proportions, workmanship, designs, use of metals, regulation, the solving of the complex problems of high speed and endurance, and the successful development of the shaft governor. Mr. Edison is preeminent in the realm of engineering."

The phenomenal growth of the copper industry was due to a rapid and ever-increasing demand, owing to the exploitation of the telephone, electric light, electric motor, and electric railway industries. Without these there might never have been the romance of "Coppers" and the rise and fall of countless fortunes. And although one cannot estimate in definite figures the extent of Edison's influence in the enormous increase of copper production, it is to be remembered that his basic inventions constitute a most important factor in the demand for the metal. Besides, one must also give him the credit, as already noted, for having recognized the necessity for a pure quality of copper for electric conductors, and for his persistence in having compelled the manufacturers of that period to introduce new and additional methods of refinement so as to bring about that result, which is now a sine qua non.

Still considering his influence on other staples and collateral trades, let us enumerate briefly and in a general manner some of the more important and additional ones that have been not merely stimulated, but in many cases the business and sales have been directly increased and new arts established through the inventions of this one man--namely, iron, steel, brass, zinc, nickel, platinum ($5 per ounce in 1878, now $26 an ounce), rubber, oils, wax, bitumen, various chemical compounds, belting, boilers, injectors, structural steel, iron tubing, glass, silk, cotton, porcelain, fine woods, slate, marble, electrical measuring instruments, miscellaneous machinery, coal, wire, paper, building materials, sapphires, and many others.

The question before us is, To what extent has Edison added to the wealth of the world by his inventions and his energy and perseverance? It will be noted from the foregoing that no categorical answer can be offered to such a question, but sufficient material can be gathered from a statistical review of the commercial arts directly influenced to afford an approximate idea of the increase in national wealth that has been affected by or has come into being through the practical application of his ideas.

First of all, as to inventions capable of fairly definite estimate, let us mention the incandescent electric light and systems of distribution of electric light, heat, and power, which may justly be considered as the crowning inventions of Edison's life. Until October 21, 1879, there was nothing in existence resembling our modern incandescent lamp. On that date, as we have seen in a previous chapter, Edison's labors culminated in his invention of a practical incandescent electric lamp embodying absolutely all the essentials of the lamp of to-day, thus opening to the world the doors of a new art and industry. To-day there are in the United States more than 41,000,000 of these lamps, connected to existing central-station circuits in active operation.

Such circuits necessarily imply the existence of central stations with their equipment. Until the beginning of 1882 there were only a few arc-lighting stations in existence for the limited distribution of current. At the present time there are over 6000 central stations in this country for the distribution of electric current for light, heat, and power, with capital obligations amounting to not less than $1,000,000,000. Besides the above-named 41,000,000 incandescent lamps connected to their mains, there are about 500,000 arc lamps and 150,000 motors, using 750,000 horse-power, besides countless fan motors and electric heating and cooking appliances.

When it is stated that the gross earnings of these central stations approximate the sum of $225,000,000 yearly, the significant import of these statistics of an art that came so largely from Edison's laboratory about thirty years ago will undoubtedly be apparent.

But the above are not by any means all the facts relating to incandescent electric lighting in the United States, for in addition to central stations there are upward of 100,000 isolated or private plants in mills, factories, steamships, hotels, theatres, etc., owned by the persons or concerns who operate them. These plants represent an approximate investment of $500,000,000, and the connection of not less than 25,000,000 incandescent lamps or their equivalent.

Then there are the factories where these incandescent lamps are made, about forty in number, representing a total investment that may be approximated at $25,000,000. It is true that many of these factories are operated by other than the interests which came into control of the Edison patents (General Electric Company), but the 150,000,000 incandescent electric lamps now annually made are broadly covered in principle by Edison's fundamental ideas and patents.

It will be noted that these figures are all in round numbers, but they are believed to be well within the mark, being primarily founded upon the special reports of the Census Bureau issued in 1902 and 1907, with the natural increase from that time computed by experts who are in position to obtain the facts. It would be manifestly impossible to give exact figures of such a gigantic and swiftly moving industry, whose totals increase from week to week.

The reader will naturally be disposed to ask whether it is intended to claim that Edison has brought about all this magnificent growth of the electric-lighting art. The answer to this is decidedly in the negative, for the fact is that he laid some of the foundation and erected a building thereon, and in the natural progressive order of things other inventors of more or less fame have laid substructures or added a wing here and a story there until the resultant great structure has attained such proportions as to evoke the admiration of the beholder; but the old foundation and the fundamental building still remain to support other parts. In other words, Edison created the incandescent electric lamp, and invented certain broad and fundamental systems of distribution of current, with all the essential devices of detail necessary for successful operation. These formed a foundation. He also spent great sums of money and devoted several years of patient labor in the early practical exploitation of the dynamo and central station and isolated plants, often under, adverse and depressing circumstances, with a dogged determination that outlived an opposition steadily threatening defeat. These efforts resulted in the firm commercial establishment of modern electric lighting. It is true that many important inventions of others have a distinguished place in the art as it is exploited today, but the fact remains that the broad essentials, such as the incandescent lamp, systems of distribution, and some important details, are not only universally used, but are as necessary to-day for successful commercial practice as they were when Edison invented them many years ago.

The electric railway next claims our consideration, but we are immediately confronted by a difficulty which seems insurmountable when we attempt to formulate any definite estimate of the value and influence of Edison's pioneer work and inventions. There is one incontrovertible fact--namely, that he was the first man to devise, construct, and operate from a central station a practicable, life-size electric railroad, which was capable of transporting and did transport passengers and freight at variable speeds over varying grades, and under complete control of the operator. These are the essential elements in all electric railroading of the present day; but while Edison's original broad ideas are embodied in present practice, the perfection of the modern electric railway is greatly due to the labors and inventions of a large number of other well-known inventors. There was no reason why Edison could not have continued the commercial development of the electric railway after he had helped to show its practicability in 1880, 1881, and 1882, just as he had completed his lighting system, had it not been that his financial allies of the period lacked faith in the possibilities of electric railroads, and therefore declined to furnish the money necessary for the purpose of carrying on the work.

With these facts in mind, we shall ask the reader to assign to Edison a due proportion of credit for his pioneer and basic work in relation to the prodigious development of electric railroading that has since taken place. The statistics of 1908 for American street and elevated railways show that within twenty-five years the electric-railway industry has grown to embrace 38,812 miles of track on streets and for elevated railways, operated under the ownership of 1238 separate companies, whose total capitalization amounted to the enormous sum of $4,123,834,598.

In the equipments owned by such companies there are included 68,636 electric cars and 17,568 trailers and others, making a total of 86,204 of such vehicles. These cars and equipments earned over $425,000,000 in 1907, in giving the public transportation, at a cost, including transfers, of a little over three cents per passenger, for whom a fifteen-mile ride would be possible. It is the cheapest transportation in the world.

Some mention should also be made of the great electrical works of the country, in which the dynamos, motors, and other varied paraphernalia are made for electric lighting, electric railway, and other purposes. The largest of these works is undoubtedly that of the General Electric Company at Schenectady, New York, a continuation and enormous enlargement of the shops which Edison established there in 1886. This plant at the present time embraces over 275 acres, of which sixty acres are covered by fifty large and over one hundred small buildings; besides which the company also owns other large plants elsewhere, representing a total investment approximating the sum of $34,850,000 up to 1908. The productions of the General Electric Company alone average annual sales of nearly $75,000,000, but they do not comprise the total of the country's manufactures in these lines.

Turning our attention now to the telephone, we again meet a condition that calls for thoughtful consideration before we can properly appreciate how much the growth of this industry owes to Edison's inventive genius. In another place there has already been told the story of the telephone, from which we have seen that to Alexander Graham Bell is due the broad idea of transmission of speech by means of an electrical circuit; also that he invented appropriate instruments and devices through which he accomplished this result, although not to that extent which gave promise of any great commercial practicability for the telephone as it then existed. While the art was in this inefficient condition, Edison went to work on the subject, and in due time, as we have already learned, invented and brought out the carbon transmitter, which is universally acknowledged to have been the needed device that gave to the telephone the element of commercial practicability, and has since led to its phenomenally rapid adoption and world-wide use. It matters not that others were working in the same direction, Edison was legally adjudicated to have been the first to succeed in point of time, and his inventions were put into actual use, and may be found in principle in every one of the 7,000,000 telephones which are estimated to be employed in the country at the present day. Basing the statements upon facts shown by the Census reports of 1902 and 1907, and adding thereto the growth of the industry since that time, we find on a conservative estimate that at this writing the investment has been not less than $800,000,000 in now existing telephone systems, while no fewer than 10,500,000,000 talks went over the lines during the year 1908. These figures relate only to telephone systems, and do not include any details regarding the great manufacturing establishments engaged in the construction of telephone apparatus, of which there is a production amounting to at least $15,000,000 per annum.

Leaving the telephone, let us now turn our attention to the telegraph, and endeavor to show as best we can some idea of the measure to which it has been affected by Edison's inventions. Although, as we have seen in a previous part of this book, his earliest fame arose from his great practical work in telegraphic inventions and improvements, there is no way in which any definite computation can be made of the value of his contributions in the art except, perhaps, in the case of his quadruplex, through which alone it is estimated that there has been saved from $15,000,000 to $20,000,000 in the cost of line construction in this country. If this were the only thing that he had ever accomplished, it would entitle him to consideration as an inventor of note. The quadruplex, however, has other material advantages, but how far they and the natural growth of the business have contributed to the investment and earnings of the telegraph companies, is beyond practicable computation.

It would, perhaps, be interesting to speculate upon what might have been the growth of the telegraph and the resultant benefit to the community had Edison's automatic telegraph inventions been allowed to take their legitimate place in the art, but we shall not allow ourselves to indulge in flights of fancy, as the value of this chapter rests not upon conjecture, but only upon actual fact. Nor shall we attempt to offer any statistics regarding Edison's numerous inventions relating to telegraphs and kindred devices, such as stock tickers, relays, magnets, rheotomes, repeaters, printing telegraphs, messenger calls, etc., on which he was so busily occupied as an inventor and manufacturer during the ten years that began with January, 1869. The principles of many of these devices are still used in the arts, but have become so incorporated in other devices as to be inseparable, and cannot now be dealt with separately. To show what they mean, however, it might be noted that New York City alone has 3000 stock "tickers," consuming 50,000 miles of record tape every year.

Turning now to other important arts and industries which have been created by Edison's inventions, and in which he is at this time taking an active personal interest, let us visit Orange, New Jersey. When his present laboratory was nearing completion in 1887, he wrote to Mr. J. Hood Wright, a partner in the firm of Drexel, Morgan & Co.: "My ambition is to build up a great industrial works in the Orange Valley, starting in a small way and gradually working up."

In this plant, which represents an investment approximating the sum of $4,000,000, are grouped a number of industrial enterprises of which Edison is either the sole or controlling owner and the guiding spirit. These enterprises are the National Phonograph Company, the Edison Business Phonograph Company, the Edison Phonograph Works, the Edison Manufacturing Company, the Edison Storage Battery Company, and the Bates Manufacturing Company. The importance of these industries will be apparent when it is stated that at this plant the maximum pay-roll shows the employment of over 4200 persons, with annual earnings in salaries and wages of more than $2,750,000.

In considering the phonograph in its commercial aspect, and endeavoring to arrive at some idea of the world's estimate of the value of this invention, we feel the ground more firm under our feet, for Edison has in later years controlled its manufacture and sale. It will be remembered that the phonograph lay dormant, commercially speaking, for about ten years after it came into being, and then later invention reduced it to a device capable of more popular utility. A few years of rather unsatisfactory commercial experience brought about a reorganization, through which Edison resumed possession of the business. It has since been continued under his general direction and ownership, and he has made a great many additional inventions tending to improve the machine in all its parts.

The uses made of the phonograph up to this time have been of four kinds, generally speaking--first, and principally, for amusement; second, for instruction in languages; third, for business, in the dictation of correspondence; and fourth, for sentimental reasons in preserving the voices of friends. No separate figures are available to show the extent of its employment in the second and fourth classes, as they are probably included in machines coming under the first subdivision. Under this head we find that there have been upward of 1,310,000 phonographs sold during the last twenty years, with and for which there have been made and sold no fewer than 97,845,000 records of a musical or other character. Phonographic records are now being manufactured at Orange at the rate of 75,000 a day, the annual sale of phonographs and records being approximately $7,000,000, including business phonographs. This does not include blank records, of which large numbers have also been supplied to the public.

The adoption of the business phonograph has not been characterized by the unanimity that obtained in the case of the one used merely for amusement, as its use involves some changes in methods that business men are slow to adopt until they realize the resulting convenience and economy. Although it is only a few years since the business phonograph has begun to make some headway, it is not difficult to appreciate that Edison's prediction in 1878 as to the value of such an appliance is being realized, when we find that up to this time the sales run up to 12,695 in number. At the present time the annual sales of the business phonographs and supplies, cylinders, etc., are not less than $350,000.

We must not forget that the basic patent of Edison on the phonograph has long since expired, thus throwing open to the world the wonderful art of reproducing human speech and other sounds. The world was not slow to take advantage of the fact, hence there are in the field numerous other concerns in the same business. It is conservatively estimated by those who know the trade and are in position to form an opinion, that the figures above given represent only about one-half of the entire business of the country in phonographs, records, cylinders, and supplies.

Taking next his inventions that pertain to a more recently established but rapidly expanding branch of business that provides for the amusement of the public, popularly known as "motion pictures," we also find a general recognition of value created. Referring the reader to a previous chapter for a discussion of Edison's standing as a pioneer inventor in this art, let us glance at the commercial proportions of this young but lusty business, whose ramifications extend to all but the most remote and primitive hamlets of our country.

The manufacture of the projecting machines and accessories, together with the reproduction of films, is carried on at the Orange Valley plant, and from the inception of the motion-picture business to the present time there have been made upward of 16,000 projecting machines and many million feet of films carrying small photographs of moving objects. Although the motion-picture business, as a commercial enterprise, is still in its youth, it is of sufficient moment to call for the annual production of thousands of machines and many million feet of films in Edison's shops, having a sale value of not less than $750,000. To produce the originals from which these Edison films are made, there have been established two "studios," the largest of which is in the Bronx, New York City.

In this, as well as in the phonograph business, there are many other manufacturers in the field. Indeed, the annual product of the Edison Manufacturing Company in this line is only a fractional part of the total that is absorbed by the 8000 or more motion-picture theatres and exhibitions that are in operation in the United States at the present time, and which represent an investment of some $45,000,000. Licensees under Edison patents in this country alone produce upward of 60,000,000 feet of films annually, containing more than a billion and a half separate photographs. To what extent the motion-picture business may grow in the not remote future it is impossible to conjecture, for it has taken a place in the front rank of rapidly increasing enterprises.

The manufacture and sale of the Edison-Lalande primary battery, conducted by the Edison Manufacturing Company at the Orange Valley plant, is a business of no mean importance. Beginning about twenty years ago with a battery that, without polarizing, would furnish large currents specially adapted for gas-engine ignition and other important purposes, the business has steadily grown in magnitude until the present output amounts to about 125,000 cells annually; the total number of cells put into the hands of the public up to date being approximately 1,500,000. It will be readily conceded that to most men this alone would be an enterprise of a lifetime, and sufficient in itself to satisfy a moderate ambition. But, although it has yielded a considerable profit to Edison and gives employment to many people, it is only one of the many smaller enterprises that owe an existence to his inventive ability and commercial activity.

So it also is in regard to the mimeograph, whose forerunner, the electric pen, was born of Edison's brain in 1877. He had been long impressed by the desirability of the rapid production of copies of written documents, and, as we have seen by a previous chapter, he invented the electric pen for this purpose, only to improve upon it later with a more desirable device which he called the mimeograph, that is in use, in various forms, at this time. Although the electric pen had a large sale and use in its time, the statistics relating to it are not available. The mimeograph, however, is, and has been for many years, a standard office appliance, and is entitled to consideration, as the total number put into use up to this time is approximately 180,000, valued at $3,500,000, while the annual output is in the neighborhood of 9000 machines, sold for about $150,000, besides the vast quantity of special paper and supplies which its use entails in the production of the many millions of facsimile letters and documents. The extent of production and sale of supplies for the mimeograph may be appreciated when it is stated that they bring annually an equivalent of three times the amount realized from sales of machines. The manufacture and sale of the mimeograph does not come within the enterprises conducted under Edison's personal direction, as he sold out the whole thing some years ago to Mr. A. B. Dick, of Chicago.

In making a somewhat radical change of subject, from duplicating machines to cement, we find ourselves in a field in which Edison has made a most decided impression. The reader has already learned that his entry into this field was, in a manner, accidental, although logically in line with pronounced convictions of many years' standing, and following up the fund of knowledge gained in the magnetic ore-milling business. From being a new-comer in the cement business, his corporation in five years has grown to be the fifth largest producer in the United States, with a still increasing capacity. From the inception of this business there has been a steady and rapid development, resulting in the production of a grand total of over 7,300,000 barrels of cement up to the present date, having a value of about $6,000,000, exclusive of package. At the time of this writing, the rate of production is over 8000 barrels of cement per day, or, say, 2,500,000 barrels per year, having an approximate selling value of a little less than $2,000,000, with prospects of increasing in the near future to a daily output of 10,000 barrels. This enterprise is carried on by a corporation called the Edison Portland Cement Company, in which he is very largely interested, and of which he is the active head and guiding spirit.

Had not Edison suspended the manufacture and sale of his storage battery a few years ago because he was not satisfied with it, there might have been given here some noteworthy figures of an extensive business, for the company's books show an astonishing number of orders that were received during the time of the shut-down. He was implored for batteries, but in spite of the fact that good results had been obtained from the 18,000 or 20,000 cells sold some years ago, he adhered firmly to his determination to perfect them to a still higher standard before resuming and continuing their manufacture as a regular commodity. As we have noted in a previous chapter, however, deliveries of the perfected type were begun in the summer of 1909, and since that time the business has continued to grow in the measure indicated by the earlier experience.

Thus far we have concerned ourselves chiefly with those figures which exhibit the extent of investment and production, but there is another and humanly important side that presents itself for consideration namely, the employment of a vast industrial army of men and women, who earn a living through their connection with some of the arts and industries to which our narrative has direct reference. To this the reader's attention will now be drawn.

The following figures are based upon the Special Reports of the Census Bureau, 1902 and 1907, with additions computed upon the increase that has subsequently taken place. In the totals following is included the compensation paid to salaried officials and clerks. Details relating to telegraph systems are omitted.

Taking the electric light into consideration first, we find that in the central stations of the United States there are not less than an average of 50,000 persons employed, requiring an aggregate yearly payroll of over $40,000,000. This does not include the 100,000 or more isolated electric-light plants scattered throughout the land. Many of these are quite large, and at least one-third of them require one additional helper, thus adding, say, 33,000 employees to the number already mentioned. If we assume as low a wage as $10 per week for each of these helpers, we must add to the foregoing an additional sum of over $17,000,000 paid annually for wages, almost entirely in the isolated incandescent electric lighting field.

Central stations and isolated plants consume over 100,000,000 incandescent electric lamps annually, and in the production of these there are engaged about forty factories, on whose pay-rolls appear an average of 14,000 employees, earning an aggregate yearly sum of $8,000,000.

Following the incandescent lamp we must not forget an industry exclusively arising from it and absolutely dependent upon it--namely, that of making fixtures for such lamps, the manufacture of which gives employment to upward of 6000 persons, who annually receive at least $3,750,000 in compensation.

The detail devices of the incandescent electric lighting system also contribute a large quota to the country's wealth in the millions of dollars paid out in salaries and wages to many thousands of persons who are engaged in their manufacture.

The electric railways of our country show even larger figures than the lighting stations and plants, as they employ on the average over 250,000 persons, whose annual compensation amounts to not less than $155,000,000.

In the manufacture of about $50,000,000 worth of dynamos and motors annually, for central-station equipment, isolated plants, electric railways, and other purposes, the manufacturers of the country employ an average of not less than 30,000 people, whose yearly pay-roll amounts to no less a sum than $20,000,000.

The growth of the telephone systems of the United States also furnishes us with statistics of an analogous nature, for we find that the average number of employees engaged in this industry is at least 140,000, whose annual earnings aggregate a minimum of $75,000,000; besides which the manufacturers of telephone apparatus employ over 12,000 persons, to whom is paid annually about $5,500,000.

No attempt is made to include figures of collateral industries, such, for instance, as copper, which is very closely allied with the electrical arts, and the great bulk of which is refined electrically.

The 8000 or so motion-picture theatres of the country employ no fewer than 40,000 people, whose aggregate annual income amounts to not less than $37,000,000.

Coming now to the Orange Valley plant, we take a drop from these figures to the comparatively modest ones which give us an average of 3600 employees and calling for an annual pay-roll of about $2,250,000. It must be remembered, however, that the sums mentioned above represent industries operated by great aggregations of capital, while the Orange Valley plant, as well as the Edison Portland Cement Company, with an average daily number of 530 employees and over $400,000 annual pay-roll, represent in a large measure industries that are more in the nature of closely held enterprises and practically under the direction of one mind.

The table herewith given summarizes the figures that have just been presented, and affords an idea of the totals affected by the genius of this one man. It is well known that many other men and many other inventions have been needed for the perfection of these arts; but it is equally true that, as already noted, some of these industries are directly the creation of Edison, while in every one of the rest his impress has been deep and significant. Before he began inventing, only two of them were known at all as arts--telegraphy and the manufacture of cement. Moreover, these figures deal only with the United States, and take no account of the development of many of the Edison inventions in Europe or of their adoption throughout the world at large. Let it suffice

STATISTICAL RESUME (APPROXIMATE) OF SOME OF THE INDUSTRIES IN THE UNITED STATES DIRECTLY FOUNDED UPON OR AFFECTED BY INVENTIONS OF THOMAS A. EDISON

Class of Industry	Investment	Annual Gross Revenue or sales	Number of Employees	Annual Pay-Rolls
Central station lighting and power	$1,000,000,000	$125,000,000	50,000	$40,000,000
Isolated incandescent lighting	500,000,000	--	33,000	17,000 000
Incandescent lamps	25,000,000	20,000,000	14,000	8,000 000
Electric fixtures	8,000,000	5,000,000	6,000	3,750,000
Dynamos and motors	60,000,000	50,000,000	30,000	20,000,000
Electric railways	4,000,000,000	430,000,000	250,000	155,000,000
Telephone systems	800,000,000	175,000,000	140,000	75,000,000
Telephone apparatus	30,000,000	15,000,000	12,000	5,500,000
Phonograph and motion pictures	10,000,000	15,000,000	5,000	6,000,000
Motion picture theatres	40,000,000	80,000,000	40,000	37,000,000
Edison Portland cement	4,000,000	2,000,000	530	400,000
Telegraphy	250,000,000	60,000,000	100,000	30,000,000
Totals	6,727,000,000	1,077,000,000	680,530	397,650,000

that in America alone the work of Edison has been one of the most potent factors in bringing into existence new industries now capitalized at nearly $ 7,000,000,000, earning annually over $1,000,000,000, and giving employment to an army of more than six hundred thousand people.

A single diamond, prismatically flashing from its many facets the beauties of reflected light, comes well within the limits of comprehension of the human mind and appeals to appreciation by the finer sensibilities; but in viewing an exhibition of thousands of these beautiful gems, the eye and brain are simply bewildered with the richness of a display which tends to confuse the intellect until the function of analysis comes into play and leads to more adequate apprehension.

So, in presenting the mass of statistics contained in this chapter, we fear that the result may have been the bewilderment of the reader to some extent. Nevertheless, in writing a biography of Edison, the main object is to present the facts as they are, and leave it to the intelligent reader to classify, apply, and analyze them in such manner as appeals most forcibly to his intellectual processes. If in the foregoing pages there has appeared to be a tendency to attribute to Edison the entire credit for the growth to which many of the above-named great enterprises have in these latter days attained, we must especially disclaim any intention of giving rise to such a deduction. No one who has carefully followed the course of this narrative can deny, however, that Edison is the father of some of the arts and industries that have been mentioned, and that as to some of the others it was the magic of his touch that helped make them practicable. Not only to his work and ingenuity is due the present magnitude of these arts and industries, but it is attributable also to the splendid work and numerous contributions of other great inventors, such as Brush, Bell, Elihu Thomson, Weston, Sprague, and many others, as well as to the financiers and investors who in the past thirty years have furnished the vast sums of money that were necessary to exploit and push forward these enterprises.

The reader may have noticed in a perusal of this chapter the lack of autobiographical quotations, such as have appeared in other parts of this narrative. Edison's modesty has allowed us but one remark on the subject. This was made by him to one of the writers a short time ago, when, after an interesting indulgence in reminiscences of old times and early inventions, he leaned back in his chair, and with a broad smile on his face, said, reflectively: "Say, I HAVE been mixed up in a whole lot of things, haven't I?"

CHAPTER XXVIII

THE BLACK FLAG

THROUGHOUT the forty-odd years of his creative life, Edison has realized by costly experience the truth of the cynical proverb that "A patent is merely a title to a lawsuit." It is not intended, however, by this statement to lead to any inference on the part of the reader that HE stands peculiarly alone in any such experience, for it has been and still is the common lot of every successful inventor, sooner or later.

To attribute dishonesty or cupidity as the root of the defence in all patent litigation would be aiming very wide of the mark, for in no class of suits that come before the courts are there any that present a greater variety of complex, finely shaded questions, or that require more delicacy of interpretation, than those that involve the construction of patents, particularly those relating to electrical devices. Indeed, a careful study of legal procedure of this character could not be carried far without discovery of the fact that in numerous instances the differences of opinion between litigants were marked by the utmost bona fides.

On the other hand, such study would reveal many cases of undoubted fraudulent intent, as well as many bold attempts to deprive the inventor of the fruits of his endeavors by those who have sought to evade, through subtle technicalities of the law, the penalty justly due them for trickery, evasion, or open contempt of the rights of others.

In the history of science and of the arts to which the world has owed its continued progress from year to year there is disclosed one remarkable fact, and that is, that whenever any important discovery or invention has been made and announced by one man, it has almost always been disclosed later that other men--possibly widely separated and knowing nothing of the other's work--have been following up the same general lines of investigation, independently, with the same object in mind. Their respective methods might be dissimilar while tending to the same end, but it does not necessarily follow that any one of these other experimenters might ever have achieved the result aimed at, although, after the proclamation of success by one, it is easy to believe that each of the other independent investigators might readily persuade himself that he would ultimately have reached the goal in just that same way.

This peculiar coincidence of simultaneous but separate work not only comes to light on the bringing out of great and important discoveries or inventions, but becomes more apparent if a new art is disclosed, for then the imagination of previous experimenters is stimulated through wide dissemination of the tidings, sometimes resulting in more or less effort to enter the newly opened field with devices or methods that resemble closely the original and fundamental ones in principle and application. In this and other ways there arises constantly in the United States Patent Office a large number of contested cases, called "Interferences," where applications for patents covering the invention of a similar device have been independently filed by two or even more persons. In such cases only one patent can be issued, and that to the inventor who on the taking of testimony shows priority in date of invention. [20]

[Footnote 20: A most remarkable instance of contemporaneous invention and without a parallel in the annals of the United States Patent Office, occurred when, on the same day, February 15, 1876, two separate descriptions were filed in that office, one a complete application and the other a caveat, but each covering an invention for "transmitting vocal sounds telegraphically." The application was made by Alexander Graham Bell, of Salem, Massachusetts, and the caveat by Elisha Gray, of Chicago, Illinois. On examination of the two papers it was found that both of them covered practically the same ground, hence, as only one patent could be granted, it became necessary to ascertain the precise hour at which the documents were respectively filed, and put the parties in interference. This was done, with the result that the patent was ultimately awarded to Bell.]

In the opening up and development of any new art based upon a fundamental discovery or invention, there ensues naturally an era of supplemental or collateral inventive activity--the legitimate outcome of the basic original ideas. Part of this development may be due to the inventive skill and knowledge of the original inventor and his associates, who, by reason of prior investigation, would be in better position to follow up the art in its earliest details than others, who might be regarded as mere outsiders. Thus a new enterprise may be presented before the world by its promoters in the belief that they are strongly fortified by patent rights which will protect them in a degree commensurate with the risks they have assumed.

Supplemental inventions, however, in any art, new or old, are not limited to those which emanate from the original workers, for the ingenuity of man, influenced by the spirit of the times, seizes upon any novel line of action and seeks to improve or enlarge upon it, or, at any rate, to produce more or less variation of its phases. Consequently, there is a constant endeavor on the part of a countless host of men possessing some degree of technical skill and inventive ability, to win fame and money by entering into the already opened fields of endeavor with devices and methods of their own, for which subsidiary patents may be obtainable. Some of such patents may prove to be valuable, while it is quite certain that in the natural order of things others will be commercially worthless, but none may be entirely disregarded in the history and development of the art.

It will be quite obvious, therefore, that the advent of any useful invention or discovery, great or small, is followed by a clashing of many interests which become complex in their interpretation by reason of the many conflicting claims that cluster around the main principle. Nor is the confusion less confounded through efforts made on the part of dishonest persons, who, like vultures, follow closely on the trail of successful inventors and (sometimes through information derived by underhand methods) obtain patents on alleged inventions, closely approximating the real ones, solely for the purpose of harassing the original patentee until they are bought up, or else, with the intent of competing boldly in the new business, trust in the delays of legal proceedings to obtain a sure foothold in their questionable enterprise.

Then again there are still others who, having no patent rights, but waving aside all compunction and in downright fraud, simply enter the commercial field against the whole world, using ruthlessly whatever inventive skill and knowledge the original patentee may have disclosed, and trusting to the power of money, rapid movement, and mendacious advertising to build up a business which shall presently assume such formidable proportions as to force a compromise, or stave off an injunction until the patent has expired. In nine cases out of ten such a course can be followed with relative impunity; and guided by skilful experts who may suggest really trivial changes here and there over the patented structure, and with the aid of keen and able counsel, hardly a patent exists that could not be invaded by such infringers. Such is the condition of our laws and practice that the patentee in seeking to enforce his rights labors under a terrible handicap.

And, finally, in this recital of perplexing conditions confronting the inventor, there must not be forgotten the commercial "shark," whose predatory instincts are ever keenly alert for tender victims. In the wake of every newly developed art of world-wide importance there is sure to follow a number of unscrupulous adventurers, who hasten to take advantage of general public ignorance of the true inwardness of affairs. Basing their operations on this lack of knowledge, and upon the tendency of human nature to give credence to widely advertised and high-sounding descriptions and specious promises of vast profits, these men find little difficulty in conjuring money out of the pockets of the unsophisticated and gullible, who rush to become stockholders in concerns that have "airy nothings" for a foundation, and that collapse quickly when the bubble is pricked. [21]

[Footnote 21: A notable instance of the fleecing of unsuspecting and credulous persons occurred in the early eighties, during the furor occasioned by the introduction of Mr. Edison's electric-light system. A corporation claiming to have a self-generating dynamo (practically perpetual motion) advertised its preposterous claims extensively, and actually succeeded in selling a large amount of stock, which, of course, proved to be absolutely worthless.]

To one who is unacquainted with the trying circumstances attending the introduction and marketing of patented devices, it might seem unnecessary that an inventor and his business associates should be obliged to take into account the unlawful or ostensible competition of pirates or schemers, who, in the absence of legal decision, may run a free course for a long time. Nevertheless, as public patronage is the element vitally requisite for commercial success, and as the public is not usually in full possession of all the facts and therefore cannot discriminate between the genuine and the false, the legitimate inventor must avail himself of every possible means of proclaiming and asserting his rights if he desires to derive any benefit from the results of his skill and labor. Not only must he be prepared to fight in the Patent Office and pursue a regular course of patent litigation against those who may honestly deem themselves to be protected by other inventions or patents of similar character, and also proceed against more palpable infringers who are openly, defiantly, and illegitimately engaged in competitive business operations, but he must, as well, endeavor to protect himself against the assaults of impudent fraud by educating the public mind to a point of intelligent apprehension of the true status of his invention and the conflicting claims involved.

When the nature of a patent right is considered it is difficult to see why this should be so. The inventor creates a new thing--an invention of utility--and the people, represented by the Federal Government, say to him in effect: "Disclose your invention to us in a patent so that we may know how to practice it, and we will agree to give you a monopoly for seventeen years, after which we shall be free to use it. If the right thus granted is invaded, apply to a Federal Court and the infringer will be enjoined and required to settle in damages." Fair and false promise! Is it generally realized that no matter how flagrant the infringement nor how barefaced and impudent the infringer, no Federal Court will grant an injunction UNTIL THE PATENT SHALL HAVE BEEN FIRST LITIGATED TO FINAL HEARING AND SUSTAINED? A procedure, it may be stated, requiring years of time and thousands of dollars, during which other infringers have generally entered the field, and all have grown fat.

Thus Edison and his business associates have been forced into a veritable maelstrom of litigation during the major part of the last forty years, in the effort to procure for themselves a small measure of protection for their interests under the numerous inventions of note that he has made at various times in that period. The earlier years of his inventive activity, while productive of many important contributions to electrical industries, such as stock tickers and printers, duplex, quadruplex, and automatic telegraphs, were not marked by the turmoil of interminable legal conflicts that arose after the beginning of the telephone and electric-light epochs. In fact, his inventions; up to and including his telephone improvements (which entered into already existing arts), had been mostly purchased by the Western Union and other companies, and while there was more or less contesting of his claims (especially in respect of the telephone), the extent of such litigation was not so conspicuously great as that which centred subsequently around his patents covering incandescent electric lighting and power systems.

Through these inventions there came into being an entirely new art, complete in its practicability evolved by Edison after protracted experiments founded upon most patient, thorough, and original methods of investigation extending over several years. Long before attaining the goal, he had realized with characteristic insight the underlying principles of the great and comprehensive problem he had started out to solve, and plodded steadily along the path that he had marked out, ignoring the almost universal scientific disbelief in his ultimate success. "Dreamer," "fool," "boaster" were among the appellations bestowed upon him by unbelieving critics. Ridicule was heaped upon him in the public prints, and mathematics were called into service by learned men to settle the point forever that he was attempting the utterly impossible.

But, presto! no sooner had he accomplished the task and shown concrete results to the world than he found himself in the anomalous position of being at once surrounded by the conditions which inevitably confront every inventor. The path through the trackless forest had been blazed, and now every one could find the way. At the end of the road was a rich prize belonging rightfully to the man who had opened a way to it, but the struggles of others to reach it by more or less honest methods now began and continued for many years. If, as a former commissioner once said, "Edison was the man who kept the path to the Patent Office hot with his footsteps," there were other great inventors abreast or immediately on his heels, some, to be sure, with legitimate, original methods and vital improvements representing independent work; while there were also those who did not trouble to invent, but simply helped themselves to whatever ideas were available, and coming from any source.

Possibly events might have happened differently had Edison been able to prevent the announcement of his electric-light inventions until he was entirely prepared to bring out the system as a whole, ready for commercial exploitation, but the news of his production of a practical and successful incandescent lamp became known and spread like wild-fire to all corners of the globe. It took more than a year after the evolution of the lamp for Edison to get into position to do actual business, and during that time his laboratory was the natural Mecca of every inquiring person. Small wonder, then, that when he was prepared to market his invention he should find others entering that market, at home and abroad, at the same time, and with substantially similar merchandise.

Edison narrates two incidents that may be taken as characteristic of a good deal that had to be contended with, coming in the shape of nefarious attack. "In the early days of my electric light," he says, "curiosity and interest brought a great many people to Menlo Park to see it. Some of them did not come with the best of intentions. I remember the visit of one expert, a well-known electrician, a graduate of Johns Hopkins University, and who then represented a Baltimore gas company. We had the lamps exhibited in a large room, and so arranged on a table as to illustrate the regular layout of circuits for houses and streets. Sixty of the men employed at the laboratory were used as watchers, each to keep an eye on a certain section of the exhibit, and see there was no monkeying with it. This man had a length of insulated No. 10 wire passing through his sleeves and around his back, so that his hands would conceal the ends and no one would know he had it. His idea, of course, was to put this wire across the ends of the supplying circuits, and short-circuit the whole thing--put it all out of business without being detected. Then he could report how easily the electric light went out, and a false impression would be conveyed to the public. He did not know that we had already worked out the safety-fuse, and that every group of lights was thus protected independently. He put this jumper slyly in contact with the wires--and just four lamps went out on the section he tampered with. The watchers saw him do it, however, and got hold of him and just led him out of the place with language that made the recording angels jump for their typewriters."

The other incident is as follows: "Soon after I had got out the incandescent light I had an interference in the Patent Office with a man from Wisconsin. He filed an application for a patent and entered into a conspiracy to 'swear back' of the date of my invention, so as to deprive me of it. Detectives were put on the case, and we found he was a 'faker,' and we took means to break the thing up. Eugene Lewis, of Eaton & Lewis, had this in hand for me. Several years later this same man attempted to defraud a leading firm of manufacturing chemists in New York, and was sent to State prison. A short time after that a syndicate took up a man named Goebel and tried to do the same thing, but again our detective-work was too much for them. This was along the same line as the attempt of Drawbaugh to deprive Bell of his telephone. Whenever an invention of large prospective value comes out, these cases always occur. The lamp patent was sustained in the New York Federal Court. I thought that was final and would end the matter, but another Federal judge out in St. Louis did not sustain it. The result is I have never enjoyed any benefits from my lamp patents, although I fought for many years." The Goebel case will be referred to later in this chapter.

The original owner of the patents and inventions covering his electric-lighting system, the Edison Electric Light Company (in which Edison was largely interested as a stockholder), thus found at the outset that its commercial position was imperilled by the activity of competitors who had sprung up like mushrooms. It became necessary to take proper preliminary legal steps to protect the interests which had been acquired at the cost of so much money and such incessant toil and experiment. During the first few years in which the business of the introduction of the light was carried on with such strenuous and concentrated effort, the attention of Edison and his original associates was constantly focused upon the commercial exploitation and the further development of the system at home and abroad. The difficult and perplexing situation at that time is thus described by Major S. B. Eaton:

"The reason for the delay in beginning and pushing suits for infringements of the lamp patent has never been generally understood. In my official position as president of the Edison Electric Light Company I became the target, along with Mr. Edison, for censure from the stockholders and others on account of this delay, and I well remember how deep the feeling was. In view of the facts that a final injunction on the lamp patent was not obtained until the life of the patent was near its end, and, next, that no damages in money were ever paid by the guilty infringers, it has been generally believed that Mr. Edison sacrificed the interest of his stockholders selfishly when he delayed the prosecution of patent suits and gave all his time and energies to manufacturing. This belief was the stronger because the manufacturing enterprises belonged personally to Mr. Edison and not to his company. But the facts render it easy to dispel this false belief. The Edison inventions were not only a lamp; they comprised also an entire system of central stations. Such a thing was new to the world, and the apparatus, as well as the manufacture thereof, was equally new. Boilers, engines, dynamos, motors, distribution mains, meters, house-wiring, safety-devices, lamps, and lamp-fixtures--all were vital parts of the whole system. Most of them were utterly novel and unknown to the arts, and all of them required quick, and, I may say, revolutionary thought and invention. The firm of Babcock & Wilcox gave aid on the boilers, Armington & Sims undertook the engines, but everything else was abnormal. No factories in the land would take up the manufacture. I remember, for instance, our interviews with Messrs. Mitchell, Vance & Co., the leading manufacturers of house gas-lighting fixtures, such as brackets and chandeliers. They had no faith in electric lighting, and rejected all our overtures to induce them to take up the new business of making electric-light fixtures. As regards other parts of the Edison system, notably the Edison dynamo, no such machines had ever existed; there was no factory in the world equipped to make them, and, most discouraging of all, the very scientific principles of their construction were still vague and experimental.

"What was to be done? Mr. Edison has never been greater than when he met and solved this crisis. 'If there are no factories,' he said, 'to make my inventions, I will build the factories myself. Since capital is timid, I will raise and supply it. The issue is factories or death.' Mr. Edison invited the cooperation of his leading stockholders. They lacked confidence or did not care to increase their investments. He was forced to go on alone. The chain of Edison shops was then created. By far the most perplexing of these new manufacturing problems was the lamp. Not only was it a new industry, one without shadow of prototype, but the mechanical devices for making the lamps, and to some extent the very machines to make those devices, were to be invented. All of this was done by the courage, capital, and invincible energy and genius of the great inventor. But Mr. Edison could not create these great and diverse industries and at the same time give requisite attention to litigation. He could not start and develop the new and hard business of electric lighting and yet spare one hour to pursue infringers. One thing or the other must wait. All agreed that it must be the litigation. And right there a lasting blow was given to the prestige of the Edison patents. The delay was translated as meaning lack of confidence; and the alert infringer grew strong in courage and capital. Moreover, and what was the heaviest blow of all, he had time, thus unmolested, to get a good start.

"In looking back on those days and scrutinizing them through the years, I am impressed by the greatness, the solitary greatness I may say, of Mr. Edison. We all felt then that we were of importance, and that our contribution of effort and zeal were vital. I can see now, however, that the best of us was nothing but the fly on the wheel. Suppose anything had happened to Edison? All would have been chaos and ruin.. To him, therefore, be the glory, if not the profit."

The foregoing remarks of Major Eaton show authoritatively how the much-discussed delay in litigating the Edison patents was so greatly misunderstood at the time, and also how imperatively necessary it was for Edison and his associates to devote their entire time and energies to the commercial development of the art. As the lighting business increased, however, and a great number of additional men were initiated into its mysteries, Edison and his experts were able to spare some time to legal matters, and an era of active patent litigation against infringers was opened about the year 1885 by the Edison company, and thereafter continued for many years.

While the history of this vast array of legal proceedings possesses a fascinating interest for those involved, as well as for professional men, legal and scientific, it could not be expected that it would excite any such feeling on the part of a casual reader. Hence, it is not proposed to encumber this narrative with any detailed record of the numerous suits that were brought and conducted through their complicated ramifications by eminent counsel. Suffice it to say that within about sixteen years after the commencement of active patent litigation, there had been spent by the owners of the Edison lighting patents upward of two million dollars in prosecuting more than two hundred lawsuits brought against persons who were infringing many of the patents of Edison on the incandescent electric lamp and component parts of his system. Over fifty separate patents were involved in these suits, including the basic one on the lamp (ordinarily called the "Filament" patent), other detail lamp patents, as well as those on sockets, switches, dynamos, motors, and distributing systems.

The principal, or "test," suit on the "Filament" patent was that brought against "The United States Electric Lighting Company," which became a cause celebre in the annals of American jurisprudence. Edison's claims were strenuously and stubbornly contested throughout a series of intense legal conflicts that raged in the courts for a great many years. Both sides of the controversy were represented by legal talent of the highest order, under whose examination and cross-examination volumes of testimony were taken, until the printed record (including exhibits) amounted to more than six thousand pages. Scientific and technical literature and records in all parts of the civilized world were subjected to the most minute scrutiny of opposing experts in the endeavor to prove Edison to be merely an adapter of methods and devices already projected or suggested by others. The world was ransacked for anything that might be claimed as an anticipation of what he had done. Every conceivable phase of ingenuity that could be devised by technical experts was exercised in the attempt to show that Edison had accomplished nothing new. Everything that legal acumen could suggest--every subtle technicality of the law--all the complicated variations of phraseology that the novel nomenclature of a young art would allow--all were pressed into service and availed of by the contestors of the Edison invention in their desperate effort to defeat his claims. It was all in vain, however, for the decision of the court was in favor of Edison, and his lamp patent was sustained not only by the tribunal of the first resort, but also by the Appellate Court some time afterward.

The first trial was had before Judge Wallace in the United States Circuit Court for the Southern District of New York, and the appeal was heard by Judges Lacombe and Shipman, of the United States Circuit Court of Appeals. Before both tribunals the cause had been fully represented by counsel chosen from among the most eminent representatives of the bar at that time, those representing the Edison interests being the late Clarence A. Seward and Grosvenor P. Lowrey, together with Sherburne Blake Eaton, Albert H. Walker, and Richard N. Dyer. The presentation of the case to the courts had in both instances been marked by masterly and able arguments, elucidated by experiments and demonstrations to educate the judges on technical points. Some appreciation of the magnitude of this case may be gained from the fact that the argument on its first trial employed a great many days, and the minutes covered hundreds of pages of closely typewritten matter, while the argument on appeal required eight days, and was set forth in eight hundred and fifty pages of typewriting. Eliminating all purely forensic eloquence and exparte statements, the addresses of counsel in this celebrated suit are worthy of deep study by an earnest student, for, taken together, they comprise the most concise, authentic, and complete history of the prior state of the art and the development of the incandescent lamp that had been made up to that time. [22]

[22] The argument on appeal was conducted with the dignity and decorum that characterize such a proceeding in that court. There is usually little that savors of humor in the ordinary conduct of a case of this kind, but in the present instance a pertinent story was related by Mr. Lowrey, and it is now reproduced. In the course of his address to the court, Mr. Lowrey said:

"I have to mention the name of one expert whose testimony will, I believe, be found as accurate, as sincere, as straightforward as if it were the preaching of the gospel. I do it with great pleasure, and I ask you to read the testimony of Charles L. Clarke along with that of Thomas A. Edison. He had rather a hard row to hoe. He is a young gentleman; he is a very well-instructed man in his profession; he is not what I have called in the argument below an expert in the art of testifying, like some of the others, he has not yet become expert; what he may descend to later cannot be known; he entered upon his first experience, I think, with my brother Duncan, who is no trifler when he comes to deal with these questions, and for several months Mr. Clarke was pursued up and down, over a range of suggestions of what he would have thought if he had thought something else had been said at some time when something else was not said."

Mr. Duncan--"I got three pages a day out of him, too."

Mr. Lowrey--"Well, it was a good result. It always recalled to me what I venture now, since my friend breaks in upon me in this rude manner, to tell the court as well illustrative of what happened there. It is the story of the pickerel and the roach. My friend, Professor Von Reisenberg, of the University of Ghent, pursued a series of investigations into the capacity of various animals to receive ideas. Among the rest he put a pickerel into a tank containing water, and separated across its middle by a transparent glass plate, and on the other side he put a red roach. Now your Honors both know how a pickerel loves a red roach, and I have no doubt you will remember that he is a fish of a very low forehead and an unlimited appetite. When this pickerel saw the red roach through the glass, he made one of those awful dashes which is usually the ruin of whatever stands in its way; but he didn't reach the red roach. He received an impression, doubtless. It was not sufficient, however, to discourage him, and he immediately tried again, and he continued to try for three-quarters of an hour. At the end of three-quarters of an hour he seemed a little shaken and discouraged, and stopped, and the red roach was taken out for that day and the pickerel left. On the succeeding day the red roach was restored, and the pickerel had forgotten the impressions of the first day, and he repeated this again. At the end of the second day the roach was taken out. This was continued, not through so long a period as the effort to take my friend Clarke and devour him, but for a period of about three weeks. At the end of the three weeks, the time during which the pickerel persisted each day had been shortened and shortened, until it was at last discovered that he didn't try at all. The plate glass was then removed, and the pickerel and the red roach sailed around together in perfect peace ever afterward. The pickerel doubtless attributed to the roach all this shaking, the rebuff which he had received. And that is about the condition in which my brother Duncan and my friend Clarke were at the end of this examination."

Mr. Duncan--"I notice on the redirect that Mr. Clarke changed his color."

Mr. Lowrey--"Well, perhaps he was a different kind of a roach then; but you didn't succeed in taking him.

"I beg your Honors to read the testimony of Mr. Clarke in the light of the anecdote of the pickerel and the roach."

Owing to long-protracted delays incident to the taking of testimony and preparation for trial, the argument before the United States Circuit Court of Appeals was not had until the late spring of 1892, and its decision in favor of the Edison Lamp patent was filed on October 4, 1892, MORE THAN TWELVE YEARS AFTER THE ISSUANCE OF THE PATENT ITSELF.

As the term of the patent had been limited under the law, because certain foreign patents had been issued to Edison before that in this country, there was now but a short time left for enjoyment of the exclusive rights contemplated by the statute and granted to Edison and his assigns by the terms of the patent itself. A vigorous and aggressive legal campaign was therefore inaugurated by the Edison Electric Light Company against the numerous infringing companies and individuals that had sprung up while the main suit was pending. Old suits were revived and new ones instituted. Injunctions were obtained against many old offenders, and it seemed as though the Edison interests were about to come into their own for the brief unexpired term of the fundamental patent, when a new bombshell was dropped into the Edison camp in the shape of an alleged anticipation of the invention forty years previously by one Henry Goebel. Thus, in 1893, the litigation was reopened, and a protracted series of stubbornly contested conflicts was fought in the courts.

Goebel's claims were not unknown to the Edison Company, for as far back as 1882 they had been officially brought to its notice coupled with an offer of sale for a few thousand dollars. A very brief examination into their merits, however, sufficed to demonstrate most emphatically that Goebel had never made a practical incandescent lamp, nor had he ever contributed a single idea or device bearing, remotely or directly, on the development of the art. Edison and his company, therefore, rejected the offer unconditionally and declined to enter into any arrangements whatever with Goebel. During the prosecution of the suits in 1893 it transpired that the Goebel claims had also been investigated by the counsel of the defendant company in the principal litigation already related, but although every conceivable defence and anticipation had been dragged into the case during the many years of its progress, the alleged Goebel anticipation was not even touched upon therein. From this fact it is quite apparent that they placed no credence on its bona fides.

But desperate cases call for desperate remedies. Some of the infringing lamp-manufacturing concerns, which during the long litigation had grown strong and lusty, and thus far had not been enjoined by the court, now saw injunctions staring them in the face, and in desperation set up the Goebel so-called anticipation as a defence in the suits brought against them.

This German watchmaker, Goebel, located in the East Side of New York City, had undoubtedly been interested, in a desultory kind of way, in simple physical phenomena, and a few trifling experiments made by him some forty or forty-five years previously were magnified and distorted into brilliant and all-comprehensive discoveries and inventions. Avalanches of affidavits of himself, "his sisters and his cousins and his aunts," practically all persons in ordinary walks of life, and of old friends, contributed a host of recollections that seemed little short of miraculous in their detailed accounts of events of a scientific nature that were said to have occurred so many years before. According to affidavits of Goebel himself and some of his family, nothing that would anticipate Edison's claim had been omitted from his work, for he (Goebel) claimed to have employed the all-glass globe, into which were sealed platinum wires carrying a tenuous carbon filament, from which the occluded gases had been liberated during the process of high exhaustion. He had even determined upon bamboo as the best material for filaments. On the face of it he was seemingly gifted with more than human prescience, for in at least one of his exhibit lamps, said to have been made twenty years previously, he claimed to have employed processes which Edison and his associates had only developed by several years of experience in making thousands of lamps!

The Goebel story was told by the affidavits in an ingenuous manner, with a wealth of simple homely detail that carried on its face an appearance of truth calculated to deceive the elect, had not the elect been somewhat prepared by their investigation made some eleven years before.

The story was met by the Edison interests with counter-affidavits, showing its utter improbabilities and absurdities from the standpoint of men of science and others versed in the history and practice of the art; also affidavits of other acquaintances and neighbors of Goebel flatly denying the exhibitions he claimed to have made. The issue thus being joined, the legal battle raged over different sections of the country. A number of contumeliously defiant infringers in various cities based fond hopes of immunity upon the success of this Goebel evidence, but were defeated. The attitude of the courts is well represented in the opinion of Judge Colt, rendered in a motion for injunction against the Beacon Vacuum Pump and Electrical Company. The defence alleged the Goebel anticipation, in support of which it offered in evidence four lamps, Nos. 1, 2, and 3 purporting to have been made before 1854, and No. 4 before 1872. After a very full review of the facts in the case, and a fair consideration of the defendants' affidavits, Judge Colt in his opinion goes on to say:

"It is extremely improbable that Henry Goebel constructed a practical incandescent lamp in 1854. This is manifest from the history of the art for the past fifty years, the electrical laws which since that time have been discovered as applicable to the incandescent lamp, the imperfect means which then existed for obtaining a vacuum, the high degree of skill necessary in the construction of all its parts, and the crude instruments with which Goebel worked.

"Whether Goebel made the fiddle-bow lamps, 1, 2, and 3, is not necessary to determine. The weight of evidence on this motion is in the direction that he made these lamp or lamps similar in general appearance, though it is manifest that few, if any, of the many witnesses who saw the Goebel lamp could form an accurate judgment of the size of the filament or burner. But assuming they were made, they do not anticipate the invention of Edison. At most they were experimental toys used to advertise his telescope, or to flash a light upon his clock, or to attract customers to his shop. They were crudely constructed, and their life was brief. They could not be used for domestic purposes. They were in no proper sense the practical commercial lamp of Edison. The literature of the art is full of better lamps, all of which are held not to anticipate the Edison patent.

"As for Lamp No. 4, I cannot but view it with suspicion. It presents a new appearance. The reason given for not introducing it before the hearing is unsatisfactory. This lamp, to my mind, envelops with a cloud of distrust the whole Goebel story. It is simply impossible under the circumstances to believe that a lamp so constructed could have been made by Goebel before 1872. Nothing in the evidence warrants such a supposition, and other things show it to be untrue. This lamp has a carbon filament, platinum leading-in wires, a good vacuum, and is well sealed and highly finished. It is said that this lamp shows no traces of mercury in the bulb because the mercury was distilled, but Goebel says nothing about distilled mercury in his first affidavit, and twice he speaks of the particles of mercury clinging to the inside of the chamber, and for that reason he constructed a Geissler pump after he moved to 468 Grand Street, which was in 1877. Again, if this lamp has been in his possession since before 1872, as he and his son swear, why was it not shown to Mr. Crosby, of the American Company, when he visited his shop in 1881 and was much interested in his lamps? Why was it not shown to Mr. Curtis, the leading counsel for the defendants in the New York cases, when he was asked to produce a lamp and promised to do so? Why did not his son take this lamp to Mr. Bull's office in 1892, when he took the old fiddle-bow lamps, 1, 2, and 3? Why did not his son take this lamp to Mr. Eaton's office in 1882, when he tried to negotiate the sale of his father's inventions to the Edison Company? A lamp so constructed and made before 1872 was worth a large sum of money to those interested in defeating the Edison patent like the American Company, and Goebel was not a rich man. Both he and one of his sons were employed in 1881 by the American Company. Why did he not show this lamp to McMahon when he called in the interest of the American Company and talked over the electrical matters? When Mr. Dreyer tried to organize a company in 1882, and procured an option from him of all his inventions relating to electric lighting for which $925 was paid, and when an old lamp of this kind was of vital consequence and would have insured a fortune, why was it not forthcoming? Mr. Dreyer asked Goebel to produce an old lamp, and was especially anxious to find one pending his negotiations with the Edison Company for the sale of Goebel's inventions. Why did he not produce this lamp in his interviews with Bohm, of the American Company, or Moses, of the Edison Company, when it was for his interest to do so? The value of such an anticipation of the Edison lamp was made known to him. He was desirous of realizing upon his inventions. He was proud of his incandescent lamps, and was pleased to talk about them with anybody who would listen. Is it conceivable under all these circumstances, that he should have had this all-important lamp in his possession from 1872 to 1893, and yet no one have heard of it or seen it except his son? It cannot be said that ignorance of the English language offers an excuse. He knew English very well although Bohm and Dreyer conversed with him in German. His children spoke English. Neither his ignorance nor his simplicity prevented him from taking out three patents: the first in 1865 for a sewing-machine hemmer, and the last in 1882 for an improvement in incandescent lamps. If he made Lamp No. 4 previous to 1872, why was it not also patented?

"There are other circumstances which throw doubt on this alleged Goebel anticipation. The suit against the United States Electric Lighting Company was brought in the Southern District of New York in 1885. Large interests were at stake, and the main defence to the Edison patent was based on prior inventions. This Goebel claim was then investigated by the leading counsel for the defence, Mr. Curtis. It was further inquired into in 1892, in the case against the Sawyer-Man Company. It was brought to the attention and considered by the Edison Company in 1882. It was at that time known to the American Company, who hoped by this means to defeat the monopoly under the Edison patent. Dreyer tried to organize a company for its purchase. Young Goebel tried to sell it. It must have been known to hundreds of people. And now when the Edison Company after years of litigation, leaving but a short time for the patent to run, have obtained a final adjudication establishing its validity, this claim is again resurrected to defeat the operation of the judgment so obtained. A court in equity should not look with favor on such a defence. Upon the evidence here presented, I agree with the first impression of Mr. Curtis and with the opinion of Mr. Dickerson that whatever Goebel did must be considered as an abandoned experiment.

"It has often been laid down that a meritorious invention is not to be defeated by something which rests in speculation or experiment, or which is rudimentary or incomplete.

"The law requires not conjecture, but certainty. It is easy after an important invention has gone into public use for persons to come forward with claims that they invented the same thing years before, and to endeavor to establish this by the recollection of witnesses as to events long past. Such evidence is to be received with great caution, and the presumption of novelty arising from the grant of the patent is not to be overcome except upon clear and convincing proof.

"When the defendant company entered upon the manufacture of incandescent lamps in May, 1891, it well knew the consequences which must follow a favorable decision for the Edison Company in the New York case."

The injunction was granted.

Other courts took practically the same view of the Goebel story as was taken by Judge Colt, and the injunctions asked in behalf of the Edison interests were granted on all applications except one in St. Louis, Missouri, in proceedings instituted against a strong local concern of that city.

Thus, at the eleventh hour in the life of this important patent, after a long period of costly litigation, Edison and his associates were compelled to assume the defensive against a claimant whose utterly baseless pretensions had already been thoroughly investigated and rejected years before by every interested party, and ultimately, on examination by the courts, pronounced legally untenable, if not indeed actually fraudulent. Irritating as it was to be forced into the position of combating a proposition so well known to be preposterous and insincere, there was nothing else to do but to fight this fabrication with all the strenuous and deadly earnestness that would have been brought to bear on a really meritorious defence. Not only did this Goebel episode divert for a long time the energies of the Edison interests from activities in other directions, but the cost of overcoming the extravagantly absurd claims ran up into hundreds of thousands of dollars.

Another quotation from Major Eaton is of interest in this connection:

"Now a word about the Goebel case. I took personal charge of running down this man and his pretensions in the section of the city where he lived and among his old neighbors. They were a typical East Side lot--ignorant, generally stupid, incapable of long memory, but ready to oblige a neighbor and to turn an easy dollar by putting a cross-mark at the bottom of a forthcoming friendly affidavit. I can say in all truth and justice that their testimony was utterly false, and that the lawyers who took it must have known it.

"The Goebel case emphasizes two defects in the court procedure in patent cases. One is that they may be spun out almost interminably, even, possibly, to the end of the life of the patent; the other is that the judge who decides the case does not see the witnesses. That adverse decision at St. Louis would never have been made if the court could have seen the men who swore for Goebel. When I met Mr. F. P. Fish on his return from St. Louis, after he had argued the Edison side, he felt keenly that disadvantage, to say nothing of the hopeless difficulty of educating the court."

In the earliest days of the art, when it was apparent that incandescent lighting had come to stay, the Edison Company was a shining mark at which the shafts of the dishonest were aimed. Many there were who stood ready to furnish affidavits that they or some one else whom they controlled had really invented the lamp, but would obligingly withdraw and leave Edison in possession of the field on payment of money. Investigation of these cases, however, revealed invariably the purely fraudulent nature of all such offers, which were uniformly declined.

As the incandescent light began to advance rapidly in public favor, the immense proportions of the future market became sufficiently obvious to tempt unauthorized persons to enter the field and become manufacturers. When the lamp became a thoroughly established article it was not a difficult matter to copy it, especially when there were employees to be hired away at increased pay, and their knowledge utilized by the more unscrupulous of these new competitors. This is not conjecture but known to be a fact, and the practice continued many years, during which new lamp companies sprang up on every side. Hence, it is not surprising that, on the whole, the Edison lamp litigation was not less remarkable for quantity than quality. Between eighty and ninety separate suits upon Edison's fundamental lamp and detail patents were brought in the courts of the United States and prosecuted to completion.

In passing it may be mentioned that in England France, and Germany also the Edison fundamental lamp patent was stubbornly fought in the judicial arena, and his claim to be the first inventor of practical incandescent lighting was uniformly sustained in all those countries.

Infringement was not, however, confined to the lamp alone, but, in America, extended all along the line of Edison's patents relating to the production and distribution of electric light, including those on dynamos, motors, distributing systems, sockets, switches, and other details which he had from time to time invented. Consequently, in order to protect its interests at all points, the Edison Company had found it necessary to pursue a vigorous policy of instituting legal proceedings against the infringers of these various patents, and, in addition to the large number of suits on the lamp alone, not less than one hundred and twenty-five other separate actions, involving some fifty or more of Edison's principal electric-lighting patents, were brought against concerns which were wrongfully appropriating his ideas and actively competing with his companies in the market.

The ramifications of this litigation became so extensive and complex as to render it necessary to institute a special bureau, or department, through which the immense detail could be systematically sifted, analyzed, and arranged in collaboration with the numerous experts and counsel responsible for the conduct of the various cases. This department was organized in 1889 by Major Eaton, who was at this time and for some years afterward its general counsel.

In the selection of the head of this department a man of methodical and analytical habit of mind was necessary, capable of clear reasoning, and at the same time one who had gained a thoroughly practical experience in electric light and power fields, and the choice fell upon Mr. W. J. Jenks, the manager of the Edison central station at Brockton, Massachusetts. He had resigned that position in 1885, and had spent the intervening period in exploiting the Edison municipal system of lighting, as well as taking an active part in various other branches of the Edison enterprises.

Thus, throughout the life of Edison's patents on electric light, power, and distribution, the interminable legal strife has continued from day to day, from year to year. Other inventors, some of them great and notable, have been coming into the field since the foundation of the art, patents have multiplied exceedingly, improvement has succeeded improvement, great companies have grown greater, new concerns have come into existence, coalitions and mergers have taken place, all tending to produce changes in methods, but not much in diminution of patent litigation. While Edison has not for a long time past interested himself particularly in electric light and power inventions, the bureau which was initiated under the old regime in 1889 still continues, enlarged in scope, directed by its original chief, but now conducted under the auspices of several allied companies whose great volumes of combined patents (including those of Edison) cover a very wide range of the electrical field.

As the general conception and theory of a lawsuit is the recovery of some material benefit, the lay mind is apt to conceive of great sums of money being awarded to a complainant by way of damages upon a favorable decision in an important patent case. It might, therefore, be natural to ask how far Edison or his companies have benefited pecuniarily by reason of the many belated victories they have scored in the courts. To this question a strict regard for truth compels the answer that they have not been benefited at all, not to the extent of a single dollar, so far as cash damages are concerned.

It is not to be denied, however, that substantial advantages have accrued to them more or less directly through the numerous favorable decisions obtained by them as a result of the enormous amount of litigation, in the prosecution of which so great a sum of money has been spent and so concentrated an amount of effort and time lavished. Indeed, it would be strange and unaccountable were the results otherwise. While the benefits derived were not directly pecuniary in their nature, they were such as tended to strengthen commercially the position of the rightful owners of the patents. Many irresponsible and purely piratical concerns were closed altogether; others were compelled to take out royalty licenses; consolidations of large interests were brought about; the public was gradually educated to a more correct view of the true merits of conflicting claims, and, generally speaking, the business has been greatly unified and brought within well-defined and controllable lines.

Not only in relation to his electric light and power inventions has the progress of Edison and his associates been attended by legal controversy all through the years of their exploitation, but also in respect to other inventions, notably those relating to the phonograph and to motion pictures.

The increasing endeavors of infringers to divert into their own pockets some of the proceeds arising from the marketing of the devices covered by Edison's inventions on these latter lines, necessitated the institution by him, some years ago, of a legal department which, as in the case of the light inventions, was designed to consolidate all law and expert work and place it under the management of a general counsel. The department is of considerable extent, including a number of resident and other associate counsel, and a general office staff, all of whom are constantly engaged from day to day in patent litigation and other legal work necessary to protect the Edison interests. Through their labors the old story is reiterated in the contesting of approximate but conflicting claims, the never-ending effort to suppress infringement, and the destruction as far as possible of the commercial pirates who set sail upon the seas of all successful enterprises. The details, circumstances, and technical questions are, of course, different from those relating to other classes of inventions, and although there has been no cause celebre concerning the phonograph and motion-picture patents, the contention is as sharp and strenuous as it was in the cases relating to electric lighting and heavy current technics.

Mr. Edison's storage battery and the poured cement house have not yet reached the stage of great commercial enterprises, and therefore have not yet risen to the dignity of patent litigation. If, however, the experience of past years is any criterion, there will probably come a time in the future when, despite present widely expressed incredulity and contemptuous sniffs of unbelief in the practicability of his ideas in these directions, ultimate success will give rise to a series of hotly contested legal conflicts such as have signalized the practical outcome of his past efforts in other lines.

When it is considered what Edison has done, what the sum and substance of his contributions to human comfort and happiness have been, the results, as measured by legal success, have been pitiable. With the exception of the favorable decision on the incandescent lamp filament patent, coming so late, however, that but little practical good was accomplished, the reader may search the law-books in vain for a single decision squarely and fairly sustaining a single patent of first order. There never was a monopoly in incandescent electric lighting, and even from the earliest days competitors and infringers were in the field reaping the benefits, and though defeated in the end, paying not a cent of tribute. The market was practically as free and open as if no patent existed. There never was a monopoly in the phonograph; practically all of the vital inventions were deliberately appropriated by others, and the inventor was laughed at for his pains. Even so beautiful a process as that for the duplication of phonograph records was solemnly held by a Federal judge as lacking invention--as being obvious to any one. The mere fact that Edison spent years of his life in developing that process counted for nothing.

The invention of the three-wire system, which, when it was first announced as saving over 60 per cent. of copper in the circuits, was

regarded as an utter impossibility--this patent was likewise held by
a Federal judge to be lacking in invention. In the motion-picture art,
infringements began with its very birth, and before the inevitable
litigation could be terminated no less than ten competitors were in the
field, with whom compromises had to be made.

In a foreign country, Edison would have undoubtedly received signal
honors; in his own country he has won the respect and admiration of
millions; but in his chosen field as an inventor and as a patentee his
reward has been empty. The courts abroad have considered his patents in
a liberal spirit and given him his due; the decisions in this country
have fallen wide of the mark. We make no criticism of our Federal
judges; as a body they are fair, able, and hard-working; but they
operate under a system of procedure that stifles absolutely the
development of inventive genius.

Until that system is changed and an opportunity offered for a final,
swift, and economical adjudication of patent rights, American inventors
may well hesitate before openly disclosing their inventions to the
public, and may seriously consider the advisability of retaining them as
"trade secrets."

CHAPTER XXIX

THE SOCIAL SIDE OF EDISON

THE title of this chapter might imply that there is an unsocial side
to Edison. In a sense this is true, for no one is more impatient
or intolerant of interruption when deeply engaged in some line of
experiment. Then the caller, no matter how important or what his
mission, is likely to realize his utter insignificance and be sent away
without accomplishing his object. But, generally speaking, Edison is
easy tolerance itself, with a peculiar weakness toward those who have
the least right to make any demands on his time. Man is a social animal,
and that describes Edison; but it does not describe accurately the
inventor asking to be let alone.

Edison never sought Society; but "Society" has never ceased to seek
him, and to-day, as ever, the pressure upon him to give up his work and
receive honors, meet distinguished people, or attend public functions,
is intense. Only two or three years ago, a flattering invitation came
from one of the great English universities to receive a degree, but at
that moment he was deep in experiments on his new storage battery, and
nothing could budge him. He would not drop the work, and while highly
appreciative of the proposed honor, let it go by rather than quit for
a week or two the stern drudgery of probing for the fact and the truth.
Whether one approves or not, it is at least admirable stoicism, of which
the world has too little. A similar instance is that of a visit paid to
the laboratory by some one bringing a gold medal from a foreign society.
It was a very hot day in summer, the visitor was in full social regalia
of silk hat and frock-coat, and insisted that he could deliver the medal
only into Edison's hands. At that moment Edison, stripped pretty nearly

down to the buff, was at the very crisis of an important experiment, and refused absolutely to be interrupted. He had neither sought nor expected the medal; and if the delegate didn't care to leave it he could take it away. At last Edison was overpersuaded, and, all dirty and perspiring as he was, received the medal rather than cause the visitor to come again. On one occasion, receiving a medal in New York, Edison forgot it on the ferry-boat and left it behind him. A few years ago, when Edison had received the Albert medal of the Royal Society of Arts, one of the present authors called at the laboratory to see it. Nobody knew where it was; hours passed before it could be found; and when at last the accompanying letter was produced, it had an office date stamp right over the signature of the royal president. A visitor to the laboratory with one of these medallic awards asked Edison if he had any others. "Oh yes," he said, "I have a couple of quarts more up at the house!" All this sounds like lack of appreciation, but it is anything else than that. While in Paris, in 1889, he wore the decoration of the Legion of Honor whenever occasion required, but at all other times turned the badge under his lapel "because he hated to have fellow-Americans think he was showing off." And any one who knows Edison will bear testimony to his utter absence of ostentation. It may be added that, in addition to the two quarts of medals up at the house, there will be found at Glenmont many other signal tokens of esteem and good-will--a beautiful cigar-case from the late Tsar of Russia, bronzes from the Government of Japan, steel trophies from Krupp, and a host of other mementos, to one of which he thus refers: "When the experiments with the light were going on at Menlo Park, Sarah Bernhardt came to America. One evening, Robert L. Cutting, of New York, brought her out to see the light. She was a terrific 'rubberneck.' She jumped all over the machinery, and I had one man especially to guard her dress. She wanted to know everything. She would speak in French, and Cutting would translate into English. She stayed there about an hour and a half. Bernhardt gave me two pictures, painted by herself, which she sent me from Paris."

Reference has already been made to the callers upon Edison; and to give simply the names of persons of distinction would fill many pages of this record. Some were mere consumers of time; others were gladly welcomed, like Lord Kelvin, the greatest physicist of the last century, with whom Edison was always in friendly communication. "The first time I saw Lord Kelvin, he came to my laboratory at Menlo Park in 1876." (He reported most favorably on Edison's automatic telegraph system at the Philadelphia Exposition of 1876.) "I was then experimenting with sending eight messages simultaneously over a wire by means of synchronizing tuning-forks. I would take a wire with similar apparatus at both ends, and would throw it over on one set of instruments, take it away, and get it back so quickly that you would not miss it, thereby taking advantage of the rapidity of electricity to perform operations. On my local wire I got it to work very nicely. When Sir William Thomson (Kelvin) came in the room, he was introduced to me, and had a number of friends with him. He said: 'What have you here?' I told him briefly what it was. He then turned around, and to my great surprise explained the whole thing to his friends. Quite a different exhibition was given two weeks later by another well-known Englishman, also an electrician, who came in with his friends, and I was trying for two hours to explain it to him and failed."

After the introduction of the electric light, Edison was more than ever in demand socially, but he shunned functions like the plague, not only because of the serious interference with work, but because of his deafness. Some dinners he had to attend, but a man who ate little and heard less could derive practically no pleasure from them. "George Washington Childs was very anxious I should go down to Philadelphia to dine with him. I seldom went to dinners. He insisted I should go--that a special car would leave New York. It was for me to meet Mr. Joseph Chamberlain. We had the private car of Mr. Roberts, President of the Pennsylvania Railroad. We had one of those celebrated dinners that only Mr. Childs could give, and I heard speeches from Charles Francis Adams and different people. When I came back to the depot, Mr. Roberts was there, and insisted on carrying my satchel for me. I never could understand that."

Among the more distinguished visitors of the electric-lighting period was President Diaz, with whom Edison became quite intimate. "President Diaz, of Mexico, visited this country with Mrs. Diaz, a highly educated and beautiful woman. She spoke very good English. They both took a deep interest in all they saw. I don't know how it ever came about, as it is not in my line, but I seemed to be delegated to show them around. I took them to railroad buildings, electric-light plants, fire departments, and showed them a great variety of things. It lasted two days." Of another visit Edison says: "Sitting Bull and fifteen Sioux Indians came to Washington to see the Great Father, and then to New York, and went to the Goerck Street works. We could make some very good pyrotechnics there, so we determined to give the Indians a scare. But it didn't work. We had an arc there of a most terrifying character, but they never moved a muscle." Another episode at Goerck Street did not find the visitors quite so stoical. "In testing dynamos at Goerck Street we had a long flat belt running parallel with the floor, about four inches above it, and travelling four thousand feet a minute. One day one of the directors brought in three or four ladies to the works to see the new electric-light system. One of the ladies had a little poodle led by a string. The belt was running so smoothly and evenly, the poodle did not notice the difference between it and the floor, and got into the belt before we could do anything. The dog was whirled around forty or fifty times, and a little flat piece of leather came out--and the ladies fainted."

A very interesting period, on the social side, was the visit paid by Edison and his family to Europe in 1889, when he had made a splendid exhibit of his inventions and apparatus at the great Paris Centennial Exposition of that year, to the extreme delight of the French, who welcomed him with open arms. The political sentiments that the Exposition celebrated were not such as to find general sympathy in monarchical Europe, so that the "crowned heads" were conspicuous by their absence. It was not, of course, by way of theatrical antithesis that Edison appeared in Paris at such a time. But the contrast was none the less striking and effective. It was felt that, after all, that which the great exposition exemplified at its best--the triumph of genius over matter, over ignorance, over superstition--met with its due recognition when Edison came to participate, and to felicitate a noble nation that could show so much in the victories of civilization and the arts, despite its long trials and its long struggle for liberty. It is no exaggeration to say that Edison was greeted with the enthusiastic homage of the whole French people. They could find no praise warm enough for the man who had "organized the echoes" and "tamed the lightning," and whose career was so picturesque with eventful and romantic development. In fact, for weeks together it seemed as though no Parisian paper was considered complete and up to date without an article on Edison. The exuberant wit and fancy of the feuilletonists seized upon his various inventions evolving from them others of the most extraordinary nature with which to bedazzle and bewilder the reader. At the close of the Exposition Edison was created a Commander of the Legion of Honor. His own exhibit, made at a personal expense of over $100,000, covered several thousand square feet in the vast Machinery Hall, and was centred around a huge Edison lamp built of myriads of smaller lamps of the ordinary size. The great attraction, however, was the display of the perfected phonograph. Several instruments were provided, and every day, all day long, while the Exposition lasted, queues of eager visitors from every quarter of the globe were waiting to hear the little machine talk and sing and reproduce their own voices. Never before was such a collection of the languages of the world made. It was the first linguistic concourse since Babel times. We must let Edison tell the story of some of his experiences:

"At the Universal Exposition at Paris, in 1889, I made a personal exhibit covering about an acre. As I had no intention of offering to sell anything I was showing, and was pushing no companies, the whole exhibition was made for honor, and without any hope of profit. But the Paris newspapers came around and wanted pay for notices of it, which we promptly refused; whereupon there was rather a stormy time for a while, but nothing was published about it.

"While at the Exposition I visited the Opera-House. The President of France lent me his private box. The Opera-House was one of the first to be lighted by the incandescent lamp, and the managers took great pleasure in showing me down through the labyrinth containing the wiring, dynamos, etc. When I came into the box, the orchestra played the 'Star-Spangled Banner,' and all the people in the house arose; whereupon I was very much embarrassed. After I had been an hour at the play, the manager came around and asked me to go underneath the stage, as they were putting on a ballet of 300 girls, the finest ballet in Europe. It seems there is a little hole on the stage with a hood over it, in which the prompter sits when opera is given. In this instance it was not occupied, and I was given the position in the prompter's seat, and saw the whole ballet at close range.

"The city of Paris gave me a dinner at the new Hotel de Ville, which was also lighted with the Edison system. They had a very fine installation of machinery. As I could not understand or speak a word of French, I went to see our minister, Mr. Whitelaw Reid, and got him to send a deputy to answer for me, which he did, with my grateful thanks. Then the telephone company gave me a dinner, and the engineers of France; and I attended the dinner celebrating the fiftieth anniversary of the discovery of photography. Then they sent to Reid my decoration, and they tried to put a sash on me, but I could not stand for that. My wife had me wear the little red button, but when I saw Americans coming I would slip it out of my lapel, as I thought they would jolly me for wearing it."

Nor was this all. Edison naturally met many of the celebrities of France: "I visited the Eiffel Tower at the invitation of Eiffel. We went to the top, where there was an extension and a small place in which was Eiffel's private office. In this was a piano. When my wife and I arrived at the top, we found that Gounod, the composer, was there. We stayed a couple of hours, and Gounod sang and played for us. We spent a day at Meudon, an old palace given by the government to Jansen, the astronomer. He occupied three rooms, and there were 300. He had the grand dining-room for his laboratory. He showed me a gyroscope he had got up which made the incredible number of 4000 revolutions in a second. A modification of this was afterward used on the French Atlantic lines for making an artificial horizon to take observations for position at sea. In connection with this a gentleman came to me a number of years afterward, and I got out a part of some plans for him. He wanted to make a gigantic gyroscope weighing several tons, to be run by an electric motor and put on a sailing ship. He wanted this gyroscope to keep a platform perfectly horizontal, no matter how rough the sea was. Upon this platform he was going to mount a telescope to observe an eclipse off the Gold Coast of Africa. But for some reason it was never completed.

"Pasteur invited me to come down to the Institute, and I went and had quite a chat with him. I saw a large number of persons being inoculated, and also the whole modus operandi, which was very interesting. I saw one beautiful boy about ten, the son of an English lord. His father was with him. He had been bitten in the face, and was taking the treatment. I said to Pasteur, 'Will he live?' 'No,' said he, 'the boy will be dead in six days. He was bitten too near the top of the spinal column, and came too late!'"

Edison has no opinion to offer as an expert on art, but has his own standard of taste: "Of course I visited the Louvre and saw the Old Masters, which I could not enjoy. And I attended the Luxembourg, with modern masters, which I enjoyed greatly. To my mind, the Old Masters are not art, and I suspect that many others are of the same opinion; and that their value is in their scarcity and in the variety of men with lots of money." Somewhat akin to this is a shrewd comment on one feature of the Exposition: "I spent several days in the Exposition at Paris. I remember going to the exhibit of the Kimberley diamond mines, and they kindly permitted me to take diamonds from some of the blue earth which they were washing by machinery to exhibit the mine operations. I found several beautiful diamonds, but they seemed a little light weight to me when I was picking them out. They were diamonds for exhibition purposes --probably glass."

This did not altogether complete the European trip of 1889, for Edison wished to see Helmholtz. "After leaving Paris we went to Berlin. The French papers then came out and attacked me because I went to Germany; and said I was now going over to the enemy. I visited all the things of

interest in Berlin; and then on my way home I went with Helmholtz
and Siemens in a private compartment to the meeting of the German
Association of Science at Heidelberg, and spent two days there. When
I started from Berlin on the trip, I began to tell American stories.
Siemens was very fond of these stories and would laugh immensely at
them, and could see the points and the humor, by his imagination; but
Helmholtz could not see one of them. Siemens would quickly, in
German, explain the point, but Helmholtz could not see it, although he
understood English, which Siemens could speak. Still the explanations
were made in German. I always wished I could have understood Siemens's
explanations of the points of those stories. At Heidelberg, my
assistant, Mr. Wangemann, an accomplished German-American, showed the
phonograph before the Association."

Then came the trip from the Continent to England, of which this will
certainly pass as a graphic picture: "When I crossed over to England
I had heard a good deal about the terrors of the English Channel as
regards seasickness. I had been over the ocean three times and did not
know what seasickness was, so far as I was concerned myself. I was told
that while a man might not get seasick on the ocean, if he met a good
storm on the Channel it would do for him. When we arrived at Calais
to cross over, everybody made for the restaurant. I did not care about
eating, and did not go to the restaurant, but my family did. I walked
out and tried to find the boat. Going along the dock I saw two small
smokestacks sticking up, and looking down saw a little boat. 'Where is
the steamer that goes across the Channel?' 'This is the boat.' There had
been a storm in the North Sea that had carried away some of the boats on
the German steamer, and it certainly looked awful tough outside. I said
to the man: 'Will that boat live in that sea?' 'Oh yes,' he said, 'but
we've had a bad storm.' So I made up my mind that perhaps I would get
sick this time. The managing director of the English railroad owning
this line was Forbes, who heard I was coming over, and placed the
private saloon at my disposal. The moment my family got in the room with
the French lady's maid and the rest, they commenced to get sick, so I
felt pretty sure I was in for it. We started out of the little inlet
and got into the Channel, and that boat went in seventeen directions
simultaneously. I waited awhile to see what was going to occur, and then
went into the smoking-compartment. Nobody was there. By-and-by the fun
began. Sounds of all kinds and varieties were heard in every direction.
They were all sick. There must have been 100 people aboard. I didn't
see a single exception except the waiters and myself. I asked one of the
waiters concerning the boat itself, and was taken to see the engineer,
and went down to look at the engines, and saw the captain. But I kept
mostly in the smoking-room. I was smoking a big cigar, and when a man
looked in I would give a big puff, and every time they saw that they
would go away and begin again. The English Channel is a holy terror, all
right, but it didn't affect me. I must be out of balance."

While in Paris, Edison had met Sir John Pender, the English "cable
king," and had received an invitation from him to make a visit to his
country residence: "Sir John Pender, the master of the cable system of
the world at that time, I met in Paris. I think he must have lived among
a lot of people who were very solemn, because I went out riding with
him in the Bois de Boulogne and started in to tell him American stories.

Although he was a Scotchman he laughed immoderately. He had the faculty of understanding and quickly seeing the point of the stories; and for three days after I could not get rid of him. Finally I made him a promise that I would go to his country house at Foot's Cray, near London. So I went there, and spent two or three days telling him stories.

"While at Foot's Cray, I met some of the backers of Ferranti, then putting up a gigantic alternating-current dynamo near London to send ten or fifteen thousand volts up into the main district of the city for electric lighting. I think Pender was interested. At any rate the people invited to dinner were very much interested, and they questioned me as to what I thought of the proposition. I said I hadn't any thought about it, and could not give any opinion until I saw it. So I was taken up to London to see the dynamo in course of construction and the methods employed; and they insisted I should give them some expression of my views. While I gave them my opinion, it was reluctantly; I did not want to do so. I thought that commercially the thing was too ambitious, that Ferranti's ideas were too big, just then; that he ought to have started a little smaller until he was sure. I understand that this installation was not commercially successful, as there were a great many troubles. But Ferranti had good ideas, and he was no small man."

Incidentally it may be noted here that during the same year (1889) the various manufacturing Edison lighting interests in America were brought together, under the leadership of Mr. Henry Villard, and consolidated in the Edison General Electric Company with a capital of no less than $12,000,000 on an eight-per-cent.-dividend basis. The numerous Edison central stations all over the country represented much more than that sum, and made a splendid outlet for the product of the factories. A few years later came the consolidation with the Thomson-Houston interests in the General Electric Company, which under the brilliant and vigorous management of President C. A. Coffin has become one of the greatest manufacturing institutions of the country, with an output of apparatus reaching toward $75,000,000 annually. The net result of both financial operations was, however, to detach Edison from the special field of invention to which he had given so many of his most fruitful years; and to close very definitely that chapter of his life, leaving him free to develop other ideas and interests as set forth in these volumes.

It might appear strange on the surface, but one of the reasons that most influenced Edison to regrets in connection with the "big trade" of 1889 was that it separated him from his old friend and ally, Bergmann, who, on selling out, saw a great future for himself in Germany, went there, and realized it. Edison has always had an amused admiration for Bergmann, and his "social side" is often made evident by his love of telling stories about those days of struggle. Some of the stories were told for this volume. "Bergmann came to work for me as a boy," says Edison. "He started in on stock-quotation printers. As he was a rapid workman and paid no attention to the clock, I took a fancy to him, and gave him piece-work. He contrived so many little tools to cheapen the work that he made lots of money. I even helped him get up tools until it occurred to me that this was too rapid a process of getting rid of my money, as I hadn't the heart to cut the price when it was originally fair. After a year or so, Bergmann got enough money to start a small shop in Wooster Street, New York, and it was at this shop that the first phonographs were made for sale. Then came the carbon telephone transmitter, a large number of which were made by Bergmann for the Western Union. Finally came the electric light. A dynamo was installed in Bergmann's shop to permit him to test the various small devices which he was then making for the system. He rented power from a Jew who owned the building. Power was supplied from a fifty-horse-power engine to other tenants on the several floors. Soon after the introduction of the big dynamo machine, the landlord appeared in the shop and insisted that Bergmann was using more power than he was paying for, and said that lately the belt on the engine was slipping and squealing. Bergmann maintained that he must be mistaken. The landlord kept going among his tenants and finally discovered the dynamo. 'Oh! Mr. Bergmann, now I know where my power goes to,' pointing to the dynamo. Bergmann gave him a withering look of scorn, and said, 'Come here and I will show you.' Throwing off the belt and disconnecting the wires, he spun the armature around by hand. 'There,' said Bergmann, 'you see it's not here that you must look for your loss.' This satisfied the landlord, and he started off to his other tenants. He did not know that that machine, when the wires were connected, could stop his engine.

"Soon after, the business had grown so large that E. H. Johnson and I went in as partners, and Bergmann rented an immense factory building at the corner of Avenue B and East Seventeenth Street, New York, six stories high and covering a quarter of a block. Here were made all the small things used on the electric-lighting system, such as sockets, chandeliers, switches, meters, etc. In addition, stock tickers, telephones, telephone switchboards, and typewriters were made the Hammond typewriters were perfected and made there. Over 1500 men were finally employed. This shop was very successful both scientifically and financially. Bergmann was a man of great executive ability and carried economy of manufacture to the limit. Among all the men I have had associated with me, he had the commercial instinct most highly developed."

One need not wonder at Edison's reminiscent remark that, "In any trade any of my 'boys' made with Bergmann he always got the best of them, no matter what it was. One time there was to be a convention of the managers of Edison illuminating companies at Chicago. There were a lot of representatives from the East, and a private car was hired. At Jersey City a poker game was started by one of the delegates. Bergmann was induced to enter the game. This was played right through to Chicago without any sleep, but the boys didn't mind that. I had gotten them immune to it. Bergmann had won all the money, and when the porter came in and said 'Chicago,' Bergmann jumped up and said: 'What! Chicago! I thought it was only Philadelphia!'"

But perhaps this further story is a better indication of developed humor and shrewdness: "A man by the name of Epstein had been in the habit of buying brass chips and trimmings from the lathes, and in some way Bergmann found out that he had been cheated. This hurt his pride, and he determined to get even. One day Epstein appeared and said: 'Good-morning, Mr. Bergmann, have you any chips to-day?' 'No,' said

Bergmann, 'I have none.' 'That's strange, Mr. Bergmann; won't you look?' No, he wouldn't look; he knew he had none. Finally Epstein was so persistent that Bergmann called an assistant and told him to go and see if he had any chips. He returned and said they had the largest and finest lot they ever had. Epstein went up to several boxes piled full of chips, and so heavy that he could not lift even one end of a box. 'Now, Mr. Bergmann,' said Epstein, 'how much for the lot?' 'Epstein,' said Bergmann, 'you have cheated me, and I will no longer sell by the lot, but will sell only by the pound.' No amount of argument would apparently change Bergmann's determination to sell by the pound, but finally Epstein got up to $250 for the lot, and Bergmann, appearing as if disgusted, accepted and made him count out the money. Then he said: 'Well, Epstein, good-bye, I've got to go down to Wall Street.' Epstein and his assistant then attempted to lift the boxes to carry them out, but couldn't; and then discovered that calculations as to quantity had been thrown out because the boxes had all been screwed down to the floor and mostly filled with boards with a veneer of brass chips. He made such a scene that he had to be removed by the police. I met him several days afterward and he said he had forgiven Mr. Bergmann, as he was such a smart business man, and the scheme was so ingenious.

"One day as a joke I filled three or four sheets of foolscap paper with a jumble of figures and told Bergmann they were calculations showing the great loss of power from blowing the factory whistle. Bergmann thought it real, and never after that would he permit the whistle to blow."

Another glimpse of the "social side" is afforded in the following little series of pen-pictures of the same place and time: "I had my laboratory at the top of the Bergmann works, after moving from Menlo Park. The building was six stories high. My father came there when he was eighty years of age. The old man had powerful lungs. In fact, when I was examined by the Mutual Life Insurance Company, in 1873, my lung expansion was taken by the doctor, and the old gentleman was there at the time. He said to the doctor: 'I wish you would take my lung expansion, too.' The doctor took it, and his surprise was very great, as it was one of the largest on record. I think it was five and one-half inches. There were only three or four could beat it. Little Bergmann hadn't much lung power. The old man said to him, one day: 'Let's run up-stairs.' Bergmann agreed and ran up. When they got there Bergmann was all done up, but my father never showed a sign of it. There was an elevator there, and each day while it was travelling up I held the stem of my Waterbury watch up against the column in the elevator shaft and it finished the winding by the time I got up the six stories." This original method of reducing the amount of physical labor involved in watch-winding brings to mind another instance of shrewdness mentioned by Edison, with regard to his newsboy days. Being asked whether he did not get imposed upon with bad bank-bills, he replied that he subscribed to a bank-note detector and consulted it closely whenever a note of any size fell into his hands. He was then less than fourteen years old.

The conversations with Edison that elicited these stories brought out some details as to peril that attends experimentation. He has confronted many a serious physical risk, and counts himself lucky to have come through without a scratch or scar. Four instances of personal danger may be noted in his own language: "When I started at Menlo, I had an electric furnace for welding rare metals that I did not know about very clearly. I was in the dark-room, where I had a lot of chloride of sulphur, a very corrosive liquid. I did not know that it would decompose by water. I poured in a beakerful of water, and the whole thing exploded and threw a lot of it into my eyes. I ran to the hydrant, leaned over backward, opened my eyes, and ran the hydrant water right into them. But it was two weeks before I could see.

"The next time we just saved ourselves. I was making some stuff to squirt into filaments for the incandescent lamp. I made about a pound of it. I had used ammonia and bromine. I did not know it at the time, but I had made bromide of nitrogen. I put the large bulk of it in three filters, and after it had been washed and all the water had come through the filter, I opened the three filters and laid them on a hot steam plate to dry with the stuff. While I and Mr. Sadler, one of my assistants, were working near it, there was a sudden flash of light, and a very smart explosion. I said to Sadler: 'What is that?' 'I don't know,' he said, and we paid no attention. In about half a minute there was a sharp concussion, and Sadler said: 'See, it is that stuff on the steam plate.' I grabbed the whole thing and threw it in the sink, and poured water on it. I saved a little of it and found it was a terrific explosive. The reason why those little preliminary explosions took place was that a little had spattered out on the edge of the filter paper, and had dried first and exploded. Had the main body exploded there would have been nothing left of the laboratory I was working in.

"At another time, I had a briquetting machine for briquetting iron ore. I had a lever held down by a powerful spring, and a rod one inch in diameter and four feet long. While I was experimenting with it, and standing beside it, a washer broke, and that spring threw the rod right up to the ceiling with a blast; and it came down again just within an inch of my nose, and went clear through a two-inch plank. That was 'within an inch of your life,' as they say.

"In my experimental plant for concentrating iron ore in the northern part of New Jersey, we had a vertical drier, a column about nine feet square and eighty feet high. At the bottom there was a space where two men could go through a hole; and then all the rest of the column was filled with baffle plates. One day this drier got blocked, and the ore would not run down. So I and the vice-president of the company, Mr. Mallory, crowded through the manhole to see why the ore would not come down. After we got in, the ore did come down and there were fourteen tons of it above us. The men outside knew we were in there, and they had a great time digging us out and getting air to us."

Such incidents brought out in narration the fact that many of the men working with him had been less fortunate, particularly those who had experimented with the Roentgen X-ray, whose ravages, like those of leprosy, were responsible for the mutilation and death of at least one expert assistant. In the early days of work on the incandescent lamp, also, there was considerable trouble with mercury. "I had a series of vacuum-pumps worked by mercury and used for exhausting experimental incandescent lamps. The main pipe, which was full of mercury, was about seven and one-half feet from the floor. Along the length of the pipe were outlets to which thick rubber tubing was connected, each tube to a pump. One day, while experimenting with the mercury pump, my assistant, an awkward country lad from a farm on Staten Island, who had adenoids in his nose and breathed through his mouth, which was always wide open, was looking up at this pipe, at a small leak of mercury, when the rubber tube came off and probably two pounds of mercury went into his mouth and down his throat, and got through his system somehow. In a short time he became salivated, and his teeth got loose. He went home, and shortly his mother appeared at the laboratory with a horsewhip, which she proposed to use on the proprietor. I was fortunately absent, and she was mollified somehow by my other assistants. I had given the boy considerable iodide of potassium to prevent salivation, but it did no good in this case.

"When the first lamp-works were started at Menlo Park, one of my experiments seemed to show that hot mercury gave a better vacuum in the lamp than cold mercury. I thereupon started to heat it. Soon all the men got salivated, and things looked serious; but I found that in the mirror factories, where mercury was used extensively, the French Government made the giving of iodide of potassium compulsory to prevent salivation. I carried out this idea, and made every man take a dose every day, but there was great opposition, and hot mercury was finally abandoned."

It will have been gathered that Edison has owed his special immunity from "occupational diseases" not only to luck but to unusual powers of endurance, and a strong physique, inherited, no doubt, from his father. Mr. Mallory mentions a little fact that bears on this exceptional quality of bodily powers. "I have often been surprised at Edison's wonderful capacity for the instant visual perception of differences in materials that were invisible to others until he would patiently point them out. This had puzzled me for years, but one day I was unexpectedly let into part of the secret. For some little time past Mr. Edison had noticed that he was bothered somewhat in reading print, and I asked him to have an oculist give him reading-glasses. He partially promised, but never took time to attend to it. One day he and I were in the city, and as Mrs. Edison had spoken to me about it, and as we happened to have an hour to spare, I persuaded him to go to an oculist with me. Using no names, I asked the latter to examine the gentleman's eyes. He did so very conscientiously, and it was an interesting experience, for he was kept busy answering Mr. Edison's numerous questions. When the oculist finished, he turned to me and said: 'I have been many years in the business, but have never seen an optic nerve like that of this gentleman. An ordinary optic nerve is about the thickness of a thread, but his is like a cord. He must be a remarkable man in some walk of life. Who is he?'"

It has certainly required great bodily vigor and physical capacity to sustain such fatigue as Edison has all his life imposed upon himself, to the extent on one occasion of going five days without sleep. In a conversation during 1909, he remarked, as though it were nothing out of the way, that up to seven years previously his average of daily working hours was nineteen and one-half, but that since then he figured it at eighteen. He said he stood it easily, because he was interested in everything, and was reading and studying all the time. For instance, he had gone to bed the night before exactly at twelve and had arisen at 4.30 A. M. to read some New York law reports. It was suggested that the secret of it might be that he did not live in the past, but was always looking forward to a greater future, to which he replied: "Yes, that's it. I don't live with the past; I am living for to-day and to-morrow. I am interested in every department of science, arts, and manufacture. I read all the time on astronomy, chemistry, biology, physics, music, metaphysics, mechanics, and other branches--political economy, electricity, and, in fact, all things that are making for progress in the world. I get all the proceedings of the scientific societies, the principal scientific and trade journals, and read them. I also read The Clipper, The Police Gazette, The Billboard, The Dramatic Mirror, and a lot of similar publications, for I like to know what is going on. In this way I keep up to date, and live in a great moving world of my own, and, what's more, I enjoy every minute of it." Referring to some event of the past, he said: "Spilt milk doesn't interest me. I have spilt lots of it, and while I have always felt it for a few days, it is quickly forgotten, and I turn again to the future." During another talk on kindred affairs it was suggested to Edison that, as he had worked so hard all his life, it was about time for him to think somewhat of the pleasures of travel and the social side of life. To which he replied laughingly: "I already have a schedule worked out. From now until I am seventy-five years of age, I expect to keep more or less busy with my regular work, not, however, working as many hours or as hard as I have in the past. At seventy five I expect to wear loud waistcoats with fancy buttons; also gaiter tops; at eighty I expect to learn how to play bridge whist and talk foolishly to the ladies. At eighty-five I expect to wear a full-dress suit every evening at dinner, and at ninety--well, I never plan more than thirty years ahead."

The reference to clothes is interesting, as it is one of the few subjects in which Edison has no interest. It rather bores him. His dress is always of the plainest; in fact, so plain that, at the Bergmann shops in New York, the children attending a parochial Catholic school were wont to salute him with the finger to the head, every time he went by. Upon inquiring, he found that they took him for a priest, with his dark garb, smooth-shaven face, and serious expression. Edison says: "I get a suit that fits me; then I compel the tailors to use that as a jig or pattern or blue-print to make others by. For many years a suit was used as a measurement; once or twice they took fresh measurements, but these didn't fit and they had to go back. I eat to keep my weight constant, hence I need never change measurements." In regard to this, Mr. Mallory furnishes a bit of chat as follows: "In a lawsuit in which I was a witness, I went out to lunch with the lawyers on both sides, and the lawyer who had been cross-examining me stated that he had for a client a Fifth Avenue tailor, who had told him that he had made all of Mr. Edison's clothes for the last twenty years, and that he had never seen him. He said that some twenty years ago a suit was sent to him from Orange, and measurements were made from it, and that every suit since had been made from these measurements. I may add, from my own personal observation, that in Mr. Edison's clothes there is no evidence but that every new suit that he has worn in that time looks as if he had been specially measured for it, which shows how very little he has changed physically in the last twenty years."

Edison has never had any taste for amusements, although he will indulge in the game of "Parchesi" and has a billiard-table in his house. The coming of the automobile was a great boon to him, because it gave him a form of outdoor sport in which he could indulge in a spirit of observation, without the guilty feeling that he was wasting valuable time. In his automobile he has made long tours, and with his family has particularly indulged his taste for botany. That he has had the usual experience in running machines will be evidenced by the following little story from Mr. Mallory: "About three years ago I had a motor-car of a make of which Mr. Edison had already two cars; and when the car was received I made inquiry as to whether any repair parts were carried by any of the various garages in Easton, Pennsylvania, near our cement works. I learned that this particular car was the only one in Easton. Knowing that Mr. Edison had had an experience lasting two or three years with this particular make of car, I determined to ask him for information relative to repair parts; so the next time I was at the laboratory I told him I was unable to get any repair parts in Easton, and that I wished to order some of the most necessary, so that, in case of breakdowns, I would not be compelled to lose the use of the car for several days until the parts came from the automobile factory. I asked his advice as to what I should order, to which he replied: 'I don't think it will be necessary to order an extra top.'" Since that episode, which will probably be appreciated by most automobilists, Edison has taken up the electric automobile, and is now using it as well as developing it. One of the cars equipped with his battery is the Bailey, and Mr. Bee tells the following story in regard to it: "One day Colonel Bailey, of Amesbury, Massachusetts, who was visiting the Automobile Show in New York, came out to the laboratory to see Mr. Edison, as the latter had expressed a desire to talk with him on his next visit to the metropolis. When he arrived at the laboratory, Mr. Edison, who had been up all night experimenting, was asleep on the cot in the library. As a rule we never wake Mr. Edison from sleep, but as he wanted to see Colonel Bailey, who had to go, I felt that an exception should be made, so I went and tapped him on the shoulder. He awoke at once, smiling, jumped up, was instantly himself as usual, and advanced and greeted the visitor. His very first question was: 'Well, Colonel, how did you come out on that experiment?'--referring to some suggestions he had made at their last meeting a year before. For a minute Colonel Bailey did not recall what was referred to; but a few words from Mr. Edison brought it back to his remembrance, and he reported that the results had justified Mr. Edison's expectations."

It might be expected that Edison would have extreme and even radical ideas on the subject of education--and he has, as well as a perfect readiness to express them, because he considers that time is wasted on things that are not essential: "What we need," he has said, "are men capable of doing work. I wouldn't give a penny for the ordinary college graduate, except those from the institutes of technology. Those coming up from the ranks are a darned sight better than the others. They aren't filled up with Latin, philosophy, and the rest of that ninny stuff." A further remark of his is: "What the country needs now is the practical skilled engineer, who is capable of doing everything. In three or four centuries, when the country is settled, and commercialism is diminished, there will be time for the literary men. At present we want engineers, industrial men, good business-like managers, and railroad men." It is hardly to be marvelled at that such views should elicit warm protest, summed up in the comment: "Mr. Edison and many like him see in reverse the course of human progress. Invention does not smooth the way for the practical men and make them possible. There is always too much danger of neglecting thoughts for things, ideas for machinery. No theory of education that aggravates this danger is consistent with national well-being."

Edison is slow to discuss the great mysteries of life, but is of reverential attitude of mind, and ever tolerant of others' beliefs. He is not a religious man in the sense of turning to forms and creeds, but, as might be expected, is inclined as an inventor and creator to argue from the basis of "design" and thence to infer a designer. "After years of watching the processes of nature," he says, "I can no more doubt the existence of an Intelligence that is running things than I do of the existence of myself. Take, for example, the substance water that forms the crystals known as ice. Now, there are hundreds of combinations that form crystals, and every one of them, save ice, sinks in water. Ice, I say, doesn't, and it is rather lucky for us mortals, for if it had done so, we would all be dead. Why? Simply because if ice sank to the bottoms of rivers, lakes, and oceans as fast as it froze, those places would be frozen up and there would be no water left. That is only one example out of thousands that to me prove beyond the possibility of a doubt that some vast Intelligence is governing this and other planets."

A few words as to the domestic and personal side of Edison's life, to which many incidental references have already been made in these pages. He was married in 1873 to Miss Mary Stillwell, who died in 1884, leaving three children--Thomas Alva, William Leslie, and Marion Estelle.

Mr. Edison was married again in 1886 to Miss Mina Miller, daughter of Mr. Lewis Miller, a distinguished pioneer inventor and manufacturer in the field of agricultural machinery, and equally entitled to fame as the father of the "Chautauqua idea," and the founder with Bishop Vincent of the original Chautauqua, which now has so many replicas all over the country, and which started in motion one of the great modern educational and moral forces in America. By this marriage there are three children--Charles, Madeline, and Theodore.

For over a score of years, dating from his marriage to Miss Miller, Edison's happy and perfect domestic life has been spent at Glenmont, a beautiful property acquired at that time in Llewellyn Park, on the higher slopes of Orange Mountain, New Jersey, within easy walking distance of the laboratory at the foot of the hill in West Orange. As noted already, the latter part of each winter is spent at Fort Myers, Florida, where Edison has, on the banks of the Calahoutchie River, a plantation home that is in many ways a miniature copy of the home and laboratory up North. Glenmont is a rather elaborate and florid building in Queen Anne English style, of brick, stone, and wooden beams showing on the exterior, with an abundance of gables and balconies. It is set in an environment of woods and sweeps of lawn, flanked by unusually large conservatories, and always bright in summer with glowing flower beds. It would be difficult to imagine Edison in a stiffly formal house, and this big, cozy, three-story, rambling mansion has an easy freedom about it, without and within, quite in keeping with the genius of the inventor, but revealing at every turn traces of feminine taste and culture. The ground floor, consisting chiefly of broad drawing-rooms, parlors, and dining-hall, is chiefly noteworthy for the "den," or lounging-room, at the end of the main axis, where the family and friends are likely to be found in the evening hours, unless the party has withdrawn for more intimate social intercourse to the interesting and fascinating private library on the floor above. The lounging-room on the ground floor is more or less of an Edison museum, for it is littered with souvenirs from great people, and with mementos of travel, all related to some event or episode. A large cabinet contains awards, decorations, and medals presented to Edison, accumulating in the course of a long career, some of which may be seen in the illustration opposite. Near by may be noticed a bronze replica of the Edison gold medal which was founded in the American Institute of Electrical Engineers, the first award of which was made to Elihu Thomson during the present year (1910). There are statues of serpentine marble, gifts of the late Tsar of Russia, whose admiration is also represented by a gorgeous inlaid and enamelled cigar-case.

There are typical bronze vases from the Society of Engineers of Japan, and a striking desk-set of writing apparatus from Krupp, all the pieces being made out of tiny but massive guns and shells of Krupp steel. In addition to such bric-a-brac and bibelots of all kinds are many pictures and photographs, including the original sketches of the reception given to Edison in 1889 by the Paris Figaro, and a letter from Madame Carnot, placing the Presidential opera-box at the disposal of Mr. and Mrs. Edison. One of the most conspicuous features of the room is a phonograph equipment on which the latest and best productions by the greatest singers and musicians can always be heard, but which Edison himself is everlastingly experimenting with, under the incurable delusion that this domestic retreat is but an extension of his laboratory.

The big library--semi-boudoir--up-stairs is also very expressive of the home life of Edison, but again typical of his nature and disposition, for it is difficult to overlay his many technical books and scientific periodicals with a sufficiently thick crust of popular magazines or current literature to prevent their outcropping into evidence. In like manner the chat and conversation here, however lightly it may begin, turns invariably to large questions and deep problems, especially in the fields of discovery and invention; and Edison, in an easy-chair, will sit through the long evenings till one or two in the morning, pulling meditatively at his eyebrows, quoting something he has just read pertinent to the discussion, hearing and telling new stories with gusto, offering all kinds of ingenious suggestions, and without fail getting hold of pads and sheets of paper on which to make illustrative sketches. He is wonderfully handy with the pencil, and will sometimes amuse himself, while chatting, with making all kinds of fancy bits of penmanship, twisting his signature into circles and squares, but always writing straight lines--so straight they could not be ruled truer. Many a night it is a question of getting Edison to bed, for he would much rather probe a problem than eat or sleep; but at whatever hour the visitor retires or gets up, he is sure to find the master of the house on hand, serene and reposeful, and just as brisk at dawn as when he allowed the conversation to break up at midnight. The ordinary routine of daily family life is of course often interrupted by receptions and parties, visits to the billiard-room, the entertainment of visitors, the departure to and return from college, at vacation periods, of the young people, and matters relating to the many social and philanthropic causes in which Mrs. Edison is actively interested; but, as a matter of fact, Edison's round of toil and relaxation is singularly uniform and free from agitation, and that is the way he would rather have it.

Edison at sixty-three has a fine physique, and being free from serious ailments of any kind, should carry on the traditions of his long-lived ancestors as to a vigorous old age. His hair has whitened, but is still thick and abundant, and though he uses glasses for certain work, his gray-blue eyes are as keen and bright and deeply lustrous as ever, with the direct, searching look in them that they have ever worn. He stands five feet nine and one-half inches high, weighs one hundred and seventy-five pounds, and has not varied as to weight in a quarter of a century, although as a young man he was slim to gauntness. He is very abstemious, hardly ever touching alcohol, caring little for meat, but fond of fruit, and never averse to a strong cup of coffee or a good cigar. He takes extremely little exercise, although his good color and quickness of step would suggest to those who do not know better that he is in the best of training, and one who lives in the open air.

His simplicity as to clothes has already been described. One would be startled to see him with a bright tie, a loud checked suit, or a fancy waistcoat, and yet there is a curious sense of fastidiousness about the plain things he delights in. Perhaps he is not wholly responsible personally for this state of affairs. In conversation Edison is direct, courteous, ready to discuss a topic with anybody worth talking to, and, in spite of his sore deafness, an excellent listener. No one ever goes away from Edison in doubt as to what he thinks or means, but he is ever shy and diffident to a degree if the talk turns on himself rather than on his work.

If the authors were asked, after having written the foregoing pages, to explain here the reason for Edison's success, based upon their observations so far made, they would first answer that he combines with a vigorous and normal physical structure a mind capable of clear and logical thinking, and an imagination of unusual activity. But this would by no means offer a complete explanation. There are many men of equal bodily and mental vigor who have not achieved a tithe of his accomplishment. What other factors are there to be taken into consideration to explain this phenomenon? First, a stolid, almost phlegmatic, nervous system which takes absolutely no notice of ennui--a system like that of a Chinese ivory-carver who works day after day and month after month on a piece of material no larger than your hand. No better illustration of this characteristic can be found than in the development of the nickel pocket for the storage battery, an element the size of a short lead-pencil, on which upward of five years were spent in experiments, costing over a million dollars, day after day, always apparently with the same tubes but with small variations carefully tabulated in the note-books. To an ordinary person the mere sight of such a tube would have been as distasteful, certainly after a week or so, as the smell of a quail to a man striving to eat one every day for a month, near the end of his gastronomic ordeal. But to Edison these small perforated steel tubes held out as much of a fascination at the end of five years as when the search was first begun, and every morning found him as eager to begin the investigation anew as if the battery was an absolutely novel problem to which his thoughts had just been directed.

Another and second characteristic of Edison's personality contributing so strongly to his achievements is an intense, not to say courageous, optimism in which no thought of failure can enter, an optimism born of self-confidence, and becoming--after forty or fifty years of experience more and more a sense of certainty in the accomplishment of success. In the overcoming of difficulties he has the same intellectual pleasure as the chess-master when confronted with a problem requiring all the efforts of his skill and experience to solve. To advance along smooth and pleasant paths, to encounter no obstacles, to wrestle with no difficulties and hardships--such has absolutely no fascination to him. He meets obstruction with the keen delight of a strong man battling with the waves and opposing them in sheer enjoyment, and the greater and more apparently overwhelming the forces that may tend to sweep him back, the more vigorous his own efforts to forge through them. At the conclusion of the ore-milling experiments, when practically his entire fortune was sunk in an enterprise that had to be considered an impossibility, when at the age of fifty he looked back upon five or six years of intense activity expended apparently for naught, when everything seemed most black and the financial clouds were quickly gathering on the horizon, not the slightest idea of repining entered his mind. The main experiment had succeeded--he had accomplished what he sought for. Nature at another point had outstripped him, yet he had broadened his own sum of knowledge to a prodigious extent. It was only during the past summer (1910) that one of the writers spent a Sunday with him riding over the beautiful New Jersey roads in an automobile, Edison in the highest spirits and pointing out with the keenest enjoyment the many beautiful views of valley and wood. The wanderings led to the old ore-milling plant at Edison, now practically a mass of deserted buildings all going to decay. It was a depressing sight, marking such titanic but futile struggles with nature. To Edison, however, no trace of sentiment or regret occurred, and the whole ruins were apparently as much a matter of unconcern as if he were viewing the remains of Pompeii. Sitting on the porch of the White House, where he lived during that period, in the light of the setting sun, his fine face in repose, he looked as placidly over the scene as a happy farmer over a field of ripening corn. All that he said was: "I never felt better in my life than during the five years I worked here. Hard work, nothing to divert my thought, clear air and simple food made my life very pleasant. We learned a great deal. It will be of benefit to some one some time." Similarly, in connection with the storage battery, after having experimented continuously for three years, it was found to fall below his expectations, and its manufacture had to be stopped. Hundreds of thousands of dollars had been spent on the experiments, and, largely without Edison's consent, the battery had been very generally exploited in the press. To stop meant not only to pocket a great loss already incurred, facing a dark and uncertain future, but to most men animated by ordinary human feelings, it meant more than anything else, an injury to personal pride. Pride? Pooh! that had nothing to do with the really serious practical problem, and the writers can testify that at the moment when his decision was reached, work stopped and the long vista ahead was peered into, Edison was as little concerned as if he had concluded that, after all, perhaps peach-pie might be better for present diet than apple-pie. He has often said that time meant very little to him, that he had but a small realization of its passage, and that ten or twenty years were as nothing when considering the development of a vital invention.

These references to personal pride recall another characteristic of Edison wherein he differs from most men. There are many individuals who derive an intense and not improper pleasure in regalia or military garments, with plenty of gold braid and brass buttons, and thus arrayed, in appearing before their friends and neighbors. Putting at the head of the procession the man who makes his appeal to public attention solely because of the brilliancy of his plumage, and passing down the ranks through the multitudes having a gradually decreasing sense of vanity in their personal accomplishment, Edison would be placed at the very end. Reference herein has been made to the fact that one of the two great English universities wished to confer a degree upon him, but that he was unable to leave his work for the brief time necessary to accept the honor. At that occasion it was pointed out to him that he should make every possible sacrifice to go, that the compliment was great, and that but few Americans had been so recognized. It was hopeless--an appeal based on sentiment. Before him was something real--work to be accomplished--a problem to be solved. Beyond, was a prize as intangible as the button of the Legion of Honor, which he concealed from his friends that they might not feel he was "showing off." The fact is that Edison cares little for the approval of the world, but that he cares everything for the approval of himself. Difficult as it may be--perhaps impossible--to trace its origin, Edison possesses what he would probably call a well-developed case of New England conscience, for whose approval he is incessantly occupied.

These, then, may be taken as the characteristics of Edison that have enabled him to accomplish more than most men--a strong body, a clear and active mind, a developed imagination, a capacity of great mental and physical concentration, an iron-clad nervous system that knows no ennui, intense optimism, and courageous self-confidence. Any one having these capacities developed to the same extent, with the same opportunities for use, would probably accomplish as much. And yet there is a peculiarity about him that so far as is known has never been referred to before in print. He seems to be conscientiously afraid of appearing indolent, and in consequence subjects himself regularly to unnecessary hardship. Working all night is seldom necessary, or until two or three o'clock in the morning, yet even now he persists in such tests upon his strength. Recently one of the writers had occasion to present to him a long typewritten document of upward of thirty pages for his approval. It was taken home to Glenmont. Edison had a few minor corrections to make, probably not more than a dozen all told. They could have been embodied by interlineations and marginal notes in the ordinary way, and certainly would not have required more than ten or fifteen minutes of his time. Yet what did he do? HE COPIED OUT PAINSTAKINGLY THE ENTIRE PAPER IN LONG HAND, embodying the corrections as he went along, and presented the result of his work the following morning. At the very least such a task must have occupied several hours. How can such a trait--and scores of similar experiences could be given--be explained except by the fact that, evidently, he felt the need of special schooling in industry--that under no circumstances must he allow a thought of indolence to enter his mind?

Undoubtedly in the days to come Edison will not only be recognized as an intellectual prodigy, but as a prodigy of industry--of hard work. In his field as inventor and man of science he stands as clear-cut and secure as the lighthouse on a rock, and as indifferent to the tumult around. But as the "old man"--and before he was thirty years old he was affectionately so called by his laboratory associates--he is a normal, fun-loving, typical American. His sense of humor is intense, but not of the hothouse, overdeveloped variety. One of his favorite jokes is to enter the legal department with an air of great humility and apply for a job as an inventor! Never is he so preoccupied or fretted with cares as not to drop all thought of his work for a few moments to listen to a new story, with a ready smile all the while, and a hearty, boyish laugh at the end. His laugh, in fact, is sometimes almost aboriginal; slapping his hands delightedly on his knees, he rocks back and forth and fairly shouts his pleasure. Recently a daily report of one of his companies that had just been started contained a large order amounting to several thousand dollars, and was returned by him with a miniature sketch of a small individual viewing that particular item through a telescope! His facility in making hasty but intensely graphic sketches is proverbial. He takes great delight in imitating the lingo of the New York street gamin. A dignified person named James may be greeted with: "Hully Gee! Chimmy, when did youse blow in?" He likes to mimic and imitate types, generally, that are distasteful to him. The sanctimonious hypocrite, the sleek speculator, and others whom he has probably encountered in life are done "to the queen's taste."

One very cold winter's day he entered the laboratory library in fine spirits, "doing" the decayed dandy, with imaginary cane under his arm, struggling to put on a pair of tattered imaginary gloves, with a self-satisfied smirk and leer that would have done credit to a real comedian. This particular bit of acting was heightened by the fact that even in the coldest weather he wears thin summer clothes, generally acid-worn and more or less disreputable. For protection he varies the number of his suits of underclothing, sometimes wearing three or four sets, according to the thermometer.

If one could divorce Edison from the idea of work, and could regard him separate and apart from his embodiment as an inventor and man of science, it might truly be asserted that his temperament is essentially mercurial. Often he is in the highest spirits, with all the spontaneity of youth, and again he is depressed, moody, and violently angry. Anger with him, however, is a good deal like the story attributed to Napoleon:

"Sire, how is it that your judgment is not affected by your great rage?"

asked one of his courtiers.

"Because," said the Emperor, "I never allow it to rise above this line," drawing his hand across his throat. Edison has been seen sometimes almost beside himself with anger at a stupid mistake or inexcusable oversight on the part of an assistant, his voice raised to a high pitch, sneeringly expressing his feelings of contempt for the offender; and yet when the culprit, like a bad school-boy, has left the room, Edison has immediately returned to his normal poise, and the incident is a thing of the past. At other times the unsettled condition persists, and his spleen is vented not only on the original instigator but upon others who may have occasion to see him, sometimes hours afterward. When such a fit is on him the word is quickly passed around, and but few of his associates find it necessary to consult with him at the time. The genuine anger can generally be distinguished from the imitation article by those who know him intimately by the fact that when really enraged his forehead between the eyes partakes of a curious rotary movement that cannot be adequately described in words. It is as if the storm-clouds within are moving like a whirling cyclone. As a general rule, Edison does not get genuinely angry at mistakes and other human weaknesses of his subordinates; at best he merely simulates anger. But woe betide the one who has committed an act of bad faith, treachery, dishonesty, or ingratitude; THEN Edison can show what it is for a strong man to get downright mad. But in this respect he is singularly free, and his spells of anger are really few. In fact, those who know him best are continually surprised at his moderation and patience, often when there has been great provocation. People who come in contact with him and who may have occasion to oppose his views, may leave with the impression that he is hot-tempered; nothing could be further from the truth. He argues his point with great vehemence, pounds on the table to emphasize his views, and illustrates his theme with a wealth of apt similes; but, on account of his deafness, it is difficult to make the argument really two-sided. Before the visitor can fully explain his side of the matter some point is brought up that starts Edison off again, and new arguments from his viewpoint are poured forth. This constant interruption is taken by many to mean that Edison has a small opinion of any arguments that oppose him; but he is only intensely in earnest in presenting his own side. If the visitor persists until Edison has seen both sides of the controversy, he is always willing to frankly admit that his own views may be unsound and that his opponent is right. In fact, after such a controversy, both parties going after each other hammer and tongs, the arguments TO HIM being carried on at the very top of one's voice to enable him to hear, and FROM HIM being equally loud in the excitement of the discussion, he has often said: "I see now that my position was absolutely rotten."

Obviously, however, all of these personal characteristics have nothing to do with Edison's position in the world of affairs. They show him to be a plain, easy-going, placid American, with no sense of self-importance, and ready at all times to have his mind turned into a lighter channel. In private life they show him to be a good citizen, a good family man, absolutely moral, temperate in all things, and of great charitableness to all mankind. But what of his position in the age in which he lives? Where does he rank in the mountain range of great

Americans?

It is believed that from the other chapters of this book the reader can formulate his own answer to the question.

INTRODUCTION TO THE APPENDIX

THE reader who has followed the foregoing narrative may feel that inasmuch as it is intended to be an historical document, an appropriate addendum thereto would be a digest of all the inventions of Edison. The desirability of such a digest is not to be denied, but as there are some twenty-five hundred or more inventions to be considered (including those covered by caveats), the task of its preparation would be stupendous. Besides, the resultant data would extend this book into several additional volumes, thereby rendering it of value chiefly to the technical student, but taking it beyond the bounds of biography.

We should, however, deem our presentation of Mr. Edison's work to be imperfectly executed if we neglected to include an intelligible exposition of the broader theoretical principles of his more important inventions. In the following Appendix we have therefore endeavored to present a few brief statements regarding Mr. Edison's principal inventions, classified as to subject-matter and explained in language as free from technicalities as is possible. No attempt has been made to conform with strictly scientific terminology, but, for the benefit of the general reader, well-understood conventional expressions, such as "flow of current," etc., have been employed. It should be borne in mind that each of the following items has been treated as a whole or class, generally speaking, and not as a digest of all the individual patents relating to it. Any one who is sufficiently interested can obtain copies of any of the patents referred to for five cents each by addressing the Commissioner of Patents, Washington, D. C.

APPENDIX

I. THE STOCK PRINTER

IN these modern days, when the Stock Ticker is in universal use, one seldom, if ever, hears the name of Edison coupled with the little instrument whose chatterings have such tremendous import to the whole world. It is of much interest, however, to remember the fact that it was by reason of his notable work in connection with this device that he first became known as an inventor. Indeed, it was through the intrinsic merits of his improvements in stock tickers that he made his real entree into commercial life.

The idea of the ticker did not originate with Edison, as we have already seen in Chapter VII of the preceding narrative, but at the time of his employment with the Western Union, in Boston, in 1868, the crudities of the earlier forms made an impression on his practical mind, and he got out an improved instrument of his own, which he introduced in Boston through the aid of a professional promoter. Edison, then only twenty-one, had less business experience than the promoter, through whose manipulation he soon lost his financial interest in this early ticker enterprise. The narrative tells of his coming to New York in 1869, and immediately plunging into the business of gold and stock reporting. It was at this period that his real work on stock printers commenced, first individually, and later as a co-worker with F. L. Pope. This inventive period extended over a number of years, during which time he took out forty-six patents on stock-printing instruments and devices, two of such patents being issued to Edison and Pope as joint inventors. These various inventions were mostly in the line of development of the art as it progressed during those early years, but out of it all came the Edison universal printer, which entered into very extensive use, and which is still used throughout the United States and in some foreign countries to a considerable extent at this very day.

Edison's inventive work on stock printers has left its mark upon the art as it exists at the present time. In his earlier work he directed his attention to the employment of a single-circuit system, in which only one wire was required, the two operations of setting the type-wheels and of printing being controlled by separate electromagnets which were actuated through polarized relays, as occasion required, one polarity energizing the electromagnet controlling the type-wheels, and the opposite polarity energizing the electromagnet controlling the printing. Later on, however, he changed over to a two-wire circuit, such as shown in Fig. 2 of this article in connection with the universal stock printer. In the earliest days of the stock printer, Edison realized the vital commercial importance of having all instruments recording precisely alike at the same moment, and it was he who first devised (in 1869) the "unison stop," by means of which all connected instruments could at any moment be brought to zero from the central transmitting station, and thus be made to work in correspondence with the central instrument and with one another. He also originated the idea of using only one inking-pad and shifting it from side to side to ink the type-wheels. It was also in Edison's stock printer that the principle of shifting type-wheels was first employed. Hence it will be seen that, as in many other arts, he made a lasting impression in this one by the intrinsic merits of the improvements resulting from his work therein.

We shall not attempt to digest the forty-six patents above named, nor to follow Edison through the progressive steps which led to the completion of his universal printer, but shall simply present a sketch of the instrument itself, and follow with a very brief and general explanation of its theory. The Edison universal printer, as it virtually appears in practice, is illustrated in Fig. 1 below, from which it will be seen that the most prominent parts are the two type-wheels, the inking-pad, and the paper tape feeding from the reel, all appropriately placed in a substantial framework.

The electromagnets and other actuating mechanism cannot be seen plainly in this figure, but are produced diagrammatically in Fig. 2, and somewhat enlarged for convenience of explanation.

It will be seen that there are two electromagnets, one of which, TM, is known as the "type-magnet," and the other, PM, as the "press-magnet," the former having to do with the operation of the type-wheels, and the latter with the pressing of the paper tape against them. As will be seen from the diagram, the armature, A, of the type-magnet has an extension arm, on the end of which is an escapement engaging with a toothed wheel placed at the extremity of the shaft carrying the type-wheels. This extension arm is pivoted at B. Hence, as the armature is alternately attracted when current passes around its electromagnet, and drawn up by the spring on cessation of current, it moves up and down, thus actuating the escapement and causing a rotation of the toothed wheel in the direction of the arrow. This, in turn, brings any desired letters or figures on the type-wheels to a central point, where they may be impressed upon the paper tape. One type-wheel carries letters, and the other one figures. These two wheels are mounted rigidly on a sleeve carried by the wheel-shaft. As it is desired to print from only one type-wheel at a time, it becomes necessary to shift them back and forth from time to time, in order to bring the desired characters in line with the paper tape. This is accomplished through the movements of a three-arm rocking-lever attached to the wheel-sleeve at the end of the shaft. This lever is actuated through the agency of two small pins carried by an arm projecting from the press-lever, PL. As the latter moves up and down the pins play upon the under side of the lower arm of the rocking-lever, thus canting it and pushing the type-wheels to the right or left, as the case may be. The operation of shifting the type-wheels will be given further on.

The press-lever is actuated by the press-magnet. From the diagram it will be seen that the armature of the latter has a long, pivoted extension arm, or platen, trough-like in shape, in which the paper tape runs. It has already been noted that the object of the press-lever is to press this tape against that character of the type-wheel centrally located above it at the moment. It will at once be perceived that this action takes place when current flows through the electromagnet and its armature is attracted downward, the platen again dropping away from the type-wheel as the armature is released upon cessation of current. The paper "feed" is shown at the end of the press-lever, and consists of a push "dog," or pawl, which operates to urge the paper forward as the press-lever descends.

The worm-gear which appears in the diagram on the shaft, near the toothed wheel, forms part of the unison stop above referred to, but this device is not shown in full, in order to avoid unnecessary complications of the drawing.

At the right-hand side of the diagram (Fig. 2) is shown a portion of the transmitting apparatus at a central office. Generally speaking, this consists of a motor-driven cylinder having metallic pins placed at intervals, and arranged spirally, around its periphery. These pins correspond in number to the characters on the type-wheels. A keyboard (not shown) is arranged above the cylinder, having keys lettered and numbered corresponding to the letters and figures on the type-wheels. Upon depressing any one of these keys the motion of the cylinder is arrested when one of its pins is caught and held by the depressed key. When the key is released the cylinder continues in motion. Hence, it is evident that the revolution of the cylinder may be interrupted as often as desired by manipulation of the various keys in transmitting the letters and figures which are to be recorded by the printing instrument. The method of transmission will presently appear.

In the sketch (Fig. 2) there will be seen, mounted upon the cylinder shaft, two wheels made up of metallic segments insulated from each other, and upon the hubs of these wheels are two brushes which connect with the main battery. Resting upon the periphery of these two segmental wheels there are two brushes to which are connected the wires which carry the battery current to the type-magnet and press-magnet, respectively, as the brushes make circuit by coming in contact with the metallic segments. It will be remembered that upon the cylinder there are as many pins as there are characters on the type-wheels of the ticker, and one of the segmental wheels, W, has a like number of metallic segments, while upon the other wheel, W', there are only one-half that number. The wheel W controls the supply of current to the press-magnet, and the wheel W' to the type-magnet. The type-magnet advances the letter and figure wheels one step when the magnet is energized, and a succeeding step when the circuit is broken. Hence, the metallic contact surfaces on wheel W' are, as stated, only half as many as on the wheel W, which controls the press-magnet.

It should be borne in mind, however, that the contact surfaces and insulated surfaces on wheel W' are together equal in number to the characters on the type-wheels, but the retractile spring of TM does half the work of operating the escapement. On the other hand, the wheel W has the full number of contact surfaces, because it must provide for the operative closure of the press-magnet circuit whether the brush B' is in engagement with a metallic segment or an insulated segment of the wheel W'. As the cylinder revolves, the wheels are carried around with its shaft and current impulses flow through the wires to the magnets as the brushes make contact with the metallic segments of these wheels.

One example will be sufficient to convey to the reader an idea of the operation of the apparatus. Assuming, for instance, that it is desired to send out the letters AM to the printer, let us suppose that the pin corresponding to the letter A is at one end of the cylinder and near the upper part of its periphery, and that the letter M is about the centre of the cylinder and near the lower part of its periphery. The operator at the keyboard would depress the letter A, whereupon the cylinder would in its revolution bring the first-named pin against the key. During the rotation of the cylinder a current would pass through wheel W' and actuate TM, drawing down the armature and operating the escapement, which would bring the type-wheel to a point where the letter A would be central as regards the paper tape When the cylinder came to rest, current would flow through the brush of wheel W to PM, and its armature would be attracted, causing the platen to be lifted and thus bringing the paper tape in contact with the type-wheel and printing the letter A. The operator next sends the letter M by depressing the appropriate key. On account of the position of the corresponding pin, the cylinder would make nearly half a revolution before bringing the pin to the key. During this half revolution the segmental wheels have also been turning, and the brushes have transmitted a number of current impulses to TM, which have caused it to operate the escapement a corresponding number of times, thus turning the type-wheels around to the letter M. When the cylinder stops, current once more goes to the press-magnet, and the operation of lifting and printing is repeated. As a matter of fact, current flows over both circuits as the cylinder is rotated, but the press-magnet is purposely made to be comparatively "sluggish" and the narrowness of the segments on wheel W tends to diminish the flow of current in the press circuit until the cylinder comes to rest, when the current continuously flows over that circuit without interruption and fully energizes the press-magnet. The shifting of the type-wheels is brought about as follows: On the keyboard of the transmitter there are two characters known as "dots"--namely, the letter dot and the figure dot. If the operator presses one of these dot keys, it is engaged by an appropriate pin on the revolving cylinder. Meanwhile the type-wheels are rotating, carrying with them the rocking-lever, and current is pulsating over both circuits. When the type-wheels have arrived at the proper point the rocking-lever has been carried to a position where its lower arm is directly over one of the pins on the arm extending from the platen of the press-lever. The cylinder stops, and current operates the sluggish press-magnet, causing its armature to be attracted, thus lifting the platen and its projecting arm. As the arm lifts upward, the pin moves along the under side of the lower arm of the rocking-lever, thus causing it to cant and shift the type-wheels to the right or left, as desired. The principles of operation of this apparatus have been confined to a very brief and general description, but it is believed to be sufficient for the scope of this article.

NOTE.--The illustrations in this article are reproduced from American Telegraphy and Encyclopedia of the Telegraph, by William Maver, Jr., by permission of Maver Publishing Company, New York.

II. THE QUADRUPLEX AND PHONOPLEX

EDISON'S work in stock printers and telegraphy had marked him as a rising man in the electrical art of the period but his invention of quadruplex telegraphy in 1874 was what brought him very prominently before the notice of the public. Duplex telegraphy, or the sending of two separate messages in opposite directions at the same time over one line was known and practiced previous to this time, but quadruplex telegraphy, or the simultaneous sending of four separate messages, two in each direction, over a single line had not been successfully accomplished, although it had been the subject of many an inventor's dream and the object of anxious efforts for many long years.

In the early part of 1873, and for some time afterward, the system invented by Joseph Stearns was the duplex in practical use. In April of that year, however, Edison took up the study of the subject and filed two applications for patents. One of these applications [23] embraced an invention by which two messages could be sent not only duplex, or in opposite directions as above explained, but could also be sent "diplex"--that is to say, in one direction, simultaneously, as separate and distinct messages, over the one line. Thus there was introduced a new feature into the art of multiplex telegraphy, for, whereas duplexing (accomplished by varying the strength of the current) permitted messages to be sent simultaneously from opposite stations, diplexing (achieved by also varying the direction of the current) permitted the simultaneous transmission of two messages from the same station and their separate reception at the distant station.

[Footnote 23: Afterward issued as Patent No. 162,633, April 27, 1875.]

The quadruplex was the tempting goal toward which Edison now constantly turned, and after more than a year's strenuous work he filed a number of applications for patents in the late summer of 1874. Among them was one which was issued some years afterward as Patent No. 480,567, covering his well-known quadruplex. He had improved his own diplex, combined it with the Stearns duplex and thereby produced a system by means of which four messages could be sent over a single line at the same time, two in each direction.

As the reader will probably be interested to learn something of the theoretical principles of this fascinating invention, we shall endeavor to offer a brief and condensed explanation thereof with as little technicality as the subject will permit. This explanation will necessarily be of somewhat elementary character for the benefit of the lay reader, whose indulgence is asked for an occasional reiteration introduced for the sake of clearness of comprehension. While the apparatus and the circuits are seemingly very intricate, the principles are really quite simple, and the difficulty of comprehension is more apparent than real if the underlying phenomena are studied attentively.

At the root of all systems of telegraphy, including multiplex systems, there lies the single basic principle upon which their performance depends--namely, the obtaining of a slight mechanical movement at the more or less distant end of a telegraph line. This is accomplished through the utilization of the phenomena of electromagnetism. These phenomena are easy of comprehension and demonstration. If a rod of soft iron be wound around with a number of turns of insulated wire, and a current of electricity be sent through the wire, the rod will be instantly magnetized and will remain a magnet as long as the current flows; but when the current is cut off the magnetic effect instantly ceases. This device is known as an electromagnet, and the charging and discharging of such a magnet may, of course, be repeated indefinitely. Inasmuch as a magnet has the power of attracting to itself pieces of iron or steel, the basic importance of an electromagnet in telegraphy will be at once apparent when we consider the sounder, whose clicks are familiar to every ear. This instrument consists essentially of an electro-magnet of horseshoe form with its two poles close together, and with its armature, a bar of iron, maintained in close proximity to the poles, but kept normally in a retracted position by a spring. When the distant operator presses down his key the circuit is closed and a current passes along the line and through the (generally two) coils of the electromagnet, thus magnetizing the iron core. Its attractive power draws the armature toward the poles. When the operator releases the pressure on his key the circuit is broken, current does not flow, the magnetic effect ceases, and the armature is drawn back by its spring. These movements give rise to the clicking sounds which represent the dots and dashes of the Morse or other alphabet as transmitted by the operator. Similar movements, produced in like manner, are availed of in another instrument known as the relay, whose office is to act practically as an automatic transmitter key, repeating the messages received in its coils, and sending them on to the next section of the line, equipped with its own battery; or, when the message is intended for its own station, sending the message to an adjacent sounder included in a local battery circuit. With a simple circuit, therefore, between two stations and where an intermediate battery is not necessary, a relay is not used.

Passing on to the consideration of another phase of the phenomena of electromagnetism, the reader's attention is called to Fig. 1, in which will be seen on the left a simple form of electromagnet consisting of a bar of soft iron wound around with insulated wire, through which a current is flowing from a battery. The arrows indicate the direction of flow.

All magnets have two poles, north and south. A permanent magnet (made of steel, which, as distinguished from soft iron, retains its magnetism for long periods) is so called because it is permanently magnetized and its polarity remains fixed. In an electromagnet the magnetism exists only as long as current is flowing through the wire, and the polarity of the soft-iron bar is determined by the DIRECTION of flow of current around it for the time being. If the direction is reversed, the polarity will also be reversed. Assuming, for instance, the bar to be end-on toward the observer, that end will be a south pole if the current is flowing from left to right, clockwise, around the bar; or a north pole if flowing in the other direction, as illustrated at the right of the figure. It is immaterial which way the wire is wound around the bar, the determining factor of polarity being the DIRECTION of the current. It will be clear, therefore, that if two EQUAL currents be passed around a bar in opposite directions (Fig. 3) they will tend to produce exactly opposite polarities and thus neutralize each other. Hence, the bar would remain non-magnetic.

As the path to the quadruplex passes through the duplex, let us consider the Stearns system, after noting one other principle--namely, that if more than one path is presented in which an electric current may complete its circuit, it divides in proportion to the resistance of each path. Hence, if we connect one pole of a battery with the earth, and from the other pole run to the earth two wires of equal resistance as illustrated in Fig. 2, equal currents will traverse the wires.

The above principles were employed in the Stearns differential duplex system in the following manner: Referring to Fig. 3, suppose a wire, A, is led from a battery around a bar of soft iron from left to right, and another wire of equal resistance and equal number of turns, B, around from right to left. The flow of current will cause two equal opposing actions to be set up in the bar; one will exactly offset the other, and no magnetic effect will be produced. A relay thus wound is known as a differential relay--more generally called a neutral relay.

The non-technical reader may wonder what use can possibly be made of an apparently non-operative piece of apparatus. It must be borne in mind, however, in considering a duplex system, that a differential relay is used AT EACH END of the line and forms part of the circuit; and that while each relay must be absolutely unresponsive to the signals SENT OUT FROM ITS HOME OFFICE, it must respond to signals transmitted by a DISTANT OFFICE. Hence, the next figure (4), with its accompanying explanation, will probably make the matter clear. If another battery, D, be introduced at the distant end of the wire A the differential or neutral relay becomes actively operative as follows: Battery C supplies wires A and B with an equal current, but battery D doubles the strength of the current traversing wire A. This is sufficient to not only neutralize the magnetism which the current in wire B would tend to set up, but also--by reason of the excess of current in wire A--to make the bar a magnet whose polarity would be determined by the direction of the flow of current around it.

In the arrangement shown in Fig. 4 the batteries are so connected that current flow is in the same direction, thus doubling the amount of current flowing through wire A. But suppose the batteries were so connected that the current from each set flowed in an opposite direction? The result would be that these currents would oppose and neutralize each other, and, therefore, none would flow in wire A. Inasmuch, however, as there is nothing to hinder, current would flow from battery C through wire B, and the bar would therefore be magnetized. Hence, assuming that the relay is to be actuated from the distant end, D, it is in a sense immaterial whether the batteries connected with wire A assist or oppose each other, as, in either case, the bar would be magnetized only through the operation of the distant key.

A slight elaboration of Fig. 4 will further illustrate the principle of the differential duplex. In Fig. 5 are two stations, A the home end, and B the distant station to which a message is to be sent. The relay at each end has two coils, 1 and 2, No. 1 in each case being known as the "main-line coil" and 2 as the "artificial-line coil." The latter, in each case, has in its circuit a resistance, R, to compensate for the resistance of the main line, so that there shall be no inequalities in the circuits. The artificial line, as well as that to which the two coils are joined, are connected to earth. There is a battery, C, and a key, K. When the key is depressed, current flows through the relay coils at A, but no magnetism is produced, as they oppose each other. The current, however, flows out through the main-line coil over the line and through the main-line coil 1 at B, completing its circuit to earth and magnetizing the bar of the relay, thus causing its armature to be attracted. On releasing the key the circuit is broken and magnetism instantly ceases.

It will be evident, therefore, that the operator at A may cause the relay at B to act without affecting his own relay. Similar effects would be produced from B to A if the battery and key were placed at the B end.

If, therefore, like instruments are placed at each end of the line, as in Fig. 6, we have a differential duplex arrangement by means of which two operators may actuate relays at the ends distant from them, without causing the operation of the relays at their home ends. In practice this is done by means of a special instrument known as a continuity preserving transmitter, or, usually, as a transmitter. This consists of an electromagnet, T, operated by a key, K, and separate battery. The armature lever, L, is long, pivoted in the centre, and is bent over at the end. At a point a little beyond its centre is a small piece of insulating material to which is screwed a strip of spring metal, S. Conveniently placed with reference to the end of the lever is a bent metallic piece, P, having a contact screw in its upper horizontal arm, and attached to the lower end of this bent piece is a post, or standard, to which the main battery is electrically connected. The relay coils are connected by wire to the spring piece, S, and the armature lever is connected to earth. If the key is depressed, the armature is attracted and its bent end is moved upward, depressing the spring which makes contact with the upper screw, which places the battery to the line, and simultaneously breaks the ground connection between the spring and the upturned end of the lever, as shown at the left. When the key is released the battery is again connected to earth. The compensating resistances and condensers necessary for a duplex arrangement are shown in the diagram.

In Fig. 6 one transmitter is shown as closed, at A, while the other one is open. From our previous illustrations and explanations it will be readily seen that, with the transmitter closed at station A, current flows via post P, through S, and to both relay coils at A, thence over the main line to main-line coil at B, and down to earth through S and the armature lever with its grounded wire. The relay at A would be unresponsive, but the core of the relay at B would be magnetized and its armature respond to signals from A. In like manner, if the transmitter at B be closed, current would flow through similar parts and thus cause the relay at A to respond. If both transmitters be closed simultaneously, both batteries will be placed to the line, which would practically result in doubling the current in each of the main-line coils, in consequence of which both relays are energized and their armatures attracted through the operation of the keys at the distant ends. Hence, two messages can be sent in opposite directions over the same line simultaneously.

The reader will undoubtedly see quite clearly from the above system, which rests upon varying the STRENGTH of the current, that two messages could not be sent in the same direction over the one line at the same time. To accomplish this object Edison introduced another and distinct feature--namely, the using of the same current, but ALSO varying its DIRECTION of flow; that is to say, alternately reversing the POLARITY of the batteries as applied to the line and thus producing corresponding changes in the polarity of another specially constructed type of relay, called a polarized relay. To afford the reader a clear conception of such a relay we would refer again to Fig. 1 and its explanation, from which it appears that the polarity of a soft-iron bar is determined not by the strength of the current flowing around it but by the direction thereof.

With this idea clearly in mind, the theory of the polarized relay, generally called "polar" relay, as presented in the diagram (Fig. 7), will be readily understood.

A is a bar of soft iron, bent as shown, and wound around with insulated copper wire, the ends of which are connected with a battery, B, thus forming an electromagnet. An essential part of this relay consists of a swinging PERMANENT magnet, C, whose polarity remains fixed, that end between the terminals of the electromagnet being a north pole. Inasmuch as unlike poles of magnets are attracted to each other and like poles repelled, it follows that this north pole will be repelled by the north pole of the electromagnet, but will swing over and be attracted by its south pole. If the direction of flow of current be reversed, by reversing the battery, the electromagnetic polarity also reverses and the end of the permanent magnet swings over to the other side. This is shown in the two figures of Fig. 7. This device being a relay, its purpose is to repeat transmitted signals into a local circuit, as before explained. For this purpose there are provided at D and E a contact and a back stop, the former of which is opened and closed by the swinging permanent magnet, thus opening and closing the local circuit.

Manifestly there must be provided some convenient way for rapidly transposing the direction of the current flow if such a device as the polar relay is to be used for the reception of telegraph messages, and this is accomplished by means of an instrument called a pole-changer, which consists essentially of a movable contact piece connected permanently to the earth, or grounded, and arranged to connect one or the other pole of a battery to the line and simultaneously ground the other pole. This action of the pole-changer is effected by movements of the armature of an electromagnet through the manipulation of an ordinary telegraph key by an operator at the home station, as in the operation of the "transmitter," above referred to.

By a combination of the neutral relay and the polar relay two operators, by manipulating two telegraph keys in the ordinary way, can simultaneously send two messages over one line in the SAME direction with the SAME current, one operator varying its strength and the other operator varying its polarity or direction of flow. This principle was covered by Edison's Patent No. 162,633, and was known as the "diplex" system, although, in the patent referred to, Edison showed and claimed the adaptation of the principle to duplex telegraphy. Indeed, as a matter of fact, it was found that by winding the polar relay differentially and arranging the circuits and collateral appliances appropriately, the polar duplex system was more highly efficient than the neutral system, and it is extensively used to the present day.

Thus far we have referred to two systems, one the neutral or differential duplex, and the other the combination of the neutral and polar relays, making a diplex system. By one of these two systems a single wire could be used for sending two messages in opposite directions, and by the other in the same direction or in opposite directions. Edison followed up his work on the diplex and combined the two systems into the quadruplex, by means of which FOUR messages could be sent and received simultaneously over the one wire, two in each direction, thus employing eight operators--four at each end--two sending and two receiving. The general principles of quadruplex telegraphy are based upon the phenomena which we have briefly outlined in connection with the neutral relay and the polar relay. The equipment of such a system at each end of the line consists of these two instruments, together with the special form of transmitter and the pole-changer and their keys for actuating the neutral and polar relays at the other, or distant, end. Besides these there are the compensating resistances and condensers. All of these will be seen in the diagram (Fig. 8). It will be understood, of course, that the polar relay, as used in the quadruplex system, is wound differentially, and therefore its operation is somewhat similar in principle to that of the differentially wound neutral relay, in that it does not respond to the operation of the key at the home office, but only operates in response to the movements of the distant key.

Our explanation has merely aimed to show the underlying phenomena and principles in broad outline without entering into more detail than was deemed absolutely necessary. It should be stated, however, that between the outline and the filling in of the details there was an enormous amount of hard work, study, patient plodding, and endless experiments before Edison finally perfected his quadruplex system in the year 1874.

If it were attempted to offer here a detailed explanation of the varied and numerous operations of the quadruplex, this article would assume the proportions of a treatise. An idea of their complexity may be gathered from the following, which is quoted from American Telegraphy and Encyclopedia of the Telegraph, by William Maver, Jr.:

"It may well be doubted whether in the whole range of applied electricity there occur such beautiful combinations, so quickly made, broken up, and others reformed, as in the operation of the Edison quadruplex. For example, it is quite demonstrable that during the making of a simple dash of the Morse alphabet by the neutral relay at the home station the distant pole-changer may reverse its battery several times; the home pole-changer may do likewise, and the home transmitter may increase and decrease the electromotive force of the home battery repeatedly. Simultaneously, and, of course, as a consequence of the foregoing actions, the home neutral relay itself may have had its magnetism reversed several times, and the SIGNAL, that is, the dash, will have been made, partly by the home battery, partly by the distant and home batteries combined, partly by current on the main line, partly by current on the artificial line, partly by the main-line 'static' current, partly by the condenser static current, and yet, on a well-adjusted circuit the dash will have been produced on the quadruplex sounder as clearly as any dash on an ordinary single-wire sounder."

We present a diagrammatic illustration of the Edison quadruplex, battery key system, in Fig. 8, and refer the reader to the above or other text-books if he desires to make a close study of its intricate operations. Before finally dismissing the quadruplex, and for the benefit of the inquiring reader who may vainly puzzle over the intricacies of the circuits shown in Fig. 8, a hint as to an essential difference between the neutral relay, as used in the duplex and as used in the quadruplex, may be given. With the duplex, as we have seen, the current on the main line is changed in strength only when both keys at OPPOSITE stations are closed together, so that a current due to both batteries flows over the main line. When a single message is sent from one station to the other, or when both stations are sending messages that do not conflict, only one battery or the other is connected to the main line; but with the quadruplex, suppose one of the operators, in New York for instance, is sending reversals of current to Chicago; we can readily see how these changes in polarity will operate the polar relay at the distant station, but why will they not also operate the neutral relay at the distant station as well? This difficulty was solved by dividing the battery at each station into two unequal parts, the smaller battery being always in circuit with the pole-changer ready to have its polarity reversed on the main line to operate the distant polar relay, but the spring retracting the armature of the neutral relay is made so stiff as to resist these weak currents. If, however, the transmitter is operated at the same end, the entire battery is connected to the main line, and the strength of this current is sufficient to operate the neutral relay. Whether the part or all the battery is alternately connected to or disconnected from the main line by the transmitter, the current so varied in strength is subject to reversal of polarity by the pole-changer; but the variations in strength have no effect upon the distant polar relay, because that relay being responsive to changes in polarity of a weak current is obviously responsive to corresponding changes in polarity of a powerful current. With this distinction before him, the reader will have no difficulty in following the circuits of Fig. 8, bearing always in mind that by reason of the differential winding of the polar and neutral relays, neither of the relays at one station will respond to the home battery, and can only respond to the distant battery--the polar relay responding when the polarity of the current is reversed, whether the current be strong or weak, and the neutral relay responding when the line-current is increased, regardless of its polarity. It should be added that besides the system illustrated in Fig. 8, which is known as the differential principle, the quadruplex was also arranged to operate on the Wheatstone bridge principle; but it is not deemed necessary to enter into its details. The underlying phenomena were similar, the difference consisting largely in the arrangement of the circuits and apparatus. [24]

[Footnote 24: Many of the illustrations in this article are reproduced from American Telegraphy and Encyclopedia of the Telegraph, by William Maver, Jr., by permission of Maver Publishing Company, New York.]

Edison made another notable contribution to multiplex telegraphy some years later in the Phonoplex. The name suggests the use of the telephone, and such indeed is the case. The necessity for this invention arose out of the problem of increasing the capacity of telegraph lines employed in "through" and "way" service, such as upon railroads. In a railroad system there are usually two terminal stations and a number of way stations. There is naturally much intercommunication, which would be greatly curtailed by a system having the capacity of only a single message at a time. The duplexes above described could not be used on a railroad telegraph system, because of the necessity of electrically balancing the line, which, while entirely feasible on a through line, would not be practicable between a number of intercommunicating points. Edison's phonoplex normally doubled the capacity of telegraph lines, whether employed on way business or through traffic, but in actual practice made it possible to obtain more than double service. It has been in practical use for many years on some of the leading railroads of the United States.

The system is a combination of telegraphic apparatus and telephone receiver, although in this case the latter instrument is not used in the generally understood manner. It is well known that the diaphragm of a telephone vibrates with the fluctuations of the current energizing the magnet beneath it. If the make and break of the magnetizing current be rapid, the vibrations being within the limits of the human ear, the diaphragm will produce an audible sound; but if the make and break be as slow as with ordinary Morse transmission, the diaphragm will be merely flexed and return to its original form without producing a sound. If, therefore, there be placed in the same circuit a regular telegraph relay and a special telephone, an operator may, by manipulating a key, operate the relay (and its sounder) without producing a sound in the telephone, as the makes and breaks of the key are far below the limit of audibility. But if through the same circuit, by means of another key suitably connected there is sent the rapid changes in current from an induction-coil, it will cause a series of loud clicks in the telephone, corresponding to the signals transmitted; but this current is too weak to affect the telegraph relay. It will be seen, therefore, that this method of duplexing is practiced, not by varying the strength or polarity, but by sending TWO KINDS OF CURRENT over the wire. Thus, two sets of Morse signals can be transmitted by two operators over one line at the same time without interfering with each other, and not only between terminal offices, but also between a terminal office and any intermediate office, or between two intermediate offices alone.

III

AUTOMATIC TELEGRAPHY

FROM the year 1848, when a Scotchman, Alexander Bain, first devised a scheme for rapid telegraphy by automatic methods, down to the beginning of the seventies, many other inventors had also applied themselves to the solution of this difficult problem, with only indifferent success. "Cheap telegraphy" being the slogan of the time, Edison became arduously interested in the subject, and at the end of three years of hard work produced an entirely successful system, a public test of which was made on December 11, 1873 when about twelve thousand (12,000) words were transmitted over a single wire from Washington to New York. in twenty-two and one-half minutes. Edison's system was commercially exploited for several years by the Automatic Telegraph Company, as related in the preceding narrative.

As a premise to an explanation of the principles involved it should be noted that the transmission of telegraph messages by hand at a rate of fifty words per minute is considered a good average speed; hence, the availability of a telegraph line, as thus operated, is limited to this capacity except as it may be multiplied by two with the use of the duplex, or by four, with the quadruplex. Increased rapidity of transmission may, however, be accomplished by automatic methods, by means of which, through the employment of suitable devices, messages may be stamped in or upon a paper tape, transmitted through automatically acting instruments, and be received at distant points in visible characters, upon a similar tape, at a rate twenty or more times greater--a speed far beyond the possibilities of the human hand to transmit or the ear to receive.

In Edison's system of automatic telegraphy a paper tape was perforated with a series of round holes, so arranged and spaced as to represent Morse characters, forming the words of the message to be transmitted. This was done in a special machine of Edison's invention, called a perforator, consisting of a series of punches operated by a bank of keys--typewriter fashion. The paper tape passed over a cylinder, and was kept in regular motion so as to receive the perforations in proper sequence.

The perforated tape was then placed in the transmitting instrument, the essential parts of which were a metallic drum and a projecting arm carrying two small wheels, which, by means of a spring, were maintained in constant pressure on the drum. The wheels and drum were electrically connected in the line over which the message was to be sent. current being supplied by batteries in the ordinary manner.

When the transmitting instrument was in operation, the perforated tape was passed over the drum in continuous, progressive motion. Thus, the paper passed between the drum and the two small wheels, and, as dry paper is a non-conductor, current was prevented from passing until a perforation was reached. As the paper passed along, the wheels dropped into the perforations, making momentary contacts with the drum beneath and causing momentary impulses of current to be transmitted over the line in the same way that they would be produced by the manipulation of the telegraph key, but with much greater rapidity. The perforations being so arranged as to regulate the length of the contact, the result would be the transmission of long and short impulses corresponding with the dots and dashes of the Morse alphabet.

The receiving instrument at the other end of the line was constructed upon much the same general lines as the transmitter, consisting of a metallic drum and reels for the paper tape. Instead of the two small contact wheels, however, a projecting arm carried an iron pin or stylus, so arranged that its point would normally impinge upon the periphery of the drum. The iron pin and the drum were respectively connected so as to be in circuit with the transmission line and batteries. As the principle involved in the receiving operation was electrochemical decomposition, the paper tape upon which the incoming message was to be received was moistened with a chemical solution readily decomposable by the electric current. This paper, while still in a damp condition, was passed between the drum and stylus in continuous, progressive motion. When an electrical impulse came over the line from the transmitting end, current passed through the moistened paper from the iron pin, causing chemical decomposition, by reason of which the iron would be attacked and would mark a line on the paper. Such a line would be long or short, according to the duration of the electric impulse. Inasmuch as a succession of such impulses coming over the line owed their origin to the perforations in the transmitting tape, it followed that the resulting marks upon the receiving tape would correspond thereto in their respective lengths. Hence, the transmitted message was received on the tape in visible dots and dashes representing characters of the Morse alphabet.

The system will, perhaps, be better understood by reference to the following diagrammatic sketch of its general principles:

Some idea of the rapidity of automatic telegraphy may be obtained when we consider the fact that with the use of Edison's system in the early seventies it was common practice to transmit and receive from three to four thousand words a minute over a single line between New York and Philadelphia. This system was exploited through the use of a moderately paid clerical force.

In practice, there was employed such a number of perforating machines as the exigencies of business demanded. Each machine was operated by a clerk, who translated the message into telegraphic characters and prepared the transmitting tape by punching the necessary perforations therein. An expert clerk could perforate such a tape at the rate of fifty to sixty words per minute. At the receiving end the tape was taken by other clerks who translated the Morse characters into ordinary words, which were written on message blanks for delivery to persons for whom the messages were intended.

This latter operation--"copying." as it was called--was not consistent with truly economical business practice. Edison therefore undertook the task of devising an improved system whereby the message when received would not require translation and rewriting, but would automatically appear on the tape in plain letters and words, ready for instant delivery.

The result was his automatic Roman letter system, the basis for which included the above-named general principles of perforated transmission tape and electrochemical decomposition. Instead of punching Morse characters in the transmission tape however, it was perforated with a series of small round holes forming Roman letters. The verticals of these letters were originally five holes high. The transmitting instrument had five small wheels or rollers, instead of two, for making contacts through the perforations and causing short electric impulses to pass over the lines. At first five lines were used to carry these impulses to the receiving instrument, where there were five iron pins impinging on the drum. By means of these pins the chemically prepared tape was marked with dots corresponding to the impulses as received, leaving upon it a legible record of the letters and words transmitted.

For purposes of economy in investment and maintenance, Edison devised subsequently a plan by which the number of conducting lines was reduced to two, instead of five. The verticals of the letters were perforated only four holes high, and the four rollers were arranged in pairs, one pair being slightly in advance of the other. There were, of course, only four pins at the receiving instrument. Two were of iron and two of tellurium, it being the gist of Edison's plan to effect the marking of the chemical paper by one metal with a positive current, and by the other metal with a negative current. In the following diagram, which shows the theory of this arrangement, it will be seen that both the transmitting rollers and the receiving pins are arranged in pairs, one pair in each case being slightly in advance of the other. Of these receiving pins, one pair--1 and 3--are of iron, and the other pair--2 and 4--of tellurium. Pins 1-2 and 3-4 are electrically connected together in other pairs, and then each of these pairs is connected with one of the main lines that run respectively to the middle of two groups of batteries at the transmitting end. The terminals of these groups of batteries are connected respectively to the four rollers which impinge upon the transmitting drum, the negatives being connected to 5 and 7, and the positives to 6 and 8, as denoted by the letters N and P. The transmitting and receiving drums are respectively connected to earth.

In operation the perforated tape is placed on the transmission drum, and the chemically prepared tape on the receiving drum. As the perforated tape passes over the transmission drum the advanced rollers 6 or 8 first close the circuit through the perforations, and a positive current passes from the batteries through the drum and down to the ground; thence through the earth at the receiving end up to the other drum and back to the batteries via the tellurium pins 2 or 4 and the line wire. With this positive current the tellurium pins make marks upon the paper tape, but the iron pins make no mark. In the merest fraction of a second, as the perforated paper continues to pass over the transmission drum, the rollers 5 or 7 close the circuit through other perforations and t e current passes in the opposite direction, over the line wire, through pins 1 or 3, and returns through the earth. In this case the iron pins mark the paper tape, but the tellurium pins make no mark. It will be obvious, therefore, that as the rollers are set so as to allow of currents of opposite polarity to be alternately and rapidly sent by means of the perforations, the marks upon the tape at the receiving station will occupy their proper relative positions, and the aggregate result will be letters corresponding to those perforated in the transmission tape.

Edison subsequently made still further improvements in this direction, by which he reduced the number of conducting wires to one, but the principles involved were analogous to the one just described.

This Roman letter system was in use for several years on lines between

New York, Philadelphia, and Washington, and was so efficient that a speed of three thousand words a minute was attained on the line between the two first-named cities.

Inasmuch as there were several proposed systems of rapid automatic telegraphy in existence at the time Edison entered the field, but none of them in practical commercial use, it becomes a matter of interest to inquire wherein they were deficient, and what constituted the elements of Edison's success.

The chief difficulties in the transmission of Morse characters had been two in number, the most serious of which was that on the receiving tape the characters would be prolonged and run into one another, forming a draggled line and thus rendering the message unintelligible. This arose from the fact that, on account of the rapid succession of the electric impulses, there was not sufficient time between them for the electric action to cease entirely. Consequently the line could not clear itself, and became surcharged, as it were; the effect being an attenuated prolongation of each impulse as manifested in a weaker continuation of the mark on the tape, thus making the whole message indistinct. These secondary marks were called "tailings."

For many years electricians had tried in vain to overcome this difficulty. Edison devoted a great deal of thought and energy to the question, in the course of which he experimented through one hundred and twenty consecutive nights, in the year 1873, on the line between New York and Washington. His solution of the problem was simple but effectual. It involved the principle of inductive compensation. In a shunt circuit with the receiving instrument he introduced electromagnets. The pulsations of current passed through the helices of these magnets, producing an augmented marking effect upon the receiving tape, but upon the breaking of the current, the magnet, in discharging itself of the induced magnetism, would set up momentarily a counter-current of opposite polarity. This neutralized the "tailing" effect by clearing the line between pulsations, thus allowing the telegraphic characters to be clearly and distinctly outlined upon the tape. Further elaboration of this method was made later by the addition of rheostats, condensers, and local opposition batteries on long lines.

The other difficulty above referred to was one that had also occupied considerable thought and attention of many workers in the field, and related to the perforating of the dash in the transmission tape. It involved mechanical complications that seemed to be insurmountable, and up to the time Edison invented his perforating machine no really good method was available. He abandoned the attempt to cut dashes as such, in the paper tape, but instead punched three round holes so arranged as to form a triangle. A concrete example is presented in the illustration below, which shows a piece of tape with perforations representing the word "same."

The philosophy of this will be at once perceived when it is remembered that the two little wheels running upon the drum of the transmitting instrument were situated side by side, corresponding in distance to the two rows of holes. When a triangle of three holes, intended to form the dash, reached the wheels, one of them dropped into a lower hole. Before it could get out, the other wheel dropped into the hole at the apex of the triangle, thus continuing the connection, which was still further prolonged by the first wheel dropping into the third hole. Thus, an extended contact was made, which, by transmitting a long impulse, resulted in the marking of a dash upon the receiving tape.

This method was in successful commercial use for some time in the early seventies, giving a speed of from three to four thousand words a minute over a single line, but later on was superseded by Edison's Roman letter system, above referred to.

The subject of automatic telegraphy received a vast amount of attention from inventors at the time it was in vogue. None was more earnest or indefatigable than Edison, who, during the progress of his investigations, took out thirty-eight patents on various inventions relating thereto, some of them covering chemical solutions for the receiving paper. This of itself was a subject of much importance and a vast amount of research and labor was expended upon it. In the laboratory note-books there are recorded thousands of experiments showing that Edison's investigations not only included an enormous number of chemical salts and compounds, but also an exhaustive variety of plants, flowers, roots, herbs, and barks.

It seems inexplicable at first view that a system of telegraphy sufficiently rapid and economical to be practically available for important business correspondence should have fallen into disuse. This, however, is made clear--so far as concerns Edison's invention at any rate--in Chapter VIII of the preceding narrative.

IV. WIRELESS TELEGRAPHY

ALTHOUGH Mr. Edison has taken no active part in the development of the more modern wireless telegraphy, and his name has not occurred in connection therewith, the underlying phenomena had been noted by him many years in advance of the art, as will presently be explained. The authors believe that this explanation will reveal a status of Edison in relation to the subject that has thus far been unknown to the public.

While the term "wireless telegraphy," as now applied to the modern method of electrical communication between distant points without intervening conductors, is self-explanatory, it was also applicable, strictly speaking, to the previous art of telegraphing to and from moving trains, and between points not greatly remote from each other, and not connected together with wires.

The latter system (described in Chapter XXIII and in a succeeding article of this Appendix) was based upon the phenomena of electromagnetic or electrostatic induction between conductors separated by more or less space, whereby electric impulses of relatively low potential and low frequency set up in. one conductor were transmitted inductively across the air to another conductor, and there received through the medium of appropriate instruments connected therewith.

As distinguished from this system, however, modern wireless telegraphy--so called--has its basis in the utilization of electric or ether waves in free space, such waves being set up by electric oscillations, or surgings, of comparatively high potential and high frequency, produced by the operation of suitable electrical apparatus. Broadly speaking, these oscillations arise from disruptive discharges of an induction coil, or other form of oscillator, across an air-gap, and their character is controlled by the manipulation of a special type of circuit-breaking key, by means of which long and short discharges are produced. The electric or etheric waves thereby set up are detected and received by another special form of apparatus more or less distant, without any intervening wires or conductors.

In November, 1875, Edison, while experimenting in his Newark laboratory, discovered a new manifestation of electricity through mysterious sparks which could be produced under conditions unknown up to that time. Recognizing at once the absolutely unique character of the phenomena, he continued his investigations enthusiastically over two mouths, finally arriving at a correct conclusion as to the oscillatory nature of the hitherto unknown manifestations. Strange to say, however, the true import and practical applicability of these phenomena did not occur to his mind. Indeed, it was not until more than TWELVE YEARS AFTERWARD, in 1887, upon the publication of the notable work of Prof. H. Hertz proving the existence of electric waves in free space, that Edison realized the fact that the fundamental principle of aerial telegraphy had been within his grasp in the winter of 1875; for although the work of Hertz was more profound and mathematical than that of Edison, the principle involved and the phenomena observed were practically identical--in fact, it may be remarked that some of the methods and experimental apparatus were quite similar, especially the "dark box" with micrometer adjustment, used by both in observing the spark. [25]

[Footnote 25: During the period in which Edison exhibited his lighting system at the Paris Exposition in 1881, his representative, Mr. Charles Batchelor, repeated Edison's remarkable experiments of the winter of 1875 for the benefit of a great number of European savants, using with other apparatus the original "dark box" with micrometer adjustment.]

There is not the slightest intention on the part of the authors to detract in the least degree from the brilliant work of Hertz, but, on the contrary, to ascribe to him the honor that is his due in having given mathematical direction and certainty to so important a discovery. The adaptation of the principles thus elucidated and the subsequent development of the present wonderful art by Marconi, Branly, Lodge, Slaby, and others are now too well known to call for further remark at this place.

Strange to say, that although Edison's early experiments in "etheric force" called forth extensive comment and discussion in the public prints of the period, they seemed to have been generally overlooked when the work of Hertz was published. At a meeting of the Institution of Electrical Engineers, held in London on May 16, 1889, at which there was a discussion on the celebrated paper of Prof. (Sir) Oliver Lodge on "Lightning Conductors," however; the chairman, Sir William Thomson (Lord Kelvin), made the following remarks:

"We all know how Faraday made himself a cage six feet in diameter, hung it up in mid-air in the theatre of the Royal Institution, went into it, and, as he said, lived in it and made experiments. It was a cage with tin-foil hanging all round it; it was not a complete metallic enclosing shell. Faraday had a powerful machine working in the neighborhood, giving all varieties of gradual working-up and discharges by 'impulsive rush'; and whether it was a sudden discharge of ordinary insulated conductors, or of Leyden jars in the neighborhood outside the cage, or electrification and discharge of the cage itself, he saw no effects on his most delicate gold-leaf electroscopes in the interior. His attention was not directed to look for Hertz sparks, or probably he might have found them in the interior. Edison seems to have noticed something of the kind in what he called the etheric force. His name 'etheric' may, thirteen years ago, have seemed to many people absurd. But now we are all beginning to call these inductive phenomena 'etheric.'"

With these preliminary observations, let us now glance briefly at Edison's laboratory experiments, of which mention has been made.

Oh the first manifestation of the unusual phenomena in November, 1875, Edison's keenness of perception led him at once to believe that he had discovered a new force. Indeed, the earliest entry of this discovery in the laboratory note-book bore that caption. After a few days of further experiment and observation, however, he changed it to "Etheric Force," and the further records thereof (all in Mr. Batchelor's handwriting) were under that heading.

The publication of Edison's discovery created considerable attention at the time, calling forth a storm of general ridicule and incredulity. But a few scientific men of the period, whose experimental methods were careful and exact, corroborated his deductions after obtaining similar phenomena by repeating his experiments with intelligent precision. Among these was the late Dr. George M. Beard, a noted physicist, who entered enthusiastically into the investigation, and, in addition to a great deal of independent experiment, spent much time with Edison at his laboratory. Doctor Beard wrote a treatise of some length on the subject, in which he concurred with Edison's deduction that the phenomena were the manifestation of oscillations, or rapidly reversing waves of electricity, which did not respond to the usual tests. Edison had observed the tendency of this force to diffuse itself in various directions through the air and through matter, hence the name "Etheric" that he had provisionally applied to it.

Edison's laboratory notes on this striking investigation are fascinating and voluminous, but cannot be reproduced in full for lack of space. In view of the later practical application of the principles involved, however, the reader will probably be interested in perusing a few extracts therefrom as illustrated by facsimiles of the original sketches from the laboratory note-book.

As the full significance of the experiments shown by these extracts may not be apparent to a lay reader, it may be stated by way of premise that, ordinarily, a current only follows a closed circuit. An electric bell or electric light is a familiar instance of this rule. There is in each case an open (wire) circuit which is closed by pressing the button or turning the switch, thus making a complete and uninterrupted path in which the current may travel and do its work. Until the time of Edison's investigations of 1875, now under consideration, electricity had never been known to manifest itself except through a closed circuit. But, as the reader will see from the following excerpts, Edison discovered a hitherto unknown phenomenon--namely, that under certain conditions the rule would be reversed and electricity would pass through space and through matter entirely unconnected with its point of origin. In other words, he had found the forerunner of wireless telegraphy. Had he then realized the full import of his discovery, all he needed was to increase the strength of the waves and to provide a very sensitive detector, like the coherer, in order to have anticipated the principal developments that came many years afterward. With these explanatory observations, we will now turn to the excerpts referred to, which are as follows:

"November 22, 1875. New Force.--In experimenting with a vibrator magnet consisting of a bar of Stubb's steel fastened at one end and made to vibrate by means of a magnet, we noticed a spark coming from the cores of the magnet. This we have noticed often in relays, in stock-printers, when there were a little iron filings between the armature and core, and more often in our new electric pen, and we have always come to the conclusion that it was caused by strong induction. But when we noticed it on this vibrator it seemed so strong that it struck us forcibly there might be something more than induction. We now found that if we touched any metallic part of the vibrator or magnet we got the spark. The larger the body of iron touched to the vibrator the larger the spark. We now connected a wire to X, the end of the vibrating rod, and we found we could get a spark from it by touching a piece of iron to it, and one of the most curious phenomena is that if you turn the wire around on itself and let the point of the wire touch any other portion of itself you get a spark. By connecting X to the gas-pipe we drew sparks from the gas-pipes in any part of the room by drawing an iron wire over the brass jet of the cock. This is simply wonderful, and a good proof that the cause of the spark is a TRUE UNKNOWN FORCE."

"November 23, 1815. New Force.--The following very curious result was obtained with it. The vibrator shown in Fig. 1 and battery were placed on insulated stands; and a wire connected to X (tried both copper and iron) carried over to the stove about twenty feet distant. When the end of the wire was rubbed on the stove it gave out splendid sparks. When permanently connected to the stove, sparks could be drawn from the stove by a piece of wire held in the hand. The point X of vibrator was now connected to the gas-pipe and still the sparks could be drawn from the stove."

. . . .

"Put a coil of wire over the end of rod X and passed the ends of spool through galvanometer without affecting it in any way. Tried a 6-ohm spool add a 200-ohm. We now tried all the metals, touching each one in turn to the point X." [Here follows a list of metals and the character of spark obtained with each.]

. . . .

"By increasing the battery from eight to twelve cells we get a spark when the vibrating magnet is shunted with 3 ohms. Cannot taste the least shock at B, yet between carbon points the spark is very vivid. As will be seen, X has no connection with anything. With a glass rod four feet long, well rubbed with a piece of silk over a hot stove, with a piece of battery carbon secured to one end, we received vivid sparks into the carbon when the other end was held in the hand with the handkerchief, yet the galvanometer, chemical paper, the sense of shock in the tongue, and a gold-leaf electroscope which would diverge at two feet from a half-inch spark plate-glass machine were not affected in the least by it.

"A piece of coal held to the wire showed faint sparks.

"We had a box made thus: whereby two points could be brought together within a dark box provided with an eyepiece. The points were iron, and we found the sparks were very irregular. After testing some time two lead-pencils found more regular and very much more vivid. We then substituted the graphite points instead of iron." [26]

[Footnote 26: The dark box had micrometer screws for delicate adjustment of the carbon points, and was thereafter largely used in this series of investigations for better study of the spark. When Mr. Edison's experiments were repeated by Mr. Batchelor, who represented him at the Paris Exposition of 1881, the dark box was employed for a similar purpose.]

. . . .

After recording a considerable number of other experiments, the laboratory notes go on to state:

"November 30, 1875. Etheric Force.--We found the addition of battery to the Stubb's wire vibrator greatly increased the volume of spark. Several persons could obtain sparks from the gas-pipes at once, each spark being equal in volume and brilliancy to the spark drawn by a single person.... Edison now grasped the (gas) pipe, and with the other hand holding a piece of metal, he touched several other metallic substances, obtained sparks, showing that the force passed through his body."

. . . .

"December 3, 1875. Etheric Force.--Charley Edison hung to the gas-pipe with feet above the floor, and with a knife got a spark from the pipe he was hanging on. We now took the wire from the vibrator in one hand and stood on a block of paraffin eighteen inches square and six inches thick; holding a knife in the other hand, we drew sparks from the stove-pipe. We now tried the crucial test of passing the etheric current through the sciatic nerve of a frog just killed. Previous to trying, we tested its sensibility by the current from a single Bunsen cell. We put in resistance up to 500,000 ohms, and the twitching was still perceptible. We tried the induced current from our induction coil having one cell on primary,, the spark jumping about one-fiftieth of an inch, the terminal of the secondary connected to the frog and it straightened out with violence. We arranged frog's legs to pass etheric force through. We placed legs on an inverted beaker, and held the two ends of the wires on glass rods eight inches long. On connecting one to the sciatic nerve and the other to the fleshy part of the leg no movement could be discerned, although brilliant sparks could be obtained on the graphite points when the frog was in circuit. Doctor Beard was present when this was tried."

. . . .

"December 5, 1875. Etheric Force.--Three persons grasping hands and standing upon blocks of paraffin twelve inches square and six thick drew sparks from the adjoining stove when another person touched the sounder with any piece of metal.... A galvanoscopic frog giving contractions with one cell through two water rheostats was then placed in circuit. When the wires from the vibrator and the gas-pipe were connected, slight contractions were noted, sometimes very plain and marked, showing the apparent presence of electricity, which from the high insulation seemed improbable. Doctor Beard, who was present, inferred from the way the leg contracted that it moved on both opening and closing the circuit. To test this we disconnected the wire between the frog and battery, and placed, instead of a vibrating sounder, a simple Morse key and a sounder taking the 'etheric' from armature. The spark was now tested in dark box and found to be very strong. It was then connected to the nerves of the frog, BUT NO MOVEMENT OF ANY KIND COULD BE DETECTED UPON WORKING THE KEY, although the brilliancy and power of the spark were undiminished. The thought then occurred to Edison that the movement of the frog was due to mechanical vibrations from the vibrator (which gives probably two hundred and fifty vibrations per second), passing through the wires and irritating the sensitive nerves of the frog. Upon disconnecting the battery wires and holding a tuning-fork giving three hundred and twenty-six vibrations per second to the base of the sounder, the vibrations over the wire made the frog contract nearly every time.... The contraction of the frog's legs may with considerable safety be said to be caused by these mechanical vibrations being transmitted through the conducting wires."

Edison thought that the longitudinal vibrations caused by the sounder produced a more marked effect, and proceeded to try out his theory. The very next entry in the laboratory note-book bears the same date as the above (December 5, 1875), and is entitled "Longitudinal Vibrations," and reads as follows:

"We took a long iron wire one-sixteenth of an inch in diameter and rubbed it lengthways with a piece of leather with resin on for about three feet, backward and forward. About ten feet away we applied the wire to the back of the neck and it gives a horrible sensation, showing the vibrations conducted through the wire."

. . . .

The following experiment illustrates notably the movement of the electric waves through free space:

"December 26, 1875. Etheric Force.--An experiment tried to-night gives a curious result. A is a vibrator, B, C, D, E are sheets of tin-foil hung on insulating stands. The sheets are about twelve by eight inches. B and C are twenty-six inches apart, C and D forty-eight inches and D and E twenty-six inches. B is connected to the vibrator and E to point in dark box, the other point to ground. We received sparks at intervals, although insulated by such space."

With the above our extracts must close, although we have given but a few of the interesting experiments tried at the time. It will be noticed, however, that these records show much progression in a little over a month. Just after the item last above extracted, the Edison shop became greatly rushed on telegraphic inventions, and not many months afterward came the removal to Menlo Park; hence the etheric-force investigations were side-tracked for other matters deemed to be more important at that time.

Doctor Beard in his previously mentioned treatise refers, on page 27, to the views of others who have repeated Edison's experiments and observed the phenomena, and in a foot-note says:

"Professor Houston, of Philadelphia, among others, has repeated some of these physical experiments, has adopted in full and after but a partial study of the subject, the hypothesis of rapidly reversed electricity as suggested in my letter to the Tribune of December 8th, and further claims priority of discovery, because he observed the spark of this when experimenting with a Ruhmkorff coil four years ago. To this claim, if it be seriously entertained, the obvious reply is that thousands of persons, probably, had seen this spark before it was DISCOVERED by Mr. Edison; it had been seen by Professor Nipher, who supposed, and still supposes, it is the spark of the extra current; it has been seen by my friend, Prof. J. E. Smith, who assumed, as he tells me, without examination, that it was inductive electricity breaking through bad insulation; it had been seen, as has been stated, by Mr. Edison many times before he thought it worthy of study, it was undoubtedly seen by Professor Houston, who, like so many others, failed to even suspect its meaning and thus missed an important discovery. The honor of a scientific discovery belongs, not to him who first sees a thing, but to him who first sees it with expert eyes; not to him even who drops an original suggestion, but to him who first makes, that suggestion fruitful of results. If to see with the eyes a phenomenon is to discover the law of which that phenomenon is a part, then every schoolboy who, before the time of Newton, ever saw an apple fall, was a discoverer of the law of gravitation...."

Edison took out only one patent on long-distance telegraphy without wires. While the principle involved therein (induction) was not precisely analogous to the above, or to the present system of wireless telegraphy, it was a step forward in the progress of the art. The application was filed May 23, 1885, at the time he was working on induction telegraphy (two years before the publication of the work of Hertz), but the patent (No. 465,971) was not issued until December 29, 1891. In 1903 it was purchased from him by the Marconi Wireless Telegraph Company. Edison has always had a great admiration for Marconi and his work, and a warm friendship exists between the two men. During the formative period of the Marconi Company attempts were made to influence Edison to sell this patent to an opposing concern, but his regard for Marconi and belief in the fundamental nature of his work were so strong that he refused flatly, because in the hands of an enemy the patent might be used inimically to Marconi's interests.

Edison's ideas, as expressed in the specifications of this patent, show very clearly the close analogy of his system to that now in vogue. As they were filed in the Patent Office several years before the possibility of wireless telegraphy was suspected, it will undoubtedly be of interest to give the following extract therefrom:

"I have discovered that if sufficient elevation be obtained to overcome the curvature of the earth's surface and to reduce to the minimum the earth's absorption, electric telegraphing or signalling between distant points can be carried on by induction without the use of wires connecting such distant points. This discovery is especially applicable to telegraphing across bodies of water, thus avoiding the use of submarine cables, or for communicating between vessels at sea, or between vessels at sea and points on land, but it is also applicable to electric communication between distant points on land, it being necessary, however, on land (with the exception of communication over open prairie) to increase the elevation in order to reduce to the minimum the induction-absorbing effect of houses, trees, and elevations in the land itself. At sea from an elevation of one hundred feet I can communicate electrically a great distance, and since this elevation or one sufficiently high can be had by utilizing the masts of ships, signals can be sent and received between ships separated a considerable distance, and by repeating the signals from ship to ship communication can be established between points at any distance apart or across the largest seas and even oceans. The collision of ships in fogs can be prevented by this character of signalling, by the use of which, also, the safety of a ship in approaching a dangerous coast in foggy weather can be assured. In communicating between points on land, poles of great height can be used, or captive balloons. At these elevated points, whether upon the masts of ships, upon poles or balloons, condensing surfaces of metal or other conductor of electricity are located. Each condensing surface is connected with earth by an electrical conducting wire. On land this earth connection would be one of usual character in telegraphy. At sea the wire would run to one or more metal plates on the bottom of the vessel, where the earth connection would be made with the water. The high-resistance secondary circuit of an induction coil is located in circuit between the condensing surface and the ground. The primary circuit of the induction coil includes a battery and a device for transmitting signals, which may be a revolving circuit-breaker operated continually by a motor of any suitable kind, either electrical or mechanical, and a key normally short-circuiting the circuit-breaker or secondary coil. For receiving signals I locate in said circuit between the condensing surface and the ground a diaphragm sounder, which is preferably one of my electromotograph telephone receivers. The key normally short-circuiting the revolving circuit-breaker, no impulses are produced in the induction coil until the key is depressed, when a large number of impulses are produced in the primary, and by means of the secondary corresponding impulses or variations in tension are produced at the elevated condensing surface, producing thereat electrostatic impulses. These electrostatic impulses are transmitted inductively to the elevated condensing surface at the distant point, and are made audible by the electromotograph connected in the ground circuit with such distant condensing surface."

The accompanying illustrations are reduced facsimiles of the drawings attached to the above patent, No. 465,971.

V. THE ELECTROMOTOGRAPH

IN solving a problem that at the time was thought to be insurmountable, and in the adaptability of its principles to the successful overcoming of apparently insuperable difficulties subsequently arising in other lines of work, this invention is one of the most remarkable of the many that Edison has made in his long career as an inventor.

The object primarily sought to be accomplished was the repeating of telegraphic signals from a distance without the aid of a galvanometer or an electromagnetic relay, to overcome the claims of the Page patent referred to in the preceding narrative. This object was achieved in the device described in Edison's basic patent No. 158,787, issued January 19, 1875, by the substitution of friction and anti-friction for the presence and absence of magnetism in a regulation relay.

It may be observed, parenthetically, for the benefit of the lay reader, that in telegraphy the device known as the relay is a receiving instrument containing an electromagnet adapted to respond to the weak line-current. Its armature moves in accordance with electrical impulses, or signals, transmitted from a distance, and, in so responding, operates mechanically to alternately close and open a separate local circuit in which there is a sounder and a powerful battery. When used for true relaying purposes the signals received from a distance are in turn repeated over the next section of the line, the powerful local battery furnishing current for this purpose. As this causes a loud repetition of the original signals, it will be seen that relaying is an economic method of extending a telegraph circuit beyond the natural limits of its battery power.

At the time of Edison's invention, as related in Chapter IX of the preceding narrative, there existed no other known method than the one just described for the repetition of transmitted signals, thus limiting the application of telegraphy to the pleasure of those who might own any patent controlling the relay, except on simple circuits where a single battery was sufficient. Edison's previous discovery of differential friction of surfaces through electrochemical decomposition was now adapted by him to produce motion at the end of a circuit without the intervention of an electromagnet. In other words, he invented a telegraph instrument having a vibrator controlled by electrochemical decomposition, to take the place of a vibrating armature operated by an electromagnet, and thus opened an entirely new and unsuspected avenue in the art.

Edison's electromotograph comprised an ingeniously arranged apparatus in which two surfaces, normally in contact with each other, were caused to alternately adhere by friction or slip by reason of electrochemical decomposition. One of these surfaces consisted of a small drum or cylinder of chalk, which was kept in a moistened condition with a suitable chemical solution, and adapted to revolve continuously by clockwork. The other surface consisted of a small pad which rested with frictional pressure on the periphery of the drum. This pad was carried on the end of a vibrating arm whose lateral movement was limited between two adjustable points. Normally, the frictional pressure between the drum and pad would carry the latter with the former as it revolved, but if the friction were removed a spring on the end of the vibrator arm would draw it back to its starting-place.

In practice, the chalk drum was electrically connected with one pole of an incoming telegraph circuit, and the vibrating arm and pad with the other pole. When the drum rotated, the friction of the pad carried the vibrating arm forward, but an electrical impulse coming over the line would decompose the chemical solution with which the drum was moistened, causing an effect similar to lubrication, and thus allowing the pad to slip backward freely in response to the pull of its retractile spring. The frictional movements of the pad with the drum were comparatively long or short, and corresponded with the length of the impulses sent in over the line. Thus, the transmission of Morse dots and dashes by the distant operator resulted in movements of corresponding length by the frictional pad and vibrating arm.

This brings us to the gist of the ingenious way in which Edison substituted the action of electrochemical decomposition for that of the electromagnet to operate a relay. The actual relaying was accomplished through the medium of two contacts making connection with the local or relay circuit. One of these contacts was fixed, while the other was carried by the vibrating arm; and, as the latter made its forward and backward movements, these contacts were alternately brought together or separated, thus throwing in and out of circuit the battery and sounder in the local circuit and causing a repetition of the incoming signals. The other side of the local circuit was permanently connected to an insulated block on the vibrator. This device not only worked with great rapidity, but was extremely sensitive, and would respond to currents too weak to affect the most delicate electromagnetic relay. It should be stated that Edison did not confine himself to the working of the electromotograph by the slipping of surfaces through the action of incoming current, but by varying the character of the surfaces in contact the frictional effect might be intensified by the electrical current. In such a case the movements would be the reverse of those above indicated, but the end sought--namely, the relaying of messages--would be attained with the same certainty.

While the principal object of this invention was to accomplish the repetition of signals without the aid of an electromagnetic relay, the instrument devised by Edison was capable of use as a recorder also, by employing a small wheel inked by a fountain wheel and attached to the vibrating arm through suitable mechanism. By means of this adjunct the dashes and dots of the transmitted impulses could be recorded upon a paper ribbon passing continuously over the drum.

The electromotograph is shown diagrammatically in Figs. 1 and 2, in plan and vertical section respectively. The reference letters in each case indicate identical parts: A being the chalk drum, B the paper tape, C the auxiliary cylinder, D the vibrating arm, E the frictional pad, F the spring, G and H the two contacts, I and J the two wires leading to local circuit, K a battery, and L an ordinary telegraph key. The two last named, K and L, are shown to make the sketch complete but in practice would be at the transmitting end, which might be hundreds of miles away. It will be understood, of course, that the electromotograph is a receiving and relaying instrument.

Another notable use of the electromotograph principle was in its adaptation to the receiver in Edison's loud-speaking telephone, on which United States Patent No. 221,957 was issued November 25, 1879. A chalk cylinder moistened with a chemical solution was revolved by hand or a small motor. Resting on the cylinder was a palladium-faced pen or spring, which was attached to a mica diaphragm in a resonator. The current passed from the main line through the pen to the chalk and to the battery. The sound-waves impinging upon the distant transmitter varied the resistance of the carbon button therein, thus causing corresponding variations in the strength of the battery current. These variations, passing through the chalk cylinder produced more or less electrochemical decomposition, which in turn caused differences of adhesion between the pen and cylinder and hence gave rise to mechanical vibrations of the diaphragm by reason of which the speaker's words were reproduced. Telephones so operated repeated speaking and singing in very loud tones. In one instance, spoken words and the singing of songs originating at a distance were heard perfectly by an audience of over five thousand people.

The loud-speaking telephone is shown in section, diagrammatically, in the sketch (Fig. 3), in which A is the chalk cylinder mounted on a shaft, B. The palladium-faced pen or spring, C, is connected to diaphragm D. The instrument in its commercial form is shown in Fig. 4.

VI. THE TELEPHONE

ON April 27, 1877, Edison filed in the United States Patent Office an application for a patent on a telephone, and on May 3, 1892, more than fifteen years afterward, Patent No. 474,230 was granted thereon. Numerous other patents have been issued to him for improvements in telephones, but the one above specified may be considered as the most important of them, since it is the one that first discloses the principle of the carbon transmitter.

This patent embodies but two claims, which are as follows:

"1. In a speaking-telegraph transmitter, the combination of a metallic diaphragm and disk of plumbago or equivalent material, the contiguous faces of said disk and diaphragm being in contact, substantially as described.

"2. As a means for effecting a varying surface contact in the circuit of a speaking-telegraph transmitter, the combination of two electrodes, one of plumbago or similar material, and both having broad surfaces in vibratory contact with each other, substantially as described."

The advance that was brought about by Edison's carbon transmitter will be more apparent if we glance first at the state of the art of telephony prior to his invention.

Bell was undoubtedly the first inventor of the art of transmitting speech over an electric circuit, but, with his particular form of telephone, the field was circumscribed. Bell's telephone is shown in the diagrammatic sectional sketch (Fig. 1).

In the drawing M is a bar magnet contained in the rubber case, L. A bobbin, or coil of wire, B, surrounds one end of the magnet. A diaphragm of soft iron is shown at D, and E is the mouthpiece. The wire terminals of the coil, B, connect with the binding screws, C C.

The next illustration shows a pair of such telephones connected for use, the working parts only being designated by the above reference letters.

It will be noted that the wire terminals are here put to their proper uses, two being joined together to form a line of communication, and the other two being respectively connected to "ground."

Now, if we imagine a person at each one of the instruments (Fig. 2) we shall find that when one of them speaks the sound vibrations impinge upon the diaphragm and cause it to act as a vibrating armature. By reason of its vibrations, this diaphragm induces very weak electric impulses in the magnetic coil. These impulses, according to Bell's theory, correspond in form to the sound-waves, and, passing over the line, energize the magnet coil at the receiving end, thus giving rise to corresponding variations in magnetism by reason of which the receiving diaphragm is similarly vibrated so as to reproduce the sounds. A single apparatus at each end is therefore sufficient, performing the double function of transmitter and receiver. It will be noticed that in this arrangement no battery is used The strength of the impulses transmitted is therefore limited to that of the necessarily weak induction currents generated by the original sounds minus any loss arising by reason of resistance in the line.

Edison's carbon transmitter overcame this vital or limiting weakness by providing for independent power on the transmission circuit, and by introducing the principle of varying the resistance of that circuit with changes in the pressure. With Edison's telephone there is used a closed circuit on which a battery current constantly flows, and in that circuit is a pair of electrodes, one or both of which is carbon. These electrodes are always in contact with a certain initial pressure, so that current will be always flowing over the circuit. One of the electrodes is connected with the diaphragm on which the sound-waves impinge, and the vibrations of this diaphragm cause corresponding variations in pressure between the electrodes, and thereby effect similar variations in the current which is passing over the line to the receiving end. This current, flowing around the receiving magnet, causes corresponding impulses therein, which, acting upon its diaphragm, effect a reproduction of the original vibrations and hence of the original sounds.

In other words, the essential difference is that with Bell's telephone the sound-waves themselves generate the electric impulses, which are therefore extremely faint. With Edison's telephone the sound-waves simply actuate an electric valve, so to speak, and permit variations in a current of any desired strength.

A second distinction between the two telephones is this: With the Bell apparatus the very weak electric impulses generated by the vibration of the transmitting diaphragm pass over the entire line to the receiving end, and, in consequence, the possible length of line is limited to a few miles, even under ideal conditions. With Edison's telephone the battery current does not flow on the main line, but passes through the primary circuit of an induction-coil, from the secondary of which corresponding impulses of enormously higher potential are sent out on the main line to the receiving end. In consequence, the line may be hundreds of miles in length. No modern telephone system is in use to-day that does not use these characteristic features: the varying resistance and the induction-coil. The system inaugurated by Edison is shown by the diagram (Fig. 3), in which the carbon transmitter, the induction-coil, the line, and the distant receiver are respectively indicated.

In Fig. 4 an early form of the Edison carbon transmitter is represented in sectional view.

The carbon disk is represented by the black portion, E, near the diaphragm, A, placed between two platinum plates D and G, which are connected in the battery circuit, as shown by the lines. A small piece of rubber tubing, B, is attached to the centre of the metallic diaphragm, and presses lightly against an ivory piece, F, which is placed directly over one of the platinum plates. Whenever, therefore, any motion is given to the diaphragm, it is immediately followed by a corresponding pressure upon the carbon, and by a change of resistance in the latter, as described above.

It is interesting to note the position which Edison occupies in the telephone art from a legal standpoint. To this end the reader's attention is called to a few extracts from a decision of Judge Brown in two suits brought in the United States Circuit Court, District of Massachusetts, by the American Bell Telephone Company against the National Telephone Manufacturing Company, et al., and Century Telephone Company, et al., reported in Federal Reporter, 109, page 976, et seq. These suits were brought on the Berliner patent, which, it was claimed, covered broadly the electrical transmission of speech by variations of pressure between opposing electrodes in constant contact. The Berliner patent was declared invalid, and in the course of a long and exhaustive opinion, in which the state of art and the work of Bell, Edison, Berliner, and others was fully discussed, the learned Judge made the following remarks: "The carbon electrode was the invention of Edison.... Edison preceded Berliner in the transmission of speech.... The carbon transmitter was an experimental invention of a very high order of merit.... Edison, by countless experiments, succeeded in advancing the art. . . . That Edison did produce speech with solid electrodes before Berliner is clearly proven.... The use of carbon in a transmitter is, beyond controversy, the invention of Edison. Edison was the first to make apparatus in which carbon was used as one of the electrodes.... The carbon transmitter displaced Bell's magnetic transmitter, and, under several forms of construction, remains the only commercial instrument.... The advance in the art was due to the carbon electrode of Edison.... It is conceded that the Edison transmitter as apparatus is a very important invention.... An immense amount of painstaking and highly ingenious experiment preceded Edison's successful result. The discovery of the availability of carbon was unquestionably invention, and it resulted in the 'first practical success in the art.'"

VII. EDISON'S TASIMETER

THIS interesting and remarkable device is one of Edison's many inventions not generally known to the public at large, chiefly because the range of its application has been limited to the higher branches of science. He never applied for a patent on the instrument, but dedicated it to the public.

The device was primarily intended for use in detecting and measuring infinitesimal degrees of temperature, however remote, and its conception followed Edison's researches on the carbon telephone transmitter. Its principle depends upon the variable resistance of carbon in accordance with the degree of pressure to which it is subjected. By means of this instrument, pressures that are otherwise inappreciable and undiscoverable may be observed and indicated.

The detection of small variations of temperatures is brought about through the changes which heat or cold will produce in a sensitive material placed in contact with a carbon button, which is put in circuit with a battery and delicate galvanometer. In the sketch (Fig. 1) there is illustrated, partly in section, the form of tasimeter which Edison took with him to Rawlins, Wyoming, in July, 1878, on the expedition to observe the total eclipse of the sun.

The substance on whose expansion the working of the instrument depends is a strip of some material extremely sensitive to heat, such as vulcanite. shown at A, and firmly clamped at B. Its lower end fits into a slot in a metal plate, C, which in turn rests upon a carbon button. This latter and the metal plate are connected in an electric circuit which includes a battery and a sensitive galvanometer. A vulcanite or other strip is easily affected by differences of temperature, expanding and contracting by reason of the minutest changes. Thus, an infinitesimal variation in its length through expansion or contraction changes the pressure on the carbon and affects the resistance of the circuit to a corresponding degree, thereby causing a deflection of the galvanometer; a movement of the needle in one direction denoting expansion, and in the other contraction. The strip, A, is first put under a slight pressure, deflecting the needle a few degrees from zero. Any subsequent expansion or contraction of the strip may readily be noted by further movements of the needle. In practice, and for measurements of a very delicate nature, the tasimeter is inserted in one arm of a Wheatstone bridge, as shown at A in the diagram (Fig. 2). The galvanometer is shown at B in the bridge wire, and at C, D, and E there are shown the resistances in the other arms of the bridge, which are adjusted to equal the resistance of the tasimeter circuit. The battery is shown at F. This arrangement tends to obviate any misleading deflections that might arise through changes in the battery.

The dial on the front of the instrument is intended to indicate the exact amount of physical expansion or contraction of the strip. This is ascertained by means of a micrometer screw, S, which moves a needle, T, in front of the dial. This screw engages with a second and similar screw which is so arranged as to move the strip of vulcanite up or down. After a galvanometer deflection has been obtained through the expansion or contraction of the strip by reason of a change of temperature, a similar deflection is obtained mechanically by turning the screw, S, one way or the other. This causes the vulcanite strip to press more or less upon the carbon button, and thus produces the desired change in the resistance of the circuit. When the galvanometer shows the desired deflection, the needle, T, will indicate upon the dial, in decimal fractions of an inch, the exact distance through which the strip has been moved.

With such an instrument as the above, Edison demonstrated the existence of heat in the corona at the above-mentioned total eclipse of the sun, but exact determinations could not be made at that time, because the tasimeter adjustment was too delicate, and at the best the galvanometer deflections were so marked that they could not be kept within the limits of the scale. The sensitiveness of the instrument may be easily comprehended when it is stated that the heat of the hand thirty feet away from the cone-like funnel of the tasimeter will so affect the galvanometer as to cause the spot of light to leave the scale.

This instrument can also be used to indicate minute changes of moisture in the air by substituting a strip of gelatine in place of the vulcanite. When so arranged a moistened piece of paper held several feet away will cause a minute expansion of the gelatine strip, which effects a pressure on the carbon, and causes a variation in the circuit sufficient to throw the spot of light from the galvanometer mirror off the scale.

The tasimeter has been used to demonstrate heat from remote stars (suns), such as Arcturus.

VIII. THE EDISON PHONOGRAPH

THE first patent that was ever granted on a device for permanently recording the human voice and other sounds, and for reproducing the same audibly at any future time, was United States Patent No. 200,251, issued to Thomas A. Edison on February 19, 1878, the application having been filed December 24, 1877. It is worthy of note that no references whatever were cited against the application while under examination in the Patent Office. This invention therefore, marked the very beginning of an entirely new art, which, with the new industries attendant upon its development, has since grown to occupy a position of worldwide reputation.

That the invention was of a truly fundamental character is also evident from the fact that although all "talking-machines" of to-day differ very widely in refinement from the first crude but successful phonograph of Edison, their performance is absolutely dependent upon the employment of the principles stated by him in his Patent No. 200,251. Quoting from the specification attached to this patent, we find that Edison said:

"The invention consists in arranging a plate, diaphragm or other flexible body capable of being vibrated by the human voice or other sounds, in conjunction with a material capable of registering the movements of such vibrating body by embossing or indenting or altering such material, in such a manner that such register marks will be sufficient to cause a second vibrating plate or body to be set in motion by them, and thus reproduce the motions of the first vibrating body."

It will be at once obvious that these words describe perfectly the basic principle of every modern phonograph or other talking-machine, irrespective of its manufacture or trade name.

Edison's first model of the phonograph is shown in the following illustration.

It consisted of a metallic cylinder having a helical indenting groove cut upon it from end to end. This cylinder was mounted on a shaft supported on two standards. This shaft at one end was fitted with a handle, by means of which the cylinder was rotated. There were two diaphragms, one on each side of the cylinder, one being for recording and the other for reproducing speech or other sounds. Each diaphragm had attached to it a needle. By means of the needle attached to the recording diaphragm, indentations were made in a sheet of tin-foil stretched over the peripheral surface of the cylinder when the diaphragm was vibrated by reason of speech or other sounds. The needle on the other diaphragm subsequently followed these indentations, thus reproducing the original sounds.

Crude as this first model appears in comparison with machines of later development and refinement, it embodied their fundamental essentials, and was in fact a complete, practical phonograph from the first moment of its operation.

The next step toward the evolution of the improved phonograph of to-day was another form of tin-foil machine, as seen in the illustration.

It will be noted that this was merely an elaborated form of the first model, and embodied several mechanical modifications, among which was the employment of only one diaphragm for recording and reproducing. Such was the general type of phonograph used for exhibition purposes in America and other countries in the three or four years immediately succeeding the date of this invention.

In operating the machine the recording diaphragm was advanced nearly to the cylinder, so that as the diaphragm was vibrated by the voice the needle would prick or indent a wave-like record in the tin-foil that was on the cylinder. The cylinder was constantly turned during the recording, and in turning, was simultaneously moved forward. Thus the record would be formed on the tin-foil in a continuous spiral line. To reproduce this record it was only necessary to again start at the beginning and cause the needle to retrace its path in the spiral line. The needle, in passing rapidly in contact with the recorded waves, was vibrated up and down, causing corresponding vibrations of the diaphragm. In this way sound-waves similar to those caused by the original sounds would be set up in the air, thus reproducing the original speech.

The modern phonograph operates in a precisely similar way, the only difference being in details of refinement. Instead of tin-foil, a wax cylinder is employed, the record being cut thereon by a cutting-tool attached to a diaphragm, while the reproduction is effected by means of a blunt stylus similarly attached.

The cutting-tool and stylus are devices made of sapphire, a gem next in hardness to a diamond, and they have to be cut and formed to an exact nicety by means of diamond dust, most of the work being performed under high-powered microscopes. The minute proportions of these devices will be apparent by a glance at the accompanying illustrations, in which the object on the left represents a common pin, and the objects on the right the cutting-tool and reproducing stylus, all actual sizes.

In the next illustration (Fig. 4) there is shown in the upper sketch, greatly magnified, the cutting or recording tool in the act of forming the record, being vibrated rapidly by the diaphragm; and in the lower sketch, similarly enlarged, a representation of the stylus travelling over the record thus made, in the act of effecting a reproduction.

From the late summer of 1878 and to the fall of 1887 Edison was intensely busy on the electric light, electric railway, and other problems, and virtually gave no attention to the phonograph. Hence, just prior to the latter-named period the instrument was still in its tin-foil age; but he then began to devote serious attention to the development of an improved type that should be of greater commercial importance. The practical results are too well known to call for further comment. That his efforts were not limited in extent may be inferred from the fact that since the fall of 1887 to the present writing he has been granted in the United States one hundred and four patents relating to the phonograph and its accessories.

Interesting as the numerous inventions are, it would be a work of supererogation to digest all these patents in the present pages, as they represent not only the inception but also the gradual development and growth of the wax-record type of phonograph from its infancy to the present perfected machine and records now so widely known all over the world. From among these many inventions, however, we will select two or three as examples of ingenuity and importance in their bearing upon present perfection of results.

One of the difficulties of reproduction for many years was the trouble experienced in keeping the stylus in perfect engagement with the wave-like record, so that every minute vibration would be reproduced. It should be remembered that the deepest cut of the recording tool is only about one-third the thickness of tissue-paper. Hence, it will be quite apparent that the slightest inequality in the surface of the wax would be sufficient to cause false vibration, and thus give rise to distorted effects in such music or other sounds as were being reproduced. To remedy this, Edison added an attachment which is called a "floating weight," and is shown at A in the illustration above.

The function of the floating weight is to automatically keep the stylus in close engagement with the record, thus insuring accuracy of reproduction. The weight presses the stylus to its work, but because of its mass it cannot respond to the extremely rapid vibrations of the stylus. They are therefore communicated to the diaphragm.

Some of Edison's most remarkable inventions are revealed in a number of interesting patents relating to the duplication of phonograph records. It would be obviously impossible, from a commercial standpoint, to obtain a musical record from a high-class artist and sell such an original to the public, as its cost might be from one hundred to several thousand dollars. Consequently, it is necessary to provide some way by which duplicates may be made cheaply enough to permit their purchase by the public at a reasonable price.

The making of a perfect original musical or other record is a matter of no small difficulty, as it requires special technical knowledge and skill gathered from many years of actual experience; but in the exact copying, or duplication, of such a record, with its many millions of microscopic waves and sub-waves, the difficulties are enormously increased. The duplicates must be microscopically identical with the original, they must be free from false vibrations or other defects, although both original and duplicates are of such easily defacable material as wax; and the process must be cheap and commercial not a scientific laboratory possibility.

For making duplicates it was obviously necessary to first secure a mold carrying the record in negative or reversed form. From this could be molded, or cast, positive copies which would be identical with the original. While the art of electroplating would naturally suggest itself as the means of making such a mold, an apparently insurmountable obstacle appeared on the very threshold. Wax, being a non-conductor, cannot be electroplated unless a conducting surface be first applied. The coatings ordinarily used in electro-deposition were entirely out of the question on account of coarseness, the deepest waves of the record being less than one-thousandth of an inch in depth, and many of them probably ten to one hundred times as shallow. Edison finally decided to apply a preliminary metallic coating of infinitesimal thinness, and accomplished this object by a remarkable process known as the vacuous deposit. With this he applied to the original record a film of gold probably no thicker than one three-hundred-thousandth of an inch, or several hundred times less than the depth of an average wave. Three hundred such layers placed one on top of the other would make a sheet no thicker than tissue-paper.

The process consists in placing in a vacuum two leaves, or electrodes, of gold, and between them the original record. A constant discharge of electricity of high tension between the electrodes is effected by means of an induction-coil. The metal is vaporized by this discharge, and is carried by it directly toward and deposited upon the original record, thus forming the minute film of gold above mentioned. The record is constantly rotated until its entire surface is coated. A sectional diagram of the apparatus (Fig. 6.) will aid to a clearer understanding of this ingenious process.

After the gold film is formed in the manner described above, a heavy backing of baser metal is electroplated upon it, thus forming a substantial mold, from which the original record is extracted by breakage or shrinkage.

Duplicate records in any quantity may now be made from this mold by surrounding it with a cold-water jacket and dipping it in a molten wax-like material. This congeals on the record surface just as melted butter would collect on a cold knife, and when the mold is removed the surplus wax falls out, leaving a heavy deposit of the material which forms the duplicate record. Numerous ingenious inventions have been made by Edison providing for a variety of rapid and economical methods of duplication, including methods of shrinking a newly made copy to facilitate its quick removal from the mold; methods of reaming, of forming ribs on the interior, and for many other important and essential details, which limits of space will not permit of elaboration. Those mentioned above are but fair examples of the persistent and effective work he has done to bring the phonograph to its present state of perfection.

In perusing Chapter X of the foregoing narrative, the reader undoubtedly noted Edison's clear apprehension of the practical uses of the phonograph, as evidenced by his prophetic utterances in the article written by him for the North American Review in June, 1878. In view of the crudity of the instrument at that time, it must be acknowledged that Edison's foresight, as vindicated by later events was most remarkable. No less remarkable was his intensely practical grasp of mechanical possibilities of future types of the machine, for we find in one of his early English patents (No. 1644 of 1878) the disk form of phonograph which, some ten to fifteen years later, was supposed to be a new development in the art. This disk form was also covered by Edison's application for a United States patent, filed in 1879. This application met with some merely minor technical objections in the Patent Office, and seems to have passed into the "abandoned" class for want of prosecution, probably because of being overlooked in the tremendous pressure arising from his development of his electric-lighting system.

IX. THE INCANDESCENT LAMP

ALTHOUGH Edison's contributions to human comfort and progress are extensive in number and extraordinarily vast and comprehensive in scope and variety, the universal verdict of the world points to his incandescent lamp and system of distribution of electrical current as the central and crowning achievements of his life up to this time. This view would seem entirely justifiable when we consider the wonderful changes in the conditions of modern life that have been brought about by the wide-spread employment of these inventions, and the gigantic industries that have grown up and been nourished by their world-wide application. That he was in this instance a true pioneer and creator is evident as we consider the subject, for the United States Patent No. 223,898, issued to Edison on January 27, 1880, for an incandescent lamp, was of such fundamental character that it opened up an entirely new and tremendously important art--the art of incandescent electric lighting. This statement cannot be successfully controverted, for it has been abundantly verified after many years of costly litigation. If further proof were desired, it is only necessary to point to the fact that, after thirty years of most strenuous and practical application in the art by the keenest intellects of the world, every incandescent lamp that has ever since been made, including those of modern days, is still dependent upon the employment of the essentials disclosed in the above-named patent--namely, a filament of high resistance enclosed in a sealed glass globe exhausted of air, with conducting wires passing through the glass.

An incandescent lamp is such a simple-appearing article--merely a filament sealed into a glass globe--that its intrinsic relation to the art of electric lighting is far from being apparent at sight. To the lay mind it would seem that this must have been THE obvious device to make in order to obtain electric light by incandescence of carbon or other material. But the reader has already learned from the preceding narrative that prior to its invention by Edison such a device was NOT obvious, even to the most highly trained experts of the world at that period; indeed, it was so far from being obvious that, for some time after he had completed practical lamps and was actually lighting them up twenty-four hours a day, such a device and such a result were declared by these same experts to be an utter impossibility. For a short while the world outside of Menlo Park held Edison's claims in derision. His lamp was pronounced a fake, a myth, possibly a momentary success magnified to the dignity of a permanent device by an overenthusiastic inventor.

Such criticism, however, did not disturb Edison. He KNEW that he had reached the goal. Long ago, by a close process of reasoning, he had clearly seen that the only road to it was through the path he had travelled, and which was now embodied in the philosophy of his incandescent lamp--namely, a filament, or carbon, of high resistance and small radiating surface, sealed into a glass globe exhausted of air to a high degree of vacuum. In originally committing himself to this line of investigation he was well aware that he was going in a direction diametrically opposite to that followed by previous investigators. Their efforts had been confined to low-resistance burners of large radiating surface for their lamps, but he realized the utter futility of such devices. The tremendous problems of heat and the prohibitive quantities of copper that would be required for conductors for such lamps would be absolutely out of the question in commercial practice.

He was convinced from the first that the true solution of the problem lay in a lamp which should have as its illuminating body a strip of material which would offer such a resistance to the flow of electric current that it could be raised to a high temperature--incandescence--and be of such small cross-section that it would radiate but little heat. At the same time such a lamp must require a relatively small amount of current, in order that comparatively small conductors could be used, and its burner must be capable of withstanding the necessarily high temperatures without disintegration.

It is interesting to note that these conceptions were in Edison's mind at an early period of his investigations, when the best expert opinion was that the subdivision of the electric current was an ignis fatuus. Hence we quote the following notes he made, November 15, 1878, in one of the laboratory note-books:

"A given straight wire having 1 ohm resistance and certain length is brought to a given degree of temperature by given battery. If the same wire be coiled in such a manner that but one-quarter of its surface radiates, its temperature will be increased four times with the same battery, or, one-quarter of this battery will bring it to the temperature of straight wire. Or the same given battery will bring a wire whose total resistance is 4 ohms to the same temperature as straight wire.

"This was actually determined by trial.

"The amount of heat lost by a body is in proportion to the radiating surface of that body. If one square inch of platina be heated to 100 degrees it will fall to, say, zero in one second, whereas, if it was at 200 degrees it would require two seconds.

"Hence, in the case of incandescent conductors, if the radiating surface be twelve inches and the temperature on each inch be 100, or 1200 for all, if it is so coiled or arranged that there is but one-quarter, or three inches, of radiating surface, then the temperature on each inch will be 400. If reduced to three-quarters of an inch it will have on that three-quarters of an inch 1600 degrees Fahr., notwithstanding the original total amount was but 1200, because the radiation has been reduced to three-quarters, or 75 units; hence, the effect of the lessening of the radiation is to raise the temperature of each remaining inch not radiating to 125 degrees. If the radiating surface should be reduced to three-thirty-seconds of an inch, the temperature would reach 6400 degrees Fahr. To carry out this law to the best advantage in regard to platina, etc., then with a given length of wire to quadruple the heat we must lessen the radiating surface to one-quarter, and to do this in a spiral, three-quarters must be within the spiral and one-quarter outside for radiating; hence, a square wire or other means, such as a spiral within a spiral, must be used. These results account for the enormous temperature of the Electric Arc with one horse-power; as, for instance, if one horse-power will heat twelve inches of wire to 1000 degrees Fahr., and this is concentrated to have one-quarter of the radiating surface, it would reach a temperature of 4000 degrees or sufficient to melt it; but, supposing it infusible, the further concentration to one-eighth its surface, it would reach a temperature of 16,000 degrees, and to one-thirty-second its surface, which would be about the radiating surface of the Electric Arc, it would reach 64,000 degrees Fahr. Of course, when Light is radiated in great quantities not quite these temperatures would be reached.

"Another curious law is this: It will require a greater initial battery to bring an iron wire of the same size and resistance to a given temperature than it will a platina wire in proportion to their specific heats, and in the case of Carbon, a piece of Carbon three inches long and one-eighth diameter, with a resistance of 1 ohm, will require a greater battery power to bring it to a given temperature than a cylinder of thin platina foil of the same length, diameter, and resistance, because the specific heat of Carbon is many times greater; besides, if I am not mistaken, the radiation of a roughened body for heat is greater than a polished one like platina."

Proceeding logically upon these lines of thought and following them out through many ramifications, we have seen how he at length made a filament of carbon of high resistance and small radiating surface, and through a concurrent investigation of the phenomena of high vacua and occluded gases was able to produce a true incandescent lamp. Not only was it a lamp as a mere article--a device to give light--but it was also an integral part of his great and complete system of lighting, to every part of which it bore a fixed and definite ratio, and in relation to which it was the keystone that held the structure firmly in place.

The work of Edison on incandescent lamps did not stop at this fundamental invention, but extended through more than eighteen years of a most intense portion of his busy life. During that period he was granted one hundred and forty-nine other patents on the lamp and its manufacture. Although very many of these inventions were of the utmost importance and value, we cannot attempt to offer a detailed exposition of them in this necessarily brief article, but must refer the reader, if interested, to the patents themselves, a full list being given at the end of this Appendix. The outline sketch will indicate the principal patents covering the basic features of the lamp.

The litigation on the Edison lamp patents was one of the most determined and stubbornly fought contests in the history of modern jurisprudence. Vast interests were at stake. All of the technical, expert, and professional skill and knowledge that money could procure or experience devise were availed of in the bitter fights that raged in the courts for many years. And although the Edison interests had spent from first to last nearly $2,000,000, and had only about three years left in the life of the fundamental patent, Edison was thoroughly sustained as to priority by the decisions in the various suits. We shall offer a few brief extracts from some of these decisions.

In a suit against the United States Electric Lighting Company, United States Circuit Court for the Southern District of New York, July 14, 1891, Judge Wallace said, in his opinion: "The futility of hoping to maintain a burner in vacuo with any permanency had discouraged prior inventors, and Mr. Edison is entitled to the credit of obviating the mechanical difficulties which disheartened them.... He was the first to make a carbon of materials, and by a process which was especially designed to impart high specific resistance to it; the first to make a carbon in the special form for the special purpose of imparting to it high total resistance; and the first to combine such a burner with the necessary adjuncts of lamp construction to prevent its disintegration and give it sufficiently long life. By doing these things he made a lamp which was practically operative and successful, the embryo of the best lamps now in commercial use, and but for which the subdivision of the electric light by incandescence would still be nothing but the ignis fatuus which it was proclaimed to be in 1879 by some of the reamed experts who are now witnesses to belittle his achievement and show that it did not rise to the dignity of an invention.... It is impossible to resist the conclusion that the invention of the slender thread of carbon as a substitute for the burners previously employed opened the path to the practical subdivision of the electric light."

An appeal was taken in the above suit to the United States Circuit Court of Appeals, and on October 4, 1892, the decree of the lower court was affirmed. The judges (Lacombe and Shipman), in a long opinion reviewed the facts and the art, and said, inter alia: "Edison's invention was practically made when he ascertained the theretofore unknown fact that carbon would stand high temperature, even when very attenuated, if operated in a high vacuum, without the phenomenon of disintegration. This fact he utilized by the means which he has described, a lamp having a filamentary carbon burner in a nearly perfect vacuum."

In a suit against the Boston Incandescent Lamp Company et al., in the United States Circuit Court for the District of Massachusetts, decided in favor of Edison on June 11, 1894, Judge Colt, in his opinion, said, among other things: "Edison made an important invention; he produced the first practical incandescent electric lamp; the patent is a pioneer in the sense of the patent law; it may be said that his invention created the art of incandescent electric lighting."

Opinions of other courts, similar in tenor to the foregoing, might be cited, but it would be merely in the nature of reiteration. The above are sufficient to illustrate the direct clearness of judicial decision on Edison's position as the founder of the art of electric lighting by incandescence.

X. EDISON'S DYNAMO WORK

AT the present writing, when, after the phenomenally rapid electrical development of thirty years, we find on the market a great variety of modern forms of efficient current generators advertised under the names of different inventors (none, however, bearing the name of Edison), a young electrical engineer of the present generation might well inquire whether the great inventor had ever contributed anything to the art beyond a mere TYPE of machine formerly made and bearing his name, but not now marketed except second hand.

For adequate information he might search in vain the books usually regarded as authorities on the subject of dynamo-electric machinery, for with slight exceptions there has been a singular unanimity in the omission of writers to give Edison credit for his great and basic contributions to heavy-current technics, although they have been universally acknowledged by scientific and practical men to have laid the foundation for the efficiency of, and to be embodied in all modern generators of current.

It might naturally be expected that the essential facts of Edison's work would appear on the face of his numerous patents on dynamo-electric machinery, but such is not necessarily the case, unless they are carefully studied in the light of the state of the art as it existed at the time. While some of these patents (especially the earlier ones) cover specific devices embodying fundamental principles that not only survive to the present day, but actually lie at the foundation of the art as it now exists, there is no revelation therein of Edison's preceding studies of magnets, which extended over many years, nor of his later systematic investigations and deductions.

Dynamo-electric machines of a primitive kind had been invented and were in use to a very limited extent for arc lighting and electroplating for some years prior to the summer of 1819, when Edison, with an embryonic lighting SYSTEM in mind, cast about for a type of machine technically and commercially suitable for the successful carrying out of his plans. He found absolutely none. On the contrary, all of the few types then obtainable were uneconomical, indeed wasteful, in regard to efficiency. The art, if indeed there can be said to have been an art at that time, was in chaotic confusion, and only because of Edison's many years' study of the magnet was he enabled to conclude that insufficiency in quantity of iron in the magnets of such machines, together with poor surface contacts, rendered the cost of magnetization abnormally high. The heating of solid armatures, the only kind then known, and poor insulation in the commutators, also gave rise to serious losses. But perhaps the most serious drawback lay in the high-resistance armature, based upon the highest scientific dictum of the time that in order to obtain the maximum amount of work from a machine, the internal resistance of the armature must equal the resistance of the exterior circuit, although the application of this principle entailed the useless expenditure of at least 50 per cent. of the applied energy.

It seems almost incredible that only a little over thirty years ago the sum of scientific knowledge in regard to dynamo-electric machines was so meagre that the experts of the period should settle upon such a dictum as this, but such was the fact, as will presently appear. Mechanical generators of electricity were comparatively new at that time; their theory and practice were very imperfectly understood; indeed, it is quite within the bounds of truth to say that the correct principles were befogged by reason of the lack of practical knowledge of their actual use. Electricians and scientists of the period had been accustomed for many years past to look to the chemical battery as the source from which to obtain electrical energy; and in the practical application of such energy to telegraphy and kindred uses, much thought and ingenuity had been expended in studying combinations of connecting such cells so as to get the best results. In the text-books of the period it was stated as a settled principle that, in order to obtain the maximum work out of a set of batteries, the internal resistance must approximately equal the resistance of the exterior circuit. This principle and its application in practice were quite correct as regards chemical batteries, but not as regards dynamo machines. Both were generators of electrical current, but so different in construction and operation, that rules applicable to the practical use of the one did not apply with proper commercial efficiency to the other. At the period under consideration, which may be said to have been just before dawn of the day of electric light, the philosophy of the dynamo was seen only in mysterious, hazy outlines--just emerging from the darkness of departing night. Perhaps it is not surprising, then, that the dynamo was loosely regarded by electricians as the practical equivalent of a chemical battery; that many of the characteristics of performance of the chemical cell were also attributed to it, and that if the maximum work could be gotten out of a set of batteries when the internal and external resistances were equal (and this was commercially the best thing to do), so must it be also with a dynamo.

It was by no miracle that Edison was far and away ahead of his time when he undertook to improve the dynamo. He was possessed of absolute KNOWLEDGE far beyond that of his contemporaries. This he ad acquired by the hardest kind of work and incessant experiment with magnets of all kinds during several years preceding, particularly in connection with his study of automatic telegraphy. His knowledge of magnets was tremendous. He had studied and experimented with electromagnets in enormous variety, and knew their peculiarities in charge and discharge, lag, self-induction, static effects, condenser effects, and the various other phenomena connected therewith. He had also made collateral studies of iron, steel, and copper, insulation, winding, etc. Hence, by reason of this extensive work and knowledge, Edison was naturally in a position to realize the utter commercial impossibility of the then best dynamo machine in existence, which had an efficiency of only about 40 per cent., and was constructed on the "cut-and-try" principle.

He was also naturally in a position to assume the task he set out to accomplish, of undertaking to plan and-build an improved type of machine that should be commercial in having an efficiency of at least 90 per cent. Truly a prodigious undertaking in those dark days, when from the standpoint of Edison's large experience the most practical and correct electrical treatise was contained in the Encyclopaedia Britannica, and in a German publication which Mr. Upton had brought with him after he had finished his studies with the illustrious Helmholtz. It was at this period that Mr. Upton commenced his association with Edison, bringing to the great work the very latest scientific views and the assistance of the higher mathematics, to which he had devoted his attention for several years previously.

As some account of Edison's investigations in this connection has already been given in Chapter XII of the narrative, we shall not enlarge upon them here, but quote from An Historical Review, by Charles L. Clarke, Laboratory Assistant at Menlo Park, 1880-81; Chief Engineer of the Edison Electric Light Company, 1881-84:

"In June, 1879, was published the account of the Edison dynamo-electric machine that survived in the art. This machine went into extensive commercial use, and was notable for its very massive and powerful field-magnets and armature of extremely low resistance as compared with the combined external resistance of the supply-mains and lamps. By means of the large masses of iron in the field-magnets, and closely fitted joints between the several parts thereof, the magnetic resistance (reluctance) of the iron parts of the magnetic circuit was reduced to a minimum, and the required magnetization effected with the maximum economy. At the same time Mr. Edison announced the commercial necessity of having the armature of the dynamo of low resistance, as compared with the external resistance, in order that a large percentage of the electrical energy developed should be utilized in the lamps, and only a small percentage lost in the armature, albeit this procedure reduced the total generating capacity of the machine. He also proposed to make the resistance of the supply-mains small, as compared with the combined resistance of the lamps in multiple arc, in order to still further increase the percentage of energy utilized in the lamps. And likewise to this end the combined resistance of the generator armatures in multiple arc was kept relatively small by adjusting the number of generators operating in multiple at any time to the number of lamps then in use. The field-magnet circuits of the dynamos were connected in multiple with a separate energizing source; and the field-current; and strength of field, were regulated to maintain the required amount of electromotive force upon the supply-mains under all conditions of load from the maximum to the minimum number of lamps in use, and to keep the electromotive force of all machines alike."

Among the earliest of Edison's dynamo experiments were those relating to the core of the armature. He realized at once that the heat generated in a solid core was a prolific source of loss. He experimented with bundles of iron wires variously insulated, also with sheet-iron rolled cylindrically and covered with iron wire wound concentrically. These experiments and many others were tried in a great variety of ways, until, as the result of all this work, Edison arrived at the principle which has remained in the art to this day. He split up the iron core of the armature into thin laminations, separated by paper, thus practically suppressing Foucault currents therein and resulting heating effect. It was in his machine also that mica was used for the first time as an insulating medium in a commutator. [27]

[Footnote 27: The commercial manufacture of built-up sheets of mica for electrical purposes was first established at the Edison Machine Works, Goerck Street, New York, in 1881.]

Elementary as these principles will appear to the modern student or engineer, they were denounced as nothing short of absurdity at the time of their promulgation--especially so with regard to Edison's proposal to upset the then settled dictum that the armature resistance should be equal to the external resistance. His proposition was derided in the technical press of the period, both at home and abroad. As public opinion can be best illustrated by actual quotation, we shall present a characteristic instance.

In the Scientific American of October 18, 1879, there appeared an illustrated article by Mr. Upton on Edison's dynamo machine, in which Edison's views and claims were set forth. A subsequent issue contained a somewhat acrimonious letter of criticism by a well-known maker of dynamo machines. At the risk of being lengthy, we must quote nearly all this letter: "I can scarcely conceive it as possible that the article on the above subject '(Edison's Electric Generator)' in last week's Scientific American could have been written from statements derived from Mr. Edison himself, inasmuch as so many of the advantages claimed for the machine described and statements of the results obtained are so manifestly absurd as to indicate on the part of both writer and prompter a positive want of knowledge of the electric circuit and the principles governing the construction and operation of electric machines.

"It is not my intention to criticise the design or construction of the machine (not because they are not open to criticism), as I am now and have been for many years engaged in the manufacture of electric machines, but rather to call attention to the impossibility of obtaining the described results without destroying the doctrine of the conservation and correlation of forces.

. . . . .

"It is stated that 'the internal resistance of the armature' of this machine 'is only 1/2 ohm.' On this fact and the disproportion between this resistance and that of the external circuit, the theory of the alleged efficiency of the machine is stated to be based, for we are informed that, 'while this generator in general principle is the same as in the best well-known forms, still there is an all-important difference, which is that it will convert and deliver for useful work nearly double the number of foot-pounds that any other machine will under like conditions.'" The writer of this critical letter then proceeds to quote Mr. Upton's statement of this efficiency: "'Now the energy converted is distributed over the whole resistance, hence if the resistance of the machine be represented by 1 and the exterior circuit by 9, then of the total energy converted nine-tenths will be useful, as it is outside of the machine, and one-tenth is lost in the resistance of the machine.'"

After this the critic goes on to say:

"How any one acquainted with the laws of the electric circuit can make such statements is what I cannot understand. The statement last quoted is mathematically absurd. It implies either that the machine is CAPABLE OF INCREASING ITS OWN ELECTROMOTIVE FORCE NINE TIMES WITHOUT AN INCREASED EXPENDITURE OF POWER, or that external resistance is NOT resistance to the current induced in the Edison machine.

"Does Mr. Edison, or any one for him, mean to say that r/n enables him to obtain nE, and that C IS NOT $= E / (r/n + R)$? If so Mr. Edison has discovered something MORE than perpetual motion, and Mr. Keely had better retire from the field.

"Further on the writer (Mr. Upton) gives us another example of this mode of reasoning when, emboldened and satisfied with the absurd theory above exposed, he endeavors to prove the cause of the inefficiency of the Siemens and other machines. Couldn't the writer of the article see that since $C = E/(r + R)$ that by R/n or by making $R = r$, the machine would, according to his theory, have returned more useful current to the circuit than could be due to the power employed (and in the ratio indicated), so that there would actually be a creation of force! . . . .

"In conclusion allow me to say that if Mr Edison thinks he has accomplished so much by the REDUCTION OF THE INTERNAL RESISTANCE of his machine, that he has much more to do in this direction before his machine will equal IN THIS RESPECT others already in the market."

Another participant in the controversy on Edison's generator was a scientific gentleman, who in a long article published in the Scientific American, in November, 1879, gravely undertook to instruct Edison in the A B C of electrical principles, and then proceeded to demonstrate mathematically the IMPOSSIBILITY of doing WHAT EDISON HAD ACTUALLY DONE. This critic concludes with a gentle rebuke to the inventor for ill-timed jesting, and a suggestion to furnish AUTHENTIC information!

In the light of facts, as they were and are, this article is so full of humor that we shall indulge in a few quotations It commences in A B C fashion as follows: "Electric machines convert mechanical into electrical energy.... The ratio of yield to consumption is the expression of the efficiency of the machine.... How many foot-pounds of electricity can be got out of 100 foot-pounds of mechanical energy? Certainly not more than 100: certainly less.... The facts and laws of physics, with the assistance of mathematical logic, never fail to furnish precious answers to such questions."

The would-be critic then goes on to tabulate tests of certain other dynamo machines by a committee of the Franklin Institute in 1879, the results of which showed that these machines returned about 50 per cent. of the applied mechanical energy, ingenuously remarking: "Why is it that when we have produced the electricity, half of it must slip away? Some persons will be content if they are told simply that it is a way which electricity has of behaving. But there is a satisfactory rational explanation which I believe can be made plain to persons of ordinary intelligence. It ought to be known to all those who are making or using machines. I am grieved to observe that many persons who talk and write glibly about electricity do not understand it; some even ignore or deny the fact to be explained."

Here follows HIS explanation, after which he goes on to say: "At this point plausibly comes in a suggestion that the internal part of the circuit be made very small and the external part very large. Why not (say) make the internal part 1 and the external 9, thus saving nine-tenths and losing only one-tenth? Unfortunately, the suggestion is not practical; a fallacy is concealed in it."

He then goes on to prove his case mathematically, to his own satisfaction, following it sadly by condoling with and a warning to Edison: "But about Edison's electric generator! . . . No one capable of making the improvements in the telegraph and telephone, for which we are indebted to Mr. Edison, could be other than an accomplished electrician. His reputation as a scientist, indeed, is smirched by the newspaper exaggerations, and no doubt he will be more careful in future. But there is a danger nearer home, indeed, among his own friends and in his very household.

". . . The writer of page 242" (the original article) "is probably a friend of Mr. Edison, but possibly, alas! a wicked partner. Why does he say such things as these? 'Mr. Edison claims that he realizes 90 per cent. of the power applied to this machine in external work.' . . . Perhaps the writer is a humorist, and had in his mind Colonel Sellers, etc., which he could not keep out of a serious discussion; but such jests are not good.

"Mr. Edison has built a very interesting machine, and he has the opportunity of making a valuable contribution to the electrical arts by furnishing authentic accounts of its capabilities."

The foregoing extracts are unavoidably lengthy, but, viewed in the light of facts, serve to illustrate most clearly that Edison's conceptions and work were far and away ahead of the comprehension of his contemporaries in the art, and that his achievements in the line of efficient dynamo design and construction were indeed truly fundamental and revolutionary in character. Much more of similar nature to the above could be quoted from other articles published elsewhere, but the foregoing will serve as instances generally representing all. In the controversy which appeared in the columns of the Scientific American, Mr. Upton, Edison's mathematician, took up the question on his side, and answered the critics by further elucidations of the principles on which Edison had founded such remarkable and radical improvements in the art. The type of Edison's first dynamo-electric machine, the description of which gave rise to the above controversy, is shown in Fig. 1.

Any account of Edison's work on the dynamo would be incomplete did it omit to relate his conception and construction of the great direct-connected steam-driven generator that was the prototype of the colossal units which are used throughout the world to-day.

In the demonstrating plant installed and operated by him at Menlo Park in 1880 ten dynamos of eight horse-power each were driven by a slow-speed engine through a complicated system of counter-shafting, and, to quote from Mr. Clarke's Historical Review, "it was found that a considerable percentage of the power of the engine was necessarily wasted in friction by this method of driving, and to prevent this waste and thus increase the economy of his system, Mr. Edison conceived the idea of substituting a single large dynamo for the several small dynamos, and directly coupling it with the driving engine, and at the same time preserve the requisite high armature speed by using an engine of the high-speed type. He also expected to realize still further gains in economy from the use of a large dynamo in place of several small machines by a more than correspondingly lower armature resistance, less energy for magnetizing the field, and for other minor reasons. To the same end, he intended to supply steam to the engine under a much higher boiler pressure than was customary in stationary-engine driving at that time."

The construction of the first one of these large machines was commenced late in the year 1880. Early in 1881 it was completed and tested, but some radical defects in armature construction were developed, and it was also demonstrated that a rate of engine speed too high for continuously safe and economical operation had been chosen. The machine was laid aside. An accurate illustration of this machine, as it stood in the engine-room at Menlo Park, is given in Van Nostrand's Engineering Magazine, Vol. XXV, opposite page 439, and a brief description is given on page 450.

With the experience thus gained, Edison began, in the spring of 1881, at the Edison Machine Works, Goerck Street, New York City, the construction of the first successful machine of this type. This was the great machine known as "Jumbo No. 1," which is referred to in the narrative as having been exhibited at the Paris International Electrical Exposition, where it was regarded as the wonder of the electrical world. An intimation of some of the tremendous difficulties encountered in the construction of this machine has already been given in preceding pages, hence we shall not now enlarge on the subject, except to note in passing that the terribly destructive effects of the spark of self-induction and the arcing following it were first manifested in this powerful machine, but were finally overcome by Edison after a strenuous application of his powers to the solution of the problem.

It may be of interest, however, to mention some of its dimensions and electrical characteristics, quoting again from Mr. Clarke: "The field-magnet had eight solid cylindrical cores, 8 inches in diameter and 57 inches long, upon each of which was wound an exciting-coil of 3.2 ohms resistance, consisting of 2184 turns of No. 10 B. W. G. insulated copper wire, disposed in six layers. The laminated iron core of the armature, formed of thin iron disks, was 33 3/4 inches long, and had an internal diameter of 12 1/2 inches, and an external diameter of 26 7/16 inches. It was mounted on a 6-inch shaft. The field-poles were 33 3/4 inches long, and 27 1/2 inches inside diameter The armature winding consisted of 146 copper bars on the face of the core, connected into a closed-coil winding by means of 73 copper disks at each end of the core. The cross-sectional area of each bar was 0.2 square inch their average length was 42.7 inches, and the copper end-disks were 0.065 inch thick. The commutator had 73 sections. The armature resistance was 0.0092 ohm, [28] of which 0.0055 ohm was in the armature bars and 0.0037 ohm in the end-disks." An illustration of the next latest type of this machine is presented in Fig. 2.

[Footnote 28: Had Edison in Upton's Scientific American article in 1879 proposed such an exceedingly low armature resistance for this immense generator (although its ratio was proportionate to the original machine), his critics might probably have been sufficiently indignant as to be unable to express themselves coherently.]

The student may find it interesting to look up Edison's United States Patents Nos. 242,898, 263,133, 263,146, and 246,647, bearing upon the construction of the "Jumbo"; also illustrated articles in the technical journals of the time, among which may be mentioned: Scientific American, Vol. XLV, page 367; Engineering, London, Vol. XXXII, pages 409 and 419,

The Telegraphic Journal and Electrical Review, London, Vol. IX, pages 431-433, 436-446; La Nature, Paris, 9th year, Part II, pages 408-409; Zeitschrift fur Angewandte Elektricitaatslehre, Munich and Leipsic, Vol. IV, pages 4-14; and Dredge's Electric Illumination, 1882, Vol. I, page 261.

The further development of these great machines later on, and their extensive practical use, are well known and need no further comment, except in passing it may be noted that subsequent machines had each a capacity of 1200 lamps of 16 candle-power, and that the armature resistance was still further reduced to 0.0039 ohm.

Edison's clear insight into the future, as illustrated by his persistent advocacy of large direct-connected generating units, is abundantly vindicated by present-day practice. His Jumbo machines, of 175 horse-power, so enormous for their time, have served as prototypes, and have been succeeded by generators which have constantly grown in size and capacity until at this time (1910) it is not uncommon to employ such generating units of a capacity of 14,000 kilowatts, or about 18,666 horse-power.

We have not entered into specific descriptions of the many other forms of dynamo machines invented by Edison, such as the multipolar, the disk dynamo, and the armature with two windings, for sub-station distribution; indeed, it is not possible within our limited space to present even a brief digest of Edison's great and comprehensive work on the dynamo-electric machine, as embodied in his extensive experiments and in over one hundred patents granted to him. We have, therefore, confined ourselves to the indication of a few salient and basic features, leaving it to the interested student to examine the patents and the technical literature of the long period of time over which Edison's labors were extended.

Although he has not given any attention to the subject of generators for many years, an interesting instance of his incisive method of overcoming minor difficulties occurred while the present volumes were under preparation (1909). Carbon for commutator brushes has been superseded by graphite in some cases, the latter material being found much more advantageous, electrically. Trouble developed, however, for the reason that while carbon was hard and would wear away the mica insulation simultaneously with the copper, graphite, being softer, would wear away only the copper, leaving ridges of mica and thus causing sparking through unequal contact. At this point Edison was asked to diagnose the trouble and provide a remedy. He suggested the cutting out of the mica pieces almost to the bottom, leaving the commutator bars separated by air-spaces. This scheme was objected to on the ground that particles of graphite would fill these air-spaces and cause a short-circuit. His answer was that the air-spaces constituted the value of his plan, as the particles of graphite falling into them would be thrown out by the action of centrifugal force as the commutator revolved. And thus it occurred as a matter of fact, and the trouble was remedied. This idea was subsequently adopted by a great manufacturer of generators.

XI. THE EDISON FEEDER SYSTEM

TO quote from the preamble of the specifications of United States Patent No. 264,642, issued to Thomas A. Edison September 19, 1882: "This invention relates to a method of equalizing the tension or 'pressure' of the current through an entire system of electric lighting or other translation of electric force, preventing what is ordinarily known as a 'drop' in those portions of the system the more remote from the central station...."

The problem which was solved by the Edison feeder system was that relating to the equal distribution of current on a large scale over extended areas, in order that a constant and uniform electrical pressure could be maintained in every part of the distribution area without prohibitory expenditure for copper for mains and conductors.

This problem had a twofold aspect, although each side was inseparably bound up in the other. On the one hand it was obviously necessary in a lighting system that each lamp should be of standard candle-power, and capable of interchangeable use on any part of the system, giving the same degree of illumination at every point, whether near to or remote from the source of electrical energy. On the other hand, this must be accomplished by means of a system of conductors so devised and arranged that while they would insure the equal pressure thus demanded, their mass and consequent cost would not exceed the bounds of practical and commercially economical investment.

The great importance of this invention can be better understood and appreciated by a brief glance at the state of the art in 1878-79, when Edison was conducting the final series of investigations which culminated in his invention of the incandescent lamp and SYSTEM of lighting. At this time, and for some years previously, the scientific world had been working on the "subdivision of the electric light," as it was then termed. Some leading authorities pronounced it absolutely impossible of achievement on any extended scale, while a very few others, of more optimistic mind, could see no gleam of light through the darkness, but confidently hoped for future developments by such workers as Edison.

The earlier investigators, including those up to the period above named, thought of the problem as involving the subdivision of a FIXED UNIT of current, which, being sufficient to cause illumination by one large lamp, might be divided into a number of small units whose aggregate light would equal the candle-power of this large lamp. It was found, however, in their experiments that the contrary effect was produced, for with every additional lamp introduced in the circuit the total candle-power decreased instead of increasing. If they were placed in series the light varied inversely as the SQUARE of the number of lamps in circuit; while if they were inserted in multiple arc, the light diminished as the CUBE of the number in circuit. [29] The idea of maintaining a constant potential and of PROPORTIONING THE CURRENT to the number of lamps in circuit did not occur to most of these early investigators as a feasible method of overcoming the supposed difficulty.

[Footnote 29: M. Fontaine, in his book on Electric Lighting (1877), showed that with the current of a battery composed of sixteen elements, one lamp gave an illumination equal to 54 burners; whereas two similar lamps, if introduced in parallel or multiple arc, gave the light of only 6 1/2 burners in all; three lamps of only 2 burners in all; four lamps of only 3/4 of one burner, and five lamps of 1/4 of a burner.]

It would also seem that although the general method of placing experimental lamps in multiple arc was known at this period, the idea of "drop" of electrical pressure was imperfectly understood, if, indeed, realized at all, as a most important item to be considered in attempting the solution of the problem. As a matter of fact, the investigators preceding Edison do not seem to have conceived the idea of a "system" at all; hence it is not surprising to find them far astray from the correct theory of subdivision of the electric current. It may easily be believed that the term "subdivision" was a misleading one to these early experimenters. For a very short time Edison also was thus misled, but as soon as he perceived that the problem was one involving the MULTIPLICATION OF CURRENT UNITS, his broad conception of a "system" was born.

Generally speaking, all conductors of electricity offer more or less resistance to the passage of current through them and in the technical terminology of electrical science the word "drop" (when used in reference to a system of distribution) is used to indicate a fall or loss of initial electrical pressure arising from the resistance offered by the copper conductors leading from the source of energy to the lamps. The result of this resistance is to convert or translate a portion of the electrical energy into another form--namely, heat, which in the conductors is USELESS and wasteful and to some extent inevitable in practice, but is to be avoided and remedied as far as possible.

It is true that in an electric-lighting system there is also a fall or loss of electrical pressure which occurs in overcoming the much greater resistance of the filament in an incandescent lamp. In this case there is also a translation of the energy, but here it accomplishes a USEFUL purpose, as the energy is converted into the form of light through the incandescence of the filament. Such a conversion is called "work" as distinguished from "drop," although a fall of initial electrical pressure is involved in each case.

The percentage of "drop" varies according to the quantity of copper used in conductors, both as to cross-section and length. The smaller the cross-sectional area, the greater the percentage of drop. The practical effect of this drop would be a loss of illumination in the lamps as we go farther away from the source of energy. This may be illustrated by a simple diagram in which G is a generator, or source of energy, furnishing current at a potential or electrical pressure of 110 volts; 1 and 2 are main conductors, from which 110-volt lamps, L, are taken in derived circuits. It will be understood that the circuits represented in Fig. 1 are theoretically supposed to extend over a large area. The main conductors are sufficiently large in cross-section to offer but little resistance in those parts which are comparatively near the generator, but as the current traverses their extended length there is a gradual increase of resistance to overcome, and consequently the drop increases, as shown by the figures. The result of the drop in such a case would be that while the two lamps, or groups, nearest the generator would be burning at their proper degree of illumination, those beyond would give lower and lower candle-power, successively, until the last lamp, or group, would be giving only about two-thirds the light of the first two. In other words, a very slight drop in voltage means a disproportionately great loss in illumination. Hence, by using a primitive system of distribution, such as that shown by Fig. 1, the initial voltage would have to be so high, in order to obtain the proper candle-power at the end of the circuit, that the lamps nearest the generator would be dangerously overheated. It might be suggested as a solution of this problem that lamps of different voltages could be used. But, as we are considering systems of extended distribution employing vast numbers of lamps (as in New York City, where millions are in use), it will be seen that such a method would lead to inextricable confusion, and therefore be absolutely out of the question. Inasmuch as the percentage of drop decreases in proportion to the increased cross-section of the conductors, the only feasible plan would seem to be to increase their size to such dimensions as to eliminate the drop altogether, beginning with conductors of large cross-section and tapering off as necessary. This would, indeed, obviate the trouble, but, on the other hand, would give rise to a much more serious difficulty--namely, the enormous outlay for copper; an outlay so great as to be absolutely prohibitory in considering the electric lighting of large districts, as now practiced.

Another diagram will probably make this more clear. The reference figures are used as before, except that the horizontal lines extending from square marked G represent the main conductors. As each lamp requires and takes its own proportion of the total current generated, it is obvious that the size of the conductors to carry the current for a number of lamps must be as large as the sum of ALL the separate conductors which would be required to carry the necessary amount of current to each lamp separately. Hence, in a primitive multiple-arc system, it was found that the system must have conductors of a size equal to the aggregate of the individual conductors necessary for every lamp. Such conductors might either be separate, as shown above (Fig. 2), or be bunched together, or made into a solid tapering conductor, as shown in the following figure:

The enormous mass of copper needed in such a system can be better appreciated by a concrete example. Some years ago Mr. W. J. Jenks made a comparative calculation which showed that such a system of conductors (known as the "Tree" system), to supply 8640 lamps in a territory extending over so small an area as nine city blocks, would require 803,250 pounds of copper, which at the then price of 25 cents per pound would cost $200,812.50!

Such, in brief, was the state of the art, generally speaking, at the period above named (1878-79). As early in the art as the latter end of the year 1878, Edison had developed his ideas sufficiently to determine that the problem of electric illumination by small units could be solved by using incandescent lamps of high resistance and small radiating surface, and by distributing currents of constant potential thereto in multiple arc by means of a ramification of conductors, starting from a central source and branching therefrom in every direction. This was an equivalent of the method illustrated in Fig. 3, known as the "Tree" system, and was, in fact, the system used by Edison in the first and famous exhibition of his electric light at Menlo Park around the Christmas period of 1879. He realized, however, that the enormous investment for copper would militate against the commercial adoption of electric lighting on an extended scale. His next inventive step covered the division of a large city district into a number of small sub-stations supplying current through an interconnected network of conductors, thus reducing expenditure for copper to some extent, because each distribution unit was small and limited the drop.

His next development was the radical advancement of the state of the art to the feeder system, covered by the patent now under discussion. This invention swept away the tree and other systems, and at one bound brought into being the possibility of effectively distributing large currents over extended areas with a commercially reasonable investment for copper.

The fundamental principles of this invention were, first, to sever entirely any direct connection of the main conductors with the source of energy; and, second, to feed current at a constant potential to central points in such main conductors by means of other conductors, called "feeders," which were to be connected directly with the source of energy at the central station. This idea will be made more clear by reference to the following simple diagram, in which the same letters are used as before, with additions:

In further elucidation of the diagram, it may be considered that the mains are laid in the street along a city block, more or less distant from the station, while the feeders are connected at one end with the source of energy at the station, their other extremities being connected to the mains at central points of distribution. Of course, this system was intended to be applied in every part of a district to be supplied with current, separate sets of feeders running out from the station to the various centres. The distribution mains were to be of sufficiently large size that between their most extreme points the loss would not be more than 3 volts. Such a slight difference would not make an appreciable variation in the candle-power of the lamps.

By the application of these principles, the inevitable but useless loss, or "drop," required by economy might be incurred, but was LOCALIZED IN THE FEEDERS, where it would not affect the uniformity of illumination of the lamps in any of the circuits, whether near to or remote from the station, because any variations of loss in the feeders would not give rise to similar fluctuations in any lamp circuit. The feeders might be operated at any desired percentage of loss that would realize economy in copper, so long as they delivered current to the main conductors at the potential represented by the average voltage of the lamps.

Thus the feeders could be made comparatively small in cross-section. It will be at once appreciated that, inasmuch as the mains required to be laid ONLY along the blocks to be lighted, and were not required to be run all the way to the central station (which might be half a mile or more away), the saving of copper by Edison's feeder system was enormous. Indeed, the comparative calculation of Mr. Jenks, above referred to, shows that to operate the same number of lights in the same extended area of territory, the feeder system would require only 128,739 pounds of copper, which, at the then price of 25 cents per pound, would cost only $39,185, or A SAVING of $168,627.50 for copper in this very small district of only nine blocks.

An additional illustration, appealing to the eye, is presented in the following sketch, in which the comparative masses of copper of the tree and feeder systems for carrying the same current are shown side by side:

XII. THE THREE-WIRE SYSTEM

THIS invention is covered by United States Patent No. 274,290, issued to Edison on March 20, 1883. The object of the invention was to provide for increased economy in the quantity of copper employed for the main conductors in electric light and power installations of considerable extent at the same time preserving separate and independent control of each lamp, motor, or other translating device, upon any one of the various distribution circuits.

Immediately prior to this invention the highest state of the art of electrical distribution was represented by Edison's feeder system, which has already been described as a straight parallel or multiple-arc system wherein economy of copper was obtained by using separate sets of conductors--minus load--feeding current at standard potential or electrical pressure into the mains at centres of distribution.

It should be borne in mind that the incandescent lamp which was accepted at the time as a standard (and has so remained to the present day) was a lamp of 110 volts or thereabouts. In using the word "standard," therefore, it is intended that the same shall apply to lamps of about that voltage, as well as to electrical circuits of the approximate potential to operate them.

Briefly stated, the principle involved in the three-wire system is to provide main circuits of double the standard potential, so as to operate standard lamps, or other translating devices, in multiple series of two to each series; and for the purpose of securing independent, individual control of each unit, to divide each main circuit into any desired number of derived circuits of standard potential (properly balanced) by means of a central compensating conductor which would be normally neutral, but designed to carry any minor excess of current that might flow by reason of any temporary unbalancing of either side of the main circuit.

Reference to the following diagrams will elucidate this principle more clearly than words alone can do. For the purpose of increased lucidity we will first show a plain multiple-series system.

In this diagram G<1S> and G<2S> represent two generators, each producing current at a potential of 110 volts. By connecting them in series this potential is doubled, thus providing a main circuit (P and N) of 220 volts. The figures marked L represent eight lamps of 110 volts each, in multiple series of two, in four derived circuits. The arrows indicate the flow of current. By this method each pair of lamps takes, together, only the same quantity or volume of current required by a single lamp in a simple multiple-arc system; and, as the cross-section of a conductor depends upon the quantity of current carried, such an arrangement as the above would allow the use of conductors of only one-fourth the cross-section that would be otherwise required. From the standpoint of economy of investment such an arrangement would be highly desirable, but considered commercially it is impracticable because the principle of independent control of each unit would be lost, as the turning out of a lamp in any series would mean the extinguishment of its companion also. By referring to the diagram it will be seen that each series of two forms one continuous path between the main conductors, and if this path be broken at any one point current will immediately cease to flow in that particular series.

Edison, by his invention of the three-wire system, overcame this difficulty entirely, and at the same time conserved approximately, the saving of copper, as will be apparent from the following illustration of that system, in its simplest form.

The reference figures are similar to those in the preceding diagram, and all conditions are also alike except that a central compensating, or balancing, conductor, PN, is here introduced. This is technically termed the "neutral" wire, and in the discharge of its functions lies the solution of the problem of economical distribution. Theoretically, a three-wire installation is evenly balanced by wiring for an equal number of lamps on both sides. If all these lamps were always lighted, burned, and extinguished simultaneously the central conductor would, in fact, remain neutral, as there would be no current passing through it, except from lamp to lamp. In practice, however, no such perfect conditions can obtain, hence the necessity of the provision for balancing in order to maintain the principle of independent control of each unit.

It will be apparent that the arrangement shown in Fig. 2 comprises practically two circuits combined in one system, in which the central conductor, PN, in case of emergency, serves in two capacities--namely, as negative to generator G<1S> or as positive to generator G<2S>, although normally neutral. There are two sides to the system, the positive side being represented by the conductors P and PN, and the negative side by the conductors PN and N. Each side, if considered separately, has a potential of about 110 volts, yet the potential of the two outside conductors, P and N, is 220 volts. The lamps are 110 volts.

In practical use the operation of the system is as follows: If all the lamps were lighted the current would flow along P and through each pair of lamps to N, and so back to the source of energy. In this case the balance is preserved and the central wire remains neutral, as no return current flows through it to the source of energy. But let us suppose that one lamp on the positive side is extinguished. None of the other lamps is affected thereby, but the system is immediately thrown out of balance, and on the positive side there is an excess of current to this extent which flows along or through the central conductor and returns to the generator, the central conductor thus becoming the negative of that side of the system for the time being. If the lamp extinguished had been one of those on the negative side of the system results of a similar nature would obtain, except that the central conductor would for the time being become the positive of that side, and the excess of current would flow through the negative, N, back to the source of energy. Thus it will be seen that a three-wire system, considered as a whole, is elastic in that it may operate as one when in balance and as two when unbalanced, but in either event giving independent control of each unit.

For simplicity of illustration a limited number of circuits, shown in Fig. 2, has been employed. In practice, however, where great numbers of lamps are in use (as, for instance, in New York City, where about 7,000,000 lamps are operated from various central stations), there is constantly occurring more or less change in the balance of many circuits extending over considerable distances, but of course there is a net result which is always on one side of the system or the other for the time being, and this is met by proper adjustment at the appropriate generator in the station.

In order to make the explanation complete, there is presented another diagram showing a three-wire system unbalanced:

The reference figures are used as before, but in this case the vertical lines represent branches taken from the main conductors into buildings or other spaces to be lighted, and the loops between these branch wires represent lamps in operation. It will be seen from this sketch that there are ten lamps on the positive side and twelve on the negative side. Hence, the net result is an excess of current equal to that required by two lamps flowing through the central or compensating conductor, which is now acting as positive to generator G<2S> The arrows show the assumed direction of flow of current throughout the system, and the small figures at the arrow-heads the volume of that current expressed in the number of lamps which it supplies.

The commercial value of this invention may be appreciated from the fact that by the application of its principles there is effected a saving of 62 1/2 per cent. of the amount of copper over that which would be required for conductors in any previously devised two-wire system carrying the same load. This arises from the fact that by the doubling of potential the two outside mains are reduced to one-quarter the cross-section otherwise necessary. A saving of 75 per cent. would thus be assured, but the addition of a third, or compensating, conductor of the same cross-section as one of the outside mains reduces the total saving to 62 1/2 per cent.

The three-wire system is in universal use throughout the world at the present day.

XIII. EDISON'S ELECTRIC RAILWAY

AS narrated in Chapter XVIII, there were two electric railroads installed by Edison at Menlo Park--one in 1880, originally a third of a mile long, but subsequently increased to about a mile in length, and the other in 1882, about three miles long. As the 1880 road was built very soon after Edison's notable improvements in dynamo machines, and as the art of operating them to the best advantage was then being developed, this early road was somewhat crude as compared with the railroad of 1882; but both were practicable and serviceable for the purpose of hauling passengers and freight. The scope of the present article will be confined to a description of the technical details of these two installations.

The illustration opposite page 454 of the preceding narrative shows the first Edison locomotive and train of 1880 at Menlo Park.

For the locomotive a four-wheel iron truck was used, and upon it was mounted one of the long "Z" type 110-volt Edison dynamos, with a capacity of 75 amperes, which was to be used as a motor. This machine was laid on its side, its armature being horizontal and located toward the front of the locomotive.

We now quote from an article by Mr. E. W. Hammer, published in the Electrical World, New York, June 10, 1899, and afterward elaborated and reprinted in a volume entitled Edisonia, compiled and published under the auspices of a committee of the Association of Edison Illuminating Companies, in 1904: "The gearing originally employed consisted of a friction-pulley upon the armature shaft, another friction-pulley upon the driven axle, and a third friction-pulley which could be brought in contact with the other two by a suitable lever. Each wheel of the locomotive was made with metallic rim and a centre portion made of wood or papier-mache. A three-legged spider connected the metal rim of each front wheel to a brass hub, upon which rested a collecting brush. The other wheels were subsequently so equipped. It was the intention, therefore, that the current should enter the locomotive wheels at one side, and after passing through the metal spiders, collecting brushes and motor, would pass out through the corresponding brushes, spiders, and wheels to the other rail."

As to the road: "The rails were light and were spiked to ordinary sleepers, with a gauge of about three and one-half feet. The sleepers were laid upon the natural grade, and there was comparatively no effort made to ballast the road. . . . No special precautions were taken to insulate the rails from the earth or from each other."

The road started about fifty feet away from the generating station, which in this case was the machine shop. Two of the "Z" type dynamos were used for generating the current, which was conveyed to the two rails of the road by underground conductors.

On Thursday, May 13, 1880, at 4 o'clock in the afternoon, this historic locomotive made its first trip, packed with as many of the "boys" as could possibly find a place to hang on. "Everything worked to a charm, until, in starting up at one end of the road, the friction gearing was brought into action too suddenly and it was wrecked. This accident demonstrated that some other method of connecting the armature with the driven axle should be arranged.

"As thus originally operated, the motor had its field circuit in permanent connection as a shunt across the rails, and this field circuit was protected by a safety-catch made by turning up two bare ends of the wire in its circuit and winding a piece of fine copper wire across from one bare end to the other. The armature circuit had a switch in it which permitted the locomotive to be reversed by reversing the direction of current flow through the armature.

"After some consideration of the gearing question, it was decided to employ belts instead of the friction-pulleys." Accordingly, Edison installed on the locomotive a system of belting, including an idler-pulley which was used by means of a lever to tighten the main driving-belt, and thus power was applied to the driven axle. This involved some slipping and consequent burning of belts; also, if the belt were prematurely tightened, the burning-out of the armature. This latter event happened a number of times, "and proved to be such a serious annoyance that resistance-boxes were brought out from the laboratory and placed upon the locomotive in series with the armature. This solved the difficulty. The locomotive would be started with these resistance-boxes in circuit, and after reaching full speed the operator could plug the various boxes out of circuit, and in that way increase the speed." To stop, the armature circuit was opened by the main switch and the brake applied.

This arrangement was generally satisfactory, but the resistance-boxes scattered about the platform and foot-rests being in the way, Edison directed that some No. 8 B. & S. copper wire be wound on the lower leg of the motor field-magnet. "By doing this the resistance was put where it would take up the least room, and where it would serve as an additional field-coil when starting the motor, and it replaced all the resistance-boxes which had heretofore been in plain sight. The boxes under the seat were still retained in service. The coil of coarse wire was in series with the armature, just as the resistance-boxes had been, and could be plugged in or out of circuit at the will of the locomotive driver. The general arrangement thus secured was operated as long as this road was in commission."

On this short stretch of road there were many sharp curves and steep grades, and in consequence of the high speed attained (as high as forty-two miles an hour) several derailments took place, but fortunately without serious results. Three cars were in service during the entire time of operating this 1880 railroad: one a flat-car for freight; one an open car with two benches placed back to back; and the third a box-car, familiarly known as the "Pullman." This latter car had an interesting adjunct in an electric braking system (covered by Edison's Patent No. 248,430). "Each car axle had a large iron disk mounted on and revolving with it between the poles of a powerful horseshoe electromagnet. The pole-pieces of the magnet were movable, and would be attracted to the revolving disk when the magnet was energized, grasping the same and acting to retard the revolution of the car axle."

Interesting articles on Edison's first electric railroad were published in the technical and other papers, among which may be mentioned the New York Herald, May 15 and July 23, 1880; the New York Graphic, July 27, 1880; and the Scientific American, June 6, 1880.

Edison's second electric railroad of 1882 was more pretentious as regards length, construction, and equipment. It was about three miles long, of nearly standard gauge, and substantially constructed. Curves were modified, and grades eliminated where possible by the erection of numerous trestles. This road also had some features of conventional railroads, such as sidings, turn-tables, freight platform, and car-house. "Current was supplied to the road by underground feeder cables from the dynamo-room of the laboratory. The rails were insulated from the ties by giving them two coats of japan, baking them in the oven, and then placing them on pads of tar-impregnated muslin laid on the ties. The ends of the rails were not japanned, but were electroplated, to give good contact surfaces for fish-plates and copper bonds."

The following notes of Mr. Frederick A. Scheffler, who designed the passenger locomotive for the 1882 road, throw an interesting light on its technical details:

"In May, 1881, I was engaged by Mr. M. F. Moore, who was the first General Manager of the Edison Company for Isolated Lighting, as a draftsman to undertake the work of designing and building Edison's electric locomotive No. 2.

"Previous to that time I had been employed in the engineering department of Grant Locomotive Works, Paterson, New Jersey, and the Rhode Island Locomotive Works, Providence, Rhode Island....

"It was Mr. Edison's idea, as I understood it at that time, to build a locomotive along the general lines of steam locomotives (at least, in outward appearance), and to combine in that respect the framework, truck, and other parts known to be satisfactory in steam locomotives at the same time.

"This naturally required the services of a draftsman accustomed to steam-locomotive practice.... Mr. Moore was a man of great railroad and locomotive experience, and his knowledge in that direction was of great assistance in the designing and building of this locomotive.

"At that time I had no knowledge of electricity.... One could count so-called electrical engineers on his fingers then, and have some fingers left over.

"Consequently, the ELECTRICAL equipment was designed by Mr. Edison and his assistants. The data and parts, such as motor, rheostat, switches, etc., were given to me, and my work was to design the supporting frame, axles, countershafts, driving mechanism, speed control, wheels and boxes, cab, running board, pilot (or 'cow-catcher'), buffers, and even supports for the headlight. I believe I also designed a bell and supports. From this it will be seen that the locomotive had all the essential paraphernalia to make it LOOK like a steam locomotive.

"The principal part of the outfit was the electric motor. At that time motors were curiosities. There were no electric motors even for stationary purposes, except freaks built for experimental uses. This motor was made from the parts--such as fields, armature, commutator, shaft and bearings, etc., of an Edison 'Z,' or 60-light dynamo. It was the only size of dynamo that the Edison Company had marketed at that time.... As a motor, it was wound to run at maximum speed to develop a torque equal to about fifteen horse-power with 220 volts. At the generating station at Menlo Park four Z dynamos of 110 volts were used, connected two in series, in multiple arc, giving a line voltage of 220.

"The motor was located in the front part of the locomotive, on its side, with the armature shaft across the frames, or parallel with the driving axles.

"On account of the high speed of the armature shaft it was not possible to connect with driving-axles direct, but this was an advantage in one way, as by introducing an intermediate counter-shaft (corresponding to the well-known type of double-reduction motor used on trolley-cars since 1885), a fairly good arrangement was obtained to regulate the speed of the locomotive, exclusive of resistance in the electric circuit.

"Endless leather belting was used to transmit the power from the motor to the counter-shaft, and from the latter to the driving-wheels, which were the front pair. A vertical idler-pulley was mounted in a frame over the belt from motor to counter-shaft, terminating in a vertical screw and hand-wheel for tightening the belt to increase speed, or the reverse to lower speed. This hand-wheel was located in the cab, where it was easily accessible....

"The rough outline sketched below shows the location of motor in relation to counter-shaft, belting, driving-wheels, idler, etc.:

"On account of both rails being used for circuits, . . . the driving-wheels had to be split circumferentially and completely insulated from the axles. This was accomplished by means of heavy wood blocks well shellacked or otherwise treated to make them water and weather proof, placed radially on the inside of the wheels, and then substantially bolted to the hubs and rims of the latter.

"The weight of the locomotive was distributed over the driving-wheels in the usual locomotive practice by means of springs and equalizers.

"The current was taken from the rims of the driving-wheels by a three-pronged collector of brass, against which flexible copper brushes were pressed--a simple manner of overcoming any inequalities of the road-bed.

"The late Mr. Charles T. Hughes was in charge of the track construction at Menlo Park.... His work was excellent throughout, and the results were highly satisfactory so far as they could possibly be with the arrangement originally planned by Mr. Edison and his assistants.

"Mr. Charles L. Clarke, one of the earliest electrical engineers employed by Mr. Edison, made a number of tests on this 1882 railroad. I believe that the engine driving the four Z generators at the power-house indicated as high as seventy horse-power at the time the locomotive was actually in service."

The electrical features of the 1882 locomotive were very similar to those of the earlier one, already described. Shunt and series field-windings were added to the motor, and the series windings could be plugged in and out of circuit as desired. The series winding was supplemented by resistance-boxes, also capable of being plugged in or out of circuit. These various electrical features are diagrammatically shown in Fig. 2, which also illustrates the connection with the generating plant.

We quote again from Mr. Hammer, who says: "The freight-locomotive had single reduction gears, as is the modern practice, but the power was applied through a friction-clutch The passenger-locomotive was very speedy, and ninety passengers have been carried at a time by it; the freight-locomotive was not so fast, but could pull heavy trains at a good speed. Many thousand people were carried on this road during 1882." The general appearance of Edison's electric locomotive of 1882 is shown in the illustration opposite page 462 of the preceding narrative. In the picture Mr. Edison may be seen in the cab, and Mr. Insull on the front platform of the passenger-car.

XIV. TRAIN TELEGRAPHY

WHILE the one-time art of telegraphing to and from moving trains was essentially a wireless system, and allied in some of its principles to the art of modern wireless telegraphy through space, the two systems cannot, strictly speaking be regarded as identical, as the practice of the former was based entirely on the phenomenon of induction.

Briefly described in outline, the train telegraph system consisted of an induction circuit obtained by laying strips of metal along the top or roof of a railway-car, and the installation of a special telegraph line running parallel with the track and strung on poles of only medium height. The train, and also each signalling station, was equipped with regulation telegraph apparatus, such as battery, key, relay, and sounder, together with induction-coil and condenser. In addition, there was a special transmitting device in the shape of a musical reed, or "buzzer." In practice, this buzzer was continuously operated at a speed of about five hundred vibrations per second by an auxiliary battery. Its vibrations were broken by means of a telegraph key into long and short periods, representing Morse characters, which were transmitted inductively from the train circuit to the pole line or vice versa, and received by the operator at the other end through a high-resistance telephone receiver inserted in the secondary circuit of the induction-coil.

The accompanying diagrammatic sketch of a simple form of the system, as installed on a car, will probably serve to make this more clear.

An insulated wire runs from the metallic layers on the roof of the car to switch S, which is shown open in the sketch. When a message is to be received on the car from a station more or less remote, the switch is thrown to the left to connect with a wire running to the telephone receiver, T. The other wire from this receiver is run down to one of the axles and there permanently connected, thus making a ground. The operator puts the receiver to his ear and listens for the message, which the telephone renders audible in the Morse characters.

If a message is to be transmitted from the car to a receiving station, near or distant, the switch, S, is thrown to the other side, thus connecting with a wire leading to one end of the secondary of induction-coil C. The other end of the secondary is connected with the grounding wire. The primary of the induction-coil is connected as shown, one end going to key K and the other to the buzzer circuit. The other side of the key is connected to the transmitting battery, while the opposite pole of this battery is connected in the buzzer circuit. The buzzer, R, is maintained in rapid vibration by its independent auxiliary battery, B<1S>.

When the key is pressed down the circuit is closed, and current from the transmitting battery, B, passes through primary of the coil, C, and induces a current of greatly increased potential in the secondary. The current as it passes into the primary, being broken up into short impulses by the tremendously rapid vibrations of the buzzer, induces similarly rapid waves of high potential in the secondary, and these in turn pass to the roof and thence through the intervening air by induction to the telegraph wire. By a continued lifting and depression of the key in the regular manner, these waves are broken up into long and short periods, and are thus transmitted to the station, via the wire, in Morse characters, dots and dashes.

The receiving stations along the line of the railway were similarly equipped as to apparatus, and, generally speaking the operations of sending and receiving messages were substantially the same as above described.

The equipment of an operator on a car was quite simple consisting merely of a small lap-board, on which were mounted the key, coil, and buzzer, leaving room for telegraph blanks. To this board were also attached flexible conductors having spring clips, by means of which connections could be made quickly with conveniently placed terminals of the ground, roof, and battery wires. The telephone receiver was held on the head with a spring, the flexible connecting wire being attached to the lap board, thus leaving the operator with both hands free.

The system, as shown in the sketch and elucidated by the text, represents the operation of train telegraphy in a simple form, but combining the main essentials of the art as it was successfully and commercially practiced for a number of years after Edison and Gilliland entered the field. They elaborated the system in various ways, making it more complete; but it has not been deemed necessary to enlarge further upon the technical minutiae of the art for the purpose of this work.

XV. KINETOGRAPH AND PROJECTING KINETOSCOPE

ALTHOUGH many of the arts in which Edison has been a pioneer have been enriched by his numerous inventions and patents, which were subsequent to those of a fundamental nature, the (so-called) motion-picture art is an exception, as the following, together with three other additional patents [30] comprise all that he has taken out on this subject: United States Patent No. 589,168, issued August 31, 1897, reissued in two parts--namely, No. 12,037, under date of September 30,1902, and No. 12,192, under date of January 12, 1904. Application filed August 24, 1891.

[Footnote 30: Not 491,993, issued February 21, 1893; No. 493,426, issued March 14, 1893; No. 772,647, issued October 18, 1904.]

There is nothing surprising in this, however, as the possibility of photographing and reproducing actual scenes of animate life are so thoroughly exemplified and rendered practicable by the apparatus and methods disclosed in the patents above cited, that these basic inventions in themselves practically constitute the art--its development proceeding mainly along the line of manufacturing details. That such a view of his work is correct, the highest criterion--commercial expediency--bears witness; for in spite of the fact that the courts have somewhat narrowed the broad claims of Edison's patents by reason of the investigations of earlier experimenters, practically all the immense amount of commercial work that is done in the motion-picture field to-day is accomplished through the use of apparatus and methods licensed under the Edison patents.

The philosophy of this invention having already been described in Chapter XXI, it will be unnecessary to repeat it here. Suffice it to say by way of reminder that it is founded upon the physiological phenomenon known as the persistence of vision, through which a series of sequential photographic pictures of animate motion projected upon a screen in rapid succession will reproduce to the eye all the appearance of the original movements.

Edison's work in this direction comprised the invention not only of a special form of camera for making original photographic exposures from a single point of view with very great rapidity, and of a machine adapted to effect the reproduction of such pictures in somewhat similar manner but also of the conception and invention of a continuous uniform, and evenly spaced tape-like film, so absolutely essential for both the above objects.

The mechanism of such a camera, as now used, consists of many parts assembled in such contiguous proximity to each other that an illustration from an actual machine would not help to clearness of explanation to the general reader. Hence a diagram showing a sectional view of a simple form of such a camera is presented below.

In this diagram, A represents an outer light-tight box containing a lens, C, and the other necessary mechanism for making the photographic exposures, H<1S> and H<2S> being cases for holding reels of film before and after exposure, F the long, tape-like film, G a sprocket whose teeth engage in perforations on the edges of the film, such sprocket being adapted to be revolved with an intermittent or step-by-step movement by hand or by motor, and B a revolving shutter having an opening and connected by gears with G, and arranged to expose the film during the periods of rest. A full view of this shutter is also represented, with its opening, D, in the small illustration to the right.

In practice, the operation would be somewhat as follows, generally speaking: The lens would first be focussed on the animate scene to be photographed. On turning the main shaft of the camera the sprocket, G, is moved intermittently, and its teeth, catching in the holes in the sensitized film, draws it downward, bringing a new portion of its length in front of the lens, the film then remaining stationary for an instant. In the mean time, through gearing connecting the main shaft with the shutter, the latter is rotated, bringing its opening, D, coincident with the lens, and therefore exposing the film while it is stationary, after which the film again moves forward. So long as the action is continued these movements are repeated, resulting in a succession of enormously rapid exposures upon the film during its progress from reel H<1S> to its automatic rewinding on reel H<2S>. While the film is passing through the various parts of the machine it is guided and kept straight by various sets of rollers between which it runs, as indicated in the diagram.

By an ingenious arrangement of the mechanism, the film moves intermittently so that it may have a much longer period of rest than of motion. As in practice the pictures are taken at a rate of twenty or more per second, it will be quite obvious that each period of rest is infinitesimally brief, being generally one-thirtieth of a second or less. Still it is sufficient to bring the film to a momentary condition of complete rest, and to allow for a maximum time of exposure, comparatively speaking, thus providing means for taking clearly defined pictures. The negatives so obtained are developed in the regular way, and the positive prints subsequently made from them are used for reproduction.

The reproducing machine, or, as it is called in practice, the Projecting Kinetoscope, is quite similar so far as its general operations in handling the film are concerned. In appearance it is somewhat different; indeed, it is in two parts, the one containing the lighting arrangements and condensing lens, and the other embracing the mechanism and objective lens. The "taking" camera must have its parts enclosed in a light-tight box, because of the undeveloped, sensitized film, but the projecting kinetoscope, using only a fully developed positive film, may, and, for purposes of convenient operation, must be accessibly open. The illustration (Fig. 2) will show the projecting apparatus as used in practice.

The philosophy of reproduction is very simple, and is illustrated diagrammatically in Fig. 3, reference letters being the same as in Fig. 1. As to the additional reference letters, I is a condenser J the source of light, and K a reflector.

The positive film is moved intermittently but swiftly throughout its length between the objective lens and a beam of light coming through the condenser, being exposed by the shutter during the periods of rest. This results in a projection of the photographs upon a screen in such rapid succession as to present an apparently continuous photograph of the successive positions of the moving objects, which, therefore, appear to the human eye to be in motion.

The first claim of Reissue Patent No. 12,192 describes the film. It reads as follows:

"An unbroken transparent or translucent tape-like photographic film having thereon uniform, sharply defined, equidistant photographs of successive positions of an object in motion as observed from a single point of view at rapidly recurring intervals of time, such photographs being arranged in a continuous straight-line sequence, unlimited in number save by the length of the film, and sufficient in number to represent the movements of the object throughout an extended period of time."

XVI. EDISON'S ORE-MILLING INVENTIONS

THE wide range of Edison's activities in this department of the arts is well represented in the diversity of the numerous patents that have been issued to him from time to time. These patents are between fifty and sixty in number, and include magnetic ore separators of ten distinct types; also breaking, crushing, and grinding rolls, conveyors, dust-proof bearings, screens, driers, mixers, bricking apparatus and machines, ovens, and processes of various kinds.

A description of the many devices in each of these divisions would require more space than is available; hence, we shall confine ourselves to a few items of predominating importance, already referred to in the narrative, commencing with the fundamental magnetic ore separator, which was covered by United States Patent No. 228,329, issued June 1, 1880.

The illustration here presented is copied from the drawing forming part of this patent. A hopper with adjustable feed is supported several feet above a bin having a central partition. Almost midway between the hopper and the bin is placed an electromagnet whose polar extension is so arranged as to be a little to one side of a stream of material falling from the hopper. Normally, a stream of finely divided ore falling from the hopper would fall into that portion of the bin lying to the left of the partition. If, however, the magnet is energized from a source of current, the magnetic particles in the falling stream are attracted by and move toward the magnet, which is so placed with relation to the falling material that the magnetic particles cannot be attracted entirely to the magnet before gravity has carried them past. Hence, their trajectory is altered, and they fall on the right-hand side of the partition in the bin, while the non-magnetic portion of the stream continues in a straight line and falls on the other side, thus effecting a complete separation.

This simple but effective principle was the one employed by Edison in his great concentrating plant already described. In practice, the numerous hoppers, magnets, and bins were many feet in length; and they were arranged in batteries of varied magnetic strength, in order that the intermingled mass of crushed rock and iron ore might be more thoroughly separated by being passed through magnetic fields of successively increasing degrees of attracting power. Altogether there were about four hundred and eighty of these immense magnets in the plant, distributed in various buildings in batteries as above mentioned, the crushed rock containing the iron ore being delivered to them by conveyors, and the gangue and ore being taken away after separation by two other conveyors and delivered elsewhere. The magnetic separators at first used by Edison at this plant were of the same generality as the ones employed some years previously in the separation of sea-shore sand, but greatly enlarged and improved. The varied experiences gained in the concentration of vast quantities of ore led naturally to a greater development, and several new types and arrangements of magnetic separators were evolved and elaborated by him from first to last, during the progress of the work at the concentrating plant.

The magnetic separation of iron from its ore being the foundation idea of the inventions now under discussion, a consideration of the separator has naturally taken precedence over those of collateral but inseparable interest. The ore-bearing rock, however, must first be ground to powder before it can be separated; hence, we will now begin at the root of this operation and consider the "giant rolls," which Edison devised for breaking huge masses of rock. In his application for United States Patent No. 672,616, issued April 23, 1901, applied for on July 16, 1897, he says: "The object of my invention is to produce a method for the breaking of rock which will be simple and effective, will not require the hand-sledging or blasting of the rock down to pieces of moderate size, and will involve the consumption of a small amount of power."

While this quotation refers to the method as "simple," the patent under consideration covers one of the most bold and daring projects that Edison has ever evolved. He proposed to eliminate the slow and expensive method of breaking large boulders manually, and to substitute therefor momentum and kinetic energy applied through the medium of massive machinery, which, in a few seconds, would break into small pieces a rock as big as an ordinary upright cottage piano, and weighing as much as six tons. Engineers to whom Edison communicated his ideas were unanimous in declaring the thing an impossibility; it was like driving two express-trains into each other at full speed to crack a great rock placed between them; that no practical machinery could be built to stand the terrific impact and strains. Edison's convictions were strong, however, and he persisted. The experiments were of heroic size, physically and financially, but after a struggle of several years and an expenditure of about $100,000, he realized the correctness and practicability of his plans in the success of the giant rolls, which were the outcome of his labors.

The giant rolls consist of a pair of iron cylinders of massive size and weight, with removable wearing plates having irregular surfaces formed by projecting knobs. These rolls are mounted side by side in a very heavy frame (leaving a gap of about fourteen inches between them), and are so belted up with the source of power that they run in opposite directions. The giant rolls described by Edison in the above-named patent as having been built and operated by him had a combined weight of 167,000 pounds, including all moving parts, which of themselves weighed about seventy tons, each roll being six feet in diameter and five feet long. A top view of the rolls is shown in the sketch, one roll and one of its bearings being shown in section.

In Fig. 2 the rolls are illustrated diagrammatically. As a sketch of this nature, even if given with a definite scale, does not always carry an adequate idea of relative dimensions to a non-technical reader, we present in Fig. 3 a perspective illustration of the giant rolls as installed in the concentrating plant.

In practice, a small amount of power is applied to run the giant rolls gradually up to a surface speed of several thousand feet a minute. When this high speed is attained, masses of rock weighing several tons in one or more pieces are dumped into a hopper which guides them into the gap between the rapidly revolving rolls. The effect is to partially arrest the swift motion of the rolls instantaneously, and thereby develop and expend an enormous amount of kinetic energy, which with pile-driver effect cracks the rocks and breaks them into pieces small enough to pass through the fourteen-inch gap. As the power is applied to the rolls through slipping friction-clutches, the speed of the driving-pulleys is not materially reduced; hence the rolls may again be quickly speeded up to their highest velocity while another load of rock is being hoisted in position to be dumped into the hopper. It will be obvious from the foregoing that if it were attempted to supply the great energy necessary for this operation by direct application of steam-power, an engine of enormous horse-power would be required, and even then it is doubtful if one could be constructed of sufficient strength to withstand the terrific strains that would ensue. But the work is done by the great momentum and kinetic energy obtained by speeding up these tremendous masses of metal, and then suddenly opposing their progress, the engine being relieved of all strain through the medium of the slipping friction-clutches. Thus, this cyclopean operation may be continuously conducted with an amount of power prodigiously inferior, in proportion, to the results accomplished.

The sketch (Fig. 4) showing a large boulder being dumped into the hopper, or roll-pit, will serve to illustrate the method of feeding these great masses of rock to the rolls, and will also enable the reader to form an idea of the rapidity of the breaking operation, when it is stated that a boulder of the size represented would be reduced by the giant rolls to pieces a trifle larger than a man's head in a few seconds.

After leaving the giant rolls the broken rock passed on through other crushing-rolls of somewhat similar construction. These also were invented by Edison, but antedated those previously described; being covered by Patent No. 567,187, issued September 8, 1896. These rolls were intended for the reducing of "one-man-size" rocks to small pieces, which at the time of their original inception was about the standard size of similar machines. At the Edison concentrating plant the broken rock, after passing through these rolls, was further reduced in size by other rolls, and was then ready to be crushed to a fine powder through the medium of another remarkable machine devised by Edison to meet his ever-recurring and well-defined ideas of the utmost economy and efficiency.

NOTE.--Figs. 3 and 4 are reproduced from similar sketches on pages 84 and 85 of McClure's Magazine for November, 1897, by permission of S. S. McClure Co.

The best fine grinding-machines that it was then possible to obtain were so inefficient as to involve a loss of 82 per cent. of the power applied. The thought of such an enormous loss was unbearable, and he did not rest until he had invented and put into use an entirely new grinding-machine, which was called the "three-high" rolls. The device was covered by a patent issued to him on November 21, 1899, No. 637,327. It was a most noteworthy invention, for it brought into the art not only a greater efficiency of grinding than had ever been dreamed of before, but also a tremendous economy by the saving of power; for whereas the previous efficiency had been 18 per cent. and the loss 82 per cent., Edison reversed these figures, and in his three-high rolls produced a working efficiency of 84 per cent., thus reducing the loss of power by friction to 16 per cent. A diagrammatic sketch of this remarkable machine is shown in Fig. 5, which shows a front elevation with the casings, hopper, etc., removed, and also shows above the rolls the rope and pulleys, the supports for which are also removed for the sake of clearness in the illustration.

For the convenience of the reader, in referring to Fig. 5, we will repeat the description of the three-high rolls, which is given on pages 487 and 488 of the preceding narrative.

In the two end-pieces of a heavy iron frame were set three rolls, or cylinders--one in the centre, another below, and the other above--all three being in a vertical line. These rolls were about three feet in diameter, made of cast-iron, and had face-plates of chilled-iron. [31] The lowest roll was set in a fixed bearing at the bottom of the frame, and, therefore, could only turn around on its axis. The middle and top rolls were free to move up or down from and toward the lower roll, and the shafts of the middle and upper rolls were set in a loose bearing which could slip up and down in the iron frame. It will be apparent, therefore, that any material which passed in between the top and the middle rolls, and the middle and bottom rolls, could be ground as fine as might be desired, depending entirely upon the amount of pressure applied to the loose rolls. In operation the material passed first through the upper and middle rolls, and then between the middle and lowest rolls.

[Footnote 31: The faces of these rolls were smooth, but as three-high rolls came into use later in Edison's Portland cement operations the faces were corrugated so as to fit into each other, gear-fashion, to provide for a high rate of feed]

This pressure was applied in a most ingenious manner. On the ends of the shafts of the bottom and top rolls there were cylindrical sleeves, or bearings, having seven sheaves in which was run a half-inch endless wire rope. This rope was wound seven times over the sheaves as above, and led upward and over a single-groove sheave, which was operated by the piston of an air-cylinder, and in this manner the pressure was applied to the rolls. It will be seen, therefore that the system consisted in a single rope passed over sheaves and so arranged that it could be varied in length, thus providing for elasticity in exerting pressure and regulating it as desired. The efficiency of this system was incomparably greater than that of any other known crusher or grinder, for while a pressure of one hundred and twenty-five thousand pounds could be exerted by these rolls, friction was almost entirely eliminated, because the upper and lower roll bearings turned with the rolls and revolved in the wire rope, which constituted the bearing proper.

Several other important patents have been issued to Edison for crushing and grinding rolls, some of them being for elaborations and improvements of those above described but all covering methods of greater economy and effectiveness in rock-grinding.

Edison's work on conveyors during the period of his ore-concentrating labors was distinctively original, ingenious and far in advance of the times. His conception of the concentrating problem was broad and embraced an entire system, of which a principal item was the continuous transfer of enormous quantities of material from place to place at the lowest possible cost. As he contemplated the concentration of six thousand tons daily, the expense of manual labor to move such an immense quantity of rock, sand, and ore would be absolutely prohibitive. Hence, it became necessary to invent a system of conveyors that would be capable of transferring this mass of material from one place to another. And not only must these conveyors be capable of carrying the material, but they must also be devised so that they would automatically receive and discharge their respective loads at appointed places. Edison's ingenuity, engineering ability, and inventive skill were equal to the task, however, and were displayed in a system and variety of conveyors that in practice seemed to act with almost human discrimination. When fully installed throughout the plant, they automatically transferred daily a mass of material equal to about one hundred thousand cubic feet, from mill to mill, covering about a mile in the transit. Up and down, winding in and out, turning corners, delivering material from one to another, making a number of loops in the drying-oven, filling up bins and passing on to the next when they were full, these conveyors in automatic action seemingly played their part with human intelligence, which was in reality the reflection of the intelligence and ingenuity that had originally devised them and set them in motion.

Six of Edison's patents on conveyors include a variety of devices that have since came into broad general use for similar work, and have been the means of effecting great economies in numerous industries of widely varying kinds. Interesting as they are, however, we shall not attempt to describe them in detail, as the space required would be too great. They are specified in the list of patents following this Appendix, and may be examined in detail by any interested student.

In the same list will also be found a large number of Edison's patents on apparatus and methods of screening, drying, mixing, and briquetting, as well as for dust-proof bearings, and various types and groupings of separators, all of which were called forth by the exigencies and magnitude of his great undertaking, and without which he could not possibly have attained the successful physical results that crowned his labors. Edison's persistence in reducing the cost of his operations is noteworthy in connection with his screening and drying inventions, in which the utmost advantage is taken of the law of gravitation. With its assistance, which cost nothing, these operations were performed perfectly. It was only necessary to deliver the material at the top of the chambers, and during its natural descent it was screened or dried as the case might be.

All these inventions and devices, as well as those described in detail above (except magnetic separators and mixing and briquetting machines), are being used by him to-day in the manufacture of Portland cement, as that industry presents many of the identical problems which presented themselves in relation to the concentration of iron ore.

XVII. THE LONG CEMENT KILN

IN this remarkable invention, which has brought about a striking innovation in a long-established business, we see another characteristic instance of Edison's incisive reasoning and boldness of conception carried into practical effect in face of universal opinions to the contrary.

For the information of those unacquainted with the process of manufacturing Portland cement, it may be stated that the material consists preliminarily of an intimate mixture of cement rock and limestone, ground to a very fine powder. This powder is technically known in the trade as "chalk," and is fed into rotary kilns and "burned"; that is to say, it is subjected to a high degree of heat obtained by the combustion of pulverized coal, which is injected into the interior of the kiln. This combustion effects a chemical decomposition of the chalk, and causes it to assume a plastic consistency and to collect together in the form of small spherical balls, which are known as "clinker." Kilns are usually arranged with a slight incline, at the upper end of which the chalk is fed in and gradually works its way down to the interior flame of burning fuel at the other end. When it arrives at the lower end, the material has been "burned," and the clinker drops out into a receiving chamber below. The operation is continuous, a constant supply of chalk passing in at one end of the kiln and a continuous dribble of clinker-balls dropping out at the other. After cooling, the clinker is ground into very fine powder, which is the Portland cement of commerce.

It is self-evident that an ideal kiln would be one that produced the maximum quantity of thoroughly clinkered material with a minimum amount of fuel, labor, and investment. When Edison was preparing to go into the cement business, he looked the ground over thoroughly, and, after considerable investigation and experiment, came to the conclusion that prevailing conditions as to kilns were far from ideal.

The standard kilns then in use were about sixty feet in length, with an internal diameter of about five feet. In all rotary kilns for burning cement, the true clinkering operation takes place only within a limited portion of their total length, where the heat is greatest; hence the interior of the kiln may be considered as being divided longitudinally into two parts or zones--namely, the combustion, or clinkering, zone, and the zone of oncoming raw material. In the sixty-foot kiln the length of the combustion zone was about ten feet, extending from a point six or eight feet from the lower, or discharge, end to a point about eighteen feet from that end. Consequently, beyond that point there was a zone of only about forty feet, through which the heated gases passed and came in contact with the oncoming material, which was in movement down toward the clinkering zone. Since the bulk of oncoming material was small, the gases were not called upon to part with much of their heat, and therefore passed on up the stack at very high temperatures, ranging from 1500 degrees to 1800 degrees Fahr. Obviously, this heat was entirely lost.

An additional loss of efficiency arose from the fact that the material moved so rapidly toward the combustion zone that it had not given up all its carbon dioxide on reaching there; and by the giving off of large quantities of that gas within the combustion zone, perfect and economical combustion of coal could not be effected.

The comparatively short length of the sixty-foot kiln not only limited the amount of material that could be fed into it, but the limitation in length of the combustion zone militated against a thorough clinkering of the material, this operation being one in which the elements of time and proper heat are prime considerations. Thus the quantity of good clinker obtainable was unfavorably affected. By reason of these and other limitations and losses, it had been possible, in practice, to obtain only about two hundred and fifty barrels of clinker per day of twenty-four hours; and that with an expenditure for coal proportionately equal to about 29 to 33 per cent. of the quantity of clinker produced, even assuming that all the clinker was of good quality.

Edison realized that the secret of greater commercial efficiency and improvement of quality lay in the ability to handle larger quantities of material within a given time, and to produce a more perfect product without increasing cost or investment in proportion. His reasoning led him to the conclusion that this result could only be obtained through the use of a kiln of comparatively great length, and his investigations and experiments enabled him to decide upon a length of one hundred and fifty feet, but with an increase in diameter of only six inches to a foot over that of the sixty-foot kiln.

The principal considerations that influenced Edison in making this radical innovation may be briefly stated as follows:

First. The ability to maintain in the kiln a load from five to seven times greater than ordinarily employed, thereby tending to a more economical output.

Second. The combustion of a vastly increased bulk of pulverized coal and a greatly enlarged combustion zone, extending about forty feet longitudinally into the kiln--thus providing an area within which the material might be maintained in a clinkering temperature for a sufficiently long period to insure its being thoroughly clinkered from periphery to centre.

Third. By reason of such a greatly extended length of the zone of oncoming material (and consequently much greater bulk), the gases and other products of combustion would be cooled sufficiently between the combustion zone and the stack so as to leave the kiln at a comparatively low temperature. Besides, the oncoming material would thus be gradually raised in temperature instead of being heated abruptly, as in the shorter kilns.

Fourth. The material having thus been greatly raised in temperature before reaching the combustion zone would have parted with substantially all its carbon dioxide, and therefore would not introduce into the combustion zone sufficient of that gas to disturb the perfect character of the combustion.

Fifth. On account of the great weight of the heavy load in a long kiln, there would result the formation of a continuous plastic coating on that portion of the inner surface of the kiln where temperatures are highest. This would effectively protect the fire-brick lining from the destructive effects of the heat.

Such, in brief, were the essential principles upon which Edison based his conception and invention of the long kiln, which has since become so well known in the cement business.

Many other considerations of a minor and mechanical nature, but which were important factors in his solution of this difficult problem, are worthy of study by those intimately associated with or interested in the art. Not the least of the mechanical questions was settled by Edison's decision to make this tremendously long kiln in sections of cast-iron, with flanges, bolted together, and supported on rollers rotated by electric motors. Longitudinal expansion and thrust were also important factors to be provided for, as well as special devices to prevent the packing of the mass of material as it passed in and out of the kiln. Special provision was also made for injecting streams of pulverized coal in such manner as to create the largely extended zone of combustion. As to the details of these and many other ingenious devices, we must refer the curious reader to the patents, as it is merely intended in these pages to indicate in a brief manner the main principles of Edison's notable inventions. The principal United States patent on the long kiln was issued October 24, 1905, No. 802,631.

That his reasonings and deductions were correct in this case have been indubitably proven by some years of experience with the long kiln in its ability to produce from eight hundred to one thousand barrels of good clinker every twenty-four hours, with an expenditure for coal proportionately equal to about only 20 per cent. of the quantity of clinker produced.

To illustrate the long cement kiln by diagram would convey but little to the lay mind, and we therefore present an illustration (Fig. 1) of actual kilns in perspective, from which sense of their proportions may be gathered.

XVIII. EDISON'S NEW STORAGE BATTERY

GENERICALLY considered, a "battery" is a device which generates electric current. There are two distinct species of battery, one being known as "primary," and the other as "storage," although the latter is sometimes referred to as a "secondary battery" or "accumulator." Every type of each of these two species is essentially alike in its general make-up; that is to say, every cell of battery of any kind contains at least two elements of different nature immersed in a more or less liquid electrolyte of chemical character. On closing the circuit of a primary battery an electric current is generated by reason of the chemical action which is set up between the electrolyte and the elements. This involves a gradual consumption of one of the elements and a corresponding exhaustion of the active properties of the electrolyte. By reason of this, both the element and the electrolyte that have been used up must be renewed from time to time, in order to obtain a continued supply of electric current.

The storage battery also generates electric current through chemical action, but without involving the constant repriming with active materials to replace those consumed and exhausted as above mentioned. The term "storage," as applied to this species of battery, is, however, a misnomer, and has been the cause of much misunderstanding to nontechnical persons. To the lay mind a "storage" battery presents itself in the aspect of a device in which electric energy is STORED, just as compressed air is stored or accumulated in a tank. This view, however, is not in accordance with facts. It is exactly like the primary battery in the fundamental circumstance that its ability for generating electric current depends upon chemical action. In strict terminology it is a "reversible" battery, as will be quite obvious if we glance briefly at its philosophy. When a storage battery is "charged," by having an electric current passed through it, the electric energy produces a chemical effect, adding oxygen to the positive plate, and taking oxygen away from the negative plate. Thus, the positive plate becomes oxidized, and the negative plate reduced. After the charging operation is concluded the battery is ready for use, and upon its circuit being closed through a translating device, such as a lamp or motor, a reversion ("discharge") takes place, the positive plate giving up its oxygen, and the negative plate being oxidized. These chemical actions result in the generation of an electric current as in a primary battery. As a matter of fact, the chemical actions and reactions in a storage battery are much more complex, but the above will serve to afford the lay reader a rather simple idea of the general result arrived at through the chemical activity referred to.

The storage battery, as a commercial article, was introduced into the market in the year 1881. At that time, and all through the succeeding years, until about 1905, there was only one type that was recognized as commercially practicable--namely, that known as the lead-sulphuric-acid cell, consisting of lead plates immersed in an electrolyte of dilute sulphuric acid. In the year last named Edison first brought out his new form of nickel-iron cell with alkaline electrolyte, as we have related in the preceding narrative. Early in the eighties, at Menlo Park, he had given much thought to the lead type of storage battery, and during the course of three years had made a prodigious number of experiments in the direction of improving it, probably performing more experiments in that time than the aggregate of those of all other investigators. Even in those early days he arrived at the conclusion that the lead-sulphuric-acid combination was intrinsically wrong, and did not embrace the elements of a permanent commercial device. He did not at that time, however, engage in a serious search for another form of storage battery, being tremendously occupied with his lighting system and other matters.

It may here be noted, for the information of the lay reader, that the lead-acid type of storage battery consists of two or more lead plates immersed in dilute sulphuric acid and contained in a receptacle of glass, hard rubber, or other special material not acted upon by acid. The plates are prepared and "formed" in various ways, and the chemical actions are similar to those above stated, the positive plate being oxidized and the negative reduced during "charge," and reversed during "discharge." This type of cell, however, has many serious disadvantages inherent to its very nature. We will name a few of them briefly. Constant dropping of fine particles of active material often causes short-circuiting of the plates, and always necessitates occasional washing out of cells; deterioration through "sulphation" if discharge is continued too far or if recharging is not commenced quickly enough; destruction of adjacent metalwork by the corrosive fumes given out during charge and discharge; the tendency of lead plates to "buckle" under certain conditions; the limitation to the use of glass, hard rubber, or similar containers on account of the action of the acid; and the immense weight for electrical capacity. The tremendously complex nature of the chemical reactions which take place in the lead-acid storage battery also renders it an easy prey to many troublesome diseases.

In the year 1900, when Edison undertook to invent a storage battery, he declared it should be a new type into which neither sulphuric nor any other acid should enter. He said that the intimate and continued companionship of an acid and a metal was unnatural, and incompatible with the idea of durability and simplicity. He furthermore stated that lead was an unmechanical metal for a battery, being heavy and lacking stability and elasticity, and that as most metals were unaffected by alkaline solutions, he was going to experiment in that direction. The soundness of his reasoning is amply justified by the perfection of results obtained in the new type of storage battery bearing his name, and now to be described.

The essential technical details of this battery are fully described in an article written by one of Edison's laboratory staff, Walter E. Holland, who for many years has been closely identified with the inventor's work on this cell The article was published in the Electrical World, New York, April 28, 1910; and the following extracts therefrom will afford an intelligent comprehension of this invention:

"The 'A' type Edison cell is the outcome of nine years of costly experimentation and persistent toil on the part of its inventor and his associates....

"The Edison invention involves the use of an entirely new voltaic combination in an alkaline electrolyte, in place of the lead-lead-peroxide combination and acid electrolyte, characteristic of all other commercial storage batteries. Experience has proven that this not only secures durability and greater output per unit-weight of battery, but in addition there is eliminated a long list of troubles and diseases inherent in the lead-acid combination....

"The principle on which the action of this new battery is based is the oxidation and reduction of metals in an electrolyte which does not combine with, and will not dissolve, either the metals or their oxides; and an electrolyte, furthermore, which, although decomposed by the action of the battery, is immediately re-formed in equal quantity; and therefore in effect is a CONSTANT element, not changing in density or in conductivity.

"A battery embodying this basic principle will have features of great value where lightness and durability are desiderata. For instance, the electrolyte, being a constant factor, as explained, is not required in any fixed and large amount, as is the case with sulphuric acid in the lead battery; thus the cell may be designed with minimum distancing of plates and with the greatest economy of space that is consistent with safe insulation and good mechanical design. Again, the active materials of the electrodes being insoluble in, and absolutely unaffected by, the electrolyte, are not liable to any sort of chemical deterioration by action of the electrolyte--no matter how long continued....

"The electrolyte of the Edison battery is a 21 per cent. solution of potassium hydrate having, in addition, a small amount of lithium hydrate. The active metals of the electrodes--which will oxidize and reduce in this electrolyte without dissolution or chemical deterioration--are nickel and iron. These active elements are not put in the plates AS METALS; but one, nickel, in the form of a hydrate, and the other, iron, as an oxide.

"The containing cases of both kinds of active material (Fig. 1), and their supporting grids (Fig. 2), as well as the bolts, washers, and nuts used in assembling (Fig. 3), and even the retaining can and its cover (Fig. 4), are all made of nickel-plated steel--a material in which lightness, durability and mechanical strength are most happily combined, and a material beyond suspicion as to corrosion in an alkaline electrolyte....

"An essential part of Edison's discovery of active masetials for an alkaline storage battery was the PREPARATION of these materials. Metallic powder of iron and nickel, or even oxides of these metals, prepared in the ordinary way, are not chemically active in a sufficient degree to work in a battery. It is only when specially prepared iron oxide of exceeding fineness, and nickel hydrate conforming to certain physical, as well as chemical, standards can be made that the alkaline battery is practicable. Needless to say, the working out of the conditions and processes of manufacture of the materials has involved great ingenuity and endless experimentation."

The article then treats of Edison's investigations into means for supporting and making electrical connection with the active materials, showing some of the difficulties encountered and the various discoveries made in developing the perfected cell, after which the writer continues his description of the "A" type cell, as follows:

"It will be seen at once that the construction of the two kinds of plate is radically different. The negative or iron plate (Fig. 5) has the familiar flat-pocket construction. Each negative contains twenty-four pockets--a pocket being 1/2 inch wide by 3 inches long, and having a maximum thickness of a little more than 1/8 inch. The positive or nickel plate (Fig. 6) is seen to consist of two rows of round rods or pencils, thirty in number, held in a vertical position by a steel support-frame.

The pencils have flat flanges at the ends (formed by closing in the metal case), by which they are supported and electrical connection is made. The frame is slit at the inner horizontal edges, and then folded in such a way as to make individual clamping-jaws for each end-flange. The clamping-in is done at great pressure, and the resultant plate has great rigidity and strength.

"The perforated tubes into which the nickel active material is loaded are made of nickel-plated steel of high quality. They are put together with a double-lapped spiral seam to give expansion-resisting qualities, and as an additional precaution small metal rings are slipped on the outside. Each tube is 1/4 inch in diameter by 4 1/8 inches long, add has eight of the reinforcing rings.

"It will be seen that the 'A' positive plate has been given the theoretically best design to prevent expansion and overcome trouble from that cause. Actual tests, long continued under very severe conditions, have shown that the construction is right, and fulfils the most sanguine expectations."

Mr. Holland in his article then goes on to explain the development of the nickel flakes as the conducting factor in the positive element, but as this has already been described in Chapter XXII, we shall pass on to a later point, where he says:

"An idea of the conditions inside a loaded tube can best be had by microscopic examination. Fig. 7 shows a magnified section of a regularly loaded tube which has been sawed lengthwise. The vertical bounding walls are edges of the perforated metal containing tube; the dark horizontal lines are layers of nickel flake, while the light-colored thicker layers represent the nickel hydrate. It should be noted that the layers of flake nickel extend practically unbroken across the tube and make contact with the metal wall at both sides. These metal layers conduct current to or from the active nickel hydrate in all parts of the tube very efficiently. There are about three hundred and fifty layers of each kind of material in a 4 1/8-inch tube, each layer of nickel hydrate being about 0.01 inch thick; so it will be seen that the current does not have to penetrate very far into the nickel hydrate--one-half a layer's thickness being the maximum distance. The perforations of the containing tube, through which the electrolyte reaches the active material, are also shown in Fig. 7."

In conclusion, the article enumerates the chief characteristics of the Edison storage battery which fit it preeminently for transportation service, as follows: 1. No loss of active material, hence no sediment short-circuits. 2. No jar breakage. 3. Possibility of quick disconnection or replacement of any cell without employment of skilled labor. 4. Impossibility of "buckling" and harmlessness of a dead short-circuit. 5. Simplicity of care required. 6. Durability of materials and construction. 7. Impossibility of "sulphation." 8. Entire absence of corrosive fumes. 9. Commercial advantages of light weight.

10. Duration on account of its dependability. 11. Its high practical efficiency.

XIX. EDISON'S POURED CEMENT HOUSE

THE inventions that have been thus far described fall into two classes--first, those that were fundamental in the great arts and industries which have been founded and established upon them, and, second, those that have entered into and enlarged other arts that were previously in existence. On coming to consider the subject now under discussion, however, we find ourselves, at this writing, on the threshold of an entirely new and undeveloped art of such boundless possibilities that its ultimate extent can only be a matter of conjecture.

Edison's concrete house, however, involves two main considerations, first of which was the conception or creation of the IDEA--vast and comprehensive--of providing imperishable and sanitary homes for the wage-earner by molding an entire house in one piece in a single operation, so to speak, and so simply that extensive groups of such dwellings could be constructed rapidly and at very reasonable cost. With this idea suggested, one might suppose that it would be a simple matter to make molds and pour in a concrete mixture. Not so, however. And here the second consideration presents itself. An ordinary cement mixture is composed of crushed stone, sand, cement, and water. If such a mixture be poured into deep molds the heavy stone and sand settle to the bottom. Should the mixture be poured into a horizontal mold, like the floor of a house, the stone and sand settle, forming an ununiform mass. It was at this point that invention commenced, in order to produce a concrete mixture which would overcome this crucial difficulty. Edison, with characteristic thoroughness, took up a line of investigation, and after a prolonged series of experiments succeeded in inventing a mixture that upon hardening remained uniform throughout its mass. In the beginning of his experimentation he had made the conditions of test very severe by the construction of forms similar to that shown in the sketch below.

This consisted of a hollow wooden form of the dimensions indicated. The mixture was to be poured into the hopper until the entire form was filled, such mixture flowing down and along the horizontal legs and up the vertical members. It was to be left until the mixture was hard, and the requirement of the test was that there should be absolute uniformity of mixture and mass throughout. This was finally accomplished, and further invention then proceeded along engineering lines looking toward the devising of a system of molds with which practicable dwellings might be cast.

Edison's boldness and breadth of conception are well illustrated in his idea of a poured house, in which he displays his accustomed tendency to reverse accepted methods. In fact, it is this very reversal of usual procedure that renders it difficult for the average mind to instantly grasp the full significance of the principles involved and the results attained.

Up to this time we have been accustomed to see the erection of a house begun at the foundation and built up slowly, piece by piece, of solid materials: first the outer frame, then the floors and inner walls, followed by the stairways, and so on up to the putting on of the roof. Hence, it requires a complete rearrangement of mental conceptions to appreciate Edison's proposal to build a house FROM THE TOP DOWNWARD, in a few hours, with a freely flowing material poured into molds, and in a few days to take away the molds and find a complete indestructible sanitary house, including foundation, frame, floors, walls, stairways, chimneys, sanitary arrangements, and roof, with artistic ornamentation inside and out, all in one solid piece, as if it were graven or bored out of a rock.

To bring about the accomplishment of a project so extraordinarily broad involves engineering and mechanical conceptions of a high order, and, as we have seen, these have been brought to bear on the subject by Edison, together with an intimate knowledge of compounded materials.

The main features of this invention are easily comprehensible with the aid of the following diagrammatic sectional sketch:

It should be first understood that the above sketch is in broad outline, without elaboration, merely to illustrate the working principle; and while the upright structure on the right is intended to represent a set of molds in position to form a three-story house, with cellar, no regular details of such a building (such as windows, doors, stairways, etc.) are here shown, as they would only tend to complicate an explanation.

It will be noted that there are really two sets of molds, an inside and an outside set, leaving a space between them throughout. Although not shown in the sketch, there is in practice a number of bolts passing through these two sets of molds at various places to hold them together in their relative positions. In the open space between the molds there are placed steel rods for the purpose of reinforcement; while all through the entire structure provision is made for water and steam pipes, gas-pipes and electric-light wires being placed in appropriate positions as the molds are assembled.

At the centre of the roof there will be noted a funnel-shaped opening. Into this there is delivered by the endless chain of buckets shown on the left a continuous stream of a special free-flowing concrete mixture. This mixture descends by gravity, and gradually fills the entire space between the two sets of molds. The delivery of the material--or "pouring," as it is called--is continued until every part of the space is filled and the mixture is even with the tip of the roof, thus completing the pouring, or casting, of the house. In a few days afterward the concrete will have hardened sufficiently to allow the molds to be taken away leaving an entire house, from cellar floor to the peak of the roof, complete in all its parts, even to mantels and picture molding, and requiring only windows and doors, plumbing, heating, and lighting fixtures to make it ready for habitation.

In the above sketch the concrete mixers, A, B, are driven by the electric motor, C. As the material is mixed it descends into the tank, D, and flows through a trough into a lower tank, E, in which it is constantly stirred, and from which it is taken by the endless chain of buckets and dumped into the funnel-shaped opening at the top of the molds, as above described.

The molds are made of cast-iron in sections of such size and weight as will be most convenient for handling, mostly in pieces not exceeding two by four feet in rectangular dimensions. The subjoined sketch shows an exterior view of several of these molds as they appear when bolted together, the intersecting central portions representing ribs, which are included as part of the casting for purposes of strength and rigidity.

The molds represented above are those for straight work, such as walls and floors. Those intended for stairways, eaves, cornices, windows, doorways, etc., are much more complicated in design, although the same general principles are employed in their construction.

While the philosophy of pouring or casting a complete house in its entirety is apparently quite simple, the development of the engineering and mechanical questions involves the solution of a vast number of most intricate and complicated problems covering not only the building as a whole, but its numerous parts, down to the minutest detail. Safety, convenience, duration, and the practical impossibility of altering a one-piece solid dwelling are questions that must be met before its construction, and therefore Edison has proceeded calmly on his way toward the goal he has ever had clearly in mind, with utter indifference to the criticisms and jeers of those who, as "experts," have professed positive knowledge of the impossibility of his carrying out this daring scheme.

LIST OF UNITED STATES PATENTS

List of United States patents granted to Thomas A. Edison, arranged according to dates of execution of applications for such patents. This list shows the inventions as Mr. Edison has worked upon them from year to year

1868

NO.	TITLE OF PATENT DATE EXECUTED	DATE EXECUTED
90,646,	Electrographic Vote Recorder . . . . .Oct. 13, 1868	

1869

| 91,527 | Printing Telegraph (reissued October 25, 1870, numbered 4166, and August 5, 1873, numbered 5519). . . . . . .Jan. 25, 1869 |
| 96,567 | Apparatus for Printing Telegraph (reissued |

200,994   Automatic Telegraph Perforator and
          Transmitter. . . . . .Oct. 30, 1876

1877
205,370   Pneumatic Stencil Pens . . . . Feb. 3, 1877
213,554   Automatic Telegraphs . . . . Feb. 3, 1877
196,747   Stencil Pens . . . . April 18, 1877
203,329   Perforating Pens . . . . April 18, 1877
474,230   Speaking Telegraph . . . . April 18, 1877
217,781   Sextuplex Telegraph. . . . . .May 8, 1877
230,621   Addressing Machine . . . . .May 8, 1877
377,374   Telegraphy . . . . .May 8, 1877
453,601   Sextuplex Telegraph. . . . . May 31, 1877
452,913   Sextuplex Telegraph. . . . . May 31, 1877
512,872   Sextuplex Telegraph. . . . . May 31, 1877
474,231   Speaking Telegraph . . . . July 9, 1877
203,014   Speaking Telegraph . . . . .July 16, 1877
208,299   Speaking Telegraph . . . . .July 16, 1877
203,015   Speaking Telegraph . . . . .Aug. 16, 1877
420,594   Quadruplex Telegraph . . . . .Aug. 16, 1877
492,789   Speaking Telegraph . . . . .Aug. 31, 1877
203,013   Speaking Telegraph . . . . Dec. 8, 1877
203 018   Telephone or Speaking Telegraph. . . . Dec. 8, 1877
200 521   Phonograph or Speaking Machine . . . .Dec. 15, 1877

1878

203,019   Circuit for Acoustic or Telephonic
          Telegraphs . . . . .Feb. 13, 1878
201,760   Speaking Machines. . . . . .Feb. 28, 1878
203,016   Speaking Machines. . . . . .Feb. 28, 1878
203,017   Telephone Call Signals . . . . .Feb. 28, 1878
214,636   Electric Lights. . . . . Oct. 5, 1878
222,390   Carbon Telephones. . . . . Nov. 8, 1878
217,782   Duplex Telegraphs. . . . . .Nov. 11, 1878
214,637   Thermal Regulator for Electric Lights.Nov. 14, 1878
210,767   Vocal Engines. . . . . .Aug. 31, 1878
218,166   Magneto Electric Machines. . . . . . . Dec. 3, 1878
218,866   Electric Lighting Apparatus. . . . . . Dec. 3, 1878
219,628   Electric Lights. . . . . Dec. 3, 1878
295,990   Typewriter . . . . Dec. 4, 1878
218,167   Electric Lights. . . . . .Dec. 31, 1878

1879

224,329   Electric Lighting Apparatus. . . . . .Jan. 23, 1879
227,229   Electric Lights. . . . . .Jan. 28, 1879
227,227   Electric Lights. . . . . Feb. 6, 1879
224.665   Autographic Stencils for Printing. . March 10, 1879
227.679   Phonograph . . . . March 19, 1879
221,957   Telephone. . . . . March 24, 1879
227,229   Electric Lights. . . . . April 12, 1879
264,643   Magneto Electric Machines. . . . . . April 21, 1879
219,393   Dynamo Electric Machines . . . . July 7, 1879

476,993 Electric Arc . . . . .July 31, 1891
484,183 Electrical Depositing Meter. . . . . .July 31, 1891
485,840 Bricking Fine Iron Ores. . . . . . .July 31, 1891
493,426 Apparatus for Exhibiting Photographs
    of Moving Objects. . . . . .July 31, 1891
509,518 Electric Railway . . . . .July 31, 1891
589,168 Kinetographic Camera (reissued September
    30, 1902, numbered 12,037
    and 12,038, and January 12, 1904,
    numbered 12,192) . . . . .July 31, 1891
470,929 Magnetic Separator . . . . .Aug. 28, 1891
471,268 Ore Conveyor and Method of Arranging
    Ore Thereon. . . . . .Aug. 28, 1891
472,288 Dust-Proof Bearings for Shafts . . . .Aug. 28, 1891
472,752 Dust-Proof Journal Bearings. . . . . .Aug. 28, 1891
472,753 Ore-Screening Apparatus. . . . . . .Aug. 28, 1891
474,592 Ore-Conveying Apparatus. . . . . . .Aug. 28, 1891
474,593 Dust-Proof Swivel Shaft Bearing. . . .Aug. 28, 1891
498,385 Rollers for Ore-Crushing or Other
    Material . . . . .Aug. 28, 1891
470,930 Dynamo Electric Machine. . . . . . . .Oct 8, 1891
476,532 Ore-Screening Apparatus. . . . . . . .Oct 8, 1891
491,992 Cut-Out for Incandescent Electric Lamps Nov. 10, 1891

1892

491,993 Stop Device. . . . . April 5 1892
564,423 Separating Ores. . . . . .June 2;, 1892
485,842 Magnetic Ore Separation. . . . . July 9, 1892
485,841 Mechanically Separating Ores . . . . . July 9, 1892
513,096 Method of and Apparatus for Mixing
    Materials. . . . . .Aug. 24, 1892

1893

509,428 Composition Brick and Making Same. . March 15, 1893
513,097 Phonograph . . . . May 22, 1893
567,187 Crushing Rolls . . . . .Dec. 13, 1893
602 064 Conveyor . . . . .Dec. 13, 1893
534 206 Filament for Incandescent Lamps. . . .Dec. 15, 1893

1896

865,367 Fluorescent Electric Lamp. . . . . . May 16, 1896

1897

604.740 Governor for Motors. . . . . .Jan. 25, 1897
607,588 Phonograph . . . . .Jan. 25, 1897
637,327 Rolls. . . . . May 14, 1897
672,616 Breaking Rock. . . . . May 14, 1897
675,056 Magnetic Separator . . . . May 14, 1897
676,618 Magnetic Separator . . . . May 14, 1897
605,475 Drying Apparatus . . . . .June 10, 1897

758,432   Stock House Conveyor . . . . .Dec. 18, 1902

873,219   Feed Regulators for Grinding Machines. Dec. 18, 1902

832,046   Automatic Weighing and Mixing Apparatus Dec. 18, 1902

1903

772,647   Photographic Film for Moving Picture
Machine. . . . . .Jan. 13, 1903

841,677   Apparatus for Separating and Grinding
Fine Materials . . . . .Jan. 22, 1903

790,351   Duplicating Phonograph Records . . . .Jan. 30. 1903

831,269   Storage Battery Electrode Plate. . . .Jan. 30, 1903

775,965   Dry Separator. . . . . April 27, 1903

754,756   Process of Treating Ores from Magnetic
Gangue . . . . May 25, 1903

775,600   Rotary Cement Kilns. . . . . .July 20, 1903

767,216   Apparatus for Vacuously Depositing
Metals . . . . July 30 1903

796,629   Lamp Guard . . . . July 30 1903

772,648   Vehicle Wheel. . . . . .Aug. 25, 1903

850,912   Making Articles by Electro-Plating . . .Oct 3, 1903

857,041   Can or Receptacle for Storage Batteries.Oct 3, 1903

766,815   Primary Battery. . . . . .Nov. 16, 1903

943,664   Sound Recording Apparatus. . . . . .Nov. 16, 1903

873,220   Reversible Galvanic Battery. . . . . .Nov. 20, 1903

898,633   Filling Apparatus for Storage Battery
Jars . . . . Dec. 8, 1903

1904

767,554   Rendering Storage Battery Gases Non-
Explosive. . . . . June 8, 1904

861,241   Portland Cement and Manufacturing Same June 20, 1904

800,800   Phonograph Records and Making Same . .June 24, 1904

821,622   Cleaning Metallic Surfaces . . . . . .June 24, 1904

879,612   Alkaline Storage Batteries . . . . . .June 24, 1904

880,484   Process of Producing Very Thin Sheet
Metal. . . . . .June 24, 1904

827,297   Alkaline Batteries . . . . .July 12, 1904

797,845   Sheet Metal for Perforated Pockets of
Storage Batteries. . . . . .July 12, 1904

847,746   Electrical Welding Apparatus . . . . .July 12, 1904

821,032   Storage Battery. . . . . Aug 10, 1904

861,242   Can or Receptacle for Storage Battery. Aug 10, 1904

970,615   Methods and Apparatus for Making
Sound Records. . . . . .Aug. 23, 1904

817,162   Treating Alkaline Storage Batteries. Sept. 26, 1904

948,542   Method of Treating Cans of Alkaline
Storage Batteries. . . . . Sept. 28, 1904

813,490   Cement Kiln. . . . . .Oct 29, 1904

821,625   Treating Alkaline Storage Batteries. . Oct 29, 1904

821,623   Storage Battery Filling Apparatus. . . Nov. 1, 1904

821,624   Gas Separator for Storage Battery. . .Oct. 29, 1904

1905

1906

964,221   Sound Records. . . . . .Dec. 28, 1906

1907

865,688   Making Metallic Films or Flakes. . . .Jan. 11, 1907
936,267   Feed Mechanism for Phonographs and
           Other Machines . . . . .Jan. 11, 1907
936,525   Making Metallic Films or Flakes. . . .Jan. 17, 1907
865,687   Making Nickel Films. . . . . .Jan. 18, 1907
939,817   Cement Kiln. . . . . Feb. 8, 1907
855,562   Diaphragm for Talking Machines . . . .Feb. 23, 1907
939,992   Phonographic Recording and Reproducing
           Machine. . . . . .Feb. 25, 1907
941,630   Process and Apparatus for Artificially
           Aging or Seasoning Portland Cement . .Feb. 25, 1907
876,445   Electrolyte for Alkaline Storage Batteries May 8, 1907
914,343   Making Storage Battery Electrodes. . . May 15, 1907
861,819   Discharging Apparatus for Belt Conveyors June 11, 1907
954,789   Sprocket Chain Drives. . . . . . . .June 11, 1907
909,877   Telegraphy . . . . .June 18, 1907

1908

896,811   Metallic Film for Use with Storage Batteries
           and Process. . . . . Feb. 4, 1908
940,635   Electrode Element for Storage Batteries Feb. 4,
1908
909,167   Water-Proofing Paint for Portland
           Cement Buildings . . . . Feb. 4, 1908
896,812   Storage Batteries. . . . . March 13, 1908
944,481   Processes and Apparatus for Artificially
           Aging or Seasoning Portland Cement. March 13,1908
947,806   Automobiles. . . . . March 13,-1908
909,168   Water-Proofing Fibres and Fabrics. . . May 27, 1908
909,169   Water-Proofing Paint for Portland
           Cement Structures. . . . . May 27, 1908
970,616   Flying Machines. . . . . .Aug. 20, 1908

1909
930,947   Gas Purifier . . . . .Feb. 15, 1909
40,527   Design Patent for Phonograph Cabinet. Sept. 13, 1909

FOREIGN PATENTS

In addition to the United States patents issued to Edison, as above
enumerated, there have been granted to him (up to October, 1910) by
foreign governments 1239 patents, as follows:

Argentine. 1
Australia. 6
Austria. 101
Belgium. 88

Brazil 1
Canada 129
Cape of Good Hope. 5
Ceylon 4
Cuba 12
Denmark. 9
France 111
Germany. 130
Great Britain. 131
Hungary. 30
India. 44
Italy. 83
Japan. 5
Mexico 14
Natal. 5
New South Wales. 38
New Zealand. 31
Norway 16
Orange Free State. 2
Portugal 10
Queensland 29
Russia 17
South African Republic 4
South Australia. 1
Spain. 54
Sweden 61
Switzerland. 13
Tasmania 8
Victoria 42
West Australia 4

Total of Edison's Foreign Patents. . . 1239